THE
BEDFORD
READER

FIFTH EDITION

THE BEDFORD READER

FIFTH EDITION

X. J. Kennedy · Dorothy M. Kennedy

Jane E. Aaron

Bedford Books *of* St. Martin's Press

Boston

For Bedford Books

Publisher: Charles H. Christensen
Associate Publisher/General Manager: Joan E. Feinberg
Managing Editor: Elizabeth M. Schaaf
Developmental Editor: Ellen M. Kuhl
Production Editor: John Amburg
Copyeditor: Carol H. Blumentritt
Text Design: Anna George
Cover Design: Hannus Design Associates
Cover Art: American Beech, Sugar Maple, and Yellow Birch, Gatineau Park, Quebec. Copyright Tim Fitzharris.

Library of Congress Catalog Card Number: 92–75303
Copyright © 1994 by Bedford Books of St. Martin's Press

Manufactured in the United States of America.
8 7 6 5 4
f   e   d   c

For information, write: St. Martin's Press, Inc.
175 Fifth Avenue, New York, NY 10010

Editorial Offices: Bedford Books of St. Martin's Press
29 Winchester Street, Boston, MA 02116

ISBN: 0–312–08637–7

ACKNOWLEDGMENTS

Maya Angelou. "Champion of the World." From *I Know Why the Caged Bird Sings* by Maya Angelou. Copyright © 1969 by Maya Angelou. Reprinted by permission of Random House, Inc. In "Maya Angelou on Writing," excerpts from Sheila Weller, "Work in Progress/Maya Angelou," in *Intellectual Digest,* June 1973. Reprinted by permission.

Barbara Lazear Ascher. "On Compassion." From *The Habit of Loving* by Barbara Ascher. Copyright © 1986, 1987, 1989 by Barbara Lazear Ascher. Reprinted by permission of Random House, Inc.

Acknowledgments and copyrights are continued at the back of the book on pages 723–29, which constitute an extension of the copyright page.

PREFACE
FOR INSTRUCTORS

The Bedford Reader has always had but a single aim: to get students writing, and writing well. "A writer," says Saul Bellow, "is a reader moved to emulation." For emulation, we assemble the best, liveliest essays we can find. Before and after these essays, we show how effective writing is written — not just theoretically, but in the working practice of good writers.

In this edition of *The Bedford Reader,* we have strengthened these core features, providing thirty-one new essays out of sixty-nine and emphasizing critical reading and the writing process. With new material on "mixed methods," we have also strengthened the book's focus on the rhetorical methods, which we show to be natural forms that assist invention and fruition. Knowing, however, that more and more instructors emphasize the topics of the essays as much as their structures, we have multiplied the thematic connections. The result is a book both familiar and fresh, a reader both rhetorical and thematic.

WHAT'S NEW

Over 150 instructors and students told us what they thought of the previous *Bedford Reader,* and we listened. The changes in this new edition are extensive.

PART TWO, "MIXING THE METHODS." Perhaps the most significant change is the addition of sixteen essays with a dual focus. First, all these essays illustrate a truth repeated often in the book: that the methods of development are not ends in themselves but strategies used to achieve a purpose. The introduction to Part Two, the head-notes before the essays, and the "Other Methods" questions after all the essays in the book help students analyze how the methods work together.

The second focus of these essays is thematic. The selections fall in chapters headed "The Power of Family," "Language and Truth," "Our Place in the Environment," and "Diversity in the Curriculum." Each chapter's introduction, end-of-essay "Connections" questions, and end-of-chapter writing topics relate these selections to one another and reinforce and extend their thematic connections to essays in earlier chapters.

NEW SELECTIONS. The essays in *The Bedford Reader* combine time-proven favorites by James Thurber, Jessica Mitford, Judy Brady, and others with more recent pieces that we're confident will rouse a class and inspire writing — essays by Amy Tan, Alan M. Dershowitz, June Jordan, Barbara Ehrenreich, Arthur M. Schlesinger, Jr., Linda Hogan, and others.

CRITICAL THINKING, READING, AND WRITING. *The Bedford Reader* now takes a thorough and consistent approach to critical thinking, reading, and writing. The book's introduction lays the groundwork with a discussion of analysis, inference, synthesis, and evaluation. A student's annotation of part of an essay by M. F. K. Fisher illustrates the material on reading strategy. And a student critique of Fisher's essay demonstrates critical writing. Then, following each essay in the book, topics labeled "Critical Writing" help students formulate their own critiques of the essays.

THE WRITING PROCESS. A new discussion of the writing process ties reading directly to writing. Students receive important advice on discovery, drafting, and revising. Then they observe the development of a paper, from notes about M. F. K. Fisher's essay through first draft and revision to a final draft, each stage accompanied by the student writer's own comments.

WHAT'S THE SAME

Some elements of *The Bedford Reader* have proved so popular that we knew better than to tamper with them.

RHETORICAL ORGANIZATION. At the core of the book, ten chapters treat ten methods of development. Each chapter introduces the method, illustrates it in two paragraphs (one on television, one on an academic discipline), and includes four or more essays developed by the method. Throughout, we stress that the rhetorical methods are not boxes to be stuffed full of verbiage but flexible forms that can help students discover how much they have to say.

VARIETY OF SELECTIONS. The essays in *The Bedford Reader* vary in authorship, subject, even length. Half the selections are by women, and more than 40 percent touch on cultural diversity. There are three essays by students, including a researched argument that is fully documented in MLA style. A story by Shirley Jackson and a poem by Emily Dickinson represent literature. Some selections deal with sports, popular culture, and family; others represent history, anthropology, psychology, and many other academic disciplines. Running from two to thirteen pages, the selections provide a range of depth and complexity.

THEMATIC PAIRS. At least two essays in each rhetorical chapter deal with a common theme, such as popular culture, conversation, homelessness, or sports. These and other common threads are highlighted in writing topics labeled "Connections" after every selection.

WRITERS ON WRITING. After their essays, fifty-one of the book's writers offer comments on everything from grammar to outlining, finding a subject to revising. Besides providing rock-solid advice, these comments also prove that for the pros, too, writing is usually a challenge.

EXTENSIVE EDITORIAL APPARATUS. We've surrounded the essays with a wealth of material designed to get students reading, thinking, and writing. To help structure students' critical approach to the essays, each one comes with two headnotes (on the author and the selection), three sets of questions (on meaning, writing strategy, and language), and at least three writing topics. Additional writing topics appear at the end of every chapter.

Two useful aids conclude the book. A glossary ("Useful Terms") contains definitions of all the terms used in the book (including all those printed in SMALL CAPITAL LETTERS), such as INTRODUCTIONS and CONCLUSIONS; and an index alphabetizes authors and titles and refers to discussions of important topics, such as revision or tone (including those in the Writers on Writing segments).

INSTRUCTOR'S MANUAL. *Notes and Resources for Teaching The Bedford Reader,* bound with the book's Instructor's Edition, features an index of thematic connections among essays and a discussion of every method, selection, and Writer on Writing.

TWO VERSIONS. As before, *The Bedford Reader* has a sibling: A shorter edition, *The Brief Bedford Reader,* features forty-two instead of sixty-nine selections and omits the four thematic, mixed-methods chapters.

ACKNOWLEDGMENTS

With each edition, our debt to teachers and students who help us shape *The Bedford Reader* grows. This time dozens of teachers, answering detailed questionnaires, showed us new directions we might take and kept us from missteps. We heartily thank Susan Ahrens, Donna Alden, Susan Amper, Jeffrey Anderson, Ursula F. Appelt, Mailin Barlow, Tim Bellows, Richard Bernard, Shirley Borud, Barbara Broer, Jeffrey Brooks, Carole Brown, Victor L. Cahn, Rita Carey, Michael Chappell, Saul Cohen, Patricia Combies, Thomas F. Connolly, Lillian Cook, James A. Cowan, Adriana Craciun, Mary Cross, Elizabeth Cullinan, Ingrid Daemmrich, John Darling, Helene Davis, Lynne H. Davis, Sheila Donnelly, Marc Falkoff, Lara R. Farina, Cheryl Fenno, R. FitzGerald, O. Joe Fleming, R. Rolph Fletcher, Richard J. Follett, Elaine Foster, Ed Fryzel, Reginald L. Gerlica, Sid Gershgoren, Eileen Godollei, Christine Godwin, Norma W. Goldstein, Claudia Gottschall, Emily Grady, Louis Graham, James Griffith, Geraldine Grunow, Lydia Hamilton, Robert Allen Harkreader, Eleanor Hartmann, Lori Haslem, Brian Heavey, Don Hendricks, Jeff Hobbs, Elizabeth Hoit-Thetford, Daniel T. Holt, Cornelius G. House, Bob Hughes, Lucy Hulme, Richard G. Johnson, Scott Kassner, Frances Kestler, Zaka Khan, Ann Kimbrough, Mary Nell King, Frances Kirkpatrick, Evan Klein, Joseph L. Kolpacke, Michael J. Kraft, Elmer Kurrus, Frank LaFerriere, Edward Lemay, Charles Lewis, Jack Longmate, Gerald F. Luboff, Deborah Luster, Betty J. Lyke, James Lynch, Joy M. Lynch, Liliane MacPherson, Diane M. Marion, C. K. Mathey, Jay K. Maurer, Jeanne Mauzy, Jeffrey McMahon, June J. McManus, Robert McManus, Robert C. Milliken, Mike Mills, Genevieve Morgan, Mary V. Morriss, Brian T. Murphy, Robin Newcomer, Julie Noble, Richard Nordquist, Jim O'Neill, Gary Pak, Christopher M. Patterson, Gail Pearlman, Suzanne Radigan, Carol C. Reposa, Mary A. Sadler, Cindy Schroeder, Pat Schutjer, Patricia Sculley, William L. Scurrah, John Simpson, Paulette Smith, J. Solonche, Bill M. Stiffler, Stephanie J. Stiles, Richard Strugala, Mary Ann Taylor, Michael C. Tighe, Nancy Tuinstra, Paul Vaccaro, K. J. Walters, Lawrence Watson, Fredrika Weisenthal, Douglas W. Werden, Jani Decena White, J. Peter Williams, Laurel V. Williamson, Brenda J. Willis, Kathleen R. Winter, Gerald Wisz, Joe Zimmerman, and Sander Zulauf.

At Bedford Books, as usual, support was generous, warm, and vital. Charles H. Christensen devised some of the book's best features. Ellen Kuhl devised the rest, kept a gentle hand on the controls, and could always be relied on for a laugh. Beth Castrodale helped out in the earlier stages of development; Mark Reimold attended brightly to the later stages. Andrea Goldman was a quick and inventive researcher. John Amburg guided the manuscript through production without a hitch. Beth Chapman, Michèle Biscoe, and Karen Baart provided sturdy support. And beyond Bedford, Patrice Boyer Claeys, David Gibbs, and Julia Sullivan contributed their talents. To all, our deep and happy thanks.

CONTENTS

PREFACE FOR INSTRUCTORS   v

THEMATIC TABLE OF CONTENTS   xxvii

INTRODUCTION   1

    WHY READ? WHY WRITE? WHY NOT PHONE?   1
    USING *THE BEDFORD READER*   2
      The Essays
      The Organization
      The Questions, Writing Topics, and Glossary
      Writers on Writing
    READING AN ESSAY   6
      The Preliminaries
        The Title / The Author / Where the Essay Was First Published / When the Essay Was First Published
      The First Reading

M. F. K. FISHER • *The Broken Chain*   **10**

An incident in the writer's childhood proves the occasion for a revelation about her father's past and a lesson on the nature of violence.

Rereadings   **14**
Writing While Reading / Summarizing / Reading Critically / Meaning / Writing Strategy / Language
WRITING   **24**
Suggestions for Writing
The Writing Process
An Essay-in-Progress
Notes on Reading / First Draft / Revised Draft / Edited Paragraph / Final Draft

CHRISTINE D'ANGELO • *Has the Chain Been Broken? Two Ideas of Violence in "The Broken Chain"*   **34**

A student questions M. F. K. Fisher's acceptance of physical punishment as a justifiable form of violence.

PART ONE
THE METHODS
37

1. NARRATION: Telling a Story   39

THE METHOD   **39**
THE PROCESS   **41**
NARRATION IN A PARAGRAPH: TWO ILLUSTRATIONS   **47**
Using Narration to Write About Television
Using Narration in an Academic Discipline

MAYA ANGELOU • *Champion of the World*   **49**

◄► She didn't dare ring up a sale while that epic battle was on. A noted black writer remembers from her early childhood the night when a people's fate hung on a pair of boxing gloves.

Maya Angelou on Writing   **53**

◄► Indicates thematic pair in each chapter.

RALPH ELLISON • *On Being the Target of Discrimination*　**55**

◄► "You'll have to leave. Both you and your chillun too." For a prominent black writer, these words spoken by a zoo guard encoded the childhood experience of racial discrimination.

Ralph Ellison on Writing　**63**

JAMES THURBER • *University Days*　**64**

Ohio State's famed alumnus tells in embarrassing detail of his struggles with a microscope, a swimming test, and an ROTC general who snaps, "You are the main trouble with this university!"

James Thurber on Writing　**71**

JUDITH ORTIZ COFER • *Casa: A Partial Remembrance of a Puerto Rican Childhood*　**73**

A story within a story: Her grandmother's "cautionary tale" about men and marriage leads Cofer to reflect on her own experience as an outsider in both Puerto Rico and America.

SHIRLEY JACKSON • *The Lottery*　**80**

Tension builds imperceptibly in this classic short story as folks gather for their town's annual lottery. "It isn't fair. It isn't right," exclaims the winner.

Shirley Jackson on Writing　**90**

ADDITIONAL WRITING TOPICS　**92**

2. DESCRIPTION: Writing with Your Senses　**93**

THE METHOD　**93**
THE PROCESS　**95**
DESCRIPTION IN A PARAGRAPH: TWO ILLUSTRATIONS　**98**
　Using Description to Write About Television
　Using Description in an Academic Discipline

VIRGINIA WOOLF • *The Death of the Moth*　**101**

◄► For a perceptive writer, a simple day moth comes to symbolize "a tiny bead of pure life," a radiant force consumed in a heroic struggle against death.

Virginia Woolf on Writing　**105**

ANNIE DILLARD • *Death of a Moth*   107

◄► "A flame-faced virgin gone to God." No mere insect in the eyes of this master describer, a moth reaches a fiery end in a candle.

Annie Dillard on Writing   111

JOAN DIDION • *Marrying Absurd*   113

A well-known writer paints an ironic portrait of the instant wedding industry in Las Vegas, a city where there is "no night and no day and no past and no future."

Joan Didion on Writing   117

E. B. WHITE • *Once More to the Lake*   120

A father takes his young son on a pilgrimage to a favorite summertime scene from his own childhood, a lake in Maine. There, he arrives at a startling realization.

E. B. White on Writing   127

EMILY DICKINSON • *A narrow Fellow in the Grass*   129

A celebrated American poet gives a quick-eyed, resonant description of a creature of mystery, and an account of her reaction to it.

Emily Dickinson on Writing   132

ADDITIONAL WRITING TOPICS   133

3. EXAMPLE: Pointing to Instances   135

THE METHOD   135
THE PROCESS   136
EXAMPLE IN A PARAGRAPH: TWO ILLUSTRATIONS   138
Using Example to Write About Television
Using Example in an Academic Discipline

BARBARA LAZEAR ASCHER • *On Compassion*   140

◄► Where do we find the compassion to help the desperate, the homeless? It's "not a character trait like a sunny disposition," says this essayist. "It must be learned, and it is learned by having adversity at our windows."

ANNA QUINDLEN • *Homeless*   **145**

◄► A journalist who confesses an aversion for "looking at the big picture, taking the global view," insists on seeing homelessness as an individual crisis.

Anna Quindlen on Writing   **148**

STEPHANIE COONTZ • *A Nation of Welfare Families*   **150**

Dispelling a myth of self-reliance, a historian shows that pioneers and suburbanites were more dependent on the government than today's "welfare family" is.

Stephanie Coontz on Writing   **156**

BRENT STAPLES • *Black Men and Public Space*   **159**

In near-deserted streets at night, a black writer finds to his surprise that women flee from him. Relating case histories, he tells us what he has discovered about "public space."

Brent Staples on Writing   **163**

ADDITIONAL WRITING TOPICS   **166**

4. COMPARISON AND CONTRAST: Setting Things Side by Side   167

THE METHOD   167
THE PROCESS   169
COMPARISON AND CONTRAST IN A PARAGRAPH:
    TWO ILLUSTRATIONS   172
        Using Comparison and Contrast to Write About Television
        Using Comparison and Contrast in an Academic Discipline

SUZANNE BRITT • *Neat People vs. Sloppy People*   **174**

"Neat people are lazier and meaner than sloppy people," asserts a light-hearted writer, who, as she compares and contrasts, takes up a cudgel and chooses sides.

Suzanne Britt on Writing   **178**

BRUCE CATTON • *Grant and Lee: A Study in Contrasts*   **180**

Face to face at Appomattox, Ulysses S. Grant and Robert E. Lee clearly personified their opposing traditions. But what the two Civil War generals had in common was more vital by far.

Bruce Catton on Writing   **186**

AMY TAN • *The Language of Discretion*   187

Tan draws on her experience as a bilingual Chinese American to ponder the idea that a person's language shapes his or her reality.

Amy Tan on Writing   197

JEFF GREENFIELD • *The Black and White Truth About Basketball*   199

◀▶ In an updated version of his classic essay, a well-known columnist and television commentator explains the dramatic differences between two basketball styles by where and how the players grew up.

Jeff Greenfield on Writing   206

MURRAY ROSS • *Football Red and Baseball Green*   209

◀▶ For this fan, the distinctly American sports of football and baseball enact fundamental myths of heroism and harmony. Watching the sports, we, too, become part of their myths.

Murray Ross on Writing   218

ADDITIONAL WRITING TOPICS   220

5. PROCESS ANALYSIS: Explaining Step by Step   221

THE METHOD   221
THE PROCESS   223
PROCESS ANALYSIS IN A PARAGRAPH:
  TWO ILLUSTRATIONS   225
    Using Process Analysis to Write About Television
    Using Process Analysis in an Academic Discipline

MERRILL MARKOE • *Conversation Piece*   227

◀▶ This humorist walks step by step through the minefield of conversation, defined as "any exchange of more than two remarks that does not end in an act of violence."

BRENDA UELAND • *Tell Me More*   233

◀▶ A revered writer urges readers to become better listeners, not only for their friends and relatives but for themselves.

Brenda Ueland on Writing   240

MARVIN HARRIS • *How Our Skins Got Their Color*   **241**

Brown, white, black, yellow—whatever its hue, skin color is beautiful. It is a beautiful adaptation to environmental conditions. An eminent anthropologist explains how.

PETER ELBOW • *Desperation Writing*   **246**

Your writing assignment is due in the morning, and you haven't a thought in the world. Here's advice from an expert: how to generate ideas and write without tearing out your hair.

Peter Elbow on Writing   **251**

JESSICA MITFORD • *Behind the Formaldehyde Curtain*   **253**

With sardonic wit, the writer, whom *Time* called "Queen of the Muckrakers," details the stages through which a sallow corpse becomes a masterwork of American mortuary art.

Jessica Mitford on Writing   **263**

ADDITIONAL WRITING TOPICS   **265**

6. DIVISION OR ANALYSIS: Slicing into Parts   **267**

THE METHOD   **267**
THE PROCESS   **270**
DIVISION OR ANALYSIS IN A PARAGRAPH:
    TWO ILLUSTRATIONS   **271**
    Using Division or Analysis to Write About Television
    Using Division or Analysis in an Academic Discipline

JUDY BRADY • *I Want a Wife*   **273**

In this feminist view of marriage, the work of a wife is divided into its roles and functions. What a wonderful boon a wife is! Shouldn't every woman have one of her own?

MARK CRISPIN MILLER • *Dow Recycles Reality*   **277**

Dissecting a television commercial, a critic shows how a major corporation whitewashes its image with symbols of family and patriotism.

Mark Crispin Miller on Writing   **281**

GAIL SHEEHY • *Predictable Crises of Adulthood*   283

A typical life, between the ages of eighteen and fifty, may be divided into six stages of growth. Among these, very likely, is the one you are writhing through right now.

BARBARA EHRENREICH • *The Wretched of the Hearth*   292

◄► Depicting one of the few working-class women on television, Roseanne Barr Arnold represents America's "neglected underside," and her no-holds-barred approach has much to teach daintier feminists.

Barbara Ehrenreich on Writing   301

BELL HOOKS • *Madonna*   303

◄► Does her appropriation of African American culture make the rock star Madonna a "soul sister" or a "plantation mistress"? The writer bell hooks admires Madonna's promotion of liberation but condemns her exploitiveness.

bell hooks on Writing   312

ADDITIONAL WRITING TOPICS   314

7. CLASSIFICATION: Sorting into Kinds   315

THE METHOD   315
THE PROCESS   317
CLASSIFICATION IN A PARAGRAPH: TWO ILLUSTRATIONS   319
    Using Classification to Write About Television
    Using Classification in an Academic Discipline

RUSSELL BAKER • *The Plot Against People*   321

The goal of inanimate objects, declares the renowned humorist, is nothing short of the destruction of the human race.

Russell Baker on Writing   325

FRAN LEBOWITZ • *The Sound of Music: Enough Already*   328

"Good music is music that I want to hear. Bad music is music that I don't want to hear." As far as this caustic writer is concerned, the only difference between most music and Muzak is the spelling.

Fran Lebowitz on Writing   332

CAMILO JOSÉ VERGARA • *A Guide to the Ghettos*   **334**

Urban ghettos are more diverse than most people realize, argues Vergara, but all types can and should be abolished.

RALPH WHITEHEAD, JR. • *Class Acts: America's Changing Middle Class*   **342**

◄► The expanding middle class used to link the upper and lower classes, says this journalist and political analyst. Now the shrinking middle class is "caught in the crossfire" between rich and poor.

Ralph Whitehead, Jr., on Writing   **348**

ROBERT B. REICH • *Why the Rich Are Getting Richer and the Poor Poorer*   **350**

◄► Symbolic-analytic services, routine production services, or routine personal services: Which will you perform in the new global economy? And which social and economic class will that place you in?

Robert B. Reich on Writing   **359**

ADDITIONAL WRITING TOPICS   **361**

8. CAUSE AND EFFECT: Asking Why   363

THE METHOD   **363**
THE PROCESS   **365**
CAUSE AND EFFECT IN A PARAGRAPH:
   TWO ILLUSTRATIONS   **368**
    Using Cause and Effect to Write About Television
    Using Cause and Effect in an Academic Discipline

GORE VIDAL • *Drugs*   **371**

◄► A critic and novelist presents a radical idea for dealing with drug abuse: Legalize drugs. The effects will be less addiction and less crime.

Gore Vidal on Writing   **374**

A. M. ROSENTHAL • *The Case for Slavery*   **376**

◄► Would Americans today agree to legalize slavery? If not, why are some Americans proposing to legalize enslaving drugs?

A. M. Rosenthal on Writing   **379**

LAWRENCE A. BEYER • *The Highlighter Crisis*   **382**

> Are you holding a highlighter in your hand? Throw it out, advises this writer, before it reduces your reading to "a mindless swallowing of words."

JUNE JORDAN • *Requiem for the Champ*   **386**

> This African American writer doesn't condemn the rape conviction of boxer Mike Tyson, but she can't rejoice over it either. She understands too much about Tyson.

June Jordan on Writing   **392**

STEPHEN JAY GOULD • *Sex, Drugs, Disasters, and the Extinction of Dinosaurs*   **393**

> What caused the dinosaurs to disappear from earth? A scientist with a flair for explanation considers possible answers and selects the most likely.

Stephen Jay Gould on Writing   **402**

ADDITIONAL WRITING TOPICS   **404**

9. DEFINITION: Tracing a Boundary   407

THE METHOD   **407**
THE PROCESS   **409**
DEFINITION IN A PARAGRAPH: TWO ILLUSTRATIONS   **412**
    Using Definition to Write About Television
    Using Definition in an Academic Discipline

TOM WOLFE • *Pornoviolence*   **414**

◄► Swiftly and steadily, a new form of pornography has oozed into our films, television programs, books, and magazines. It's the kind that stacks the bodies deep and puts "hair on the walls."

Tom Wolfe on Writing   **422**

GLORIA STEINEM • *Erotica and Pornography*   **424**

◄► A founder of the American women's movement distinguishes between two representations of sex: erotica, which is about mutually pleasurable acts; and pornography, which is about "power and sex-as-weapon."

Gloria Steinem on Writing   **430**

JAMAICA KINCAID • *The Tourist*   **432**

What does it mean to be a tourist in a beautiful but impoverished country? Kincaid, a native of just such a place, has a bitter answer.

Jamaica Kincaid on Writing   **436**

BRUNO BETTELHEIM • *The Holocaust*   **438**

We use language to shield ourselves from feeling, says this renowned psychiatrist. But murder must be called murder.

JOSEPH EPSTEIN • *What Is Vulgar?*   **443**

Uncle Jake the junk man swilled soup from a tureen while sweating into it. Yet, claims the editor of *The American Scholar*, Jake doesn't fit the definition of *vulgar*. What does?

Joseph Epstein on Writing   **457**

ADDITIONAL WRITING TOPICS   **459**

10. ARGUMENT AND PERSUASION: Stating Opinions and Proposals   461

THE METHOD   **461**
    Basic Considerations
    Reasoning
        Data, Claim, and Warrant / Deductive and Inductive Reasoning / Logical Fallacies
THE PROCESS   **471**
ARGUMENT AND PERSUASION IN A PARAGRAPH:
    FOUR ILLUSTRATIONS   **473**
    Stating an Opinion About Television
    Stating a Proposal About Television
    Stating an Opinion in an Academic Discipline
    Stating a Proposal in an Academic Discipline

OPINIONS   **477**

H. L. MENCKEN • *The Penalty of Death*   **477**

◀▶ Just what do we gain when a murderer dies on the gallows? Here is a highly original view — one that you will have to look into your heart to confirm or deny.

H. L. Mencken on Writing   **482**

ALAN M. DERSHOWITZ • *Don't Pull the Plug on Televised Executions* **484**

◄► Deeply committed to First Amendment freedoms, the famous trial lawyer argues for protection of televised executions even though he fears they will increase public demand for capital punishment.

Alan M. Dershowitz on Writing **488**

NANCY MAIRS • *Disability* **489**

A writer with multiple sclerosis thinks she knows why the media carry so few images of disabled people like herself: viewers might conclude, correctly, that "there is something ordinary about disability itself."

Nancy Mairs on Writing **493**

CURTIS CHANG • *Streets of Gold: The Myth of the Model Minority* **495**

This prize-winning student research paper challenges the media's depiction of Asian Americans as a "model minority." The facts, the author says, tell a different story.

Curtis Chang on Writing **506**

PROPOSALS **507**

WILLIAM F. BUCKLEY, JR. • *Why Don't We Complain?* **507**

Most of us let ourselves be pushed around like patsies, argues an outspoken conservative, urging us to stand up and speak out against little oppressions and to make greater nuisances of ourselves.

William F. Buckley, Jr., on Writing **514**

MARTIN LUTHER KING, JR. • *I Have a Dream* **516**

◄► With force and eloquence, an inspired leader champions the rights of blacks and equality for all.

JONATHAN SWIFT • *A Modest Proposal* **522**

◄► The rich devour the poor—so why not commercialize cannibalism? With scathing irony, the supreme English satirist states his views in a fit of bitter indignation.

Jonathan Swift on Writing **532**

ADDITIONAL WRITING TOPICS **534**

PART TWO
MIXING THE METHODS
537

11. THE POWER OF FAMILY   541

VIVIAN GORNICK • *Mama Went to Work*   **542**

Spending her adolescence in the grip of her mother's grim, obsessive depression, the author barely understood the changes occurring within herself.

Vivian Gornick on Writing   547

CLIFFORD CHASE • *My Brother on the Shoulder of the Road*   **549**

The death of a brother from AIDS transforms this simple story of a shared childhood into a powerfully understated portrait of brotherly love.

Clifford Chase on Writing   561

RICHARD RODRIGUEZ • *Aria: A Memoir of a Bilingual Childhood*   **563**

Recalling both pleasures and pains of his boyhood, a Mexican American writer reflects on his two languages, Spanish and English, and his two cultures. His argument against bilingual education may provoke debate.

Richard Rodriguez on Writing   576

DAVID UPDIKE • *The Colorings of Childhood*   **578**

A white American married to a black African considers what life will be like for their son when his country, America, has such difficulty with color.

MAXINE HONG KINGSTON • *No Name Woman*   **589**

An adulterous woman is driven to suicide by her unforgiving family and village in China. A generation later, her American-born niece seeks to understand the story of someone whose name she has never dared to ask.

Maxine Hong Kingston on Writing   602

ADDITIONAL WRITING TOPICS   603

12. LANGUAGE AND TRUTH   605

GEORGE ORWELL • *Politics and the English Language*   606

Starting with the assumption that the English language is in trouble, Orwell urges action to rescue it. Here is a classic attack on smoke screens, murk, and verbosity in prose.

George Orwell on Writing   620

STEPHANIE ERICSSON • *The Ways We Lie*   623

Most of us couldn't get by without little lies, the writer acknowledges, but even these little lies corrupt, until "moral garbage becomes as invisible to us as water is to a fish."

DAVID SEGAL • *Excuuuse Me*   634

This commentator makes a surprising case for ethnic and other off-color humor. Misguidedly banished by "political correctness," these jokes in fact help keep us sane.

David Segal on Writing   638

MICHIKO KAKUTANI • *The Word Police*   640

Can changing the words we use alter our reality? This *New York Times* critic holds that "political correctness," while aiming for justice and inclusiveness, has hardened into a rigid, often absurd orthodoxy.

ADDITIONAL WRITING TOPICS   648

13. OUR PLACE IN THE ENVIRONMENT   649

ALBERT GORE, JR. • *Ships in the Desert*   650

Human activity is radically and rapidly transforming the earth. For Al Gore, now the nation's vice-president, the message is clear: The future of the planet is ours to decide.

LINNEA SAUKKO • *How to Poison the Earth*   659

A prize-winning student writer sets forth the process by which the earth can be polluted — and often is. What moves her to share such knowledge with her readers?

Linnea Saukko on Writing   663

SLAVENKA DRAKULIĆ • *Some Doubts About Fur Coats*   **664**

Like other environmental causes, this East European writer argues, the animal rightists' crusade against fur coats asks the world's poorer peoples to give up advantages they've never had.

LINDA HOGAN • *Waking Up the Rake*   **672**

A task as simple as raking an injured bird's enclosure can help repair what this Native American writer calls "the severed trust we humans hold with the earth."

Linda Hogan on Writing   678

ADDITIONAL WRITING TOPICS   679

14. DIVERSITY IN THE CURRICULUM   681

ISHMAEL REED • *America: The Multinational Society*   **682**

To all those defending the United States as a homogeneous culture, this controversial writer holds out an image of diversity: "The world is here. The world has been arriving at these shores for at least ten thousand years."

Ishmael Reed on Writing   688

ARTHUR M. SCHLESINGER, JR. • *The Cult of Ethnicity, Good and Bad*   **689**

A respected historian worries that the values that bound the American melting pot are evaporating in "the hullabaloo over 'multiculturalism' and 'political correctness.'"

Arthur M. Schlesinger, Jr., on Writing   693

KATHA POLLITT • *Why Do We Read?*   **695**

The debate over opening the literary canon to more works by women and minorities is almost beside the point, this writer says. The real issue is not what students *should* read but whether they *do* read.

ADDITIONAL WRITING TOPICS   705

USEFUL TERMS   707

INDEX   731

THEMATIC
TABLE OF CONTENTS

AUTOBIOGRAPHY

Maya Angelou, "Champion of the World"   49
William F. Buckley, Jr., "Why Don't We Complain?"   507
Clifford Chase, "My Brother on the Shoulder of the Road"   549
Judith Ortiz Cofer, "*Casa:* A Partial Remembrance of a Puerto Rican
    Childhood"   73
Annie Dillard, "Death of a Moth"   107
Slavenka Drakulić, "Some Doubts About Fur Coats"   664
Ralph Ellison, "On Being the Target of Discrimination"   55
M. F. K. Fisher, "The Broken Chain"   10
Vivian Gornick, "Mama Went to Work"   542
Nancy Mairs, "Disability"   489
Richard Rodriguez, "Aria: A Memoir of a Bilingual Childhood"   563
Brent Staples, "Black Men and Public Space"   159
Amy Tan, "The Language of Discretion"   187
James Thurber, "University Days"   64
E. B. White, "Once More to the Lake"   120

BIOGRAPHY

Bruce Catton, "Grant and Lee: A Study in Contrasts"   180
Barbara Ehrenreich, "The Wretched of the Hearth"   292
Maxine Hong Kingston, "No Name Woman"   589
June Jordan, "Requiem for the Champ"   386

CAPITAL PUNISHMENT

Alan M. Dershowitz, "Don't Pull the Plug on Televised Executions"   48
H. L. Mencken, "The Penalty of Death"   477

CHILDREN, FAMILY, AND GROWING UP

Maya Angelou, "Champion of the World"   49
Judy Brady, "I Want a Wife"   273
Clifford Chase, "My Brother on the Shoulder of the Road"   549
Judith Ortiz Cofer, "Casa: A Partial Remembrance of a Puerto Rican
    Childhood"   73
Stephanie Coontz, "A Nation of Welfare Families"   150
Christine D'Angelo, "Has the Chain Been Broken?"   34
Ralph Ellison, "On Being the Target of Discrimination"   55
M. F. K. Fisher, "The Broken Chain"   10
Vivian Gornick, "Mama Went to Work"   542
Maxine Hong Kingston, "No Name Woman"   589
Richard Rodriguez, "Aria: A Memoir of a Bilingual Childhood"   563
Jonathan Swift, "A Modest Proposal"   522
David Updike, "The Colorings of Childhood"   578
E. B. White, "Once More to the Lake"   120

CLASS

Barbara Lazear Ascher, "On Compassion"   140
Stephanie Coontz, "A Nation of Welfare Families"   150
Barbara Ehrenreich, "The Wretched of the Hearth"   292
Joseph Epstein, "What Is Vulgar?"   443
Martin Luther King, Jr., "I Have a Dream"   516
Robert B. Reich, "Why the Rich Are Getting Richer and the Poor
    Poorer"   350
Camilo José Vergara, "A Guide to the Ghettos"   334
Ralph Whitehead, Jr., "Class Acts: America's Changing Middle
    Class"   342

COMMUNITY

Maya Angelou, "Champion of the World"   49
Judith Ortiz Cofer, "Casa: A Partial Remembrance of a Puerto Rican
    Childhood"   73

Stephanie Coontz, "A Nation of Welfare Families"   150
Ralph Ellison, "On Being the Target of Discrimination"   55
Shirley Jackson, "The Lottery"   80
Martin Luther King, Jr., "I Have a Dream"   516
Maxine Hong Kingston, "No Name Woman"   589
Richard Rodriguez, "Aria: A Memoir of a Bilingual Childhood"   563
Arthur M. Schlesinger, Jr., "The Cult of Ethnicity, Good and Bad"   689
Camilo José Vergara, "A Guide to the Ghettos"   334

CULTURAL DIVERSITY

Curtis Chang, "Streets of Gold: The Myth of the Model Minority"   495
Judith Ortiz Cofer, "Casa: A Partial Remembrance of a Puerto Rican
     Childhood"   73
Ralph Ellison, "On Being the Target of Discrimination"   55
bell hooks, "Madonna"   303
June Jordan, "Requiem for the Champ"   386
Michiko Kakutani, "The Word Police"   640
Katha Pollitt, "Why Do We Read?"   695
Ishmael Reed, "America: The Multinational Society"   682
Richard Rodriguez, "Aria: A Memoir of a Bilingual Childhood"   563
Arthur M. Schlesinger, Jr., "The Cult of Ethnicity, Good and Bad"   689
David Segal, "Excuuuse Me"   634
Brent Staples, "Black Men and Public Space"   159
Amy Tan, "The Language of Discretion"   187
David Updike, "The Colorings of Childhood"   578

DEATH

Bruno Bettelheim, "The Holocaust"   438
Clifford Chase, "My Brother on the Shoulder of the Road"   549
Alan M. Dershowitz, "Don't Pull the Plug on Televised Executions"   484
Annie Dillard, "Death of a Moth"   107
Vivian Gornick, "Mama Went to Work"   542
Stephen Jay Gould, "Sex, Drugs, Disasters, and the Extinction of
     Dinosaurs"   393
Shirley Jackson, "The Lottery"   80
Linda Hogan, "Waking Up the Rake"   672
Maxine Hong Kingston, "No Name Woman"   589
H. L. Mencken, "The Penalty of Death"   477
Jessica Mitford, "Behind the Formaldehyde Curtain"   253
Jonathan Swift, "A Modest Proposal"   522
Virginia Woolf, "The Death of the Moth"   101

ENVIRONMENT

Slavenka Drakulić, "Some Doubts About Fur Coats"   664
Albert Gore, Jr., "Ships in the Desert"   650

Stephen Jay Gould, "Sex, Drugs, Disasters, and the Extinction of
    Dinosaurs"   393
Marvin Harris, "How Our Skins Got Their Color"   241
Linda Hogan, "Waking Up the Rake"   672
Mark Crispin Miller, "Dow Recycles Reality"   277
Linnea Saukko, "How to Poison the Earth"   659

HEALTH

Clifford Chase, "My Brother on the Shoulder of the Road"   549
Nancy Mairs, "Disability"   489

HISTORY

Bruno Bettelheim, "The Holocaust"   438
Bruce Catton, "Grant and Lee: A Study in Contrasts"   180
Stephanie Coontz, "A Nation of Welfare Families"   150
Martin Luther King, Jr., "I Have a Dream"   516
Ishmael Reed, "America: The Multinational Society"   682
Murray Ross, "Football Red and Baseball Green"   209
Arthur M. Schlesinger, Jr., "The Cult of Ethnicity, Good and Bad"   689
Gloria Steinem, "Erotica and Pornography"   424
Jonathan Swift, "A Modest Proposal"   522

HOMELESSNESS

Barbara Lazear Ascher, "On Compassion"   140
Anna Quindlen, "Homeless"   145
Camilo José Vergara, "A Guide to the Ghettos"   334

HUMOR AND SATIRE

Russell Baker, "The Plot Against People"   321
Judy Brady, "I Want a Wife"   273
Suzanne Britt, "Neat People vs. Sloppy People"   174
Joan Didion, "Marrying Absurd"   113
Barbara Ehrenreich, "The Wretched of the Hearth"   292
Fran Lebowitz, "The Sound of Music: Enough Already"   328
Merrill Markoe, "Conversation Piece"   227
H. L. Mencken, "The Penalty of Death"   477
Jessica Mitford, "Behind the Formaldehyde Curtain"   253
Linnea Saukko, "How to Poison the Earth"   659
David Segal, "Excuuuse Me"   634
Jonathan Swift, "A Modest Proposal"   522
James Thurber, "University Days"   64

LAW

Alan M. Dershowitz, "Don't Pull the Plug on Televised Executions"   484
H. L. Mencken, "The Penalty of Death"   477
A. M. Rosenthal, "The Case for Slavery"   376
Gore Vidal, "Drugs"   371

MANNERS AND MORALS

Barbara Lazear Ascher, "On Compassion"   140
Joan Didion, "Marrying Absurd"   113
Joseph Epstein, "What Is Vulgar?"   443
Stephanie Ericsson, "The Ways We Lie"   623
June Jordan, "Requiem for the Champ"   386
Michiko Kakutani, "The Word Police"   640
Jamaica Kincaid, "The Tourist"   432
Maxine Hong Kingston, "No Name Woman"   589
Merrill Markoe, "Conversation Piece"   227
Anna Quindlen, "Homeless"   145
A. M. Rosenthal, "The Case for Slavery"   376
David Segal, "Excuuuse Me"   634
Gloria Steinem, "Erotica and Pornography"   424
Brenda Ueland, "Tell Me More"   233
David Updike, "The Colorings of Childhood"   578
Gore Vidal, "Drugs"   371
Tom Wolfe, "Pornoviolence"   414

MARRIAGE

Judy Brady, "I Want a Wife"   273
Judith Ortiz Cofer, "*Casa:* A Partial Remembrance of a Puerto Rican
    Childhood"   73
Joan Didion, "Marrying Absurd"   113
Barbara Ehrenreich, "The Wretched of the Hearth"   292
M. F. K. Fisher, "The Broken Chain"   10
Vivian Gornick, "Mama Went to Work"   542
Maxine Hong Kingston, "No Name Woman"   589
David Updike, "The Colorings of Childhood"   578

MEDIA AND IMAGE

Curtis Chang, "Streets of Gold: The Myth of the Model Minority"   495
Alan M. Dershowitz, "Don't Pull the Plug on Televised Executions"   484
Barbara Ehrenreich, "The Wretched of the Hearth"   292
bell hooks, "Madonna"   303
Fran Lebowitz, "The Sound of Music: Enough Already"   328

Nancy Mairs, "Disability" 489
Mark Crispin Miller, "Dow Recycles Reality" 277
David Segal, "Excuuuse Me" 634
Gloria Steinem, "Erotica and Pornography" 424
David Updike, "The Colorings of Childhood" 578
Tom Wolfe, "Pornoviolence" 414

MINORITY EXPERIENCE

Maya Angelou, "Champion of the World" 49
Bruno Bettelheim, "The Holocaust" 438
Curtis Chang, "Streets of Gold: The Myth of the Model Minority" 495
Clifford Chase, "My Brother on the Shoulder of the Road" 549
Judith Ortiz Cofer, "*Casa:* A Partial Remembrance of a Puerto Rican
    Childhood" 73
Slavenka Drakulić, "Some Doubts About Fur Coats" 664
Ralph Ellison, "On Being the Target of Discrimination" 63
Jeff Greenfield, "The Black and White Truth About Basketball" 199
bell hooks, "Madonna" 303
June Jordan, "Requiem for the Champ" 386
Martin Luther King, Jr., "I Have a Dream" 516
Maxine Hong Kingston, "No Name Woman" 589
Nancy Mairs, "Disability" 489
Ishmael Reed, "America: The Multinational Society" 682
Richard Rodriguez, "Aria: A Memoir of a Bilingual Childhood" 563
Brent Staples, "Black Men and Public Space" 159
Amy Tan, "The Language of Discretion" 187
David Updike, "The Colorings of Childhood" 578
Camilo José Vergara, "A Guide to the Ghettos" 334

THE NATURAL WORLD

Emily Dickinson, "A narrow Fellow in the Grass" 129
Annie Dillard, "Death of a Moth" 107
Albert Gore, Jr., "Ships in the Desert" 650
Stephen Jay Gould, "Sex, Drugs, Disasters, and the Extinction of
    Dinosaurs" 393
Marvin Harris, "How Our Skins Got Their Color" 241
Linda Hogan, "Waking Up the Rake" 672
Linnea Saukko, "How to Poison the Earth" 659
E. B. White, "Once More to the Lake" 120
Virginia Woolf, "The Death of the Moth" 101

OTHER PEOPLES, OTHER COUNTRIES

Bruno Bettelheim, "The Holocaust" 438
Curtis Chang, "Streets of Gold: The Myth of the Model Minority" 495

Judith Ortiz Cofer, "*Casa:* A Partial Remembrance of a Puerto Rican
    Childhood"   73
Slavenka Drakulić, "Some Doubts About Fur Coats"   664
Jamaica Kincaid, "The Tourist"   432
Maxine Hong Kingston, "No Name Woman"   589
Ishmael Reed, "America: The Multinational Society"   682
Jonathan Swift, "A Modest Proposal"   522
Amy Tan, "The Language of Discretion"   187
David Updike, "The Colorings of Childhood"   578

PLACES

Judith Ortiz Cofer, "*Casa:* A Partial Remembrance of a Puerto Rican
    Childhood"   73
Joan Didion, "Marrying Absurd"   113
Annie Dillard, "Death of a Moth"   107
Ralph Ellison, "On Being the Target of Discrimination"   55
June Jordan, "Requiem for the Champ"   386
Jamaica Kincaid, "The Tourist"   432
Camilo José Vergara, "A Guide to the Ghettos"   334
E. B. White, "Once More to the Lake"   120
Virginia Woolf, "The Death of the Moth"   101

PSYCHOLOGY AND BEHAVIOR

Barbara Lazear Ascher, "On Compassion"   140
Suzanne Britt, "Neat People vs. Sloppy People"   174
William F. Buckley, Jr., "Why Don't We Complain?"   507
Christine D'Angelo, "Has the Chain Been Broken?"   34
Slavenka Drakulić, "Some Doubts About Fur Coats"   664
Ralph Ellison, "On Being the Target of Discrimination"   55
Stephanie Ericsson, "The Ways We Lie"   623
M. F. K. Fisher, "The Broken Chain"   10
Vivian Gornick, "Mama Went to Work"   542
bell hooks, "Madonna"   303
Shirley Jackson, "The Lottery"   80
June Jordan, "Requiem for the Champ"   386
Michiko Kakutani, "The Word Police"   640
Jamaica Kincaid, "The Tourist"   432
Maxine Hong Kingston, "No Name Woman"   589
Merrill Markoe, "Conversation Piece"   227
David Segal, "Excuuuse Me"   634
Gail Sheehy, "Predictable Crises of Adulthood"   283
Brent Staples, "Black Men and Public Space"   159
Gloria Steinem, "Erotica and Pornography"   424
Amy Tan, "The Language of Discretion"   187
Brenda Ueland, "Tell Me More"   233

READING, WRITING, AND LANGUAGE

Bruno Bettelheim, "The Holocaust"   438
Lawrence A. Beyer, "The Highlighter Crisis"   382
Annie Dillard, "Death of a Moth"   107
Peter Elbow, "Desperation Writing"   246
Stephanie Ericsson, "The Ways We Lie"   623
Michiko Kakutani, "The Word Police"   640
Merrill Markoe, "Conversation Piece"   227
George Orwell, "Politics and the English Language"   606
Katha Pollitt, "Why Do We Read?"   695
Richard Rodriguez, "Aria: A Memoir of a Bilingual Childhood"   563
David Segal, "Excuuuse Me"   634
Amy Tan, "The Language of Discretion"   187
Brenda Ueland, "Tell Me More"   233
Tom Wolfe, "Pornoviolence,"   414
Writers on Writing: See Index for specific writers and topics.

SCHOOL AND COLLEGE

Lawrence A. Beyer, "The Highlighter Crisis"   382
Peter Elbow, "Desperation Writing"   246
Katha Pollitt, "Why Do We Read?"   695
Richard Rodriguez, "Aria: A Memoir of a Bilingual Childhood"   563
James Thurber, "University Days"   64

SCIENCE AND TECHNOLOGY

Russell Baker, "The Plot Against People"   321
Albert Gore, Jr., "Ships in the Desert"   650
Stephen Jay Gould, "Sex, Drugs, Disasters, and the Extinction of
    Dinosaurs"   393
Mark Crispin Miller, "Dow Recycles Reality"   277
Linnea Saukko, "How to Poison the Earth"   659

SELF-DISCOVERY

Clifford Chase, "My Brother on the Shoulder of the Road"   549
Annie Dillard, "Death of a Moth"   107
Slavenka Drakulić, "Some Doubts About Fur Coats"   664
Ralph Ellison, "On Being the Target of Discrimination"   55
Stephanie Ericsson, "The Ways We Lie"   623
M. F. K. Fisher, "The Broken Chain"   10
Vivian Gornick, "Mama Went to Work"   542
Linda Hogan, "Waking Up the Rake"   672
June Jordan, "Requiem for the Champ"   386

Jamaica Kincaid, "The Tourist"   432
Maxine Hong Kingston, "No Name Woman"   589
Richard Rodriguez, "Aria: A Memoir of a Bilingual Childhood"   563
Gail Sheehy, "Predictable Crises of Adulthood"   283
Brent Staples, "Black Men and Public Space"   159
Amy Tan, "The Language of Discretion"   187
Brenda Ueland, "Tell Me More"   233
E. B. White, "Once More to the Lake"   120

SEXUALITY

Clifford Chase, "My Brother on the Shoulder of the Road"   549
bell hooks, "Madonna"   303
June Jordan, "Requiem for the Champ"   386
Maxine Hong Kingston, "No Name Woman"   589
Gloria Steinem, "Erotica and Pornography"   424
Tom Wolfe, "Pornoviolence"   414

SOCIAL CUSTOMS

Judith Ortiz Cofer, "*Casa:* A Partial Remembrance of a Puerto Rican
    Childhood"   73
Joan Didion, "Marrying Absurd"   113
Slavenka Drakulić, "Some Doubts About Fur Coats"   664
Joseph Epstein, "What Is Vulgar?"   443
Stephanie Ericsson, "The Ways We Lie"   623
bell hooks, "Madonna"   303
Shirley Jackson, "The Lottery"   80
June Jordan, "Requiem for the Champ"   386
Jamaica Kincaid, "The Tourist"   432
Maxine Hong Kingston, "No Name Woman"   589
Fran Lebowitz, "The Sound of Music: Enough Already"   328
Merrill Markoe, "Conversation Piece"   227
Jessica Mitford, "Behind the Formaldehyde Curtain"   253
Amy Tan, "The Language of Discretion"   187
Gloria Steinem, "Erotica and Pornography"   424
Brenda Ueland, "Tell Me More"   233
David Updike, "The Colorings of Childhood"   578
E. B. White, "Once More to the Lake"   120

SPORTS AND LEISURE

Maya Angelou, "Champion of the World"   49
Jeff Greenfield, "The Black and White Truth About Basketball"   199
June Jordan, "Requiem for the Champ"   386
Jamaica Kincaid, "The Tourist"   432

Fran Lebowitz, "The Sound of Music: Enough Already"   328
Murray Ross, "Football Red and Baseball Green"   209
E. B. White, "Once More to the Lake"   120

VIOLENCE

Christine D'Angelo, "Has the Chain Been Broken?"   34
M. F. K. Fisher, "The Broken Chain"   10
Linda Hogan, "Waking Up the Rake"   672
June Jordan, "Requiem for the Champ"   386
Maxine Hong Kingston, "No Name Woman"   589
Gloria Steinem, "Erotica and Pornography"   424
Tom Wolfe, "Pornoviolence"   414

WOMEN AND MEN

Judy Brady, "I Want a Wife"   273
Clifford Chase, "My Brother on the Shoulder of the Road"   549
Judith Ortiz Cofer, "*Casa:* A Partial Remembrance of a Puerto Rican
    Childhood"   73
Barbara Ehrenreich, "The Wretched of the Hearth"   292
bell hooks, "Madonna"   303
June Jordan, "Requiem for the Champ"   386
Maxine Hong Kingston, "No Name Woman"   589
Gloria Steinem, "Erotica and Pornography"   424
Brenda Ueland, "Tell Me More"   233

WORK

Stephanie Coontz, "A Nation of Welfare Families"   150
Barbara Ehrenreich, "The Wretched of the Hearth"   292
Vivian Gornick, "Mama Went to Work"   542
Robert B. Reich, "Why the Rich Are Getting Richer and the Poor
    Poorer"   350
Gail Sheehy, "Predictable Crises of Adulthood"   283
Camilo José Vergara, "A Guide to the Ghettos"   334
Ralph Whitehead, Jr., "Class Acts: America's Changing Middle Class"
    342

THE
BEDFORD
READER

FIFTH EDITION

INTRODUCTION

WHY READ? WHY WRITE?
WHY NOT PHONE?

Many prophets have forecast the doom of the word on paper. Soon, they have argued, books and magazines will be read on pocket computers. Newspapers will be found only in attics, supplanted by interactive television. The mails will be replaced by electronic message boards.

The prophets have been making such forecasts for many decades, but book sales remain high, magazines and newspapers keep publishing, and the Postal Service has trouble keeping up with volume. In the electronic office, the computer workstation is an island in a sea of paper: Evidently, the permanent, word-on-paper record still has its advantages.

Even if the day comes when we throw away pens and paper, it is doubtful that the basic aims and methods of writing will completely change. Whether on paper or on screens, we will need to arrange our thoughts in a clear order. We will still have to explain them to others plainly and forcefully.

That is why, in almost any career or profession you may enter, you will be expected to read continually and also to write. This book assumes that reading and writing are a unity. Deepen your mastery of one, and you deepen your mastery of the other. The experience of carefully reading an excellent writer, noticing not only what the writer has to say but also the quality of its saying, rubs off (if you are patient and perceptive) on your own writing. "We go to college," said the poet Robert Frost, "to be given one more chance to learn to read in case we haven't learned in high school. Once we have learned to read, the rest can be trusted to add itself *unto us.*"

For any writer, reading is indispensable. It turns up fresh ideas; it stocks the mind with information, understanding, examples, and illustrations; it instills critical awareness of one's surroundings. When you have a well-stocked and girded mental storehouse, you tell truths, even small and ordinary truths, and so write what most readers will find worth reading, instead of building shimmering spires of words in an attempt to make a reader think, "Wow, what a grade A writer." Thornton Wilder, playwright and novelist, put this advice memorably: "If you write to *impress* it will always be bad, but if you write to *express* it will be good."

USING *THE BEDFORD READER*

The Essays

In this book, we trust, you'll find at least a few essays you will enjoy and care to remember. *The Bedford Reader* features work by many of the finest nonfiction writers, past and present.

The essays deal with more than just writing and literature and such usual concerns of English courses; they cut broadly across a college curriculum. You'll find writings on science, history, business, law, religion, popular culture, women's studies, sociology, education, adult development, the environment, music, sports, cities, politics, the media, and minority experience. Some writers recall their childhoods, their families, their own college days, their problems and challenges. Some explore matters likely to spark controversy: drug use, funerals, sex roles, race relations, class distinctions, bilingual schooling, pornography, conservation, the death penalty. Some writers are intently serious; others, funny. In all, these sixty-nine selections — including one story and one poem — reveal kinds of reading you will meet in other college courses. Such reading is the usual diet of well-informed people with lively minds — who, to be sure, aren't found only on campuses.

The essays have been chosen with one main purpose in mind: to show you how good writers write. Don't feel glum if at first you find an immense gap in quality between E. B. White's writing and yours. Of course there's a gap: White is an immortal with a unique style that he perfected over half a century. You don't have to judge your efforts by comparison. The idea is to gain whatever writing techniques you can. If you're going to learn from other writers, why not go to the best of them? Do you want to know how to define an idea so that the definition is vivid and clear? Read Tom Wolfe on "porno-violence." Do you want to know how to tell a story about your childhood and make it stick in someone's memory? Read Maya Angelou. Incidentally, not all the selections in this book are the work of professional writers: As Christine D'Angelo, Curtis Chang, and Linnea Saukko prove, students, too, write essays worth studying.

This book has another aim: to encourage you in critical reading, meaning thoughtful, open-minded, questioning reading. Like everyone else, you face a daily barrage of words — from the information and advertisements on television, from course texts and lectures, even from relatives and friends. Mulling over the views of the writers in this book, figuring out their motives and strategies, agreeing or disagreeing with their ideas, will help you learn to manage, digest, and use, in your own writing, what you read and hear.

The Organization

As a glance over the table of contents will show, the essays in *The Bedford Reader* fall into fourteen chapters: Each of the first ten explains a familiar method of developing ideas, such as DESCRIPTION or CLASSIFICATION or DEFINITION, and the essays illustrate the method; each of the last four chapters focuses on a subject, such as family or the environment, and the essays illustrate how, most often, the methods work together.

These methods of development aren't empty jugs to pour full of any old, dull words. Neither are they straitjackets woven by fiendish English teachers to pin your writing arm to your side and keep you from expressing yourself naturally. Amazingly, these methods can be ways to discover what you know, what you need to know, how to say what you have to say, and how to shape it.

Suppose, for example, you set out to write about two popular singers — their sounds, their styles, their looks, what they are like offstage — by the method of COMPARISON AND CONTRAST. With luck, you may find the method prompting you to notice similarities and differences between the two singers that you hadn't dreamed of noticing. Using the methods, such little miracles of creating and finding take place with heartening regularity. Give the methods a try. See if they don't help you find more to say, more that you feel is worth saying.

Reading the illustrations in *The Bedford Reader*, you'll discover two important facts about the methods of development. First, they are flexible: Just about any method can point a way into just about any subject, and two writers using the same method will probably approach the same subject very differently. To demonstrate this flexibility, in each method chapter we offer a sample paragraph on television, a sample paragraph drawn from a college textbook, and a pair of essays by different authors on the same general subject (such as sports or conversation or capital punishment).

The second thing you'll discover about the methods of development is that a writer never sticks to just one method all the way through an essay. Even when one method predominates, as in all the essays in the methods chapters (1–10), you'll see the writer pick up another method, let it shape a passage, and then move on to yet another method — all to achieve some overriding aim. In "The Black and White Truth About Basketball," Jeff Greenfield mainly compares and contrasts the styles of black and white players, but he begins with a paragraph that follows another method: giving EXAMPLES. Later, he gives still more examples; he briefly describes famous players in action; he defines the terms *rhythm, "black" basketball,* and *"white" basketball*; he examines the CAUSES AND EFFECTS of each style of play. The point is that Greenfield employs whatever methods suit his purpose: to explain the differences between two playing styles.

So the methods are like oxygen, iron, and other elements that make up substances in nature: all around us, indispensable to us, but seldom found alone and isolated, in laboratory-pure states. When you read an essay in a chapter called "Description" or "Classification," don't expect it to describe or classify in every line, but do notice how the method is central to the writer's purpose. Then, when you read the essays in the last four, thematic chapters, notice how the "elements" of description, example, comparison, definition, and so on rise to prominence and recede as the writer's need dictates.

The Questions, Writing Topics, and Glossary

Following every essay, you'll find questions on meaning, writing strategy, and language that can help you analyze the selection and learn from it. (You can see a sample of how these questions work when we analyze M. F. K. Fisher's "The Broken Chain," starting on p. 10.) These questions are followed by at least three suggestions for writing. One of them, labeled "Connections," links the essay with one or two others in the book. Another, labeled "Critical Writing," asks you to read the essay and write about it with your critical faculties alert (more on this in a moment). More writing topics conclude each chapter.

In the material surrounding the essays, certain terms appear in CAPITAL LETTERS. These are words helpful in discussing both the essays in this book and the essays you write. If you'd like to see such a term defined and illustrated, you can find it in the glossary at the back of the book: Useful Terms. This section offers more than just brief definitions. It is there to provide you with further information and support.

Writers on Writing

We have tried to give this book another dimension. We want to show that the writers represented here do not produce their readable and informative prose on the first try, as if by magic, leaving the rest of us to cope with writer's block, awkward sentences, and all the other difficulties of writing. Take comfort and cheer: These writers, too, struggled to make themselves interesting and clear. In proof, we visit their workshops littered with crumpled paper and forgotten coffee cups. Later in this introduction, when we discuss the writing process briefly and include an essay by a student, Christine D'Angelo, we also include her drafts and her thoughts about them. Then after most of the other essays are statements by the writers, revealing how they write (or wrote), offering their tricks, setting forth things they admire about good writing.

No doubt you'll soon notice some contradictions in these statements: The writers disagree about when and how to think about their readers, about whether outlines have any value, about whether style follows subject or vice versa. The reason for the difference of opinion is, simply, that no two writers follow the same path to finished work. Even the same writer may take the left instead of the customary right fork if the writing situation demands a change. A key aim of providing D'Angelo's drafts and the other writers' statements on writing, then, is to suggest the sheer variety of routes open to you, the many approaches to writing and strategies for succeeding at it. At the very end of the book, an index points you toward the writers' comments on such practical matters as writing introductions, finding your point, and revising sentences.

READING AN ESSAY

Whatever career you enter, much of the reading you will do — for business, not for pleasure — will probably be hasty. You'll skim: glance at words here and there, find essential facts, catch the drift of an argument. To cross oceans of print, you won't have time to paddle: You'll need to hop a jet. By skimming, you'll be able to tear through screens full of electronic mail or quickly locate the useful parts of a long report.

But other reading that you do for work, most that you do in college, and all that you do in this book call for reading word for word. You may be trying to understand how a new company policy affects you, or researching a complicated historical treaty, or (in using this book) looking for pointers to sharpen your reading and writing skills. To learn from the essays here how to write better yourself, expect to spend an hour or two in the company of each one. Does the essay assigned for today remain unread, and does class start in five minutes? "I'll just breeze through this little item," you might tell yourself. But no, give up. You're a goner.

Good writing, as every writer knows, demands toil, and so does CRITICAL READING — reading that looks beneath the surface of the writing, that seeks to understand how the piece works and whether it succeeds. Never try to gulp down a rich and potent essay without chewing; all it will give you is indigestion. When you're going to read an essay in depth, seek out some quiet place — a library, a study cubicle, your room (provided it doesn't also hold a cranky baby or two roommates playing poker). Flick off the radio, stereo, or television. What writer can outsing Aretha Franklin or Luciano Pavarotti, or outshout a kung fu movie? The fewer the distractions, the easier your task will be and the more you'll enjoy it.

How do you read an essay? Exactly how, that is, do you read it critically, master its complexities, learn how a good writer writes, and so write better yourself? To find out, we'll be taking a close look at an actual essay, M. F. K. Fisher's "The Broken Chain." You'll find it rewards the time you spend on it.

The Preliminaries

Critical reading starts before you read the first word of the essay. Like a pilot circling an airfield, you take stock of what's before you, locating clues to the essay's content and the writer's biases.

The Title

Often the title will tell you the writer's subject, as in H. L. Mencken's "The Penalty of Death" or Marvin Harris's "How Our Skins Got Their Color." Sometimes the title immediately states the THESIS, the main point the writer will make: "I Want a Wife." The title may set forth the thesis as a question: "Why Don't We Complain?" Some titles spell out the method a writer proposes to follow: "Grant and Lee: A Study in Contrasts." The TONE of the title may also reveal the writer's attitude toward the material. If a work is named "Why the Rich Are Getting Richer and the Poor Poorer," the title gives you an idea of the writer's approach, all right; and so does that of an informal, irritable essay such as "The Sound of Music: Enough Already." The reader, in turn, approaches each work in a different way — with serious intent, or set to chuckle. Some titles reveal more than others. M. F. K. Fisher's title, "The Broken Chain," is a bit mysterious. We may suspect that the author does not mean "chain" literally (a bicycle chain) but figuratively (like a chain of events or a chain reaction). The title hints at change (a chain breaks), so we may guess that this broken chain lies at the heart of a story. The rest is for us to find out.

Whatever it does, a title sits atop its essay like a neon sign. It tells you what's inside or makes you want to venture in. To pick an alluring title for an essay of your own is a skill worth cultivating.

The Author

Whatever you know about a writer — background, special training, previous works, outlook, or ideology — often will help you guess something about the essay before you read a word of it. Is the writer on new taxes a political conservative? Expect an argument against added "revenue enhancement." Is the writer a liberal? Expect an argument that new social programs are worth the price. Is the writer a feminist? An athlete? An internationally renowned philosopher? A popular television comedian? By knowing something about a writer's background or beliefs, you may know beforehand a little of what he or she will say.

To help provide such knowledge, this book supplies biographical notes. The one on M. F. K. Fisher before "The Broken Chain" (p. 10) tells us that Fisher often wrote about food but that she told other stories as well. You won't know until you read it whether "The Broken Chain" is about food. But if you guess from the note that the essay will be thought provoking, enjoyable, and readily understandable, you will be right.

Where the Essay Was First Published

Clearly, it matters to a writer's credibility whether an article called "Living Mermaids: An Amazing Discovery" first saw print in *Scientific American,* a magazine for scientists and interested nonscientists, or in a popular tabloid weekly, sold at supermarket checkout counters, that is full of eye-popping sensations. But no less important, finding out where an essay first appeared can tell you for whom the writer was writing. In this book we'll strongly urge you as a writer to think of your AUDIENCE, your readers, and to try looking at what you write as if through their eyes. To help you develop this ability, we tell you something about the sources and thus the original readers of each essay you study, in a note just before the essay. (Such a note precedes "The Broken Chain" on p. 10.) After you have read the sample essay, we'll further consider how having a sense of your readers helps you write.

When the Essay Was First Published

Knowing in what year an essay was first printed may give you another key to understanding it. A 1988 essay on mermaids will contain statements of fact more recent and more reliable than an essay printed in 1700 — although the older essay might contain valuable information, too, and perhaps some delectable language, folklore, and poetry. In *The Bedford Reader,* the brief introductory note on every essay tells you not only where but also when the essay was originally printed. If you're reading an essay elsewhere — say, in one of the writer's books — you can usually find this information on the copyright page.

The First Reading

On first reading an essay, you don't want to bog down over every troublesome particular. "The Broken Chain" is written for an educated audience, and that means the author may use a few large words when they seem necessary. If you meet any words that look intimidating, take them in your stride. When, in reading a rich essay, you run into an unfamiliar word or name, see if you can figure it out from its surroundings. If a word stops you cold and you feel lost, circle it in pencil; you can always look it up later. (In a little while we'll come back to the helpful habit of reading with a pencil. Indeed, some readers feel more confident with pencil in hand from the start.)

The first time you read an essay, size up the forest; later, you can squint at the acorns all you like. Glimpse the essay in its entirety. When you start to read "The Broken Chain," don't even think about dissecting it. Just see what Fisher has to say.

M. F. K. FISHER

MARY FRANCES KENNEDY FISHER was born in 1908 and began telling stories at age four. Raised in California and educated there and in Illinois and France, Fisher became renowned for her writing about food. Her first book, *Serve It Forth* (1937), was followed by more than sixteen others before her death at eighty-three in 1992. Not all of them concerned eating, and even those on food, such as *How to Cook a Wolf* (1942), expanded the subject to encompass needs and pleasures of all sorts. Besides writing her books, Fisher produced essays, poetry, and a screenplay, kept house, tended a vineyard in Switzerland, and translated a French gastronomical classic, Brillat-Savarin's *The Physiology of Taste*. Her works reveal a keen sense of story, a sharply observant, independent mind, and a search for the truths in her own and others' lives.

The Broken Chain

"The Broken Chain" was written in 1983 and first published in Fisher's last book, *To Begin Again* (1992). Taking her lead from news headlines, Fisher flashes back to an incident in 1920 that transformed her and her father, Rex, and could perhaps help others as well.

There has been more talk than usual lately about the abuse and angry beating of helpless people, mostly children and many women. I think about it. I have never been beaten, so empathy is my only weapon against the ugliness I know vicariously. On the radio someone talks about a chain of violence. When is it broken? he asks. How?

When I was growing up, I was occasionally spanked and always by my father. I often had to go upstairs with him when he came home from the *News* for lunch, and pull down my panties and lay myself obediently across his long bony knees, and then steel my emotions against the ritualistic whack of five or eight or even ten sharp taps from a wooden hairbrush. They were counted by my age, and by nine or ten he began to use his hand, in an expert upward slap that stung more than the hairbrush. I often cried a little, to prove that I had learned my lesson.

I knew that Rex disliked this duty very much, but that it was part of being Father. Mother could not or would not punish us.

Instead, she always said, by agreement with him and only when she felt that things were serious enough to drag him into it, that she would have to speak with him about the ugly matter when he came home at noon.

This always left me a cooling-off period of thought and regret and conditioned dread, even though I knew that I had been the cause, through my own stupidity, of involving both my parents in the plot. 4

Maybe it was a good idea. I always felt terrible that it was dragged out. I wished that Mother would whack me or something and get it over with. And as I grew older I resented having to take several undeserved blows because I was the older child and was solemnly expected to be a model to my younger sister, Anne. She was a comparatively sickly child, and spoiled and much cleverer than I, and often made it bitterly clear to me that I was an utter fool to take punishment for her own small jaunty misdoings. I continued to do this, far past the fatherly spankings and other parental punishments, because I loved her and agreed that I was not as clever as she. 5

Once Rex hit me. I deserved it, because I had vented stupid petulance on my helpless little brother David. He was perhaps a year old, and I was twelve. We'd all left the lunch table for the living room and had left him sitting alone in his high chair, and Father spotted him through the big doors and asked me to get him down. I felt sulky about something, and angered, and I stamped back to the table and pulled up the wooden tray that held the baby in his chair, and dumped him out insolently on the floor. David did not even cry out, but Rex saw it and in a flash leapt across the living room toward the dining table and the empty high chair and gave me a slap across the side of my head that sent me halfway across the room against the big old sideboard. He picked up David and stood staring at me. Mother ran in. A couple of cousins came, looking flustered and embarrassed at the sudden ugliness. 6

I picked myself up from the floor by the sideboard, really raging with insulted anger, and looked disdainfully around me and then went silently up the stairs that rose from the dining room to all our sleeping quarters. Behind me I could hear Mother crying, and then a lot of talk. 7

I sat waiting for my father to come up to the bedroom that Anne and I always shared, from her birth until I was twenty, in our two family homes in Whittier, and in Laguna in the summers, and then when we went away to three different schools. I knew I was going to be punished. 8

Finally Father came upstairs, looking very tired. "Daughter," he 9 said, "your mother wants you to be spanked. You have been bad. Pull down your panties and lie across my knees."

I was growing very fast and was almost as tall as I am now, with small growing breasts. I looked straight at him, not crying, and got into the old position, all long skinny arms and legs, with my bottom bared to him. I felt insulted and full of fury. He gave me twelve expert upward stinging whacks. I did not even breathe fast, on purpose. Then I stood up insolently, pulled up my sensible Munsingwear panties, and stared down at him as he sat on the edge of my bed.   10

"That's the last time," he said.   11

"Yes," I said. "And you hit me."   12

"I apologize for that," he said, and stood up slowly, so that once again I had to look up into his face as I had always done. He went out of the room and downstairs, and I stayed alone in the little room under the eaves of the Ranch house, feeling my insult and anger drain slowly out and away forever. I knew that a great deal had happened, and I felt ashamed of behaving so carelessly toward my helpless little brother and amazed at the way I had simply blown across the room and into the sideboard under my own father's wild stinging blow across my cheek. I wished that I would be maimed, so that he would feel shame every time he looked at my poor face. I tried to forget how silly I'd felt, baring my pubescent bottom to his heavy dutiful slaps across it. I was full of scowling puzzlements.   13

My mother came into the room, perhaps half an hour later, and wrapped her arms around me with a tenderness I had never felt from her before, although she had always been quietly free with her love and her embraces. She had been crying but was very calm with me, as she told me that Father had gone back to the *News* and that the cousins were playing with the younger children. I wanted to stay haughty and abused with her, but sat there on the bed quietly, while she told me about Father.   14

She said that he had been beaten when he was a child and then as a growing boy, my age, younger, older. His father beat him, almost every Saturday, with a long leather belt. He beat all four of his boys until they were big enough to tell him that it was the last time. They were all of them tall strong people, and Mother said without any quivering in her voice that they were all about sixteen before they could make it clear that if it ever happened again, they would beat their father worse than he had ever done it to them.   15

He did it, she said, because he believed that he was ridding them of the devil, of sin. Grandfather, she said quietly, was not a brute or a beast, not sinful, not a devil. But he lived in the wild prairies and   16 raised strong sons to survive, as he had, the untold dangers of frontier life. When he was starting his family, as a wandering newspaperman and printer of political broadsides, he got religion. He was born again. He repented of all his early wildness and tried to keep his four sons from "sinning," as he came to call what he had done before he accepted God as his master.

I sat close to Mother as she explained to me how horrible it had been only a few minutes or hours before in my own short life, when Rex had broken a long vow and struck his own child in unthinking anger. She told me that before they married, he had told her that he had vowed when he was sixteen to break the chain of violence and that never would he strike anyone in anger. She must help him. They promised each other that they would break the chain. And then today he had, for the first time in his whole life, struck out, and he had struck his oldest child.   17

I could feel my mother trembling. I was almost overwhelmed by pity for the two people whom I had betrayed into this by my stupidity. "Then why did he hit me?" I almost yelled suddenly. She said that he hardly remembered doing it, because he was so shocked by my dumping the helpless baby out onto the floor. "Your father does not remember," she repeated. "He simply had to stop you, stop the unthinking way you acted toward a helpless baby. He was . . . He suddenly acted violently. And it is dreadful for him now to see that, after so long, he can be a raging animal. He thought it would never happen. That is why he has never struck any living thing in anger. Until today."   18

We talked for a long time. It was a day of spiritual purging, obviously. I have never been the same — still stupid but never unthinking, because of the invisible chains that can be forged in all of us, without our knowing it. Rex knew of the chain of violence that was forged in him by his father's whippings, brutal no matter how mistakenly committed in the name of God. I learned of what violence could mean as I sat beside my mother, that day when I was twelve, and felt her tremble as she put her arm over my skinny shoulders and pulled me toward her in an embrace that she was actually giving to her husband.   19

It is almost certain that I stayed aloof and surly, often, in the next years with my parents. But I was never spanked again. And I know as surely as I do my given name that Rex no longer feared the chain of violence that had bound him when he was a boy. Perhaps it is as well that he hit me, the one time he found that it had not been broken for him.   20

Rereadings

When first looking into an essay, you are like a person who arrives at the doorway of a large and lively room, surveying a party going on inside. Glancing around the room, you catch the overall picture: the locations of the food and the drinks, of people you know, of people you don't know but would certainly like to. You have just taken such an overview of Fisher's essay. Now, stepping through the doorway of the essay and going on in, you can head for whatever beckons most strongly.

Well, what will it be? If it is writing skills you want, then go for those elements that took skill or flair or thoughtful decision on the writer's part. Most likely, you'll need to reread the essay more than once, go over the difficult parts several times, with all the care of someone combing a snag from the mane of an admirable horse.

Writing While Reading

In giving an essay this going-over, many students — some of the best — find a pencil in hand as good as a currycomb for a horse's mane. The pencil concentrates the attention wonderfully. If the book is yours, you can underline any idea that strikes you as essential. You can score things with vertical lines; you can bracket passages. You can vent your feelings ("Bull!" "Yes!" "Says who?"). You can write notes in the margins. (If the book is borrowed, you can accomplish the same thing with just a bit more effort by making notes on a separate sheet of paper.)

Here, as an example, are the jottings of one student, Christine D'Angelo, on a paragraph of Fisher's essay:

> "I apologize for that," he said, and stood up slowly, so that once again I had to look up into <u>his face</u> as I had always done. *What was his expression?*
> He went out of the room and downstairs, and I stayed alone in the little room under the eaves of the Ranch house, <u>feeling my insult and anger drain slowly out and away forever.</u> I knew that a great deal had happened, and I felt ashamed of behaving so carelessly toward my helpless little brother and amazed at the way I had simply blown across the room and into the sideboard under my own father's <u>wild stinging blow</u> across my cheek. I wished that I would be maimed, so that he would feel shame every time he looked at my poor face. I tried to forget how silly I'd felt, baring my (pubescent) bottom to his heavy dutiful slaps across it. I was full of <u>scowling puzzlements.</u>
>
> *already forgives father?*
>
> *← difference in blow and spanking (to author and father)*
>
> (?)
>
> *Good phrase for child's mixed emotions*

Such pencilwork, you'll find, helps you behold the very spine of the essay, as if in an X-ray view. You'll feel you have put your own two cents into it. While reading this way, you're being a writer. Your pencil tracks will jog your memory, too, when you review for a test, when you take part in class discussion, or when you want to write about what you've read. Some readers favor markers that roll pink or yellow ink over a word or line, leaving it legible, but you can't make notes with a highlighter. (In his essay "The Highlighter Crisis," p. 382, Lawrence A. Beyer scorns these markers for making reading a "mindless swallowing of words.")

Summarizing

It's usually good practice, especially with more difficult essays, to SUMMARIZE the content in writing to be sure you understand it or, as often happens, to come to understand it. We use summary all the time to fill friends in on the gist of a story — shrinking a two-hour movie to a single sentence, "This woman is recruited to be a spy, and she stops a ring of double agents." In summarizing a work of writing, you digest, *in your own words,* what the author says: You take the essence of the author's meaning, without the supporting evidence and other details that make that gist convincing or interesting. When you are practicing reading and the work is short (the case with the reading you do in this book), you may want to make this a two-step procedure: first write a summary sentence for every paragraph or related group of paragraphs; then summarize those sentences in two or three others that capture the heart of the author's meaning.

Here is a two-step summary of "The Broken Chain." (The numbers in parentheses refer to paragraph numbers in the essay.) First, the longer version:

(1) Fisher wonders about the "chain of violence" against children and women. (2–3) As a child, she was sometimes spanked on her bare bottom by her father, who carried out the job reluctantly as a father's responsibility. (4–5) The spanking did not occur immediately after the bad behavior, and the delay left Fisher feeling sorry and afraid and often resentful of her younger sister, who escaped such punishment. (6) Then once Fisher peevishly dropped her baby brother on the floor, and her father struck her suddenly and violently in anger. (7–13) She was simply furious at first, but she became remorseful, vindictive, and embarrassed as well when her father later spanked her for her deed and apologized for striking her. (14–16) Her mother then comforted her and explained that her father had been regularly beaten by his own father.

(17–18) Her father had sworn that he would "break the chain of violence" by never hitting another person out of anger, and now he was horrified to discover that he, too, could be violent. (19) The incident helped Fisher understand her father and violence. (20) It also broke the chain by releasing her father from his fear that any violence in him must control him as it had his own father.

Now the short summary:

Fisher's father sometimes reluctantly spanked her as punishment, but once when she deliberately dropped her baby brother he struck her suddenly and violently. Her father had not escaped the "chain of violence" begun by his own father's regular beatings, but the incident released him from his fear that the chain must control him.

(We're suggesting that you write summaries for your personal use, but the technique is also useful when you discuss other people's works in your writing. Using a summary in such writing, you must use your own words or use quotation marks for the author's words, and either way you must acknowledge the source in a citation.)

Reading Critically

Summarizing will start you toward understanding the author's meaning, but it won't take you as far as you're capable of going, or as far as you'll need to go in school or work or just to live well in our demanding Information Age. Passive, rote learning (such as memorizing the times tables in arithmetic) won't do. You require techniques for comprehending what you encounter. But more: You need tools for discovering what's beneath the surface of an essay or case study or business letter or political message. You need ways to discriminate between the trustworthy and the not so and to apply what's valid in your own work and life.

We're talking here about critical thinking, reading, and writing — not "negative," the common conception of *critical*, but "thorough, thoughtful, question-asking, judgment-forming." When you approach something critically, you harness your faculties, your fund of knowledge, and your experiences to understand, appreciate, and evaluate the object. Using this book — guided by questions on meaning, writing strategy, and language — you'll read an essay and ask what the author's purpose and main idea are, how clear they are, and how well supported. You'll isolate which writing techniques the author has used to special advantage, what hits you as particularly fresh, clever, or wise — and what *doesn't* work, too. You'll discover exactly what the writer is saying, how he or she says it, and whether, in the end, it was worth saying. In class discussions and in writing, you'll tell others what you think and why.

Critical reading is a process involving several overlapping operations: analysis, inference, synthesis, and evaluation. Say you're listening to a new album by a band called the Alley Cats. Without thinking much about it, you isolate melodies, song lyrics, and instrumentals — in other words, you ANALYZE the album by separating it into its parts. Analysis is a way of thinking so basic to us that it has its own chapter (6) in this book. For reading in this book, you'll consciously analyze essays by looking at the author's main idea, support for the idea, special writing strategies, and other elements.

Say that after listening to the Alley Cats' new album, you conclude that it reveals a preoccupation with traditional blues music and themes. Now you are using INFERENCE, drawing conclusions about a work based on your store of information and experience, your knowledge of the creator's background and biases, and your analysis. When you infer, you add to the work, making explicit what was only implicit. In critical reading, inference is especially important in discovering a writer's ASSUMPTIONS: opinions or beliefs, often unstated, that direct the writer's choices of ideas, support, writing strategies, and language. A writer who favors gun control may assume without saying so that some individual rights (such as the right to bear arms) may be infringed for the good of the community. A writer who opposes gun control may assume the opposite — that in this case the individual's right is superior to the community's.

Back to the Alley Cats: What are they trying to accomplish with their new album? Is it different from their previous album in its understanding of the blues? Answering such questions leads you into SYNTHESIS, linking elements into a whole, or linking two or more wholes. During synthesis, you use your special aptitudes, interests, and training to reconstitute the analyzed work so that it now contains not just the original elements but also your sense of their underpinnings and relationships. About an essay you might ask why the author elicits contradictory feelings from readers, or what this essay has to do with that other essay, or what this essay has to do with your life.

Analysis, inference, and synthesis overlap — so much so that it's often impossible to distinguish one from the other during critical reading. To stave off confusion, in this book we use the word *analysis* to cover all three of these operations: separating elements, drawing conclusions about them, *and* reconstituting them.

That leaves a separate category for EVALUATION, judging the quality of the work, which is not always part of critical reading. You'll probably form a judgment of the Alley Cats' new album (Is the band getting better or just standing still?), but often you (and your teachers) will be satisfied with a nonjudgmental reading of a work. ("Nonjudgmental" does not mean "uncritical": you will still be expected to analyze, infer, and synthesize.) When you *do* evaluate, you determine adequacy, significance, value. You answer questions such as whether an essay moves you as it was intended to, or whether the author has proved a case, or whether the argument is even worthwhile.

The following comments on M. F. K. Fisher's "The Broken Chain" show how a critical reading can work.

Meaning

"No man but a blockhead," declared Samuel Johnson, "ever wrote except for money." Perhaps the industrious critic, journalist, and dictionary maker was remembering his own days as a literary drudge in London's Grub Street; but surely most people who write often do so for other reasons.

When you read an essay, you'll find it rewarding to ask, "What is this writer's PURPOSE?" By purpose, we mean the writer's apparent reason for writing: what he or she was trying to achieve with readers. A purpose is as essential to a good, pointed essay as a destination is to a trip. It affects every choice or decision the writer makes. (On vacation, of course, carefree people sometimes climb into a car without a thought and go happily rambling around; but if a writer rambles like that in an essay, the reader may plead, "Let me out!") In making a simple statement of a writer's purpose, we might say that the writer writes *to entertain* readers, or *to explain* something to them, or *to persuade* them. To state a purpose more fully, we might say that a writer writes not just to persuade but "to tell readers a story to illustrate the point that when you are being cheated it's a good idea to complain," or not just to entertain but "to tell a horror story to make chills shoot down readers' spines." If the essay is an argument meant to convince, a fuller statement of its writer's purpose might be "to win readers over to the writer's opinion that San Antonio is the most livable city in the United States," or "to persuade readers to take action: write their representatives and urge more federal spending for the rehabilitation of criminals."

"But," the skeptic might object, "how can I know a writer's purpose? I'm no mind reader, and even if I were, how could I tell what Jonathan Swift was trying to do? He's dead and buried." And yet writers living and dead reveal their purposes in what they write, just as visibly as a hiker leaves footprints.

What is M. F. K. Fisher's purpose in writing? If you want to be more exact, you can speak of her *main purpose* or *central purpose,* for "The Broken Chain" fulfills more than one. Fisher clearly wants to tell her readers something about her parents and herself as a child. She is not averse to entertaining readers with details capturing the fierce moodiness of a twelve-year-old. But Fisher's main purpose is larger than these and encompasses them. She has heard much lately of child abuse, and a recollection from her own childhood might throw some light on the problem. She wants to help.

How can you tell a writer's purpose? This is where analysis, inference, and synthesis come in. Fisher hints at her purpose in the first paragraph, asking "When is [the chain of violence] broken? . . . How?" The rest of her essay answers these questions: At least for her father, the chain broke when he no longer feared it (para. 20). The opening questions and last paragraph form the THESIS of the essay — the point made for a purpose, the overwhelming idea that the writer communicates. Some writers will come right out, early on, and sum up this central idea in a sentence or two. George Orwell, in his essay "Politics and the English Language," states the gist of his argument in his second paragraph:

> Modern English, especially written English, is full of bad habits which spread by imitation and which can be avoided if one is willing to take the necessary trouble. If one gets rid of these habits one can think more clearly, and to think clearly is a necessary first step towards political regeneration.

Orwell's thesis is obvious early on. Sometimes, however, like Fisher, a writer will introduce and conclude the thesis at the beginning and end. Other writers won't come out and state their theses in any neat Orwellian capsule at all. Even so, the main point of a well-written essay will make itself clear to you — so clear that you can sum it up in a sentence of your own. What might that sentence be for Fisher's essay? Perhaps this: The chain of violence against children may be broken when a former victim understands that violence need not take control even when it is expressed.

It's part of your job as an active reader to answer questions like these: What is the writer's purpose? How does it govern the writer's choices? Is it actually achieved? Does the thesis come through? How is it supported? Is the support adequate to convince you of the author's sincerity and truthfulness? (Such conviction is a basic transaction between writer and reader, even when the writer isn't seeking the reader's outright agreement or action.) Sometimes you'll be confused by a writer's point — "What *is* this about?" — and sometimes your confusion won't yield to repeated careful readings. That's when you'll want to toss the book or magazine aside in exasperation, but you won't always have the choice: A school or work assignment or just an urge to figure out the writer's problem may keep you at it. Then it'll be up to you to figure out why the writer fails — in essence, to clarify what's unclear — by, say, digging for buried assumptions that you may not agree with or by spotting where facts and examples fall short.

With some reservations, we think M. F. K. Fisher achieves her purpose. Her essay is engaging. She gives plenty of details to place us in her shoes, to experience what she experienced. Her story about her father rings true, as does the lesson to be learned from it. The story and the lesson do lean on certain assumptions, though, and these are bound to influence a reader's response. One is that the father's spankings are justified and, because they are reluctant and unemotional, do not constitute violence — at least not the abusive violence that concerns Fisher. Even if the spankings are justified, a second, more ticklish assumption is that their manner is appropriate. Fisher describes hereself merely as feeling "silly . . . baring my pubescent bottom" for the spanking (para. 13), but these days many readers might condemn her father for expecting her to undress. If you are one of these readers, the essay may be hard to accept. For us, such objections are understandable but ultimately irrelevant because Fisher was writing of a time (1920) when spankings and whippings (even on bare bottoms) were common methods of disciplining children.

Analyzing writers' purposes and their successes and failures makes you an alert and critical reader. Applied to your own writing, this analysis also gives you a decided advantage, for when you write with a clear-cut purpose in mind, aware of your assumptions, you head toward a goal. Of course, sometimes you just can't know what you are going to say until you say it, to echo the English novelist E. M. Forster. In such a situation, your purpose emerges as you write. But the earlier and more exactly you define your purpose, the easier you'll find it to fulfill.

Writing Strategy

To the extent that M. F. K. Fisher holds our interest and engages our sympathies, it pays to ask, How does she succeed? (When a writer bores or angers us, we ask why he or she fails.) As we've already hinted, success and failure lie in the eye of the beholder: The reader knows. Almost all writing is a *transaction* between a writer and an audience, maybe one reader, maybe millions. Conscious writers make choices intended to get their audience on their side so that they can achieve their purpose. These choices are what we mean by STRATEGY in writing.

Fisher's audience was the readers of her memoir, *To Begin Again*. She might have assumed that many of these readers would be familiar with her earlier writing and predisposed to like her work. But even for such an appreciative audience, and certainly for newcomers, Fisher would have to be interesting and focused, making readers (us) care about *this* piece. She grabs our attention right at the start by connecting with the disturbing and controversial issue of physical abuse. She doesn't oversell, though — she hasn't been abused herself — so she whets our appetites without setting us up for disappointment. When she begins her story, she keeps involving us by referring to common feelings and experiences in memorably specific terms. Even if we've never been spanked, we can feel her father's "long bony knees" and the "sharp taps" of the brush (para. 2). We share Fisher's resentment of her sister, who "made it bitterly clear to me that I was an utter fool to take punishment for her own small jaunty misdoings" (5). We know that adolescent feeling of "stupid petulance" that caused Fisher to drop her brother (6) and her "raging with insulted anger" at being struck by her father (7). We see that "little room under the eaves" where Fisher found herself "full of scowling puzzlements" (13). We submit as her mother "wrapped her arms around me with a tenderness I had never felt from her before" (14), "an embrace that she was actually giving to her husband" (19). We believe Fisher because of how vivid and precise she is all along.

Part of a writer's strategy — Fisher's, too — is in the methods used to elicit and arrange details such as these. Fisher draws mainly on two methods: narration (telling a story) and description (conveying the evidence of the senses). But she also gives examples of spankings and her feelings about them (2 5), contrasts the "heavy dutiful slaps" of a spanking with the "wild stinging blow" of being struck (13), analyzes her own reactions (13), defines the "chain of violence" (17, 19), and examines the causes and effects of child abuse (15–20). In short, Fisher uses nearly every method discussed in this book, asking each one to perform the work it's best suited for. As we noted earlier, one method or another may predominate in an essay (as narration and description do in Fisher's), but other methods will help the writer explore the subject in paragraphs or shorter passages.

Aside from the details and the methods used to develop them, probably no writing strategy is as crucial to success as finding an appropriate structure. Writing that we find interesting and clear and convincing almost always has UNITY (everything relates to the main idea) and COHERENCE (the relations between parts are clear). When we find an essay wanting, it may be because the writer got lost in digressions or couldn't make the parts fit together.

Sometimes structure almost takes care of itself. When she chose the method of narration, for instance, Fisher also chose a chronological sequence (reporting events as they occurred in time). But she still had to emphasize certain events and de-emphasize others. She lingers over the important moments: dropping her brother and being struck by her father (6–7), the following encounters with her father (8–13) and her mother (14–18). She compresses all the events that contribute background but are not the heart of the story, notably the previous spankings (2–4) and taking the blame for her sister (5).

This kind of handiwork will be even more evident in essays where the method of development doesn't dictate an overall structure. Then the writer must mold and shape ideas and details to pique, hold, and direct our interest. One writer may hit us with the big idea right at the start and then fill us in on the details. Another writer may gradually unfold the idea, leading to a surprise. One writer may arrange information in order of increasing importance; another may do the opposite. Like all other choices in writing, these come out of the writer's purpose: What is the aim? What do I want readers to think or feel? What's the best way to achieve that? As you'll see in this book, there are as many options as there are writers.

Language

To examine the element of language is often to go even more deeply into an essay and how it was made. Fisher, you'll notice, is a writer whose language is rich and varied. It isn't bookish. Many expressions from common speech lend her prose vigor and naturalness. "I always felt terrible that it was dragged out," she writes (5). Her father "gave me a slap across the side of my head that sent me halfway across the room against the big old sideboard" (6). When spanked, she says, "I did not even breathe fast, on purpose" (10). "I have never been the same —" she concludes, "still stupid but never unthinking" (19). These relaxed sentences suit the material: Fisher's recollections of herself as a fresh, moody adolescent. At the same time, Fisher is an adult addressing adults, and her vocabulary reflects as much. Consult a dictionary if you need help defining *vicariously* (1), *ritualistic* (2), *conditioned* (4), *petulance, insolently* (6), *disdainfully* (7), *pubescent* (13), or *haughty* (14).

Fisher's words and sentence structures not only sharpen and animate her meaning but also convey her attitudes and elicit them from readers. They create a TONE, the equivalent of tone of voice in speaking. Whether it's angry, sarcastic, or sad, joking or serious, tone carries almost as much information about a writer's purpose as the words themselves do. Fisher's tone is sincere, matter-of-fact. In true adolescent fashion, she occasionally veers into indignation or embarrassment or compassion; but she never indulges in histrionics, which would overwhelm the sensations and make her account untrustworthy.

With everything you read, as with "The Broken Chain," it's instructive to study the writer's tone so that you are aware of whether and how it affects you. Pay particular attention to the CONNOTATIONS of words — their implied meanings, their associations. We sympathize when Fisher takes those "twelve expert upward stinging whacks" (10) — stinging whacks *hurt*. We identify with her "scowling puzzlements" (13) — the anger and hurt are there and also the confusion. When one writer calls the homeless "society's downtrodden" and another calls them "human refuse," we know something of their attitudes and can use that knowledge to analyze and evaluate what they say about homelessness.

One other use of language is worth noting in Fisher's essay and in many others in this book: FIGURES OF SPEECH, bits of colorful language not meant to be taken literally. In one instance, Fisher makes her adolescent gangliness vivid with HYPERBOLE, or exaggeration, describing herself as "all skinny arms and legs" (10). Most memorable is the extended METAPHOR of the "chain of violence" (17, 19–20) — not an actual, physical chain, of course, but a pattern of behavior passed from generation to generation. This chain is "invisible"; it had "bound" Fisher's father since childhood; and finally, as the title tells us, it was "broken." Such a colorful comparison — a chain and a destructive behavior — gives Fisher's essay flavor and force. (More examples of figures of speech can be found under Useful Terms, p. 707.)

Many questions in this book point to such figures, to oddities of tone, or to troublesome or unfamiliar words. We don't wish to swamp you in details or make you a slave to your dictionary, only to get you thinking about how meaning and effect begin at the most basic level, with the word. As a writer, you can have no traits more valuable to you than a fondness and respect for words and a yen to experiment with them.

WRITING

Suggestions for Writing

Throughout this book every essay is followed by several "Suggestions for Writing." Usually at least one encourages you to write something similar to the essay you have just read (same subject, perhaps, or different subject but same approach). Always one suggestion, labeled "Critical Writing," asks you to take a deliberate, critical look at the essay. And always one suggestion, labeled "Connections," helps you relate the essay to one or two other essays in the book. You may not wish to take these suggestions exactly as worded; they may merely urge your own thoughts toward what you want to say. Here are four possibilities for M. F. K. Fisher's "The Broken Chain."

1. Following Fisher's example, recount an incident from your childhood or adolescence that changed you or someone you know or both. Provide plenty of specific details so that the reader understands the incident and its effects.
2. If you have had some experience with physical abuse (as a counselor, bystander, victim, abuser) and you care to write about it, compose an essay that develops a thesis about the problem. You do not have to write in the first person (*I*) unless you want to. Draw on personal experience, observation, or reading as needed to support your thesis. (If you draw on reading, be sure to acknowledge your sources.)
3. CRITICAL WRITING. Write an essay in which you analyze and evaluate Fisher's attitudes toward physical punishment. Consider what Fisher actually says about spanking and what her words convey about her feelings. (You will have to infer some of her assumptions.) When you are sure you understand Fisher's point of view, explain it and then evaluate it, using specific evidence from the essay and from your own sources (experience, observation, reading). Do you agree with Fisher? Does she omit any important considerations? In your view, do her attitudes toward physical punishment weaken or strengthen the essay? Why?
4. CONNECTIONS. Both Fisher's "The Broken Chain" and Judith Ortiz Cofer's "*Casa:* A Partial Remembrance of a Puerto Rican Childhood" (p. 73) address the ways love, cultural knowledge, and standards of behavior are passed from one generation to another. Compare and contrast these two essays, looking closely at how Fisher's parents and Ortiz's grandmother love and educate their children and grandchildren. Be specific in your analysis, using evidence from the essays and, if you

wish, your own experience. (If you need help with the method of comparison and contrast, see Chap. 4.)

The Writing Process

To complete an assignment like those above, you need in a way to duplicate the reading process, moving from sketchy impressions to rich understandings as you gain mastery over your material. Like critical reading, writing is no snap: As this book's Writers on Writing attest, even professionals do not produce thoughtful, well-ordered, detailed, attention-getting essays in a single draft. Writing well demands, and rewards, a willingness to work recursively — to begin tentatively, perhaps, and then to double back, to welcome change and endure frustration, to recognize and exploit progress. Something of this recursive process is captured in the case study beginning on page 27. A student, Christine D'Angelo, wrote this piece for *The Bedford Reader* in response to M. F. K. Fisher's essay. D'Angelo provided us with her notes and drafts, along with her comments on her progress at each stage.

For you, as for D'Angelo and most writers, the recursive writing process may proceed through three rough stages. First is a DISCOVERY period, when you feel your way into an assignment. If you're writing about something you've read (such as an essay in this book), you'll spend this stage reading and rereading, coming to understand the work, figuring out what you think of it, figuring out what you have to *say* about it. From notes during reading to jotted phrases, lists, or half-finished paragraphs after reading, this stage should always be a writing stage. You may even produce a rough draft. The important thing is to let yourself go: Do not, above all, concern yourself with making beautiful sentences or correcting errors. Such self-consciousness at this stage will only jam the flow of thoughts. If your idea of "audience" is "teacher with sharp pencil" (not, by the way, a fair picture), then temporarily blank out your audience, too.

Sooner or later, this discovery stage yields to DRAFTING: arranging ideas in sequence, filling in their details, spelling out their relationships. For most, this is the occasion for further exploration, but with a sharper focus. Here you may be concerned with clarifying your purpose, isolating your thesis. You may experiment with tone. You may try out different structures. It's best to stay fairly loose during drafting so that you're free to wander down promising avenues or consider changing direction altogether. As during discovery, you'll want to keep your eyes on what's ahead, not obsess over the pebbles underfoot — the possible mistakes, "wrong" words, and bumpy sentences that you can attend to later. This is an important message that many inexperienced writers miss: It's okay to make mistakes. You can fix them later.

If it helps you produce writing, you may view your draft as a kind of dialog with readers, fulfilling their expectations, answering the questions you imagine they would ask. But some writers save this kind of thinking for the next stage, REVISION. Literally "re-seeing," revision is the price you pay for the freedom to experiment and explore. Initially the work centers on you and your material, but gradually it shifts into that transaction we spoke of earlier between you and your reader. And that means stepping outside the intense circle of you-and-the-material to see the work as a reader, with whatever qualities you imagine that reader to have. Questions after most essays in this book ask you to analyze how the writers' ideas of their readers have influenced their writing strategies, and how you as a reader react to the writers' choices. These analyses will teach you much about responding to your own readers.

Like many writers, you will be able to concentrate better if you approach revision as at least a two-step process. First you question fundamental matters, asking questions like these:

Will my purpose be clear to readers? Have I achieved it?
What is my thesis? Have I proved it?
Is the essay unified (all parts relate to the thesis)?
Is the essay coherent (the parts relate clearly)?
Will readers be able to follow the organization?
Have I given enough details, examples, and other specifics for readers to understand me and stay with me?
Is the tone appropriate for my purpose?
Have I used the methods of development to full advantage?

When these deeper issues are resolved, then you look at the surface of the writing:

Do PARAGRAPH breaks help readers grasp related information?
Do TRANSITIONS tell readers where I am making connections, additions, and other changes?
Are sentences smooth and concise? Do they use PARALLELISM, EMPHASIS, and other techniques to clarify meaning?
Do words say what I mean, and are they as vivid as I can make them?

Are my grammar and punctuation correct?
Are any words misspelled?

Two-step revision is like inspecting a ship before it sails. First check underwater for holes to make sure the boat will stay afloat. Then look above water at what will move the boat and please the passengers: intact sails, sparkling hardware, gleaming decks.

An Essay-in-Progress

In the following pages, watch Christine D'Angelo as she develops an essay through several drafts. Her topic is the third one on page 24, about M. F. K. Fisher's attitudes toward physical punishment. Besides her drafts, D'Angelo has also given us some comments that enlighten us about her thinking at various stages in the writing process.

Notes on Reading

"I have never been beaten"— she doesn't consider her father's punishment as beating. (¶ 1)

Very conscious of how to play role of victim (excellent description of kids that age).

— "I often cried a little, to prove that I had learned my lesson" (¶ 2)

— wishes she were maimed (¶ 13)

— "I wanted to stay haughty and abused with her" (¶ 14)

"Your mother wants you to be spanked": typical of fathers' tendency not to take responsibility for feelings. More common when trying to express tenderness: "Your mother was worried sick about you," "Your mother and I are going to miss you," "You know we love you," etc. The potentially embarrassing feelings are diluted.

She doesn't seem to consider spankings
as violent
     "<u>Once</u> Rex hit me" (¶ 6)
     "<u>And</u> you hit me" (¶ 12)

Calling father first name: distancing?
("Father" vs. "Rex")

Justifies father's actions
    — he "disliked this duty very much" (¶ 3)
    — "fatherly spankings" (¶ 5)
    — "two people whom I had betrayed
      into this" (¶ 18)

Is father's reaction justified by narrator's act?
Both are acts of violence. It's easy to
understand his anger.

"Once Rex hit me" and "and you hit me"
literally confusing until you become aware that
she doesn't count spanking as "hitting."

Mother shares same refusal to see spanking as violent.

Fisher's ideas about physical punishment outdated.

D'Angelo's Comments on Reading Notes. I think I have a lot of evidence
here to answer question 3, about Fisher's attitudes toward physical
punishment and whether they weaken or strengthen the essay.

It's clear that she doesn't think of the spankings as violent. I like
the idea of talking about how Fisher's assumptions confuse the reader
who doesn't share them. I was confused that she opened with "I have
never been beaten" and then recounted many spankings. (This could
be a good introduction.)

Even though they're interesting ideas, I don't think I'll be able
to use anything about the narrator knowing how to play the victim
or fathers' inability to express their emotions. (Not in this paper at
least.)

First Draft

How is the reader of "The Broken Chain" to reconcile the   1
narrator's account of the physical punishment she suffered from
her father up to the age of twelve with her assumption in the
very first paragraph that "I have never been beaten"?

Knowing that the father has a history of spanking the narra-   2
tor, the reader has a hard time interpreting her statement
"Once Rex hit me." Why does she say "once" if he actually hit
her quite often? In the key scene in which the narrator is
spanked for having dropped her baby brother on the floor, her
father says "That's the last time," after he has finished
spanking her. To which she responds, "Yes. And you hit me."
"Once" and "and" make no sense. Until we realize that spanking
seems to fall under the realm of just punishment but on the
other hand violence outside the clear realm of punishment is
unjustifiable.

The narrator's mother shares this distinction. Describing   3
her husband's history of violence in the family, she maintains
that up until now he had succeeded in breaking the chain. "He
has never struck any living thing in anger," she says, "Until
today." In other words, the spankings have never counted as
part of the chain of violence.

It is interesting to note that narrator never questions why   4
it should be the father who struggles constantly to keep his
violence in check, who has this "duty" rather than the mother.
After all, isn't such a choice rather like putting a dieter in
charge of guarding the refrigerator?

When we understand that the narrator does not consider her   5
father's spankings to be violent, we can only call this assumption into question, in fact it is easier to justify the father's response to the dumping of the baby on the floor, itself
a violent act that could have been deadly, than his more calculated, repeated capital punishment. If the father is so concerned with breaking the "chain of violence" in his family, why
can he not look to alternative methods of punishment? And
again, why is it him and not the mother who must carry out this
punishment?

```
     I can only speculate on Fisher's reasons for not classifying   6
her father's spankings as violent. But capital punishment is no
longer considered an acceptable form of punishment--it is rec-
ognized as violence in its own right. In writing this essay,
Fisher's purpose was to expose in a family the "chain of vio-
lence" against children passed down from generation to genera-
tion. But she herself is too blind to see that spanking is a
form of violence too.
```

D'Angelo's Comments on First Draft. This gets at what I want to say pretty well, but there are some big holes. I need an explicit thesis — an answer to the question I pose in the first paragraph — to tie the whole thing together. The last sentence of paragraph 2 is really my thesis: that the narrator makes a distinction between two kinds of violence — one kind (the spankings) being OK, the other (the slap) unjustified. The rest of the paper goes on to explain this distinction and call it into question. I just need to make this thesis clearer and bring it up into the first paragraph.

Paragraph 2 needs to be developed more, probably expanded into two paragraphs. I think the first paragraph can pretty much stay the way it is, talking about readers' confusion. But the idea of the last sentence — now the thesis — needs to be fleshed out, expanded into an entire paragraph. Need to *define* the narrator's distinction between justified and unjustified violence.

Paragraph 4 goes nowhere. It's an interesting point, but doesn't fit in with the rest of the paper. Think it's going to have to be cut. (Same for last sentence of paragraph 5.)

The last sentence of the conclusion is too angry and judgmental. Instead, I could say something about how the very fact that Fisher doesn't see the spankings as violent just goes to show how subtle the "chain" is.

Title??? It should work in the thesis somehow.

Big mistake: spanking is *corporal,* not *capital,* punishment.

Revised Draft

Has the Chain Been Broken?
Two Ideas of Violence in "The Broken Chain"

How is the reader of "The Broken Chain" to reconcile the
narrator's account of the physical punishment she suffered from
her father up to the age of twelve with her assumption in the
very first paragraph that "I have never been beaten"? *The
answer lies in the difference she makes between
what is in her view justified and unjustified
violence.*   1

(¶) *This distinction is never made explicit in the essay
and is apt to lead to confusion on the readers' part.*   2

Λ Knowing that the father has a history of spanking the narrator, the reader has a hard time interpreting her statement
"Once Rex hit me." ~~Why does she say "once" if he actually hit~~
Likewise,   i
~~her quite often?~~ /n the key scene in which the narrator is
spanked for having dropped her baby brother on the floor, her
father says "That's the last time," after he has finished
spanking her. To which she responds, "Yes. And you hit me."
What does she mean by "and"?
~~"Once" and "and" make no sense. Until we realize that spanking~~
~~seems to fall under the realm of just punishment but on the~~
~~other hand violence outside the clear realm of punishment is~~
~~unjustifiable.~~

*The "once" and "and" make no sense until we
realize that they do not refer to the fathers
spankings. They refer to his violent, immediate
reaction to the narrator's dropping the baby.
It becomes clear that "spanking" and "hitting" have
different values for the narrator depending on
the intention behind it. Spanking, in her
eyes, falls under the realm of just
punishment, unpleasant though it may be,*   3

she sees it as an appropriate response to
her own crime. On the other hand, violence
outside the clear realm of punishment, in
this case the blow, is unjustifiable,
despite the fact that both are responses
to the same wrongdoing (and each probably
hurts about as much as the other!).

The narrator's mother shares this distinction. Describing   4
between "just" and "unjust" violence.
her husband's history of violence in the family, she maintains
that up until now he had succeeded in breaking the chain. "He
has never struck any living thing in anger," she says, "Until
today." In other words, the spankings have never counted as
part of the chain of violence.

~~It is interesting to note that narrator never questions why
it should be the father who struggles constantly to keep his
violence in check, who has this "duty" rather than the mother.
After all, isn't such a choice rather like putting a dieter in
charge of guarding the refrigerator?~~

When we understand that the narrator does not consider her   5
father's spankings to be violent, we can only call this assumption into question, in fact it is easier to justify the father's response to the dumping of the baby on the floor, itself
a violent act that could have been deadly, than his more calculated, repeated corporal ~~capital~~ punishment. If the father is so concerned with breaking the "chain of violence" in his family, why
can he not look to alternative methods of punishment? ~~And
again, why is it him and not the mother who must carry out this
punishment?~~ In law, a premeditated crime is more serious than one committed on the spur of the moment.

I can only speculate on Fisher's reasons for not classifying   6
her father's spankings as violent. Perhaps she
loved and respected her parents too
much to judge them objectively, even
sixty years after the essay.

corporal

But ~~capital~~ punishment is no longer considered an acceptable form of punishment—it is recognized as violence in its own right. In writing this essay, Fisher's purpose was to expose in a family the "chain of violence" against children passed down from generation to generation. But ~~she herself is too blind to see that spanking is a form of violence too.~~ *her refusal to recognize corporal punishment as a form of violence is a good example of how subtle the chain is, and why it is so hard to break.*

D'Angelo's Comments on Revised Draft. Hangs together much better now; more coherent. Every paragraph has something to do with the distinction between "good" and "bad" violence. The new title incorporates both the thesis (the two standards of violence) and the hint in the conclusion about the chain not necessarily being broken.

The first sentence is abrupt. Need a "cushion" to ease the reader into the paper.

I think saying "the narrator" is too impersonal for an autobiographical essay. Since this is a personal essay, not fiction, I could just say "Fisher." And since the events in the essay really happened, I should change them to the past tense, keeping present tense when referring to Fisher as writer, in 1983. This will help make it clear that there are really two "Fishers" in question.

Conclusion: Last sentence is still too angry. I could change "refusal" to "inability," taking some of the blame off Fisher.

Need to edit for rough or awkward sentences, spelling and grammar mistakes, and poor word choice.

Edited Paragraph

The "once" and "and" make no sense until we realize that they ~~do not~~ refer *not* to the fathers spankings*,* ~~They refer~~ *but* to his violent, immediate reaction to ~~the narrator's~~ *Fisher's* dropping the baby. It becomes clear that "spanking" and "hitting" have different values for ~~the narrator~~ *Fisher* depending on the intention behind ~~it.~~ *them.* Spanking, in her eyes, falls under the realm of just punishment*;* ~~U~~npleasant though it may ~~be,~~ *have been,* she sees it as an appropriate response to her own ~~crime. On the other hand,~~ *misconduct. But* violence outside the ~~clear~~ *well-defined* realm of punishment*/* in this case the blow*,* is unjustifiable, despite the fact that both are re—sponses to the same wrongdoing*/* (and ~~each~~ probably hurt*s* ~~about as much as the other!~~) *the same!).*

Final Draft

Has the Chain Been Broken?

Two Ideas of Violence in "The Broken Chain"

There is a problem of definition in "The Broken Chain." How   1
is the reader to reconcile M. F. K. Fisher's account of the
physical punishment she suffered from her father up to the age
of twelve with her assertion in the very first paragraph that
"I have never been beaten"? The answer lies in her distinction
between justified and unjustified violence.

This distinction is never made explicit in the essay. Know—   2
ing that the father had a history of spanking Fisher, the
reader has a hard time interpreting her statement "Once Rex hit
me." Then after Fisher was spanked for dropping her baby
brother on the floor and her father said, "That's the last
time," she responded, "Yes. And you hit me." What did she mean
by "and"?

The "once" and "and" make no sense until we realize that   3
they refer not to the father's spankings but to his violent,
immediate reaction to Fisher's dropping the baby. It becomes
clear that "spanking" and "hitting" have different values for
Fisher depending on the intention behind them. Spanking, in her
eyes, falls under the realm of just punishment. Unpleasant
though it may have been, she sees it as an appropriate response
to her own misconduct. But violence outside the well—defined
realm of punishment—in this case the blow—is unjustifiable,
despite the fact that both are responses to the same wrongdoing
(and probably hurt the same!).

The mother shared Fisher's distinction between "just" and   4
"unjust" violence. Describing the "chain of violence" passed
down from generation to generation in her husband's family, she
maintained that up until then he had succeeded in breaking the
chain. "He has never struck any living thing in anger," she
said. "Until today." In other words, the spankings never
counted.

Once we understand that Fisher does not consider her father's spankings to be violent, we can only call this assumption into question. In fact, it is easier to justify the father's heated response to the dumping of the baby on the floor, a violent act that could have been deadly, than his more calculated, repeated corporal punishment. In law, a premeditated crime is more serious than one committed on the spur of the moment.

One can only speculate on Fisher's reasons for not classifying her father's spankings as violent. Perhaps she loves and respects her parents too much to judge them objectively, even sixty years after the events of the essay. But physical punishment is no longer universally considered acceptable; it is recognized as violence in its own right. In writing this essay, Fisher intends to expose the "chain of violence" against children passed from generation to generation in a family. But her inability to recognize corporal punishment as a form of violence is a good example of how subtle the chain is, and why it is so hard to break.

PART ONE

THE METHODS

1

NARRATION
Telling a Story

THE METHOD

"What happened?" you ask a friend who sports a luminous black eye. Unless he merely grunts, "A golf ball," he may answer you with a narrative — a story, true or fictional.

"OK," he sighs, "you know The Tenth Round? That nightclub down by the docks that smells of formaldehyde? Last night I heard they were giving away $500 to anybody who could stand up for three minutes against this karate expert, the Masked Samurai. And so . . ."

You lean forward. At least, you lean forward *if* you love a story. Most of us do, particularly if the story tells us of people in action or in conflict, and if it is told briskly, vividly, and with insight into the human heart. Narration, or storytelling, is therefore a powerful method by which to engage and hold the attention of listeners — readers as well. A little of its tremendous power flows to the public speaker who starts off with a joke, even a stale joke ("A funny thing happened to me on my way over here . . ."), and to the preacher who at the beginning of a sermon tells of some funny or touching incident. In its opening paragraph, an article in a popular magazine ("Vampires Live Today!") will give us a brief, arresting narrative:

perhaps the case history of a car dealer who noticed, one moonlit night, his incisors strangely lengthening.

The term *narrative* takes in abundant territory. A narrative may be short or long, factual or imagined, as artless as a tale told in a locker room or as artful as a novel by Henry James. A narrative may instruct and inform, or simply divert and regale. It may set forth some point or message, or it may be as devoid of significance as a comic yarn or a horror tale whose sole aim is to curdle your blood.

At least a hundred times a year, you probably resort to narration, not always for the purpose of telling an entertaining story, but often to explain, to illustrate a point, to report information, to argue, or to persuade. That is, although a narrative can run from the beginning of an essay to the end, more often in your writing (as in your speaking) a narrative is only a part of what you have to say. It is there because it serves a larger purpose. In truth, because narration is such an effective way to put across your ideas, the ability to tell a compelling story — on paper, as well as in conversation — may be one of the most useful skills you can acquire.

A novel is a narrative, but a narrative doesn't have to be long. Sometimes an essay will include several brief stories. See, for instance, William F. Buckley, Jr.'s argument "Why Don't We Complain?" (p. 507). A type of story often used to illustrate a point is the ANECDOTE, a short, entertaining account of a single incident. Sometimes told of famous persons, anecdotes add color and life to history, biography, autobiography, and every issue of *People* magazine. Besides being fun to read, an anecdote can be deeply revealing. W. Jackson Bate, in his biography of Samuel Johnson, traces the growth of the great eighteenth-century critic and scholar's ideas and, with the aid of anecdotes, he shows that his subject was human and lovable. As Bate tells us, Dr. Johnson, a portly and imposing gentleman of fifty-five, had walked with some friends to the crest of a hill, where the great man,

> delighted by its steepness, said he wanted to "take a roll down." They tried to stop him. But he said he "had not had a roll for a long time," and taking out of his pockets his keys, a pencil, a purse, and other objects, lay down parallel at the edge of the hill, and rolled down its full length, "turning himself over and over till he came to the bottom."

However small the event it relates, this anecdote is memorable — partly because of its attention to detail, such as the exact list of the contents of Johnson's pockets. In such a brief story, a superhuman figure comes down to human size. In one stroke, Bate reveals an essential part of Johnson: his boisterous, hearty, and boyish sense of fun.

An anecdote may be used to explain a point. Asked why he had appointed to a cabinet post Josephus Daniels, the harshest critic of his policies, President Woodrow Wilson replied with an anecdote of a woman he knew. On spying a strange man urinating through her picket fence into her flower garden, she invited the offender into her yard because, as she explained to him, "I'd a whole lot rather have you inside pissing out than have you outside pissing in." By telling this story, Wilson made clear his situation in regard to his political enemy more succinctly and pointedly than if he had given a more abstract explanation. As a statesman, Woodrow Wilson may have had his flaws; but as a storyteller, he is surely among the less forgettable.

THE PROCESS

So far, we have considered a few uses of narration. Now let us see how you tell an effective story.

Every good story has a purpose. Perhaps the storyteller seeks to explain what it was like to be an African American in a certain time and place (as Maya Angelou does in "Champion of the World" in this chapter); perhaps the teller seeks merely to entertain us. Whatever the reason for its telling, an effective story holds the attention of readers or listeners; and to do so, the storyteller shapes that story to appeal to its audience. If, for instance, you plan to tell a few friends of an embarrassing moment you had on your way to campus — you tripped and spilled a load of books into the arms of a passing dean — you know how to proceed. Simply to provide a laugh is your purpose, and your listeners, who need no introduction to you or the dean, need to be told only the bare events of the story. Perhaps you'll use some vivid words to convey the surprise on the dean's face when sixty pounds of literary lumber hit her. Perhaps you'll throw in a little surprise of your own. At first, you didn't take in the identity of this passerby on whom you'd dumped a load of literary lumber. Then you realized: It was the dean!

Such simple, direct storytelling is so common and habitual that we do it without planning in advance. The NARRATOR (or teller) of such a personal experience is the speaker, the one who was there. (Four selections in this chapter — by Maya Angelou, Ralph Ellison,

James Thurber, and Judith Ortiz Cofer — tell of such experiences. All except Ellison use the first PERSON *I*.) The telling is usually SUBJECTIVE, with details and language chosen to express the writer's feelings. Of course, a personal experience told in the first person can use some artful telling and some structuring. (In the course of this discussion, we'll offer advice on telling stories of different kinds.)

When a story isn't your own experience but a recital of someone else's, or of events that are public knowledge, then you proceed differently. Without expressing opinions, you step back and report, content to stay invisible. Instead of saying, "I did this; I did that," you use the third person, *he, she, it,* or *they*: "The runner did this; he did that." You may have been on the scene; if so, you will probably write as a spectator, from your own POINT OF VIEW (or angle of seeing). If you put together what happened from the testimony of others, you tell the story from the point of view of a nonparticipant (a witness who didn't take part). Generally, a nonparticipant is OBJECTIVE in setting forth events: unbiased, as accurate and dispassionate as possible.

When you narrate a story in the third person, you aren't a character central in the eyes of your audience. Unlike the first-person writer of a personal experience, you aren't the main actor; you are the camera operator, whose job is to focus on what transpires. Most history books and news stories are third-person narratives, and so is much fiction. (In this chapter, the story by Shirley Jackson illustrates third-person narration.) In narrating actual events, writers stick to the facts and do not invent the thoughts of participants (historical novels, though, do mingle fact and fancy in this way). And even writers of fiction and anecdote imagine the thoughts of their characters only if they want to explore psychology. Note how much Woodrow Wilson's anecdote would lose if the teller had gone into the thoughts of his characters: "The woman was angry and embarrassed at seeing the stranger. . . ."

Whether you tell of your own experience or of someone else's, even if it is brief, you need a whole story to tell. If the story is complex, do some searching and discovering in writing. One trusty method to test your memory (or to make sure you have all the necessary elements of a story) is that of a news reporter. Ask yourself:

1. *What* happened?
2. *Who* took part?
3. *When?*
4. *Where?*

5. *Why* did this event (or these events) take place?
6. *How* did it (or they) happen?

That last *how* isn't merely another way of asking what happened. It means: In exactly what way or under what circumstances? If the event was a murder, how was it done — with an ax or with a bulldozer? Journalists call this handy list of questions "the five *W*'s and the *H*."

Well-prepared storytellers, those who first search their memories (or do some research and legwork), have far more information on hand than they can use. The writing of a good story calls for careful choice. In choosing, remember your purpose and your audience. If you're writing that story of the dean and the books to give pleasure to readers who are your friends, delighted to hear about the discomfort of a pompous administrator, you will probably dwell lovingly on each detail of her consternation. You would tell the story differently if your audience were strangers who didn't know the dean from Eve. They would need more information on her background, reputation for stiffness, and appearance. If, suspected of having deliberately contrived the dean's humiliation, you were writing a report of the incident for the campus police, you'd want to give the plainest possible account of the story — without drama, without adornment, without background, and certainly without any humor whatsoever.

Your purpose and your audience, then, clearly determine which of the two main strategies of narration you're going to choose: to tell a story by SCENE or to tell it by SUMMARY. When you tell a story in a scene, or in scenes, you visualize each event as vividly and precisely as if you were there — as though it were a scene in a film, and your reader sat before the screen. This is the strategy of most fine novels and short stories — and of much excellent nonfiction as well. Instead of just mentioning people, you portray them. You recall dialogue as best you can, or you invent some that could have been spoken. You include DESCRIPTION (a mode of writing to be dealt with fully in our next chapter).

For a lively example of a well-drawn scene, see Maya Angelou's account of a tense crowd's behavior as, jammed into a small-town store, they listen to a fight broadcast (in "Champion of the World," beginning on page 49). Angelou prolongs one scene for almost her entire essay. Sometimes, though, a writer will draw a scene in only two or three sentences. This is the brevity we find in W. Jackson Bate's glimpse of the hill-rolling Johnson. Unlike Angelou, Bate evidently seeks not to weave a tapestry of detail, but to show, in telling of one brief event, a trait of his hero's character.

When, on the other hand, you tell a story by the method of summary, you relate events concisely. Instead of depicting people and their surroundings in great detail, you set down just the essentials of what happened. Most of us employ this method in most stories we tell, for it takes less time and fewer words. A summary is to a scene, then, as a simple stick figure is to a portrait in oils. This is not to dismiss simple stick figures as inferior. A story told in summary may be as effective as a story told in scenes, in lavish detail.

Again, your choice of a method depends on your answer to the questions you ask yourself: What is my purpose? Who is my audience? How fully to flesh out a scene, how much detail to include — these choices depend on what you seek to do, and on how much your audience needs to know to follow you. Read the life of some famous person in an encyclopedia, and you will find the article telling its story in summary form. Its writer's purpose, evidently, is to recount the main events of a whole life in a short space. But glance through a book-length biography of the same celebrity, and you will probably find scenes in it. A biographer writes with a different purpose: to present a detailed portrait roundly and thoroughly, bringing the subject vividly to life.

To be sure, you can use both methods in telling a single story. Often, summary will serve a writer who passes briskly from one scene to the next, or hurries over events of lesser importance. Were you to write, let's say, the story of a man's fiendish passion for horse racing, you might decide to give short shrift to most other facts of his life. To emphasize what you consider essential, you might begin a scene with a terse summary: "Seven years went by, and after three marriages and two divorces, Lars found himself again back at Hialeah." (A detailed scene might follow.)

Good storytellers know what to emphasize. They do not fall into a boring drone: "And then I went down to the club and I had a few beers and I noticed this sign, Go 3 Minutes with the Masked Samurai and Win $500, so I went and got knocked out and then I had pizza and went home." In this lazily strung-out summary, the narrator reduces all events to equal unimportance. A more adept storyteller might leave out the pizza and dwell in detail on the big fight.

Some storytellers assume that to tell a story in the present tense (instead of the past tense, traditionally favored) gives events a sense of immediacy. Presented as though everything were happening right now, the story of the Masked Samurai might begin: "I duck between the ropes and step into the ring. My heart is thudding fast." You can try the present tense, if you like, and see how immediate it seems to you. Be warned, however, that nowadays so many fiction writers write in this fashion that to use the past tense may make your work seem almost fresh and original.

In *The Bedford Reader*, we are concerned with the kind of writing you do every day in college: nonfiction writing in which you generally explain ideas, organize information you have learned, analyze other people's ideas, or argue a case. In fiction, though, we find an enormously popular and appealing use of narration and certain devices of storytelling from which all storytellers can learn. For these reasons, this chapter includes one celebrated short story by a master storyteller, Shirley Jackson. As Maya Angelou does in her true memoir "Champion of the World," Jackson strives to make the people in her story come alive for us. Both authors use a tool that academic writers generally do not: dialogue. Reported speech, in quotation marks, is indispensable for writers of fiction and many writers of personal narrative — not only Angelou but Ellison, Thurber, and Cofer in this chapter. With dialogue, Jackson lets conversation advance the story and reveal her characters' feelings.

In any kind of narration, the simplest approach is to set down events in CHRONOLOGICAL ORDER, the way they happened. To do so is to have your story already organized for you. A chronological order is therefore an excellent sequence to follow unless you can see some special advantage in violating it. Ask: What am I trying to do? If you are trying to capture your readers' attention right away, you might begin *in medias res* (Latin, "in the middle of things") and open with a colorful, dramatic event, even though it took place late in the chronology. If trying for dramatic effect, you might save the most exciting or impressive event for last, even though it actually happened early. By this means, you can keep your readers in suspense for as long as possible. (You can return to earlier events by a FLASHBACK, an earlier scene recalled.) Let your purpose be your guide.

The writer Calvin Trillin has recalled why, in a narrative titled "The Tunica Treasure," he deliberately chose not to follow a chronology:

> I wrote a story on the discovery of the Tunica treasure which I couldn't begin by saying, "Here is a man who works as a prison guard in Angola State Prison, and on his weekends he sometimes looks for buried treasure that is rumored to be around the Indian village." Because the real point of the story centered around the problems caused when an amateur wanders onto professional territory, I thought it would be much better to open with how momentous the discovery was, that it was the most important arche-

ological discovery about Indian contact with the European settlers
to date, and *then* to say that it was discovered by a prison guard.
So I made a conscious choice *not* to start with Leonard Charrier
working as a prison guard, not to go back to his boyhood in Bunkie,
Louisiana, not to talk about how he'd always been interested in
treasure hunting — hoping that the reader would assume I was
about to say that the treasure was found by an archeologist from
the Peabody Museum at Harvard.

Trillin, by saving the fact that a prison guard made the earthshaking
discovery, effectively took his reader by surprise.

No matter what order you choose, either following chronology or
departing from it, make sure your audience can follow it. The sequence of events has to be clear. This calls for TRANSITIONS of time,
whether they are brief phrases that point out exactly when each event
happened ("Seven years later," "A moment earlier"), or whole sentences that announce an event and clearly locate it in time ("If you
had known Leonard Charrier ten years earlier, you would have found
him voraciously poring over every archeology text he could lay his
hands on in the public library").

In writing a news story, a reporter often begins with the conclusion, placing the main event in the opening paragraph (called the
lead). Dramatically, this may be the weakest method to tell the story;
yet it is effective in this case because the reporter's purpose is not to
entertain but rather to tell quickly what happened, for an audience
impatient to learn the essentials. In most other kinds of narration,
however, whether fiction or nonfiction, whether to entertain or to
make an idea clear, the storyteller builds toward a memorable CON-
CLUSION. In a story Mark Twain liked to tell aloud, a woman's ghost
returns to claim her artificial arm made of gold, which she wore in
life and which her greedy husband had unscrewed from her corpse.
Carefully, Twain would build up suspense as the ghost pursued the
husband upstairs to his bedroom, stood by his bed, breathed her cold
breath on him, and intoned, *"Who's got my golden arm?"* Twain used
to end his story by suddenly yelling at a member of the audience,
"You've got it!" — and enjoying the victim's shriek of surprise. That
final punctuating shriek may be a technique that will work only in
oral storytelling; yet, like Twain, most storytellers like to end with a
bang if they can. The final impact, however, need not be so obvious.
As Maya Angelou demonstrates in her story in this chapter, you can
achieve impact just by leading to a point. In an effective written
narrative, a writer usually hits the main events of a story especially
hard, often saving the best punch (or the best karate chop) for the
very end.

NARRATION IN A PARAGRAPH:
TWO ILLUSTRATIONS

Using Narration to Write About Television

Oozing menace from beyond the stars or from the deeps, televised horror powerfully stimulates a child's already frisky imagination. As parents know, a "Creature Double Feature" has an impact that lasts long after the click of the *off* button. Recently a neighbor reported the strange case of her eight-year-old. Discovered late at night in the game room watching *The Exorcist*, the girl was promptly sent to bed. An hour later, her parents could hear her chanting something in the darkness of her bedroom. On tiptoe, they stole to her door to listen. The creak of springs told them that their daughter was swaying rhythmically to and fro and the smell of acrid smoke warned them that something was burning. At once, they shoved open the door to find the room flickering with shadows cast by a lighted candle. Their daughter was sitting in bed, rocking back and forth as she intoned over and over, "Fiend in human form . . . Fiend in human form . . ." This case may be unique; still, it seems likely that similar events take place each night all over the screen-watching world.

COMMENT. This paragraph, addressed to a general audience — that is, most readers, those who read nonspecialized books or magazines — puts a story to work to support a TOPIC SENTENCE. A brief anecdote, the story of the mesmerized child backs up the claim (in the first sentence) that TV horror excites children's imaginations. The story relates a small, ordinary, but disquieting experience taken from the writer's conversation with friends. A bit of suspense is introduced, and the reader's curiosity is whetted, when the parents steal to the bedroom door to learn why the child isn't asleep. The crisis — the dramatic high moment in the story when our curiosity is about to be gratified — is a sensory detail: the smell of smoke. At the end of the paragraph, the writer stresses the importance of these events by suggesting that they are probably universal. In a way, he harks back to his central idea, reminding us of his reason for telling the story. Narration, as you can see, is a method for dramatizing your ideas.

Using Narration in an Academic Discipline

The news media periodically relate the terrifying and often grim details of landslides. On May 31, 1970, one such event occurred when a gigantic rock avalanche buried more than 20,000 people in Yungay and Ranrahirca, Peru. There was little warning of the impending disaster; it began and ended in just a matter of a few minutes. The avalanche started 14 kilometers from Yungay, near the summit of 6,700-meter-high Nevados Huascaran, the loftiest peak in the Peruvian Andes. Triggered by the ground motion from a strong offshore earthquake, a huge mass of rock and ice broke free from the precipitous north face of the mountain. After plunging nearly one kilometer, the material pulverized on impact and immediately began rushing down the mountainside, made fluid by trapped air and melted ice. The initial mass ripped loose additional millions of tons of debris as it roared downhill. The shock waves produced by the event created thunderlike noise and stripped nearby hillsides of vegetation. Although the material followed a previously eroded gorge, a portion of the debris jumped a 200–300-meter-high bedrock ridge that had protected Yungay from past rock avalanches and buried the entire city. After inundating another town in its path, Ranrahirca, the mass of debris finally reached the bottom of the valley where its momentum carried it across the Rio Santa and tens of meters up the opposite bank.

COMMENT. This paragraph of vivid narration enlivens a college textbook, *The Earth: An Introduction to Physical Geology*, by Edward J. Tarbuck and Frederick K. Lutgens. To illustrate the awesome power of a landslide, the writers give this one-paragraph example, choosing one of the most horrendous such catastrophes in history. Not all landslides are so spectacular, of course, and yet this brief narrative serves to set forth traits typical of landslides in general: sudden beginning, fast movement, irresistible force. This paragraph shows another way in which narration can serve: as a memorable example, making the point that landslides concern people and can cost lives, and as a means to enlist the reader's immediate attention to a discussion that otherwise might seem dry and abstract.

MAYA ANGELOU

Maya Angelou was born Marguerite Johnson in Saint Louis in 1928. After an unpleasantly eventful youth by her account ("from a broken family, raped at eight, unwed mother at sixteen"), she went on to join a dance company, star in an off-Broadway play (*The Blacks*), write six books of poetry, produce a series on Africa for PBS-TV, act in the television-special series *Roots*, serve as a coordinator for the Southern Christian Leadership Conference, and accept several honorary doctorates. She is best known, however, for the five books of her searching, frank, and joyful autobiography — beginning with *I Know Why the Caged Bird Sings* (1970), which she adapted for television, through *All God's Children Need Traveling Shoes* (1986). Her latest book is a collection of essays, *Wouldn't Take Nothing for My Journey Now* (1993). Angelou is Reynolds Professor of American Studies at Wake Forest University. In 1993 she read a specially commissioned poem, "On the Pulse of Morning," at the inauguration of President Bill Clinton.

Champion of the World

"Champion of the World" is the nineteenth chapter in *I Know Why the Caged Bird Sings*; the title is a phrase taken from the chapter. Remembering her childhood, the writer tells how she and her older brother, Bailey, grew up in a town in Arkansas. The center of their lives was Grandmother and Uncle Willie's store, a gathering place for the black community. On the night when this story takes place, Joe Louis, the "Brown Bomber" and the hero of his people, defends his heavyweight boxing title against a white contender.

The last inch of space was filled, yet people continued to wedge 1
themselves along the walls of the Store. Uncle Willie had turned the radio up to its last notch so that youngsters on the porch wouldn't miss a word. Women sat on kitchen chairs, dining-room chairs, stools, and upturned wooden boxes. Small children and babies perched on every lap available and men leaned on the shelves or on each other.

The apprehensive mood was shot through with shafts of gaiety, 2
as a black sky is streaked with lightning.

"I ain't worried 'bout this fight. Joe's gonna whip that cracker 3
like it's open season."

"He gone whip him till that white boy call him Momma." 4

49

At last the talking finished and the string-along songs about razor ₅
blades were over and the fight began.

"A quick jab to the head." In the Store the crowd grunted. "A ₆
left to the head and a right and another left." One of the listeners
cackled like a hen and was quieted.

"They're in a clinch, Louis is trying to fight his way out." ₇

Some bitter comedian on the porch said, "That white man don't ₈
mind hugging that niggah now, I betcha."

"The referee is moving in to break them up, but Louis finally ₉
pushed the contender away and it's an uppercut to the chin. The
contender is hanging on, now he's backing away. Louis catches him
with a short left to the jaw."

A tide of murmuring assent poured out the door and into the ₁₀
yard.

"Another left and another left. Louis is saving that mighty right ₁₁
. . ." The mutter in the Store had grown into a baby roar and it was
pierced by the clang of a bell and the announcer's "That's the bell
for round three, ladies and gentlemen."

As I pushed my way into the Store I wondered if the announcer ₁₂
gave any thought to the fact that he was addressing as "ladies and
gentlemen" all the Negroes around the world who sat sweating and
praying, glued to their "Master's voice."[1]

There were only a few calls for RC Colas, Dr Peppers, and Hires ₁₃
root beer. The real festivities would begin after the fight. Then even
the old Christian ladies who taught their children and tried themselves to practice turning the other cheek would buy soft drinks, and
if the Brown Bomber's victory was a particularly bloody one they
would order peanut patties and Baby Ruths also.

Bailey and I laid the coins on top of the cash register. Uncle ₁₄
Willie didn't allow us to ring up sales during a fight. It was too noisy
and might shake up the atmosphere. When the gong rang for the
next round we pushed through the near-sacred quiet to the herd of
children outside.

"He's got Louis against the ropes and now it's a left to the body ₁₅
and a right to the ribs. Another right to the body, it looks like it was
low . . . Yes, ladies and gentlemen, the referee is signaling but the
contender keeps raining the blows on Louis. It's another to the body,
and it looks like Louis is going down."

[1]"His master's voice," accompanied by a picture of a little dog listening to a
phonograph, was a familiar advertising slogan. (The picture still appears on some
RCA recordings.) — EDS.

My race groaned. It was our people falling. It was another lynch- 16
ing, yet another Black man hanging on a tree. One more woman
ambushed and raped. A Black boy whipped and maimed. It was
hounds on the trail of a man running through slimy swamps. It was
a white woman slapping her maid for being forgetful.

The men in the Store stood away from the walls and at attention. 17
Women greedily clutched the babes on their laps while on the porch
the shufflings and smiles, flirtings and pinching of a few minutes
before were gone. This might be the end of the world. If Joe lost we
were back in slavery and beyond help. It would all be true, the
accusations that we were lower types of human beings. Only a little
higher than apes. True that we were stupid and ugly and lazy and
dirty and, unlucky and worst of all, that God Himself hated us and ordained us to be hewers of wood and drawers of water, forever and
ever, world without end.

We didn't breathe. We didn't hope. We waited. 18

"He's off the ropes, ladies and gentlemen. He's moving towards 19
the center of the ring." There was no time to be relieved. The worst
might still happen.

"And now it looks like Joe is mad. He's caught Carnera with a 20
left hook to the head and a right to the head. It's a left jab to the
body and another left to the head. There's a left cross and a right to
the head. The contender's right eye is bleeding and he can't seem to
keep his block up. Louis is penetrating every block. The referee is
moving in, but Louis sends a left to the body and it's an uppercut to
the chin and the contender is dropping. He's on the canvas, ladies
and gentlemen."

Babies slid to the floor as women stood up and men leaned toward 21
the radio.

"Here's the referee. He's counting. One, two, three, four, five, 22
six, seven . . . Is the contender trying to get up again?"

All the men in the store shouted, "NO." 23

" — eight, nine, ten." There were a few sounds from the audi- 24
ence, but they seemed to be holding themselves in against tremendous
pressure.

"The fight is all over, ladies and gentlemen. Let's get the micro- 25
phone over to the referee . . . Here he is. He's got the Brown
Bomber's hand, he's holding it up . . . Here he is . . ."

Then the voice, husky and familiar, came to wash over us — 26
"The winnah, and still heavyweight champeen of the world . . . Joe
Louis."

Champion of the world. A Black boy. Some Black mother's son. 27

He was the strongest man in the world. People drank Coca-Colas like ambrosia and ate candy bars like Christmas. Some of the men went behind the Store and poured white lightning in their soft-drink bottles, and a few of the bigger boys followed them. Those who were not chased away came back blowing their breath in front of themselves like proud smokers.

It would take an hour or more before the people would leave the   28
Store and head for home. Those who lived too far had made arrangements to stay in town. It wouldn't do for a Black man and his family to be caught on a lonely country road on a night when Joe Louis had proved that we were the strongest people in the world.

—————

QUESTIONS ON MEANING

1. What do you take to be the author's PURPOSE in telling this story?
2. What connection does Angelou make between the outcome of the fight and the pride of African Americans? To what degree do you think the author's view is shared by the others in the store listening to the broadcast?
3. To what extent are the statements in paragraphs 16 and 17 to be taken literally? What function do they serve in Angelou's narrative?
4. Primo Carnera was probably *not* the Brown Bomber's opponent on the night Maya Angelou recalls. Louis fought Carnera only once, on June 25, 1935, and it was not a title match; Angelou would have been no more than seven years old at the time. Does the author's apparent error detract from her story?

QUESTIONS ON WRITING STRATEGY

1. What details in the opening paragraphs indicate that an event of crucial importance is about to take place?
2. How does Angelou build up SUSPENSE in her account of the fight? At what point were you able to predict the winner?
3. Comment on the IRONY in Angelou's final paragraph.
4. What EFFECT does the author's use of direct quotation have on her narrative?
5. **OTHER METHODS.** Besides narration, Angelou also relies heavily on the method of DESCRIPTION. Analyze how narration depends on description in paragraph 27 alone.

QUESTIONS ON LANGUAGE

1. Explain what the author means by "string-along songs about razor blades" (para. 5).
2. How does Angelou's use of NONSTANDARD ENGLISH contribute to her narrative?
3. Be sure you know the meanings of these words: apprehensive (para. 2); assent (10); ambushed, maimed (16); ordained (17); ambrosia, white lightning (27).

SUGGESTIONS FOR WRITING

1. In a brief essay, write about the progress and outcome of a recent sporting event and your reaction to the outcome. Include enough illustrative detail to bring the contest to life.
2. Write an essay based on some childhood experience of your own, still vivid in your memory.
3. CRITICAL WRITING. Angelou does not directly describe relations between African Americans and whites, yet her essay implies quite a lot. Write a brief essay about what you can INFER from the exaggeration of paragraphs 16–17 and the obliqueness of paragraph 28. Focus on Angelou's details and the language she uses to present them.
4. CONNECTIONS. Compare Angelou's narrative with Ralph Ellison's "On Being the Target of Discrimination" (p. 55). Using details and quotations from both works as evidence, write an essay on the ways group identity — even, or perhaps especially, identity with an oppressed group such as African Americans — strengthens and binds the group's members.

MAYA ANGELOU ON WRITING

Maya Angelou's writings have shown great variety: She has done notable work as an autobiographer, poet, short-story writer, screenwriter, journalist, and song lyricist. Asked by interviewer Sheila Weller, "Do you start each project with a specific idea?" Angelou replied:

"It starts with a definite subject, but it might end with something entirely different. When I start a project, the first thing I do is write down, in longhand, everything I know about the subject, every thought I've ever had on it. This may be twelve or fourteen pages. Then I read it back through, for quite a few days, and find — given that subject — what its rhythm is. 'Cause everything in the universe has a rhythm. So if it's free form, it still has a rhythm. And once I hear the rhythm of the piece, then I try to find out what are the salient points that I must make. And then it begins to take shape.

"I try to set myself up in each chapter by saying: 'This is what I want to go from — from B to, say, G-sharp. Or from D to L.' And then I find the hook. It's like the knitting, where, after you knit a certain amount, there's one thread that begins to pull. You know, you can see it right along the cloth. Well, in writing, I think: 'Now where is that one hook, that one little thread?' It may be a sentence. If I can catch that, then I'm home-free. It's the one that tells me where I'm going. It may not even turn out to be in the final chapter. I may throw it out later or change it. But if I follow it through, it leads me right out."

FOR DISCUSSION

1. How would you define the word *rhythm* as Maya Angelou uses it?
2. What response would you give a student who said, "Doesn't Angelou's approach to writing waste more time and thought than it's worth?"

RALPH ELLISON

RALPH WALDO ELLISON is best known for his award-winning novel *Invisible Man* (1952), about a black man who seeks his identity somewhere beyond white and black stereotypes. Born in 1919, Ellison studied music and read literature at Tuskegee Institute in Alabama but left before graduating for lack of money. He began publishing stories in the late 1930s and has written essays of autobiography, criticism, and cultural history that have been collected in *Shadow and Act* (1964) and *Going to the Territory* (1986). At New York University, Ellison was Albert Schweitzer Professor in Humanities for almost a decade, and he has lectured at Rutgers, Yale, and many other universities. His second novel, long awaited by his readers, has appeared in tantalizing excerpts over the years. Ellison lives in New York City and western Massachusetts.

On Being the Target of Discrimination

Ellison grew up in Oklahoma, where he felt that "relationships between the races were more fluid and thus more human than in the old slave states." Still, as a boy he knew discrimination in "brief impersonal encounters, stares, vocal inflections, hostile laughter, or public reversals of private expectations." Some of these slights are recounted in this essay, which first appeared in 1989 in *A World of Difference*, a special *New York Times* supplement devoted to reducing racial and ethnic prejudice.

It got to you first at the age of six, and through your own curiosity. 1 With kindergarten completed and the first grade ahead, you were eagerly anticipating your first day of public school. For months you had been imagining your new experience and the children, known and unknown, with whom you would study and play. But the physical framework of your imagining, an elementary school in the process of construction, lay close at hand on the block-square site across the street from your home. For over a year you had watched it rise and spread in the air to become a handsome structure of brick and stone, then seen its broad encircling grounds arrayed with seesaws, swings, and baseball diamonds. You had imagined this picture-book setting as the scene of your new experience, and when enrollment day arrived, with its grounds astir with bright colors and voices of kids like yourself, it did, indeed, become the site of your very first lesson in public schooling — though not within its classrooms, as you had imagined, but well outside its walls. For while located within a fairly mixed neighborhood this new public school was exclusively for whites.

It was then you learned that you would attend a school located 2 far to the south of your neighborhood, and that reaching it involved a journey which took you over, either directly or by way of a viaduct which arched head-spinning high above, a broad expanse of railroad tracks along which a constant traffic of freightcars, switch engines, and passenger trains made it dangerous for a child to cross. And that once the tracks were safely negotiated you continued past warehouses, factories, and loading docks, and then through a notorious red-light district where black prostitutes in brightly colored housecoats and Mary Jane shoes supplied the fantasies and needs of a white clientele. Considering the fact that you couldn't attend school with white kids this made for a confusion that was further confounded by the giggling jokes which older boys whispered about the district's peculiar form of integration. For you it was a grown-up's mystery, but streets being no less schools than routes to schools, the district would soon add a few forbidden words to your vocabulary.

It took a bit of time to forget the sense of incongruity aroused by 3 your having to walk *past* a school to get *to* a school, but soon you came to like your school, your teachers, and most of your schoolmates. Indeed, you soon enjoyed the long walks and anticipated the sights you might see, the adventures you might encounter, and the many things not taught in school that could be learned along the way. Your school was not nearly so fine as that which faced your home but it had its attractions. Among them its nearness to a park, now abandoned by whites, in which you picnicked and played. And there were the two tall cylindrical fire-escapes on either wing of its main building down which it was a joy to lie full-length and slide, spiraling down and around three stories to the ground — providing no outraged teacher was waiting to strap your legs once you sailed out of its chute like a shot off a fireman's shovel. Besides, in your childish way you were learning that it was better to take self-selected risks and pay the price than be denied the joy or pain of risk-taking by those who begrudged your existence.

Beginning when you were four or five you had known the joy of 4 trips to the city's zoo, but one day you would ask your mother to take you there and have her sigh and explain that it was now against the law for Negro kids to view the animals. Had someone done something bad to the animals? No. Had someone tried to steal them or feed them poison? No. Could white kids still go? Yes! So why? Quit asking questions, it's the law and only because some white folks are out to turn this state into a part of the South.

This sudden and puzzling denial of a Saturday's pleasure was   5 disappointing and so angered your mother that later, after the zoo was moved north of the city, she decided to do something about it. Thus one warm Saturday afternoon with you and your baby brother dressed in your best she took you on a long streetcar ride which ended at a strange lakeside park, in which you found a crowd of noisy white people. Having assumed that you were on your way to the integrated cemetery where at the age of three you had been horrified beyond all tears or forgetting when you saw your father's coffin placed in the ground, you were bewildered. But now as your mother herded you and your brother in to the park you discovered that you'd come to the zoo and were so delighted that soon you were laughing and babbling as excitedly as the kids around you.

Your mother was pleased and as you moved through the crowd of   6 white parents and children she held your brother's hand and allowed as much time for staring at the cages of rare animals as either of you desired. But once your brother began to tire she herded you out of the park and toward the streetcar line. And then it happened.

Just as you reached the gate through which crowds of whites were   7 coming and going you had a memorable lesson in the strange ways of segregated-democracy as instructed by a guard in civilian clothes. He was a white man dressed in a black suit and a white straw hat, and when he looked at the fashion in which your mother was dressed, then down to you and your brother, he stiffened, turned red in the face, and stared as though at something dangerous.

"Girl," he shouted, "where are your *white* folks!"   8

"*White* folks," your mother said, "What white folks? I don't *have*   9 any white folks, I'm a Negro!"

"Now don't you get smart with me, colored gal," the white man   10 said, "I mean where are the white folks you come *out* here with!"

"But I just told you that I didn't come here with any white   11 people," your mother said, "I came here with my boys . . ."

"Then what are you doing in this park," the white man said.   12

And now when your mother answered you could hear the familiar   13 sound of anger in her voice.

"I'm here," she said, "because I'm a *taxpayer*, and I thought it was   14 about time that my boys have a look at those animals. And for that I didn't *need* any *white* folks to show me the way!"

"Well," the white man said, "*I'm* here to tell you that you're   15 breaking the law! So now you'll have to leave. Both you and your chillun too. The rule says no niggers is allowed in the zoo. That's the law and I'm enforcing it!"

"Very well," your mother said, "we've seen the animals anyway 16 and were on our way to the streetcar line when you stopped us."

"That's fine," the white man said, "and when that car comes you 17 be sure that you get on it, you hear? You and your chillun too!"

So it was quite a day. You had enjoyed the animals with your 18 baby brother and had another lesson in the sudden ways good times could be turned into bad when white people looked at your color instead of *you*. But better still, you had learned something of your mother's courage and were proud that she had broken an unfair law and stood up for her right to do so. For while the white man kept staring until the streetcar arrived she ignored him and answered your brother's questions about the various animals. Then the car came with its crowd of white parents and children, and when you were entrained and rumbling home past the fine lawns and houses your mother gave way to a gale of laughter; in which, hesitantly at first, and then with assurance and pride, you joined. And from that day the incident became the source of a family joke that was sparked by accidents, faux pas, or obvious lies. Then one of you was sure to frown and say, "Well, I think you'll have to go now, both you and your chillun too!" And the family would laugh hilariously. Discrimination teaches one to discriminate between discriminators while countering absurdity with black (Negro? Afro-American? African-American?) comedy.

When you were eight you would move to one of the white sections 19 through which you often passed on the way to your father's grave and your truly last trip to the zoo. For now your mother was the custodian of several apartments located in a building which housed on its street floor a drug store, a tailor shop, a Piggly Wiggly market, and a branch post office. Built on a downward slope, the building had at its rear a long driveway which led from the side street past an empty lot to a group of garages in which the apartments' tenants stored their cars. Built at an angle with wings facing north and east, the structure supported a servant's quarters which sat above its angle like a mock watchtower atop a battlement, and it was there that you now lived.

Reached by a flight of outside stairs, it consisted of four small 20 rooms, a bath, and a kitchen. Windows on three of its sides provided a view across the empty frontage to the street, of the back yards behind it, and of the back wall and windows of the building in which your mother worked. It was quite comfortable but you secretly disliked the idea of your mother living in service and missed your friends who now lived far away. Nevertheless, the neighborhood was pleasant, served by a sub-station of the streetcar line, and marked by a variety of activities which challenged your curiosity. Even its affluent alleys were more exciting to explore than those of your old neighborhood, and the one white friend you were to acquire in the area lived nearby.

This friend was a brilliant but sickly boy who was tutored at 21 home, and with him you shared your new interest in building radios, a hobby at which he was quite skilled. Your friendship eased your loneliness and helped dispel some of the mystery and resentment imposed by segregation. Through access to his family, headed by an important Episcopalian minister, you learned more about whites and thus about yourself. With him you could make comparisons that were not so distorted by the racial myths which obstructed your thrust toward self-perception; compare their differences in taste, discipline, and manners with those of Negro families of comparable status and income; observe variations between your friend's boyish lore and your own, and measure his intelligence, knowledge, and ambitions against your own. For you this was a most important experience and a rare privilege, because up to now the prevailing separation of the races had made it impossible to learn how you and your Negro friends compared with boys who lived on the white side of the color line. It was said by word of mouth, proclaimed in newsprint, and dramatized by acts of discriminatory law that you were inferior. You were barred from vying with them in sports and games, competing in the classroom or the world of art. Yet what you saw, heard, and smelled of them left irrepressible doubts. So you ached for objective proof, for a fair field of testing.

Even your school's proud marching band was denied participation 22 in the statewide music contests so popular at the time, as though so airy and earth-transcending an art as music would be contaminated if performed by musicians of different races.

Which was especially disturbing because after the father of a friend 23 who lived next door in your old neighborhood had taught you the beginner's techniques required to play valved instruments you had decided to become a musician. Then shortly before moving among whites your mother had given you a brass cornet, which in the isolation of the servant's quarters you practiced hours on end. But you yearned to play with other musicians and found none available. Now you lived less than a block from a white school with a famous band, but there was no one in the neighborhood with whom to explore the mysteries of the horn. You could hear the school band's music and watch their marching, but joining in making the thrilling sounds was impossible. Nor did it help that you owned the scores to a few of their marches and could play with a certain facility and fairly good tone. So there, surrounded by sounds but unable to share a sound, you went it alone. You turned yourself into a one-man band.

You played along as best you could with the phonograph, read 24
the score to *The Carnival of Venice* while listening to Del Steigers executing triple-tongue variations on its themes; played the trumpet parts of your bandbook's marches while humming in your head the supporting voices of horns and reeds. And since your city was a seedbed of Southwestern jazz you played Kansas City riffs, bugle calls, and wha-wha-muted imitations of blues singers' pleas. But none of this made up for your lack of fellow musicians. And then, late one Saturday afternoon when your mother and brother were away, and when you had dozed off while reading, you awoke to the nearby sound of live music. At first you thought you were dreaming, and then that you were listening to the high school band, but that couldn't be the source because, instead of floating over building tops and bouncing off wall and windowpane, the sounds you heard rose up, somewhat muffled, from below.

With that you ran to a window which faced the driveway, and 25
looking down through the high windowpane of the lighted post office you could see the metal glint of instruments. Then you were on your feet and down the stairs, keeping to the shadows as you drew close and peeped below. And there you looked down upon a room full of men and women postal workers who were playing away at a familiar march. It was like the answer to a silent prayer because you could tell by the sound that they were beginners like yourself and the covers of the thicket of bandbooks revealed that they were of the same set as yours. For a while you listened and hummed along, unseen but shaking with excitement in the dimming twilight. And then, hardly before the idea formed in your head, you were skipping up the stairs to grab your cornet, lyre, and bandbook and hurtling down again to the drive.

For a while you listened, hearing the music come to a pause and 26
the sound of the conductor's voice. Then came a rap on a music stand and once again the music. And now turning to the march by the light from the window, you snapped score to lyre, raised horn to lip, and began to play; at first silently tonguing the notes through the mouthpiece and then, carried away with the thrill of stealing a part of the music, you tensed your diaphragm and blew. And as you played, keeping time with your foot on the concrete drive, you realized that you were a better cornetist than some in the band and grew bold in

the pride of your sound. Now in your mind you were marching along a downtown street to the flying of flags, the tramping of feet, and the cheering of excited crowds. For at last by an isolated act of brassy cunning you had become a member of the band.

Yes, but unfortunately you then let yourself become so carried 27 away that you forgot to listen for the conductor's instructions which you were too high and hidden to see. Suddenly the music faded and you opened your ears to the fact that you were now rendering a lonely solo in the startled quietness. And before you could fully return to reality there came the sound of table legs across a floor and a rustle of movement ending in the appearance of a white startled face in the opened window. Then you heard a man's voice exclaim, "I'll be damn, it's a little nigger!" whereupon you took off like quail at the sound of sudden shotgun fire.

Next thing you knew, you were up the stairs and on your bed, 28 crying away in the dark your guilt and embarrassment. You cried and cried, asking yourself how could you have been so lacking in pride as to shame yourself and your entire race by butting in where you weren't wanted. And this just to make some amateur music. To this you had no answers but then and there you made a vow that it would never happen again. And then, slowly, slowly, as you lay in the dark, your earlier lessons in the absurd nature of racial relations came to your aid. And suddenly you found yourself laughing, both at the way you'd run away and the shock you'd caused by joining unasked in the music.

Then you could hear yourself intoning in your eight-year-old's 29 imitation of a white Southern accent. "Well boy, you broke the law, so you have to go, and that means you and your chillun too!"

QUESTIONS ON MEANING

1. What do you see as Ellison's PURPOSE in writing this essay?
2. What does the phrase "You and your chillun too" mean in paragraph 17? What does it come to mean in the writer's family? What does it mean at the end of the essay?
3. How does the writer's self-image change from the beginning of the narrative to the end?

QUESTIONS ON WRITING STRATEGY

1. What is the narrator's POINT OF VIEW? What PERSON does the narrator use? What EFFECT does this choice of person have on you as reader?

2. Why do you think this essay was published in a newspaper supplement designed to reduce discrimination (see the note on the essay, p. 55)? How did the essay affect your understanding of or attitude toward discrimination?
3. Why does Ellison narrate several events instead of just one? What is the point of each incident?
4. How do we learn that the narrator's father is dead? Is this fact important to the narrative? Is the narrator's handling of it effective?
5. **OTHER METHODS.** Comment on Ellison's use of EXAMPLES in paragraphs 3 and 24. What do they add?

QUESTIONS ON LANGUAGE

1. What do the description and dialogue in paragraphs 7–17 tell you about Ellison's attitude toward the white zoo guard?
2. What is generally meant by "black comedy" or "black humor"? What joke is Ellison making at the end of paragraph 18?
3. Define: astir (para. 1); viaduct, clientele (2); incongruity, begrudged (3); faux pas (18); battlement (19); lore, vying (21); intoning (29).

SUGGESTIONS FOR WRITING

1. Write a narrative about a childhood event in which you discovered something about your place in the world. Give careful consideration to POINT OF VIEW and the use of dialogue.
2. Relate an incident from your childhood that illustrates how you felt about a particular environment — a house, rooftop, school, neighborhood, clearing in the woods. Use DESCRIPTION to create a clear picture of the place.
3. **CRITICAL WRITING.** Ellison's use of *you* for the participant in his story is unusual; we might expect *I* or, less commonly, *he*. To ANALYZE this strategy, first rewrite paragraph 28, substituting *I/my* and then *he/his* for *you/your*. (You'll need to change verbs to match the new pronouns.) Read the paragraphs aloud, analyzing the EFFECT of each pronoun: Does it create distance or immediacy? Does it elicit more or less sympathy for the narrator? Is it clear or confusing? What can you INFER about Ellison's reasons for choosing *you*? In an essay, EVALUATE Ellison's choice on the basis of your analysis, supporting your ideas with examples from the essay or your rewrites.
4. **CONNECTIONS.** If you haven't already, read Maya Angelou's "Champion of the World" (p. 49). Compare and contrast the ways the African Americans in Ellison's and Angelou's essays find their value as human beings.

RALPH ELLISON ON WRITING

In his introduction to his collection of essays, *Shadow and Act* (1964), Ralph Ellison talks about how he came to be a writer. "When the first of these essays [reprinted in *Shadow and Act*] was published I regarded myself — in my most secret heart at least — a musician. . . . Writing was far from a serious matter. . . . Nor had I invested in writing any long hours of practice and study. Rather it was a reflex of reading, an extension of a source of pleasure, escape, and instruction. . . . It was not, then, the *process* of writing which initially claimed my attention, but the finished creations, the artifacts — poems, plays, novels. . . . The pleasure I derived from reading had long been a necessity, and in the *act* of reading, that marvelous collaboration between the writer's artful vision and the reader's sense of life, I had become acquainted with other possible selves — freer, more courageous and ingenuous and, during the course of the narrative at least, even wise."

The process of writing did not attract Ellison as strongly until he actually started writing. "Once involved," he says, "I soon became consciously concerned with craft, with technique. . . . I was gradually led, often reluctantly, to become consciously concerned with the nature of the culture and the society out of which American fiction is fabricated."

For Ellison, "the act of writing requires a constant plunging back into the shadow of the past where time hovers ghostlike. . . . [It is] the agency of my efforts to answer the question: Who am I, what am I, how did I come to be? What shall I make of the life around me, what celebrate, what reject, how confront the snare of good and evil which is inevitable? What does American society *mean* when regarded out of my *own* eyes, when informed by my *own* sense of the past and viewed by my *own* complex sense of the present? How, in other words, should I think of myself and my pluralistic sense of the world, how express my vision of the human predicament?"

FOR DISCUSSION

1. How did reading prepare Ellison for writing?
2. What connection does Ellison see between writing and personal identity?

JAMES THURBER

James Thurber (1894–1961), a native of Columbus, Ohio, made himself immortal with his humorous stories of shy, bumbling men (such as "The Secret Life of Walter Mitty") and his cartoons of men, women, and dogs that look as though he had drawn them with his foot. (In fact, Thurber suffered from weak eyesight and had to draw his cartoons in crayon on sheets of paper two or three feet wide.) As Thurber aged and approached blindness, he drew less and less and wrote more and more. His first book, written with his friend E. B. White, is a takeoff on self-help manuals, *Is Sex Necessary?* (1929). His later prose includes *My Life and Hard Times* (1933), from which "University Days" is taken; *The Thirteen Clocks,* a fable for children (1950); and *The Years with Ross* (1959), a memoir of his years on the staff of *The New Yorker.*

University Days

Ohio State University during World War I may seem remote from your own present situation, but see if you don't agree that this story of campus frustration is as fresh as the day it was first composed. Notice how, with beautiful brevity, Thurber draws a scene, introduces bits of revealing dialogue, and shifts briskly from one scene to another.

I passed all the other courses that I took at my university, but I   1
could never pass botany. This was because all botany students had to spend several hours a week in a laboratory looking through a microscope at plant cells, and I could never see through a microscope. I never once saw a cell through a microscope. This used to enrage my instructor. He would wander around the laboratory pleased with the progress all the students were making in drawing the involved and, so I am told, interesting structure of flower cells, until he came to me. I would just be standing there. "I can't see anything," I would say. He would begin patiently enough, explaining how anybody can see through a microscope, but he would always end up in a fury, claiming that I could *too* see through the microscope but just pretended that I couldn't. "It takes away from the beauty of flowers anyway," I used to tell him. "We are not concerned with beauty in this course," he would say. "We are concerned solely with what I may call the *mechanics* of flars." "Well," I'd say, "I can't see anything."

"Try it just once again," he'd say, and I would put my eye to the microscope and see nothing at all, except now and again a nebulous milky substance — a phenomenon of maladjustment. You were supposed to see a vivid, restless clockwork of sharply defined plant cells. "I see what looks like a lot of milk," I would tell him. This, he claimed, was the result of my not having adjusted the microscope properly, so he would readjust it for me, or rather, for himself. And I would look again and see milk.

I finally took a deferred pass, as they called it, and waited a year 2 and tried again. (You had to pass one of the biological sciences or you couldn't graduate.) The professor had come back from vacation brown as a berry, bright-eyed, and eager to explain cell-structure again to his classes. "Well," he said to me, cheerily, when we met in the first laboratory hour of the semester, "we're going to see cells this time, aren't we?" "Yes, sir," I said. Students to right of me and to left of me and in front of me were seeing cells; what's more, they were quietly drawing pictures of them in their notebooks. Of course, I didn't see anything.

"We'll try it," the professor said to me, grimly, "with every ad- 3 justment of the microscope known to man. As God is my witness, I'll arrange this glass so that you see cells through it or I'll give up teaching. In twenty-two years of botany, I — " He cut off abruptly for he was beginning to quiver all over, like Lionel Barrymore,[1] and he genuinely wished to hold onto his temper; his scenes with me had taken a great deal out of him.

So we tried it with every adjustment of the microscope known to 4 man. With only one of them did I see anything but blackness or the familiar lacteal opacity, and that time I saw, to my pleasure and amazement, a variegated constellation of flecks, specks, and dots. These I hastily drew. The instructor, noting my activity, came back from an adjoining desk, a smile on his lips and his eyebrows high in hope. He looked at my cell drawing. "What's that?" he demanded, with a hint of a squeal in his voice. "That's what I saw," I said. "You didn't, you didn't, you *didn't!*" he screamed, losing control of his temper instantly, and he bent over and squinted into the microscope. His head snapped up. "That's your eye!" he shouted. "You've fixed the lens so that it reflects! You've drawn your eye!"

Another course that I didn't like, but somehow managed to pass, 5 was economics. I went to that class straight from the botany class, which didn't help me any in understanding either subject. I used to

[1]A noted American stage, radio, and screen actor (1878–1954). — EDS.

get them mixed up. But not as mixed up as another student in my economics class who came there direct from a physics laboratory. He was a tackle on the football team, named Bolenciecwcz. At that time Ohio State University had one of the best football teams in the country, and Bolenciecwcz was one of its outstanding stars. In order to be eligible to play it was necessary for him to keep up in his studies, a very difficult matter, for while he was not dumber than an ox he was not any smarter. Most of his professors were lenient and helped him along. None gave him more hints in answering questions or asked him simpler ones than the economics professor, a thin, timid man named Bassum. One day when we were on the subject of transportation and distribution, it came Bolenciecwcz's turn to answer a question. "Name one means of transportation," the professor said to him. No light came into the big tackle's eyes. "Just any means of transportation," said the professor. Bolenciecwcz sat staring at him. "That is," pursued the professor, "any medium, agency, or method of going from one place to another." Bolenciecwcz had the look of a man who is being led into a trap. "You may choose among steam, horse-drawn, or electrically propelled vehicles," said the instructor. "I might suggest the one which we commonly take in making long journeys across land." There was a profound silence in which everybody stirred uneasily, including Bolenciecwcz and Mr. Bassum. Mr. Bassum abruptly broke this silence in an amazing manner. "Choo-choo-choo," he said, in a low voice, and turned instantly scarlet. He glanced appealingly around the room. All of us, of course, shared Mr. Bassum's desire that Bolenciecwcz should stay abreast of the class in economics, for the Illinois game, one of the hardest and most important of the season, was only a week off. "Toot, too, too-toooooooot!" some student with a deep voice moaned, and we all looked encouragingly at Bolenciecwcz. Somebody else gave a fine imitation of a locomotive letting off steam. Mr. Bassum himself rounded off the little show. "Ding, dong, ding, dong," he said, hopefully. Bolenciecwcz was staring at the floor now, trying to think, his great brow furrowed, his huge hands rubbing together, his face red.

"How did you come to college this year, Mr. Bolenciecwcz?" asked 6 the professor. "*Chuffa* chuffa, *chuffa* chuffa."

"M'father sent me," said the football player. 7

"What on?" asked Bassum. 8

"I git an 'lowance," said the tackle, in a low, husky voice, ob- 9 viously embarrassed.

"No, no," said Bassum. "Name a means of transportation. What 10 did you *ride* here on?"

"Train," said Bolenciecwcz. 11

"Quite right," said the professor. "Now, Mr. Nugent, will you tell 12
us — "

If I went through anguish in botany and economics — for differ- 13
ent reasons — gymnasium work was even worse. I don't even like to
think about it. They wouldn't let you play games or join the exercises
with your glasses on and I couldn't see with mine off. I bumped into
professors, horizontal bars, agricultural students, and swinging iron
rings. Not being able to see, I could take it but I couldn't dish it out.
Also, in order to pass gymnasium (and you had to pass it to graduate)
you had to learn to swim if you didn't know how. I didn't like the
swimming pool, I didn't like swimming, and I didn't like the swimming instructor, and after all these years I still don't. I never swam
but I passed my gym work anyway, by having another student give
my gymnasium number (978) and swim across the pool in my place.
He was a quiet, amiable blond youth, number 473, and he would
have seen through a microscope for me if we could have got away
with it, but we couldn't get away with it. Another thing I didn't like
about gymnasium work was that they made you strip the day you
registered. It is impossible for me to be happy when I am stripped
and being asked a lot of questions. Still, I did better than a lanky
agricultural student who was cross-examined just before I was. They
asked each student what college he was in — that is, whether Arts,
Engineering, Commerce, or Agriculture. "What college are you in?"
the instructor snapped at the youth in front of me. "Ohio State
University," he said promptly.

It wasn't that agricultural student but it was another a whole lot 14
like him who decided to take up journalism, possibly on the ground
that when farming went to hell he could fall back on newspaper work.
He didn't realize, of course, that that would be very much like falling
back full-length on a kit of carpenter's tools. Haskins didn't seem cut
out for journalism, being too embarrassed to talk to anybody and
unable to use a typewriter, but the editor of the college paper assigned
him to the cow barns, the sheep house, the horse pavilion, and the
animal husbandry department generally. This was a genuinely big
"beat," for it took up five times as much ground and got ten times as
great a legislative appropriation as the College of Liberal Arts. The
agricultural student knew animals, but nevertheless his stories were
dull and colorlessly written. He took all afternoon on each of them,
on account of having to hunt for each letter on the typewriter. Once
in a while he had to ask somebody to help him hunt. C and L, in
particular, were hard letters for him to find. His editor finally got
pretty much annoyed at the farmer-journalist because his pieces were
so uninteresting. "See here, Haskins," he snapped at him one day,

"why is it we never have anything hot from you on the horse pavilion? Here we have two hundred head of horses on this campus — more than any other university in the Western Conference except Purdue — and yet you never get any real lowdown on them. Now shoot over to the horse barns and dig up something lively." Haskins shambled out and came back in about an hour; he said he had something. "Well, start if off snappily," said the editor. "Something people will read." Haskins set to work and in a couple of hours brought a sheet of typewritten paper to the desk; it was a two-hundred-word story about some disease that had broken out among the horses. Its opening sentence was simple but arresting. It read: "Who has noticed the sores on the tops of the horses in the animal husbandry building?"

Ohio State was a land grant university and therefore two years of 15 military drill was compulsory. We drilled with old Springfield rifles and studied the tactics of the Civil War even though the World War was going on at the time. At 11 o'clock each morning thousands of freshmen and sophomores used to deploy over the campus, moodily creeping up on the old chemistry building. It was good training for the kind of warfare that was waged at Shiloh but it had no connection with what was going on in Europe. Some people used to think there was German money behind it, but they didn't say so or they would have been thrown in jail as German spies. It was a period of muddy thought and marked, I believe, the decline of higher education in the Middle West.

As a soldier I was never any good at all. Most of the cadets were 16 glumly indifferent soldiers, but I was no good at all. Once General Littlefield, who was commandant of the cadet corps, popped up in front of me during regimental drill and snapped, "You are the main trouble with this university!" I think he meant that my type was the main trouble with the university but he may have meant me individually. I was mediocre at drill, certainly — that is, until my senior year. By that time I had drilled longer than anybody else in the Western Conference, having failed at military at the end of each preceding year so that I had to do it all over again. I was the only senior still in uniform. The uniform which, when new, had made me look like an interurban railway conductor, now that it had become faded and too tight made me look like Bert Williams in his bellboy act.[2] This had a definitely bad effect on my morale. Even so, I had become by sheer practice little short of wonderful at squad maneuvers.

---

[2]A popular vaudeville and silent-screen comedian of the time, Williams in one routine played a hotel porter in a shrunken suit. — Eds.

One day General Littlefield picked our company out of the whole   17
regiment and tried to get it mixed up by putting it through one
movement after another as fast as we could execute them: squads
right, squads left, squads on right into line, squads right about, squads
left front into line, etc. In about three minutes one hundred and
nine men were marching in one direction and I was marching away
from them at an angle of forty degrees all alone. "Company, halt!"
shouted General Littlefield. "That man is the only man who has it
right!" I was made a corporal for my achievement.

The next day General Littlefield summoned me to his office. He   18
was swatting flies when I went in. I was silent and he was silent too,
for a long time. I don't think he remembered me or why he had sent
for me, but he didn't want to admit it. He swatted some more flies,
keeping his eyes on them narrowly before he let go with the swatter.
"Button up your coat!" he snapped. Looking back on it now I can
see that he meant me although he was looking at a fly, but I just
stood there. Another fly came to rest on a paper in front of the
general and began rubbing its hind legs together. The General lifted
the swatter cautiously. I moved restlessly and the fly flew away. "You
startled him!" barked General Littlefield, looking at me severely. I
said I was sorry. "That won't help the situation!" snapped the General,
with cold military logic. I didn't see what I could do except offer to
chase some more flies toward his desk, but I didn't say anything. He
stared out the window at the faraway figures of co-eds crossing the
campus toward the library. Finally, he told me I could go. So I went.
He either didn't know which cadet I was or else he forgot what he
wanted to see me about. It may have been that he wished to apologize
for having called me the main trouble with the university; or maybe
he had decided to compliment me on my brilliant drilling of the day
before and then at the last minute decided not to. I don't know. I
don't think about it much any more.

QUESTIONS ON MEANING

1. In what light does Thurber portray himself in "University Days"? Is his
   self-portrait sympathetic?
2. Are Bolenciecwcz and Haskins stereotypes? Discuss.
3. To what extent does Thurber sacrifice believability for humorous EFFECT?
   What is his main PURPOSE?

QUESTIONS ON WRITING STRATEGY

1. How do Thurber's INTRODUCTION, his TRANSITIONS, and his CONCLU-SION heighten the humor of his essay?
2. Criticize the opening sentence of the story Haskins writes about horse disease (quoted in para. 14).
3. Thurber does not explain in "University Days" how he ever did fulfill his biological science requirement for graduation. Is this an important omission? Explain.
4. OTHER METHODS. Each of Thurber's anecdotes is also an EXAMPLE, but the GENERALIZATION illustrated by these examples is not stated. How would you phrase this generalization? What idea do the examples add up to? (Avoid a vague assertion like "College can be frustrating.") Does the absence of a stated generalization weaken or strengthen the essay?

QUESTIONS ON LANGUAGE

1. Be sure to know what the following words mean: nebulous (para. 1); lacteal opacity, variegated (4).
2. Explain how Thurber's word choices heighten the IRONY in the following phrases: "like falling back full-length on a kit of carpenter's tools" (para. 14); "a genuinely big 'beat'" (14); "the decline of higher education in the Middle West" (15).
3. What is a land grant university (para. 15)?
4. Where in his essay does Thurber use colloquial DICTION? What is its effect?

SUGGESTIONS FOR WRITING

1. How does Thurber's picture of campus life during the days of World War I compare with campus life today? What has changed? What has stayed the same? Develop your own ideas in a brief essay.
2. Write an essay called "High-School Days" in which, with a light touch, you recount two or three related anecdotes from your own experience, educational or otherwise.
3. CRITICAL WRITING. ANALYZE the details and language Thurber uses to exploit a stereotype in the football player Bolenciecwcz (paras. 5–12). (If you need help defining stereotype, see p. 470.) In an essay, explain your analysis and EVALUATE the characterization: Do you, for instance, find it funny or offensive? Why?
4. CONNECTIONS. James Thurber and E. B. White were friends and colleagues at The New Yorker, and both are here represented by reminiscences. But Thurber's "University Days" and White's "Once More to the Lake" (p. 120) are very different in substance and TONE. After reading White's essay, write an essay of your own comparing these two works. What attitudes does each author convey, and how does he do

it? (Use quotations and PARAPHRASES from both essays to support your points.)

JAMES THURBER ON WRITING

In an interview with writers George Plimpton and Max Steele, James Thurber fielded some revealing questions. "Is the act of writing easy for you?" the interviewers wanted to know.

"For me," Thurber replied, "it's mostly a question of rewriting. It's part of a constant attempt on my part to make the finished version smooth, to make it seem effortless. A story I've been working on — 'The Train on Track Six,' it's called — was rewritten fifteen complete times. There must have been close to 240,000 words in all the manuscripts put together, and I must have spent two thousand hours working at it. Yet the finished version can't be more than twenty thousand words."

"Then it's rare that your work comes out right the first time?"

"Well," said Thurber, "my wife took a look at the first version of something I was doing not long ago and said, 'Goddamn it, Thurber, that's high-school stuff.' I have to tell her to wait until the seventh draft, it'll work out all right. I don't know why that should be so, that the first or second draft of everything I write reads as if it was turned out by a charwoman. I've only written one piece quickly. I wrote a thing called 'File and Forget' in one afternoon — but only because it was a series of letters just as one would ordinarily dictate. And I'll have to admit that the last letter of the series, after doing all the others that one afternoon, took me a week. It was the end of the piece and I had to fuss over it."

"Does the fact that you're dealing with humor slow down the production?"

"It's possible. With humor you have to look out for traps. You're likely to be very gleeful with what you've first put down, and you think it's fine, very funny. One reason you go over and over it is to make the piece sound less as if you were having a lot of fun with it yourself."

In his own book *Thurber Country*, Thurber set forth, with tongue in cheek, some general principles for comic writing. "I have established a few standing rules of my own about humor," he wrote, "after receiving dozens of humorous essays and stories from strangers over a period of twenty years. (1) The reader should be able to find out what the story is about. (2) Some inkling of the general idea should be apparent in the first five hundred words. (3) If the writer has decided to change the name of his protagonist from Ketcham to McTavish, Ketcham should not keep bobbing up in the last five pages. A good way to eliminate this confusion is to read the piece over before sending it out, and remove Ketcham completely. He is a nuisance. (4) The word "I'll" should not be divided so that the "I" is on one line and "'ll" on the next. The reader's attention, after the breaking up of "I'll," can never be successfully recaptured. (5) It also never recovers from such names as Ann S. Thetic, Maud Lynn, Sally Forth, Bertha Twins, and the like. (6) Avoid comic stories about plumbers who are mistaken for surgeons, sheriffs who are terrified by gunfire, psychiatrists who are driven crazy by women patients, doctors who faint at the sight of blood, adolescent girls who know more about sex than their fathers do, and midgets who turn out to be the parents of a two-hundred-pound wrestler."

FOR DISCUSSION

1. By what means does Thurber make his writing look "effortless"?
2. Is there any serious advice to be extracted from Thurber's "standing rules about humor"? If so, what is it?

JUDITH ORTIZ COFER

A native of Puerto Rico who has lived most of her life in the United States, JUDITH ORTIZ COFER writes about heritage and the balancing of two cultures. Born in 1952, she earned a B.A. from Augusta College in 1974 and an M.A. from Florida Atlantic University in 1977, the same year she attended Oxford University as scholar of the English Speaking Union. Cofer started out as a bilingual teacher in the schools of Palm Beach County, Florida, and she has taught English at several colleges and universities. Her publications include collections of poetry, among them *Peregrina* (1986) and *Terms of Survival* (1987); a novel, *The Line of the Sun* (1989); and a book of essays, *Silent Dancing* (1990). As a native Spanish speaker who challenged herself to learn English, she is always experimenting, she says, with "the 'infinite variety' and power of language."

Casa: *A Partial Remembrance of a Puerto Rican Childhood*

First published in the literary magazine *Prairie Schooner* in 1989, this essay recounts hours Cofer spent literally at the knee of her grandmother, listening to her talk. What Cofer has said of her poetry applies equally to this essay: She writes of her relatives to understand the "process of change, assimilation, and transformation" that they, and she herself, experienced in moving between cultures.

At three or four o'clock in the afternoon, the hour of *café con leche*, the women of my family gathered in Mamá's living room to speak of important things and retell familiar stories meant to be overheard by us young girls, their daughters. In Mamá's house (everyone called my grandmother Mamá) was a large parlor built by my grandfather to his wife's exact specifications so that it was always cool, facing away from the sun. The doorway was on the side of the house so no one could walk directly into her living room. First they had to take a little stroll through and around her beautiful garden where prize-winning orchids grew in the trunk of an ancient tree she had hollowed out for that purpose. This room was furnished with several mahogany rocking chairs, acquired at the births of her children, and one intricately carved rocker that had passed down to Mamá at the death of her own mother.

73

It was on these rockers that my mother, her sisters, and my   2
grandmother sat on these afternoons of my childhood to tell their
stories, teaching each other, and my cousin and me, what it was like
to be a woman, more specifically, a Puerto Rican woman. They talked
about life on the island, and life in *Los Nueva Yores*, their way of
referring to the United States from New York City to California: the
other place, not home, all the same. They told real-life stories though,
as I later learned, always embellishing them with a little or a lot of
dramatic detail. And they told *cuentos*, the morality and cautionary
tales told by the women in our family for generations: stories that
became a part of my subconscious as I grew up in two worlds, the
tropical island and the cold city, and that would later surface in my
dreams and in my poetry.

One of these tales was about the woman who was left at the altar.   3
Mamá liked to tell that one with histrionic intensity. I remember the
rise and fall of her voice, the sighs, and her constantly gesturing
hands, like two birds swooping through her words. This particular
story usually would come up in a conversation as a result of someone
mentioning a forthcoming engagement or wedding. The first time I
remember hearing it, I was sitting on the floor at Mamá's feet,
pretending to read a comic book. I may have been eleven or twelve
years old, at that difficult age when a girl was no longer a child who
could be ordered to leave the room if the women wanted freedom to
take their talk into forbidden zones, nor really old enough to be
considered a part of their conclave. I could only sit quietly, pretending
to be in another world, while absorbing it all in a sort of unspoken
agreement of my status as silent auditor. On this day, Mamá had
taken my long, tangled mane of hair into her ever-busy hands. Without looking down at me and with no interruption of her flow of words,
she began braiding my hair, working at it with the quickness and
determination that characterized her all actions. My mother was
watching us impassively from her rocker across the room. On her lips
played a little ironic smile. I would never sit still for *her* ministrations,
but even then, I instinctively knew that she did not possess Mamá's
matriarchal power to command and keep everyone's attention. This
was never more evident than in the spell she cast when telling a
story.

"It is not like it used to be when I was a girl," Mamá announced.   4
"Then, a man could leave a girl standing at the church altar with a
bouquet of fresh flowers in her hands and disappear off the face of
the earth. No way to track him down if he was from another town.
He could be a married man, with maybe even two or three families

all over the island. There was no way to know. And there were men who did this. Hombres with the devil in their flesh who would come to a pueblo, like this one, take a job at one of the haciendas, never meaning to stay, only to have a good time and to seduce the women."

5 The whole time she was speaking, Mamá would be weaving my hair into a flat plait that required pulling apart the two sections of hair with little jerks that made my eyes water; but knowing how grandmother detested whining and *boba* (sissy) tears, as she called them, I just sat up as straight and stiff as I did at La Escuela San Jose, where the nuns enforced good posture with a flexible plastic ruler they bounced off of slumped shoulders and heads. As Mamá's story progressed, I noticed how my young Aunt Laura lowered her eyes, refusing to meet Mamá's meaningful gaze. Laura was seventeen, in her last year of high school, and already engaged to a boy from another town who had staked his claim with a tiny diamond ring, then left for Los Nueva Yores to make his fortune. They were planning to get married in a year. Mamá had expressed serious doubts that the wedding would ever take place. In Mamá's eyes, a man set free without a legal contract was a man lost. She believed that marriage was not something men desired, but simply the price they had to pay for the privilege of children and, of course, for what no decent (synonymous with "smart") woman would give away for free.

6 "María La Loca was only seventeen when *it* happened to her." I listened closely at the mention of this name. María was a town character, a fat middle-aged woman who lived with her old mother on the outskirts of town. She was to be seen around the pueblo delivering the meat pies the two women made for a living. The most peculiar thing about María, in my eyes, was that she walked and moved like a little girl though she had the thick body and wrinkled face of an old woman. She would swing her hips in an exaggerated, clownish way, and sometimes even hop and skip up to someone's house. She spoke to no one. Even if you asked her a question, she would just look at you and smile, showing her yellow teeth. But I had heard that if you got close enough, you could hear her humming a tune without words. The kids yelled out nasty things to her, calling her *La Loca*, and the men who hung out at the bodega playing dominoes sometimes whistled mockingly as she passed by with her funny, outlandish walk. But María seemed impervious to it all, carrying her basket of *pasteles* like a grotesque Little Red Riding Hood through the forest.

7 María La Loca interested me, as did all the eccentrics and crazies of our pueblo. Their weirdness was a measuring stick I used in my

serious quest for a definition of normal. As a Navy brat shuttling between New Jersey and the pueblo, I was constantly made to feel like an oddball by my peers, who made fun of my two-way accent: a Spanish accent when I spoke English, and when I spoke Spanish I was told that I sounded like a *Gringa*. Being the outsider had already turned my brother and me into cultural chameleons. We developed early on the ability to blend into a crowd, to sit and read quietly in a fifth story apartment building for days and days when it was too bitterly cold to play outside, or, set free, to run wild in Mamá's realm, where she took charge of our lives, releasing Mother for a while from the intense fear for our safety that our father's absences instilled in her. In order to keep us from harm when Father was away, Mother kept us under strict surveillance. She even walked us to and from Public School No. 11, which we attended during the months we lived in Paterson, New Jersey, our home base in the states. Mamá freed all three of us like pigeons from a cage. I saw her as my liberator and my model. Her stories were parables from which to glean the *Truth*.

"María La Loca was once a beautiful girl. Everyone thought she would marry the Méndez boy." As everyone knew, Rogelio Méndez was the richest man in town. "But," Mamá continued, knitting my hair with the same intensity she was putting into her story, "this *macho* made a fool out of her and ruined her life." She paused for the effect of her use of the word *macho*, which at that time had not yet become a popular epithet for an unliberated man. This word had for us the crude and comical connotation of "male of the species," stud; a *macho* was what you put in a pen to increase your stock. 8

I peeked over my comic book at my mother. She too was under Mamá's spell, smiling conspiratorially at this little swipe at men. She was safe from Mamá's contempt in this area. Married at an early age, an unspotted lamb, she had been accepted by a good family of strict Spaniards whose name was old and respected, though their fortune had been lost long before my birth. In a rocker Papá had painted sky blue sat Mamá's oldest child, Aunt Nena. Mother of three children, step-mother of two more, she was a quiet woman who liked books but had married an ignorant and abusive widower whose main interest in life was accumulating wealth. He too was in the mainland working on his dream of returning home rich and triumphant to buy the *finca* of his dreams. She was waiting for him to send for her. She would leave her children with Mamá for several years while the two of them slaved away in factories. He would one day be a rich man, and she a sadder woman. Even now her life-light was dimming. She spoke little, an aberration in Mamá's house, and she read avidly, as if storing 9 up spiritual food for the long winters that awaited her in Los Nueva Yores without her family. But even Aunt Nena came alive to Mamá's words, rocking gently, her hands over a thick book in her lap.

Her daughter, my cousin Sara, played jacks by herself on the tile 10 porch outside the room where we sat. She was a year older than I. We shared a bed and all our family's secrets. Collaborators in search of answers, Sara and I discussed everything we heard the women say, trying to fit it all together like a puzzle that, once assembled, would reveal life's mysteries to us. Though she and I still enjoyed taking part in boys' games — chase, volleyball, and even *vaqueros*, the island version of cowboys and Indians involving cap-gun battles and violent shoot-outs under the mango tree in Mamá's backyard — we loved best the quiet hours in the afternoon when the men were still at work, and the boys had gone to play serious baseball at the park. Then Mamá's house belonged only to us women. The aroma of coffee perking in the kitchen, the mesmerizing creaks and groans of the rockers, and the women telling their lives in *cuentos* are forever woven into the fabric of my imagination, braided like my hair that day I felt my grandmother's hands teaching me about strength, her voice convincing me of the power of storytelling.

That day Mamá told how the beautiful María had fallen prey to 11 a man whose name was never the same in subsequent versions of the story; it was Juan one time, José, Rafael, Diego, another. We understood that neither the name nor any of the *facts* were important, only that a woman had allowed love to defeat her. Mamá put each of us in María's place by describing her wedding dress in loving detail: how she looked like a princess in her lace as she waited at the altar. Then, as Mamá approached the tragic denouement of her story, I was distracted by the sound of my Aunt Laura's violent rocking. She seemed on the verge of tears. She knew the fable was intended for her. That week she was going to have her wedding gown fitted, though no firm date had been set for the marriage. Mamá ignored Laura's obvious discomfort, digging out a ribbon from the sewing basket she kept by her rocker while describing María's long illness, "a fever that would not break for days." She spoke of a mother's despair: "that woman climbed the church steps on her knees every morning, wore only black as a *promesa* to the Holy Virgin in exchange for her daughter's health." By the time María returned from her honeymoon with death, she was ravished, no longer young or sane. "As you can see, she is almost as old as her mother already," Mamá lamented while tying the ribbon to the ends of my hair, pulling it back with such force that I just knew I would never be able to close my eyes completely again.

"That María is getting crazier every day." Mamá's voice would 12 take a lighter tone now, expressing satisfaction, either for the perfection of my braid, or for a story well told — it was hard to tell. "You know that tune María is always humming?" Carried away by her enthusiasm, I tried to nod, but Mamá still had me pinned between her knees.

"Well, that's the wedding march." Surprising us all, Mamá sang out, "Da, da, dara . . . da, da, dara." Then lifting me off the floor by my skinny shoulders, she would lead me around the room in an impromptu waltz — another session ending with the laughter of women, all of us caught up in the infectious joke of our lives.   13

QUESTIONS ON MEANING

1. What is Cofer's PURPOSE in re-creating one particular afternoon from her childhood?
2. How do we know that Mamá's tale of the abandoned bride is not actually true? In what way is the story "true"?
3. Why do Cofer and her brother feel like "cultural chameleons" (para. 7)?
4. Did Cofer's relatives see the mainland United States — "*Los Nueva Yores*" (para. 2) — as a familiar, welcoming place?

QUESTIONS ON WRITING STRATEGY

1. Why does Cofer alternate between telling the story of the bride left at the altar, as her grandmother told it, and giving character sketches of her mother and aunts?
2. The only person quoted directly in Cofer's memoir is her grandmother. Why might this be?
3. Discuss Cofer's POINT OF VIEW. Is her perspective that of a girl of "eleven or twelve years old" (para. 3) or that of an adult writer reflecting on her childhood experience?
4. OTHER METHODS. What is the function of the DESCRIPTION of Mamá's house that opens the essay? What sensations does Cofer evoke?

QUESTIONS ON LANGUAGE

1. What is the EFFECT of Cofer's use of Spanish? Look up the following Spanish words and phrases: casa (title); café con leche (para. 1); Los Nueva Yores, cuentos (2); hombres, haciendas (4); boba, escuela (5); loca, bodega, pasteles (6); pueblo, gringa (7); macho (8); finca (9); vaqueros (10); promesa (11).

2. Be sure you know the meaning of these words: histrionic, conclave, impassively, ministrations, matriarchal (para. 3); plait (5); impervious (6); parables (7); epithet (8); aberration (9); mesmerizing (10); denouement, ravished (11); impromptu (13).

3. What is the EFFECT of the animal IMAGES Cofer uses to describe human beings — for instance, "cultural chameleons" and freed "like pigeons from a cage" (para. 7), "an unspotted lamb" (9), and "what you put in a pen to increase your stock" (8)?

SUGGESTIONS FOR WRITING

1. Think of a story told to you in your childhood that affected how you view the world. Using the first PERSON, retell the story, including a description of its teller.

2. What roles do the women in Cofer's family expect to play in life? How would you characterize Cofer's depictions of masculinity and femininity? In a short essay, discuss the views of men and women expressed in this selection. How do your views differ?

3. CRITICAL WRITING. Cofer says that her grandmother's stories "were parables from which to glean the *Truth*" (para. 7). Judging from the story related here, would you agree with that characterization? Why or why not? In a brief essay, discuss what Cofer might mean by "the *Truth*." What ASSUMPTIONS does this truth rest on?

4. CONNECTIONS. Cofer's "*Casa*" and E. B. White's "Once More to the Lake" (p. 120) both concern the transfer of cultural knowledge from one generation to another. But the narrators have different POINTS OF VIEW, and the cultures are very different. Write an essay about the similarities and differences in the reasons for transmitting cultural knowledge, the ways it's transmitted, and the actual content.

SHIRLEY JACKSON

SHIRLEY JACKSON was a fiction writer best known for horror stories that probe the dark side of human nature and social behavior. But she also wrote humorously about domestic life, a subject she knew well as a wife and the mother of four children. Born in 1919 in California, Jackson moved as a teenager to Syracuse, New York, and graduated from Syracuse University in 1940. She started writing as a young girl and was highly disciplined and productive all her life. She began publishing stories in 1941, and eventually her fiction appeared in *The New Yorker, Harper's, Good Housekeeping,* and many other magazines. Her tales of family life appeared in two books, *Life among the Savages* (1953) and *Raising Demons* (1957). Her more popular (and to her more significant) suspense novels included *The Haunting of Hill House* (1959) and *We Have Always Lived in the Castle* (1962). After Jackson's death in 1965, her husband, the literary critic Stanley Edgar Hyman, published two volumes of her stories, novels, and lectures, *The Magic of Shirley Jackson* (1966) and *Come Along with Me* (1968).

The Lottery

By far Jackson's best-known work and indeed one of the best-known short stories ever, "The Lottery" first appeared in *The New Yorker* in 1948 to loud applause and louder cries of outrage. Jackson's husband, denying that her work purveyed "neurotic fantasies," argued instead that it was fitting "for our distressing world of concentration camps and The Bomb." See if you agree.

The morning of June 27th was clear and sunny, with the fresh 1
warmth of a full-summer day; the flowers were blossoming profusely and the grass was richly green. The people of the village began to gather in the square, between the post office and the bank, around ten o'clock; in some towns there were so many people that the lottery took two days and had to be started on June 26th, but in this village, where there were only about three hundred people, the whole lottery took less than two hours, so it could begin at ten o'clock in the morning and still be through in time to allow the villagers to get home for noon dinner.

The children assembled first, of course. School was recently over 2 for the summer, and the feeling of liberty sat uneasily on most of them; they tended to gather together quietly for a while before they broke into boisterous play, and their talk was still of the classroom and the teacher, of books and reprimands. Bobby Martin had already stuffed his pockets full of stones, and the other boys soon followed his example, selecting the smoothest and roundest stones; Bobby and Harry Jones and Dickie Delacroix — the villagers pronounced this name "Dellacroy" — eventually made a great pile of stones in one corner of the square and guarded it against the raids of the other boys. The girls stood aside, talking among themselves, looking over their shoulders at the boys, and the very small children rolled in the dust or clung to the hands of their older brothers or sisters.

Soon the men began to gather, surveying their own children,   3
speaking of planting and rain, tractors and taxes. They stood together, away from the pile of stones in the corner, and their jokes were quiet and they smiled rather than laughed. The women, wearing faded house dresses and sweaters, came shortly after their menfolk. They greeted one another and exchanged bits of gossip as they went to join their husbands. Soon the women, standing by their husbands, began to call to their children, and the children came reluctantly, having to be called four or five times. Bobby Martin ducked under his mother's grasping hand and ran, laughing, back to the pile of stones. His father spoke up sharply, and Bobby came quickly and took his place between his father and his oldest brother.

The lottery was conducted — as were the square dances, the   4
teenage club, the Halloween program — by Mr. Summers, who had time and energy to devote to civic activities. He was a round-faced, jovial man and he ran the coal business, and people were sorry for him, because he had no children and his wife was a scold. When he arrived in the square, carrying the black wooden box, there was a murmur of conversation among the villagers, and he waved and called, "Little late today, folks." The postmaster, Mr. Graves, followed him, carrying a three-legged stool, and the stool was put in the center of the square and Mr. Summers set the black box down on it. The villagers kept their distance, leaving a space between themselves and the stool, and when Mr. Summers said, "Some of you fellows want to give me a hand?" there was a hesitation before two men, Mr. Martin and his oldest son, Baxter, came forward to hold the box steady on the stool while Mr. Summers stirred up the papers inside it.

The original paraphernalia for the lottery had been lost long ago,   5
and the black box now resting on the stool had been put into use

even before Old Man Warner, the oldest man in town, was born. Mr. Summers spoke frequently to the villagers about making a new box, but no one liked to upset even as much tradition as was represented by the black box. There was a story that the present box had been made with some pieces of the box that had preceded it, the one that had been constructed when the first people settled down to make a village here. Every year, after the lottery, Mr. Summers began talking again about a new box, but every year the subject was allowed to fade off without anything's being done. The black box grew shabbier each year; by now it was no longer completely black but splintered badly along one side to show the original wood color, and in some places faded or stained.

Mr. Martin and his oldest son, Baxter, held the black box securely   6
on the stool until Mr. Summers had stirred the papers thoroughly with his hand. Because so much of the ritual had been forgotten or discarded, Mr. Summers had been successful in having slips of paper substituted for the chips of wood that had been used for generations. Chips of wood, Mr. Summers had argued, had been all very well when the village was tiny, but now that the population was more than three hundred and likely to keep on growing, it was necessary to use something that would fit more easily into the black box. The night before the lottery, Mr. Summers and Mr. Graves made up the slips of paper and put them in the box, and it was then taken to the safe of Mr. Summers' coal company and locked up until Mr. Summers was ready to take it to the square next morning. The rest of the year, the box was put away, sometimes one place, sometimes another; it had spent one year in Mr. Graves's barn and another year underfoot in the post office, and sometimes it was set on a shelf in the Martin grocery and left there.

There was a great deal of fussing to be done before Mr. Summers   7
declared the lottery open. There were the lists to make up — of heads of families, heads of households in each family, members of each household in each family. There was the proper swearing-in of Mr. Summers by the postmaster, as the official of the lottery; at one time, some people remembered, there had been a recital of some sort, performed by the official of the lottery, a perfunctory, tuneless chant that had been rattled off duly each year; some people believed that the official of the lottery used to stand just so when he said or sang it, others believed that he was supposed to walk among the people, but years and years ago this part of the ritual had been allowed to lapse. There had been, also, a ritual salute, which the official of the lottery had had to use in addressing each person who came up to

draw from the box, but this also had changed with time, until now it was felt necessary only for the official to speak to each person approaching. Mr. Summers was very good at all this; in his clean white shirt and blue jeans, with one hand resting carelessly on the black box, he seemed very proper and important as he talked interminably to Mr. Graves and the Martins.

Just as Mr. Summers finally left off talking and turned to the   8 assembled villagers, Mrs. Hutchinson came hurriedly along the path to the square, her sweater thrown over her shoulders, and slid into place in the back of the crowd. "Clean forgot what day it was," she said to Mrs. Delacroix, who stood next to her, and they both laughed softly. "Thought my old man was out back stacking wood," Mrs. Hutchinson went on, "and then I looked out the window and the kids was gone, and then I remembered it was the twenty-seventh and came a-running." She dried her hands on her apron, and Mrs. Delacroix said, "You're in time, though. They're still talking away up there."

Mrs. Hutchinson craned her neck to see through the crowd and   9 found her husband and children standing near the front. She tapped Mrs. Delacroix on the arm as a farewell and began to make her way through the crowd. The people separated good-humoredly to let her through, two or three people said, in voices just loud enough to be heard across the crowd, "Here comes your Missus, Hutchinson," and "Bill, she made it after all." Mrs. Hutchinson reached her husband, and Mr. Summers, who had been waiting, said cheerfully, "Thought we were going to have to get on without you, Tessie." Mrs. Hutchinson said, grinning, "Wouldn't have me leave m'dishes in the sink, now, would you, Joe?" and soft laughter ran through the crowd as the people stirred back into position after Mrs. Hutchinson's arrival.

"Well now," Mr. Summers said soberly, "guess we better get   10 started, get this over with, so's we can go back to work. Anybody ain't here?"

"Dunbar," several people said. "Dunbar, Dunbar."   11

Mr. Summers consulted his list. "Clyde Dunbar," he said. "That's   12 right. He's broke his leg, hasn't he? Who's drawing for him?"

"Me, I guess," a woman said, and Mr. Summers turned to look   13 at her. "Wife draws for her husband," Mr. Summers said. "Don't you have a grown boy to do it for you, Janey?" Although Mr. Summers and everyone else in the village knew the answer perfectly well, it was the business of the official of the lottery to ask such questions formally. Mr. Summers waited with an expression of polite interest while Mrs. Dunbar answered.

"Horace's not but sixteen yet," Mrs. Dunbar said regretfully. 14 "Guess I gotta fill in for the old man this year."

"Right," Mr. Summers said. He made a note on the list he was 15 holding. Then he asked, "Watson boy drawing this year?"

A tall boy in the crowd raised his hand. "Here," he said. "I'm 16 drawing for m'mother and me." He blinked his eyes nervously and ducked his head as several voices in the crowd said things like "Good fellow, Jack," and "Glad to see your mother's got a man to do it."

"Well," Mr. Summers said, "guess that's everyone. Old Man 17 Warner make it?"

"Here," a voice said, and Mr. Summers nodded. 18

A sudden hush fell on the crowd as Mr. Summers cleared his 19 throat and looked at the list. "All ready?" he called. "Now, I'll read the names — heads of families first — and the men come up and take a paper out of the box. Keep the paper folded in your hand without looking at it until everyone has had a turn. Everything clear?"

The people had done it so many times that they only half listened 20 to the directions, most of them were quiet, wetting their lips, not looking around. Then Mr. Summers raised one hand high and said, "Adams." A man disengaged himself from the crowd and came forward. "Hi, Steve," Mr. Summers said, and Mr. Adams said, "Hi, Joe." They grinned at one another humorlessly and nervously. Then Mr. Adams reached into the black box and took out a folded paper. He held it firmly by one corner as he turned and went hastily back to his place in the crowd, where he stood a little apart from his family, not looking down at his hand.

"Allen," Mr. Summers said, "Anderson. . . . Bentham." 21

"Seems like there's no time at all between lotteries any more," 22 Mrs. Delacroix said to Mrs. Graves in the back row. "Seems like we got through with the last one only last week."

"Time sure goes fast," Mrs. Graves said. 23

"Clark. . . . Delacroix." 24

"There goes my old man," Mrs. Delacroix said. She held her 25 breath while her husband went forward.

"Dunbar," Mr. Summers said, and Mrs. Dunbar went steadily to 26 the box while one of the women said, "Go on Janey," and another said, "There she goes."

"We're next," Mrs. Graves said. She watched while Mr. Graves 27 came around from the side of the box, greeted Mr. Summers gravely, and selected a slip of paper from the box. By now, all through the crowd there were men holding the small folded papers in their large hands, turning them over and over nervously. Mrs. Dunbar and her two sons stood together, Mrs. Dunbar holding the slip of paper.

"Harburt. . . . Hutchinson." 28

"Get up there, Bill," Mrs. Hutchinson said, and the people near her laughed. 29

"Jones." 30

"They do say," Mr. Adams said to Old Man Warner, who stood next to him, "that over in the north village they're talking of giving up the lottery." 31

Old Man Warner snorted. "Pack of crazy fools," he said. "Listening to the young folks, nothing's good enough for *them*. Next thing you know, they'll be wanting to go back to living in caves, nobody work any more, live *that* way for a while. Used to be a saying about 'Lottery in June, corn be heavy soon.' First thing you know, we'd all be eating stewed chickweed and acorns. There's *always* been a lottery," he added petulantly. "Bad enough to see young Joe Summers up there joking with everybody." 32

"Some places have already quit lotteries," Mrs. Adams said. 33

"Nothing but trouble in *that*," Old Man Warner said stoutly. "Pack of young fools." 34

"Martin." And Bobby Martin watched his father go forward. "Overdyke. . . . Percy." 35

"I wish they'd hurry," Mrs. Dunbar said to her older son. "I wish they'd hurry." 36

"They're almost through," her son said. 37

"You get ready to run tell Dad," Mrs. Dunbar said. 38

Mr. Summers called his own name and then stepped forward precisely and selected a slip from the box. Then he called, "Warner." 39

"Seventy-seventh year I been in the lottery," Old Man Warner said as he went through the crowd. "Seventy-seventh time." 40

"Watson." The tall boy came awkwardly through the crowd. Someone said, "Don't be nervous, Jack," and Mr. Summers said, "Take your time, son." 41

"Zanini." 42

After that, there was a long pause, a breathless pause, until Mr. Summers, holding his slip of paper in the air, said, "All right, fellows." For a minute, no one moved, and then all the slips of paper were opened. Suddenly, all the women began to speak at once, saying, "Who is it?" "Who's got it?" "Is it the Dunbars?" "Is it the Watsons?" Then the voices began to say, "It's Hutchinson. It's Bill," "Bill Hutchinson's got it." 43

"Go tell your father," Mrs. Dunbar said to her older son.   44

People began to look around to see the Hutchinsons. Bill Hutch-   45
inson was standing quiet, staring down at the paper in his hand.
Suddenly, Tessie Hutchinson shouted to Mr. Summers, "You didn't
give him time enough to take any paper he wanted. I saw you. It
wasn't fair!"

"Be a good sport, Tessie," Mrs. Delacroix called, and Mrs. Graves   46
said, "All of us took the same chance."

"Shut up, Tessie," Bill Hutchinson said.   47

"Well, everyone," Mr. Summers said, "that was done pretty fast,   48
and now we've got to be hurrying a little more to get done in time."
He consulted his next list. "Bill," he said, "you draw for the Hutchinson family. You got any other households in the Hutchinsons?"

"There's Don and Eva," Mrs. Hutchinson yelled. "Make *them*   49
take their chance!"

"Daughters drew with their husband's families, Tessie," Mr. Sum-   50
mers said gently. "You know that as well as anyone else."

"It wasn't *fair*," Tessie said.   51

"I guess not, Joe," Bill Hutchinson said regretfully. "My daughter 52
draws with her husband's family, that's only fair. And I've got no
other family except the kids."

"Then, as far as drawing for families is concerned, it's you," Mr. 53
Summers said in explanation, "and as far as drawing for households
is concerned, that's you, too. Right?"

"Right," Bill Hutchinson said.   54

"How many kids, Bill?" Mr. Summers asked formally.   55

"Three," Bill Hutchinson said. "There's Bill, Jr., and Nancy, and   56
little Dave. And Tessie and me."

"All right, then," Mr. Summer said. "Harry, you got their tickets   57
back?"

Mr. Graves nodded and held up the slips of paper. "Put them in   58
the box, then," Mr. Summers directed. "Take Bill's and put it in."

"I think we ought to start over," Mrs. Hutchinson said, as quietly 59
as she could. "I tell you it wasn't *fair*. You didn't give him time
enough to choose. *Every*body saw that."

Mr. Graves had selected the five slips and put them in the box,   60
and he dropped all the papers but those onto the ground, where the
breeze caught them and lifted them off.

"Listen, everybody," Mrs. Hutchinson was saying to the people   61
around her.

"Ready, Bill?" Mr. Summers asked, and Bill Hutchinson, with   62
one quick glance around at his wife and children, nodded.

"Remember," Mr. Summers said, "take the slips and keep them 63 folded until each person has taken one. Harry, you help little Dave." Mr. Graves took the hand of the little boy, who came willingly with him up to the box. "Take a paper out of the box, Davy," Mr. Summers said. Davy put his hand into the box and laughed. "Take just *one* paper," Mr. Summers said. "Harry, you hold it for him." Mr. Graves took the child's hand and removed the folded paper from the tight fist and held it while little Dave stood next to him and looked up at him wonderingly.

"Nancy next," Mr. Summers said. Nancy was twelve, and her 64 school friends breathed heavily as she went forward, switching her skirt, and took a slip daintily from the box. "Bill, Jr.," Mr. Summers said, and Billy, his face red and his feet overlarge, nearly knocked the box over as he got a paper out. "Tessie," Mr. Summers said. She hesitated for a minute, looking around defiantly, and then set her lips and went up to the box. She snatched a paper out and held it behind her.

"Bill," Mr. Summers said, and Bill Hutchinson reached into the 65 box and felt around, bringing his hand out at last with the slip of paper in it.

The crowd was quiet. A girl whispered, "I hope it's not Nancy," 66 and the sound of the whisper reached the edges of the crowd.

"It's not the way it used to be," Old Man Warner said clearly. 67 "People ain't the way they used to be."

"All right," Mr. Summers said. "Open the papers. Harry, you 68 open little Dave's."

Mr. Graves opened the slip of paper and there was a general sigh 69 through the crowd as he held it up and everyone could see that it was blank. Nancy and Bill, Jr., opened theirs at the same time, and both beamed and laughed, turning around to the crowd and holding their slips of paper above their heads.

"Tessie," Mr. Summers said. There was a pause, and then Mr. 70 Summers looked at Bill Hutchinson, and Bill unfolded his paper and showed it. It was blank.

"It's Tessie," Mr. Summers said, and his voice was hushed. "Show 71 us her paper, Bill."

Bill Hutchinson went over to his wife and forced the slip of paper 72 out of her hand. It had a black spot on it, the black spot Mr. Summers had made the night before with the heavy pencil in the coal-company office. Bill Hutchinson held it up and there was a stir in the crowd.

"All right, folks," Mr. Summers said. "Let's finish quickly." 73

Although the villagers had forgotten the ritual and lost the orig- 74 inal black box, they still remembered to use stones. The pile of stones the boys had made earlier was ready; there were stones on the ground with the blowing scraps of paper that had come out of the box. Mrs. Delacroix selected a stone so large she had to pick it up with both hands and turned to Mrs. Dunbar. "Come on," she said. "Hurry up."

Mrs. Dunbar had small stones in both hands, and she said, gasping 75 for breath, "I can't run at all. You'll have to go ahead and I'll catch up with you."

The children had stones already, and someone gave little Davy 76 Hutchinson a few pebbles.

Tessie Hutchinson was in the center of a cleared space by now, 77 and she held her hands out desperately as the villagers moved in on her. "It isn't fair," she said. A stone hit her on the side of the head.

Old Man Warner was saying, "Come on, come on, everyone." 78 Steve Adams was in front of the crowd of villagers, with Mrs. Graves beside him.

"It isn't fair, it isn't right," Mrs. Hutchinson screamed and then 79 they were upon her.

QUESTIONS ON MEANING

1. The PURPOSE of all fiction might be taken as entertainment or self-expression. Does Jackson have any other purpose in "The Lottery"?
2. When does the reader know what is actually going to occur?
3. Describe this story's community on the basis of what Jackson says of it.
4. What do the villagers' attitudes toward the black box indicate about their feelings toward the lottery?

QUESTIONS ON WRITING STRATEGY

1. Jackson uses the third PERSON (he, she, it, they) to narrate the story, and she does not enter the minds of her characters. Why do you think she keeps this distant POINT OF VIEW?
2. On your first reading of the story, what did you make of the references to rocks in paragraphs 2–3? Do you think they effectively forecast the ending?
3. Jackson has a character introduce a controversial notion in paragraph 31. Why does she do this?
4. OTHER METHODS. Jackson is exploring — or inviting us to explore — CAUSES AND EFFECTS. Why do the villagers participate in the lottery

every year? What does paragraph 32 hint might have been the original reason for it?

QUESTIONS ON LANGUAGE

1. Dialogue provides much information not stated elsewhere in the story. Give three examples of such information about the community and its interactions.
2. Check a dictionary for definitions of the following words: profusely (para. 1); boisterous, reprimand (2); jovial, scold, paraphernalia (4); perfunctory, duly, interminably (7); petulantly (32).
3. Jackson admits to setting the story in her Vermont village in the present time (that is, 1948). Judging from the names of the villagers, where did these people's ancestors originally come from? What do you make of the names Delacroix and Zanini? What is their significance?
4. Unlike much fiction, "The Lottery" contains few FIGURES OF SPEECH. Why do you think this is?

SUGGESTIONS FOR WRITING

1. Write an imaginary narrative, perhaps set in the future, of a ritual that demonstrates something about the people who participate in it. The ritual can be but need not be as sinister as Jackson's lottery; yours could concern bathing, eating, dating, going to school, driving, growing older.
2. Choose an actual ritual familiar to you concerning a holiday, a meal, a religion, an observance, a vacation — anything repeated and traditional. Write a narrative about the last time you participated in this ritual. Use description and dialogue to convey the signifance of the ritual and your own and other participants' attitudes toward it.
3. In his 1974 book *Obedience to Authority*, the psychologist Stanley Milgram reported and analyzed the results of a study he had conducted that caused a furor among psychologists and the general public. Under orders from white-coated "experimenters," many subjects administered what they believed to be life-threatening electric shocks to other people whom they could hear but not see. In fact, the "victims" were actors and received no shocks, but the subjects thought otherwise and many continued to administer stronger and stronger "shocks" when ordered to do so. Find *Obedience to Authority* in the library and compare and contrast the circumstances of Milgram's experiment with those of Jackson's lottery. For instance, who or what is the order-giving authority in the lottery? What is the significance of seeing or not seeing one's victim?
4. CRITICAL WRITING. In a 1960 lecture (which we quote more from in "Shirley Jackson on Writing"), Jackson said that a common response she received to "The Lottery" was "What does this story mean?" (She never answered the question.) In an essay, interpret the meaning of the story as *you* understand it. (What does it say, for instance, about social

customs, conformity, guilt, obliviousness, or good and evil?) You will have to INFER meaning from such features as Jackson's own TONE as narrator, the tone of the villagers' dialogue, and, of course, the events of the story. Your essay should be supported with specific EVIDENCE from the story.

5. CONNECTIONS. As its title might suggest, "Why Don't We Complain?" by William F. Buckley, Jr. (p. 507), touches on some of the same issues as "The Lottery." Write an essay applying Buckley's explanations for why we don't complain to the situation in Jackson's story — or arguing that they don't apply.

SHIRLEY JACKSON ON WRITING

Come Along with Me, a posthumous collection of her work, contains a lecture by Shirley Jackson titled "Biography of a Story" — specifically, a biography of "The Lottery." Far from being born in cruelty or cynicism, the story had quite benign origins. Jackson wrote the story, she recalled, "on a bright June morning when summer seemed to have come at last, with blue skies and warm sun and no heavenly signs to warn me that my morning's work was anything but just another story. The idea had come to me while I was pushing my daughter up the hill in her stroller — it was, as I say, a warm morning, and the hill was steep, and beside my daughter the stroller held the day's groceries — and perhaps the effort of that last fifty yards up the hill put an edge on the story; at any rate, I had the idea fairly clearly in my mind when I put my daughter in her playpen and the frozen vegetables in the refrigerator, and, writing the story, I found that it went quickly and easily, moving from beginning to end without pause. As a matter of fact, when I read it over later I decided that except for one or two minor corrections, it needed no changes, and the story I finally typed up and sent off to my agent the next day was almost word for word the original draft. This, as any writer of stories can tell you, is not a usual thing. All I know is that when I came to read the story over I felt strongly that I didn't want to fuss with it. I didn't think it was perfect, but I didn't want to fuss with it. It was, I thought, a serious, straightforward story, and I was pleased and a little surprised at the ease with which it had been written; I was reasonably proud of it, and hoped that my agent would sell it to some magazine and I would have the gratification of seeing it in print."

After the story was published, however, Jackson was surprised to find both it and herself the subject of "bewilderment, speculation, and plain old-fashioned abuse." She wrote that "one of the most terrifying aspects of publishing stories and books is the realization that they are going to be read, and read by strangers. I had never fully realized this before, although I had of course in my imagination dwelt lovingly upon the thought of the millions and millions of people who were going to be uplifted and enriched and delighted by the stories I wrote. It had simply never occurred to me that these millions and millions of people might be so far from being uplifted that they would sit down and write me letters I was downright scared to open; of the three-hundred-odd letters that I received that summer I can count only thirteen that spoke kindly to me, and they were mostly from friends."

Jackson's favorite letter was one concluding, "Our brothers feel that Miss Jackson is a true prophet and disciple of the true gospel of the redeeming light. When will the next revelation be published?" Jackson's answer: "Never. I am out of the lottery business for good."

FOR DISCUSSION

1. What lesson can we draw about creative inspiration from Jackson's anecdote about the origins of "The Lottery"?
2. What seems to have alarmed Jackson about readers' reactions to her story? Do you think she was naive in expecting otherwise?

ADDITIONAL WRITING TOPICS

Narration

1. Write a narrative with one of the following as your subject. It may be (as your instructor may advise) either a first-PERSON memoir or a story written in the third person, observing the experience of someone else. Decide before you begin what your PURPOSE is and whether you are writing (1) an anecdote; (2) an essay consisting mainly of a single narrative; or (3) an essay that includes more than one story.

    A memorable experience from your early life
    A lesson you learned the hard way
    A trip into unfamiliar territory
    An embarrassing moment that taught you something
    A monumental misunderstanding
    An accident
    An unexpected encounter
    A story about a famous person, or someone close to you
    A conflict or contest
    A destructive storm
    An assassination attempt
    A historic event of significance

2. Tell a true story of your early or recent school days, either humorous or serious, showing what a struggle school or college has been for you. (For comparable stories, see Ellison's "On Being the Target of Discrimination" and Thurber's "University Days.")

Note: Writing topics combining narration and description appear on pages 133–34.

2

DESCRIPTION
Writing with Your Senses

THE METHOD

Like narration, description is a familiar method of expression, already a working part of you. In any talk-fest with friends, you probably do your share of describing. You depict in words someone you've met by describing her clothes, the look on her face, the way she walks. You describe somewhere you've been, something you admire, something you just can't abide. In a diary or in a letter to a friend, you describe your college (cast concrete buildings, crowded walks, pigeons rattling their wings); or perhaps you describe your brand-new secondhand car, from the snakelike glitter of its hubcaps to the odd antiques in its trunk, bequeathed by its previous owner. You hardly can live a day without describing (or hearing described) some person, place, or thing. Small wonder that, in written discourse, description is almost as indispensable as paper.

Description reports the testimony of your senses. It invites your readers to imagine that they, too, not only see but perhaps also hear, taste, smell, and touch the subject you describe. Usually, you write a description for either of two purposes: (1) to convey information without bias or emotion; or (2) to convey it with feeling.

In writing with the first purpose in mind, you write an OBJECTIVE (or *impartial, public,* or *functional*) description. You describe your subject so clearly and exactly that your reader will understand it or recognize it, and you leave your emotions out. Technical or scientific descriptive writing is usually objective: a manual detailing the parts of an internal combustion engine, a biologist's report of a previously unknown species of frog. You write this kind of description in sending a friend directions for finding your house: "Look for the green shutters on the windows and a new garbage can at the front door." Although in a personal letter describing your house you might very well become emotionally involved with it (and call it, perhaps, a "fleabag"), in writing an objective description your purpose is not to convey your feelings. You are trying to make the house easily recognized.

The other type of descriptive writing is SUBJECTIVE (or *emotional, personal,* or *impressionistic*) description. This is the kind included in a magazine advertisement for a new car. It's what you write in your letter to a friend setting forth what your college is like — whether you are pleased or displeased with it. In this kind of description, you may use biases and personal feelings — in fact, they are essential. Let us consider a splendid example: a subjective description of a storm at sea. Charles Dickens, in his memoir *American Notes,* conveys his passenger's-eye view of an Atlantic steamship on a morning when the ocean is wild:

> Imagine the ship herself, with every pulse and artery of her huge body swollen and bursting . . . sworn to go on or die. Imagine the wind howling, the sea roaring, the rain beating; all in furious array against her. Picture the sky both dark and wild, and the clouds in fearful sympathy with the waves, making another ocean in the air. Add to all this the clattering on deck and down below; the tread of hurried feet; the loud hoarse shouts of seamen; the gurgling in and out of water through the scuppers; with every now and then the striking of a heavy sea upon the planks above, with the deep, dead, heavy sound of thunder heard within a vault; and there is the head wind of that January morning.
>
> I say nothing of what may be called the domestic noises of the ship; such as the breaking of glass and crockery, the tumbling down of stewards, the gambols, overhead, of loose casks and truant dozens of bottled porter, and the very remarkable and far from exhilarating sounds raised in their various staterooms by the seventy passengers who were too ill to get up to breakfast.

Notice how many *sounds* are included in this primarily ear-minded description. We can infer how Dickens feels about the storm. It is a terrifying event that reduces the interior of the vessel to chaos; and yet the writer (in hearing the loose barrels and beer bottles merrily gambol, in finding humor in the seasick passengers' plight) apparently delights in it. Writing subjectively, he intrudes his feelings. Think of what a starkly different description of the very same storm the captain might set down — objectively — in the ship's log: "At 0600 hours, watch reported a wind from due north of 70 knots. Whitecaps were noticed, in height two ells above the bow. Below deck, much gear was reported adrift, and ten casks of ale were broken and their staves strewn about. Mr. Liam Jones, chief steward, suffered a compound fracture of the left leg. . . ." But Dickens, not content simply to record information, strives to ensure that the mind's eye is dazzled and the mind's ear regaled.

Description is usually found in the company of other methods of writing. Often, for instance, it will enliven NARRATION and make the people in the story and the setting unmistakably clear. Writing an ARGUMENT in his essay "Why Don't We Complain?" William F. Buckley, Jr., begins with a description of eighty suffering commuters perspiring in an overheated train; the description makes the argument more powerful. Description will help a writer in examining the EF-FECTS of a flood, or in COMPARING AND CONTRASTING two towns. Keep the method of description in mind when you come to try expository and argumentative writing.

THE PROCESS

Understand, first of all, your purpose in writing a description. Are you going to write a subjective description, expressing your personal feelings? Or, instead, do you want to write an objective description, trying only to see and report, leaving out your emotions and biases?

Give a little thought to your AUDIENCE. What do your readers need to be told, if they are to share the feelings you would have them share, if they are clearly to behold what you want them to? If, let's say, you are describing a downtown street on a Saturday night for an audience of fellow students who live in the same city and know it well, then you need not dwell on the street's familiar geography. What must you tell? Only those details that make the place different on a Saturday night. But if you are remembering your home city, and writing for readers who don't know it, you'll need to establish a few central landmarks to sketch (in their minds) an unfamiliar street on a Saturday night.

Before you begin to write a description, go look at your subject.

If that is not possible, your next best course is to spend a few minutes imagining the subject until, in your mind's eye, you can see every flyspeck on it.

Then, having fixed your subject in mind, ask yourself which of its features you'll need to report to your particular audience, for your particular purpose. If you plan to write a subjective description of an old house, laying weight on its spooky atmosphere for readers you wish to make shiver, then you might mention its squeaking bats and its shadowy halls, leaving out any reference to its busy swimming pool and the stomping dance music that billows from its interior. If, however, you are describing the house in a classified ad, for an audience of possible buyers, you might focus instead on its eat-in kitchen, working fireplace, and proximity to public transportation. Details have to be carefully selected. Feel no grim duty to include every perceptible detail. To do so would only invite chaos — or perhaps, for the reader, mere tedium. Pick out the features that matter most. One revealing, hard-to-forget detail (such as Dickens's truant porter bottles) is, like a single masterly brush stroke, worth a whole coat of dull paint. In selecting or discarding details, ask, What am I out to accomplish? What main impression of my subject am I trying to give?

Let your description, as a whole, convey this one DOMINANT IMPRESSION. (The swimming pool and the dance music might be details useful in a description meant to convey that the house is full of merriment.) Perhaps many details will be worth noticing; if so, you will want to arrange them so that your reader will see which matter most. In his description of the storm at sea — a subjective description — Charles Dickens sorts out the pandemonium for us. He groups the various sounds into two classes: those of sea and sailors, and the "domestic noises" of the ship's passengers — their smashing dishes, their rolling bottles, the crashing of stewards who wait on them. Like many effective descriptions, this one clearly reveals a principle of organization.

In organizing your description, you may find it helpful to be aware of your POINT OF VIEW — the physical angle from which you're perceiving and describing. In the previous chapter, on narration, we spoke of point of view: how essential it is for a story to have a narrator — one who, from a certain position, reports what takes place. A description, too, needs a consistent point of view: that of an observer who stays put and observes steadily. For instance, when describing a landscape as seen from the air, do not swoop suddenly to earth.

You can organize a description in several ways. Some writers, as

they describe something, make a carefully planned inspection tour of
its details, moving spatially (from left to right, from near to far, from
top to bottom, from center to periphery), or perhaps moving from
prominent objects to tiny ones, from dull to bright, from commonplace to extraordinary — or vice versa. The plan you choose is the
one that best fulfills your purpose. If you were to describe, for instance,
a chapel in the middle of a desert, you might begin with the details
of the lonely terrain. Then, as if approaching the chapel with the
aid of a zoom lens, you might detail its exterior and then go on
inside. That might be a workable method to write a description *if*
your purpose were to emphasize the sense that the chapel is an island
of beauty and warmth in the midst of desolation. Say, however, that
your purpose was quite different: to emphasize the interior design of
the chapel. You might then begin your description inside the structure, perhaps with its most prominent feature, the stained glass windows. You might mention the surrounding desert later in your description, but only incidentally. An effective description makes a
definite impression. The writer arranges details so that the reader is
firmly left with the feeling the writer intends to convey.

Whatever method you follow in arranging details, stick with it
all the way through. Don't start out describing a group of cats by
going from old cats to kittens, then switch in the middle of your
description and line up the cats according to color. If your arrangement would cause any difficulty for the reader, you need to rearrange
your details. If a writer, in describing a pet shop, should skip about
wildly from clerks to cats to customers to cat food to customers to
cat food to clerks, the reader may quickly be lost. Instead, the writer
might group clerks together with customers, and cats together with
cat food (or in some other clear order). But suppose (the writer might
protest) it's a wildly confused pet shop I'm trying to describe? No
matter — the writer nevertheless has to write in an orderly manner,
if the reader is to understand. Dickens describes a scene of shipboard
chaos, yet his prose is orderly.

Luckily, to write a memorable description, you don't need a storm
at sea or any other awe-inspiring subject. As E. B. White demonstrates in his essay in this chapter, "Once More to the Lake," you
can write about a summer cabin on a lake as effectively as you can
write about a tornado. The secret is in the vividness, the evocative-
ness, of the details. Like most masters of description, White relies
heavily on IMAGES (language calling up concrete sensory experiences),
including FIGURES OF SPEECH (expressions that do not mean literally
what they say, often describing one thing in terms of another). White

writes of motorboats that "whined about one's ears like mosquitoes" (a SIMILE) and of "small waves . . . chucking the rowboat under the chin" (a METAPHOR). Another writer, the humorist S. J. Perelman, uses metaphor to convey the garish brightness of a certain low-rent house. Notice how he makes clear the spirit of the place: "After a few days, I could have sworn that our faces began to take on the hue of Kodachromes, and even the dog, an animal used to bizarre surroundings, developed a strange, off-register look, as if he were badly printed in overlapping colors."

When you, too, write an effective description, you'll convey your sensory experience as exactly as possible. Find vigorous, specific words, and you will enable your reader to behold with the mind's eye — and to feel with the mind's fingertips.

DESCRIPTION IN A PARAGRAPH:
TWO ILLUSTRATIONS

Using Description to Write About Television

At 2:59 this Monday afternoon, a thick hush settles like cigarette smoke inside the sweat-scented TV room of Harris Hall. First to arrive, freshman Lee Ann squashes down into the catbird seat in front of the screen. Soon she is flanked by roommates Lisa and Kate, silent, their mouths straight lines, their upturned faces lit by the nervous flicker of a detergent ad. To the left and right of the couch, Pete and Anse crouch on the floor, leaning forward like runners awaiting a starting gun. Behind them, stiff standees line up at attention. Farther back still, English majors and jocks compete for an unobstructed view. Fresh from class, shirttail flapping, arm crooking a bundle of books, Dave barges into the room demanding, "Has it started? Has it started yet?" He is shushed. Somebody shushes a popped-open can of Dr Pepper whose fizz is distractingly loud. What do these students so intently look forward to — the announcement of World War III? A chord of music climbs and the screen dissolves to a title: *General Hospital.*

COMMENT. Although in the end the anticipated mind-blower turns out to be merely an installment of a gripping soap opera, the purpose of this description is to build one definite impression: that something vital is about to arrive. Details are selected accordingly: "thick hush," "nervous flicker," people jostling one another for a better view. The watchers are portrayed as tense and expectant, their mouths straight lines, their faces upturned, the men on the floor crouching forward. The chief appeal is to our visual imaginations, but a few details address our auditory imaginations (the fizz of a can of soda, people saying *Shhh-h-h!*) and our olfactory imaginations ("sweat-scented").

In organizing this description, the writer's scrutiny moves outward from the television screen: first to the students immediately in front of it, then to those on either side, next to the second row, then to the third, and finally to the last anxious arrival. By this arrangement, the writer presents the details to the reader in a natural order. The main impression is enforced, since the TV screen is the center for all eyes.

Using Description in an Academic Discipline

While working on *The Battle of Anghiari*, Leonardo painted his most famous portrait, the *Mona Lisa*. The delicate *sfumato* already noted in the *Madonna of the Rocks* is here so perfected that it seemed miraculous to the artist's contemporaries. The forms are built from layers of glazes so gossamer-thin that the entire panel seems to glow with a gentle light from within. But the fame of the *Mona Lisa* comes not from this pictorial subtlety alone; even more intriguing is the psychological fascination of the sitter's personality. Why, among all the smiling faces ever painted, has this particular one been singled out as "mysterious"? Perhaps the reason is that, as a portrait, the picture does not fit our expectations. The features are too individual for Leonardo to have simply depicted an ideal type, yet the element of idealization is so strong that it blurs the sitter's character. Once again the artist has brought two opposites into harmonious balance. The smile, too, may be read in two ways: as the echo of a momentary mood, and as a timeless, symbolic expression (somewhat like the "Archaic smile" of the Greeks . . .). Clearly, the *Mona Lisa* embodies a quality of maternal tenderness which was to Leonardo the essence of womanhood. Even the landscape in the background, composed mainly of rocks and water, suggests elemental generative forces.

COMMENT. Taken from H. W. Janson's *History of Art: A Survey of the Major Visual Arts from the Dawn of History to the Present Day*, this paragraph describes the world's most famous portrait in oils, the *Mona Lisa*. In a section of the book dealing with the achievement of Leonardo da Vinci, the author makes clear that this painting amply demonstrates the artist's genius. He does so by describing both the picture's subject and some of the painting techniques that bring it alive — the *sfumato*, or soft gradations of lights and darks, the layering of glazes, the tension the viewer can discern between Mona

Lisa the individual and Mona Lisa the ideal type. Note the words and phrases he uses that appeal to the senses: "delicate," "gossamer-thin," "glow with a gentle light." By directing readers' attention to the painting's details, Janson has used description as a teaching tool of tremendous usefulness.

VIRGINIA WOOLF

Generally regarded as one of the greatest twentieth-century writers, VIRGINIA WOOLF earned her acclaim by producing uncommon fiction and nonfiction, the first sensitive and complex, the second poetic and immediate. Born Virginia Stephen in London in 1882, Woolf and her sister Vanessa were educated at home, largely by their father, Sir Leslie Stephen, an author and editor. The two sisters were central to the Bloomsbury Group, an informal society of writers and artists that included the economist John Maynard Keynes and the novelist E. M. Forster. Virginia married Leonard Woolf, a member of the group, in 1912, and the two soon founded the Hogarth Press, publisher of Virginia Woolf and many other notable writers of the day. Woolf's most innovative novels include *Mrs. Dalloway* (1925), *To the Lighthouse* (1927), *Orlando* (1928), *The Waves* (1931), and *Between the Acts* (1941). Her exemplary critical and meditative essays appear in *The Common Reader* (1925), *The Second Common Reader* (1933), and many other collections. Subject to severe depression all her adult life, in 1941 Woolf committed suicide.

The Death of the Moth

One of Woolf's most famous works of nonfiction, "The Death of the Moth" was published for the first time in *The Death of the Moth and Other Essays* (1942). Though brief as the life of the moth Woolf observes, the essay is typically evocative, intense, and enduring.

Moths that fly by day are not properly to be called moths; they 1 do not excite that pleasant sense of dark autumn nights and ivy-blossom which the commonest yellow-underwing asleep in the shadow of the curtain never fails to rouse in us. They are hybrid creatures, neither gay like butterflies nor somber like their own species. Nevertheless the present specimen, with his narrow hay-colored wings, fringed with a tassel of the same color, seemed to be content with life. It was a pleasant morning, mid-September, mild, benignant, yet with a keener breath than that of the summer months. The plough was already scoring the field opposite the window, and where the share had been, the earth was pressed flat and gleamed with moisture. Such vigor came rolling in from the fields and the down beyond that it was difficult to keep the eyes strictly turned upon the book. The rooks too were keeping one of their annual festivities; soaring round the tree tops until it looked as if a vast net with thousands of black knots in it had been cast up into the air; which, after a few moments sank slowly down upon the trees until every twig seemed to have a knot at the end of it. Then suddenly, the net would be thrown into the air again in a wider circle this time, with the utmost clamor and vociferation, as though to be thrown into the air and settle slowly down upon the tree tops were a tremendously exciting experience.

The same energy which inspired the rooks, the ploughmen, the   2 horses, and even, it seemed, the lean bare-backed downs, sent the moth fluttering from side to side of his square of the windowpane. One could not help watching him. One was, indeed, conscious of a queer feeling of pity for him. The possibilities of pleasure seemed that morning so enormous and so various that to have only a moth's part in life, and a day moth's at that, appeared a hard fate, and his zest in enjoying his meager opportunities to the full, pathetic. He flew vigorously to one corner of his compartment, and, after waiting there a second, flew across to the other. What remained for him but to fly to a third corner and then to a fourth? That was all he could do, in spite of the size of the downs, the width of the sky, the far-off smoke of houses, and the romantic voice, now and then, of a steamer out at sea. What he could do he did. Watching him, it seemed as if a fiber, very thin but pure, of the enormous energy of the world had been thrust into his frail and diminutive body. As often as he crossed the pane, I could fancy that a thread of vital light became visible. He was little or nothing but life.

Yet, because he was so small, and so simple a form of the energy   3 that was rolling in at the open window and driving its way through so many narrow and intricate corridors in my own brain and in those of other human beings, there was something marvelous as well as pathetic about him. It was as if someone had taken a tiny bead of pure life and decking it as lightly as possible with down and feathers, had set it dancing and zigzagging to show us the true nature of life. Thus displayed one could not get over the strangeness of it. One is apt to forget all about life, seeing it humped and bossed and garnished and cumbered so that it has to move with the greatest circumspection and dignity. Again, the thought of all that life might have been had he been born in any other shape caused one to view his simple activities with a kind of pity.

After a time, tired by his dancing apparently, he settled on the   4 window ledge in the sun, and, the queer spectacle being at an end,

I forgot about him. Then, looking up, my eye was caught by him. He was trying to resume his dancing, but seemed either so stiff or so awkward that he could only flutter to the bottom of the windowpane; and when he tried to fly across it he failed. Being intent on other matters I watched these futile attempts for a time without thinking, unconsciously waiting for him to resume his flight, as one waits for a machine, that has stopped momentarily, to start again without considering the reason of its failure. After perhaps a seventh attempt he slipped from the wooden ledge and fell, fluttering his wings, on to his back on the windowsill. The helplessness of his attitude roused me. It flashed upon me that he was in difficulties; he could no longer raise himself; his legs struggled vainly. But, as I stretched out a pencil, meaning to help him to right himself, it came over me that the failure and awkwardness were the approach of death. I laid the pencil down again.

The legs agitated themselves once more. I looked as if for the   5 enemy against which he struggled. I looked out of doors. What had happened there? Presumably it was midday, and work in the fields had stopped. Stillness and quiet had replaced the previous animation. The birds had taken themselves off to feed in the brooks. The horses stood still. Yet the power was there all the same, massed outside, indifferent, impersonal, not attending to anything in particular. Somehow it was opposed to the little hay-colored moth. It was useless to try to do anything. One could only watch the extraordinary efforts made by those tiny legs against an oncoming doom which could, had it chosen, have submerged an entire city, not merely a city, but masses of human beings; nothing, I knew, had any chance against death. Nevertheless after a pause of exhaustion the legs fluttered again. It was superb this last protest, and so frantic that he succeeded at last in righting himself. One's sympathies, of course, were all on the side of life. Also, when there was nobody to care or to know, this gigantic effort on the part of an insignificant little moth, against a power of such magnitude, to retain what no one else valued or desired to keep, moved one strangely. Again, somehow, one saw life, a pure bead. I lifted the pencil again, useless though I knew it to be. But even as I did so, the unmistakable tokens of death showed themselves. The body relaxed, and instantly grew stiff. The struggle was over. The insignificant little creature now knew death. As I looked at the dead moth, this minute wayside triumph of so great a force over so mean an antagonist filled me with wonder. Just as life had been strange a few minutes before, so death was now as strange. The moth having righted himself now lay most decently and uncomplainingly composed. O yes, he seemed to say, death is stronger than I am. *Resignation to death*

QUESTIONS ON MEANING

1. Why does Woolf choose to write about something as insignificant as a moth's death? Does she have a PURPOSE other than relating a simple observation?
2. Why, in paragraph 2, does Woolf say that the moth was "little or nothing but life"? Why is the moth pitiable?
3. What does the moth in his square windowpane represent to the author? How does Woolf's description in the essay make this clear?
4. How does Woolf's outlook change in paragraph 5? Why? *personal/ panel*

QUESTIONS ON WRITING STRATEGY

1. Is Woolf's essay an OBJECTIVE or a SUBJECTIVE description? Give details from the essay to support your answer.
2. What is the EFFECT of Woolf's scene-setting in paragraph 1? How does this description influence our perception of the moth?
3. Which of the five senses does Woolf's description principally rely on? Why, do you think? *visual, intuilerse*
4. OTHER METHODS. This essay is a description in the framework of a NARRATIVE. SUMMARIZE the changes in Woolf's perceptions of the moth that occur in the narrative.

QUESTIONS ON LANGUAGE

1. Analyze the writing in paragraph 5. How do sentence structure and words create a mood different from that in earlier paragraphs?
2. Analyze Woolf's IMAGES in describing the moth and her substitutions for the word *moth*, such as "the present specimen" (para. 1). How do these reinforce Woolf's changing perceptions as you outlined them in question 4 above?
3. You may find Woolf's vocabulary more difficult than that of some other writers in this book. Look up any unfamiliar words in the following list: rouse, hybrid, benignant, plough, share, down, rooks, clamor, vociferation (para. 1); meager, pathetic, diminutive (2); decking, cumbered, circumspection (3); spectacle, futile, vainly (4); animation, righting, magnitude, minute, mean, antagonist (5).

objective — biological part

SUGGESTIONS FOR WRITING

1. In an essay of your own, respond to the ideas about life and death in Woolf's essay. First explain what you understand these ideas to be. Then use examples from your reading and experience to support or contest Woolf's ideas.
2. Watch something over an extended period of time and describe it — its physical attributes, movements, surroundings. Draw on as many of your five senses as you like, but make your description as OBJECTIVE as possible by keeping your feelings out of it.
3. Use the same subject as in the previous suggestion, or choose a new one. This time, write a SUBJECTIVE description in which your feelings influence your selection of details and what you say about them. Again, draw on as many senses as you like. Use word IMAGES to convey your perceptions.
4. CRITICAL WRITING. Write a brief essay ANALYZING Woolf's use of language to describe the moth and its struggle. Concentrate on how the language changes over the course of the essay and what those changes add to Woolf's factual statements about the moth's progress. (This suggestion gives you a chance to draw and elaborate on your answers to the first and second "Questions on Language.")
5. CONNECTIONS. Read Annie Dillard's "Death of a Moth," which follows this essay. Of the two highly subjective essays, which is more personal? Write a brief essay answering this question, and support your answer with quotations and PARAPHRASES from both essays.

VIRGINIA WOOLF ON WRITING

A diary keeper from her youth, Virginia Woolf used the form not only to record and reflect on events but also to do a kind of "rough & random" writing she otherwise had little chance for. (Today this kind of writing is often called *freewriting*.) Woolf wrote in her diary on April 20, 1919, that "the habit of writing thus for my own eye only is good practice. It loosens the ligaments. Never mind the misses & the stumbles. Going at such a pace as I do I must make the most direct & instant shots at my object, & thus have to lay hands on words, choose them, & shoot them with no more pause than is needed to put my pen in the ink. I believe that during the past year I can trace some increase of ease in my professional writing which I attribute to my casual half hours after tea."

Thirteen years later, Woolf felt just as strongly about the value of writing freely, without censorship. In "A Letter to a Young Poet," she advises against writing solely for "a severe and intelligent public."

Follow the excitement of "actual life," she urges. "Write then, now that you are young, nonsense by the ream. Be silly, be sentimental, imitate Shelley, imitate Samuel Smiles; give the rein to every impulse; commit every fault of style, grammar, taste, and syntax; pour out; tumble over; loose anger, love, satire, in whatever words you can catch, coerce, or create, in whatever meter, prose, poetry, or gibberish that comes to hand. Thus you will learn to write."

FOR DISCUSSION

1. What does Woolf gain from diary writing? What does she mean that such writing "loosens the ligaments"?
2. Do you think Woolf seriously believed that young writers should write "nonsense by the ream"? (A *ream*, incidentally, is about five hundred sheets of paper.) What might the young writer learn from such freedom?
3. These excerpts do not discuss the writer's work between the loose, private writing Woolf recommends and writing for others. In your view, what does that work consist of?

ANNIE DILLARD

ANNIE DILLARD is accomplished as a prose writer, poet, and literary critic. Born in 1945, she earned a B.A. (1967) and an M.A. (1968) from Hollins College in Virginia. She now teaches writing at Wesleyan University in Connecticut. Dillard's first published prose, *Pilgrim at Tinker Creek* (1974), is a work alive with close, intense, and poetic descriptions of the natural world. It won her a Pulitzer Prize and comparison with Thoreau. Since then, Dillard's entranced and entrancing writing has appeared regularly in *Harper's, American Scholar, The Atlantic Monthly,* and other magazines and in her books: *Tickets for a Prayer Wheel* (1975), poems; *Holy the Firm* (1978), a prose poem; *Living by Fiction* (1982), literary criticism; *Teaching a Stone to Talk* (1982), nonfiction; *Encounters with Chinese Writers* (1984), an account of a trip to China; *An American Childhood* (1987), an autobiography; and *The Writing Life* (1989), anecdotes and metaphors about writing. Dillard's acclaimed first novel, *The Living* (1992), tells the saga of Native Americans and pioneers in the Pacific Northwest.

Death of a Moth

Early in life, Annie Dillard began training her powers of description. "When I worked as a detective in Pittsburgh," she recalls, "(strictly freelance, because I was only ten years old), I drew suspects' faces from memory." These powers are evident in all Dillard's writing, including this essay, first published in 1976 in *Harper's.*

I live alone with two cats, who sleep on my legs. There is a 1 yellow one, and a black one whose name is Small. In the morning I joke to the black one, Do you remember last night? Do you remember? I throw them both out before breakfast, so I can eat.

There is a spider, too, in the bathroom, of uncertain lineage, 2 bulbous at the abdomen and drab, whose six-inch mess of web works, works somehow, works miraculously, to keep her alive and me amazed. The web is in a corner behind the toilet, connecting tile wall to tile wall. The house is new, the bathroom immaculate, save for the spider, her web, and the sixteen or so corpses she's tossed to the floor.

The corpses appear to be mostly sow bugs, those little armadillo 3 creatures who live to travel flat out in houses, and die round. In addition to sow-bug husks, hollow and sipped empty of color, there are what seem to be two or three wingless moth bodies, one new flake of earwig, and three spider carcasses crinkled and clenched.

I wonder on what fool's errand an earwig, or a moth, or a sow   4
bug, would visit that clean corner of the house behind the toilet; I have not noticed any blind parades of sow bugs blundering into corners. Yet they do hazard there, at a rate of more than one a week, and the spider thrives. Yesterday she was working on the earwig, mouth on gut; today he's on the floor. It must take a certain genius to throw things away from there, to find a straight line through that sticky tangle to the floor.

Today the earwig shines darkly, and gleams, what there is of him;   5
a dorsal curve of thorax and abdomen, and a smooth pair of pincers by which I knew his name. Next week, if the other bodies are any indication, he'll be shrunk and gray, webbed to the floor with dust. The sow bugs beside him are curled and empty, fragile, a breath away from brittle fluff. The spiders lie on their sides, translucent and ragged, their legs drying in knots. The moths stagger against each other, headless, in a confusion of arcing strips of chitin like peeling varnish, like a jumble of buttresses for cathedral vaults, like nothing resembling moths, so that I would hestitate to call them moths, except that I have had some experience with the figure Moth reduced to a nub.

Two summers ago I was camped alone in the Blue Ridge Moun-   6
tains of Virginia. I had hauled myself and gear up there to read, among other things, *The Day on Fire*, by James Ullman, a novel about Rimbaud[1] that had made me want to be a writer when I was sixteen; I was hoping it would do it again. So I read every day sitting under a tree by my tent, while warblers sang in the leaves overhead and bristle worms trailed their inches over the twiggy dirt at my feet; and I read every night by candlelight, while barred owls called in the forest and pale moths seeking mates massed round my head in the clearing, where my light made a ring.

Moths kept flying into the candle. They would hiss and recoil,   7
reeling upside down in the shadows among my cooking pans. Or they would singe their wings and fall, and their hot wings, as if melted, would stick to the first thing they touched — a pan, a lid, a spoon — so that the snagged moths could struggle only in tiny arcs, unable to flutter free. These I could release by a quick flip with a stick; in the morning I would find my cooking stuff decorated with torn flecks of

[1]Arthur Rimbaud (1854–1891) was a French poet, adventurer, and merchant-trader. — Eds.

moth wings, ghostly triangles of shiny dust here and there on the aluminum. So I read, and boiled water, and replenished candles, and read on.

One night a moth flew into the candle, was caught, burnt dry, and held. I must have been staring at the candle, or maybe I looked up when a shadow crossed my page; at any rate, I saw it all. A golden female moth, a biggish one with a two-inch wingspread, flapped into the fire, drooped abdomen into the wet wax, stuck, flamed, and frazzled in a second. Her moving wing ignited like tissue paper, like angel's wings, enlarging the circle of light in the clearing and creating out of the darkness the sudden blue sleeves of my sweater, the green leaves of jewelweed by my side, the ragged red trunk of a pine; at once the light contracted again and the moth's wings vanished in a fine, foul smoke. At the same time, her six legs clawed, curled, blackened, and ceased, disappearing utterly. And her head jerked in spasms, making a spattering noise; her antennae crisped and burnt away and her heaving mouthparts cracked like pistol fire. When it was all over, her head was, so far as I could determine, gone, gone the long way of her wings and legs. Her head was a hole lost to time. All that was left was the glowing horn shell of her abdomen and thorax — a fraying, partially collapsed gold tube jammed upright in the candle's round pool.

And then this moth-essence, this spectacular skeleton, began to act as a wick. She kept burning. The wax rose in the moth's body from her soaking abdomen to her thorax to the shattered hole where her head should have been, and widened into flame, a saffron-yellow flame that robed her to the ground like an immolating monk. That candle had two wicks, two winding flames of identical light, side by side. The moth's head was fire. She burned for two hours, until I blew her out.

She burned for two hours without changing, without swaying or kneeling — only glowing within, like a building fire glimpsed through silhouetted walls, like a hollow saint, like a flame-faced virgin gone to God, while I read by her light, kindled, while Rimbaud in Paris burnt out his brain in a thousand poems, while night pooled wetly at my feet.

So. That is why I think those hollow shreds on the bathroom floor are moths. I believe I know what moths look like, in any state.

I have three candles here on the table which I disentangle from the plants and light when visitors come. The cats avoid them, although Small's tail caught fire once; I rubbed it out before she noticed.

I don't mind living alone. I like eating alone and reading. I don't mind sleeping alone. The only time I mind being alone is when something is funny; then, when I am laughing at something funny, I wish someone were around. Sometimes I think it is pretty funny that I sleep alone.

QUESTIONS ON MEANING

1. Why did Dillard retreat to the mountains? What is the significance of this information to the essay?
2. What or whom does the burning moth represent? How does Dillard reveal her meaning?
3. What would you say is the unstated THESIS of this essay? What point is Dillard making?
4. In the beginning and end of her essay, Dillard emphasizes that she lives alone. Why? How does this fact relate to the idea of the essay?

QUESTIONS ON WRITING STRATEGY

1. Why do you think Dillard devotes so much of this essay to her domestic arrangements?
2. Dillard's IMAGES are mostly visual. Find three images that belong to other senses. What is their EFFECT?
3. Pick out all the SIMILES in paragraphs 8–10, the episode of the moth. How do they change?
4. The preceding essay, by Virginia Woolf, is titled "The Death of the Moth" (p. 101). Dillard's title — undoubtedly written in full knowledge of Woolf's essay — is "Death of a Moth." What is the significance of the difference?
5. OTHER METHODS. In "Death of a Moth" Dillard offers a kind of DEFI-NITION. What does she define?

QUESTIONS ON LANGUAGE

1. Analyze the TONE of paragraphs 1–5 and 8–10. How does vocabulary alone contribute to the difference in these two sections?
2. What are "sudden blue sleeves" (para. 8)? How can this be said more conventionally? Why is the author's phrase more effective?
3. Define the following: lineage, immaculate (para. 2); earwig (3); dorsal, thorax, pincers, translucent, chitin, buttresses (5); singe, replenished (7); spasms, antennae (8); robed, immolating (9); silhouetted (10).

SUGGESTIONS FOR WRITING

1. Write an essay describing a thing (object, animal, plant) that serves as a SYMBOL of an important event or period in your life — a pet, a flannel shirt, a spider plant, a bottle cap, whatever. Describe both the circumstances and the object so that readers grasp and care about the relationship.
2. In a few paragraphs, describe a friend, relative, or acquaintance in terms of an animal or plant. This topic will require liberal use of FIGURES OF SPEECH.
3. CRITICAL WRITING. As noted in questions above, Dillard's essay shifts between mundane domestic concerns and ecstatic transformations, between matter-of-fact, almost scientific language and highly charged poetic images. In an essay, ANALYZE and EVALUATE these shifts. What do they accomplish? Do they strengthen or weaken the essay? Be sure to use EVIDENCE from the essay to support your views.
4. CONNECTIONS. Both "The Death of the Moth" by Virginia Woolf (p. 101) and "Death of a Moth" by Annie Dillard are ostensibly about a moth's death. Compare and contrast the moths in both essays as symbols.

ANNIE DILLARD ON WRITING

"Description's not too hard," according to Annie Dillard, "if you mind your active verbs, keep ticking off as many sense impressions as you can, and omit feelings." In descriptive writing, apparently, she believes in paying attention first of all to the world outside herself.

Writing for *The Bedford Reader,* Dillard has testified to her work habits. Rarely satisfied with an essay until it has gone through many drafts, she sometimes goes on correcting and improving it even after it has been published. "I always have to condense or toss openings," she affirms; "I suspect most writers do. When you begin something, you're so grateful to have begun you'll write down anything, just to prolong the sensation. Later, when you've learned what the writing is really about, you go back and throw away the beginning and start over."

Often she replaces a phrase or sentence with a shorter one. In one essay, to tell how a drop of pond water began to evaporate on a microscope slide, she first wrote, "Its contours pulled together." But that sentence seemed to suffer from "tortured abstraction." She made the sentence read instead, "Its edges shrank." Dillard observes, "I like short sentences. They're forceful, and they can get you out of big trouble."

FOR DISCUSSION

1. Why, according to Dillard, is it usually necessary for writers to revise the opening paragraphs of what they write?
2. Dillard says that short sentences "can get you out of big trouble." What kinds of "big trouble" do you suppose she means?

JOAN DIDION

A writer whose fame is fourfold — as novelist, essayist, journalist, and screenwriter — JOAN DIDION was born in 1934 in California, where her family has lived for five generations. After graduation from the University of California, Berkeley, she spent a few years in New York, working as a feature editor for *Vogue*, a fashion magazine. In 1964 she returned to California, where she worked as a freelance journalist and wrote four much-discussed novels: *River Run* (1963), *Play It As It Lays* (1971), *A Book of Common Prayer* (1977), and *Democracy* (1984). *Salvador* (1983), her book-length essay based on a visit to war-torn El Salvador, and *Miami* (1987), a study of Cuban exiles in Florida, also received wide attention. With her husband, John Gregory Dunne, Didion has coauthored screenplays, notably for *True Confessions* (1981) and the Barbra Streisand film *A Star Is Born* (1976). *After Henry*, Didion's latest collection of essays, appeared in 1992.

Marrying Absurd

"Marrying Absurd" appeared originally in 1967 in *The Saturday Evening Post*, a general-interest magazine, and was reprinted in a book of Didion's essays, *Slouching Towards Bethlehem* (1968). As you will see, the essay is no aged relic of the 1960s. Didion's descriptions of Las Vegas and the people who marry there are enduringly fresh and funny.

To be married in Las Vegas, Clark County, Nevada, a bride must   1
swear that she is eighteen or has parental permission and a bride-groom that he is twenty-one or has parental permission. Someone must put up five dollars for the license. (On Sundays and holidays, fifteen dollars. The Clark County Courthouse issues marriage licenses at any time of the day or night except between noon and one in the afternoon, between eight and nine in the evening, and between four and five in the morning.) Nothing else is required. The State of Nevada, alone among these United States, demands neither a premarital blood test nor a waiting period before or after the issuance of a marriage license. Driving in across the Mojave from Los Angeles, one sees the signs way out on the desert, looming up from the moonscape of rattlesnakes and mesquite, even before the Las Vegas lights appear like a mirage on the horizon: "GETTING MARRIED? Free

License Information First Strip Exit." Perhaps the Las Vegas wedding industry achieved its peak operational efficiency between 9:00 P.M. and midnight of August 26, 1965, an otherwise unremarkable Thursday which happened to be, by Presidential order, the last day on which anyone could improve his draft status merely by getting married. One hundred and seventy-one couples were pronounced man and wife in the name of Clark County and the State of Nevada that night, sixty-seven of them by a single justice of the peace, Mr. James A. Brennan. Mr. Brennan did one wedding at the Dunes and the other sixty-six in his office, and charged each couple eight dollars. One bride lent her veil to six others. "I got it down from five to three minutes," Mr. Brennan said later of his feat. "I could've married them *en masse*, but they're people, not cattle. People expect more when they get married."

What people who get married in Las Vegas actually do expect — 2 what, in the largest sense, their "expectations" are — strikes one as a curious and self-contradictory business. Las Vegas is the most extreme and allegorical of American settlements, bizarre and beautiful in its venality and in its devotion to immediate gratification, a place the tone of which is set by mobsters and call girls and ladies' room attendants with amyl nitrate poppers in their uniform pockets. Almost everyone notes that there is no "time" in Las Vegas, no night and no day and no past and no future (no Las Vegas casino, however, has taken the obliteration of the ordinary time sense quite so far as Harold's Club in Reno, which for a while issued, at odd intervals in the day and night, mimeographed "bulletins" carrying news from the world outside); neither is there any logical sense of where one is. One is standing on a highway in the middle of a vast hostile desert looking at an eighty-foot sign which blinks "STARDUST" or "CAESAR'S PALACE." Yes, but what does that explain? This geographical implausibility reinforces the sense that what happens there has no connection with "real" life; Nevada cities like Reno and Carson are ranch towns, Western towns, places behind which there is some historical imperative. But Las Vegas seems to exist only in the eye of the beholder. All of which makes it an extraordinarily stimulating and interesting place, but an odd one in which to want to wear a candlelight satin Priscilla of Boston wedding dress with Chantilly lace insets, tapered sleeves and a detachable modified train.

And yet the Las Vegas wedding business seems to appeal to 3 precisely that impulse. "Sincere and Dignified Since 1954," one wedding chapel advertises. There are nineteen such wedding chapels in Las Vegas, intensely competitive, each offering better, faster, and, by implication, more sincere services than the next: Our Photos Best Anywhere, Your Wedding on a Phonograph Record, Candlelight with Your Ceremony, Honeymoon Accommodations, Free Transportation from Your Motel to Courthouse to Chapel and Return to Motel, Religious or Civil Ceremonies, Dressing Rooms, Flowers, Rings, Announcements, Witnesses Available, and Ample Parking. All of these services, like most others in Las Vegas (sauna baths, payroll-check cashing, chinchilla coats for sale or rent) are offered twenty-four hours a day, seven days a week, presumably on the premise that marriage, like craps, is a game to be played when the table seems hot.

But what strikes one most about the Strip chapels, with their 4 wishing wells and stained-glass paper windows and their artificial bouvardia, is that so much of their business is by no means a matter of simple convenience, of late-night liaisons between show girls and baby Crosbys. Of course there is some of that. (One night about eleven o'clock in Las Vegas I watched a bride in an orange minidress and masses of flame-colored hair stumble from a Strip chapel on the arm of her bridegroom, who looked the part of the expendable nephew in movies like *Miami Syndicate*. "I gotta get the kids," the bride whimpered. "I gotta pick up the sitter, I gotta get to the midnight show." "What you gotta get," the bridegroom said, opening the door of a Cadillac Coupe de Ville and watching her crumple on the seat, "is sober.") But Las Vegas seems to offer something other than "convenience"; it is merchandising "niceness," the facsimile of proper ritual, to children who do not know how else to find it, how to make the arrangements, how to do it "right." All day and evening long on the Strip, one sees actual wedding parties, waiting under the harsh lights at a crosswalk, standing uneasily in the parking lot of the Frontier while the photographer hired by The Little Church of the West ("Wedding Place of the Stars") certifies the occasion, takes the picture: the bride in a veil and white satin pumps, the bridegroom usually in a white dinner jacket, and even an attendant or two, a sister or a best friend in hot-pink *peau de soie*, a flirtation veil, a carnation nosegay. "When I Fall in Love It Will Be Forever," the organist plays, and then a few bars of Lohengrin. The mother cries; the stepfather, awkward in his role, invites the chapel hostess to join them for a drink at the Sands. The hostess declines with a professional smile; she has already transferred her interest to the group waiting outside. One bride out, another in, and again the sign goes up on the chapel door: "One moment please — Wedding."

I sat next to one such wedding party in a Strip restaurant the last 5 time I was in Las Vegas. The marriage had just taken place; the bride still wore her dress, the mother her corsage. A bored waiter poured out a few swallows of pink champagne ("on the house") for everyone but the bride, who was too young to be served. "You'll need something with more kick than that," the bride's father said with heavy jocularity to his new son-in-law; the ritual jokes about the wedding night had a certain Panglossian character, since the bride was clearly several months pregnant. Another round of pink champagne, this time not on the house, and the bride began to cry. "It was just as nice," she sobbed, "as I hoped and dreamed it would be."

QUESTIONS ON MEANING

1. Why do people from other states choose to get married in Nevada?
2. Why does Didion feel that in Las Vegas there is "no night and no day" (para. 2)?
3. What is Didion's THESIS in this essay? Where is it stated?
4. Does Didion seem sympathetic to her subjects?

QUESTIONS ON WRITING STRATEGY

1. To which of our senses does Didion's description primarily appeal? Why might that be? *visual*
2. What kinds of EVIDENCE does Didion use to support her impressions?
3. How would you characterize Didion's POINT OF VIEW in this essay? Note her use of pronouns — she is "one" until the middle of paragraph 4, when she appears as "I."
4. What is the essay's DOMINANT IMPRESSION? *cynical*
5. OTHER METHODS. Over the course of her essay, Didion offers a PROCESS ANALYSIS of the Las Vegas wedding. Outline this process.

QUESTIONS ON LANGUAGE

1. Is Didion's DICTION well matched to her subject matter? How would you describe it?
2. What is the TONE of this essay? Give examples to support your opinion.
3. What is the EFFECT of Didion's use of brand names, place names, and business slogans? Look closely at paragraphs 3 and 4. How do strings of commercial phrases help reinforce Didion's THESIS?
4. What does Didion ALLUDE to with the expression "Panglossian character" (para. 5)?

5. Check a dictionary for the meanings of the following words: allegorical, venality, implausibility, imperative (para. 2); chinchilla (3); bouvardia, peau de soie (4); jocularity (5).

SUGGESTIONS FOR WRITING

1. Didion's description of Las Vegas weddings illustrates some contemporary attitudes toward marriage. Along the same lines, write an essay describing another ritual or social custom (for example, a graduation, military induction, presidential inauguration, religious service). What does the conduct of this custom tell us about our attitudes toward it? Try to convey a strong DOMINANT IMPRESSION.
2. CRITICAL WRITING. Didion is well known for her detached, wryly IRONIC TONE. Reread the essay, making note of how its tone is set. Write a brief essay analyzing Didion's use of words and sentence structures to create this tone.
3. CONNECTIONS. After reading Didion's essay, turn to Jessica Mitford's "Behind the Formaldehyde Curtain" (p. 253). How are the wedding and funeral industries similar or different? Use quotations from both essays to support your comparison. (If you need help with COMPARISON AND CONTRAST, see Chap. 4.)

JOAN DIDION ON WRITING

In "Why I Write," an essay published by the *New York Times Book Review,* adapted from her Regents' Lecture at the University of California, Berkeley, Joan Didion writes, "Of course I stole the title for this talk, from George Orwell [excerpts of which appear on pages 620–21]. One reason I stole it was that I like the sound of the words: Why I Write. There you have three short unambiguous words that share a sound, and the sound they share is this:

I

I

I

In many ways writing is the act of saying *I,* of imposing oneself upon other people, of saying *listen to me, see it my way, change your mind. . . .*"

Didion's "way," though, comes not from notions of how the world works or should work but from its observable details. She writes, "I am not in the least an intellectual, which is not to say that when I hear the word 'intellectual' I reach for my gun, but only to say that

I do not think in abstracts. During the years when I was an under-graduate at Berkeley I tried, with a kind of hopeless late-adolescent energy, to buy some temporary visa into the world of ideas, to forge for myself a mind that could deal with the abstract. . . . In short, I tried to think. I failed. My attention veered inexorably back to the specific, to the tangible, to what was generally considered, by every-one I knew then and for that matter have known since, the periph-eral. I would try to contemplate the Hegelian dialectic and would find myself concentrating instead on the flowering pear tree outside my window and the particular way the petals fell on my floor."

Later in the essay, Didion writes, "During those years I was traveling on what I knew to be a very shaky passport, forged papers: I knew that I was no legitimate resident in any world of ideas. I knew I couldn't think. All I knew then was what I wasn't, and it took me some years to discover what I was.

"Which was a writer.

"By which I mean not a 'good' writer or a 'bad' writer but simply a writer, a person whose most absorbed and passionate hours are spent arranging words on pieces of paper. Had my credentials been in order I would never have become a writer. Had I been blessed with even limited access to my own mind there would have been no reason to write. I write entirely to find out what I'm thinking, what I'm looking at, what I see, and what it means. What I want and what I fear. . . . *What is going on in these pictures in my mind?*"

In the essay, Didion emphasizes that these mental pictures have a grammar. "Grammar is a piano I play by ear, since I seem to have been out of school the year the rules were mentioned. All I know about grammar is its infinite power. To shift the structure of a sentence alters the meaning of that sentence, as definitely and inflexibly as the position of a camera alters the meaning of the object photographed. Many people know about camera angles now, but not so many know about sentences. The arrangement of the words matters, and the arrangement you want can be found in the picture in your mind. The picture dictates the arrangement. The picture dictates whether this will be a sentence with or without clauses, a sentence that ends hard or a dying-fall sentence, long or short, active or passive. The picture tells you how to arrange the words and the arrangement of the words tells you, or tells me, what's going on in the picture."

FOR DISCUSSION

1. What is Didion's definition of thinking? Do you agree with it?
2. To what extent does Didion's writing support her remarks about how and why she writes?
3. What does Didion mean when she says that grammar has "infinite power"? Power to do what?

E. B. WHITE

ELWYN BROOKS WHITE (1899–1985) for half a century was a regular contributor to *The New Yorker*, and his essays, editorials, anonymous features for "The Talk of the Town," and fillers helped build the magazine a reputation for wit and good writing. If as a child you read *Charlotte's Web* (1952), you have met E. B. White before. The book reflects some of his own life on a farm in North Brooklin, Maine. His *Letters* were collected in 1976, his *Essays* in 1977, and his *Poems and Sketches* in 1981. On July 4, 1963, President Kennedy named White in the first group of Americans to receive the Presidential Medal of Freedom, with a citation that called him "an essayist whose concise comment . . . has revealed to yet another age the vigor of the English sentence."

Once More to the Lake

"Once More to the Lake" first appeared in *Harper's* magazine in 1941. Perhaps if a duller writer had written the essay, or an essay with the same title, we wouldn't much care about it, for at first its subject seems as personal and ordinary as a letter home. White's loving and exact description, however, brings this lakeside camp to life for us. In the end, the writer arrives at an awareness that shocks him — shocks us, too, with a familiar sensory detail.

August 1941

One summer, along about 1904, my father rented a camp on a 1 lake in Maine and took us all there for the month of August. We all got ringworm from some kittens and had to rub Pond's Extract on our arms and legs night and morning, and my father rolled over in a canoe with all his clothes on; but outside of that the vacation was a success and from then on none of us ever thought there was any place in the world like that lake in Maine. We returned summer after summer — always on August 1 for one month. I have since become a salt-water man, but sometimes in summer there are days when the restlessness of the tides and the fearful cold of the sea water and the incessant wind that blows across the afternoon and into the evening make me wish for the placidity of a lake in the woods. A few weeks ago this feeling got so strong I bought myself a couple of bass hooks and a spinner and returned to the lake where we used to go, for a week's fishing and to revisit old haunts.

I took along my son, who had never had any fresh water up his 2 nose and who had seen lily pads only from train windows. On the journey over to the lake I began to wonder what it would be like. I wondered how time would have marred this unique, this holy spot — the coves and streams, the hills that the sun set behind, the camps and the paths behind the camps. I was sure that the tarred road would have found it out, and I wondered in what other ways it would be desolated. It is strange how much you can remember about places like that once you allow your mind to return into the grooves that lead back. You remember one thing, and that suddenly reminds you of another thing. I guess I remembered clearest of all the early mornings, when the lake was cool and motionless, remembered how the bedroom smelled of the lumber it was made of and of the wet woods whose scent entered through the screen. The partitions in the camp were thin and did not extend clear to the top of the rooms, and as I was always the first up I would dress softly so as not to wake the others, and sneak out into the sweet outdoors and start out in the canoe, keeping close along the shore in the long shadows of the pines. I remembered being very careful never to rub my paddle against the gunwale for fear of disturbing the stillness of the cathedral.

The lake had never been what you would call a wild lake. There 3 were cottages sprinkled around the shores, and it was in farming country although the shores of the lake were quite heavily wooded. Some of the cottages were owned by nearby farmers, and you would live at the shore and eat your meals at the farmhouse. That's what our family did. But although it wasn't wild, it was a fairly large and undisturbed lake and there were places in it that, to a child at least, seemed infinitely remote and primeval.

I was right about the tar: It led to within half a mile of the shore. 4 But when I got back there, with my boy, and we settled into a camp near a farmhouse and into the kind of summertime I had known, I could tell that it was going to be pretty much the same as it had been before — I knew it, lying in bed the first morning smelling the bedroom and hearing the boy sneak quietly out and go off along the shore in a boat. I began to sustain the illusion that he was I, and therefore, by simple transposition, that I was my father. This sensation persisted, kept cropping up all the time we were there. It was not an entirely new feeling, but in this setting it grew much stronger. I seemed to be living a dual existence. I would be in the middle of some simple act, I would be picking up a bait box or laying down a table fork, or I would be saying something and suddenly it would be not I but my father who was saying the words or making the gesture. It gave me a creepy sensation.

We went fishing the first morning. I felt the same damp moss 5 covering the worms in the bait can, and saw the dragonfly alight on the tip of my rod as it hovered a few inches from the surface of the water. It was the arrival of this fly that convinced me beyond any doubt that everything was as it always had been, that the years were a mirage and that there had been no years. The small waves were the same, chucking the rowboat under the chin as we fished at anchor, and the boat was the same boat, the same color green and the ribs broken in the same places, and under the floorboards the same fresh water leavings and debris — the dead hellgrammite, the wisps of moss, the rusty discarded fishhook, the dried blood from yesterday's catch. We stared silently at the tips of our rods, at the dragonflies that came and went. I lowered the tip of mine into the water, tentatively, pensively dislodging the fly, which darted two feet away, poised, darted two feet back, and came to rest again a little farther up the rod. There had been no years between the ducking of this dragonfly and the other one — the one that was part of memory. I looked at the boy, who was silently watching his fly, and it was my hands that held his rod, my eyes watching. I felt dizzy and didn't know which rod I was at the end of.

We caught two bass, hauling them in briskly as though they were   6
mackerel, pulling them over the side of the boat in a businesslike manner without any landing net, and stunning them with a blow on the back of the head. When we got back for a swim before lunch, the lake was exactly where we had left it, the same number of inches from the dock, and there was only the merest suggestion of a breeze. This seemed an utterly enchanted sea, this lake you could leave to its own devices for a few hours and come back to, and find that it had not stirred, this constant and trustworthy body of water. In the shallows, the dark, water-soaked sticks and twigs, smooth and old, were undulating in clusters on the bottom against the clean ribbed sand, and the track of the mussel was plain. A school of minnows swam by, each minnow with its small individual shadow, doubling the attendance, so clear and sharp in the sunlight. Some of the other campers were in swimming, along the shore, one of them with a cake of soap, and the water felt thin and clear and unsubstantial. Over the years there had been this person with the cake of soap, this cultist, and here he was. There had been no years.

Up to the farmhouse to dinner through the teeming dusty field,   7
the road under our sneakers was only a two-track road. The middle track was missing, the one with the marks of the hooves and the splotches of dried, flaky manure. There had always been three tracks to choose from in choosing which track to walk in; now the choice

was narrowed down to two. For a moment I missed terribly the middle alternative. But the way led past the tennis court, and something about the way it lay there in the sun reassured me; the tape had loosened along the backline, the alleys were green with plantains and other weeds, and the net (installed in June and removed in September) sagged in the dry noon, and the whole place steamed with midday heat and hunger and emptiness. There was a choice of pie for dessert, and one was blueberry and one was apple, and the waitresses were the same country girls, there having been no passage of time, only the illusion of it as in a dropped curtain — the waitresses were still fifteen; their hair had been washed, that was the only difference — they had been to the movies and seen the pretty girls with the clean hair.

Summertime, oh, summertime, pattern of life indelible with fade- 8 proof lake, the wood unshatterable, the pasture with the sweetfern and the juniper forever and ever, summer without end; this was the background, and the life along the shore was the design, the cottages with their innocent and tranquil design, their tiny docks with the flagpole and the American flag floating against the white clouds in the blue sky, the little paths over the roots of the trees leading from camp to camp and the paths leading back to the outhouses and the can of lime for sprinkling, and at the souvenir counters at the store the miniature birchbark canoes and the postcards that showed things looking a little better than they looked. This was the American family at play, escaping the city heat, wondering whether the newcomers in the camp at the head of the cove were "common" or "nice," wondering whether it was true that the people who drove up for Sunday dinner at the farmhouse were turned away because there wasn't enough chicken.

It seemed to me, as I kept remembering all this, that those times 9 and those summers had been infinitely precious and worth saving. There had been jollity and peace and goodness. The arriving (at the beginning of August) had been so big a business in itself, at the railway station the farm wagon drawn up, the first smell of the pine-laden air, the first glimpse of the smiling farmer, and the great importance of the trunks and your father's enormous authority in such matters, and the feel of the wagon under you for the long ten-mile haul, and at the top of the last long hill catching the first view of the lake after eleven months of not seeing this cherished body of water. The shouts and cries of the other campers when they saw you, and the trunks to be unpacked, to give up their rich burden. (Arriving was less exciting nowadays, when you sneaked up in your car and

parked it under a tree near the camp and took out the bags and in
five minutes it was all over, no fuss, no loud wonderful fuss about
trunks.)

Peace and goodness and jollity. The only thing that was wrong   10
now, really, was the sound of the place, an unfamiliar nervous sound
of the outboard motors. This was the note that jarred, the one thing
that would sometimes break the illusion and set the years moving. In
those other summertimes all motors were inboard; and when they
were at a little distance, the noise they made was a sedative, an
ingredient of summer sleep. They were one-cylinder and two-cylinder
engines, and some were make-and-break and some were jump-spark,
but they all made a sleepy sound across the lake. The one-lungers
throbbed and fluttered, and the twin-cylinder ones purred and purred,
and that was a quiet sound, too. But now the campers all had
outboards. In the daytime, in the hot mornings, these motors made
a petulant irritable sound; at night in the still evening when the
afterglow lit the water, they whined about one's ears like mosquitoes.
My boy loved our rented outboard, and his great desire was to achieve
single-handed mastery over it, and authority, and he soon learned
the trick of choking it a little (but not too much), and the adjustment
of the needle valve. Watching him I would remember the things you
could do with the old one-cylinder engine with the heavy flywheel,
how you could have it eating out of your hand if you got really close
to it spiritually. Motorboats in those days didn't have clutches, and
you would make a landing by shutting off the motor at the proper
time and coasting in with a dead rudder. But there was a way of
reversing them, if you learned the trick, by cutting the switch and
putting it on again exactly on the final dying revolution of the
flywheel, so that it would kick back against compression and begin
reversing. Approaching a dock in a strong following breeze, it was
difficult to slow up sufficiently by the ordinary coasting method, and
if a boy felt he had complete mastery over his motor, he was tempted
to keep it running beyond its time and then reverse it a few feet from
the dock. It took a cool nerve, because if you threw the switch a
twentieth of a second too soon you would catch the flywheel when
it still had speed enough to go up past center, and the boat would
leap ahead, charging bull-fashion at the dock.

We had a good week at the camp. The bass were biting well and   11
the sun shone endlessly, day after day. We would be tired at night
and lie down in the accumulated heat of the little bedrooms after the
long hot day and the breeze would stir almost imperceptibly outside
and the smell of the swamp drift in through the rusty screens. Sleep
would come easily and in the morning the red squirrel would be on

the roof, tapping out his gay routine. I kept remembering everything, lying in bed in the mornings — the small steamboat that had a long rounded stern like the lip of a Ubangi, and how quietly she ran on the moonlight sails, when the older boys played their mandolins and the girls sang and we ate doughnuts dipped in sugar, and how sweet the music was on the water in the shining night, and what it had felt like to think about girls then. After breakfast we would go up to the store and the things were in the same place — the minnows in a bottle, the plugs and spinners disarranged and pawed over by the youngsters from the boys' camp, the Fig Newtons and the Beeman's gum. Outside, the road was tarred and cars stood in front of the store. Inside, all was just as it had always been, except there was more Coca-Cola and not so much Moxie and root beer and birch beer and sarsaparilla. We would walk out with the bottle of pop apiece and sometimes the pop would backfire up our noses and hurt. We explored the streams, quietly, where the turtles slid off the sunny logs and dug their way into the soft bottom; and we lay on the town wharf and fed worms to the tame bass. Everywhere we went I had trouble making out which was I, the one walking at my side, the one walking in my pants.

One afternoon while we were at the lake a thunderstorm came   12 up. It was like the revival of an old melodrama that I had seen long ago with childish awe. The second-act climax of the drama of the electrical disturbance over a lake in America had not changed in any important respect. This was the big scene, still the big scene. The whole thing was so familiar, the first feeling of oppression and heat and a general air around camp of not wanting to go very far away. In midafternoon (it was all the same) a curious darkening of the sky, and a lull in everything that had made life tick; and then the way the boats suddenly swung the other way at their moorings with the coming of a breeze out of the new quarter, and the premonitory rumble. Then the kettle drum, then the snare, then the bass drum and cymbals, then crackling light against the dark, and the gods grinning and licking their chops in the hills. Afterward the calm, the rain steadily rustling in the calm lake, the return of light and hope and spirits, and the campers running out in joy and relief to go swimming in the rain, their bright cries perpetuating the deathless joke about how they were getting simply drenched, and the children screaming with delight at the new sensation of bathing in the rain, and the joke about getting drenched linking the generations in a strong indestructible chain. And the comedian who waded in carrying an umbrella.

When the others went swimming my son said he was going in,   13

too. He pulled his dripping trunks from the line where they had hung
all through the shower and wrung them out. Languidly, and with no
thought of going in, I watched him, his hard little body, skinny and
bare, saw him wince slightly as he pulled up around his vitals the
small, soggy, icy garment. As he buckled the swollen belt, suddenly
my groin felt the chill of death.

QUESTIONS ON MEANING

1. How do you account for the distortions that creep into the author's
   sense of time?
2. What does the discussion of inboard and outboard motors (para. 10)
   have to do with the author's divided sense of time?
3. To what degree does White make us aware of his son's impression of
   this trip to the lake?
4. What do you take to be White's main PURPOSE in the essay? At what
   point do you become aware of it?

QUESTIONS ON WRITING STRATEGY

1. In paragraph 4, the author first introduces his confused feeling that he
   has gone back in time to his own childhood, an idea that he repeats
   and expands throughout his account. What is the function of these
   repetitions?
2. Try to describe the impact of the essay's final paragraph. By what means
   is it achieved?
3. To what extent is this essay written to appeal to any but middle-aged
   readers? Is it comprehensible to anyone whose vacations were never
   spent at a Maine summer cottage?
4. What is the TONE of White's essay?
5. OTHER METHODS. White's essay is both a description and a COMPARI-
   SON of the lake when he was a boy and when he revisits it with his
   son. What changes does he find at the lake? What things have stayed
   the same?

QUESTIONS ON LANGUAGE

1. Be sure you know the meanings of the following words: incessant,
   placidity (para. 1); gunwale (2); primeval (3); transposition (4); hellgrammite (5); undulating, cultist (6); indelible, tranquil (8); petulant
   (10); imperceptibly (11); premonitory (12); languidly (13).

2. Comment on White's DICTION in his reference to the lake as "this unique, this holy spot" (para. 2).
3. Explain what White is describing in the sentence that begins, "Then the kettle drum . . ." (para. 12). Where else does the author use METAPHORS?
4. Find effective IMAGES that are not FIGURES OF SPEECH.

SUGGESTIONS FOR WRITING

1. In a descriptive paragraph, try to appeal to each of your reader's five senses.
2. Describe in a brief essay a place you loved as a child. Or, if you have ever returned to a favorite old haunt, describe the experience. Was it pleasant or painful — or both? What, exactly, made it so?
3. CRITICAL WRITING. While on the vacation he describes, White wrote to his wife, Katharine, "This place is as American as a drink of Coca Cola. The white collar family having its annual liberty." Obviously, not everyone has a chance at the lakeside summers White enjoyed. To what extent, if at all, does White's privileged POINT OF VIEW deprive his essay of universal meaning and significance? Write an essay answering this question. Back up your ideas with EVIDENCE from White's essay.
4. CONNECTIONS. As he depicts it in "Once More to the Lake," White experienced a very different childhood from that portrayed in Ralph Ellison's "On Being the Target of Discrimination" (p. 55). Write about the differing childhoods of Ellison and White, focusing on each one's feelings about family, sense of security, and sense of place. Use examples from each essay as EVIDENCE for your ideas. If you want to explore this topic further, use the two essays as the basis for a broader examination of whether and why one experience of childhood is preferable to another.

E. B. WHITE ON WRITING

"You asked me about writing — how I did it," E. B. White replied to a seventeen-year-old who had written to him, wanting to become a professional writer but feeling discouraged. "There is no trick to it. If you like to write and want to write, you write, no matter where you are or what else you are doing or whether anyone pays any heed. I must have written half a million words (mostly in my journal) before I had anything published, save for a couple of short items in St. Nicholas.[1] If you want to write about feelings, about the end of the

---

[1]A magazine for children, popular early in the century. — EDS.

summer, about growing, write about it. A great deal of writing is not 'plotted' — most of my essays have no plot structure, they are a ramble in the woods, or a ramble in the basement of my mind. You ask, 'Who cares?' Everybody cares. You say, 'It's been written before.' Everything has been written before. . . . Henry Thoreau, who wrote *Walden*, said, 'I learned this at least by my experiment: that if one advances confidently in the direction of his dreams and endeavors to live the life which he has imagined, he will meet with a success unexpected in common hours.' The sentence, after more than a hundred years, is still alive. So, advance confidently."

In trying to characterize his own writing, White was modest in his claims. To his brother Stanley Hart White, he once remarked, "I discovered a long time ago that writing of the small things of the day, the trivial matters of the heart, the inconsequential but near things of this living, was the only kind of creative work which I could accomplish with any sincerity or grace. As a reporter, I was a flop, because I always came back laden not with facts about the case, but with a mind full of the little difficulties and amusements I had encountered in my travels. Not till *The New Yorker* came along did I ever find any means of expressing those impertinences and irrelevancies. Thus yesterday, setting out to get a story on how police horses are trained, I ended by writing a story entitled "How Police Horses Are Trained" which never even mentions a police horse, but has to do entirely with my own absurd adventures at police headquarters. The rewards of such endeavor are not that I have acquired an audience or a following, as you suggest (fame of any kind being a Pyrrhic victory), but that sometimes in writing of myself — which is the only subject anyone knows intimately — I have occasionally had the exquisite thrill of putting my finger on a little capsule of truth, and heard it give the faint squeak of mortality under my pressure, an antic sound."

FOR DISCUSSION

1. Sometimes young writers are counseled to study the market and then try to write something that will sell. How would you expect E. B. White to have reacted to such advice?
2. What, exactly, does White mean when he says, "Everything has been written before"? How might an aspiring writer take this remark as encouragement?
3. What interesting distinction does White make between reporting and essay writing?

EMILY DICKINSON

For most of her life, EMILY DICKINSON (1830–86) kept to the shadowy privacy of her family mansion in Amherst, Massachusetts, a farming village and the site of Amherst College. Her father, an eminent lawyer, was for a time a United States congressman. One brief trip to Philadelphia and Washington, two semesters at New England Female Seminary (ending with Emily's refusal to declare herself a Christian despite pressure on her), and a few months with nieces in Cambridge, Massachusetts, while having her eyes treated, were all the poet's travels away from home. Her work on her brilliantly original poems intensified in the years 1858–62. In later years, Emily Dickinson withdrew more and more from the life of the town into her private thoughts, correspondence with friends, and the society of only her closest family. After her death, her poems were discovered in manuscript (stitched into little booklets), and a first selection was published in 1890. Since then, her personal legend and the devotion of readers have grown vastly and steadily.

A narrow Fellow
in the Grass

In her lifetime, Emily Dickinson published only seven of her more than a thousand poems. "A narrow Fellow in the Grass," one of this handful, was first printed anonymously in 1866 in a newspaper, the *Springfield Republican*. There, without the poet's consent, it was titled "The Snake" and rearranged into eight-line stanzas. Such high-handed treatment seems to have confirmed Dickinson in her dread of publication. For the rest of her life, she preferred to store her poems in the attic. In shape, this poem and most of her others owe much to hymn tunes she had heard in church as a girl. Like "A narrow Fellow in the Grass," about half her poems fall into "common meter": stanzas of four lines, alternating eight syllables and six syllables, the shorter lines rhyming either exactly or roughly. Notice the lively verbs in this poem, its images, its sense of the physical world. On first reading it, Samuel Bowles, the poem's first editor, admiringly wondered aloud: "How did that girl ever know that a boggy field wasn't good for corn?"

A narrow Fellow in the Grass   1
Occasionally rides–
You may have met Him–did you not
His notice sudden is–

The Grass divides as with a Comb–   5
A spotted shaft is seen–
And then it closes at your feet
And opens further on–

He likes a Boggy Acre
A Floor too cool for Corn–   10
Yet when a Boy, and Barefoot–
I more than once at Noon

Have passed, I thought, a Whip lash
Unbraiding in the Sun
When stooping to secure it   15
It wrinkled, and was gone–

Several of Nature's People
I know, and they know me–
I feel for them a transport
Of cordiality–   20

But never met this Fellow
Attended, or alone
Without a tighter breathing
And Zero at the Bone–

QUESTIONS ON MEANING

1. How would you sum up the poet's attitude toward this Fellow? Is she playful, serious, or both? Point to lines in the poem to support your view.
2. Recast in your own words the thought in Dickinson's lines 17–24.

QUESTIONS ON WRITING STRATEGY

1. By what details does the poet make the snake seem elusive and mysterious?
2. What does the poem gain from the speaker's claim to have once been

a barefoot boy? By her PERSONIFICATION of the snake as a Fellow, one of Nature's People?

2. **OTHER METHODS.** Dickinson is NARRATING as well as describing her encounters with the snake. What EFFECT does she achieve by using present-tense verbs such as *is* and *closes*?

QUESTIONS ON LANGUAGE

1. In addition to PERSONIFICATION, can you locate examples of SIMILE, METAPHOR, and HYPERBOLE?
2. Which pairs of rhyming words chime exactly? Which rhymes seem rough or far out? Dickinson's early editors tried to regularize her inexact rhymes. But how might these rhymes be defended?
3. Can you see any justification for the poet's personal, homemade system of punctuation — the half-dashes?

SUGGESTIONS FOR WRITING

1. What do you feel about snakes? Write a brief essay describing a snake. (If you haven't got one already in mind, go to the zoo or look in a book or tip over a rock.) Agree or disagree with Dickinson's IMAGES if you like.
2. Have you written poetry? Try it now, choosing as your subject an object or animal to describe — something you (like Dickinson) have strong feelings about, such as a favorite tree, a beloved cat, a loathed cockroach. Don't worry too much about meter and rhyme; concentrate instead on images.
3. **CRITICAL WRITING.** In a paragraph, ANALYZE Dickinson's last two lines. In your own words, what sensations does each image conjure up? What is the poet's feeling?
4. **CONNECTIONS.** In two or three paragraphs, analyze Emily Dickinson's and E. B. White's final images — Dickinson's in lines 23–24 and White's in the last two sentences of "Once More to the Lake" (p. 126). What do their images have in common? How are they different? Which do you find more effective, and why?

EMILY DICKINSON ON WRITING

Although Emily Dickinson never spelled out in detail her methods of writing, her practices are clear to us from the work of scholars who have studied her manuscripts. Evidently she liked to rewrite extensively both poetry and prose, with the result that many poems and some letters exist in multiple versions. Usually, a poem proceeded through three stages: a first, worksheet draft; a semifinal draft; and final copy. Occasionally, in later years, she would return to a poem, tinkering, striving for improvements. (In a few cases, she reduced a previously finished poem to a permanent confusion.)

Her admiration for the work of writer and lecturer Thomas Wentworth Higginson began after he published his "Letter to a Young Contributor" in *The Atlantic Monthly* in 1862. In it, he advised novice writers, "Charge your style with life." Echoing Higginson's remark with approval, Dickinson sent him some of her poems and asked, "Are you too deeply occupied to say if my Verse is alive?" Writers might attain liveliness, Higginson had maintained, by choosing plain words, as few of them as possible. We might expect this advice to find favor with Emily Dickinson, who once wrote:

> A word is dead
> When it is said,
> Some say.
> I say it just
> Begins to live
> That day.

FOR DISCUSSION

1. In what sense might a word "begin to live" when it's said?
2. If *you* had been advised to "charge your style with life," how would you go about it?

ADDITIONAL WRITING TOPICS

Description

1. This is an in-class writing experiment. Describe another person in the room so clearly and unmistakably that when you read your description aloud, your subject will be recognized. (Be OBJECTIVE. No insulting descriptions, please!)
2. Write a paragraph describing one subject from *each* of the following categories. It will be up to you to make the general subject refer to a particular person, place, or thing. Write at least one paragraph as an OBJECTIVE description and at least one as a SUBJECTIVE description. (Identify your method in each case, so that your instructor can see how well you carry it out.)

Person

A friend or roommate
A typical rap, heavy metal, or country musician
One of your parents
An elderly person you know
A prominent politician
A historical figure

Place

An office
A classroom
A college campus
A vacation spot
A hospital emergency room
A forest

Thing

A dentist's drill
A painting or photograph
A foggy day
A season of the year
A musical instrument
A train

3. In a brief essay, describe your ideal place: an apartment, a bookstore, a dorm room, a vacation spot, a classroom, a restaurant, a gym, a supermarket or convenience store, a garden, a golf course. With concrete details, try to make the ideal seem actual.

Narration and Description

4. Use a combination of narration and description to develop any one of the following topics:

   Your first day on the job
   Your first day at college
   Returning to an old neighborhood
   Getting lost
   A brush with a celebrity
   Delivering bad (or good) news

3

EXAMPLE

Pointing to Instances

THE METHOD

"There have been many women runners of distinction," a writer begins, and quickly goes on, "among them Joan Benoit, Grete Waitz, Florence Griffith Joyner. . . ."

You have just seen examples at work. An *example* (from the Latin *exemplum:* "one thing selected from among many") is an instance that reveals a whole type. By selecting an example, a writer shows the nature or character of the group from which it is taken. In a written essay, an example will often serve to illustrate a general statement, or GENERALIZATION. Here, for instance, the writer Linda Wolfe makes a point about the food fetishes of Roman emperors (Domitian and Claudius ruled in the first century A.D.).

The emperors used their gastronomical concerns to indicate their contempt of the country and the whole task of governing it. Domitian humiliated his cabinet by forcing them to attend him at his villa to help solve a serious problem. When they arrived he kept them waiting for hours. The problem, it finally appeared, was that the emperor had just purchased a giant fish, too large for any dish he owned, and he needed the learned brains of his ministers

135

to decide whether the fish should be minced or whether a larger pot should be sought. The emperor Claudius one day rode hurriedly to the Senate and demanded they deliberate the importance of a life without pork. Another time he sat in his tribunal ostensibly administering justice but actually allowing the litigants to argue and orate while he grew dreamy, interrupting the discussions only to announce, "Meat pies are wonderful. We shall have them for dinner."

Wolfe might have allowed the opening sentence of her paragraph — the TOPIC SENTENCE — to remain a vague generalization. Instead, she supports it with three examples, each an anecdote briefly narrating an instance of an emperor's contemptuous behavior. With these examples, Wolfe not only explains and supports her generalization, she animates it.

The method of giving examples — of illustrating what you're saying with a "for instance" — is not merely helpful to practically all kinds of writing, it is indispensable. Bad writers — those who bore us, or lose us completely — often have an ample supply of ideas; their trouble is that they never pull their ideas down out of the clouds. A dull writer, for instance, might declare, "The emperors used food to humiliate their governments," and then, instead of giving examples, go on, "They also manipulated their families," or something — adding still another large, unillustrated idea. Specific examples are *needed* elements in good prose. Not only do they make ideas understandable, but they also keep readers awake. (The previous paragraphs have tried — by giving examples from Linda Wolfe and from "a dull writer" — to illustrate this point.)

THE PROCESS

Where do you find examples? In anything you know — or care to learn. Start close to home. Seek examples in your own immediate knowledge and experience. When assigned an elephant-sized subject that you think you know nothing about — ethical dilemmas, for instance — rummage your memory and you may discover that you know more than you thought. In what ethical dilemmas have you ever found yourself? Deciding whether or not to date your best friend's fiancé (or fiancée) when your best friend is out of town? Being tempted to pilfer from the jelly jar of a small boy's Kool-Aid stand when you need a quarter for a bus? No doubt you can supply your own examples. It is the method — exemplifying — that matters. To bring some huge and ethereal concept down to earth may just set your expository

Example   **137**

faculties galloping over the plains of your own life to the sound of "hi-ho, Silver!" For different examples, you can explore your conversations with others, your studies, and the storehouse of information you have gathered from books, newspapers, magazines, radio, and TV, and from popular hearsay: proverbs and sayings, bits of wisdom you've heard voiced in your family, folklore, popular song.

Now and again, you may feel an irresistible temptation to make up an example out of thin air. This procedure is risky, but can work wonderfully — if, that is, you have a wonder-working imagination. When Henry David Thoreau, in *Walden*, attacks Americans' smug pride in the achievements of nineteenth-century science and industry, he wants to illustrate that kind of invention or discovery "which distracts our attention from serious things." And so he makes up the examples — farfetched at the time, but pointed — of a transatlantic speaking tube and what it might convey: "We are eager to tunnel under the Atlantic and bring the Old World some weeks nearer to the New; but perchance the first news that will leak through into the broad, flapping American ear will be that the Princess Adelaide has the whooping cough." (Thoreau would be appalled at our immersion in the British Royal Family via just the sort of communication he imagined.)

Thoreau's examples (and the sarcastic phrase about the American ear) bespeak genius; but, of course, not every writer can be a Thoreau — or needs to be. A hypothetical example may well be better than no example at all; yet, as a rule, an example from fact or experience is likely to carry more weight. Suppose you have to write about the benefits — any benefits — that recent science has conferred upon the nation. You might imagine one such benefit: the prospect of one day being able to vacation in outer space and drift about in free-fall like a soap bubble. That imagined benefit would be all right, but it is obviously a conjecture that you dreamed up without going to the library. Do a little digging in recent books and magazines (for the latter, with the aid of the *Readers' Guide to Periodical Literature*). Your reader will feel better informed to be told that science — specifically, the NASA space program — has produced useful inventions. You add:

> Among these are the smoke detector, originally developed as Skylab equipment; the inflatable air bag to protect drivers and pilots, designed to cushion astronauts in splashdowns; a walking chair that enables paraplegics to mount stairs and travel over uneven ground, derived from the moonwalkers' surface buggy; the technique of cryosurgery, the removal of cancerous tissue by fast freezing.

By using specific examples like these, you render the idea of "benefits to society" more concrete and more definite. Such examples are not prettifications of your essay; they are necessary if you are to hold your readers' attention and convince them that you are worth listening to.

When giving examples, you'll find other methods useful. Sometimes, as in the paragraph by Linda Wolfe, an example takes the form of a NARRATIVE (Chap. 1): a brief story, an ANECDOTE, or a case history. Sometimes an example embodies a vivid DESCRIPTION of a person, place, or thing (Chap. 2).

Lazy writers think, "Oh well, I can't come up with any example here — I'll just leave it to the reader to find one." The flaw in this assumption is that the reader may be as lazy as the writer. As a result, a perfectly good idea may be left suspended in the stratosphere. The linguist and writer S. I. Hayakawa tells the story of a professor who, in teaching a philosophy course, spent a whole semester on the theory of beauty. When students asked him for a few examples of beautiful paintings, symphonies, or works of nature, he refused, saying, "We are interested in principles, not in particulars." The professor himself may well have been interested in principles, but it is a safe bet that his classroom resounded with snores. In written exposition, it is undoubtedly the particulars — the pertinent examples — that keep a reader awake and having a good time, and taking in the principles besides.

EXAMPLE IN A PARAGRAPH:
TWO ILLUSTRATIONS

Using Example to Write About Television

To simulate reality must be among television's main concerns, for the airwaves glow with programs that create a smooth and enjoyable imitation of life. Take, for example, wrestling. Stripped to their essentials (and to their gaudy tights), the heroes and villains of TV wrestling matches parade before us like walking abstractions: the Sly Braggart, the Well-Barbered Athlete, the Evil Russian. Larger than life, wrestlers are also louder. They seldom speak; they bellow instead. Part of our enjoyment comes from recognizing the phoniness of it all: When blows fail to land, the intended recipients groan anyway. Some TV simulations are less obvious than wrestling: for instance, the long-running *People's Court.* "What you're about to see is real," a voice-over tells us. In fact, the litigants are not professional actors but people who have filed to appear in a small claims court. Enticed to drop their complaints and instead appear

Example   **139**

on *People's Court* before the admirably fair Judge Wapner, they play themselves and are rewarded with instant fame and a paycheck. We enjoy the illusion that a genuine legal dispute can be as dramatic as a soap opera. And happily, it can always be settled in exactly ten minutes, between commercials.

COMMENT. To explain the general notion that television often gives us a glossy imitation of life, this paragraph uses two chief examples: wrestling and *People's Court*. (The examples come from Michael Sorkin's "Faking It," in *Watching Television*, edited by Todd Gitlin.) Inside a brief discussion of wrestling, the writer exemplifies still further, mentioning and inventing names for familiar types of wrestling champions (the Sly Braggart and others). The result is that, in only a few lines, the intangible idea of simulating life becomes clear and unmistakable. Fun to read, these examples also pack weight: They convince us that the writer knows the subject.

Using Example in an Academic Discipline

The primary function of the market is to bring together suppliers and demanders so that they can trade with one another. Buyers and sellers do not necessarily have to be in face-to-face contact; they can signal their desires and intentions through various intermediaries. For example, the demand for green beans in California is not expressed directly by the green bean consumers to the green bean growers. People who want green beans buy them at a grocery store; the store orders them from a vegetable wholesaler; the wholesaler buys them from a bean cooperative, whose manager tells local farmers of the size of the current demand for green beans. The demanders of green beans are able to signal their demand schedule to the original suppliers, the farmers who raise the beans, without any personal communication between the two parties.

COMMENT. Taken from Lewis C. Solmon's *Microeconomics*, this paragraph uses a simple example to demonstrate how the market works. By showing step-by-step how green bean growers are brought together with green bean buyers, the author can make clear in a single paragraph a concept that would take much longer to explain in abstract terms — thus doing his audience a favor. Most readers can more easily grasp a concept when they are shown rather than merely told how it works. In this case, by personalizing the three intermediaries between the buyers and sellers of green beans, the author lends life and vigor as well as clarity to his explanation.

BARBARA LAZEAR ASCHER

BARBARA LAZEAR ASCHER was born in 1946 and educated at Bennington College and Cardozo School of Law. She practiced law for two years in a private firm, where she found herself part of a power structure in which those on top resembled "the two-year-old with the biggest plastic pail and shovel on the beach. It's a life of nervous guardianship." Ascher quit the law to devote herself to writing, to explore, as she says, "what really matters." Her essays have appeared in the *New York Times,* the *Yale Review, Vogue,* and other periodicals and have been collected in *Playing after Dark* (1987) and *The Habit of Loving* (1989). Her latest book, *Landscape Without Gravity: A Memoir of Grief* (1993), is about her brother's death from AIDS. Ascher lives with her family in New York City.

On Compassion

Ascher often writes about life in New York City, where human problems sometimes seem larger and more stubborn than in other places. But this essay concerns an experience most of us have had, wherever we live: responding to those who need help. First published in *Elle* magazine in 1988, the essay was later reprinted in *The Habit of Loving.* (The essay following this one, Anna Quindlen's "Homeless," addresses the same issue.)

The man's grin is less the result of circumstance than dreams or 1 madness. His buttonless shirt, with one sleeve missing, hangs outside the waist of his baggy trousers. Carefully plaited dreadlocks bespeak a better time, long ago. As he crosses Manhattan's Seventy-ninth Street, his gait is the shuffle of the forgotten ones held in place by gravity rather than plans. On the corner of Madison Avenue, he stops before a blond baby in an Aprica stroller. The baby's mother waits for the light to change and her hands close tighter on the stroller's handle as she sees the man approach.

The others on the corner, five men and women waiting for the 2 crosstown bus, look away. They daydream a bit and gaze into the weak rays of November light. A man with a briefcase lifts and lowers the shiny toe of his right shoe, watching the light reflect, trying to catch and balance it, as if he could hold and make it his, to ease the heavy gray of coming January, February, and March. The winter months that will send snow around the feet, calves, and knees of the grinning man as he heads for the shelter of Grand Central or Pennsylvania Station.

But for now, in this last gasp of autumn warmth, he is still. His ³
eyes fix on the baby. The mother removes her purse from her shoulder
and rummages through its contents: lipstick, a lace handkerchief, an
address book. She finds what she's looking for and passes a folded
dollar over her child's head to the man who stands and stares even
though the light has changed and traffic navigates about his hips.

His hands continue to dangle at his sides. He does not know his ⁴
part. He does not know that acceptance of the gift and gratitude are
what make this transaction complete. The baby, weary of the unwavering
stare, pulls its blanket over its head. The man does not
look away. Like a bridegroom waiting at the altar, his eyes pierce the
white veil.

The mother grows impatient and pushes the stroller before her, ⁵
bearing the dollar like a cross. Finally, a black hand rises and closes
around green.

Was it fear or compassion that motivated the gift? ⁶

Up the avenue, at Ninety-first Street, there is a small French ⁷
bread shop where you can sit and eat a buttery, overpriced croissant
and wash it down with rich cappuccino. Twice when I have stopped
here to stave hunger or stay the cold, twice as I have sat and read
and felt the warm rush of hot coffee and milk, an old man has
wandered in and stood inside the entrance. He wears a stained blanket
pulled up to his chin, and a woolen hood pulled down to his gray,
bushy eyebrows. As he stands, the scent of stale cigarettes and urine
fills the small, overheated room.

The owner of the shop, a moody French woman, emerges from ⁸
the kitchen with steaming coffee in a Styrofoam cup, and a small
paper bag of . . . of what? Yesterday's bread? Today's croissant? He
accepts the offering as silently as he came, and is gone.

Twice I have witnessed this, and twice I have wondered, what ⁹
compels this woman to feed this man? Pity? Care? Compassion? Or
does she simply want to rid her shop of his troublesome presence? If
expulsion were her motivation she would not reward his arrival with
gifts of food. Most proprietors do not. They chase the homeless from
their midst with expletives and threats.

As winter approaches, the mayor of New York City is moving ¹⁰
the homeless off the streets and into Bellevue Hospital. The New
York Civil Liberties Union is watchful. They question whether the
rights of these people who live in our parks and doorways are being
violated by involuntary hospitalization.

I think the mayor's notion is humane, but I fear it is something 11
else as well. Raw humanity offends our sensibilities. We want to
protect ourselves from an awareness of rags with voices that make no
sense and scream forth in inarticulate rage. We do not wish to be
reminded of the tentative state of our own well-being and sanity.
And so, the troublesome presence is removed from the awareness of
the electorate.

Like other cities, there is much about Manhattan now that re- 12
sembles Dickensian London. Ladies in high-heeled shoes pick their
way through poverty and madness. You hear more cocktail party
complaints than usual, "I just can't take New York anymore." Our
citizens dream of the open spaces of Wyoming, the manicured exclu-
sivity of Hobe Sound.

And yet, it may be that these are the conditions that finally give 13
birth to empathy, the mother of compassion. We cannot deny the
existence of the helpless as their presence grows. It is impossible to
insulate ourselves against what is at our very doorstep. I don't believe
that one is born compassionate. Compassion is not a character trait
like a sunny disposition. It must be learned, and it is learned by
having adversity at our windows, coming through the gates of our
yards, the walls of our towns, adversity that becomes so familiar that
we begin to identify and empathize with it.

For the ancient Greeks, drama taught and reinforced compassion 14
within a society. The object of Greek tragedy was to inspire empathy
in the audience so that the common response to the hero's fall was:
"There, but for the grace of God, go I." Could it be that this was the
response of the mother who offered the dollar, the French woman
who gave the food? Could it be that the homeless, like those ancients,
are reminding us of our common humanity? Of course, there is a
difference. This play doesn't end — and the players can't go home.

QUESTIONS ON MEANING

1. What do the two men in Ascher's essay exemplify?
2. What is Ascher's THESIS? What is her PURPOSE?
3. What solution to homelessness is introduced in paragraph 10? What
   does Ascher think of this possibility?
4. How do you interpret Ascher's last sentence? Is she optimistic or pes-
   simistic about whether people will learn compassion?

QUESTIONS ON WRITING STRATEGY

1. Which comes first, the GENERALIZATIONS or the supporting examples? Why has Ascher chosen this order?
2. What assumptions does the author make about her AUDIENCE?
3. Why do the other people at the bus stop look away (para. 2)? What does Ascher's description of their activities say about them?
4. **OTHER METHODS.** Ascher explores CAUSES AND EFFECTS. Do you agree with her that exposure to others' helplessness increases our compassion? Why, or why not?

QUESTIONS ON LANGUAGE

1. What is the difference between empathy and compassion? Why does Ascher say that "empathy [is] the mother of compassion" (para. 13)?
2. Find definitions for the following words: plaited, dreadlocks, bespeaks (para. 1); stave, stay (7); expletives (9); inarticulate, electorate (11).
3. What are the implications of Ascher's ALLUSION to "Dickensian London"?
4. Examine the language Ascher uses to describe the two homeless men. Is it OBJECTIVE? Sympathetic? Negative?

SUGGESTIONS FOR WRITING

1. Write an essay on the problem of homelessness in your town or city. Use examples to support your view of the problem and a possible solution.
2. Have you had a personal experience with misfortune? Have you needed to beg on the street, been evicted from an apartment, had to scrounge for food? Have you worked in a soup kitchen, been asked for money by beggars, helped in a city hospital? Write an essay on your experience, using examples to convey the effect the experience had on you.
3. Ascher refers to the efforts of New York City to move the homeless off the streets (para. 10). In October 1987, one of New York's homeless, Joyce Brown, was taken off the sidewalk where she lived to Bellevue Hospital. The American Civil Liberties Union sued on her behalf, claiming that she was not a danger to herself or to others — the grounds for involuntary hospitalization. Although Brown was eventually released in January 1988, the issue of the city's right to hospitalize her was never resolved. Consult the *New York Times Index* and the *Times* itself for news articles and editorials on this situation. Write an essay arguing for or against Joyce Brown's freedom to live on the street, supporting your argument with evidence from the newspaper and from your own experience.
4. **CRITICAL WRITING.** In her last paragraph, Ascher mentions but does not address another key difference between the characters in Greek

tragedy and the homeless on today's streets: The former were "heroes" —
gods and goddesses, kings and queens — whereas the latter are placeless,
poor, anonymous, even reviled. Does this difference negate Ascher's
comparison between Greek theatergoers and ourselves or her larger point
about how compassion is learned? Answer in a brief essay, saying why
or why not.

5. **CONNECTIONS.** The next essay, Anna Quindlen's "Homeless," also uses
examples to make a point about homelessness. What are some of the
differences in the examples each writer uses? In a brief essay, explore
whether and how these differences create different TONES in the two
works.

ANNA QUINDLEN

ANNA QUINDLEN was born in 1952 and graduated from Barnard College in 1974. She worked as a reporter for the *New York Post* and the *New York Times* before taking over the *Times*'s "About New York" column, serving as the paper's deputy metropolitan editor, and in 1986 creating her own weekly column, "Life in the Thirties." Many of the essays from this popular column were collected in *Living Out Loud* (1988). After taking some time off to care for her third child, in 1989 Quindlen began a twice-weekly op-ed column for the *Times,* on social and political issues. Many of these essays were collected in *Thinking Out Loud: On the Personal, the Political, the Public, and the Private* (1993). Quindlen also published a suc-cessful novel, *Object Lessons* (1991).

Homeless

In this essay from *Living Out Loud,* Quindlen explores the same topic as Barbara Lazear Ascher (p. 140), but with a different slant. Typically for Quindlen, she mingles a reporter's respect for details with a passionate regard for life.

Her name was Ann, and we met in the Port Authority Bus 1
Terminal several Januarys ago. I was doing a story on homeless people. She said I was wasting my time talking to her; she was just passing through, although she'd been passing through for more than two weeks. To prove to me that this was true, she rummaged through a tote bag and a manila envelope and finally unfolded a sheet of typing paper and brought out her photographs.

They were not pictures of family, or friends, or even a dog or cat, 2
its eyes brown-red in the flashbulb's light. They were pictures of a house. It was like a thousand houses in a hundred towns, not suburb, not city, but somewhere in between, with aluminum siding and a chain-link fence, a narrow driveway running up to a one-car garage and a patch of backyard. The house was yellow. I looked on the back for a date or a name, but neither was there. There was no need for discussion. I knew what she was trying to tell me, for it was something I had often felt. She was not adrift, alone, anonymous, although her bags and her raincoat with the grime shadowing its creases had made me believe she was. She had a house, or at least once upon a time

145

had had one. Inside were curtains, a couch, a stove, potholders. You are where you live. She was somebody.

I've never been very good at looking at the big picture, taking 3 the global view, and I've always been a person with an overactive sense of place, the legacy of an Irish grandfather. So it is natural that the thing that seems most wrong with the world to me right now is that there are so many people with no homes. I'm not simply talking about shelter from the elements, or three square meals a day or a mailing address to which the welfare people can send the check — although I know that all these are important for survival. I'm talking about a home, about precisely those kinds of feelings that have wound up in cross-stitch and French knots on samplers over the years.

Home is where the heart is. There's no place like it. I love my 4 home with a ferocity totally out of proportion to its appearance or location. I love dumb things about it: the hot-water heater, the plastic rack you drain dishes in, the roof over my head, which occasionally leaks. And yet it is precisely those dumb things that make it what it is — a place of certainty, stability, predictability, privacy, for me and for my family. It is where I live. What more can you say about a place than that? That is everything.

Yet it is something that we have been edging away from gradually 5 during my lifetime and the lifetimes of my parents and grandparents. There was a time when where you lived often was where you worked and where you grew the food you ate and even where you were buried. When that era passed, where you lived at least was where your parents had lived and where you would live with your children when you became enfeebled. Then, suddenly where you lived was where you lived for three years, until you could move on to something else and something else again.

And so we have come to something else again, to children who 6 do not understand what it means to go to their rooms because they have never had a room, to men and women whose fantasy is a wall they can paint a color of their own choosing, to old people reduced to sitting on molded plastic chairs, their skin blue-white in the lights of a bus station, who pull pictures of houses out of their bags. Homes have stopped being homes. Now they are real estate.

People find it curious that those without homes would rather sleep 7 sitting up on benches or huddled in doorways than go to shelters. Certainly some prefer to do so because they are emotionally ill, because they have been locked in before and they are damned if they will be locked in again. Others are afraid of the violence and trouble they may find there. But some seem to want something that is not available in shelters, and they will not compromise, not for a cot, or oatmeal, or a shower with special soap that kills the bugs. "One room," a woman with a baby who was sleeping on her sister's floor, once told me, "painted blue." That was the crux of it; not size or location, but pride of ownership. Painted blue.

This is a difficult problem, and some wise and compassionate   8
people are working hard at it. But in the main I think we work around it, just as we walk around it when it is lying on the sidewalk or sitting in the bus terminal — the problem, that is. It has been customary to take people's pain and lessen our own participation in it by turning it into an issue, not a collection of human beings. We turn an adjective into a noun: the poor, not poor people; the homeless, not Ann or the man who lives in the box or the woman who sleeps on the subway grate.

Sometimes I think we would be better off if we forgot about the   9
broad strokes and concentrated on the details. Here is a woman without a bureau. There is a man with no mirror, no wall to hang it on. They are not the homeless. They are people who have no homes. No drawer that holds the spoons. No window to look out upon the world. My God. That is everything.

QUESTIONS ON MEANING

1. What is Quindlen's THESIS?
2. What distinction is Quindlen making in her CONCLUSION with the sentences "They are not the homeless. They are people without homes"?
3. Why does Quindlen feel a home is so important?

QUESTIONS ON WRITING STRATEGY

1. Why do you think Quindlen begins with the story of Ann? How else might Quindlen have begun her essay?
2. What is the EFFECT of Quindlen's examples of her own home?
3. What key ASSUMPTIONS does the author make about her AUDIENCE? Are the assumptions reasonable? Where does she specifically address an assumption that might undermine her view?
4. OTHER METHODS. Quindlen uses examples to support an ARGUMENT. What position does she want readers to recognize and accept?

QUESTIONS ON LANGUAGE

1. What is the EFFECT of "My God" in the last paragraph?
2. How might Quindlen be said to give new meaning to the old CLICHÉ "Home is where the heart is" (para. 4)?
3. What is meant by "crux" (para. 7)? Where does the word come from?

SUGGESTIONS FOR WRITING

1. Describe your living space — house, apartment, or room — in a way that conveys its importance or lack of importance to you.
2. Have you ever moved from one place to another? What sort of experience was it? Write an essay about leaving an old home and moving to a new one. Was there an activity or a piece of furniture that helped ease the transition?
3. Address Quindlen's contention that turning homelessness into an issue avoids the problem, that we might "be better off if we forgot about the broad strokes and concentrated on the details."
4. CRITICAL WRITING. Write a brief essay in which you agree or disagree with Quindlen's assertion that a home is "everything." Can one, for instance, be a fulfilled person without a home? In your answer, take account of the values that might underlie an attachment to home; Quindlen mentions "certainty, stability, predictability, privacy" (para. 4), but there are others, including some (such as fear) that are less positive.
5. CONNECTIONS. COMPARE AND CONTRAST the views of homelessness and its solution in Quindlen's "Homeless" and Barbara Lazear Ascher's "On Compassion" (p. 140). Use specific passages from each essay to support your comparison.

ANNA QUINDLEN ON WRITING

Anna Quindlen started her writing career as a newspaper reporter. "I had wanted to be a writer for most of my life," she recalls in the introduction to her book *Living Out Loud*, "and in the service of the writing I became a reporter. For many years I was able to observe, even to feel, life vividly, but at secondhand. I was able to stand over the chalk outline of a body on a sidewalk dappled with black blood; to stand behind the glass and look down into an operating theater where one man was placing a heart in the yawning chest of another; to sit in the park on the first day of summer and find myself professionally obligated to record all the glories of it. Every day I found answers: who, what, when, where, and why."

Quindlen was a good reporter, but the business of finding answers did not satisfy her personally. "In my own life," she continues, "I had only questions." Then she switched from reporter to columnist at the *New York Times*. It was "exhilarating," she says, that "my work became a reflection of my life. After years of being a professional observer of other people's lives, I was given the opportunity to be a professional observer of my own. I was permitted — and permitted myself — to write a column, not about my answers, but about my questions. Never did I make so much sense of my life as I did then, for it was inevitable that as a writer I would find out most clearly what I thought, and what I only thought I thought, when I saw it written down. . . . After years of feeling secondhand, of feeling the pain of the widow, the joy of the winner, I was able to allow myself to feel those emotions for myself."

FOR DISCUSSION

1. What were the advantages and disadvantages of news reporting, ac-cording to Quindlen?
2. What does Quindlen feel she can accomplish in a column that she could not accomplish in a news report? What evidence of this difference do you see in her essay "Homeless"?

STEPHANIE COONTZ

A descendant of a pioneer family in Washington State and herself a single mother, STEPHANIE COONTZ investigates traditional ideas about gender roles and the American family. Born in Seattle, she earned a B.A. from the University of California at Berkeley (1966), was a Woodrow Wilson fellow (1968–69), and earned an M.A. from the University of Washington (1970). Since 1975, Coontz has taught history and women's studies at The Evergreen State College in Olympia, Washington. She has contributed to many periodicals and has written three books: *Women's Work, Men's Property* (with Peta Henderson; 1986); *The Social Origins of Private Life: A History of America's Families* (1988); and *The Way We Never Were: American Families and the Nostalgia Trap* (1992). This last study, published at a time when "family values" was a political catch phrase, led Coontz to appear on talk shows and to testify before the House Select Committee on Children, Youth, and Families.

A Nation of Welfare Families

Appearing in *Harper's* magazine in October 1992, this essay was adapted from Coontz's book *The Way We Never Were*. In this book, as in much of her writing, Coontz focuses on misconceptions about the American family. She has warned that "nostalgia for a mythical Golden Age will not help the American families of the twenty-first century." Here, using plenty of examples, she sets about correcting the record.

The current political debate over family values, personal responsibility, and welfare takes for granted the entrenched American belief that dependence on government assistance is a recent and destructive phenomenon. Conservatives tend to blame this dependence on personal irresponsibility aggravated by a swollen welfare apparatus that saps individual initiative. Liberals are more likely to blame it on personal misfortune magnified by the harsh lot that falls to losers in our competitive market economy. But both sides believe that "winners" in America make it on their own, that dependence reflects some kind of individual or family failure, and that the ideal family is the self-reliant unit of traditional lore — a family that takes care of its own, carves out a future for its children, and never asks for handouts. Politicians at both ends of the ideological spectrum have wrapped themselves in the mantle of these "family values," arguing over *why* the poor have not been able to make do without assistance, or whether aid has exacerbated their situation, but never questioning the assumption that American families traditionally achieve success by establishing their independence from the government.

The myth of family self-reliance is so compelling that our actual   2
national and personal histories often buckle under its emotional weight. "We always stood on our own two feet," my grandfather used to say about his pioneer heritage, whenever he walked me to the top of the hill to survey the property in Washington State that his family had bought for next to nothing after it had been logged off in the early 1900s. Perhaps he didn't know that the land came so cheap because much of it was part of a federal subsidy originally allotted to the railroad companies, which had received 183 million acres of the public domain in the nineteenth century. These federal giveaways were the original source of most major western logging companies' land, and when some of these logging companies moved on to virgin stands of timber, federal lands trickled down to a few early settlers who were able to purchase them inexpensively.

Like my grandparents, few families in American history — what-   3
ever their "values" — have been able to rely solely on their own resources. Instead, they have depended on the legislative, judicial and social-support structures set up by governing authorities, whether those authorities were the clan elders of Native American societies, the church courts and city officials of colonial America, or the judicial and legislative bodies established by the Constitution.

At America's inception, this was considered not a dirty little   4
secret but the norm, one that confirmed our social and personal interdependence. The idea that the family should have the sole or even primary responsibility for educating and socializing its members, finding them suitable work, or keeping them from poverty and crime was not only ludicrous to colonial and revolutionary thinkers but dangerously parochial.

Historically, one way that government has played a role in the   5
well-being of its citizens is by regulating the way that employers and civic bodies interact with families. In the early twentieth century, for example, as a response to rapid changes ushered in by a mass-production economy, the government promoted a "family wage system." This system was designed to strengthen the ability of the male bread-winner to support a family without having his wife or children work. This family wage system was not a natural outgrowth of the market.

It was a *political* response to conditions that the market had produced: child labor, rampant employment insecurity, recurring economic downturns, an earnings structure in which 45 percent of industrial workers fell below the poverty level and another 40 percent hovered barely above it, and a system in which thousands of children had been placed in orphanages or other institutions simply because their parents could not afford their keep. The state policies involved in the establishment of the family wage system included abolition of child labor, government pressure on industrialists to negotiate with unions, federal arbitration, expansion of compulsory schooling — and legislation discriminating against women workers.

But even such extensive regulation of economic and social insti- 6
tutions has never been enough: Government has always supported families with direct material aid as well. The two best examples of the government's history of material aid can be found in what many people consider the ideal models of self-reliant families: the western pioneer family and the 1950s suburban family. In both cases, the ability of these families to establish and sustain themselves required massive underwriting by the government.

Pioneer families, such as my grandparents, could never have 7
moved west without government-funded military mobilizations against the original Indian and Mexican inhabitants or state-sponsored economic investment in transportation systems. In addition, the Homestead Act of 1862 allowed settlers to buy 160 acres for $10 — far below the government's cost of acquiring the land — if the homesteader lived on and improved the land for five years. In the twentieth century, a new form of public assistance became crucial to western families: construction of dams and other federally subsidized irrigation projects. During the 1930s, for example, government electrification projects brought pumps, refrigeration, and household technology to millions of families.

The suburban family of the 1950s is another oft-cited example of 8
familial self-reliance. According to legend, after World War II a new, family-oriented generation settled down, saved their pennies, worked hard, and found well-paying jobs that allowed them to purchase homes in the suburbs. In fact, however, the 1950s suburban family was far more dependent on government assistance than any so-called underclass family of today. Federal GI benefit payments, available to 40 percent of the male population between the ages of twenty and twenty-four, permitted a whole generation of men to expand their education and improve their job prospects without forgoing marriage

and children. The National Defense Education Act retooled science education in America, subsidizing both American industry and the education of individual scientists. Government-funded research developed the aluminum clapboards, prefabricated walls and ceilings, and plywood paneling that comprised the technological basis of the postwar housing revolution. Government spending was also largely responsible for the new highways, sewer systems, utility services, and traffic-control programs that opened up suburbia.

In addition, suburban home ownership depended on an unprecedented expansion of federal regulation and financing. Before the war, banks often required a 50 percent down payment on homes and normally issued mortgages for five to ten years. In the postwar period, however, the Federal Housing Authority, supplemented by the GI Bill, put the federal government in the business of insuring and regulating private loans for single-home construction. FHA policy required down payments of only 5 to 10 percent of the purchase price and guaranteed mortgages of up to thirty years at interest rates of just 2 to 3 percent. The Veterans Administration required a mere dollar down from veterans. Almost half the housing in suburbia in the 1950s depended on such federal programs. 9

The drawback of these aid programs was that although they worked well for recipients, nonrecipients — disproportionately poor and urban — were left far behind. While the general public financed the roads that suburbanites used to commute, the streetcars and trolleys that served urban and poor families received almost no tax revenues, and our previously thriving rail system was allowed to decay. In addition, federal loan policies, which were a boon to upwardly mobile white families, tended to systematize the pervasive but informal racism that had previously characterized the housing market. FHA redlining practices, for example, took entire urban areas and declared them ineligible for loans, while the government's two new mortgage institutions, the Federal National Mortgage Association and the Government National Mortgage Association (Fannie Mae and Ginny Mae), made it possible for urban banks to transfer savings out of the cities and into new suburban developments in the South and West. 10

Despite the devastating effects on families and regions that did not receive such assistance, government aid to suburban residents during the 1950s and 1960s produced in its beneficiaries none of the demoralization usually presumed to afflict recipients of government handouts. Instead, federal subsidies to suburbia encouraged family 11 formation, residential stability, upward occupational mobility, and rising educational aspirations among youth who could look forward to receiving such aid. Seen in this light, the idea that government subsidies intrinsically induce dependence, undermine self-esteem, or break down family ties is exposed as no more than a myth.

I am not suggesting that the way to solve the problems of poverty   12
and urban decay in America is to quadruple our spending on welfare. Certainly there are major reforms needed in our current aid policies to the poor. But the debate over such reform should put welfare in the context of *all* federal assistance programs. As long as we pretend that only poor or single-parent families need outside assistance, while normal families "stand on their own two feet," we will shortchange poor families, overcompensate rich ones, and fail to come up with effective policies for helping out families in the middle. Current government housing policies are a case in point. The richest 20 percent of American households receives three times as much federal housing aid — mostly in tax subsidies — as the poorest 20 percent receives in expenditures for low-income housing.

Historically, the debate over government policies toward families   13
has never been over *whether* to intervene but *how:* to rescue or to warehouse, to prevent or to punish, to moralize about values or mobilize resources for education and job creation. Today's debate, lacking such historical perspective, caricatures the real issues. Our attempt to sustain the myth of family self-reliance in the face of all the historical evidence to the contrary has led policymakers into theoretical contortions and practical miscalculations that are reminiscent of efforts by medieval philosophers to maintain that the earth and not the sun was the center of the planetary system. In the sixteenth century, leading European thinkers insisted that the planets and the sun all revolved around the earth — much as American politicians today insist that our society revolves around family self-reliance. When evidence to the contrary mounted, defenders of the Ptolemaic universe postulated all sorts of elaborate planetary orbits in order to reconcile observed reality with their cherished theory. Similarly, rather than admit that all families need some kind of public support, we have constructed ideological orbits that explain away each instance of middle-class dependence as an "exception," an "abnormality," or even an illusion. We have distributed public aid to families through convoluted bureaucracies that have become impossible to track; in some cases the system has become so cumbersome that it threatens to collapse around our ears. It is time to break

through the old paradigm of self-reliance and substitute a new one that recognizes that assisting families is, simply, what government does.

QUESTIONS ON MEANING

1. What did Coontz's grandfather mean when he said, "We always stood on our own two feet"?
2. In the author's opinion, what groups benefited the most from federal programs in the 1950s and 1960s? What groups suffered?
3. What is this essay's PURPOSE?
4. Give a short restatement, in your own words, of Coontz's THESIS.

QUESTIONS ON WRITING STRATEGIES

1. Look closely at paragraph 5. What GENERALIZATION does Coontz make in this paragraph? What specific examples does she give to support it?
2. What is the EFFECT of Coontz's ANECDOTE from her own family's history? How does it work with her other examples?
3. How are Coontz's examples arranged? Why is this an appropriate order?
4. OTHER METHODS. In paragraphs 11 and 12, Coontz COMPARES AND CONTRASTS government spending on affluent suburban families and the urban poor. How does this comparison support her THESIS?

QUESTIONS ON LANGUAGE

1. Find definitions for any of these words you don't know: entrenched, ideological, exacerbated (para. 1); inception, parochial (4); intrinsically (11); Ptolemaic, convoluted, paradigm (13).
2. Coontz refers to common perceptions about family self-reliance as a "myth" (para. 2) and a "legend" (8). What are the CONNOTATIONS of these words? How do these connotations help Coontz make her point?
3. In her introductory paragraph, why does Coontz use quotation marks around "winners" and "family values"?

SUGGESTIONS FOR WRITING

1. Write a short essay detailing the influence of government on your own life. You may want to discuss a way in which government makes your life easier or better (student loans, public broadcasting) or a way it makes things more difficult (taxes, regulations). Use examples to support your claims.
2. Do you agree or disagree with Coontz's argument that "as long as we

pretend that only poor or single-parent families need outside assistance, while normal families 'stand on their own two feet,' we will shortchange poor families, overcompensate rich ones, and fail to come up with effective policies for helping out families in the middle" (para. 12)? In a brief essay, state your case and support it with examples. If you were elected president tomorrow, what might you do to resolve this issue?

3. CRITICAL WRITING. Coontz argues in favor of questioning "the assumption that American families traditionally achieve success by establishing their independence from the government" (para. 1). What assumptions about the role of government in family and individual life does Coontz leave unquestioned? ANALYZE her argument closely, and see what unspoken assumptions you can INFER from it.

4. CONNECTIONS. Compare this essay to Robert B. Reich's "Why the Rich Are Getting Richer and the Poor Poorer" (p. 350). To what causes does each author attribute the growing distance between rich and poor? How do their viewpoints differ? What assumptions do Coontz and Reich seem to share?

STEPHANIE COONTZ ON WRITING

"I am not a good writer," Stephanie Coontz reports in a statement written for *The Bedford Reader*. "My first drafts — frequently my third and fourth as well — lack focus. I try to pack in too many ideas and too many examples. Worse yet, I tend to choose examples that illustrate too many generalizations. While my students sometimes generalize without specific examples or multiply examples without indicating precisely what they demonstrate, I work my evidence too hard: I pick such complicated examples that they lead me into new assertions, and I end up piling onto my original thesis a load of subsidiary ideas that, I tell myself, 'just have to be pointed out.'

"The best writing help I ever received was from a newspaper editor who circled one paragraph of a six-page essay I'd written and told me to write the entire piece around the one idea and two examples I'd used there. Today I try to do this with all my drafts. First I write all the assertions I want to make about the topic and all the possible illustrations of my points; then I decide what single assertion and particular type of example I'm going to focus on.

"The only way I can bear this is by using the 'Save' key on my computer. 'It's okay,' I reassure the inner pack rat who clutches possessively at all her treasures. 'We're not throwing away your precious words, ideas, and facts; we're saving them to use somewhere else.' Sometimes this is the truth. Other times it's a necessary fiction to pry me away from some digression that 'people just have to hear.' (Even after all these maneuvers, I usually require another rewrite after I've had a week to think about what my *real* point is.)

"When writing, I think of myself as a tour guide at a large museum. I have room after room crowded with wonderful objects I'd like to show off, but most people who show up at my door have limited time to spend with me, because they're going somewhere for dinner, and they're not even sure they want a guide. So I have to choose just one point I want to get across, convince my visitors to follow me instead of poking around on their own, assure them I won't keep them all evening, and make certain I don't lose them at any of my turnings. This means I can't show them all our holdings and I can't tell them everything I think they should know about the exhibits I do include. Instead, I simply need to indicate how each piece builds on a point made at the last exhibit, and how it paves the way for the next.

"Remembering that you don't have a captive audience is a powerful impetus for being choosy about evidence. But how do you select the most effective example? For me, it is the one that does double duty. I don't want an example that merely supports my assertion; I want one that simultaneously refutes or at least disconcerts a person who may be making an opposing assertion.

"Writing teachers often advise students to anticipate the reader's questions. The problem with this is that most of us unconsciously anticipate a friendly question: 'Oh, I see what you mean, and how does that tie in with . . . ?' When we answer this kind of question, we may leap beyond our evidence, leaving the skeptical reader behind. Instead, I assume the possibility of a more adversarial relationship with my readers. I try to anticipate my readers' *objections* and to find examples that answer those.

"In 'A Nation of Welfare Families,' for instance, I was trying to make the point that government cannot expect families to go it alone. If I had thought my readers already agreed that families need more social support, then I might have begun with the fact that 22 percent of American children are now poor, a striking increase since 1970. This fact would add urgency to the proposition that government should rebuild social safety nets. But I thought my readers might not agree with me and might take this fact to prove that modern Americans lack the self-reliance, individual responsibility, and strong values of 'traditional' families. To get a hearing from such readers, I needed to show that the very families they most admire have depended on government assistance. At the very least, I hoped to knock away one of the most widespread objections to my later argument that modern families need far more help than they have received over the past two decades."

FOR DISCUSSION

1. What does Coontz see as her weakness as a writer? What does her solution involve? What is the lesson in her ANALOGY of writing and tour guiding?
2. Why does Coontz think of her readers as adversaries rather than friends? Do you agree with this approach? Do you think it is always appropriate? If not, when is it not?

BRENT STAPLES

BRENT STAPLES is a member of the editorial board of the *New York Times*. Born in 1951 in Chester, Pennsylvania, Staples has a B.A. in behavioral science from Widener University in Chester and a Ph.D. in psychology from the University of Chicago. Before joining the *New York Times* in 1985, he worked for the *Chicago Sun-Times*, the *Chicago Reader, Chicago* magazine, and *Down Beat* magazine. At the *Times*, Staples writes on culture and politics. He has also contributed to the *New York Times Magazine, New York Woman, Ms., Harper's,* and other magazines. *Parallel Time: A Memoir* appeared in 1994.

Black Men and Public Space

"Black Men and Public Space" appeared in the December 1987 issue of *Harper's* magazine. It was originally published, in a slightly different version, in *Ms.* magazine (September 1986) under the title "Just Walk on By." The essay relates incidents Staples has experienced "as a night walker in the urban landscape."

My first victim was a woman — white, well dressed, probably in her late twenties. I came upon her late one evening on a deserted street in Hyde Park, a relatively affluent neighborhood in an otherwise mean, impoverished section of Chicago. As I swung onto the avenue behind her, there seemed to be a discreet, uninflammatory distance between us. Not so. She cast back a worried glance. To her, the youngish black man — a broad six feet two inches with a beard and billowing hair, both hands shoved into the pockets of a bulky military jacket — seemed menacingly close. After a few more quick glimpses, she picked up her pace and was soon running in earnest. Within seconds she disappeared into a cross street.

That was more than a decade ago. I was twenty-two years old, a graduate student newly arrived at the University of Chicago. It was in the echo of that terrified woman's footfalls that I first began to know the unwieldy inheritance I'd come into — the ability to alter public space in ugly ways. It was clear that she thought herself the quarry of a mugger, a rapist, or worse. Suffering a bout of insomnia, however, I was stalking sleep, not defenseless wayfarers. As a softy who is scarcely able to take a knife to a raw chicken — let alone hold one to a person's throat — I was surprised, embarrassed, and

159

dismayed all at once. Her flight made me feel like an accomplice in tyranny. It also made it clear that I was indistinguishable from the muggers who occasionally seeped into the area from the surrounding ghetto. That first encounter, and those that followed, signified that a vast, unnerving gulf lay between nighttime pedestrians — particularly women — and me. And I soon gathered that being perceived as dangerous is a hazard in itself. I only needed to turn a corner into a dicey situation, or crowd some frightened, armed person in a foyer somewhere, or make an errant move after being pulled over by a policeman. Where fear and weapons meet — and they often do in urban America — there is always the possibility of death.

In that first year, my first away from my hometown, I was to 3 become thoroughly familiar with the language of fear. At dark, shadowy intersections, I could cross in front of a car stopped at a traffic light and elicit the *thunk, thunk, thunk, thunk* of the driver — black, white, male, or female — hammering down the door locks. On less traveled streets after dark, I grew accustomed to but never comfortable with people crossing to the other side of the street rather than pass me. Then there were the standard unpleasantries with policemen, doormen, bouncers, cabdrivers, and others whose business it is to screen out troublesome individuals *before* there is any nastiness.

I moved to New York nearly two years ago and I have remained 4 an avid night walker. In central Manhattan, the near-constant crowd cover minimizes tense one-on-one street encounters. Elsewhere — in SoHo, for example, where sidewalks are narrow and tightly spaced buildings shut out the sky — things can get very taut indeed.

After dark, on the warrenlike streets of Brooklyn where I live, I 5 often see women who fear the worst from me. They seem to have set their faces on neutral, and with their purse straps strung across their chests bandolier-style, they forge ahead as though bracing themselves against being tackled. I understand, of course, that the danger they perceive is not a hallucination. Women are particularly vulnerable to street violence, and young black males are drastically overrepresented among the perpetrators of that violence. Yet these truths are no solace against the kind of alienation that comes of being ever the suspect, a fearsome entity with whom pedestrians avoid making eye contact.

It is not altogether clear to me how I reached the ripe old age of 6 twenty-two without being conscious of the lethality nighttime pedestrians attributed to me. Perhaps it was because in Chester, Pennsylvania, the small, angry industrial town where I came of age in the 1960s, I was scarcely noticeable against a backdrop of gang warfare, street knifings, and murders. I grew up one of the good boys, had perhaps a half-dozen fistfights. In retrospect, my shyness of combat has clear sources.

As a boy, I saw countless tough guys locked away; I have since 7
buried several, too. They were babies, really — a teenage cousin, a brother of twenty-two, a childhood friend in his mid-twenties — all gone down in episodes of bravado played out in the streets. I came to doubt the virtues of intimidation early on. I chose, perhaps unconsciously, to remain a shadow — timid, but a survivor.

The fearsomeness mistakenly attributed to me in public places 8
often has a perilous flavor. The most frightening of these confusions occurred in the late 1970s and early 1980s, when I worked as a journalist in Chicago. One day, rushing into the office of a magazine I was writing for with a deadline story in hand, I was mistaken for a burglar. The office manager called security and, with an ad hoc posse, pursued me through the labyrinthine halls, nearly to my editor's door. I had no way of proving who I was. I could only move briskly toward the company of someone who knew me.

Another time I was on assignment for a local paper and killing 9
time before an interview. I entered a jewelry store on the city's affluent Near North Side. The proprietor excused herself and returned with an enormous red Doberman pinscher straining at the end of a leash. She stood, the dog extended toward me, silent to my questions, her eyes bulging nearly out of her head. I took a cursory look around, nodded, and bade her good night.

Relatively speaking, however, I never fared as badly as another 10
black male journalist. He went to nearby Waukegan, Illinois, a couple of summers ago to work on a story about a murderer who was born there. Mistaking the reporter for the killer, police officers hauled him from his car at gunpoint and but for his press credentials would probably have tried to book him. Such episodes are not uncommon. Black men trade tales like this all the time.

Over the years, I learned to smother the rage I felt at so often 11
being taken for a criminal. Not to do so would surely have led to madness. I now take precautions to make myself less threatening. I move about with care, particularly late in the evening. I give a wide berth to nervous people on subway platforms during the wee hours, particularly when I have exchanged business clothes for jeans. If I happen to be entering a building behind some people who appear skittish, I may walk by, letting them clear the lobby before I return, so as not to seem to be following them. I have been calm and extremely congenial on those rare occasions when I've been pulled over by the police.

And on late-evening constitutionals I employ what has proved to   12
be an excellent tension-reducing measure: I whistle melodies from
Beethoven and Vivaldi and the more popular classical composers.
Even steely New Yorkers hunching toward nighttime destinations
seem to relax, and occasionally they even join in the tune. Virtually
everybody seems to sense that a mugger wouldn't be warbling bright,
sunny selections from Vivaldi's *Four Seasons*. It is my equivalent of
the cowbell that hikers wear when they know they are in bear country.

QUESTIONS ON MEANING

1. What is the PURPOSE of this essay? Do you think Staples believes that
   he (or other African American men) will cease "to alter public space
   in ugly ways" in the near future? Does he suggest any long-term solution
   for "the kind of alienation that comes of being ever the suspect" (para.
   5)?
2. In paragraph 5, Staples says he understands that the danger women fear
   when they see him "is not a hallucination." Do you take this to mean
   that Staples perceives himself to be dangerous? Explain.
3. Staples says, "I chose, perhaps unconsciously, to remain a shadow —
   timid, but a survivor" (para. 7). What are the usual CONNOTATIONS of
   the word *survivor*? Is "timid" one of them? How can you explain this
   apparent discrepancy?

QUESTIONS ON WRITING STRATEGY

1. The concept of altering public space is relatively abstract. How does
   Staples convince you that this phenomenon really takes place?
2. The author employs a large number of examples in a fairly small space.
   He cites three specific instances that involved him, several general
   situations, and one incident involving another African American man.
   How does Staples avoid having the piece sound like a list? How does
   he establish COHERENCE among all these examples? (Look, for example,
   at details and TRANSITIONS.)
3. OTHER METHODS. Many of Staples's examples are actually ANEC-
   DOTES — brief NARRATIVES. The opening paragraph is especially notable. Why is it so effective?

QUESTIONS ON LANGUAGE

1. What does the author accomplish by using the word *victim* in the essay's
   first paragraph? Is the word used literally? What TONE does it set for the
   essay?

2. Be sure you know how to define the following words, as used in this essay: affluent, uninflammatory (para. 1); unwieldy, tyranny, pedestrians (2); intimidation (7); congenial (11); constitutionals (12).
3. The word *dicey* (para. 2) comes from British slang. Without looking it up in your dictionary, can you figure out its meaning from the context in which it appears?

SUGGESTIONS FOR WRITING

1. Write an essay using examples to show how a trait of your own or of someone you know well always seems to affect people, whether positively or negatively.
2. Are you aware of any incident in which *you* altered public space? That is, where your entry into a situation, or simply your presence, brought about changes in people's attitudes or behavior? Write a narrative essay describing this experience. Or write an essay about witnessing someone else altering public space. What changes did you observe in the behavior of the people around you? Was your behavior similarly affected? In retrospect, do you feel your reactions were justified?
3. CRITICAL WRITING. Consider, more broadly than Staples does, what it means to alter public space. Staples would rather not have the power to do so, but it *is* a power, and it could perhaps be positive in some circumstances (wielded by a street performer, for instance, or the architect of a beautiful new building on campus). Write an essay expanding on Staples's essay in which you examine the pros and cons of altering public space. Use specific examples as your EVIDENCE.
4. CONNECTIONS. Like Staples, Barbara Lazear Ascher, in "On Compassion" (p. 140), also considers how people regard and respond to "the Other," the one who is regarded as different. In an essay, compare and contrast the POINTS OF VIEW of these two authors. How does point of view affect each author's selection of details and TONE?

BRENT STAPLES ON WRITING

In comments written especially for *The Bedford Reader*, Brent Staples talks about the writing of "Black Men and Public Space." "I was only partly aware of how I felt when I began this essay. I knew only that I had this collection of experiences (facts) and that I felt uneasy with them. I sketched out the experiences one by one and strung them together. The bridge to the essay — what I wanted to say, but did not know when I started — sprang into life quite unexpectedly as I sat looking over these experiences. The crucial sentence comes right after the opening anecdote, in which my first 'victim' runs away from me: 'It was in the echo of that woman's footfalls that

I first began to know the unwieldy inheritance I'd come into — the ability to alter public space in ugly ways.' 'Aha!' I said, 'This is why I feel bothered and hurt and frustrated when this happens. I don't want people to think I'm stalking them. I want some fresh air. I want to stretch my legs. I want to be as anonymous as any other person out for a walk in the night.'"

A news reporter and editor by training and trade, Staples sees much similarity between the writing of a personal essay like "Black Men and Public Space" and the writing of, say, a murder story for a daily newspaper. "The newspaper murder," he says, "begins with standard newspaper information: the fact that the man was found dead in an alley in such-and-such a section of the city; his name, occupation, and where he lived; that he died of gunshot wounds to such-and-such a part of his body; that arrests were or were not made; that such-and-such a weapon was found at the scene; that the police have established no motive; etc.

"Personal essays take a different tack, but they, too, begin as assemblies of facts. In 'Black Men and Public Space,' I start out with an anecdote that crystalizes the issue I want to discuss — what it is like to be viewed as a criminal all the time. I devise a sentence that serves this purpose and also catches the reader's attention: 'My first victim was a woman — white, well dressed, probably in her late twenties.' The piece gives examples that are meant to illustrate the same point and discusses what those examples mean.

"The newspaper story stacks its details in a specified way, with each piece taking a prescribed place in a prescribed order. The personal essay begins often with a flourish, an anecdote, or the recounting of a crucial experience, then goes off to consider related experiences and their meanings. But both pieces rely on reporting. Both are built of facts. Reporting is the act of finding and analyzing facts.

"A fact can be a state of the world — a date, the color of someone's eyes, the arc of a body that flies through the air after having been struck by a car. A fact can also be a feeling — sorrow, grief, confusion, the sense of being pleased, offended, or frustrated. 'Black Men and Public Space' explores the relationship between two sets of facts: (1) the way people cast worried glances at me and sometimes run away from me on the streets after dark, and (2) the frustration and anger I feel at being made an object of fear as I try to go about my business in the city."

Personal essays and news stories share one other quality as well, Staples thinks: They affect the writer even when the writing is finished. "The discoveries I made in 'Black Men and Public Space' continued long after the essay was published. Writing about the experiences gave me access to a whole range of internal concerns and ideas, much the way a well-reported news story opens the door onto a given neighborhood, a situation, or set of issues."

FOR DISCUSSION

1. In recounting how his essay developed, what does Staples reveal about his writing process?
2. How, according to Staples, are essay writing and news writing similar? How are they different?
3. What does Staples mean when he says that "writing about the experiences gave me access to a whole range of internal concerns and ideas"?

ADDITIONAL WRITING TOPICS

Example

1. Select one of the following general statements, or set forth a general statement of your own that one of these inspires. Making it your central idea (or THESIS), support it in an essay full of examples. Draw your examples from your reading, your studies, your conversation, or your own experience.

   People one comes to admire don't always at first seem likable.
   Fashions this year are loonier than ever before.
   Good (or bad) habits are necessary to the nation's economy.
   Each family has its distinctive life-style.
   Certain song lyrics, closely inspected, promote violence.
   Comic books are going to the dogs.
   At some point in life, most people triumph over crushing difficulties.
   Churchgoers aren't perfect.
   TV commercials suggest: Buy this product and your love life will improve like crazy.
   Home cooking can't win over fast food.
   Ordinary lives sometimes give rise to legends.
   Some people I know are born winners (or losers).
   Books can change our lives.
   Certain machines *do* have personalities.
   Some road signs lead drivers astray.

2. In a brief essay, make some GENERALIZATION about either the terrors or the joys that ethnic minorities seem to share. To illustrate your generalization, draw examples from personal experience, from outside reading, or from two or three of the following *Bedford Reader* essays: Maya Angelou's "Champion of the World" (p. 49), Ralph Ellison's "On Being the Target of Discrimination" (p. 55), Brent Staples's "Black Men and Public Space" (p. 159), Amy Tan's "The Language of Discretion" (p. 187), June Jordan's "Requiem for the Champ" (p. 386), Curtis Chang's "Streets of Gold" (p. 495), Martin Luther King, Jr.'s "I Have a Dream" (p. 516), Richard Rodriguez's "Aria" (p. 563), and David Updike's "The Colorings of Childhood" (p. 578).

4

COMPARISON
AND CONTRAST
Setting Things Side by Side

THE METHOD

Should we pass laws to regulate pornography, or just let pornography run wild? Which team do you place your money on, the Dolphins or the Colts? To go to school full-time or part-time: What are the rewards and drawbacks of each way of life? How do the Republican and the Democratic platforms stack up against each other? How is the work of Picasso like or unlike that of Matisse? These are questions that may be addressed by the dual method of comparison and contrast. In comparing, you point to similar features of the subjects; in contrasting, to different features. (The features themselves you identify by the method of DIVISION or ANALYSIS; see Chap. 6.)

With the aid of comparison and contrast, you can show why you prefer one thing to another, one course of action to another, one idea to another. In an argument in which you support one of two possible choices, a careful and detailed comparison and contrast of the choices may be extremely convincing. In an expository essay, it can demonstrate that you understand your subjects thoroughly. That is why, on exams that call for essay answers, often you will be asked to compare and contrast. Sometimes the examiner will come right out and say, "Compare and contrast nineteenth-century methods of treating drug addiction with those of the present day." Sometimes, however, comparison and contrast won't even be mentioned by name; instead, the examiner will ask, "What resemblances and differences do you find between John Updike's short story 'A & P' and the Grimm fairy tale 'Godfather Death'?" Or, "Explain the relative desirability of holding a franchise as against going into business as an independent proprietor." But those — as you realize when you begin to plan your reply — are just other ways of asking you to compare and contrast.

In practice, the two methods are usually inseparable. A little reflection will show you why you need both. Say you intend to write a portrait-in-words of two people. No two people are in every respect exactly the same, or entirely dissimilar. Simply to compare them, or to contrast them, would not be true to life. To set them side by side and portray them accurately, you must consider both similarities and differences.

A good essay in comparing and contrasting serves a purpose. Most of the time, the writer of such an essay has one of two purposes in mind:

1. *The purpose of showing each of two subjects distinctly by considering both, side by side.* Writing with such a purpose, the writer doesn't necessarily find one of the subjects better than the other. In "The Black and White Truth About Basketball" in this chapter, Jeff Greenfield details two styles of playing the game; and his conclusion is not that either "black" or "white" basketball is the more beautiful, but that the two styles can complement each other on the same court.

2. *The purpose of choosing between two things.* In daily life, we often EVALUATE two possibilities to choose between them: which college course to elect, which movie to see, which luncheon special to take — chipped beef over green noodles or fried smelt on a bun? Our thinking on a matter such as the last is quick and informal: "Hmmmm, the smelt *looks* better. Red beef, green noodles — ugh, what a sight! Smelt has bones, but the beef is rubbery. Still, I don't like the smell of that smelt. I'll go for the beef (or maybe just grab a hamburger after class)." In essays, too, a writer, by comparing and evaluating points, decides which of two things is more admirable: "Organic Gardening, Yes; Gardening with Chemical Fertilizers, No!" — or "Skydiving Versus the Safe, Sane Life." In writing, as in thinking, you need to consider the main features of both subjects, the positive features and the negative, and to choose the subject whose positive features more clearly predominate.

THE PROCESS

The first step in comparing and contrasting is to select subjects that will display a clear basis for comparison. In other words, you have to pick two subjects that have enough in common to be worth placing side by side. You'll have the best luck if you choose two of a kind: two California wines, two mystery writers, two schools of political thought.

It can sometimes be effective to find similarities between evidently unlike subjects — a city and a country town, say — and a special form of comparison, ANALOGY, always equates two very unlike things, explaining one in terms of the other. (In an analogy you might explain how the human eye works by comparing it with a simple camera, or you might explain the forces in a thunderstorm by comparing them to armies in battle.) In any comparison of unlike things, you must have a valid reason for bringing the two together. In his essay "Grant and Lee," Bruce Catton compares the characters of the two Civil War generals. But in an essay called "General Grant and Mick Jagger" you would be hard-pressed to find any real basis for comparison. Although you might wax ingenious and claim, "Like Grant, Jagger has posed a definite threat to Nashville," the ingenuity would wear thin and soon the yoking together of general and rock star would fall apart.

The basis for a comparison has to be carefully limited. You would be overly ambitious to try to compare and contrast the Russian way of life with the American way of life in 500 words; you probably couldn't include all the important similarities and differences. In a brief paper, you would be wise to select a single point: to show, for instance, how day care centers in Russia and the United States are both alike and dissimilar.

Students occasionally groan when asked to compare and contrast things; but, in fact, this method isn't difficult. You have only to plan your paper carefully, make an outline (in your head or on paper), and then follow it. Here are two common ways to compare and contrast:

1. *Subject by subject.* Set forth all your facts about subject A, then do the same for subject B. Next, sum up their similarities and differences. In your conclusion, state what you think you have shown.

TITLE: "Jed and Jake: Two Bluegrass Banjo-Pickers"

PURPOSE: To show the distinct identities of the two musicians

INTRODUCTION: Who are Jed and Jake?

1. *Jed*

   Training
   Choice of material
   Technical dexterity
   Playing style

2. *Jake*

   Training
   Choice of material
   Technical dexterity
   Playing style

   SUMMARY
   CONCLUSION

This procedure works for a paper of a few paragraphs, but for a longer one, it has a built-in disadvantage. Readers need to remember all the facts about subject A while they read about subject B. If the essay is long and lists many facts, this procedure may be burdensome.

   2. *Point by point.* Usually more workable in writing a long paper than the first method, a different scheme is to compare and contrast as you go. You consider one point at a time, taking up your two subjects alternately. In this way, you continually bring the subjects together, perhaps in every paragraph. Notice the differences in the outline:

1. *Training*

   Jed: studied under Scruggs
   Jake: studied under Segovia

2. *Choice of material*

   Jed: traditional
   Jake: innovative

3. *Technical dexterity*

   Jed: highly skilled
   Jake: highly skilled

4. *Playing style*

   Jed: likes to show off
   Jake: keeps work simple

Another way to organize a longer paper would be to group together all the similarities, then group together all the differences. (For either the subject-by-subject or the point-by-point scheme, your conclusion might be: Although similar in degree of skill, the two differ greatly in aims and in personalities. Jed is better suited to the Grand Ol' Opry; Jake, to a concert hall.)

No matter how you group your points, they have to balance; you can't discuss Jed's on-stage manner without discussing Jake's too. If you have nothing to say about Jake's on-stage manner, then you might as well omit the point. A sure-fire loser is the paper that proposes to compare and contrast two subjects but then proceeds to discuss quite different elements in each: Jed's playing style and Jake's choice of material, Jed's fondness for smelt on a bun and Jake's hobby of antique car collecting. The writer of such a paper doesn't compare and contrast the two musicians at all, but provides two quite separate discussions.

By the way, a subject-by-subject organization works most efficiently for a *pair* of subjects. If you want to write about *three* banjo-pickers, you might first consider Jed and Jake, then Jake and Josh, then Josh and Jed — but it would probably be easiest to compare and contrast all three point by point.

As you write, an outline will help you see the shape of your paper and keep your procedure in mind. But don't be the simple tool of your outline. Few essays are more boring to read than the long comparison-and-contrast written mechanically. The reader comes to feel like a weary tennis spectator, whose head has to swivel from side to side: now Jed, now Jake; now Jed again, now back to Jake. No law decrees that an outline has to be followed in lockstep order, nor that a list of similarities and a list of differences must be of the same length, nor that if you spend fifty words discussing Jed's banjo-picking skill, you are obliged to give Jake his fifty, too. Your essay, remember, doesn't need to be as symmetrical as a pair of salt and pepper shakers. What is your outline but a simple means to organize your account of a complicated reality? As you write, keep casting your thoughts upon a living, particular world — not twisting and squeezing that world into a rigid scheme, but moving through it with open senses, being patient and faithful and exact in your telling of it.

COMPARISON AND CONTRAST
IN A PARAGRAPH: TWO ILLUSTRATIONS

Using Comparison and Contrast
to Write About Television

Seen on aged 16-millimeter film, the original production of Paddy Chayevsky's *Marty* makes clear the differences between television drama of 1953 and that of today. Today there's no weekly Goodyear Playhouse to showcase original one-hour plays; most scriptwriters write serials about familiar characters. *Marty* features no car chases, no bodice ripping, no mansions. Instead, it simply shows the awakening of love between a heavyset butcher and a mousy high-school teacher: both single, lonely, and shy, never twice dating the same person. Unlike the writer of today, Chayevsky couldn't set scenes outdoors or on location. In one small studio, in slow lingering takes (some five minutes long — not eight to twelve seconds, as we now expect), the camera probes the faces of two seated characters as Marty and his pal Angie plan Saturday night ("What do you want to do?" — "I dunno, what do *you*?"). Oddly, the effect is spellbinding. To bring such scenes to life, the actors must project with vigor; and like the finer actors of today, Rod Steiger as Marty exploits each moment. In 1953, plays were telecast live. Today, well-edited videotape may eliminate blown lines, but a chill slickness prevails. Technically, *Marty* is primitive, yet it probes souls. Most televised drama today displays a physically larger world — only to nail a box around it.

COMMENT. The writer of this closely knit paragraph compares and contrasts televised drama of today with drama of television's so-called Golden Age — in particular, *Marty*, an outstanding example. Most of the paragraph is taken up with differences. That both eras of television have actors who make the most of their time on screen is the one similarity noted. In building the paragraph, the writer followed this outline:

1. *Today:* mostly serials
   Then: Goodyear Playhouse, weekly series of new plays
2. *Today:* violence, sex, luxury
   Then: simplicity
3. *Today:* scenes outdoors, on location
   Then: one small studio
4. *Today:* brief takes
   Then: long, slow takes
5. *Today:* good acting
   Then: good acting

6. *Today:* plays videotaped
   Then: plays telecast live
7. *Conclusion:* TV drama today shows a more limited world.

In fulfilling this outline, the writer didn't proceed in a rigid, mechanical alternation of *Today* and *Then,* but took each point in
whatever order came naturally. This is a long outline, as a paragraph
so full and meaty required, and it might have sufficed for a whole
essay had the writer wanted to compare at greater length with the
aid of other examples.

Using Comparison and Contrast
in an Academic Discipline

In Russia, too, modernists fell into two camps. They squared
off against each other in public debate and in Vkhutemas, a school
of architecture organized in 1920 along lines parallel to the Bauhaus.
"The measure of architecture is architecture," went the motto of
one camp. They believed in an unfettered experimentalism of form.
The rival camp had a problem-solving orientation. The architect's
main mission, in their view, was to share in the common task of
achieving the transformation of society promised by the October
Revolution [of 1917]. They were keen on standardization, user
interviews, and ideological prompting. They worked on new building programs that would consolidate the social order of communism.
These they referred to as "social condensers."

COMMENT. Taken from *A History of Architecture* by Spiro Kostof,
this paragraph explains the key difference in the philosophies of two
groups of architects working in Russia just after the Russian Revolution in 1917. Notice how the paragraph is organized: The author first
introduces the topic; then, following a subject-by-subject structure,
he specifies the views of one group at a time. The discussion of the
"problem-solving" group comes last and is more detailed because, as
Kostof goes on to discuss, it eventually prevailed.

SUZANNE BRITT

SUZANNE BRITT was born in Winston-Salem, North Carolina, and studied at Salem College and Washington University, where she earned an M.A. in English. She writes a regular column for *North Carolina Gardens & Homes* and for the *Dickens Dispatch*, a national newsletter for Charles Dickens disciples, and she occasionally contributes to *Books and Religion*, a newspaper of social and theological comment, published by Duke University. Britt has written for the *New York Times*, *Newsweek*, the *Boston Globe*, and many other publications. She teaches English part-time at Meredith College in North Carolina and has published a history of the college and two English textbooks. Her other books are collections of her essays: *Skinny People Are Dull and Crunchy like Carrots* (1982) and *Show and Tell* (1983).

Neat People
vs.
Sloppy People

"Neat People vs. Sloppy People" appears in Britt's collection *Show and Tell*. Mingling humor with seriousness (as she often does), Britt has called the book a report on her journey into "the awful cave of self: You shout your name and voices come back in exultant response, telling you their names." In this essay about certain inescapable personality traits, you may recognize some aspects of your *own* self, awful or otherwise.

I've finally figured out the difference between neat people and   1
sloppy people. The distinction is, as always, moral. Neat people are lazier and meaner than sloppy people.

Sloppy people, you see, are not really sloppy. Their sloppiness is   2
merely the unfortunate consequence of their extreme moral rectitude. Sloppy people carry in their mind's eye a heavenly vision, a precise plan, that is so stupendous, so perfect, it can't be achieved in this world or the next.

Sloppy people live in Never-Never Land. Someday is their métier.   3
Someday they are planning to alphabetize all their books and set up home catalogs. Someday they will go through their wardrobes and mark certain items for tentative mending and certain items for passing on to relatives of similar shape and size. Someday sloppy people will

make family scrapbooks into which they will put newspaper clippings, postcards, locks of hair, and the dried corsage from their senior prom. Someday they will file everything on the surface of their desks, including the cash receipts from coffee purchases at the snack shop. Someday they will sit down and read all the back issues of *The New Yorker.*

For all these noble reasons and more, sloppy people never get   4
neat. They aim too high and wide. They save everything, planning someday to file, order, and straighten out the world. But while these ambitious plans take clearer and clearer shape in their heads, the books spill from the shelves onto the floor, the clothes pile up in the hamper and closet, the family mementos accumulate in every drawer, the surface of the desk is buried under mounds of paper and the unread magazines threaten to reach the ceiling.

Sloppy people can't bear to part with anything. They give loving   5
attention to every detail. When sloppy people say they're going to tackle the surface of a desk, they really mean it. Not a paper will go unturned; not a rubber band will go unboxed. Four hours or two weeks into the excavation, the desk looks exactly the same, primarily because the sloppy person is meticulously creating new piles of papers with new headings and scrupulously stopping to read all the old book catalogs before he throws them away. A neat person would just bulldoze the desk.

Neat people are bums and clods at heart. They have cavalier   6
attitudes toward possessions, including family heirlooms. Everything is just another dust-catcher to them. If anything collects dust, it's got to go and that's that. Neat people will toy with the idea of throwing the children out of the house just to cut down on the clutter.

Neat people don't care about process. They like results. What   7
they want to do is get the whole thing over with so they can sit down and watch the rasslin' on TV. Neat people operate on two unvarying principles: Never handle any item twice, and throw everything away.

The only thing messy in a neat person's house is the trash can.   8
The minute something comes to a neat person's hand, he will look at it, try to decide if it has immediate use and, finding none, throw it in the trash.

Neat people are especially vicious with mail. They never go   9
through their mail unless they are standing directly over a trash can. If the trash can is beside the mailbox, even better. All ads, catalogs, pleas for charitable contributions, church bulletins and money-saving coupons go straight into the trash can without being opened. All letters from home, postcards from Europe, bills and paychecks are

opened, immediately responded to, then dropped in the trash can. Neat people keep their receipts only for tax purposes. That's it. No sentimental salvaging of birthday cards or the last letter a dying relative ever wrote. Into the trash it goes.

Neat people place neatness above everything, even economics. 10 They are incredibly wasteful. Neat people throw away several toys every time they walk through the den. I knew a neat person once who threw away a perfectly good dish drainer because it had mold on it. The drainer was too much trouble to wash. And neat people sell their furniture when they move. They will sell a La-Z-Boy recliner while you are reclining in it.

Neat people are no good to borrow from. Neat people buy every- 11 thing in expensive little single portions. They get their flour and sugar in two-pound bags. They wouldn't consider clipping a coupon, saving a leftover, reusing plastic nondairy whipped cream containers or rinsing off tin foil and draping it over the unmoldy dish drainer. You can never borrow a neat person's newspaper to see what's playing at the movies. Neat people have the paper all wadded up and in the trash by 7:05 A.M.

Neat people cut a clean swath through the organic as well as the 12 inorganic world. People, animals, and things are all one to them. They are so insensitive. After they've finished with the pantry, the medicine cabinet, and the attic, they will throw out the red geranium (too many leaves), sell the dog (too many fleas), and send the children off to boarding school (too many scuff-marks on the hardwood floors).

QUESTIONS ON MEANING

1. "Suzanne Britt believes that neat people are lazy, mean, petty, callous, wasteful, and insensitive." How would you respond to this statement?
2. Is the author's main PURPOSE to make fun of neat people, to assess the habits of neat and sloppy people, to help neat and sloppy people get along better, to defend sloppy people, to amuse and entertain, or to prove that neat people are morally inferior to sloppy people? Discuss.
3. What is meant by "as always" in the sentence "The distinction is, as always, moral" (para. 1)? Does the author seem to be suggesting that any and all distinctions between people are moral?

QUESTIONS ON WRITING STRATEGY

1. What is the general TONE of this essay? What words and phrases help you determine that tone?
2. Britt mentions no similarities between neat and sloppy people. Does that mean this is not a good comparison and contrast essay? Why might a writer deliberately focus on differences and give very little or no time to similarities?
3. Consider the following GENERALIZATIONS: "For all these noble reasons and more, sloppy people never get neat" (para. 4) and "The only thing messy in a neat person's house is the trash can" (para. 8). How can you tell that these statements are generalizations? Look for other generalizations in the essay. What is the EFFECT of using so many?
4. OTHER METHODS. Although filled with generalizations, Britt's essay does not lack for EXAMPLES. Study the examples in paragraph 11 and explain how they do and don't work the way examples are supposed to, to bring the generalizations about people down to earth.

QUESTIONS ON LANGUAGE

1. Consult your dictionary for definitions of these words: rectitude (para. 2); métier, tentative (3); accumulate (4); excavation, meticulously, scrupulously (5); salvaging (9).
2. How do you understand the use of the word *noble* in the first sentence of paragraph 4? Is it meant literally? Are there other words in the essay that appear to be written in a similar tone?

SUGGESTIONS FOR WRITING

1. Write an essay in which you compare and contrast two apparently dissimilar groups of people: for example, blue-collar workers and white-collar workers, people who write letters and people who don't write letters, runners and football players, readers and TV watchers, or any other variation you choose. Your approach may be either lighthearted or serious, but make sure you come to some conclusion about your subjects. Which group do you favor? Why?
2. Analyze the similarities and differences between two characters in your favorite novel, story, film, or television show. Which aspects of their personalities make them work well together, within the context in which they appear? Which characteristics work against each other, and therefore provide the necessary conflict to hold the readers' or viewers' attention?
3. CRITICAL WRITING. Britt's essay is remarkable for its exaggeration of the two types. Write a brief essay ANALYZING and contrasting the ways Britt characterizes sloppy people and neat people. Be sure to consider

the CONNOTATIONS of the words, such as "moral rectitude" for sloppy people (para. 2) and "cavalier" for neat people (6).

4. CONNECTIONS. Write an essay about the humor gained from exaggeration, relying on Britt's essay and James Thurber's "University Days" (p. 64) for examples. Consider why exaggeration is often funny and what qualities humorous exaggeration often has. Use quotations and PARAPHRASES from Britt's and Thurber's essays as your support.

SUZANNE BRITT ON WRITING

Asked to tell how she writes, Suzanne Britt contributed the following comment to *The Bedford Reader.*

"The question 'How do you write?' gets a snappy, snappish response from me. The first commandment is 'Live!' And the second is like unto it: 'Pay attention!' I don't mean that you have to live high or fast or deep or wise or broad. And I certainly don't mean you have to live true and upright. I just mean that you have to suck out all the marrow of whatever you do, whether it's picking the lint off the navy-blue suit you'll be wearing to Cousin Ione's funeral or popping an Aunt Jemimah frozen waffle into the toaster oven or lying between sand dunes, watching the way the sea oats slice the azure sky. The ominous question put to me by students on all occasions of possible accountability is 'Will this count?' My answer is rock bottom and hard: 'Everything counts,' I say, and silence falls like prayers across the room.

"The same is true of writing. Everything counts. Despair is good. Numbness can be excellent. Misery is fine. Ecstasy will work — or pain or sorrow or passion. The only thing that won't work is indifference. A writer refuses to be shocked and appalled by anything going or coming, rising or falling, singing or soundless. The only thing that shocks me, truth to tell, is indifference. How dare you not fight for the right to the crispy end piece on the standing-rib roast? How dare you let the fragrance of Joy go by without taking a whiff of it? How dare you not see the old woman in the snap-front housedress and the rolled-down socks, carrying her Polident and Charmin in a canvas tote that says, simply, elegantly, Le Bag?

"After you have lived, paid attention, seen connections, felt the harmony, writhed under the dissonance, fixed a Diet Coke, popped a big stick of Juicy Fruit in your mouth, gathered your life around you as a mother hen gathers her brood, as a queen settles the folds in her purple robes, you are ready to write. And what you will write about, even if you have one of those teachers who makes you write about, say, Guatemala, will be something very exclusive and intimate — something just between you and Guatemala. All you have to find out is what that small intimacy might be. It is there. And having found it, you have to make it count.

"There is no rest for a writer. But there is no boredom either. A Sunday morning with a bottle of extra-strength aspirin within easy reach and an ice bag on your head can serve you very well in writing. So can a fly buzzing at your ear or a heart-stopping siren in the night or an interminable afternoon in a biology lab in front of a frog's innards.

"All you need, really, is the audacity to believe, with your whole being, that if you tell it right, tell it truly, tell it so we can all see it, the 'it' will play in Peoria, Poughkeepsie, Pompeii, or Podunk. In the South we call that conviction, that audacity, an act of faith. But you can call it writing."

FOR DISCUSSION

1. What advice does Britt offer a student assigned to write a paper about, say, Guatemala? If you were that student, how would you go about taking her advice?
2. Where in her comment does the author use colorful and effective FIGURES OF SPEECH?
3. What is the TONE of Britt's remarks? Sum up her attitude toward her subject, writing.

BRUCE CATTON

BRUCE CATTON (1899–1978) became America's best-known historian of the Civil War. As a boy in Benzonia, Michigan, Catton acted out historical battles on local playing fields. In his memoir *Waiting for the Morning Train* (1972), he recalls how he would listen by the hour to the memories of Union Army veterans. His studies at Oberlin College interrupted by service in World War I, Catton never finished his bachelor's degree. Instead, he worked as a reporter, columnist, and editorial writer for the *Cleveland Plain Dealer* and other newspapers, then became a speechwriter and information director for government agencies. Of Catton's eighteen books, seventeen were written after his fiftieth year. *A Stillness at Appomattox* (1953) won him both a Pulitzer Prize for history and a National Book Award; other notable works include *This Hallowed Ground* (1956) and *Gettysburg: The Final Fury* (1974). From 1954 until his death, Catton edited *American Heritage*, a magazine of history. President Gerald Ford awarded him a Medal of Freedom for his life's accomplishment.

Grant and Lee:
A Study in Contrasts

"Grant and Lee: A Study in Contrasts" first appeared in *The American Story*, a book of essays written by eminent historians for interested general readers. In his discussion of the two great Civil War generals, Catton contrasts not only two very different men, but the conflicting traditions they represented. Catton's essay builds toward the conclusion that, in one outstanding way, the two leaders were more than a little alike.

When Ulysses S. Grant and Robert E. Lee met in the parlor of   1
a modest house at Appomattox Court House, Virginia, on April 9,
1865, to work out the terms for the surrender of Lee's Army of
Northern Virginia, a great chapter in American life came to a close,
and a great new chapter began.

These men were bringing the Civil War to its virtual finish. To   2
be sure, other armies had yet to surrender, and for a few days the
fugitive confederate government would struggle desperately and
vainly, trying to find some way to go on living now that its chief
support was gone. But in effect it was all over when Grant and Lee

signed the papers. And the little room where they wrote out the terms was the scene of one of the poignant, dramatic contrasts in American history.

They were two strong men, these oddly different generals, and they represented the strengths of two conflicting currents that, through them, had come into final collision. 3

Back of Robert E. Lee was the notion that the old aristocratic concept might somehow survive and be dominant in American life. 4

Lee was tidewater Virginia, and in his background were family, culture, and tradition . . . the age of chivalry transplanted to a New World which was making its own legends and its own myths. He embodied a way of life that had come down through the age of knighthood and the English country squire. America was a land that was beginning all over again, dedicated to nothing much more complicated than the rather hazy belief that all men had equal rights, and should have an equal chance in the world. In such a land Lee stood for the feeling that it was somehow of advantage to human society to have a pronounced inequality in the social structure. There should be a leisure class, backed by ownership of land; in turn, society itself should be keyed to the land as the chief source of wealth and influence. It would bring forth (according to this ideal) a class of men with a strong sense of obligation to the community; men who lived not to gain advantage for themselves, but to meet the solemn obligations which had been laid on them by the very fact that they were privileged. From them the country would get its leadership; to them it could look for the higher values — of thought, of conduct, of personal deportment — to give it strength and virtue. 5

Lee embodied the noblest elements of this aristocratic ideal. Through him, the landed nobility justified itself. For four years, the Southern states had fought a desperate war to uphold the ideals for which Lee stood. In the end, it almost seemed as if the Confederacy fought for Lee; as if he himself was the Confederacy . . . the best thing that the way of life for which the Confederacy stood could ever have to offer. He had passed into legend before Appomattox. Thousands of tired, underfed, poorly clothed Confederate soldiers, long-since past the simple enthusiasm of the early days of the struggle, somehow considered Lee the symbol of everything for which they had been willing to die. But they could not quite put this feeling into words. If the Lost Cause, sanctified by so much heroism and so many deaths, had a living justification, its justification was General Lee. 6

Grant, the son of a tanner on the Western frontier, was everything Lee was not. He had come up the hard way, and embodied 7 nothing in particular except the eternal toughness and sinewy fiber of the men who grew up beyond the mountains. He was one of a body of men who owed reverence and obeisance to no one, who were self-reliant to a fault, who cared hardly anything for the past but who had a sharp eye for the future.

These frontier men were the precise opposites of the tidewater 8 aristocrats. Back of them, in the great surge that had taken people over the Alleghenies and into the opening Western country, there was a deep, implicit dissatisfaction with a past that had settled into grooves. They stood for democracy, not from any reasoned conclusion about the proper ordering of human society, but simply because they had grown up in the middle of democracy and knew how it worked. Their society might have privileges, but they would be privileges each man had won for himself. Forms and patterns meant nothing. No man was born to anything, except perhaps to a chance to show how far he could rise. Life was competition.

Yet along with this feeling had come a deep sense of belonging 9 to a national community. The Westerner who developed a farm, opened a shop, or set up in business as a trader could hope to prosper only as his own community prospered — and his community ran from the Atlantic to the Pacific and from Canada down to Mexico. If the land was settled, with towns and highways and accessible markets, he could better himself. He saw his fate in terms of the nation's own destiny. As its horizons expanded, so did his. He had, in other words, an acute dollars-and-cents stake in the continued growth and development of his country.

And that, perhaps, is where the contrast between Grant and Lee 10 becomes most striking. The Virginia aristocrat, inevitably, saw himself in relation to his own region. He lived in a static society which could endure almost anything except change. Instinctively, his first loyalty would go to the locality in which that society existed. He would fight to the limit of endurance to defend it, because in defending it he was defending everything that gave his own life its deepest meaning.

The Westerner, on the other hand, would fight with an equal 11 tenacity for the broader concept of society. He fought so because everything he lived by was tied to growth, expansion, and a constantly widening horizon. What he lived by would survive or fall with the nation itself. He could not possibly stand by unmoved in the face of an attempt to destroy the Union. He would combat it with everything he had, because he could only see it as an effort to cut the ground out from under his feet.

So Grant and Lee were in complete contrast, representing two 12
diametrically opposed elements in American life. Grant was the modern man emerging; beyond him, ready to come on the stage, was the
great age of steel and machinery, of crowded cities and a restless,
burgeoning vitality. Lee might have ridden down from the old age of
chivalry, lance in hand, silken banner fluttering over his head. Each
man was the perfect champion of his cause, drawing both his strengths
and his weaknesses from the people he led.

Yet it was not all contrast, after all. Different as they were — in 13
background, in personality, in underlying aspiration — these two
great soldiers had much in common. Under everything else, they
were marvelous fighters. Furthermore, their fighting qualities were
really very much alike.

Each man had, to begin with, the great virtue of utter tenacity 14
and fidelity. Grant fought his way down the Mississippi Valley in
spite of acute personal discouragement and profound military handicaps. Lee hung on in the trenches at Petersburg after hope itself had
died. In each man there was an indomitable quality . . . the born
fighter's refusal to give up as long as he can still remain on his feet
and lift his two fists.

Daring and resourcefulness they had, too; the ability to think 15
faster and move faster than the enemy. These were the qualities
which gave Lee the dazzling campaigns of Second Manassas and
Chancellorsville and won Vicksburg for Grant.

Lastly, and perhaps greatest of all, there was the ability, at the 16
end, to turn quickly from war to peace once the fighting was over.
Out of the way these two men behaved at Appomattox came the
possibility of a peace of reconciliation. It was a possibility not wholly
realized, in the years to come, but which did, in the end, help the
two sections to become one nation again . . . after a war whose
bitterness might have seemed to make such a reunion wholly impossible. No part of either man's life became him more than the part he
played in their brief meeting in the McLean house at Appomattox.
Their behavior there put all succeeding generations of Americans in
their debt. Two great Americans, Grant and Lee — very different,
yet under everything very much alike. Their encounter at Appomattox was one of the great moments of American history.

QUESTIONS ON MEANING

1. What is Bruce Catton's PURPOSE in writing: to describe the meeting of two generals at a famous moment in history; to explain how the two men stood for opposing social forces in America; or to show how the two differed in personality?
2. SUMMARIZE the background and the way of life that produced Robert E. Lee; then do the same for Ulysses S. Grant. According to Catton, what ideals did each man represent?
3. In the historian's view, what essential traits did the two men have in common? Which trait does Catton think most important of all? For what reason?
4. How does this essay help you understand why Grant and Lee were such determined fighters?

QUESTIONS ON WRITING STRATEGY

1. From the content of this essay, and from knowing where it first appeared, what can you infer about Catton's original AUDIENCE? At what places in his essay does the writer expect of his readers a familiarity with United States history?
2. What effect does the writer achieve by setting both his INTRODUCTION and his CONCLUSION in Appomattox?
3. For what reasons does Catton contrast the two generals *before* he compares them? Suppose he had reversed his outline, and had dealt first with Grant and Lee's mutual resemblances. Why would his essay have been less effective?
4. Pencil in hand, draw a single line down the margin of every paragraph in which you find the method of contrast. Then draw a *double* line next to every paragraph in which you find the method of comparison. How much space does Catton devote to each method? Why didn't he give comparison and contrast equal time?
5. Closely read the first sentence of every paragraph and underline each word or phrase in it that serves as a TRANSITION. Then review your underlinings. How much COHERENCE has Catton given his essay?
6. What is the TONE of this essay — that is, what is the writer's attitude toward his two subjects? Is Catton poking fun at Lee by imagining the Confederate general as a knight of the Middle Ages, "lance in hand, silken banner fluttering over his head" (para. 12)?
7. OTHER METHODS. In identifying "two conflicting currents," Catton uses CLASSIFICATION to sort Civil War–era Americans into two groups represented by Lee and Grant. Catton then uses ANALYSIS to tease out the characteristics of each current, each type. How do classification and analysis serve Catton's comparison and contrast?

QUESTIONS ON LANGUAGE

1. In his opening paragraph, Catton uses a METAPHOR: American life is a book containing chapters. Find other FIGURES OF SPEECH in his essay. What do they contribute?
2. Look up *poignant* in the dictionary. Why is it such a fitting word in paragraph 2? Why wouldn't *touching, sad,* or *teary* have been as good?
3. What information do you glean from the sentence, "Lee was tidewater Virginia" (para. 5)?
4. Define *aristocratic* as Catton uses it in paragraphs 4 and 6.
5. Define *obeisance* (para. 7); *indomitable* (14).

SUGGESTIONS FOR WRITING

1. Compare and contrast two other figures of American history with whom you are familiar: Franklin D. Roosevelt and John F. Kennedy, Abraham Lincoln and Stephen A. Douglas, or Susan B. Anthony and Elizabeth Cady Stanton — to suggest only a few.
2. In a brief essay full of specific examples, discuss: Do the "two diametrically opposed elements in American life" (as Catton calls them) still exist in the country today? Are there still any "landed nobility"?
3. In your thinking and your attitudes, whom do you more closely resemble — Grant or Lee? Compare and contrast your outlook with that of one famous American or the other. (A serious tone for this topic isn't required.)
4. CRITICAL WRITING. Although slavery, along with other issues, helped precipitate the Civil War, Catton in this particular essay does not deal with it. Perhaps he assumes that his readers will supply the missing context themselves. Is this a fair ASSUMPTION? If Catton had recalled the facts of slavery, would he have undermined any of his assertions about Lee? (Though the general of the pro-slavery Confederacy, Lee was personally opposed to slavery.) In a brief essay, judge whether or not the omission of slavery weakens the essay, and explain why.
5. CONNECTIONS. Lee's and Grant's backgrounds positioned them in different socioeconomic classes, classes echoed in the contemporary America discussed by Ralph Whitehead, Jr., in "Class Acts" (p. 342). In a brief essay, compare and contrast Lee's outlook with that of the rich today (Whitehead's paras. 5, 21) and Grant's outlook with that of the Bright Collars today (paras. 10–12, 19). Feel free to draw on relevant information outside Catton's and Whitehead's essays.

BRUCE CATTON ON WRITING

Most of Bruce Catton's comments on writing, those that have been preserved, refer to the work of others. As editor of *American Heritage,* he was known for his blunt, succinct comments on unsuccessful manuscripts: "This article can't be repaired and wouldn't be much good if it were." Or: "The high-water mark of this piece comes at the bottom of page one, where the naked Indian nymph offers the hero strawberries. Unfortunately, this level is not maintained."

In a memoir published in *Bruce Catton's America* (1979), Catton's associate Oliver Jensen has marveled that, besides editing *American Heritage* for twenty-four years (and contributing to nearly every issue), Catton managed to produce so many substantial books. "Concentration was no doubt the secret, that and getting an early start. For many years Catton was always the first person in the office, so early that most of the staff never knew when he did arrive. On his desk the little piles of yellow sheets grew slowly, with much larger piles in the wastebasket. A neat and orderly man, he preferred to type a new page than correct very much in pencil."

His whole purpose as a writer, Catton once said, was "to reexamine [our] debt to the past."

FOR DISCUSSION

1. To which of Catton's traits does Oliver Jensen attribute the historian's impressive output?
2. Which characteristics of Catton the editor would you expect to have served him well as a writer?

AMY TAN

AMY TAN is a gifted storyteller whose first novel, *The Joy Luck Club* (1989), met with critical acclaim and huge success. The relation-ships it details between immigrant Chinese mothers and their Chinese American daughters came from Tan's firsthand experience. She was born in 1952 in Oakland, California, the daughter of immigrants who had fled China's Cultural Revolution in the late 1940s. She majored in English and linguistics at San Jose State University, where she received a B.A. in 1973 and an M.A. in 1974. After two more years of graduate work, Tan became a con-sultant in language development for disabled children and then started her own company writing reports and speeches for business corporations. Tan began writing fiction to explore her ethnic am-bivalence and to find a voice for herself. After *The Joy Luck Club*, she published *The Kitchen God's Wife* (1991), a fictional account of her mother's harrowing life in China. Tan has also contributed essays to *McCall's, Life, Glamour, The Atlantic Monthly,* and other magazines.

The Language of Discretion

With her Chinese background, American upbringing, and training in linguistics, Amy Tan is unusually well qualified to explore the connection among language, thought, and behavior. In this essay, she compares and contrasts on two fronts: misperceptions and re-alities of the Chinese language, and the qualities of the Chinese and English languages. The essay, first published in 1990, has ap-peared in several anthologies. We found it in *The State of the Language*, edited by Christopher Ricks and Leonard Michaels.

At a recent family dinner in San Francisco, my mother whispered to me: "Sau-sau [Brother's Wife] pretends too hard to be polite! Why bother? In the end, she always takes everything."

My mother thinks like a *waixiao*, an expatriate, temporarily away from China since 1949, no longer patient with ritual courtesies. As if to prove her point, she reached across the table to offer my elderly aunt from Beijing the last scallop from the Happy Family seafood dish.

Sau-sau scowled. "*B'yao, zhen b'yao!*" (I don't want it, really I don't!) she cried, patting her plump stomach.

"Take it! Take it!" scolded my mother in Chinese.

"Full, I'm already full," Sau-sau protested weakly, eyeing the   5
beloved scallop.

"Ai!" exclaimed my mother, completely exasperated. "Nobody   6
else wants it. If you don't take it, it will only rot!"

At this point, Sau-sau sighed, acting as if she were doing my   7
mother a big favor by taking the wretched scrap off her hands.

My mother turned to her brother, a high-ranking communist   8
official who was visiting her in California for the first time: "In
America a Chinese person could starve to death. If you say you don't
want it, they won't ask you again forever."

My uncle nodded and said he understood fully: Americans take   9
things quickly because they have no time to be polite.

I thought about this misunderstanding again — of social contexts   10
failing in translation — when a friend sent me an article from the
New York Times Magazine (24 April 1988). The article, on changes
in New York's Chinatown, made passing reference to the inherent
ambivalence of the Chinese language.

Chinese people are so "discreet and modest," the article stated,   11
there aren't even words for "yes" and "no."

That's not true, I thought, although I can see why an outsider   12
might think that. I continued reading.

If one is Chinese, the article went on to say, "One compromises,   13
one doesn't hazard a loss of face by an overemphatic response."

My throat seized. Why do people keep saying these things? As if   14
we truly were those little dolls sold in Chinatown tourist shops, heads
bobbing up and down in complacent agreement to anything said!

I worry about the effect of one-dimensional statements on the   15
unwary and guileless. When they read about this so-called vocabulary
deficit, do they also conclude that Chinese people evolved into a
mild-mannered lot because the language only allowed them to hobble
forth with minced words?

Something enormous is always lost in translation. Something   16
insidious seeps into the gaps, especially when amateur linguists continue to compare, one-for-one, language differences and then put
forth notions wide open to misinterpretation: that Chinese people
have no direct linguistic means to make decisions, assert or deny,
affirm or negate, just say no to drug dealers, or behave properly on
the witness stand when told, "Please answer yes or no."

Yet one can argue, with the help of renowned linguists, that the   17
Chinese are indeed up a creek without "yes" and "no." Take any
number of variations on the old language-and-reality theory stated

years ago by Edward Sapir: "Human beings . . . are very much at the mercy of the particular language which has become the medium for their society. . . . The fact of the matter is that the 'real world' is to a large extent built upon the language habits of the group."[1]

This notion was further bolstered by the famous Sapir-Whorf   18 hypothesis, which roughly states that one's perception of the world and how one functions in it depend a great deal on the language used. As Sapir, Whorf, and new carriers of the banner would have us believe, language shapes our thinking, channels us along certain patterns embedded in words, syntactic structures, and intonation patterns. Language has become the peg and the shelf that enables us to sort out and categorize the world. In English, we see "cats" and "dogs"; what if the language had also specified *glatz,* meaning "animals that leave fur on the sofa," and *glotz,* meaning "animals that leave fur and drool on the sofa"? How would language, the enabler, have changed our perceptions with slight vocabulary variations?

And if this were the case — of language being the master of   19 destined thought — think of the opportunities lost from failure to evolve two little words, *yes* and *no,* the simplest of opposites! Ghenghis Khan could have been sent back to Mongolia. Opium wars might have been averted. The Cultural Revolution could have been sidestepped.

There are still many, from serious linguists to pop psychology   20 cultists, who view language and reality as inextricably tied, one being the consequence of the other. We have traversed the range from the Sapir-Whorf hypothesis to est and neurolinguistic programming, which tell us "you are what you say."

I too have been intrigued by the theories. I can summarize, albeit   21 badly, ages-old empirical evidence: of Eskimos and their infinite ways to say "snow," their ability to *see* the differences in snowflake configurations, thanks to the richness of their vocabulary, while non-Eskimo speakers like myself founder in "snow," "more snow," and "lots more where that came from."

I too have experienced dramatic cognitive awakenings via the   22 word. Once I added "mauve" to my vocabulary I began to see it everywhere. When I learned how to pronounce *prix fixe,* I ate French food at prices better than the easier-to-say *à la carte* choices.

But just how seriously are we supposed to take this?   23

Sapir said something else about language and reality. It is the   24

[1]Edward Sapir, *Selected Writings,* ed. D. G. Mandelbaum (Berkeley and Los Angeles, 1949).

part that often gets left behind in the dot-dot-dots of quotes: ". . . No two languages are ever sufficiently similar to be considered as representing the same social reality. The worlds in which different societies live are distinct worlds, not merely the same world with different labels attached."

When I first read this, I thought, Here at last is validity for the 25 dilemmas I felt growing up in a bicultural, bilingual family! As any child of immigrant parents knows, there's a special kind of double bind attached to knowing two languages. My parents, for example, spoke to me in both Chinese and English; I spoke back to them in English.

"Amy-ah!" they'd call me.   26

"What?" I'd mumble back.   27

"Do not question us when we call," they scolded me in Chinese. 28 "It is not respectful."

"What do you mean?"   29

"Ai! Didn't we just tell you not to question?"   30

To this day, I wonder which parts of my behavior were shaped 31 by Chinese, which by English. I am tempted to think, for example, that if I am of two minds on some matter it is due to the richness of my linguistic experiences, not to any personal tendencies toward wishy-washiness. But which mind says what?

Was it perhaps patience — developed through years of decipher- 32 ing my mother's fractured English — that had me listening politely while a woman announced over the phone that I had won one of five valuable prizes? Was it respect — pounded in by the Chinese imperative to accept convoluted explanations — that had me agreeing that I might find it worthwhile to drive seventy-five miles to view a time-share resort? Could I have been at a loss for words when asked, "Wouldn't you like to win a Hawaiian cruise or perhaps a fabulous Star of India designed exclusively by Carter and Van Arpels?"

And when this same woman called back a week later, this time 33 complaining that I had missed my appointment, obviously it was my type A language that kicked into gear and interrupted her. Certainly, my blunt denial — "Frankly I'm not interested" — was as American as apple pie. And when she said, "But it's in Morgan Hill," and I shouted, "Read my lips. I don't care if it's Timbuktu," you can be sure I said it with the precise intonation expressing both cynicism and disgust.

It's dangerous business, this sorting out of language and behavior. 34 Which one is English? Which is Chinese? The categories manifest themselves: passive and aggressive, tentative and assertive, indirect and direct. And I realize they are just variations of the same theme: that Chinese people are discreet and modest.

Reject them all!   35

If my reaction is overly strident, it is because I cannot come across 36
as too emphatic. I grew up listening to the same lines over and over again, like so many rote expressions repeated in an English phrase-book. And I too almost came to believe them.

Yet if I consider my upbringing more carefully, I find there was 37
nothing discreet about the Chinese language I grew up with. My parents made everything abundantly clear. Nothing wishy-washy in their demands, no compromises accepted: "Of course you will become a famous neurosurgeon," they told me. "And yes, a concert pianist on the side."

In fact, now that I remember, it seems that the more emphatic 38
outbursts always spilled over into Chinese: "Not that way! You must wash rice so not a single grain spills out."

I do not believe that my parents — both immigrants from main- 39
land China — are an exception to the modest-and-discreet rule. I have only to look at the number of Chinese engineering students skewing minority ratios at Berkeley, MIT, and Yale. Certainly they were not raised by passive mothers and fathers who said, "It is up to you, my daughter. Writer, welfare recipient, masseuse, or molecular engineer — you decide."

And my American mind says, See, those engineering students 40
weren't able to say no to their parents' demands. But then my Chinese mind remembers: Ah, but those parents all wanted their sons and daughters to be *pre-med.*

Having listened to both Chinese and English, I also tend to be 41
suspicious of any comparisons between the two languages. Typically, one language — that of the person doing the comparing — is often used as the standard, the benchmark for a logical form of expression. And so the language being compared is always in danger of being judged deficient or superfluous, simplistic or unnecessarily complex, melodious or cacophonous. English speakers point out that Chinese is extremely difficult because it relies on variations in tone barely discernible to the human ear. By the same token, Chinese speakers tell me English is extremely difficult because it is inconsistent, a language of too many broken rules, of Mickey Mice and Donald Ducks.

Even more dangerous to my mind is the temptation to compare 42
both language and behavior *in translation.* To listen to my mother speak English, one might think she has no concept of past or future

tense, that she doesn't see the difference between singular and plural, that she is gender blind because she calls my husband "she." If one were not careful, one might also generalize that, based on the way my mother talks, all Chinese people take a circumlocutory route to get to the point. It is, in fact, my mother's idiosyncratic behavior to ramble a bit.

Sapir was right about differences between two languages and their   43
realities. I can illustrate why word-for-word translation is not enough to translate meaning and intent. I once received a letter from China which I read to non-Chinese speaking friends. The letter, originally written in Chinese, had been translated by my brother-in-law in Beijing. One portion described the time when my uncle at age ten discovered his widowed mother (my grandmother) had remarried — as a number three concubine, the ultimate disgrace for an honorable family. The translated version of my uncle's letter read in part:

> In 1925, I met my mother in Shanghai. When she came to me, I didn't have greeting to her as if seeing nothing. She pull me to a corner secretly and asked me why didn't have greeting to her. I couldn't control myself and cried, "Ma! Why did you leave us? People told me: one day you ate a beancake yourself. Your sister in-law found it and sweared at you, called your names. So . . . is it true?" She clasped my hand and answered immediately, "It's not true, don't say what like this." After this time, there was a few chance to meet her.

"What!" cried my friends. "Was eating a beancake so terrible?"   44
Of course not. The beancake was simply a euphemism; a ten-   45
year-old boy did not dare question his mother on something as shocking as concubinage. Eating a beancake was his equivalent for committing this selfish act, something inconsiderate of all family members, hence, my grandmother's despairing response to what seemed like a ludicrous charge of gluttony. And sure enough, she was banished from the family, and my uncle saw her only a few times before her death.

While the above may fuel people's argument that Chinese is   46
indeed a language of extreme discretion, it does not mean that Chinese people speak in secrets and riddles. The contexts are fully understood. It is only to those on the *outside* that the language seems cryptic, the behavior inscrutable.

I am, evidently, one of the outsiders. My nephew in Shanghai,   47
who recently started taking English lessons, has been writing me letters in English. I had told him I was a fiction writer, and so in one

letter he wrote, "Congratulate to you on your writing. Perhaps one day I should like to read it." I took it in the same vein as "Perhaps one day we can get together for lunch." I sent back a cheery note. A month went by and another letter arrived from Shanghai. "Last one perhaps I hadn't writing distinctly," he said. "In the future, you'll send a copy of your works for me."

48   I try to explain to my English-speaking friends that Chinese language use is more *strategic* in manner, whereas English tends to be more direct; an American business executive may say, "Let's make a deal," and the Chinese manager may reply, "Is your son interested in learning about your widget business?" Each to his or her own purpose, each with his or her own linguistic path. But I hesitate to add more to the pile of generalizations, because no matter how many examples I provide and explain, I fear that it appears defensive and only reinforces the image: that Chinese people are "discreet and modest" — and it takes an American to explain what they really mean.

49   Why am I complaining? The description seems harmless enough (after all, the *New York Times Magazine* writer did not say "slippery and evasive"). It is precisely the bland, easy acceptability of the phrase that worries me.

50   I worry that the dominant society may see Chinese people from a limited — and limiting — perspective. I worry that seemingly benign stereotypes may be part of the reason there are few Chinese in top management positions, in mainstream political roles. I worry about the power of language: that if one says anything enough times — in *any* language — it might become true.

51   Could this be why Chinese friends of my parents' generation are willing to accept the generalization?

52   "Why are you complaining?" one of them said to me. "If people think we are modest and polite, let them think that. Wouldn't Americans be pleased to admit they are thought of as polite?"

53   And I do believe anyone would take the description as a compliment — at first. But after a while, it annoys, as if the only things that people heard one say were phatic remarks: "I'm so pleased to meet you. I've heard many wonderful things about you. For me? You shouldn't have!"

54   These remarks are not representative of new ideas, honest emotions, or considered thought. They are what is said from the polite distance of social contexts: of greetings, farewells, wedding thank-you notes, convenient excuses, and the like.

55   It makes me wonder, though. How many anthropologists, how

many sociologists, how many travel journalists have documented so-called "natural interactions" in foreign lands, all observed with spiral notebook in hand? How many other cases are there of the long-lost primitive tribe, people who turned out to be sophisticated enough to put on the stone-age show that ethnologists had come to see?

And how many tourists fresh off the bus have wandered into 56 Chinatown expecting the self-effacing shopkeeper to admit under duress that the goods are not worth the price asked? I have witnessed it.

"I don't know," the tourist said to the shopkeeper, a Cantonese 57 woman in her fifties. "It doesn't look genuine to me. I'll give you three dollars."

"You don't like my price, go somewhere else," said the shop- 58 keeper.

"You are not a nice person," cried the shocked tourist, "not a 59 nice person at all!"

"Who say I have to be nice," snapped the shopkeeper.   60

"So how does one say 'yes' and 'no' in Chinese?" ask my friends 61 a bit warily.

And here I do agree in part with the *New York Times Magazine* 62 article. There is no one word for "yes" or "no" — but not out of necessity to be discreet. If anything, I would say the Chinese equivalent of answering "yes" or "no" is *discrete*, that is, specific to what is asked.

Ask a Chinese person if he or she has eaten, and he or she might 63 say *chrle* (eaten already) or perhaps *meiyou* (have not).

Ask, "So you had insurance at the time of the accident?" and 64 the response would be *dwei* (correct) or *meiyou* (did not have).

Ask, "Have you stopped beating your wife?" and the answer refers 65 directly to the proposition being asserted or denied: stopped already, still have not, never beat, have no wife.

What could be clearer?   66

As for those who are still wondering how to translate the language 67 of discretion, I offer this personal example.

My aunt and uncle were about to return to Beijing after a three- 68 month visit to the United States. On their last night I announced I wanted to take them out to dinner.

"Are you hungry?" I asked in Chinese.   69

"Not hungry," said my uncle promptly, the same response he once 70 gave me ten minutes before he suffered a low-blood-sugar attack.

"Not too hungry," said my aunt. "Perhaps you're hungry?"   71

"A little," I admitted.   72

"We can eat, we can eat," they both consented.   73

"What kind of food?" I asked.   74

"Oh, doesn't matter. Anything will do. Nothing fancy, just some   75
simple food is fine."

"Do you like Japanese food? We haven't had that yet," I suggested.   76

They looked at each other.   77

"We can eat it," said my uncle bravely, this survivor of the Long   78
March.

"We have eaten it before," added my aunt. "Raw fish."   79

"Oh, you don't like it?" I said. "Don't be polite. We can go   80
somewhere else."

"We are not being polite. We can eat it," my aunt insisted.   81

So I drove them to Japantown and we walked past several restau-   82
rants featuring colorful plastic displays of sushi.

"Not this one, not this one either," I continued to say, as if   83
searching for a Japanese restaurant similar to the last. "Here it is," I
finally said, turning into a restaurant famous for its Chinese fish dishes
from Shandong.

"Oh, Chinese food!" cried my aunt, obviously relieved.   84

My uncle patted my arm. "You think Chinese."   85

"It's your last night here in America," I said. "So don't be polite.   86
Act like an American."

And that night we ate a banquet.   87

QUESTIONS ON MEANING

1. What is the Sapir-Whorf hypothesis (para. 18)? Why does Tan address it?
2. What is Tan's THESIS? State it in your own words.
3. In your own words, state the essay's PURPOSE.
4. In paragraph 48, Tan says, "Chinese language use is more *strategic* in manner, whereas English tends to be more direct." What does she mean?

QUESTIONS ON WRITING STRATEGY

1. Who is the AUDIENCE Tan intends to reach with this essay? How familiar does she expect her readers to be with Chinese culture and the Chinese language? How do you know?

2. Tan's presentation of Chinese language and behavior is far more detailed than her discussion of American ways of thinking and speaking. Does this weaken her comparison?

3. Where does Tan compare the perception and reality of the Chinese language? Where does she compare Chinese and English? How are the two comparisons related?

4. OTHER METHODS. As in any comparison, Tan uses brief NARRATIVES, or ANECDOTES, to support her assertions. What is the EFFECT of these anecdotes?

QUESTIONS ABOUT LANGUAGE

1. Familiarize yourself with the meanings of the following words: expatriate (para. 2); inherent, ambivalence (9); guileless (15); insidious (16); hypothesis (18); est (20); strident (36); cacophonous (41); circumlocutory (42); euphemism (45); self-effacing, duress (56).

2. What is the EFFECT of Tan's use of Chinese words and phrases?

3. How does Tan use humor to illustrate her points? Is this a challenge to an American stereotype of Chinese culture?

4. In Tan's narration of her conversation with her aunt and uncle (paras. 67–87), how does her English indicate that the conversation took place in Chinese?

SUGGESTIONS FOR WRITING

1. In her essay, Tan challenges an overenthusiastic acceptance of the Sapir-Whorf hypothesis that "one's perception of the world and how one functions in it depend a great deal on the language used" (para. 18). Drawing on your own experience, write a brief essay agreeing or disagreeing with the Sapir-Whorf hypothesis. Does using different languages make for different ways of thinking? (Consider either different languages — for example, Spanish and English — or different styles of language — street talk versus formal speech.) Be sure to use EVIDENCE to support your view.

2. What are some of the "seemingly benign stereotypes" (para. 50) of Chinese people that Tan worries about? In an essay, discuss the stereotypes Tan mentions or alludes to in this section. How widespread are they? How many of them might, as she believes, be due to mistakes in translation? You may want to use ANECDOTES to illustrate your point.

3. CRITICAL WRITING. Tan says of the Chinese language, "It is only to those on the *outside* that the language seems cryptic, the behavior inscrutable" (para. 46). How does Tan establish her credentials as an insider? Review the essay, noting where she stakes a claim to special knowledge. EVALUATE her assertions of expertise. How convincing are they?

4. CONNECTIONS. How does Tan's depiction of a bilingual childhood and

its role in shaping identity differ from that presented by Judith Ortiz Cofer in "*Casa*: A Partial Remembrance of a Puerto Rican Childhood" (p. 73)? How are they similar? Write a short essay comparing and contrasting the two selections. What aspects of a bilingual upbringing struck each author as significant?

AMY TAN ON WRITING

Around the time she wrote "The Language of Discretion," Amy Tan delivered a lecture titled "Mother Tongue" at the State of the Language Symposium in San Francisco. The lecture, subsequently published in *The Threepenny Review* in 1990, expands on the theme of bilingualism. Tan bemoans the fact that non-Chinese speakers and Tan herself on occasion refer to her mother's English as "broken" or "fractured." Although "vivid, direct, full of observation and imagery," it is choppy and ungrammatical, giving people the impression that she doesn't think clearly. "I know this for a fact," Tan says, "because when I was growing up, my mother's 'limited' English limited *my* perception of her. I was ashamed of her English. . . .

"I think my mother's English almost had an effect on limiting my possibilities in life as well. . . . I do think that the language spoken in the family, especially in immigrant families, which are more insular, plays a large role in shaping the language of the child. And I believe that it affected my results on achievement tests, IQ tests, and the SAT. While my English skills were never judged as poor, compared to math English could not be considered my strong suit. . . . This was understandable. Math is precise; there is only one correct answer. Whereas, for me at least, the answers on English tests were always a judgment call, a matter of opinion and personal experience."

Tan goes on to say that the necessity of adapting to different styles of expression may affect other children from bilingual households. "I've been asked, as a writer, why there are not more Asian-Americans represented in American literature. Why are there few Asian-Americans enrolled in creative-writing programs? Why do so many Chinese students go into engineering? Well, these are broad sociological questions I can't begin to answer. But I have noticed in surveys . . . that Asian students, as a whole, always do significantly better on math achievement tests than in English. And this makes me think that there are other Asian-American students whose English spoken in the home might also be described as 'broken' or 'limited.' And perhaps they also have teachers who are steering them away from writing and into math and science, which is what happened to me."

Tan admits that when she first began writing fiction, she wrote "what I thought to be wittily crafted sentences, sentences that would finally prove I had mastery over the English language." But they were awkward and self-conscious, so she changed her tactic. "I later decided I should envision a reader for the stories I would write. And the reader I decided upon was my mother, because these were stories about mothers. So with this reader in mind — and in fact, she did read my early drafts — I began to write stories using all the Englishes I grew up with: the English I spoke to my mother, . . . the English she used with me, . . . my translation of her Chinese, . . . and what I imagined to be her translation of her Chinese if she could speak in perfect English, her internal language, and for that I sought to preserve the essence, but not either an English or a Chinese structure. I wanted to capture what language ability tests can never reveal: her intent, her passion, her imagery, the rhythms of her speech and the nature of her thoughts.

"Apart from what any critic had to say about my writing, I knew I had succeeded where it counted when my mother finished reading my book and gave me her verdict: 'So easy to read.'"

FOR DISCUSSION

1. How could growing up in a household of "broken" English be a handicap for a student taking an achievement test?
2. What does the author suggest is the reason why more Asian Americans enter engineering than English?
3. Why did Amy Tan's mother make a good reader?

JEFF GREENFIELD

Jeff Greenfield, born in 1943, graduated from the University of Wisconsin and Yale University School of Law. He became a sportswriter, humorist, and media commentator for CBS-TV, and now he is a political and media analyst for ABC News, a regular guest anchor on the news show *Nightline,* and a syndicated columnist. Earlier in his career, he served as a staff aide and writer of speeches for both John V. Lindsay, former mayor of New York City, and the late attorney general Robert F. Kennedy. His books include *A Populist Manifesto* (1972), *Where Have You Gone, Joe DiMaggio?* (1973), *The World's Greatest Team* (history of the Boston Celtics, 1976), *Television: The First 50 Years* (1977), *Playing to Win: An Insider's Guide to Politics* (1980), and *The Real Campaign* (1982).

The Black and White Truth About Basketball

When Jeff Greenfield's survey of "black" and "white" basketball, subtitled "A Skin-Deep Theory of Style," was first published in *Esquire* in 1975, it provoked immediate interest and controversy. Greenfield has regularly updated the essay for Bedford Books, most recently in 1993. (His thesis is unchanged.) For a complementary view of two other American sports — football and baseball — see the essay following this one, by Murray Ross.

The dominance of black athletes over professional basketball is beyond dispute. Two-thirds of the players are black, and the number would be greater were it not for the continuing practice of picking white bench warmers for the sake of balance. Over the last two decades, no more than three white players have been among the ten starting players on the National Basketball Association's All-Star team, and in the last quarter century, only two white players — Dave Cowens and Larry Bird of the Boston Celtics — have ever been chosen as the NBA's Most Valuable Player.

And at a time when a baseball executive can lose his job for asserting that blacks lack "the necessities" to become pro sports executives and when the National Football League only in 1989 had its first black head coach, the NBA stands as a pro sports league that hired its first black head coach in 1968 (Bill Russell) and its first black general manager in the early 1970s (Wayne Embry of the Milwaukee Bucks). What discrimination remains — lack of equal

opportunity for speaking engagements and product endorsements —
has more to do with society than with basketball.

This dominance reflects a natural inheritance: Basketball is a   3
pastime of the urban poor. The current generation of black athletes
are heirs to a tradition more than half a century old. In a neighborhood without the money for bats, gloves, hockey sticks and ice skates,
or shoulder pads, basketball is an eminently accessible sport. "Once
it was the game of the Irish and Italian Catholics in Rockaway and
the Jews on Fordham Road in the Bronx," writes David Wolf in his
brilliant book, *Foul!* "It was recreation, status, and a way out." But
now the ethnic names have been changed: Instead of the Red Holz-
mans, Red Auerbachs, and the McGuire brothers, there are the
Michael Jordans and Charles Barkleys, the Shaquille O'Neals and
Patrick Ewings. And professional basketball is a sport with national
television exposure and million-dollar salaries.

But the mark on basketball of today's players can be measured by   4
more than money or visibility. It is a question of style. For there is a
clear difference between "black" and "white" styles of play that is as
clear as the difference between 155th Street at Eighth Avenue and
Crystal City, Missouri. Most simply (remembering we are talking
about culture, not chromosomes), "black" basketball is the use of
superb athletic skill to adapt to the limits of space imposed by the
game. "White" ball is the pulverization of that space by sheer intensity.[1]

It takes a conscious effort to realize how constricted the space is   5
on a basketball court. Place a regulation court (ninety-four by fifty
feet) in a football field, and it will reach from the back of the end
zone to the twenty-one-yard line; its width will cover less than a third
of the field. On a baseball diamond, a basketball court will reach
from home plate to first base. Compared to its principal indoor rival,
ice hockey, basketball covers about one-fourth the playing area. Moreover, during the normal flow of the game, most of the action takes
place on the third of the court nearest the basket. It is in this
dollhouse space that ten men, each of them half a foot taller than
the average man, come together to battle each other.

---

[1]This distinction has nothing to do with the question of whether whites can
play as "well" as blacks. In 1987, the Detroit Pistons' Isiah Thomas quipped that the
Celtics' Larry Bird was "a pretty good player," but would be much less celebrated and
wealthy if he were black. As Thomas later said, Bird was one of the greatest pro
players in history. Nor is this distinction about "smart," although the ex–Los Angeles
Laker great Magic Johnson was right when he said that too many journalists attribute
brilliant strategic moves by black players to "innate" ability.

There is, thus, no room; basketball is a struggle for the edge: the ⁶ half step with which to cut around the defender for a lay-up, the half second of freedom with which to release a jump shot, the instant a head turns allowing a pass to a teammate breaking for the basket. It is an arena for the subtlest of skills: the head fake, the shoulder fake, the shift of body weight to the right and the sudden cut to the left. Deception is crucial to success; and to young men who have learned early and painfully that life is a battle for survival, basketball is one of the few pursuits in which the weapon of deception is a legitimate tactic rather than a source of trouble.

If there is, then, the need to compete in a crowd, to battle for ⁷ the edge, then the surest strategy is to develop the *unexpected:* to develop a shot that is simply and fundamentally different from the usual methods of putting the ball in the basket. Drive to the hoop, but go under it and come up the other side; hold the ball at waist level and shoot from there instead of bringing the ball up to eye level; leap into the air, but fall away from the basket instead of toward it. All these tactics, which a fan can see embodied in the astonishing play of the Chicago Bulls' Michael Jordan, take maximum advantage of the crowding on the court. They also stamp uniqueness on young men who may feel it nowhere else.

"For many young men in the slums," David Wolf writes, "the ⁸ school yard is the only place they can feel true pride in what they do, where they can move free of inhibitions and where they can, by being spectacular, rise for the moment against the drabness and an- onymity of their lives. Thus, when a player develops extraordinary 'school yard' moves and shots . . . [they] become his measure as a man."

So the moves that begin as tactics for scoring soon become calling ⁹ cards. You don't just lay the ball in for an uncontested basket; you take the ball in both hands, leap as high as you can, and slam the ball through the hoop. When you jump in the air, fake a shot, bring the ball back to your body, and throw up a shot, all without coming back down, you have proven your worth in uncontestable fashion.

This liquid grace is an integral part of "black" ball, almost exclu- ¹⁰ sively the province of the playground player. Some white stars like Bob Cousy, Billy Cunningham, Doug Collins, and Kevin McHale had it; John Stockton of the Utah Jazz has it now: the body control, the moves to the basket, the free-ranging mobility. Most of them also possessed the surface ease that is integral to the "black" style; an incorporation of the ethic of mean streets — to "make it" is not just to have wealth but to have it without strain. Whatever the muscles and organs are doing, the face of the "black" star almost never shows it. Magic Johnson of the Lakers could bring the ball downcourt with two men on him, whip a pass through an invisible opening, cut to the basket, take a return pass, and hit the shot all with no more emotion than a quick smile. So stoic was San Antonio Spurs great George Gervin that he earned the nickname "Ice Man." (Interestingly, a black coach like San Antonio's John Lucan exhibits far less emotion on the bench than a white counterpart like Portland's Rick Adelman.)

If there is a single trait that characterizes "black" ball it is leaping 11 ability. Bob Cousy, ex-Celtic great and former pro coach, says that "when coaches get together, one is sure to say, 'I've got the one black kid in the country who can't jump.' When coaches see a white boy who can jump or who moves with extraordinary quickness, they say, 'He should have been born black, he's that good.'" This pervasive belief was immortalized by the title of the hit film *White Men Can't Jump.*

Don Nelson, now a top executive with the Golden State War- 12 riors, recalls that back in 1970, Dave Cowens, then a relatively unknown graduate of Florida State, prepared for his rookie pro season by playing in the Rucker League, an outdoor competition in Harlem playgrounds that pits pros against college kids and playground stars. So ferocious was Cowens's leaping ability, Nelson says, that "when the summer was over, everyone wanted to know who the white son of a bitch was who could jump so high." That's another way to overcome a crowd around the basket — just go over it.

Speed, mobility, quickness, acceleration, "the moves" — all of 13 these are catch-phrases that surround the "black" playground athlete, the style of play. So does the most racially tinged of attributes, "rhythm." Yet rhythm is what the black stars themselves talk about: feeling the flow of the game, finding the tempo of the dribble, the step, the shot. It is an instinctive quality (although it stems from hundreds of hours of practice), and it is one that has led to difficulty between system-oriented coaches and free-form players. "Cats from the street have their own rhythm when they play," said college dropout Bill Spivey, onetime New York high school star. "It's not a matter of somebody setting you up and you shooting. You *feel* the shot. When a coach holds you back, you lose the feel and it isn't fun anymore."

When legendary Brooklyn playground star Connie Hawkins was 14 winding up his NBA career under Laker coach Bill Sharman, he chafed under the methodical style of play. "He's systematic to the point where it begins to be a little too much. It's such an action-reaction type of game that when you have to do everything the same way, I think you lose something."

There is another kind of basketball that has grown up in America. 15 It is not played on asphalt playgrounds with a crowd of kids competing for the court; it is played on macadam driveways by one boy with a ball and a backboard nailed over the garage; it is played in gyms in the frigid winter of the rural Midwest and on Southern dirt courts. It is a mechanical, precise development of skills (when Don Nelson was an Iowa farm boy, his incentive to make his shots was that an errant rebound would land in the middle of chicken droppings). It is a game without frills, without flow, but with effectiveness. It is "white" basketball: jagged, sweaty, stumbling, intense. Where a "black" player overcomes an obstacle with finesse and body control, a "white" player reacts by outrunning or overpowering the obstacle.

By this definition, the Boston Celtics have been classically 16 "white" regardless of the pigmentation of the players. They have rarely suited up a player with dazzling moves; indeed, such a player would probably have made Red Auerbach swallow his cigar. Instead, the Celtic philosophy has been to wear you down with execution, with constant running, with the same play run again and again. The rebound by Bill Russell (or Dave Cowens or Robert Parrish) triggers the fast break, as everyone races downcourt; the ball goes to Bob Cousy (or John Havlicek or Larry Bird), who pulls up and takes the shot, or who drives and then finds Sam Jones (or Kevin McHale or M. L. Carr) free for an easy basket.

Perhaps the most definitively "white" position is that of the quick 17 forward, one without great moves to the basket, without highly developed shots, without the height and mobility for rebounding effectiveness. So what does he do?

He runs. He runs from the opening jump to the final buzzer. He 18 runs up and down the court, from base line to base line, back and forth under the basket, looking for the opening, the pass, the chance to take a quick step, the high-percentage shot. To watch Detroit's Bill Laimbeer or the Suns' Dan Majerle, players without speed or obvious moves, is to wonder what they are doing in the NBA — until you see them swing free and throw up a shot that, without demanding any apparent skill, somehow goes in the basket more frequently than the shots of many of their more skilled teammates. And to have watched the New York Knicks' (now U.S. Senator) Bill Bradley, or the Celtics' John Havlicek, is to have watched "white" ball at its best.

Havlicek or Laimbeer or the Phoenix Suns' Danny Ainge stands   19
in dramatic contrast to Michael Jordan or to the Philadelphia 76ers
legend Julius Erving. Erving had the capacity to make legends come
true, leaping from the foul line and slam-dunking the ball on his way
down; going up for a lay-up, pulling the ball to his body, and driving
under and up the other side of the rim, defying gravity and probability
with impossible moves and jumps. Michael Jordan of the Chicago
Bulls has been seen by thousands spinning a full 360 degrees in midair
before slamming the ball through the hoop.

When John Havlicek played, by contrast, he was the living   20
embodiment of his small-town Ohio background. He would bring the
ball downcourt, weaving left, then right, looking for a path. He
would swing the ball to a teammate, cut behind the pick, take the
pass, and release the shot in a flicker of time. It looked plain,
unvarnished. But it was a blend of skills that not more than half a
dozen other players in the league possessed.

To former pro Jim McMillian, a black who played quick forward   21
with "white" attributes, "it's a matter of environment. Julius Erving
grew up in a different environment from Havlicek. John came from
a very small town in Ohio. There everything was done the easy way,
the shortest distance between two points. It's nothing fancy; very few
times will he go one-on-one. He hits the lay-up, hits the jump shot,
makes the free throw, and after the game you look up and say, 'How
did he hurt us that much?'"

"White" ball, then, is the basketball of patience, method, and   22
sometimes brute strength. "Black" ball is the basketball of electric
self-expression. One player has all the time in the world to perfect
his skills, the other a need to prove himself. These are slippery
categories, because a poor boy who is black can play "white" and a
white boy of middle-class parents can play "black." Charles Oakley
of the New York Knicks and John Paxson of the Chicago Bulls are
athletes who seem to defy these categories.

And what makes basketball the most intriguing of sports is how   23
these styles do not necessarily clash; how the punishing intensity of
"white" players and the dazzling moves of the "blacks" can fit together,
a fusion of cultures that seems more and more difficult in the world
beyond the out-of-bounds line.

QUESTIONS ON MEANING

1. According to Greenfield, how did black athletes come to dominate professional basketball?
2. What differences does the author discern between "black" and "white" styles of play? How do exponents of the two styles differ in showing emotion?
3. Explain the author's reference to the word *rhythm* as "the most racially tinged of attributes" (para. 13).
4. Does Greenfield stereotype black and white players? Where in his essay does he admit there are players who don't fit neatly into his two categories?

QUESTIONS ON WRITING STRATEGY

1. How much do we have to know about professional basketball to appreciate Greenfield's essay? Is it written only for basketball fans, or for a general AUDIENCE?
2. In what passage in his essay does Greenfield begin comparing and contrasting? What is the function of the paragraphs that come before this passage?
3. In paragraph 5, the author compares a basketball court to a football field, a baseball diamond, and an ice hockey arena. What is the basis for his comparison?
4. OTHER METHODS. In addition to comparison and contrast and a good deal of DESCRIPTION, Greenfield uses CAUSE AND EFFECT when he accounts for the differences in playing style. In your own words, SUMMARIZE the author's point about school yards (para. 8) and his point about macadam driveways, gyms, and dirt courts (para. 15). Explain "the ethic of mean streets" (para. 10).

QUESTIONS ON LANGUAGE

1. Consult the dictionary if you need help in defining the following words: ethnic (para. 3); constricted (5); inhibitions, anonymity (8); uncontestable (9); finesse (15); execution (16); embodiment (20).
2. Talk to someone who knows basketball if you need help in understanding the head fake, the shoulder fake (para. 6); the fast break (16); the high-percentage shot (18); the jump shot (21). What kind of DICTION do you find in these instances?
3. When Greenfield says, "We are talking about culture, not chromosomes" (para. 4), how would you expect him to define these terms?

SUGGESTIONS FOR WRITING

1. In a paragraph or two, discuss how well you think Greenfield has surmounted the difficulties facing any writer who makes GENERALIZATIONS about people.
2. Compare and contrast a college basketball and professional basketball team, or the styles of two athletes in any sport.
3. Compare and contrast the styles of two people in the same line of work, showing how their work is affected by their different personalities. You might take, for instance, two singers, two taxi drivers, two bank tellers, two evangelists, two teachers, or two symphony orchestra conductors.
4. CRITICAL WRITING. Do you agree with Greenfield's observations about basketball styles? Consider the exceptions Greenfield cites (paras. 10, 21, 22), and muster any of your own. In an essay, EVALUATE whether Greenfield's essay can withstand these exceptions: In your opinion, are Greenfield's ideas valid?
5. CONNECTIONS. The following essay, Murray Ross's "Football Red and Baseball Green," proposes that "each sport contains a fundamental myth which it elaborates for its fans." First, read Ross's essay so that you understand just what he means by the myths in sports. Then write your own interpretation of the myths represented by the "black" and "white" styles of basketball play; or, if you prefer, write about the myth represented by the entire sport of basketball.

JEFF GREENFIELD ON WRITING

For *The Bedford Reader,* Jeff Greenfield told how he gathered his information for "The Black and White Truth About Basketball" from basketball professionals, and how he tried to contrast the two styles of play with humor and goodwill. "In the early 1970s," he commented, "I was spending a good deal of time playing hooky from my work as a political consultant writing books and magazine articles; and no writing was more enjoyable than sports reporting. . . . Coming from the world of politics where everything was debatable — who would win, whose position was right, who was engaging in 'desperation smear tactics' — I relished the world of sports, where winners and losers were clearly identifiable. . . .

"It was while writing about various star basketball players of the time — men like the New York Knicks' Willis Reed, the Boston Celtics' Dave Cowens — that I first began noticing how often offhand, utterly unmalicious racial references were being thrown about. A white player in practice would miss a rebound, and a black teammate would joke, 'Come on, man, jump like a brother.' A black player would lose a footrace for a ball, and someone would quip, 'Looks black, plays white.' It slowly became clear to me that many of those in the basketball world freely acknowledged that there were different styles of play that broke down, roughly speaking, into black and white characteristics.

"At first, it did not even occur to me that this would make a publishable magazine piece. For one thing, I came from a typical postwar liberal family, repulsed by the racial stereotypes which still dominated 'respectable' conversation. In a time when black Americans were heavily portrayed as happy-go-lucky, shiftless, childlike adults, consigned to success as athletes and tap-dancers, the idea that there was anything like a 'black' or 'white' way to play basketball would have seemed something out of a segregationist manifesto.

"For another, I have always been an enthusiastic follower of the sports pages and had never seen any such analysis in the many newspapers I read. Apparently, most sportswriters felt equally uncomfortable with a foray into race; it had, after all, taken baseball more than a half a century to admit blacks into its ranks. Indeed, one of the more common assertions of bigots in the 1930s and 1940s was that blacks could not be great athletes because 'they couldn't take the pressure.' It is easy to understand why race was not a comfortable basis on which to analyze athletic grace.

"In the end, I decided to write about 'black' and 'white' basketball because it made the game more enjoyable to me. Clearly, there *were* different ways to play the game; clearly the kind of self-assertion represented by the spectacular moves of black schoolyard ball was a reflection of how important the game was to an inner-city kid, for whom the asphalt court was the cheapest — maybe the only — release from a nasty, sometimes brutish, existence. And books such as Pete Axthelm's *The City Game* and David Wolf's *Foul!* had brilliantly explored the significance of basketball in the urban black world of modern America.

"I talked with players and sportswriters alike when I wrote the article; without exception, they approached the subject as I did: with humor, un-self-consciously. Perhaps it is a measure of the progress we have made in racial matters that no one — black or white — thought it insulting or offensive to remark on the different styles of play, to note that the gravity-defying slam-dunks of a Michael Jordan and the carefully calibrated shots of a Dan Majerle are two facets of the same game."

FOR DISCUSSION

1. What gave Greenfield the idea for his essay?
2. What aspects of his topic made Greenfield hesitant to write about it?
   What persuaded him to go ahead?

MURRAY ROSS

Born in 1942 in Pasadena, California, MURRAY ROSS was educated at Williams College and the University of California at Berkeley. In 1975 he was hired by the University of Colorado at Colorado Springs to found and direct a theater program, and he has been there ever since teaching English, humanities, and theater. He has published articles on film and Elizabethan drama, but most of his creative attention, he says, goes to directing plays. As artistic director of Theatreworks, the resident theater company at Colorado Springs, he has directed fourteen of Shakespeare's plays and aspires to complete the entire canon.

Football Red and Baseball Green

By his own testimony, Murray Ross's only involvement in football and baseball "is confined to the couch." But as this essay shows, spectating can afford a powerful position from which to see and understand. Like Jeff Greenfield in "The Black and White Truth About Basketball" (p. 199), Ross perceives that sports represent more in American life than "just games." "Football Red and Baseball Green" first appeared in *Chicago Review* in 1971. Murray Ross revised and updated it for this edition of *The Bedford Reader.*

Every Superbowl ever played has rated among the top television draws of its year. By now, after nearly three decades, we know the game has a more than fair chance of being not so hot, some sort of mismatched rout. Even so, everyone — and I mean just about *every-one* — watches. This revelation is just one way of indicating how popular and compelling spectator sports are in this country. Americans, or American men anyway, seem to care about the games they watch as much as the Elizabethans cared about their plays, and I suspect for some of the same reasons. There is, in sport, some of the rudimentary drama found in popular theater: familiar plots, type characters, heroic and comic action spiced with new and unpredictable variations. And common to watching both activities is the sense of participation in a shared tradition and in shared fantasies. If sport exploits these fantasies without significantly transcending them, it seems no less satisfying for all that.

It is my guess that sport spectating involves something more than the vicarious pleasures of identifying with athletic prowess. I suspect

Thesis 1

2

209

that each sport contains a fundamental myth which it elaborates for its fans, and that our pleasure in watching such games derives in part from belonging briefly to the mythical world which the game and its players bring to life. I am especially interested in baseball and football because they are so popular and so uniquely *American;* they began here and unlike basketball they have not been widely exported. Thus whatever can be said, mythically, about these games would seem to apply to our culture.

Baseball's myth may be the easier to identify since we have a greater historical perspective on the game. It was an instant success during the Industrialization, and most probably it was a reaction to the squalor, the faster pace, and the dreariness of the new conditions. Baseball was old-fashioned right from the start; it seems conceived in nostalgia, in the resuscitation of the Jeffersonian dream. It established an artificial rural environment, one removed from the toil of an urban life, which spectators could be admitted to and temporarily breathe in. Baseball is a *pastoral* sport, and I think the game can be best understood as this kind of art. For baseball does what all good pastoral does — it creates an atmosphere in which everything exists in harmony.

Consider, for instance, the spatial organization of the game. A kind of controlled openness is created by having everything fan out from home plate, and the crowd sees the game through an arranged perspective that is rarely violated. Visually this means that the game is always seen as a constant, rather calm whole, and that the players and the playing field are viewed in relationship to each other. Each player has a certain position, a special area to tend, and the game often seems to be as much a dialogue between the fielders and the field as it is a contest between the players themselves: Will that ball get through the hole? Can that outfielder run under that fly? As a moral genre, pastoral asserts the virtue of communion with nature. As a competitive game, baseball asserts that the team which best relates to the playing field (by hitting the ball in the right places) will win.

Having established its landscape, pastoral art operates to eliminate any reference to that bigger, more disturbing, more real world it has left behind. All games are to some extent insulated from the outside by having their own rules, but baseball has a circular structure as well which furthers its comfortable feeling of self-sufficiency. By this I mean that every motion of extention is also one of return — a ball hit outside is a *home* run, a full circle. Home — familiar, peaceful, secure — it is the beginning and end. You must go out but you must come back; only the completed movement is registered.

Time is a serious threat to any form of pastoral. The genre poses   6
a timeless world of perpetual spring, and it does its best to silence
the ticking of clocks which remind us that in time the green world
fades into winter. One's sense of time is directly related to what
happens in it, and baseball is so structured as to stretch out and
ritualize whatever action it contains. Dramatic moments are few, and
they are almost always isolated by the routine texture of normal play.
It is certainly a game of climax and drama, but it is perhaps more a
game of repeated and predictable action: the foul balls, the walks,
the pitcher fussing around on the mound, the lazy fly ball to center
field. This is, I think, as it should be, for baseball exists as an
alternative to a world of too much action, struggle, and change. It is
a merciful release from a more grinding and insistent tempo, and its
time, as William Carlos Williams suggests, makes a virtue out of
idleness simply by providing it:

> The crowd at the ball game
> is moved uniformly
> by a spirit of uselessness
> Which delights them. . . .

Within this expanded and idle time the baseball fan is at liberty   7
to become a ceremonial participant and a lover of style. Because the
action is normalized, how something is done becomes as important
as the action itself. Thus baseball's most delicate and detailed aspects
are often, to the spectator, the most interesting. The pitcher's
windup, the anticipatory crouch of the infielders, the quick waggle
of the bat as it poises for the pitch — these subtle miniature movements are as meaningful as the home runs and the strikeouts. It
somehow matters in baseball that all the tiny rituals are observed:
The shortstop must kick the dirt and the umpire must brush the plate
with his pocket broom. In a sense baseball is largely a continuous
series of small gestures, and I think it characteristic that the game's
most treasured moment came when Babe Ruth pointed to where he
subsequently hit a home run.

Baseball is a game where the little things mean a lot, and this,   8
together with its clean serenity, its open space, and its ritualized
action, is enough to place it in a world of yesterday. Baseball evokes
for us a past which may never have been ours, but which we believe
was, and certainly that is enough. In the Second World War, supposedly, we fought for "Baseball, Mom, and Apple Pie," and considering what baseball means, that phrase is a good one. We fought then
for the right to believe in a green world of tranquility and uninter-
rupted contentment, where the little things would count. But now

the possibilities of such a world are more remote, and it seems that while the entertainment of such a dream has an enduring appeal, it is no longer sufficient for our fantasies. I think this may be why baseball is no longer our preeminent national pastime, and why its myth is being replaced by another more appropriate to the new realities (and fantasies) of our time.

Football, especially professional football, is the embodiment of a 9 newer myth, one which in many respects is opposed to baseball's. The fundamental difference is that football is not a pastoral game; it is a heroic one. Football wants to convert men into gods; it suggests that magnificence and glory are as desirable as happiness. Football is designed, therefore, to impress its audience rather differently than baseball.

As a pastoral game, baseball attempts to close the gap between 10 the players and the crowd. It creates the illusion, for instance, that with a lot of hard work, a little luck, and possibly some extra talent, the average spectator might well be playing, not watching. For most of us can do a few of the things the ball players do: catch a pop-up, field a ground ball, and maybe get a hit once in a while. As a heroic game, football is not concerned with a shared community of near-equals. It seeks almost the opposite relationship between its spectators and players, one which stresses the distance between them. We are not invited to identify with Thurman Thomas, Randall Cunningham, or any other of football's megaheroes any more than we are with Zeus. Football's heroes are systematically catapulted into Olympus; they are more than human. Commercial after commercial portrays them as giants of the earth, prodigies to be seen, properly, with awe. Most of us lesser beings could not begin to imagine ourselves playing their game without also imagining our instant humiliation and possible death. The players are that much bigger, that much faster than we are. Watching, we have enough problems figuring out what's going on. In baseball, most of what happens is what meets the eye, but in football each play involves twenty-two men acting simultaneously in combat: It's too much for a single pair of eyes to follow. So we now have two or three television commentators to explain the action as it unfolds, then another three at halftime to evaluate. Coaches have teams of spotters in the stands and hundreds of hours of videos to watch. There is a seemingly infinite proliferation of "meaningful" data; full comprehension remains on the horizon.

If football is distanced from its fans by its intricacy and "super- 11 human" play, it nonetheless remains a compelling and intense spectacle. Baseball, as I have implied, dissolves time and urgency in a green expanse, thereby creating a luxurious and peaceful sense of leisure. As is appropriate to a heroic enterprise, football reverses this procedure and converts space into time. The game is ideally played in an oval stadium, not in a "park," and the difference is the elimination of perspective. This makes football a perfect television game, because even at first hand it offers a flat, perpetually moving foreground (wherever the ball is). The eye in baseball viewing opens up; in football it zeroes in. There is no democratic vista in football, and spectators are not asked to relax, but to concentrate. You are encouraged to watch the drama, not a medley of ubiquitous gestures, and you are constantly reminded that this event is taking place in time. The third element in baseball is the field; in football this element is the clock. Traditionally heroes do reckon with time, and football players are no exceptions. Time in football is wound up inexorably until it reaches the breaking point in the last minutes of a close game. More often than not it is the clock which emerges as the real enemy, and it is the sense of time running out that regularly produces a pitch of tension uncommon in baseball.

A further reason for football's intensity is that the game is played 12 like a war, with television putting the fans in the war room. The idea is to win by going through, around, or over the opposing team, and the battle lines, quite literally, are drawn on every play. Violence is somewhere at the heart of the game, and the combat quality is reflected in football's army language ("blitz," "trap," "zone," "bomb," "trenches," etc.). Coaches often sound like generals when they discuss their strategy. Woody Hayes, the legendary coach of Ohio State, explained his quarterback option play as if it had been conceived in the Pentagon: "You know," he said, "the most effective kind of warfare is siege. You have to attack on broad fronts. And that's all the option is — attacking on a broad front. You know General Sherman ran an option through the South."

Football like war is an arena for action, and like war football 13 leaves little room for personal style. It seems to be a game which projects "character" more than personality, and for the most part football heroes, publicly, are a rather similar lot. They tend to become personifications rather than individuals, and, with certain exceptions, they are easily read emblematically as embodiments of heroic qualities such as "strength," "confidence," "grace," etc. — clichés really, but forceful enough when represented by the play of a Reggie White, a Troy Aikman, or a Jim Rice. Perhaps this simplification of personality results in part from the heroes' total identification with their mission, to the extent that they become more characterized by what they do

than by what they intrinsically "are." At any rate football does not
make as many allowances for the idiosyncrasies that baseball actually
seems to encourage, and as a result there have been few football
characters as eccentric and as recognizably human as, say, the pasta-
loving Tommy Lasorda, the surly Jose Canseco, the exuberant Willie
Mays.

A further reason for the underdeveloped qualities of football   14
personalities, and one which gets us to the heart of the game's
modernity, is that football is very much a game of modern technology.
Football's action is largely interaction, and the game's complexity
requires that its players mold themselves into a perfectly coordinated
unit. The smoothness and precision of play execution are insatiable
preoccupations, and most coaches believe that the team which makes
the fewest mistakes will be the team that wins. Individual identity
thus comes to be associated with the team or unit that one plays for
to a much greater extent than in baseball. Yogi Berra was not so
much a Yankee as a phenomenon unto himself, a man with his own
language and a future as a cartoon character. But Mike Ditka, though
personally forceful and particular, is mostly a Chicago Bear. Now,
relieved of his stewardship, he's a publicly displaced identity, a lost
man. The gods of football stand out not only because of their individual acts, but even more because they epitomize the style of the
groups they belong to and represent. The archetypal ideal is Camelot,
or what Camelot was advertised as: a group of men who function as
equal parts of a larger whole, dependent on each other for total
meaning.

The humanized machine as hero is something very new in sport,   15
for in baseball anything approaching a machine has always been
suspect. The famous Yankee teams of the fifties were almost flawlessly
perfect, yet they never were especially popular. Their admirers took
pains to romanticize their precision into something more natural than
plain mechanics — Joe DiMaggio, for instance, became the "Yankee
Clipper." Even so, most people seemed to want the Brooklyn Dodgers
(the "bums") to thrash them in the World Series. One of the most
memorable triumphs in recent decades — the victory of the Amazin'
Mets in 1969 — was memorable precisely because it was the triumph
of a random collection of inspired rejects over the superbly skilled,
fully integrated, and almost homogenized Baltimore Orioles. In baseball, machinery seems tantamount to villainy, whereas in football
this smooth perfection is part of the unexpected integration a cham-
pionship team must attain.

It is not surprising, really, that we should have a game which   16 asserts the heroic function of a mechanized group, since we have become a country where collective identity is a reality. Yet football's collective pattern is only one aspect of the way in which it seems to echo our contemporary environment. The game, like our society, can be thought of as a cluster of people living under great tension in a state of perpetual flux. The potential for sudden disaster or triumph is as great in football as it is in our own age, and although there is something ludicrous in equating interceptions with assassinations and long passes with moonshots, there is also something valid and appealing in the analogies. It seems to me that football does successfully reflect those salient and common conditions which affect us all, and it does so with the end of making us feel better about them and our lot. For one thing, it makes us feel that something can be released and connected in all this chaos; out of the accumulated pile of bodies something can emerge — a runner breaks into the clear or a pass finds its way to a receiver. To the spectator, plays such as these are human and dazzling. They suggest to the audience what it has hoped for (and been told) all along, that technology is still a tool and not a master. Fans get living proof of this every time a long pass is completed; they appreciate that it is the result of careful planning, perfect integration, and an effective "pattern," but they see too that it is human and that what counts as well is man, his desire, his natural skill, and his "grace under pressure." Football metaphysically yokes heroic action and technology by violence to suggest that they are mutually supportive. It's a doubtful proposition, but given how we live, it has its attractions.

Football, like the space program, is a game in the grand manner.   17
Homer would have chronicled it; Beowulf would have played fullback. Baseball's roots are at least as deep; it's a variation of the Satyr play, it's a feast of fools. But today their mythic resonance has been eroded by commercial success. Like so much else in America, their character has been modified by money.

More and more, both baseball and football are being played   18
indoors on rugs in multipurpose spaces. It doesn't make good business sense to play outside where it might rain and snow and do terrible things; it isn't really prudent to play on a natural field that can be destroyed in a single afternoon; and why build a whole stadium or park that's good for only one game? The fans in these stadiums are constantly diverted by huge whiz-bang scoreboards that dominate and describe the action, while the fans at home are constantly being reminded by at least three lively sportscasters of the other games, the other sports, and the other shows that are coming up later on the

same stations. Both pro football and pro baseball now play vastly extended seasons, so that the World Series now takes place on chilly October nights and football is well under way before the summer ends. From my point of view all this is regrettable, because these changes tend to remove the games from their intangible but palpable mythic contexts. No longer clearly set in nature, no longer given the chance to breathe and steep in their own special atmosphere, both baseball and football risk becoming demythologized. As fans we seem to participate a little less in mythic ritual these days, while being subjected even more to the statistics, the hype, and the salary disputes that proceed from a jazzed-up, inflated, yet somehow flattened sporting world — a world that looks too much like the one we live in all the time.

Still, there is much to be thankful for, and every season seems to 19 bring its own contribution to mythic lore. Some people will think this nonsense, and I must admit there are good reasons for finding both games simply varieties of decadence.

In its preoccupation with mechanization, and in its open display 20 of violence, football is the more obvious target for social moralists, but I wonder if this is finally more "corrupt" than the seductive picture of sanctuary and tranquility that baseball has so artfully drawn for us. Almost all sport is vulnerable to such criticism because it is not strictly ethical in intent, and for this reason there will always be room for puritans like the Elizabethan John Stubbes, who howled at the "wanton fruits which these cursed pastimes bring forth." As a long-time dedicated fan of almost anything athletic, I confess myself out of sympathy with most of this; which is to say, I guess, that I am vulnerable to those fantasies which these games support, and that I find happiness in the company of people who feel as I do.

A final note. It is interesting that the heroic and pastoral con- 21 ventions which underlie our most popular sports are almost classically opposed. The contrasts are familiar: city versus country, aspirations versus contentment, activity versus peace, and so on. Judging from the rise of professional football, we seem to be slowly relinquishing that unfettered rural vision of ourselves that baseball so beautifully mirrors, and we have come to cast ourselves in a genre more reflective of a nation confronted by constant and unavoidable challenges. Right now, like the Elizabethans, we seem to share both heroic and pastoral yearnings, and we reach out to both. Perhaps these divided needs account in part for the enormous attention we as a nation now give to spectator sports. For sport provides one place where we can have our football and our baseball too.

QUESTIONS ON MEANING

1. SUMMARIZE the features Ross mentions for both baseball and football. Do the two sports have any similarities?
2. What do you see as Ross's principal PURPOSE?
3. What is Ross's THESIS? Where does he state it?
4. What problem does Ross introduce in paragraph 17? To what does he attribute the coexistence of football and baseball in his CONCLUSION?

QUESTIONS ON WRITING STRATEGY

1. Does Ross give equal treatment to baseball and football? To similarities and differences? What explains his strategy?
2. What types of EVIDENCE does Ross use to support his opinions?
3. What does Ross assume about his AUDIENCE? Does he seem to address only sports fans or nonfans as well?
4. What is the author's TONE? How does he achieve it? Is it effective, do you think?
5. OTHER METHODS. Like all comparisons, Ross's depends heavily on DIVISION or ANALYSIS, the method of separating something (here two sports) into its elements. List the contrasting elements of baseball and football that Ross identifies.

QUESTIONS ON LANGUAGE

1. How does Ross use language to extend his SIMILE that football "is played like a war" (para. 12)?
2. Study Ross's ALLUSIONS — for instance, to Elizabethan theater (para. 1), the "Jeffersonian dream" (3), Babe Ruth pointing his bat (7), Zeus and Olympus (10), Homer and Beowulf (17). What does each one refer to? What do they add to the essay?
3. How much baseball and football does the reader need to know to follow Ross's essay? Did you have problems with any terms or names?
4. Consult your dictionary if any of these words are unfamiliar: revelation, rudimentary (para. 1); vicarious, prowess (2); squalor, resuscitation, pastoral (3); preeminent (8); embodiment (9); proliferation (10); inexorably (11); emblematically, idiosyncrasies (13); epitomize (14); tantamount (15); flux, ludicrous, salient (16); intangible, palpable (18); decadence (19); sanctuary (20); aspirations, relinquishing, unfettered (21).

SUGGESTIONS FOR WRITING

1. Select two sports or other activities you enjoy watching or participating in: football and hockey, dance and swimming, music and dance, whatever. Write an essay comparing and contrasting the two activities on some point, such as what they represent, what they demand, or what they give the spectator or participant.

2. Ross regrets the modernization and commercialization of sports — artificial turf, indoor multiuse stadiums, giant scoreboards, extended seasons, salary disputes, and so on (para. 18). In an essay, argue for or against some element of contemporary sports (it may be one Ross doesn't mention). Be sure to compare old and new ways of doing things and to make your THESIS clear: Why exactly is your subject a good or bad thing?

3. CRITICAL WRITING. Like all good arguers, Ross acknowledges a potential objection to his observations about baseball and football — namely, that his ideas are "nonsense," that "there are good reasons for finding both games simply varieties of decadence" (para. 19). Write an essay in which you argue for or against Ross's mythologizing of sports. (If you don't find sports decadent, you may still object on other grounds.) Support your argument with specific EVIDENCE from Ross's essay.

4. CONNECTIONS. Write an essay comparing and contrasting two essays on sport: Ross's "Football Red and Baseball Green" and Jeff Greenfield's "The Black and White Truth About Basketball" (p. 199). How are the two authors' attitudes toward sports the same or different? Which is the more ambitious essay, do you think? Which is the more successful?

MURRAY ROSS ON WRITING

Murray Ross revealed his writing habits and pleasures in these comments written especially for *The Bedford Reader*:

"Unlike many — nearly all — of the essayists in this anthology, I am not a Writer. Writing is neither my primary craft nor trade; it's something I slip into now and then, and almost always just because I want to. I am in every sense an amateur writer, a possibly vanishing breed. What I mean to say is that I actually write for the fun of it, and when I want to. This puts me in a privileged position, since neither the state of my soul nor my pocketbook critically depends on the writing I produce.

"I wrote 'Football Red and Baseball Green' years ago as a graduate student, because I had a great place to write, and I think finding your place to write is an essential part of the enterprise. Mine was on an old door I installed in a sun porch on the second floor of the Berkeley house we rented; from the desk I could see both San Francisco Bay and the Golden Gate Bridge, and I just liked sitting there. I've never had it so good since. I also began with some connections I wanted to make between a graduate course I was taking on the pastoral and sports, which I spent a lot of time watching. So I sat down in my place and worked it out. I had no idea I was writing a model comparison/contrast essay.

"Writing for me has become an occasional but essential activity. I like the control it gives me, and the solitude — a very active solitude which suits my temperament. I like the way, sitting in my place, writing takes me places, the way it sends out lines and takes on a wonderful life of its own. If you are writing as I do, as an amateur, without specific obligation, you are completely free. This is rare. Writing is one of the few activities in my life where discipline and liberty naturally reinforce each other: I like the way writing rapidly breeds my own little herd of sentences and paragraphs, and I like rounding them up, brushing them down, and putting them in order. So writing for me, in the best sense, is play.

"I consider myself a mighty lucky fellow in this respect. After years of writing drudgery (which probably helped my writing), I now write only when I want to, and only about what interests me. I do this about three times a year. I've discovered there are some things that ask to be written about, because writing gives you the chance to explore more thoroughly than conversation or meditation. When you write, eventually you may get to say, 'Oh, so *that*'s what I think!' And you may get to think it in a form that gives you pleasure. Finding your voice is a legitimate form of self-fashioning. We all should cultivate our personal styles, which then can be infinitely refined.

"No student reading this is likely to be writing as an amateur: You're here under some form of voluntary compulsion. But hang in there. Someday you too may find yourself sitting down and writing, with no external agenda. Then, to your astonishment, you may discover that writing turns out to be what you may have least expected: a fairly reliable form of happiness."

FOR DISCUSSION

1. What does Ross mean when he says, "I had no idea I was writing a model comparison/contrast essay"? What did he think he was writing?
2. What does Ross get out of writing now? What does it matter that the effort is voluntary?
3. Do you ever have a chance to do the sort of voluntary writing Ross describes? If so, do you find the same benefits he does, or are yours different?

ADDITIONAL WRITING TOPICS

Comparison and Contrast

1. In an essay replete with examples, compare and contrast the two subjects in any one of the following pairs:

   The main characters of two films, stories, or novels
   Women and men as consumers
   The styles of two runners
   Alexander Hamilton and Thomas Jefferson: their opposing views of central government
   How city dwellers and country dwellers spend their leisure time
   The presentation styles of two television news commentators

2. Approach a comparison and contrast essay on one of the following general subjects by explaining why you prefer one thing to the other:

   Two buildings on campus or in town
   Two football teams
   German-made cars and Detroit-made cars
   Two horror movies
   Television when you were a child and television today
   City life and small-town or rural life
   Malls and main streets
   Two neighborhoods
   Two sports

3. Write an essay in which you compare a reality (what actually exists) with an ideal (what should exist). Some possible topics:

   The affordable car
   Available living quarters
   A job
   The college curriculum
   Public transportation
   Financial aid to college students

5

PROCESS ANALYSIS
Explaining Step by Step

THE METHOD

A chemist working for a soft-drink firm is asked to improve on a competitor's product, Orange Quench. First, she chemically tests a sample to figure out what's in the drink. This is the method of DIVISION OR ANALYSIS, the separation of something into its parts in order to understand it (see the following chapter). Then the chemist writes a report telling her boss how to make a drink like Orange Quench, but better. This recipe is a special kind of analysis, called *process analysis:* explaining step by step how to do something or how something is done.

Like any type of analysis, process analysis divides a subject into its components. It divides a continuous action into stages. Processes much larger and more involved than the making of an orange drink also may be analyzed. When geologists explain how a formation such as the Grand Canyon occurred — a process taking several hundred million years — they describe the successive layers of sediment deposited by oceans, floods, and wind; then the great uplift of the entire region by underground forces; and then the erosion, visible to us today, by the Colorado River and its tributaries, by little streams and flash floods, by crumbling and falling rock, and by wind. Exactly what are the geologists doing in this explanation? They are taking a complicated event (or process) and dividing it into parts. They are telling us what happened first, second, and third, and what is still happening today.

Because it is useful in explaining what is complicated, process analysis is a favorite method of scientists such as geologists. The method, however, may be useful to anybody. Two kinds of process analysis are very familiar to you. The first is directive: It tells a reader how to do something or make something. You meet it when you read a set of instructions for assembling newly purchased stereo components, or follow the directions to a stereo store ("Turn right at the blinker and follow Patriot Boulevard for 2.4 miles . . ."). The second kind is informative: It tells us how something is done, or how it takes place. This is the kind we often read out of curiosity. Such an essay may tell of events beyond our control: how atoms behave when split, how lions hunt, how a fertilized egg develops into a child. In this chapter, you will find examples of both kinds of process analysis — both the "how to" and the "how." In a practical directive, Merrill Markoe, with tongue in cheek, tells you how to conduct a conversation. In a spellbinding informative essay, Jessica Mitford explains how corpses are embalmed; but, clearly, she doesn't expect you to rush down to your basement and give her instructions a try.

Sometimes the method is used very imaginatively. Foreseeing that the sun eventually will cool, the earth shrink, the oceans freeze, and all life perish, an astronomer who cannot possibly behold the end of the world nevertheless can write a process analysis of it. An exercise in learned guesswork, such an essay divides a vast and almost inconceivable event into stages that, taken one at a time, become clearer and more readily imaginable.

Whether it is useful or useless (but fun to imagine), an effective process analysis can grip readers and even hold them fascinated. Say you were proposing a change in the procedures for course registration at your school. You could argue your point until you were out of words, but you would get nowhere if you failed to tell your readers exactly how the new process would work: That's what makes your proposal sing. Leaf through a current issue of a newsstand magazine, and you will find that process analysis abounds in it. You may meet, for instance, articles telling you how to tenderize cuts of meat, sew homemade designer jeans, lose fat, cut hair, play the money markets, arouse a bored mate, and program a computer. Less practical, but not necessarily less interesting, are the informative articles: how brain surgeons work, how diamonds are formed, how cities fight crime. Readers, it seems, have an unslakable thirst for process analysis. In every issue of the *New York Times Book Review,* we find an entire best-seller list devoted to "Advice, How-to and Miscellaneous," including books on how to make money in real estate, how to lose weight, how to find a good mate, and how to lose a bad one. Evidently, if anything will still make an American crack open a book, it is a step-by-step explanation of how he or she, too, can be a success at living.

THE PROCESS

Here are suggestions for writing an effective process analysis of your own. (In fact, what you are about to read is itself a process analysis.)

1. Understand clearly the process you are about to analyze. Think it through. This preliminary survey will make the task of writing far easier for you.

2. If you are giving a set of detailed instructions, ask yourself: Are there any preparatory steps a reader ought to take? If there are, list them. (These might include, "Remove the packing from the components," or, "First, lay out three eggs, one pound of Sheboygan bratwurst. . . .")

3. List the steps or stages in the process. Try setting them down in chronological order, one at a time — if this is possible. Some processes, however, do not happen in an orderly sequence, but occur all at once. If, for instance, you are writing an account of a typical earthquake, what do you mention first? The shifting of underground rock strata? Cracks in the earth? Falling houses? Bursting water mains? Toppling trees? Mangled cars? Casualties? (Here is a subject for which the method of CLASSIFICATION, to be discussed in Chapter 7, may come to your aid. You might sort out apparently simultaneous events into categories: injury to people; damage to homes, to land, to public property.)

4. Now glance back over your list, making sure you haven't omitted anything or instructed your reader to take the steps in the wrong order. Sometimes a stage of a process may contain a number of smaller stages. Make sure none has been left out. If any seems particularly tricky or complicated, underline it on your list to remind yourself when you write your essay to slow down and detail it with extra care.

5. Ask yourself: Will I use any specialized or technical terms? If

you will, be sure to define them. You'll sympathize with your reader if you have ever tried to work a Hong Kong–made shortwave radio that comes with an instruction booklet written in translatorese, full of unexplained technical jargon; or if you have ever tried to assemble a plastic tricycle according to a directive that reads, "Position sleeve casing on wheel center in fork with shaft in tong groove, and gently but forcibly tap in medium pal nut head. . . ."

6. Use time-markers or TRANSITIONS. These words or phrases indicate *when* one stage of a process stops and the next begins, and they greatly aid your reader in following you. Here, for example, is a paragraph of plain medical prose that makes good use of the helpful time-markers printed in *italics*. (The paragraph is adapted from Alan F. Guttmacher's *Pregnancy and Birth.*)

> In the human, *thirty-six hours after* the egg is fertilized, a two-cell egg appears. A twelve-cell development takes place *in seventy-two hours.* The egg is *still* round and has increased little in diameter. In this respect it is like a real estate development. *At first* a road bisects the whole area; *then* a cross road divides it into quarters, and *later* other roads divide it into eighths and twelfths. This happens without the taking of any more land, simply by subdivision of the original tract. *On the third or fourth day,* the egg passes from the Fallopian tube into the uterus. *By the fifth day* the original single large cell has subdivided into sixty small cells and floats about the slitlike uterine cavity *a day or two longer, then* adheres to the cavity's inner lining. *By the twelfth day* the human egg is already firmly implanted. Impregnation is *now* completed, *as yet* unbeknown to the woman. *At present,* she has not even had time to miss her first menstrual period, and other symptoms of pregnancy are *still several days distant.*

Brief as these time-markers are, they define each stage of the human egg's journey. Note how the writer, after declaring in the second sentence that the egg forms twelve cells, backtracks for a moment and retraces the process by which the egg has subdivided, comparing it (by a brief ANALOGY) to a piece of real estate. When using time-markers, vary them so that they won't seem mechanical. If you can, avoid the monotonous repetition of a fixed phrase (*In the fourteenth stage . . .* , *In the fifteenth stage . . .*). Even boring time-markers, though, are better than none at all. As in any chronological narrative, words and phrases such as *in the beginning, first, second, next, after that, three seconds later, at the same time,* and *finally* can help a process to move smoothly in the telling and lodge firmly in the reader's mind.

7. When you begin writing a first draft, state your analysis in

generous detail, even at the risk of being wordy. When you revise, it will be easier to delete than to amplify.

8. Finally, when your essay is finished, reread it carefully. If it is a simple directive ("How to Eat an Ice Cream Cone without Dribbling"), ask a friend to try it out. See if somebody else can follow your instructions without difficulty. If you have written an informative process analysis ("How a New Word Enters the Dictionary"), ask others to read your essay and tell you whether the process unfolds as clearly in their minds as it does in yours.

PROCESS ANALYSIS IN A PARAGRAPH:
TWO ILLUSTRATIONS

Using Process Analysis to Write About Television

The timer on your videocassette recorder permits you to record up to eight programs over a two-week period even when you are not at home. For each program you wish to record in your absence, locate an empty program number by pushing the *P* button until a flashing number appears on the TV screen. The next four steps set the information for the program. First, push the *Day* button until the day and date show on the screen. The screen will flash *On* until you set the starting time. (Be sure the time is set correctly for A.M. or P.M.) Then push the *Off* button and set the ending time (again, watching A.M. or P.M.). When the times have been set, push the *Chan* button and set the channel using the unit's channel selector. You may review the program information by pushing the *Check* button. When you are satisfied that the settings are correct, push *Timer* to set the timer to operate. (The unit cannot be operated manually while the timer is on.)

COMMENT. In this directive process analysis adapted from a VCR user's manual, the writer neatly lays out the steps necessary to program a machine for timed recording. (Of course, drawings would accompany any such instructions in an actual manual to make the steps even clearer.) The writer introduces the purpose of the process in the first sentence, pauses once to preview "the next four steps," and provides a way of checking that the process has been performed correctly — all to help users understand the instructions and avoid mistakes. The separate steps are indicated with time-markers ("first," "until you set," "then," "When the times have been set," "When you are satisfied"). Notice that the writer avoids any temptation to digress to other functions of the machine (as, indeed, one real and almost useless VCR manual did by stopping midstream to explain three different speeds for taping). By the way, the writer's use of the second person ("you") along with sentences of command ("Push the *Day* button . . .") is quite usual in directive process analyses.

Using Process Analysis in an Academic Discipline

The generation of rain by the coalescence process depends on the occurrence of oversize water droplets that are larger than twenty micrometers in radius. An oversize droplet falls just a bit faster than the typical droplet, and it grows by colliding with and sweeping up smaller droplets in its path. Rising currents of air carry the swelling droplets upward faster than they can fall out of the cloud, allowing them more time to grow. A droplet requires about half an hour to grow to raindrop size by coalescence, and the rain cloud must be at least 2.5 km (1.6 miles) thick to contain the growing drops long enough for them to become raindrops. Thinner clouds limit the growth of drops by coalescence, resulting in *drizzle,* a form of precipitation that consists of very tiny drops that "float" rather than fall to the surface. Pavements made wet by drizzle can be very hazardous for motorists, but drizzle never produces significant quantities of precipitation.

COMMENT. This paragraph, from Robert A. Muller and Theodore M. Oberlander's *Physical Geography Today: A Portrait of a Planet,* clearly illustrates the method of informative process analysis. In it, the authors detail one of the ways in which minuscule water droplets coalesce to form raindrops large enough to fall to earth. The most interesting detail, perhaps, is that the droplets have to travel upward and collide and combine with other droplets before they have enough weight to fall down. In organizing their analysis, the authors proceed step by step, making the point as they move through the process that conditions have to be right: The clouds have to be thick enough. If they aren't, the end result will be drizzle rather than rain.

MERRILL MARKOE

A comedian and comedy writer, MERRILL MARKOE was born in New York City in 1950 and received an M.F.A. from the University of California, Berkeley, in 1974. She worked for one year as a drawing teacher and then tried stand-up comedy. While performing in Los Angeles in 1977, she met David Letterman and went on to win four Emmy Awards as a writer for *Late Night with David Letterman*. She wrote and starred in several cable TV specials, including *This Week Indoors* and *Merrill Markoe's Guide to Glamorous Living*. She won Writers' Guild and Ace awards for *Not Necessarily the News*. Markoe's essays for *New York Woman* are collected in *What the Dogs Have Taught Me* (1992). The creator of Stupid Pet Tricks lives in Malibu, California, with her four dogs.

Conversation Piece

"Conversation Piece" is one of the essays appearing originally in the magazine *New York Woman* and then in *What the Dogs Have Taught Me*. In this essay, Markoe shares one of her wryly humorous takes on contemporary social customs. Another essay about conversation, approaching the subject from quite a different angle, is Brenda Ueland's "Tell Me More" (p. 233).

I recently spent one of those weeks where I hardly spoke a word   1
out loud. This is the sort of life experience that is almost totally unimaginable in New York City, where one's proximity to complete strangers causes a regular number of pointless verbal exchanges. I call them verbal exchanges because I don't think "I was here first" "Well, what do you want? A medal?" can be classified as a conversation per se.

I have been giving some serious thought to the nature of conver-   2
sation (as serious as I am capable of) just in case I ever have one again.

First, it is important to note that men and women regard con-   3
versation quite differently. For women it is a passion, a sport, an activity even more important to life than eating because it doesn't involve weight gain. The first sign of closeness among women is when they find themselves engaging in endless, secretless rounds of conversation with one another. And as soon as a woman begins to relax and feel comfortable in a relationship with a man, she tries to have

that type of conversation with him as well. However, the first sign that a man is feeling close to a woman is when he admits that he'd rather she please quiet down so he can hear the TV. A man who feels truly intimate with a woman often reserves for her and her alone the precious gift of one-word answers. Everyone knows that the surest way to spot a successful long-term relationship is to look around a restaurant for the table where no one is talking. Ah . . . now *that's* real love.

But to get to that blissful state, the relationship usually passes   4 through a conversational stage first, which is why I thought I'd take this opportunity to present:

The Merrill Markoe Course in Conversation

What is a conversation? For our purposes, it is any exchange of   5 more than two remarks that does not end in an act of violence. The successful conversationalist always remembers to first remove all extraneous objects from the mouth (and hide them, unless you are prepared to make that the topic of the conversation, and quite frankly I have found that admitting "I just *like* the feel of packing materials between my teeth and I don't really care that they're made of toxic chemicals" is not the sort of opening remark that shows one off in the best light).

Always remember to ENUNCIATE clearly. If you notice that the   6 person to whom you are talking is reacting with a blank stare, repeat the phrases "Can you hear me?" and "Do you understand?" in louder and louder tones of voice until you ascertain that your conversational partner (a) does not have a language in common with you, or (b) is in some kind of a stupor. (The former condition is more frequent on the East Coast, the latter on the West. Either situation renders the whole thing pretty hopeless and gives you permission to call a cab.) Which brings us to another basic point: Remember that the creation of new language is the sole domain of advertising copywriters and desperate Scrabble players. And that the words created by these people, such as *Scrum-diddly-umptious, FUNtastic* and *CHOC-o-li-cious* — or, in the case of Scrabble, *zziquox* — should never be spoken aloud, even in the privacy of your own home.

Now that we have discussed form, let's move ahead to content.   7

An important part of any successful conversation is, of course, a   8 good OPENING REMARK, one that is designed to intrigue, inspire and delight. Which is why "Leave me alone," "Please leave me alone" and "Won't you please, please leave me alone" are not good opening remarks. Oddly enough, the opposite — as in "Please, I beg of you, talk to me!" — does not work either. It is considered a turnoff by many. The best opening remark, therefore, is on the surface cheering and neutral but contains an essentially truthful subtext that says, "Do you have the time to listen to me drone on ceaselessly about my problems for as long as I find it convenient?" Examples of this type of opening remark are "Hi. How are you? You look great. That's a very nice purse. Where'd you get it?" and "Hey, what's happening?"

Okay! Now that we've got the old conversational ball rolling,   9
your next important task is to figure out SOMETHING TO SAY. If you have nothing to say but still feel the need simply to hear yourself talk — maybe just for the facial exercise, or to prove that you're alive — then the appropriate outlet is, of course, talk radio, where a handsomely paid professional moderator is willing to pretend to care about your views on Barbara Bush's weight or the inflated salaries of professional athletes.

"But," you may say to me, "Merrill, Merrill, Merrill. . . . What   10
if I see someone I barely know and want to talk to them? Then what?" And I would say back to you, "First, don't ever use my name three times in a row like that. It puts you well over the legal lifetime limit for using my first name in a sentence." And then I would have to say that this is the best time to use:

The Merrill Markoe Sociological Stereotyping Chart

Clever sociological stereotyping can help you make the sweeping   11
generalizations that are useful conversation starters. Or they will get you a punch in the mouth. Either way you have had that important initial contact with the person of your choice. What I am referring to is the fact that certain types of people are more likely to be interested in certain topics. For example, if you choose "Methods of Scoring Hockey" as your topic of conversation with the average middle-class woman, you're probably making a bad choice. Which is not to say that the average middle-class woman for whom this is a passionate topic does not exist. (Okay. The woman does not exist.) But just as the average middle-class man does not like to talk about his emotions or anything of importance *except* methods of scoring hockey, there is a reason why hockey scoring is the only topic never addressed by Geraldo, Oprah, Phil and Sally Jessy Raphael.

Presented below is a short reference chart indicating some topics   12
and the corresponding demographic sampling that may find them

interesting. You will probably want to make up your own list. Or maybe not, if you have any kind of a real life.

Topic	Who Will Talk About It
What we as individuals can do to make this planet called Earth a better place to live	Students under the age of twenty-five and sit-com stars who are not getting enough media attention
The plots of highly rated network TV shows such as *Who's the Boss?* and *Full House*	No one. Being forced to listen to this is considered grounds for justifiable homicide in eighteen states
How they score televised sports	Men between the ages of twenty-five and sixty
Why the men in their life won't talk about anything but televised sports	Women between the ages of eighteen and seventy
The weather	Employees of dry-cleaning establishments or the U.S. Postal Service; your parents or, if they're not home, my parents
The deteriorating health of people you barely know	Your mother or, if she's not home, my mother
What it means that all your man will talk about is sports and all your parents will talk about is the weather and the deteriorating health of people you barely know	Mental health professionals; me

All righty, now that you have successfully initiated the conversation, another problem is likely to present itself. More and more it seems as though a person (and of course by "a person" I mean "me") runs into someone who tells the same story over and over, beat for beat. They never even bother to say, "Stop me if you've heard this one before" and do not feel the least bit deterred when they notice that you are mouthing along with them as though you were an audience member at a sing-along. What do you do?   13

I recommend an exercise that I call CREATIVE CONVERSATIONAL   14

VISUALIZATION. As the person drones on, imagine that he is being squashed flat as a bug by a giant steamroller. Now, as you gaze downward at a two-dimensional aerial view of your formerly three-dimensional friend, see if you can answer the following questions: Would he make an interesting piece of abstract art? What sort of frame would you buy for it, and where would you hang it in your home? And, while you're at it, how much do you think you could get for the piece at an art auction? While you proceed with the answers to these questions, do not forget to meet the traditional obligation of "Mmm hmm" and "I see" at five-second intervals.

"But Merrill," you say to me (and of course when I say "you" I 15 mean "me"), "what do I do if I continue to be trapped, a virtual prisoner of dull conversation that threatens to go on until the end of time? Then what?" This is the proper moment for a polite but firm remark that allows you to exit quickly, one that does not hurt the feelings of your conversational partner, such as, "I see by my oxygen sensor that there is not enough breathable air on this part of the planet, and since one of us is in danger, I will make the sacrifice and leave." Then you turn on your heel and run like the wind — after, of course, waving a polite good-bye.

QUESTIONS ON MEANING

1. Is Markoe's PURPOSE only to amuse, or is she also serious?
2. In a way, Markoe's essay has two THESES: one on the surface and another beneath the humor. What are these ideas? Do they conflict?
3. What point is Markoe making about men and women in paragraph 3? Do you agree with it?

QUESTIONS ON WRITING STRATEGY

1. What steps does Markoe identify in the process of conversation?
2. This essay is a directive process analysis. Is it meant to be taken seriously as a set of instructions on how to have a conversation? How do you know? What is the combined EFFECT of its content and method?
3. Markoe wrote for *Late Night with David Letterman* for many years. Does this essay seem aimed at an AUDIENCE similar to Letterman's? Explain your answer.
4. OTHER METHODS. In paragraph 12, Markoe uses CLASSIFICATION as a means of analyzing conversation. What classes does she identify? How are her classifications IRONIC?

QUESTIONS ON LANGUAGE

1. Markoe says that women feel conversation is "an activity even more important to life than eating because it doesn't involve weight gain" (para. 3). What language and context clues help identify her IRONY here?
2. Markoe relies quite a bit on HYPERBOLE and UNDERSTATEMENT. Point out one instance of each. How do they help establish Markoe's TONE?
3. Look up any of these words you do not know: proximity, per se (para. 1); extraneous (5); demographic (12); deterred (13).

SUGGESTIONS FOR WRITING

1. Markoe's essay is a SATIRE that simultaneously mimics how-to articles and humorously attacks the inadequacies of modern conversation. Write a short satire of your own, using the method of process analysis to make your point. You might, for example, write "How to Be a Bad Driver" or "How to Teach a Boring Class." Divide the process into steps, and give the reader careful "instructions" on how to achieve the "desired" outcome.
2. What do people really like to talk about? In a brief essay, take a serious look at Markoe's statement that "certain types of people are more likely to be interested in certain topics" (para. 11). How true is this? Support your GENERALIZATIONS with EVIDENCE from your own experience. (Do your expectations about others' interests influence the ways you make conversation with them?)
3. CRITICAL WRITING. Look closely at paragraphs 3, 11, and 12. Does Markoe's use of stereotypes serve to challenge them or to reinforce them? Support your answer with evidence from the essay as well as from your experience.
4. CONNECTIONS. In "Tell Me More" (next page), Brenda Ueland also analyzes a process of conversation, but her PURPOSE is quite different from Markoe's. In an essay, compare Markoe's light, satirical approach with Ueland's sincere, enthusiastic approach. What elements of each essay create its TONE? What can you INFER about the personality of each author? Which approach do you prefer, and why?

BRENDA UELAND

BRENDA UELAND was the first woman reporter on the *Minneapolis Tribune*. She claimed to be "the first woman in the Western World to have my hair all cut off." She dressed in men's clothing, was married and divorced three times, and attempted to run up Pike's Peak at the age of eighty-four. Born in 1891 in Minneapolis, Ueland came from a family of leaders: Her Norwegian grandfather was a legislator, her father was a judge, and her mother championed women's suffrage and child labor laws. After graduating from Barnard College in New York City, Ueland worked at the *Tribune*, traveled to Europe, and returned to New York to live among the Greenwich Village bohemians. With her daughter, she went back to Minneapolis, where she lived until her death in 1985 at the age of ninety-three. For thirty years, Ueland contributed a passionate column to the *Minneapolis Times*. She is best known as the author of two books: *If You Want to Write* (1938), inspirational advice for writers, and *ME* (1939), an autobiography. A collection of Ueland's writings, *Strength to Your Sword Arm*, was published in 1992.

Tell Me More

Brenda Ueland, observes the writer Susan Allen Toth, "is no stylist. . . . Unabashed and persistent, she talks to her readers as if to old, deeply interested friends. . . . Such friends, she somehow makes us feel, don't need or expect superficial polish — just straight, honest, compelling talk." This essay from *Strength to Your Sword Arm* is just such talk, about talk. It complements Merrill Markoe's wry "Conversation Piece" (p. 227).

I want to write about the great and powerful thing that listening 1
is. And how we forget it. And how we don't listen to our children, or those we love. And least of all   which is so important too — to those we do not love. But we should. Because listening is a magnetic and strange thing, a creative force. Think how the friends that really listen to us are the ones we move toward, and we want to sit in their radius as though it did us good, like ultraviolet rays.

This is the reason: When we are listened to, it creates us, makes 2
us unfold and expand. Ideas actually begin to grow within us and come to life. You know how if a person laughs at your jokes you become funnier and funnier, and if he does not, every tiny little joke

in you weakens up and dies. Well, that is the principle of it. It makes people happy and free when they are listened to. And if you are a listener, it is the secret of having a good time in society (because everybody around you becomes lively and interesting), of comforting people, of doing them good.

Who are the people, for example, to whom you go for advice? 3
Not to the hard, practical ones who can tell you exactly what to do, but to the listeners; that is, the kindest, least censorious, least bossy people that you know. It is because by pouring out your problem to them, you then know what to do about it yourself.

When we listen to people there is an alternating current, and 4
this recharges us so that we never get tired of each other. We are constantly being re-created. Now there are brilliant people who cannot listen much. They have no ingoing wires on their apparatus. They are entertaining, but exhausting, too. I think it is because these lecturers, these brilliant performers, by not giving us a chance to talk, do not let us express our thoughts and expand; and it is this little creative fountain inside us that begins to spring and cast up new thoughts and unexpected laughter and wisdom. That is why, when someone has listened to you, you go home rested and lighthearted.

Now this little creative fountain is in us all. It is the spirit, or 5
the intelligence, or the imagination — whatever you want to call it. If you are very tired, strained, have no solitude, run too many errands, talk to too many people, drink too many cocktails, this little fountain is muddied over and covered with a lot of debris. The result is you stop living from the center, the creative fountain, and you live from the periphery, from externals. That is, you go along on mere will power without imagination.

It is when people really listen to us, with quiet fascinated atten- 6
tion, that the little fountain begins to work again, to accelerate in the most surprising way.

I discovered all this about three years ago, and truly it made a 7
revolutionary change in my life. Before that, when I went to a party I would think anxiously: "Now try hard. Be lively. Say bright things. Talk. Don't let down." And when tired, I would have to drink a lot of coffee to keep this up.

Now before going to a party, I just tell myself to listen with 8
affection to anyone who talks to me, *to be in their shoes when they talk*; to try to know them without my mind pressing against theirs, or arguing, or changing the subject. No. My attitude is: "Tell me more. This person is showing me his soul. It is a little dry and meager and full of grinding talk just now, but presently he will begin to think,

not just automatically to talk. He will show his true self. Then he will be wonderfully alive."

Sometimes, of course, I cannot listen as well as others. But when I have this listening power, people crowd around and their heads keep turning to me as though irresistibly pulled. It is not because people are conceited and want to show off that they are drawn to me, the listener. It is because by listening I have started up their creative fountain. I do them good. 9

Now why does it do them good? I have a kind of mystical notion about this. I think it is only by expressing all that is inside that purer and purer streams come. It is so in writing. You are taught in school to put down on paper only the bright things. Wrong. Pour out the dull things on paper too — you can tear them up afterward — for only then do the bright ones come. If you hold back the dull things, you are certain to hold back what is clear and beautiful and true and lively. So it is with people who have not been listened to in the right way — with affection and a kind of jolly excitement. Their creative fountain has been blocked. Only superficial talk comes out — what is prissy or gushing or merely nervous. No one has called out of them, by wonderful listening, what is true and alive. 10

I think women have this listening faculty more than men. It is not the fault of men. They lose it because of their long habit of striving in business, of self-assertion. And the more forceful men are, the less they can listen as they grow older. And that is why women in general are more fun than men, more restful and inspiriting. 11

Now this nonlistening of able men is the cause of one of the saddest things in the world — the loneliness of fathers, of those quietly sad men who move among their grown children like remote ghosts. When my father was over seventy, he was a fiery, humorous, admirable man, a scholar, a man of great force. But he was deep in the loneliness of old age and another generation. He was so fond of me. But he could not hear me — not one word I said, really. I was just audience. I would walk around the lake with him on a beautiful afternoon and he would talk to me about Darwin and Huxley and Higher Criticism of the Bible. 12

"Yes, I see, I see," I kept saying and tried to keep my mind pinned to it, but I was restive and bored. There was a feeling of helplessness because he could not hear what I had to say about it. When I spoke I found myself shouting, as one does to a foreigner, and in a kind of despair that he could not hear me. After the walk I would feel that I had worked off my duty and I was anxious to get him settled and reading in his Morris chair, so that I could go out and have a livelier 13 time with other people. And he would sigh and look after me absentmindedly with perplexed loneliness.

For years afterward I have thought with real suffering about my 14 father's loneliness. Such a wonderful man, and reaching out to me and wanting to know me! But he could not. He could not listen. But now I think that if only I had known as much about listening then as I do now, I could have bridged that chasm between us. To give an example:

Recently, a man I had not seen for twenty years wrote me: "I 15 have a family of mature children. So did your father. They never saw him. Not in the days he was alive. Not in the days he was the deep and admirable man we now both know he was. That is man's life. When next you see me, you'll just know everything. Just your father all over again, trying to reach through, back to the world of those he loves."

Well, when I saw this man again, what had happened to him 16 after twenty years? He was an unusually forceful man and had made a great deal of money. But he had lost his ability to listen. He talked rapidly and told wonderful stories and it was just fascinating to hear them. But when I spoke — restlessness: "Just hand me that, will you? . . . Where is my pipe?" It was just a habit. He read countless books and was eager to take in ideas, but he just could not listen to people.

Well, this is what I did. I was more patient — I did not resist 17 his nonlistening talk as I did my father's. I listened and listened to him, not once pressing against him, even in thought, with my own self-assertion. I said to myself: "He has been under a driving pressure for years. His family has grown to resist his talk. But now, by listening, I will pull it all out of him. He must talk freely and on and on. When he has been really listened to enough, he will grow tranquil. He will begin to want to hear me."

And he did, after a few days. He began asking me questions. 18 And presently I was saying gently:

"You see, it has become hard for you to listen." 19

He stopped dead and stared at me. And it was because I had 20 listened with such complete, absorbed, uncritical sympathy, without one flaw of boredom or impatience, that he now believed and trusted me, although he did not know this.

"Now talk," he said. "Tell me about that. Tell me all about that." 21

Well, we walked back and forth across the lawn and I told him 22 my ideas about it.

"You love your children, but probably don't let them in. Unless 23 you listen, people are wizened in your presence; they become about a third of themselves. Unless you listen, you can't know anybody. Oh, you will know facts and what is in the newspapers and all of history, perhaps, but you will not know one single person. You know, I have come to think listening is love, that's what it really is."

Well, I don't think I would have written this article if my notions   24
had not had such an extraordinary effect on this man. For he says they have changed his whole life. He wrote me that his children at once came closer; he was astonished to see what they are: how original, independent, courageous. His wife seemed really to care about him again, and they were actually talking about all kinds of things and making each other laugh.

For just as the tragedy of parents and children is not listening, so   25
it is of husbands and wives. If they disagree they begin to shout louder and louder — if not actually, at least inwardly — hanging fiercely and deafly onto their own ideas, instead of listening and becoming quieter and quieter and more comprehending. But the most serious result of not listening is that worst thing in the world, boredom; for it is really the death of love. It seals people off from each other more than any other thing. I think that is why married people quarrel. It is to cut through the nonconduction and boredom. Because when feelings are hurt, they really begin to listen. At last their talk is a real exchange. But of course, they are just injuring their marriage forever.

Besides critical listening, there is another kind that is no good: 26
passive, censorious listening. Sometimes husbands can be this kind of listener, a kind of ungenerous eavesdropper who mentally (or aloud) keeps saying as you talk: "Bunk . . . Bunk . . . Hokum."

Now, how to listen? It is harder than you think. I don't believe   27
in critical listening, for that only puts a person in a straitjacket of hesitancy. He begins to choose his words solemnly or primly. His little inner fountain cannot spring. Critical listeners dry you up. But creative listeners are those who want you to be recklessly yourself, even at your very worst, even vituperative, bad-tempered. They are laughing and just delighted with any manifestation of yourself, bad or good. For true listeners know that if you are bad-tempered it does not mean that you are always so. They don't love you just when you are nice; they love all of you.

In order to learn to listen, here are some suggestions: Try to learn   28
tranquility, to live in the present a part of the time every day. Sometimes say to yourself: "Now. What is happening now? This friend is talking. I am quiet. There is endless time. I hear it, every word." Then suddenly you begin to hear not only what people are saying,

but what they are trying to say, and you sense the whole truth about them. And you sense existence, not piecemeal, not this object and that, but as a translucent whole.

Then watch your self-assertiveness. And give it up. Try not to 29 drink too many cocktails to give up that nervous pressure that feels like energy and wit but may be neither. And remember it is not enough just to *will* to listen to people. One must *really* listen. Only then does the magic begin.

Sometimes people cannot listen because they think that unless 30 they are talking, they are socially of no account. There are those women with an old-fashioned ballroom training that insists there must be unceasing vivacity and gyrations of talk. But this is really a strain on people.

No. We should all know this: that listening, not talking, is the 31 gifted and great role, and the imaginative role. And the true listener is much more beloved, magnetic than the talker, and he is more effective, and learns more and does more good. And so try listening. Listen to your wife, your husband, your father, your mother, your children, your friends; to those who love you and those who don't, to those who bore you, to your enemies. It will work a small miracle. And perhaps a great one.

QUESTIONS ON MEANING

1. How did Ueland convince her friend to become a listener?
2. Was Ueland always a listener herself?
3. What is Ueland's THESIS? Where does she state it?
4. What connection does Ueland make between writing and talking?
5. According to Ueland's essay, who are better listeners, women or men? Why? Do you agree?

QUESTIONS ON WRITING STRATEGY

1. In paragraphs 4–6, Ueland develops an ANALOGY of a "creative fountain." What is this image's EFFECT?
2. Ueland's essay culminates in a concise directive process analysis (paras. 28–31). What is the function of the preceding material? How does it relate to these final paragraphs?
3. Into what steps does Ueland divide the process of becoming a listener?
4. OTHER METHODS. How do Ueland's brief NARRATIVES, or ANECDOTES,

about her father (paras. 12–14) and her friend (15–24) help to make her case for listening?

QUESTIONS ON LANGUAGE

1. Consult your dictionary if any of these words are unfamiliar: censorious (para. 3); periphery (5); prissy (10); perplexed (13); tranquil (17); wizened (23); vituperative (27); vivacity, gyrations (30).
2. Ueland's STYLE is conversational rather than formal — for instance, "Well, that is the principle of it. It makes people happy and free when they are listened to" (para. 2). Locate a few other examples of conversational style. How does this style affect your impression of Ueland and your acceptance of what she says?
3. Ueland relies heavily on the first-PERSON *I*. Why, do you think? What EFFECT does it have?
4. How would you describe Ueland's TONE?

SUGGESTIONS FOR WRITING

1. Try to recall an incident in which you failed to listen to someone, or someone else failed to listen to you. Write a short NARRATIVE of the failed communication. Where did the conversation go wrong? How could the failure have been averted?
2. "I think women have this listening faculty more than men," claims Ueland (para. 11). In a brief essay, give your opinion on whether women or men are better listeners. Be sure to use EVIDENCE to support your ideas. You may want to include ANECDOTES to reinforce your argument.
3. CRITICAL WRITING. In the last paragraph of her essay, Ueland makes the claim that "listening, not talking, is the gifted and great role, and the imaginative role." What does Ueland seem to mean by "imagination" in this essay? What might her definition of "listening" be, and how does it differ from yours?
4. CONNECTIONS. In a brief essay, experiment with TONE: Write Ueland's advice in the light, satirical tone of Merrill Markoe's "Conversation Piece" (p. 227) or write Markoe's advice in the sincere, enthusiastic tone of Ueland's "Tell Me More."

BRENDA UELAND ON WRITING

Brenda Ueland has strong and abundant views on writing. In her book *If You Want to Write*, she insists that the writer trust his or her creative instincts, the fountain she speaks of in "Tell Me More." Free yourselves from self-imposed restraints, she urges writers: "Be careless, reckless! Be a lion, be a pirate! Write any old way." In an excerpt from the book, reprinted in the *Utne Reader*, Ueland insists that "the imagination needs moodling — long, inefficient, happy idling, daw-dling, and puttering. These people who are always briskly doing something and as busy as waltzing mice, they have little, sharp, staccato ideas, such as: 'I see where I can make an annual cut of $3.47 in my meat budget.' But they have no slow, big ideas. And the fewer consoling, noble, shining, free, jovial, magnanimous ideas that come, the more nervously and desperately they rush and run from office to office and up and down stairs, thinking by action at last to make life have some warmth and meaning.

"If you write, good ideas must come welling up into you so that you have something to write. If good ideas do not come at once, or for a long time, do not be troubled at all. Wait for them. Meanwhile, put down the little ideas however insignificant they are.

"Ideas come with the dreamy idleness that children have, an idleness when you walk alone for a long, long time, or take a long, dreamy time at dressing, or lie in bed at night and thoughts come and go, or dig in a garden, or drive a car for many hours alone, or play the piano, or sew, or paint alone; or an idleness — and this is what I want you to do — where you sit with pencil and paper or before a typewriter quietly putting down what you happen to be thinking, that is creative idleness. With all my heart I tell you and reassure you: At such times you are being slowly filled and recharged with warm imagination, with wonderful, living thoughts."

FOR DISCUSSION

1. What is the "moodling" Ueland refers to and how does it contribute to the writing process?
2. Have you ever tried "moodling"? If so, what were your results? If not, why not?

MARVIN HARRIS

MARVIN HARRIS is an influential and often controversial cultural anthropologist with a particular interest in how the "practical problems of earthly existence" — getting food, for instance — determine human cultures. Harris was born in Brooklyn, New York, in 1927 and received a B.A. (1949) and Ph.D. (1953) from Columbia University. He taught at Columbia for almost three decades and is now graduate research professor of anthropology at the University of Florida. Harris has traveled extensively, conducting research in South America, Africa, Asia, and East Harlem, New York City. His eighteen books comprise scholarly works such as *The Rise of Anthropological Theory* (1968) and textbooks such as *Culture, People, Nature* (now in its sixth edition). But Harris is best known for books intended for general audiences: *Cows, Pigs, Wars, and Witches: The Riddles of Culture* (1974); *Cannibals and Kings: The Origins of Cultures* (1977); and *Good to Eat* (1986) and *The Sacred Cow and the Abominable Pig* (1987), both subtitled *Riddles of Food and Culture*.

How Our Skins Got Their Color

This essay comes from Harris's book *Our Kind: Who We Are, Where We Came from, Where We Are Going* (1988). Typically for Harris's writing, the book tackles big questions about human evolution with insight and information. In this selection, Harris sets the record straight on race.

Most human beings are neither very fair nor very dark, but brown. 1
The extremely fair skin of northern Europeans and their descendants, and the very black skins of central Africans and their descendants, are probably special adaptations. Brown-skinned ancestors may have been shared by modern-day blacks and whites as recently as ten thousand years ago.

Human skin owes its color to the presence of particles known as 2
melanin. The primary function of melanin is to protect the upper levels of the skin from being damaged by the sun's ultraviolet rays. This radiation poses a critical problem for our kind because we lack the dense coat of hair that acts as a sunscreen for most mammals. Hairlessness exposes us to two kinds of radiation hazards: ordinary sunburn, with its blisters, rashes, and risk of infection; and skin

cancers, including malignant melanoma, one of the deadliest diseases known. Melanin is the body's first line of defense against these afflictions. The more melanin particles, the darker the skin, and the lower the risk of sunburn and all forms of skin cancer. This explains why the highest rates for skin cancer are found in sun-drenched lands such as Australia, where light-skinned people of European descent spend a good part of their lives outdoors wearing scanty attire. Very dark-skinned people such as heavily pigmented Africans of Zaire seldom get skin cancer, but when they do, they get it on depigmented parts of their bodies — palms and lips.

If exposure to solar radiation had nothing but harmful effects,   3
natural selection would have favored inky black as the color for all human populations. But the sun's rays do not present an unmitigated threat. As it falls on the skin, sunshine converts a fatty substance in the epidermis into vitamin D. The blood carries vitamin D from the skin to the intestines (technically making it a hormone rather than a vitamin), where it plays a vital role in the absorption of calcium. In turn, calcium is vital for strong bones. Without it, people fall victim to the crippling diseases rickets and osteomalacia. In women, calcium deficiencies can result in a deformed birth canal, which makes childbirth lethal for both mother and fetus.

Vitamin D can be obtained from a few foods, primarily the oils   4
and livers of marine fish. But inland populations must rely on the sun's rays and their own skins for the supply of this crucial substance. The particular color of a human population's skin, therefore, represents in large degree a trade-off between the hazards of too much versus too little solar radiation: acute sunburn and skin cancer on the one hand, and rickets and osteomalacia on the other. It is this trade-off that largely accounts for the preponderance of brown people in the world and for the general tendency for skin color to be darkest among equatorial populations and lightest among populations dwelling at higher latitudes.

At middle latitudes, the skin follows a strategy of changing colors   5
with the seasons. Around the Mediterranean basin, for example, exposure to the summer sun brings high risk of cancer but low risk for rickets; the body produces more melanin and people grow darker (i.e., they get suntans). Winter reduces the risk of sunburn and cancer; the body produces less melanin, and the tan wears off.

The correlation between skin color and latitude is not perfect   6
because other factors — such as the availability of foods containing vitamin D and calcium, regional cloud cover during the winter, amount of clothing worn, and cultural preferences — may work for or against

the predicted relationship. Arctic-dwelling Eskimo, for example, are not as light-skinned as expected, but their habitat and economy afford them a diet that is exceptionally rich in both vitamin D and calcium.

Northern Europeans, obliged to wear heavy garments for protec-   7
tion against the long, cold, cloudy winters, were always at risk for rickets and osteomalacia from too little vitamin D and calcium. This risk increased sometime after 6000 B.C., when pioneer cattle herders who did not exploit marine resources began to appear in northern Europe. The risk would have been especially great for the brown-skinned Mediterranean peoples who migrated northward along with the crops and farm animals. Samples of Caucasian skin (infant penile foreskin obtained at the time of circumcision) exposed to sunlight on cloudless days in Boston (42°N) from November through February produced no vitamin D. In Edmonton (52°N) this period extended from October to March. But further south (34°N) sunlight was effective in producing vitamin D in the middle of the winter. Almost all of Europe lies north of 42°N. Fair-skinned, nontanning individuals who could utilize the weakest and briefest doses of sunlight to synthesize vitamin D were strongly favored by natural selection. During the frigid winters, only a small circle of a child's face could be left to peek out at the sun through the heavy clothing, thereby favoring the survival of individuals with translucent patches of pink on their cheeks characteristic of many northern Europeans. . . .

If light-skinned individuals on the average had only 2 percent   8
more children survive per generation, the changeover in their skin color could have begun five thousand years ago and reached present levels well before the beginning of the Christian era. But natural selection need not have acted alone. Cultural selection may also have played a role. It seems likely that whenever people consciously or unconsciously had to decide which infants to nourish and which to neglect, the advantage would go to those with lighter skin, experience having shown that such individuals tended to grow up to be taller, stronger, and healthier than their darker siblings. White was beautiful because white was healthy.

To account for the evolution of black skin in equatorial latitudes,   9
one has merely to reverse the combined effects of natural and cultural selection. With the sun directly overhead most of the year, and clothing a hindrance to work and survival, vitamin D was never in short supply (and calcium was easily obtained from vegetables). Rickets and osteomalacia were rare. Skin cancer was the main problem, and what nature started, culture amplified. Darker infants were favored by parents because experience showed that they grew up to be

freer of disfiguring and lethal malignancies. Black was beautiful because black was healthy.

QUESTIONS ON MEANING

1. What is Harris's THESIS? How does process analysis develop this idea?
2. How does the author explain the development of very light-skinned and very dark-skinned people?
3. With what is skin color most closely associated? Why is this correlation not perfect?
4. What point does Harris make about cultural selection? What do you think he means by this term?

QUESTIONS ON WRITING STRATEGY

1. What historical movement of people does Harris refer to? Why does he mention this movement?
2. What kind of EVIDENCE does Harris use? Do you find the evidence convincing?
3. How does the example of Australia (para. 2) fit into Harris's process analysis?
4. What is the ALLUSION in Harris's last sentence? What does that sentence suggest about Harris's PURPOSE?
5. OTHER METHODS. Harris COMPARES AND CONTRASTS people with different skin colors. Does he have a bias — either personal or biologically based — toward any particular color?

QUESTIONS ON LANGUAGE

1. What is the TONE of this essay? Is it appropriate, do you think?
2. Examine how Harris introduces technical vocabulary. What can you tell about the meanings of the following terms from what Harris says: melanin, malignant, melanoma (para. 2); radiation, epidermis, hormone, calcium, rickets, osteomalacia (3); latitudes (4); correlation, habitat (6); siblings (8)?
3. Be sure you know the meanings of these words as well: afflictions (para. 2); unmitigated (3); preponderance (4); translucent (7).
4. When, if at all, does Harris use the words "whites" and "blacks"? What words does he use to describe skin color? Why?

SUGGESTIONS FOR WRITING

1. Write a process analysis of how something came to be the way it is —
for instance, a city street pattern, the furless bodies of humans, automated bank tellers, or the basic design of the automobile. Conduct
whatever research is necessary, and explain the process clearly and with
ample detail.

2. Respond to Harris's essay in one of several possible ways: (*a*) Explain
the EFFECT the essay had on you. (*b*) Explain how you think skin color
is viewed in this country, with examples. (*c*) List individuals or groups
of people you think should read this essay, and explain why in each
case.

3. CRITICAL WRITING. Instead of stating his PURPOSE outright, Harris
asks the reader to INFER his intention (see number 4 under "Questions
on Writing Strategy"). In an essay, ANALYZE the clues Harris provides
about his purpose and consider why he may have taken this indirect
approach. Finally, EVALUATE how well the approach works to further
Harris's purpose.

4. CONNECTIONS. Several essays in this book address perceptions of skin
color in American society — for instance, Ralph Ellison's "On Being
the Target of Discrimination" (p. 55), Brent Staples's "Black Men and
Public Space" (p. 159), and bell hooks's "Madonna" (p. 303). In an
essay of your own based on two or more of these works, analyze what
skin color seems to signify in the United States. In your opinion, to
what extent, if at all, is skin color regarded as biological?

PETER ELBOW

PETER ELBOW is well known as a director of writing programs for community groups and for college students. Born in 1935, he received his education at Williams College and at Brandeis, Harvard, and Oxford. He has taught at Wesleyan University, MIT, Franconia College, and the Harvard Graduate School of Education, as well as at Evergreen State College in Olympia, Washington. Recently he started the highly acclaimed "Workshop in Language and Thinking" at Bard College and served as director of the Writing Program at the State University of New York, Stony Brook. He is the author of many articles and of the influential *Writing Without Teachers* (1973), *Writing with Power* (1981), and *Embracing Contraries: Explorations in Learning and Teaching* (1986). Currently, he teaches at the University of Massachusetts, Amherst.

Desperation Writing

What do you do when a paper's deadline looms but you can't think of a word to say about the assigned subject? Take heart: Peter Elbow has a solution. What's more, following his advice, you may find writing much less painful than you expected. "Desperation Writing" has offered solace and help to thousands since it first appeared in *Writing Without Teachers*.

I know I am not alone in my recurring twinges of panic that I 1
won't be able to write something when I need to, I won't be able to produce coherent speech or thought. And that lingering doubt is a great hindrance to writing. It's a constant fog or static that clouds the mind. I never got out of its clutches till I discovered that it was possible to write something — not something great or pleasing but at least something usable, workable — when my mind is out of commission. The trick is that you have to do all your cooking out on the table: Your mind is incapable of doing any inside. It means using symbols and pieces of paper not as a crutch but as a wheelchair.

The first thing is to admit your condition: Because of some mood 2
or event or whatever, your mind is incapable of anything that could be called thought. It can put out a babbling kind of speech utterance, it can put a simple feeling, perception or sort-of-thought into understandable (though terrible) words. But it is incapable of considering anything in relation to anything else. The moment you try to hold

that thought or feeling up against some other to see the relationship, you simply lose the picture — you get nothing but buzzing lines or waving colors.

So admit this. Avoid anything more than one feeling, perception, or thought. Simply write as much as possible. Try simply to steer your mind in the direction or general vicinity of the thing you are trying to write about and start writing and keep writing.

Just write and keep writing. (Probably best to write on only one side of the paper in case you should want to cut parts out with scissors — but you probably won't.) Just write and keep writing. It will probably come in waves. After a flurry, stop and take a brief rest. But don't stop too long. Don't think about what you are writing or what you have written or else you will overload the circuit again. Keep writing as though you are drugged or drunk. Keep doing this till you feel you have a lot of material that might be useful; or, if necessary, till you can't stand it any more — even if you doubt that there's anything useful there.

Then take a pad of little pieces of paper — or perhaps 3 × 5 cards — and simply start at the beginning of what you were writing, and as you read over what you wrote, every time you come to any thought, feeling, perception, or image that could be gathered up into one sentence or one assertion, do so and write it by itself on a little sheet of paper. In short, you are trying to turn, say, ten or twenty pages of wandering mush into twenty or thirty hard little crab apples. Sometimes there won't be many on a page. But if it seems to you that there are none on a page, you are making a serious error — the same serious error that put you in this comatose state to start with. You are mistaking lousy, stupid, second-rate, wrong, childish, foolish, worthless ideas for no ideas at all. Your job is not to pick out *good* ideas but to pick out ideas. As long as you were conscious, your words will be full of things that could be called feelings, utterances, ideas — things that can be squeezed into one simple sentence. This is your job. Don't ask for too much.

After you have done this, take those little slips or cards, read through them a number of times — not struggling with them, simply wandering and mulling through them; perhaps shifting them around and looking through in various sequences. In a sense these are cards you are playing solitaire with, and the rules of this particular game permit shuffling the unused pile.

The goal of this procedure with the cards is to get them to distribute themselves in two or three or ten or fifteen different piles on your desk. You can get them to do this almost by themselves if

you simply keep reading through them in different orders; certain
cards will begin to feel like they go with other cards. I emphasize this
passive, thoughtless mode because I want to talk about desperation
writing in its pure state. In practice, almost invariably at some point
in the procedure, your sanity begins to return. It is often at this point.
You actually are moved to have thoughts or — and the difference
between active and passive is crucial here — to *exert* thought; to hold
two cards together and *build* or *assert* a relationship. It is a matter of
bringing energy to bear.

So you may start to be able to do something active with these   8
cards, and begin actually to think. But if not, just allow the cards to
find their own piles with each other by feel, by drift, by intuition,
by mindlessness.

You have now engaged in the two main activities that will permit   9
you to get something cooked out on the table rather than in your
brain: writing out into messy words, summing up into single assertions, and even sensing relationships between assertions. You can
simply continue to deploy these two activities.

If, for example, after the first round of writing, assertion-making,   10
and pile-making, your piles feel as though they are useful and satisfactory for what you are writing — paragraphs or sections or trains of
thought — then you can carry on from there. See if you can gather
each pile up into a single assertion. When you can, then put the
subsidiary assertions of that pile into their best order to fit with that
single unifying one. If you *can't* get the pile into one assertion, then
take the pile as the basis for doing some more writing out into words.
In the course of this writing, you may produce for yourself the single
unifying assertion you were looking for; or you may have to go through
the cycle of turning the writing into assertions and piles and so forth.
Perhaps more than once. The pile may turn out to want to be two
or more piles itself; or it may want to become part of a pile you
already have. This is natural. This kind of meshing into one configuration, then coming apart, then coming together and meshing into
a different configuration — this is growing and cooking. It makes a
terrible mess, but if you can't do it in your head, you have to put up
with a cluttered desk and a lot of confusion.

If, on the other hand, all that writing *didn't* have useful material   11
in it, it means that your writing wasn't loose, drifting, quirky, jerky,
associative enough. This time try especially to let things simply remind you of things that are seemingly crazy or unrelated. Follow these
odd associations. Make as many metaphors as you can — be as nutty
as possible — and explore the metaphors themselves — open them

out. You may have all your energy tied up in some area of your experience that you are leaving out. Don't refrain from writing about whatever else is on your mind: how you feel at the moment, what you are losing your mind over, randomness that intrudes itself on your consciousness, the pattern on the wallpaper, what those people you see out the window have on their minds — though keep coming back to the whateveritis you are supposed to be writing about. Treat it, in short, like ten-minute writing exercises. Your best perceptions and thoughts are always going to be tied up in whatever is really occupying you, and that is also where your energy is. You may end up writing a love poem — or a hate poem — in one of those little piles while the other piles will finally turn into a lab report on data processing or whatever you have to write about. But you couldn't, in your present state of having your head shot off, have written that report without also writing the poem. And the report will have some of the juice of the poem in it and vice versa.

QUESTIONS ON MEANING

1. On what assumptions does Elbow base his advice?
2. Where in his essay does the author reveal his PURPOSE?
3. What value does Elbow discern in "lousy, stupid, second-rate, wrong, childish, foolish, worthless ideas" (para. 5)?
4. In your own words, describe the role of the unconscious in the process Elbow analyzes. Where in the process does the conscious mind have to do its part?
5. How does the author justify writing a poem when the assignment is to write a lab report?

QUESTIONS ON WRITING STRATEGY

1. What EFFECT does the author achieve by opening his essay in the first PERSON (*I*)?
2. At what AUDIENCE does Elbow direct his advice?
3. Into how many steps does the author break down the process he analyzes? What are they?
4. Point to effective samples of time-markers in this essay. (Time-markers are discussed on p. 224.)
5. Point to phrases or sentences in the essay that seem to you designed to offer encouragement and comfort.
6. OTHER METHODS. When Elbow says that he wants "to talk about

desperation writing in its pure state," he calls attention to a developing DEFINITION. In your own words, what is "pure" desperation writing?

QUESTIONS ON LANGUAGE

1. Where in his essay does the author make good use of FIGURES OF SPEECH?
2. Using a dictionary if necessary, define the following words: coherent, hindrance (para. 1); assertion, comatose (5); configuration (10).

SUGGESTIONS FOR WRITING

1. Approach a writing assignment for any one of your classes by following Peter Elbow's advice. Write steadily in the manner prescribed for at least ten minutes; then sort out any ideas you may have brought forth. If you have no class assignment that involves writing, work instead on a journal entry about some recent event, book, idea, or experience that impressed you. When your exercise has been completed, write a paragraph in which you explain how well Elbow's method succeeded for you. Did it lead to any good results? Any surprises?
2. In a brief essay, explain how to tackle any job you're not in the mood for: researching a paper, preparing a speech, performing a lab experiment, studying for a test, cleaning your house, washing your car, getting up in the morning. The process should involve at least three steps.
3. CRITICAL WRITING. Write an EVALUATION of Elbow's essay as a work of directive process analysis. First try out Elbow's process, as suggested in the first writing topic. Then test Elbow's advice against your experience. Which suggestions are especially helpful? Which aren't? Why?
4. CONNECTIONS. Peter Elbow and Brenda Ueland (in "Tell Me More," p. 233) both address what Ueland calls a "creative force": For Elbow, it is desperation writing; for Ueland, it is listening. In an essay, compare and contrast these two processes as Elbow and Ueland present them. How do they work? What are their benefits? (Note that Ueland compares listening and writing, in para. 10.) If you need help with the method of comparison, see Chapter 4.

PETER ELBOW ON WRITING

Peter Elbow's best-known work is devoted, like "Desperation Writing," to encouraging people to write. Much of his advice comes from his writing experience. His own life is the source for a recent article, "Closing My Eyes as I Speak: An Argument for Ignoring Audience."

That it often helps writers to be aware of their readers is an article of faith for many college writing instructors; it is an assumption we make in *The Bedford Reader*. Without denying that a sense of audience is sometimes valuable, Elbow makes a persuasive case for sometimes trying to forget that an audience is there. "When I am talking to a person or a group," he begins, "and struggling to find words or thoughts, I often find myself involuntarily closing my eyes as I speak. I realize now that this behavior is an instinctive attempt to blot out awareness of audience when I need all my concentration for just trying to figure out or express what I want to say. Because the audience is so imperiously *present* in a speaking situation, my instinct reacts with this active attempt to avoid audience awareness. This behavior — in a sense impolite or antisocial — is not so uncommon. Even when we write, alone in a room to an absent audience, there are occasions when we are struggling to figure something out and need to push aside awareness of those absent readers."

Some audiences — like a readership of close friends — are helpful to keep in mind. "When we think about them from the start, we think of more and better things to say." But other audiences are powerfully inhibiting, and keeping them in mind as we write may put up writer's blocks. "For example, when we have to write to someone we find intimidating (and of course students often perceive teachers as intimidating), we often start thinking wholly defensively. As we write down each thought or sentence, our mind fills with thoughts of how the intended reader will criticize or object to it. So we try to qualify or soften what we've just written — or write out some answer to a possible objection. Our writing becomes tangled. Sometimes we get so tied in knots that we cannot even figure out what we think."

The solution? "We can ignore that audience altogether during the *early* stages of writing and direct our words only to ourselves or to no one in particular — or even to the 'wrong' audience, that is, to an *inviting* audience of trusted friends or allies. . . . Putting audience out of mind is of course a traditional practice: Serious writers have long used private journals for early explorations of feeling, thinking, or language." In contrast, inferior newspaper or business writing often reminds us of "the ineffective actor whose consciousness of self dis-tracts us: He makes us too aware of his own awareness of us. When we read such prose, we wish the writer would stop thinking about us — would stop trying to adjust or fit what he is saying to our frame of reference. 'Damn it, put all your attention on what you are saying,' we want to say, 'and forget about us and how we are reacting.'

"When we examine really good student or professional writing, we can often see that its goodness comes from the writer's having gotten sufficiently wrapped up in her meaning and her language as to forget all about audience needs: The writer manages to 'break through.'"

To overcome the problem of being painfully conscious of readers, if it is a problem you've met, Elbow advises writing more than one draft of everything. "*After* we have figured out our thinking in copious exploratory or draft writing — perhaps finding the right voice or stance as well — *then* we can follow the traditional rhetorical advice: Think about readers and revise carefully to adjust our words and thoughts to our intended audience."

FOR DISCUSSION

1. How closely do Peter Elbow's observations reflect your own writing experience? Do you ever worry so hard about what your reader will think that you become pen-tied? Or do you usually close your eyes to your audience, and just write?
2. What is wrong with the following attempt to state Elbow's thesis: "A writer should simply forget about audience"?
3. If you feel uncomfortable when you write, too keenly aware of the reader "looking over your shoulder," what advice of Elbow's might you follow? Can you suggest any other advice to relieve a writer's self-consciousness?

JESSICA MITFORD

Born in Batsford Mansion, England, in 1917, the daughter of Lord and Lady Redesdale, JESSICA MITFORD devoted much of her early life to defying her aristocratic upbringing. In her autobiography *Daughters and Rebels* (1960), she tells how she received a genteel schooling at home, then as a young woman moved to Loyalist Spain during the violent Spanish Civil War. Later, she emigrated to America, where for a time she worked in Miami as a bartender. She has since become one of her adopted country's most noted reporters: *Time* called her "Queen of the Muckrakers." Exposing with her typewriter what she regards as corruption, abuse, and absurdity, Mitford has written *The American Way of Death* (1963), *Kind and Unusual Punishment: The Prison Business* (1973), and *The American Way of Birth* (1992). *Poison Penmanship* (1979) collects articles from *The Atlantic, Harper's,* and other magazines. *A Fine Old Conflict* (1976) is the second volume of Mitford's autobiography. And a novel, *Grace Had an English Heart* (1989), examines how the media transform ordinary people into celebrities.

Behind the Formaldehyde Curtain

The most famous (or notorious) thing Jessica Mitford has written is *The American Way of Death*. The following essay is a self-contained selection from it. In the book, Mitford criticizes the mortuary profession; and when her work landed on bestseller lists, the author was the subject of bitter attacks from funeral directors all over North America. To finish reading the essay, you will need a stable stomach as well as an awareness of Mitford's outrageous sense of humor. "Behind the Formaldehyde Curtain" is a clear, painstaking process analysis, written with masterly style.

The drama begins to unfold with the arrival of the corpse at the   1
mortuary.

Alas, poor Yorick! How surprised he would be to see how his   2
counterpart of today is whisked off to a funeral parlor and is in short order sprayed, sliced, pierced, pickled, trussed, trimmed, creamed, waxed, painted, rouged, and neatly dressed — transformed from a common corpse into a Beautiful Memory Picture. This process is known in the trade as embalming and restorative art, and is so universally employed in the United States and Canada that the

253

funeral director does it routinely, without consulting corpse or kin.
He regards as eccentric those few who are hardy enough to suggest
that it might be dispensed with. Yet no law requires embalming, no
religious doctrine commends it, nor is it dictated by considerations
of health, sanitation, or even of personal daintiness. In no part of
the world but in Northern America is it widely used. The purpose of
embalming is to make the corpse presentable for viewing in a suitably
costly container; and here too the funeral director routinely, without
first consulting the family, prepares the body for public display.

Is all this legal? The processes to which a dead body may be   3
subjected are after all to some extent circumscribed by law. In most
states, for instance, the signature of next of kin must be obtained
before an autopsy may be performed, before the deceased may be
cremated, before the body may be turned over to a medical school
for research purposes; or such provision must be made in the decedent's will. In the case of embalming, no such permission is required
nor is it ever sought.[1] A textbook, *The Principles and Practices of
Embalming*, comments on this: "There is some question regarding the
legality of much that is done within the preparation room." The
author points out that it would be most unusual for a responsible
member of a bereaved family to instruct the mortician, in so many
words, to "embalm" the body of a deceased relative. The very term
embalming is so seldom used that the mortician must rely upon custom
in the matter. The author concludes that unless the family specifies
otherwise, the act of entrusting the body to the care of a funeral
establishment carries with it an implied permission to go ahead and
embalm.

Embalming is indeed a most extraordinary procedure, and one   4
must wonder at the docility of Americans who each year pay hundreds
of millions of dollars for its perpetuation, blissfully ignorant of what
it is all about, what is done, how it is done. Not one in ten thousand
has any idea of what actually takes place. Books on the subject are
extremely hard to come by. They are not to be found in most libraries
or bookshops.

In an era when huge television audiences watch surgical opera-   5
tions in the comfort of their living rooms, when, thanks to the
animated cartoon, the geography of the digestive system has become

---

[1]Partly because of Mitford's attack, the Federal Trade Commission now requires
the funeral industry to provide families with itemized price lists, including the price
of embalming, to state that embalming is not required, and to obtain the family's
consent to embalming before charging for it. — EDS.

familiar territory even to the nursery school set, in a land where the satisfaction of curiosity about almost all matters is a national pastime, the secrecy surrounding embalming can, surely, hardly be attributed to the inherent gruesomeness of the subject. Custom in this regard has within this century suffered a complete reversal. In the early days of American embalming, when it was performed in the home of the deceased, it was almost mandatory for some relative to stay by the embalmer's side and witness the procedure. Today, family members who might wish to be in attendance would certainly be dissuaded by the funeral director. All others, except apprentices, are excluded by law from the preparation room.

A close look at what does actually take place may explain in large measure the undertaker's intractable reticence concerning a procedure that has become his major *raison d'être*. Is it possible he fears that public information about embalming might lead patrons to wonder if they really want this service? If the funeral men are loath to discuss the subject outside the trade, the reader may, understandably, be equally loath to go on reading at this point. For those who have the stomach for it, let us part the formaldehyde curtain. . . .   6

The body is first laid out in the undertaker's morgue — or rather, Mr. Jones is reposing in the preparation room — to be readied to bid the world farewell.   7

The preparation room in any of the better funeral establishments has the tiled and sterile look of a surgery, and indeed the embalmer-restorative artist who does his chores there is beginning to adopt the term *dermasurgeon* (appropriately corrupted by some mortician-writers as "demi-surgeon") to describe his calling. His equipment, consisting of scalpels, scissors, augers, forceps, clamps, needles, pumps, tubes, bowls, and basins, is crudely imitative of the surgeon's, as is his technique, acquired in a nine- or twelve-month post-high-school course in an embalming school. He is supplied by an advanced chemical industry with a bewildering array of fluids, sprays, pastes, oils, powders, creams, to fix or soften tissue, shrink or distend it as needed, dry it here, restore the moisture there. There are cosmetics, waxes, and paints to fill and cover features, even plaster of Paris to replace entire limbs. There are ingenious aids to prop and stabilize the cadaver: a Vari-Pose Head Rest, the Edwards Arm and Hand Positioner, the Repose Block (to support the shoulders during the embalming), and the Throop Foot Positioner, which resembles an old-fashioned stocks.   8

Mr. John H. Eckels, president of the Eckels College of Mortuary Science, thus describes the first part of the embalming procedure: "In   9 the hands of a skilled practitioner, this work may be done in a comparatively short time and without mutilating the body other than by slight incision — so slight that it scarcely would cause serious inconvenience if made upon a living person. It is necessary to remove the blood, and doing this not only helps in the disinfecting, but removes the principal cause of disfigurements due to discoloration."

Another textbook discusses the all-important time element: "The 10 earlier this is done, the better, for every hour that elapses between death and embalming will add to the problems and complications encountered. . . ." Just how soon should one get going on the embalming? The author tells us, "On the basis of such scanty information made available to this profession through its rudimentary and haphazard system of technical research, we must conclude that the best results are to be obtained if the subject is embalmed before life is completely extinct — that is, before cellular death has occurred. In the average case, this would mean within an hour after somatic death." For those who feel that there is something a little rudimentary, not to say haphazard, about this advice, a comforting thought is offered by another writer. Speaking of fears entertained in early days of premature burial, he points out, "One of the effects of embalming by chemical injection, however, has been to dispel fears of live burial." How true; once the blood is removed, chances of live burial are indeed remote.

To return to Mr. Jones, the blood is drained out through the 11 veins and replaced by embalming fluid pumped in through the arteries. As noted in *The Principles and Practices of Embalming*, "every operator has a favorite injection and drainage point — a fact which becomes a handicap only if he fails or refuses to forsake his favorites when conditions demand it." Typical favorites are the carotid artery, femoral artery, jugular vein, subclavian vein. There are various choices of embalming fluid. If Flextone is used, it will produce a "mild, flexible rigidity. The skin retains a velvety softness, the tissues are rubbery and pliable. Ideal for women and children." It may be blended with B. and G. Products Company's Lyf-Lyk tint, which is guaranteed to reproduce "nature's own skin texture . . . the velvety appearance of living tissue." Suntone comes in three separate tints: Suntan; Special Cosmetic Tint, a pink shade "especially indicated for female subjects"; and Regular Cosmetic Tint, moderately pink.

About three to six gallons of a dyed and perfumed solution of 12 formaldehyde, glycerin, borax, phenol, alcohol, and water is soon circulating through Mr. Jones, whose mouth has been sewn together with a "needle directed upward between the upper lip and gum and brought out through the left nostril," with the corners raised slightly "for a more pleasant expression." If he should be bucktoothed, his teeth are cleaned with Bon Ami and coated with colorless nail polish. His eyes, meanwhile, are closed with flesh-tinted eye caps and eye cement.

The next step is to have at Mr. Jones with a thing called a trocar. 13 This is a long, hollow needle attached to a tube. It is jabbed into the abdomen, poked around the entrails and chest cavity, the contents of which are pumped out and replaced with "cavity fluid." This done, and the hole in the abdomen sewn up, Mr. Jones's face is heavily creamed (to protect the skin from burns which may be caused by leakage of the chemicals), and he is covered with a sheet and left unmolested for a while. But not for long — there is more, much more, in store for him. He has been embalmed, but not yet restored, and the best time to start the restorative work is eight to ten hours after embalming, when the tissues have become firm and dry.

The object of all this attention to the corpse, it must be remem- 14 bered, is to make it presentable for viewing in an attitude of healthy repose. "Our customs require the presentation of our dead in the semblance of normality . . . unmarred by the ravages of illness, disease, or mutilation," says Mr. J. Sheridan Mayer in his *Restorative Art.* This is rather a large order since few people die in the full bloom of health, unravaged by illness and unmarked by some disfigurement. The funeral industry is equal to the challenge: "In some cases the gruesome appearance of a mutilated or disease-ridden subject may be quite discouraging. The task of restoration may seem impossible and shake the confidence of the embalmer. This is the time for intestinal fortitude and determination. Once the formative work is begun and affected tissues are cleaned or removed, all doubts of success vanish. It is surprising and gratifying to discover the results which may be obtained."

The embalmer, having allowed an appropriate interval to elapse, 15 returns to the attack, but now he brings into play the skill and equipment of sculptor and cosmetician. Is a hand missing? Casting one in plaster of Paris is a simple matter. "For replacement purposes, only a cast of the back of the hand is necessary; this is within the ability of the average operator and is quite adequate." If a lip or two, a nose, or an ear should be missing, the embalmer has at hand a variety of restorative waxes with which to model replacements. Pores and skin texture are simulated by stippling with a little brush, and over this cosmetics are laid on. Head off? Decapitation cases are rather routinely handled. Ragged edges are trimmed, and head joined

to torso with a series of splints, wires, and sutures. It is a good idea
to have a little something at the neck — a scarf or a high collar —
when time for viewing comes. Swollen mouth? Cut out tissue as
needed from inside the lips. If too much is removed, the surface
contour can easily be restored by padding with cotton. Swollen necks
and cheeks are reduced by removing tissue through vertical incisions
made down each side of the neck. "When the deceased is casketed,
the pillow will hide the suture incisions . . . as an extra precaution
against leakage, the suture may be painted with liquid sealer."

The opposite condition is more likely to present itself — that of 16
emaciation. His hypodermic syringe now loaded with massage cream,
the embalmer seeks out and fills the hollowed and sunken areas by
injection. In this procedure the backs of the hands and fingers and
the under-chin area should not be neglected.

Positioning the lips is a problem that recurrently challenges the 17
ingenuity of the embalmer. Closed too tightly, they tend to give a
stern, even disapproving expression. Ideally, embalmers feel, the lips
should give the impression of being ever so slightly parted, the upper
lip protruding slightly for a more youthful appearance. This takes
some engineering, however, as the lips tend to drift apart. Lip drift
can sometimes be remedied by pushing one or two straight pins
through the inner margin of the lower lip and then inserting them
between the two front upper teeth. If Mr. Jones happens to have no
teeth, the pins can just as easily be anchored in his Armstrong Face
Former and Denture Replacer. Another method to maintain lip clo-
sure is to dislocate the lower jaw, which is then held in its new
position by a wire run through holes which have been drilled through
the upper and lower jaws at the midline. As the French are fond of
saying, *il faut souffrir pour être belle.*[2]

If Mr. Jones has died of jaundice, the embalming fluid will very 18
likely turn him green. Does this deter the embalmer? Not if he has
intestinal fortitude. Masking pastes and cosmetics are heavily laid on,
burial garments and casket interiors are color-correlated with particular care, and Jones is displayed beneath rose-colored lights. Friends
will say "How *well* he looks." Death by carbon monoxide, on the
other hand, can be rather a good thing from the embalmer's viewpoint: "One advantage is the fact that this type of discoloration is an
exaggerated form of a natural pink coloration." This is nice because
the healthy glow is already present and needs but little attention.

The patching and filling completed, Mr. Jones is now shaved, 19

[2]You have to suffer to be beautiful. — EDS.

washed, and dressed. Cream-based cosmetic, available in pink, flesh, suntan, brunette, and blond, is applied to his hands and face, his hair is shampooed and combed (and, in the case of Mrs. Jones, set), his hands manicured. For the horny-handed son of toil special care must be taken; cream should be applied to remove ingrained grime, and the nails cleaned. "If he were not in the habit of having them manicured in life, trimming and shaping is advised for better appearance — never questioned by kin."

Jones is now ready for casketing (this is the present participle of the verb "to casket"). In this operation his right shoulder should be depressed slightly "to turn the body a bit to the right and soften the appearance of lying flat on the back." Positioning the hands is a matter of importance, and special rubber positioning blocks may be used. The hands should be cupped slightly for a more lifelike, relaxed appearance. Proper placement of the body requires a delicate sense of balance. It should lie as high as possible in the casket, yet not so high that the lid, when lowered, will hit the nose. On the other hand, we are cautioned, placing the body too low "creates the impression that the body is in a box." [20]

Jones is next wheeled into the appointed slumber room where a few last touches may be added — his favorite pipe placed in his hand or, if he was a great reader, a book propped into position. (In the case of little Master Jones a Teddy bear may be clutched.) Here he will hold open house for a few days, visiting hours 10 A.M. to 9 P.M. [21]

All now being in readiness, the funeral director calls a staff conference to make sure that each assistant knows his precise duties. Mr. Wilber Kriege writes: "This makes your staff feel that they are a part of the team, with a definite assignment that must be properly carried out if the whole plan is to succeed. You never heard of a football coach who failed to talk to his entire team before they go on the field. They have drilled on the plays they are to execute for hours and days, and yet the successful coach knows the importance of making even the benchwarming third-string substitute feel that he is important if the game is to be won." The winning of *this* game is predicated upon glass-smooth handling of the logistics. The funeral director has notified the pallbearers whose names were furnished by the family, has arranged for the presence of clergyman, organist, and soloist, has provided transportation for everybody, has organized and listed the flowers sent by friends. In *Psychology of Funeral Service* Mr. Edward A. Martin points out, "He may not always do as much as the family thinks he is doing, but it is his helpful guidance that they appreciate in knowing they are proceeding as they should. . . . The [22] important thing is how well his services can be used to make the family believe they are giving unlimited expression to their own sentiment."

The religious service may be held in a church or in the chapel of the funeral home; the funeral director vastly prefers the latter arrangement, for not only is it more convenient for him but it affords him the opportunity to show off his beautiful facilities to the gathered mourners. After the clergyman has had his say, the mourners queue up to file past the casket for a last look at the deceased. The family is *never* asked whether they want an open-casket ceremony; in the absence of their instruction to the contrary, this is taken for granted. Consequently well over 90 per cent of all American funerals feature the open casket — a custom unknown in other parts of the world. Foreigners are astonished by it. An English woman living in San Francisco described her reaction in a letter to the writer: 23

> I myself have attended only one funeral here — that of an elderly fellow worker of mine. After the service I could not understand why everyone was walking towards the coffin (sorry, I mean casket), but thought I had better follow the crowd. It shook me rigid to get there and find the casket open and poor old Oscar lying there in his brown tweed suit, wearing a suntan makeup and just the wrong shade of lipstick. If I had not been extremely fond of the old boy, I have a horrible feeling that I might have giggled. Then and there I decided that I could never face another American funeral — even dead.

The casket (which has been resting throughout the service on a Classic Beauty Ultra Metal Casket Bier) is now transferred by a hydraulically operated device called Porto-Lift to a balloon-tired, Glide Easy casket carriage which will wheel it to yet another conveyance, the Cadillac Funeral Coach. This may be lavender, cream, light green — anything but black. Interiors, of course, are color-correlated, "for the man who cannot stop short of perfection." 24

At graveside, the casket is lowered into the earth. This office, once the prerogative of friends of the deceased, is now performed by a patented mechanical lowering device. A "Lifetime Green" artificial grass mat is at the ready to conceal the sere earth, and overhead, to conceal the sky, is a portable Steril Chapel Tent ("resists the intense heat and humidity of summer and the terrific storms of winter . . . available in Silver Gray, Rose, or Evergreen"). Now is the time for the ritual scattering of earth over the coffin, as the solemn words "earth to earth, ashes to ashes, dust to dust" are pronounced by the officiating cleric. This can today be accomplished "with a mere flick 25 of the wrist with the Gordon Leak-Proof Earth Dispenser. No grasping of a handful of dirt, no soiled fingers. Simple, dignified, beautiful, reverent! The modern way!" The Gordon Earth Dispenser (at $5) is of nickel-plated brass construction. It is not only "attractive to the eye and long wearing"; it is also "one of the 'tools' for building better public relations" if presented as "an appropriate non-commercial gift" to the clergyman. It is shaped something like a saltshaker.

Untouched by human hand, the coffin and the earth are now   26 united.

It is in the function of directing the participants through this   27 maze of gadgetry that the funeral director has assigned to himself his relatively new role of "grief therapist." He has relieved the family of every detail, he has revamped the corpse to look like a living doll, he has arranged for it to nap for a few days in a slumber room, he has put on a well-oiled performance in which the concept of *death* has played no part whatsoever — unless it was inconsiderately mentioned by the clergyman who conducted the religious service. He has done everything in his power to make the funeral a real pleasure for everybody concerned. He and his team have given their all to score an upset victory over death.

QUESTIONS ON MEANING

1. What was your emotional response to this essay? Can you analyze your feelings?
2. To what does the author attribute the secrecy that surrounds the process of embalming?
3. What, according to Mitford, is the mortician's intent? What common obstacles to fulfilling it must be surmounted?
4. What do you understand from Mitford's remark in paragraph 10, on dispelling fears of live burial: "How true; once the blood is removed, chances of live burial are indeed remote"?
5. Do you find any implied PURPOSE in this essay? Does Mitford seem primarily out to rake muck, or does she offer any positive suggestions to Americans?

QUESTIONS ON WRITING STRATEGY

1. What is Mitford's TONE? In her opening two paragraphs, exactly what shows her attitude toward her subject?

2. Why do you think Mitford goes into so much grisly detail? How does it serve her purpose?
3. What is the EFFECT of calling the body Mr. Jones (or Master Jones)?
4. Paragraph by paragraph, what time-markers does the author employ? (If you need a refresher on this point, see the discussion of time-markers on p. 224.)
5. Into what stages has the author divided the embalming process?
6. To whom does Mitford address her process analysis? How do you know she isn't writing for an AUDIENCE of professional morticians?
7. Consider one of the quotations from the journals and textbooks of professionals and explain how it serves the author's general purpose.
8. **OTHER METHODS.** In paragraph 8, Mitford uses CLASSIFICATION in listing the embalmer's equipment and supplies. What groups does she identify, and why does she bother sorting the items at all?

QUESTIONS ON LANGUAGE

1. Explain the ALLUSION to Yorick in paragraph 2.
2. What IRONY do you find in Mitford's statement in paragraph 7, "The body is first laid out in the undertaker's morgue — or rather, Mr. Jones is reposing in the preparation room"? Pick out any other words or phrases in the essay that seem ironic. Comment especially on those you find in the essay's last two sentences.
3. Why is it useful to Mitford's purpose that she cites the brand names of morticians' equipment and supplies (the Edwards Arm and Hand Positioner, Lyf-Lyk tint)? List all the brand names in the essay that are memorable.
4. Define the following words or terms: counterpart (para. 2); circumscribed, autopsy, cremated, decedent, bereaved (3); docility, perpetuation (4); inherent, mandatory (5); intractable, reticence, *raison d'être*, formaldehyde (6); "dermasurgeon," augers, forceps, distend, stocks (8); somatic (10); carotid artery, femoral artery, jugular vein, subclavian vein, pliable (11); glycerin, borax, phenol, bucktoothed (12); trocar, entrails (13); stippling, sutures (15); emaciation (16); jaundice (18); predicated (22); queue (23); hydraulically (24); cleric (25); therapist (27).

SUGGESTIONS FOR WRITING

1. With the aid of the *Readers' Guide to Periodical Literature*, find information about the recent phenomenon of quick-freezing the dead. Set forth this process, including its hoped-for result of reviving the corpses in the far future.
2. Analyze some other process whose operations may not be familiar to everyone. (Have you ever held a job, or helped out in a family business, that has taken you behind the scenes? How is fast food prepared? How

are cars serviced? How is a baby sat? How is a house constructed?)
Detail it step by step in an essay that includes time-markers.
3. CRITICAL WRITING. In attacking the funeral industry, Mitford also,
implicitly, attacks the people who pay for and comply with the industry's
attitudes and practices. What ASSUMPTIONS does Mitford seem to make
about how we ought to deal with death and the dead? (Consider, for
instance, her statements about the "docility of Americans, . . . blissfully
ignorant" [para. 4] and the funeral director's making "the funeral a real
pleasure for everybody concerned" [27].) Write an essay in which you
interpret Mitford's assumptions and agree or disagree with them, based
on your own reading and experience. If you like, defend the ritual of
the funeral, or the mortician's profession, against Mitford's attack.
4. CONNECTIONS. Mitford is not the only writer of IRONY in this book:
James Thurber (p. 64), Joan Didion (p. 113), Judy Brady (p. 273), Fran
Lebowitz (p. 328), H. L. Mencken (p. 477), and Jonathan Swift (p.
522) also employ it. Based on Mitford's essay and essays by at least two
of these others, define *irony*. If you need a boost, supplement the
definition in this book's glossary with one in a dictionary of literary or
rhetorical terms. But go beyond others' definitions to construct one of
your own, using quotations from the essays as your support.

JESSICA MITFORD ON WRITING

"Choice of subject is of cardinal importance," declares Jessica
Mitford in *Poison Penmanship*. "One does by far one's best work when
besotted by and absorbed in the matter at hand." After *The American
Way of Death* was published, Mitford received hundreds of letters
suggesting alleged rackets that ought to be exposed, and to her surprise, an overwhelming majority of these letters complained about
defective and overpriced hearing aids. But Mitford never wrote a
book blasting the hearing aid industry. "Somehow, although there
may well be need for such an exposé, I could not warm up to hearing
aids as a subject for the kind of thorough, intensive, long-range
research that would be needed to do an effective job." She once
taught a course at Yale in muckraking, with each student choosing a
subject to investigate. "Those who tackled hot issues on campus, such
as violations of academic freedom or failure to implement affirmative-
action hiring policies, turned in some excellent work; but the lad
who decided to investigate 'waste in the Yale dining halls' was pre-
dictably unable to make much of this trivial topic." (The editors
interject: We aren't sure that the topic is necessarily trivial, but
obviously not everyone would burn to write about it!)

The hardest problem Mitford faced in writing *The American Way of Death*, she recalls, was doing her factual, step-by-step account of the embalming process. She felt "determined to describe it in all its revolting details, but how to make this subject palatable to the reader?" Her solution was to cast the whole process analysis in the official jargon of the mortuary industry, drawing on lists of taboo words and their EUPHEMISMS (or acceptable synonyms), as published in the trade journal *Casket & Sunnyside*: "Mr., Mrs., Miss Blank, not corpse or body; preparation room, not morgue; reposing room, not laying-out room. . . ." The story of Mr. Jones thus took shape, and Mitford's use of jargon, she found, added macabre humor to the proceedings.

FOR DISCUSSION

1. What seem to be Mitford's criteria for an effective essay or book?
2. What is muckraking? Why do you suppose anyone would want to do it?

ADDITIONAL WRITING TOPICS

Process Analysis

1. Write a *directive* process analysis (a "how-to" essay) in which, drawing on your own knowledge, you instruct someone in doing or making something. Divide the process into steps and be sure to detail each step thoroughly. Some possible subjects (any of which may be modified or narrowed):

   How to enlist people's confidence
   How to bake bread
   How to meditate
   How to teach a child to swim
   How to select a science fiction novel
   How to drive a car in snow or rain
   How to prepare yourself to take an intelligence test
   How to compose a photograph
   How to judge cattle
   How to buy a used motorcycle
   How to enjoy an opera
   How to organize your own rock group
   How to eat an artichoke
   How to groom a horse
   How to bellydance
   How to make a movie or videotape
   How to build (or fly) a kite
   How to start weight training
   How to aid a person who is choking
   How to behave on a first date
   How to get your own way
   How to kick a habit
   How to lose weight
   How to win at poker
   How to make an effective protest or complaint

   Or, if you don't like any of those topics, what else do you know that others might care to learn from you?

2. Step by step, working in chronological order, write a careful *informative* analysis of any one of the following processes. (This is not to be a "how-to" essay, but an essay that explains how something works or happens.) Make use of DESCRIPTION wherever necessary, and be sure to include frequent time-markers. If one of these topics gives you a better idea for a paper, go with your own subject.

   How a student is processed during orientation or registration
   How the student newspaper gets published

How a professional umpire (or an insurance underwriter, or some other professional) does his or her job

How an amplifier (or other stereo component) works

How an air conditioner (or other household appliance) works

How a political candidate runs for office

How birds teach their young (or some other process in the natural world: how sharks feed, how a snake swallows an egg, how the human liver works)

How police control crowds

How people usually make up their minds when shopping for new cars (or new clothes)

3. Write a directive process analysis in which you use a light TONE. Although you need not take your subject in deadly earnest, your humor will probably be effective only if you take the method of process analysis seriously. Make clear each stage of the process and explain it in sufficient detail. Possible topics:

How to get through the month of November (or March)

How to flunk out of college swiftly and efficiently

How to outwit a pinball machine

How to choose a mate

How to go broke

How to sell something that nobody wants

6

DIVISION OR ANALYSIS
Slicing into Parts

THE METHOD

A chemist working for a soft-drink company is asked to improve on a competitor's product, Orange Quench. (In Chap. 5, the same chemist was working on a different part of the same problem.) To do the job, the chemist first has to figure out what's in the drink. She smells the stuff and tastes it. Then she tests a sample chemically to discover the actual ingredients: water, corn syrup, citric acid, sodium benzoate, coloring. Methodically, the chemist has performed *division* or *analysis*: She has separated the beverage into its components. Orange Quench stands revealed, understood, ready to be bettered.

Division or analysis (the terms are interchangeable) is a key skill in learning and in life. It is an instrument allowing you to slice a large and complicated subject into smaller parts that you can grasp and relate to one another. With analysis you comprehend — and communicate — the structure of things. And when it works, you find in the parts an idea or conclusion about the subject that makes it clearer, truer, more comprehensive, or more vivid than before you started.

If you have worked with the previous two chapters, you have already used division or analysis in explaining a process (Chap. 5) and in comparing and contrasting (Chap. 4). To make a better Orange Quench (a process), the chemist might prepare a recipe that divides the process into separate steps or actions ("First, boil a gallon of water . . ."). When the batch was done, she might taste-test the two drinks, analyzing and then comparing their orange flavor, sweetness, and acidity. As you'll see in following chapters, too, division or analysis figures in all the other methods of developing ideas, for it is basic to any concerted thought, explanation, or evaluation.

Although division or analysis always works the same way — separating a whole, singular subject into its elements, slicing it into parts — the method can be more or less difficult depending on how unfamiliar, complex, and abstract the subject is. Obviously, it's going to be much easier to analyze a chicken (wings, legs, thighs . . .) than a poem by T. S. Eliot (this image, that allusion . . .), easier to analyze why you won a swimming race than why the French and then the Americans got involved in Vietnam. Just about any subject *can* be analyzed and will be the clearer for it. In "I Want a Wife," an essay in this chapter, Judy Brady divides the role of a wife into its various functions or services. In an essay called "Teacher" from his book *Pot Shots at Poetry* (1980), Robert Francis divides the knowledge of poetry he imparted to his class into six pie sections. The first slice is what he told his students that they knew already.

> The second slice is what I told them that they could have found out just as well or better from books. What, for instance, is a sestina?
> The third slice is what I told them that they refused to accept. I could see it on their faces, and later I saw the evidence in their writing.
> The fourth slice is what I told them that they were willing to accept and may have thought they accepted but couldn't accept since they couldn't fully understand. This also I saw in their faces and in their work. Here, no doubt, I was mostly to blame.
> The fifth slice is what I told them that they discounted as whimsy or something simply to fill up time. After all, I was being paid to talk.
> The sixth slice is what I didn't tell them, for I didn't try to tell them all I knew. Deliberately I kept back something — a few professional secrets, a magic formula or two.

There are always multiple ways to divide or analyze a subject, just as there are many ways to slice a pie. Francis could have divided his knowledge of poetry into knowledge of rhyme, knowledge of meter, knowledge of imagery, and so forth — basically following the components of a poem. In other words, the outcome of an analysis depends on the rule or principle used to do the slicing. This fact accounts for some of the differences among academic disciplines: A psychologist, say, may look at the individual person primarily as a bundle of drives and needs, whereas a sociologist may emphasize the individual's roles in society. Even within disciplines, different factions analyze differently, using different principles of division or analysis. Some psychologists are interested mainly in thought, others mainly in behavior; some psychologists focus mainly on emotional development, others mainly on moral development.

Analysis plays a fundamental role in CRITICAL THINKING, READING, AND WRITING, topics discussed in this book's introduction (pp. 16–18). In fact, *analysis* and *criticism* are deeply related: The first comes from a Greek word meaning "to undo," the second from a Greek word meaning "to separate."

Critical thinking, reading, and writing go beneath the surface of the object, word, image, or whatever the subject is. When you work critically, you divide the subject into its elements, INFER the buried meanings and ASSUMPTIONS that define its essence, and SYNTHESIZE the parts into a new whole. Say a campaign brochure quotes a candidate as favoring "reasonable government expenditures on reasonable highway projects." The candidate will support new roads, right? Wrong. As a critical reader of the brochure, you quickly sense something fishy in the use (twice) of "reasonable." As an informed reader, you know (or find out) that the candidate has consistently opposed new roads, so the chances of her finding a highway project "reasonable" are slim. At the same time, her stand has been unpopular, so of course she wants to seem "reasonable" on the issue. Read critically, then, a campaign statement that seems to offer mild support for highways is actually a slippery evasion of any such commitment.

Analysis (a convenient term for the overlapping operations of analysis, inference, and synthesis) is very useful for exposing such evasiveness, but that isn't its only function. It may also help you understand a short story, perceive the importance of a sociological case study, or form a response to an environmental impact report.

If you've read this far in this book, you've already done quite a bit of analytical/critical thinking as you've read and analyzed the essays. In this chapter, several of the essays themselves — by Mark Crispin Miller, Barbara Ehrenreich, and bell hooks — show a fair range of concerted critical thinking.

THE PROCESS

Keep an eye out for writing assignments requiring division or analysis — in college and work, they won't be few or hard to find. They will probably include the word *analyze* or a word implying analysis such as *evaluate, interpret, discuss,* or *criticize.* Any time you spot such a term, you know your job is to separate the subject into its elements, to infer their meanings, to explore the relations among them, and to draw a conclusion about the subject.

Almost any coherent entity — object, person, place, concept — is a fit subject for analysis *if* the analysis will add to the subject's meaning or significance. Little is deadlier than the rote analytical exercise that leaves the parts neatly dissected and the subject comatose on the page. As a writer, you have to animate the subject, and that means finding your interest. What about your subject seems curious? What's appealing? Or mysterious? Or awful?

Such questions can help you find your analytical framework, the rule or principle you will use to divide the subject into parts. (As we mentioned before, there's more than one way to slice most subjects.) Say you're contemplating a hunk of bronze in the park. What elements of its creation and physical form make this sculpture art? Or what is the point of such public art? Or what does this sculpture do for this park? Or vice versa? Any of these questions would give you an angle of vision, a slant on your subject, a framework, and get your analysis moving.

In developing an essay by analysis, having an outline at your elbow can be a help. You don't want to overlook any parts or elements that should be included in your framework. (You needn't mention every feature in your final essay or give them all equal treatment, but any omissions or variations should be conscious.) And you want to use your framework consistently, not switching carelessly (and confusingly) from, say, the form of the sculpture to the function of public art. In writing her brief essay "I Want a Wife," Judy Brady must have needed an outline to work out carefully the different activities of a wife, so that she covered them all and clearly distinguished them.

Making a valid analysis is chiefly a matter of giving your subject thought, but for the result to seem useful and convincing to your readers, it will have to refer to the concrete world. The method requires not only cogitation, but open eyes and a willingness to provide EVIDENCE. The nature of the evidence will depend entirely on what you are analyzing — physical details for a sculpture, quotations for a poem, financial data for a business case study, statistics for a psychology case study, and so forth. The idea is to supply enough evidence to justify and support your particular slant on the subject.

Be sure your readers know what that slant is, too. Why did you go to the trouble of analyzing the sculpture, anyway, and what conclusion can you draw from the work? Usually, you'll state that conclusion as your THESIS close to the beginning of your essay — for instance, "Like much public art today, this bronze sculpture seems chiefly intended to make people feel good." It helps to reassemble your divided subject at the end of the essay, too: That gives you a chance to place your subject in a larger context or speculate on its influence or affirm its significance.

A final caution: It's possible to get carried away with one's own analysis, to become so enamored of the details that the subject itself becomes dim or distorted. You can avoid this danger by keeping the subject literally in front of you as you work (or at least imagining it vividly) and by maintaining an outline. In the end, your subject must be truly represented by your analysis, not twisted, diminished, inflated, or obliterated. The reader should be intrigued by your subject, yes, but also able to recognize it on the street.

DIVISION OR ANALYSIS IN A PARAGRAPH: TWO ILLUSTRATIONS

Using Division or Analysis to Write About Television

Most television comedies, even some that boast live audiences, rely on the laugh machine to fill too-quiet moments on the soundtrack. The effect of a canned laugh comes from its four overlapping elements. The first is style, from titter to belly laugh. The second is intensity, the volume, ranging from mild to medium to ear splitting. The third ingredient is duration, the length of the laugh, whether quick, medium, or extended. And finally, there's the number of laughers, from a lone giggler to a roaring throng. According to rumor (for its exact workings are a secret), the machine contains a bank of thirty-two tapes. Furiously working keys and tromping pedals, the operator plays the tapes singly or in combination to blend the four ingredients, as a maestro weaves a symphony out of brass, woodwinds, percussion, and strings.

COMMENT. This paragraph illustrates a fairly simple form of division or analysis: The four simultaneous parts of a canned laugh are separated out and explained. The writer's principle of analysis — the framework for dividing the subject — is clear and consistently applied: Any canned laugh has four overlapping elements. (The writer might have begun with an altogether different principle, such as the sequence of an individual laugh — beginning, crescendo, end — and that would have produced an altogether different paragraph.) Notice that each element of the laugh is adequately detailed for us to understand it clearly. Because of the analysis, we may not hear television laugh tracks — or even our own laughter — the same way again.

Using Division or Analysis in an Academic Discipline

The model of social relationship which fits these conditions [of realistic equality between patient and doctor] is that of the contract or covenant. The notion of contract should not be loaded with legalistic implications, but taken in its more symbolic form as in the traditional religious or marriage "contract" or "covenant." Here two individuals or groups are interacting in a way where there are obligations and expected benefits for both parties. The obligations and benefits are limited in scope, though, even if they are expressed in somewhat vague terms. The basic norms of freedom, dignity, truth-telling, promise-keeping, and justice are essential to a contractual relationship. The premise is trust and confidence even though it is recognized that there is not a full mutuality of interests. Social sanctions institutionalize and stand behind the relationship, in case there is a violation of the contract, but for the most part the assumption is that there will be a faithful fulfillment of the obligations.

COMMENT. This paragraph by Robert M. Veatch comes from "Models for Medicine in a Revolutionary Age," an article that first appeared in a scholarly journal, *Hastings Center Report*, and then was reprinted in a textbook on medical ethics. The author divides or analyzes the idea of the contract as it might pertain to the relation between doctor and patient. That, indeed, is the principle of analysis: What elements of a typical contractual relation might apply to the basic medical relation? The question is a complicated one, and Veatch clearly itemizes the elements: interacting individuals or groups with mutual but limited obligations and expectations; freedom, dignity, and other "norms"; trust and confidence; the support of social sanctions (meaning that society upholds the relation); and good faith. The analysis accomplishes two interlocking goals. It explains contractual arrangements such as the marriage covenant Veatch mentions. And it reconfigures the doctor-patient relation so that, as Veatch goes on to propose, patients and doctors can share decision making.

JUDY BRADY

JUDY BRADY, born in 1937 in San Francisco, where she now lives, earned a B.F.A. in painting from the University of Iowa in 1962. Drawn into political action by her work in the feminist movement, she went to Cuba in 1973, where she studied class relationships as a way of understanding change in a society. "I am not a 'writer,'" Brady declares, "but really am a disenfranchised (and fired) house-wife, now secretary." Despite her disclaimer, Brady does publish articles occasionally — on union organizing, abortion, education in Cuba, and other topics. In 1991 she also published *1 in 3: Women with Cancer Confront an Epidemic,* an anthology of writings by women.

I Want a Wife

"I Want a Wife" first appeared in the Spring 1972 issue of *Ms.* magazine and has been reprinted there, most recently in 1990. The essay is one of the best-known manifestos in popular feminist writing. In it, Brady trenchantly divides the work of a wife into its multiple duties and functions, leading to an inescapable conclusion.

I belong to that classification of people known as wives. I am A 1
Wife. And, not altogether incidentally, I am a mother.

Not too long ago a male friend of mine appeared on the scene 2
fresh from a recent divorce. He had one child, who is, of course, with his ex-wife. He is looking for another wife. As I thought about him while I was ironing one evening, it suddenly occurred to me that I, too, would like to have a wife. Why do I want a wife?

I would like to go back to school so that I can become econom- 3
ically independent, support myself, and, if need be, support those dependent upon me. I want a wife who will work and send me to school. And while I am going to school I want a wife to take care of my children. I want a wife to keep track of the children's doctor and dentist appointments. And to keep track of mine, too. I want a wife to make sure my children eat properly and are kept clean. I want a wife who will wash the children's clothes and keep them mended. I want a wife who is a good nurturant attendant to my children, who arranges for their schooling, makes sure that they have an adequate social life with their peers, takes them to the park, the zoo, etc. I want a wife who takes care of the children when they are sick, a wife

who arranges to be around when the children need special care, because, of course, I cannot miss classes at school. My wife must arrange to lose time at work and not lose the job. It may mean a small cut in my wife's income from time to time, but I guess I can tolerate that. Needless to say, my wife will arrange and pay for the care of the children while my wife is working.

I want a wife who will take care of *my* physical needs. I want a   4
wife who will keep my house clean. A wife who will pick up after my children, a wife who will pick up after me. I want a wife who will keep my clothes clean, ironed, mended, replaced when need be, and who will see to it that my personal things are kept in their proper place so that I can find what I need the minute I need it. I want a wife who cooks the meals, a wife who is a *good* cook. I want a wife who will plan the menus, do the necessary grocery shopping, prepare the meals, serve them pleasantly, and then do the cleaning up while I do my studying. I want a wife who will care for me when I am sick and sympathize with my pain and loss of time from school. I want a wife to go along when our family takes vacation so that someone can continue to care for me and my children when I need a rest and change of scene.

I want a wife who will not bother me with rambling complaints   5
about a wife's duties. But I want a wife who will listen to me when I feel the need to explain a rather difficult point I have come across in my course of studies. And I want a wife who will type my papers for me when I have written them.

I want a wife who will take care of the details of my social life.   6
When my wife and I are invited out by my friends, I want a wife who will take care of the babysitting arrangements. When I meet people at school that I like and want to entertain, I want a wife who will have the house clean, will prepare a special meal, serve it to me and my friends, and not interrupt when I talk about things that interest me and my friends. I want a wife who will have arranged that the children are fed and ready for bed before my guests arrive so that the children do not bother us. I want a wife who takes care of the needs of my guests so that they feel comfortable, who makes sure that they have an ashtray, that they are passed the hors d'oeuvres, that they are offered a second helping of the food, that their wine glasses are replenished when necessary, that their coffee is served to them as they like it. And I want a wife who knows that sometimes I need a night out by myself.

I want a wife who is sensitive to my sexual needs, a wife who   7
makes love passionately and eagerly when I feel like it, a wife who

makes sure that I am satisfied. And, of course, I want a wife who will not demand sexual attention when I am not in the mood for it. I want a wife who assumes the complete responsibility for birth control, because I do not want more children. I want a wife who will remain sexually faithful to me so that I do not have to clutter up my intellectual life with jealousies. And I want a wife who understands that *my* sexual needs may entail more than strict adherence to monogamy. I must, after all, be able to relate to people as fully as possible.

If, by chance, I find another person more suitable as a wife than   8
the wife I already have, I want the liberty to replace my present wife with another one. Naturally, I will expect a fresh, new life; my wife will take the children and be solely responsible for them so that I am left free.

When I am through with school and have a job, I want my wife   9
to quit working and remain at home so that my wife can more fully and completely take care of a wife's duties.

My God, who *wouldn't* want a wife?   10

QUESTIONS ON MEANING

1. Sum up the duties of a wife as Brady sees them.
2. To what inequities in the roles traditionally assigned to men and to women does "I Want a Wife" call attention?
3. What is the THESIS of this essay? Is it stated or implied?
4. Is Brady unfair to men?

QUESTIONS ON WRITING STRATEGY

1. What EFFECT does Brady obtain with the title "I Want a Wife"?
2. What do the first two paragraphs accomplish?
3. What is the TONE of this essay?
4. How do you explain the fact that Brady never uses the pronoun *she* to refer to a wife? Does this make her prose unnecessarily awkward?
5. What principle does Brady use to analyze the role of wife? Can you think of some other principle for analyzing the job?
6. Knowing that this essay was first published in Ms. magazine in 1972, what can you guess about its intended readers? Does "I Want a Wife" strike a college AUDIENCE today as revolutionary?
7. **OTHER METHODS.** Although she mainly divides or analyzes the role of wife, Brady also uses CLASSIFICATION to sort the many duties and responsibilities into manageable groups. What are the groups?

QUESTIONS ON LANGUAGE

1. What is achieved by the author's frequent repetition of the phrase "I want a wife"?
2. Be sure you know how to define the following words as Brady uses them: nurturant (para. 3); replenished (6); adherence, monogamy (7).
3. In general, how would you describe the DICTION of this essay? How well does it suit the essay's intended audience?

SUGGESTIONS FOR WRITING

1. Write a brief essay entitled "I Want a Husband" in which, using examples as Brady does, you enumerate the stereotyped roles traditionally assigned to men in our society.
2. Imagining that you want to employ someone to do a specific job, divide the task into its duties and functions. Then, guided by your analysis, write an accurate job description in essay form.
3. CRITICAL WRITING. In an essay, SUMMARIZE Brady's view as you understand it and then EVALUATE her essay. Consider: Is Brady fair? (If not, is unfairness justified?) Is the essay relevant today? (If not, what has changed?) Provide specific EVIDENCE from your experience, observation, and reading.
4. CONNECTIONS. Like Brady's essay, Suzanne Britt's "Neat People vs. Sloppy People" (p. 174) is also notable for a strong, uncompromising TONE. Write an analysis of the language Brady and Britt use to characterize husbands and neat people, respectively. How are their attitudes similar or different? Use specific EXAMPLES from both essays.

MARK CRISPIN MILLER

Applying his academic training as a Renaissance scholar to contemporary culture, MARK CRISPIN MILLER produces fresh and provocative cultural criticism. He was born in 1949 in Chicago and grew up there and in Boston. He received a B.A. in 1971 from Northwestern University, and an M.A. in 1973 and Ph.D. in 1977 from the Johns Hopkins University. After several years at the University of Pennsylvania, Miller now teaches in the writing seminars at Johns Hopkins. Miller's critical essays on rock music, film, television, and advertising appear frequently in *The New Republic, The Nation, Mother Jones, The New York Review of Books,* and other magazines. Some of the essays are collected in the volume *Boxed In: The Culture of TV* (1987). Miller edited *Seeing Through Movies* (1990), an anthology, and wrote *Spectacle* (1992), an examination of the media and the military during the Gulf War.

Dow Recycles Reality

Published in *Esquire* magazine in September 1990, this essay exemplifies Miller's close readings of contemporary popular culture. Television especially grabs his attention because after the 1970s, he says, "it was no longer a mere stain or imposition on some preexistent cultural environment, but had itself become the environment"; it "was not only 'on the air,' but had become the very air we breathe."

"That's my Dad." In the preteen voice-over there's just the trace 1
of an apologetic chuckle. It's understandable. This "Dad" is an overt dork. Pitching at a (Dow) company softball game, he gives up a base hit, then tries to block it with his foot. Note the look of nitwit concentration, recalling Dagwood Bumstead or Curly Howard hard at work. Dad, too, is a diverting stooge, with that potent Dow logo stamped across his cap, and his togs steeped in the brilliant white and orange of that logo. (In fact, the whole bright ball field is decked out in the same festive colors.)

"Good thing he's got a *real* job!" jokes Dad's young son, ". . . at 2
Dow!" As the subject shifts from softball to the corporation, this cherub drops the mild, ironic tone and starts promoting Dow's environmentalism in a kind of earnest kidspeak. Dad is (spoken haltingly) "a . . . plastics . . . recycling . . . engineer!" Dad "figures out

ways" to turn plastic trash "into neat stuff like those picnic tables — and Brad's bat 'n' ball!"

With this last phrase, there appears tiny "Brad," apparently a ³ baby brother, whacking a home run — and then there's Dad again, oafishly striking out: "My Dad may be a lousy ballplayer," his son concludes, "but he's a *neat guy!*" The boy then grasps Dad's hand and gazes up, with filial pathos, into the engineer's weak, boyish face, sighing, "I'm *real proud* o' ya, Dad!" "*Proud* of me?" Dad gasps, and the camera cranes up and back to reveal the father-son communion

amid the Dow-sponsored gaiety, as that hearty female voice, so reminiscent of the "the Sixties" (the Seekers), breaks, as usual, into: "Dow . . . *lets* you do *great thiiiiiings!*"

Devised for Earth Day, this ad, like most "Green ads," tries to   4
dim our awareness of foul air, mounting garbage, ozone depletion. Implicitly, Dow's sponsorship of this old-fashioned sunny fete assures us that Dow, prolific maker of (among other goodies) Styrofoam, pesticide, and chemical fertilizer, wants us all to live as we did before the rise of agribusiness, freeways, and fast food. The child, too, is reassuring. If this cool young Aryan is so moved by Dad's daily responsibilities, then Dad/Dow must be doing a heroic job indeed, with that "plastics recycling."

Not that plastic poses any danger! Certainly, each and every one   5
of us should go on using tons of it: Dad is there to help Dow make *more* plastics. And why not? Isn't plastic just as wholesome as whatever grows on trees? Note, among the items displayed on the child's left (fig. 2), that large green apple, placed there as if to blur the crucial difference between nature's bounty and the corporation's goods.

And Dow's TV spots work to sanitize not just its wares but its   6
very image. In this ad Dow seems not huge and lethal, but goofily benign, like that awkward boy/dad in his special hat and corporate colors. By softening "Dad," our usual symbol of authority, Dow appears also to champion the weak and innocent: "Brad" belts a homer while Dad strikes out — just as, in other Dow ads, the effectual one is not some steel-gray CEO, but a slightly rumpled backpacker; a lanky college student grinning on a humble bike; a slim and saintly Ph.D. gone home to save her Grandpa's farm. Dow projects itself as "caring" — yet its power seems all-pervasive. Note, in the final shot, that white-and-orange umbrella, placed protectively above the faulty employee and his adoring son.

What Dow is selling here, then, is not just a profitable myth   7
about plastics but the sense (which will become *our* sense, if we don't watch out) that certain dissident impulses of the past have been absorbed — by Dow. In its ads, the young are on Dow's side — not like, say, twenty years ago. Back then, one of Dow's products — napalm — made the company notorious, through horrifying images of children burned and screaming.[1] Those who saw, and haven't forgotten, may not feel comforted by Dow's knowing hikers, tykes,

[1]During the Vietnam War, napalm was used to destroy forests and villages. — EDS.

and Ph.D.s. Younger viewers, on the other hand, have no way of spotting the lie, since TV, thanks to Dow and others, has no memory.

QUESTIONS ON MEANING

1. What is a "Green ad"?
2. State Miller's THESIS in your own words.
3. How does the boy in the Dow ad characterize his father?
4. What is the PURPOSE of this essay?
5. Why, in Miller's opinion, does Dow want to project a "family" image?

QUESTIONS ON WRITING STRATEGY

1. What elements does Miller identify in the Dow commercial? How does what he sees in these elements lead him to his conclusion about the commercial?
2. This essay was first published in *Esquire*, a magazine aimed primarily at men. How might Miller's AUDIENCE have influenced his choice of which commercial to analyze?
3. What is the essay's TONE? Support your answer with specific examples.
4. **OTHER METHODS.** Why does Miller use NARRATION and DESCRIPTION so carefully in relating the Dow commercial? Would his analysis be as effective without the detailed presentation of the ad?

QUESTIONS ON LANGUAGE

1. Be sure you know the meaning of these words: ironic (para. 2): oafishly, filial, pathos (3); implicitly, fete, prolific, agribusiness (4); benign (6); dissident (7).
2. What is the EFFECT of Miller's juxtaposition of formal and informal language? Look at phrases like "overt dork" and "diverting stooge" (para. 1).
3. What are the CONNOTATIONS of the phrase "cool young Aryan" (para. 4)? What is Miller implying?

SUGGESTIONS FOR WRITING

1. Analyze a TV commercial or magazine ad that you find unusual or interesting. You may, but need not, follow Miller's example of analyzing the ad as image control. Some other principles of analysis you might consider: What makes an ad effective? Boring? Offensive? Informative? Worthwhile?

2. Miller takes Dow to task for its corporate hypocrisy — a company known for polluting the environment claims not to hurt, but even to help, the environment. Select an instance of hypocrisy well known to you, and present an analysis of it. (For instance, a university may champion intellectual freedom but censor its student newspapers, or a politician might claim to be a friend of the poor but advocate tax breaks for the rich.) What is the image? What is the reality? How is the image used to mask the truth?
3. CRITICAL WRITING. Do you agree with Miller's assumption that Dow tries to "sanitize its wares and its very image" — that the environmental concerns the commercial boasts of are insincere? EVALUATE Miller's argument for its ability to convince you, the reader. Where does the essay seem strong? Where does it seem weak? Be specific.
4. CONNECTIONS. Both Miller's essay and Barbara Ehrenreich's "The Wretched of the Hearth" (p. 292) depict television as a political medium. After reading both essays, write an essay of your own agreeing or disagreeing with this view. Does television shape viewers' attitudes? Does it reflect them?

MARK CRISPIN MILLER ON WRITING

Mark Miller learned the art of analysis while studying literature in graduate school. "I learned to know the poem," he recalls in the introduction to *Boxed In*, "to (try to) divine its every implication, to trace its terms and images back through their respective secret histories, and then finally to compose a reading, so that the old text might dance clear of the impediments of age. Such, at any rate, was the ideal." The procedure sometimes resembled an autopsy, Miller admits; but it "could also illuminate what had been dark, for there was, in the erotic sense, a certain madness in that method, which demanded the near-maniacal attentiveness of a yearning lover."

While thus engaged in Renaissance poetry, Miller was also attracted by "the different sort of text piling up all over the place, covering the world like snow, or uncollected trash . . . — the interminable text of television, usually somewhere in view, never out of earshot." This text, too, demanded close reading, for "TV has all but boxed us in, . . . overwhelming the mind . . . , making it only half-aware."

In his writing, Miller has attempted to set out a "critical approach that would take TV seriously (without extolling it), a method of deciphering TV's component images, requiring both a meticulous attention to concrete detail and a sense of TV's historical situation.

. . . The reading of TV contains and necessitates a reading of our moment and its past."

For Miller, "critical analysis can just as easily reclaim a marvel . . . as it can devastate a lie. . . . The critical impulse can help also to replenish the minds within its sphere. . . . Those who have grown up watching television are not, because of all that gaping, now automatically adept at visual interpretation. That spectatorial 'experience' is passive, mesmeric, undiscriminating, and therefore not conducive to the refinement of the critical faculties: logic and imagination, linguistic precision, historical awareness, and a capacity for long, intense absorption. These — and not the abilities to compute, apply, or memorize — are the true desiderata of any higher education, and it is critical thinking that can best realize them."

FOR DISCUSSION

1. How is Renaissance poetry like television?
2. In your own words, what does Miller mean by "critical analysis"?
3. What are the "desiderata of higher education"? How does critical thinking help one realize them?

GAIL SHEEHY

GAIL SHEEHY was born in 1937. She earned her B.S. degree from
the University of Vermont in 1958 and was a fellow in Columbia
University's Journalism School in 1970. A contributor to the *New
York Times Magazine, Esquire, McCall's, Ms., Cosmopolitan, Rolling
Stone,* and other magazines, she has also written a novel, *Lovesounds*
(1970), and many popular studies of contemporary life: *Speed Is of
the Essence* (1971), *Panthermania* (1971), *Hustling* (1973), *Passages*
(1976), *Pathfinders* (1981), *Character: America's Search for Leadership*
(1988), *The Man Who Changed the World: The Lives of Mikhail S.
Gorbachev* (1991), and *Silent Passage* (1992). In *The Spirit of Survival*
(1986), Sheehy has written a history of strife and deprivation in
Cambodia. The book includes a narrative told from the point of
view of Mohm, a twelve-year-old Cambodian child adopted by
Sheehy and her husband, Clay Felker, a New York editor.

Predictable Crises of Adulthood

"Predictable Crises of Adulthood" is adapted from the second chapter of *Passages*. In the essay, Sheehy identifies six stages that most
people experience between the ages of eighteen and fifty. The
author, as she herself makes clear, is not a theorist or a scholar; she
is an artful reporter, in this case of findings in adult development.
Not everyone goes through the stages Sheehy traces at exactly the
same time, but see whether any of the following crises sound familiar
to you.

We are not unlike a particularly hardy crustacean. The lobster 1
grows by developing and shedding a series of hard, protective shells.
Each time it expands from within, the confining shell must be
sloughed off. It is left exposed and vulnerable until, in time, a new
covering grows to replace the old.

With each passage from one stage of human growth to the next 2
we, too, must shed a protective structure. We are left exposed and
vulnerable — but also yeasty and embryonic again, capable of stretching in ways we hadn't known before. These sheddings may take several
years or more. Coming out of each passage, though, we enter a longer
and more stable period in which we can expect relative tranquility
and a sense of equilibrium regained. . . .

As we shall see, each person engages the steps of development 3 in his or her own characteristic *step-style*. Some people never complete the whole sequence. And none of us "solves" with one step — by jumping out of the parental home into a job or marriage, for example — the problems in separating from the caregivers of childhood. Nor do we "achieve" autonomy once and for all by converting our dreams into concrete goals, even when we attain those goals. The central issues or tasks of one period are never fully completed, tied up, and cast aside. But when they lose their primacy and the current life structure has served its purpose, we are ready to move on to the next period.

Can one catch up? What might look to others like listlessness,   4
contrariness, a maddening refusal to face up to an obvious task may be a person's own unique detour that will bring him out later on the other side. Developmental gains won can later be lost — and rewon. It's plausible, though it can't be proven, that the mastery of one set of tasks fortifies us for the next period and the next set of challenges. But it's important not to think too mechanistically. Machines work by units. The bureaucracy (supposedly) works step by step. Human beings, thank God, have an individual inner dynamic that can never be precisely coded.

Although I have indicated the ages when Americans are likely   5
to go through each stage, and the differences between men and women where they are striking, do not take the ages too seriously. The stages are the thing, and most particularly the sequence.

Here is the briefest outline of the developmental ladder.   6

Pulling Up Roots

Before 18, the motto is loud and clear: "I have to get away from   7
my parents." But the words are seldom connected to action. Generally still safely part of our families, even if away at school, we feel our autonomy to be subject to erosion from moment to moment.

After 18, we begin Pulling Up Roots in earnest. College, military   8
service, and short-term travels are all customary vehicles our society provides for the first round trips between family and a base of one's own. In the attempt to separate our view of the world from our family's view, despite vigorous protestations to the contrary — "I know exactly what I want!" — we cast about for any beliefs we can call our own. And in the process of testing those beliefs we are often drawn to fads, preferably those most mysterious and inaccessible to our parents.

Whatever tentative memberships we try out in the world, the   9 fear haunts us that we are really kids who cannot take care of ourselves. We cover that fear with acts of defiance and mimicked confidence. For allies to replace our parents, we turn to our contemporaries. They become conspirators. So long as their perspective meshes with our own, they are able to substitute for the sanctuary of the family. But that doesn't last very long. And the instant they diverge from the shaky ideals of "our group," they are seen as betrayers. Rebounds to the family are common between the ages of 18 and 22.

The tasks of this passage are to locate ourselves in a peer group 10 role, a sex role, an anticipated occupation, an ideology or world view. As a result, we gather the impetus to leave home physically and the identity to *begin* leaving home emotionally.

Even as one part of us seeks to be an individual, another part 11 longs to restore the safety and comfort of merging with another. Thus one of the most popular myths of this passage is: We can piggyback our development by attaching to a Stronger One. But people who marry during this time often prolong financial and emotional ties to the family and relatives that impede them from becoming self-sufficient.

A stormy passage through the Pulling Up Roots years will probably 12 facilitate the normal progression of the adult life cycle. If one doesn't have an identity crisis at this point, it will erupt during a later transition, when the penalties may be harder to bear.

The Trying Twenties

The Trying Twenties confront us with the question of how to 13 take hold in the adult world. Our focus shifts from the interior turmoils of late adolescence — "Who am I?" "What is truth?" — and we become almost totally preoccupied with working out the externals. "How do I put my aspirations into effect?" "What is the best way to start?" "Where do I go?" "Who can help me?" "How did *you* do it?"

In this period, which is longer and more stable compared with 14 the passage that leads to it, the tasks are as enormous as they are exhilarating: To shape a Dream, that vision of ourselves which will generate energy, aliveness, and hope. To prepare for a lifework. To find a mentor if possible. And to form the capacity for intimacy, without losing in the process whatever consistency of self we have thus far mustered. The first test structure must be erected around the life we choose to try.

Doing what we "should" is the most pervasive theme of the 15

twenties. The "shoulds" are largely defined by family models, the press
of the culture, or the prejudices of our peers. If the prevailing cultural
instructions are that one should get married and settle down behind
one's own door, a nuclear family is born. If instead the peers insist
that one should do one's own thing, the 25-year-old is likely to
harness himself onto a Harley-Davidson and burn up Route 66 in the
commitment to have no commitments.

One of the terrifying aspects of the twenties is the inner convic- 16
tion that the choices we make are irrevocable. It is largely a false
fear. Change is quite possible, and some alteration of our original
choices is probably inevitable.

Two impulses, as always, are at work. One is to build a firm, safe 17
structure for the future by making strong commitments, to "be set."
Yet people who slip into a ready-made form without much self-
examination are likely to find themselves *locked in.*

The other urge is to explore and experiment, keeping any struc- 18
ture tentative and therefore easily reversible. Taken to the extreme,
these are people who skip from one trial job and one limited personal
encounter to another, spending their twenties in the *transient* state.

Although the choices of our twenties are not irrevocable, they 19
do set in motion a Life Pattern. Some of us follow the lock-in pattern,
others the transient pattern, the wunderkind pattern, the caregiver
pattern, and there are a number of others. Such patterns strongly
influence the particular questions raised for each person during each
passage. . . .

Buoyed by powerful illusions and belief in the power of the will, 20
we commonly insist in our twenties that what we have chosen to do
is the one true course in life. Our backs go up at the merest hint that
we are like our parents, that two decades of parental training might
be reflected in our current actions and attitudes.

"Not me," is the motto, "I'm different."   21

Catch-30

Impatient with devoting ourselves to the "shoulds," a new vitality 22
springs from within as we approach 30. Men and women alike speak
of feeling too narrow and restricted. They blame all sorts of things,
but what the restrictions boil down to are the outgrowth of career
and personal choices of the twenties. They may have been choices
perfectly suited to that stage. But now the fit feels different. Some
inner aspect that was left out is striving to be taken into account.
Important new choices must be made, and commitments altered or

deepened. The work involves great change, turmoil, and often crisis — a simultaneous feeling of rock bottom and the urge to bust out.

One common response is the tearing up of the life we spent most   23
of our twenties putting together. It may mean striking out on a
secondary road toward a new vision or converting a dream of "running
for president" into a more realistic goal. The single person feels a
push to find a partner. The woman who was previously content at
home with children chafes to venture into the world. The childless
couple reconsiders children. And almost everyone who is married,
especially those married for seven years, feels a discontent.

If the discontent doesn't lead to a divorce, it will, or should, call   24
for a serious review of the marriage and of each partner's aspirations
in their Catch-30 condition. The gist of that condition was expressed
by a 29-year-old associate with a Wall Street law firm:

"I'm considering leaving the firm. I've been there four years now;   25
I'm getting good feedback, but I have no clients of my own. I feel
weak. If I wait much longer, it will be too late, too close to that
fateful time of decision on whether or not to become a partner. I'm
success-oriented. But the concept of being 55 years old and stuck in
a monotonous job drives me wild. It drives me crazy now, just a little
bit. I'd say that 85 percent of the time I thoroughly enjoy my work.
But when I get a screwball case, I come away from court saying,
'What am I doing here?' It's a *visceral* reaction that I'm wasting my
time. I'm trying to find some way to make a social contribution or a
slot in city government. I keep saying, 'There's something more.'"

Besides the push to broaden himself professionally, there is a wish   26
to expand his personal life. He wants two or three more children.
"The concept of a home has become very meaningful to me, a place
to get away from troubles and relax. I love my son in a way I could
not have anticipated. I never could live alone."

Consumed with the work of making his own critical life-steering   27
decisions, he demonstrates the essential shift at this age: an absolute
requirement to be more self-concerned. The self has new value now
that his competency has been proved.

His wife is struggling with her own age-30 priorities. She wants   28
to go to law school, but he wants more children. If she is going to
stay home, she wants him to make more time for the family instead
of taking on even wider professional commitments. His view of the
bind, of what he would most like from his wife, is this:

"I'd like not to be bothered. It sounds cruel, but I'd like not to   29
have to worry about what she's going to do next week. Which is why
I've told her several times that I think she should do something. Go

back to school and get a degree in social work or geography or whatever. Hopefully that would fulfill her, and then I wouldn't have to worry about her line of problems. I want her to be decisive about herself."

The trouble with his advice to his wife is that it comes out of 30 concern with *his* convenience, rather than with *her* development. She quickly picks up on this lack of goodwill: He is trying to dispose of her. At the same time, he refuses her the same latitude to be "selfish" in making an independent decision to broaden her horizons. Both perceive a lack of mutuality. And that is what Catch-30 is all about for the couple.

Rooting and Extending

Life becomes less provisional, more rational and orderly in the 31 early thirties. We begin to settle down in the full sense. Most of us begin putting down roots and sending out new shoots. People buy houses and become very earnest about climbing career ladders. Men in particular concern themselves with "making it." Satisfaction with marriage generally goes downhill in the thirties (for those who have remained together) compared with the highly valued, vision-supporting marriage of the twenties. This coincides with the couple's reduced social life outside the family and the inturned focus on raising their children.

The Deadline Decade

In the middle of the thirties we come upon a crossroads. We have 32 reached the halfway mark. Yet even as we are reaching our prime, we begin to see there is a place where it finishes. Time starts to squeeze.

The loss of youth, the faltering of physical powers we have always 33 taken for granted, the fading purpose of stereotyped roles by which we have thus far identified ourselves, the spiritual dilemma of having no absolute answers — any or all of these shocks can give this passage the character of crisis. Such thoughts usher in a decade between 35 and 45 that can be called the Deadline Decade. It is a time of both danger and opportunity. All of us have the chance to rework the narrow identity by which we defined ourselves in the first half of life. And those of us who make the most of the opportunity will have a full-out authenticity crisis.

To come through this authenticity crisis, we must reexamine our 34 purposes and reevaluate how to spend our resources from now on. "Why am I doing all this? What do I really believe in?" No matter what we have been doing, there will be parts of ourselves that have been suppressed and now need to find expression. "Bad" feelings will demand acknowledgment along with the good.

It is frightening to step off onto the treacherous footbridge leading   35
to the second half of life. We can't take everything with us on this journey through uncertainty. Along the way, we discover that we are alone. We no longer have to ask permission because we are the providers of our own safety. We must learn to give ourselves permission. We stumble upon feminine or masculine aspects of our natures that up to this time have usually been masked. There is grieving to be done because an old self is dying. By taking in our suppressed and even our unwanted parts, we prepare at the gut level for the reintegration of an identity that is ours and ours alone — not some artificial form put together to please the culture or our mates. It is a hard passage at the beginning. But by disassembling ourselves, we can glimpse the light and gather our parts into a renewal.

Women sense this inner crossroads earlier than men do. The time   36
pinch often prompts a woman to stop and take an all-points survey at age 35. Whatever options she has already played out, she feels a "my last chance" urgency to review those options she has set aside and those that aging and biology will close off in the *now foreseeable* future. For all her qualms and confusion about where to start looking for a new future, she usually enjoys an exhilaration of release. Assertiveness begins rising. There are so many firsts ahead.

Men, too, feel the time push in the mid-thirties. Most men   37
respond by pressing down harder on the career accelerator. It's "my last chance" to pull away from the pack. It is no longer enough to be the loyal junior executive, the promising young novelist, the lawyer who does a little *pro bono* work on the side. He wants now to become part of top management, to be recognized as an established writer, or an active politician with his own legislative program. With some chagrin, he discovers that he has been too anxious to please and too vulnerable to criticism. He wants to put together his own ship.

During this period of intense concentration on external advance-   38
ment, it is common for men to be unaware of the more difficult, gut issues that are propelling them forward. The survey that was neglected at 35 becomes a crucible at 40. Whatever rung of achievement he has reached, the man of 40 usually feels stale, restless, burdened, and unappreciated. He worries about his health. He wonders, "Is this all there is?" He may make a series of departures from well-established lifelong base lines, including marriage. More and more men are seeking second careers in midlife. Some become self-destructive. And

many men in their forties experience a major shift of emphasis away from pouring all their energies into their own advancement. A more tender, feeling side comes into play. They become interested in developing an ethical self.

Renewal or Resignation

Somewhere in the mid-forties, equilibrium is regained. A new 39 stability is achieved, which may be more or less satisfying.

If one has refused to budge through the midlife transition, the 40 sense of staleness will calcify into resignation. One by one, the safety and supports will be withdrawn from the person who is standing still. Parents will become children; children will become strangers; a mate will grow away or go away; the career will become just a job — and each of these events will be felt as an abandonment. The crisis will probably emerge again around 50. And although its wallop will be greater, the jolt may be just what is needed to prod the resigned middle-ager toward seeking revitalization.

On the other hand . . .   41

If we have confronted ourselves in the middle passage and found 42 a renewal of purpose around which we are eager to build a more authentic life structure, these may well be the best years. Personal happiness takes a sharp turn upward for partners who can now accept the fact: "I cannot expect *anyone* to fully understand me." Parents can be forgiven for the burdens of our childhood. Children can be let go without leaving us in collapsed silence. At 50, there is a new warmth and mellowing. Friends become more important than ever, but so does privacy. Since it is so often proclaimed by people past midlife, the motto of this stage might be "No more bullshit."

QUESTIONS ON MEANING

1. In your own words, summarize each of Sheehy's six predictable stages of adult life.
2. According to the author, what happens to people who fail to experience a given stage of growth at the usual time?
3. How would you characterize Sheehy's attitude toward growth and change in adult life?

QUESTIONS ON WRITING STRATEGY

1. Why does Sheehy employ the method of division or analysis? How does it serve her readers, too?
2. What, if anything, does the author gain by writing her essay in the first PERSON plural (*we, us*)?
3. What difficulties go along with making GENERALIZATIONS about human beings? To what extent does Sheehy surmount these difficulties?
4. How much knowledge of psychology does Sheehy expect of her AUDI-ENCE?
5. OTHER METHODS. Sheehy relies on CAUSE AND EFFECT to explain why needs and goals change at each stage of adulthood. SUMMARIZE the pattern of cause and effect in the "Catch-30" stage (paras. 22–30).

QUESTIONS ON LANGUAGE

1. Consult your dictionary if you need help in defining the following words: crustacean (para. 1); embryonic, tranquility, equilibrium (2); autonomy, primacy (3); plausible (4); inaccessible (8); sanctuary (9); impetus (10); exhilarating, mentor (14); pervasive (15); irrevocable (16); tentative (18); wunderkind (19); visceral (25); mutuality (30); dilemma (33); *pro bono*, chagrin, vulnerable (37); crucible (38); calcify (40).
2. What is a "nuclear family" (para. 15)?
3. The author coins a few phrases of her own. Refer to their context to help you define the following: step-style (para. 3); Stronger One (11); Catch-30 (24); authenticity crisis (33).

SUGGESTIONS FOR WRITING

1. From your experience, observation, or reading, test the accuracy of one of Sheehy's accounts of a typical period of crisis.
2. Inspired by Sheehy's division of life after 18 into phases, look back on your own earlier life or that of a younger person you know, and detail a series of phases in it. Invent names for the phases.
3. CRITICAL WRITING. In popularizing scholarly research from developmental psychology, Sheehy eliminates such features as detailed analyses of researchers' methods and results, statistical correlations and other data, source citations, and specialized terminology. Write an essay EVALUATING the advantages and disadvantages of popularizations such as Sheehy's versus scholarly books and articles like those you read for courses in the sciences, social sciences, or humanities.
4. CONNECTIONS. You may have noticed the similarity between Sheehy's characterization of the Catch-30 couple (paras. 22–30) and Judy Brady's analysis in "I Want a Wife" (p. 273). Use the information provided by Sheehy (about other stages as well, if you like) to analyze the particular crisis of the "I" who wants a wife in Brady's essay. Support your ideas with EVIDENCE from both essays.

BARBARA EHRENREICH

Barbara Ehrenreich was born in 1941 in Butte, Montana. After she graduated from Reed College, she took her Ph.D. at Rockefeller University, then taught at the State University of New York in Old Westbury in the early 1970s. She has contributed to many periodicals, among them *The New Republic, Mother Jones, Ms.*, and, most recently, *Time*, for which she writes a column. Ehrenreich's range encompasses investigative journalism, popular history, and astute social and political commentary. Her books include *Complaints and Disorders: The Sexual Politics of Sickness* (1973); *For Her Own Good: 150 Years of the Experts' Advice to Women* (with Deirdre English; 1978); *The Hearts of Men: American Dreams and the Flight from Commitment* (1983); *Fear of Falling: The Inner Life of the Middle Class* (1989); *The Worst Years of Our Lives* (1990), a collection of essays; and *Kipper's Game* (1993), a novel.

The Wretched of the Hearth

The occasion for the following essay was a review of *My Life as a Woman*, the autobiography of the comedian Roseanne Barr (now Roseanne Arnold). But Ehrenreich goes beyond a simple book review to analyze Roseanne's message and appeal. The essay was first published in *The New Republic* in April 1990. A complementary essay on another popular culture figure, bell hooks's "Madonna," begins on page 303.

In the second half of the eighties, when American conservatism had reached its masochistic zenith with the re-election of Ronald Reagan, when women's liberation had been replaced by the more delicate sensibility known as post-feminism, when everyone was a yuppie and the heartiest word of endorsement in our vocabulary was "appropriate," there was yet this one paradox: our favorite TV personages were a liberal black man and a left-wing white feminist. Cosby could be explained as a representative of America's officially pro-family mood, but Roseanne is a trickier case. Her idea of humor is to look down on her sleeping family in the eponymous sitcom and muse, "Mmmm, I wonder where we could find an all-night taxidermist."

If Zeitgeist were destiny, Roseanne would never have happened. Only a few years ago, we learn from her autobiography, Roseanne

Barr was just your run-of-the-mill radical feminist mother-of-three, writing poems involving the Great Goddess, denouncing all known feminist leaders as sellout trash, and praying for the sixties to be born again in the female body. Since the entertainment media do not normally cast about for fat, loudmouthed feminists to promote to superstardom, we must assume that Roseanne has something to say that many millions of people have been waiting to hear. Like this, upon being told of a woman who stabbed her husband thirty-seven times: "I admire her restraint."

Roseanne is the neglected underside of the eighties, bringing   3 together its great themes of poverty, obesity, and defiance. The overside is handled well enough by Candice Bergen (*Murphy Brown*) and Madonna, who exist to remind us that talented women who work out are bound to become fabulously successful. Roseanne works a whole different beat, both in her sitcom and in the movie *She-Devil*, portraying the hopeless underclass of the female sex: polyester-clad, overweight occupants of the slow track; fast-food waitresses, factory workers, housewives, members of the invisible pink-collar army; the despised, the jilted, the underpaid.

But Barr — and this may be her most appealing feature — is   4 never a victim. In the sitcom, she is an overworked mother who is tormented by her bosses at such locales as Wellman Plastics (where she works the assembly line) and Chicken Divine (a fast-food spot). But Roseanne Connor, her sitcom character, has, as we say in the blue-collar suburbs, a mouth on her. When the cute but obnoxious boss at Wellman calls the workers together and announces, "I have something to tell you," Roseanne yells out, "What? That you feel you're a woman trapped in a man's body?" In *She-Devil*, where Barr is unfortunately shorn of her trademark deadpan snarl, revenge must take more concrete forms: She organizes an army of the wretched of the earth — nursing home patients and clerical workers — to destroy her errant husband and drive the slender, beautiful, rich-and-famous Other Woman dotty.

At some point, the women's studies profession is bound to look   5 up from its deconstructions and "re-thinkings" and notice Roseanne. They will then observe, in article and lecture form, that Barr's radicalism is distributed over the two axes of gender and class. This is probably as good an approach as any. Barr's identity is first of all female — her autobiography is titled *My Life as a Woman* — but her female struggles are located in the least telegenic and most frequently overlooked of social strata — the white, blue-collar working class. In anticipation of Roseannology, let us begin with Barr's contribution to the sociology of social class, and then take up her impressive achievements in the area of what could be called feminist theory.

Roseanne the sitcom, which was inspired by Barr the stand-up   6
comic, is a radical departure simply for featuring blue-collar Americans — and for depicting them as something other than half-witted greasers and low-life louts. The working class does not usually get much of a role in the American entertainment spectacle. In the seventies mumbling, muscular blue-collar males (*Rocky, The Deer Hunter, Saturday Night Fever*) enjoyed a brief modishness on the screen, while Archie Bunker, the consummate blue-collar bigot, raved away on the tube. But even these grossly stereotyped images vanished in the eighties, as the spectacle narrowed in on the brie-and-chardonnay class. Other than *Roseanne*, I can find only one sitcom that deals consistently with the sub-yuppie condition: *Married . . . with Children,* a relentlessly nasty portrayal of a shoe salesman and his cognitively disabled family members. There may even be others, but sociological zeal has not sufficed to get me past the opening sequences of *Major Dad, Full House,* or *Doogie Howser.*

Not that *Roseanne* is free of class stereotyping. The Connors must   7
bear part of the psychic burden imposed on all working-class people by their economic and occupational betters: They inhabit a zone of glad-handed *Gemeinschaft,*[1] evocative, now and then, of the stock wedding scene (*The Godfather, The Deer Hunter, Working Girl*) that routinely signifies lost old-world values. They indulge in a manic physicality that would be unthinkable among the more controlled and genteel Huxtables. They maintain a traditional, low-fiber diet of white bread and macaroni. They are not above a fart joke.

Still, in *Roseanne* I am willing to forgive the stereotypes as markers   8
designed to remind us of where we are: in the home of a construction worker and his minimum-wage wife. Without the reminders, we might not be aware of how thoroughly the deeper prejudices of the professional class are being challenged. Roseanne's fictional husband Dan (played by the irresistibly cuddly John Goodman) drinks domestic beer and dedicates Sundays to football; but far from being a Bunkeresque boor, he looks to this feminist like the fabled "sensitive man" we have all been pining for. He treats his rotund wife like a sex goddess. He picks up on small cues signaling emotional distress. He helps with homework. And when Roseanne works overtime, he cooks, cleans, and rides herd on the kids without any of the piteous

[1]German: "community." — Eds.

whining we have come to expect from upscale males in their rare, and lavishly documented, encounters with soiled Pampers.

Roseanne Connor has her own way of defying the stereotypes. 9 Variously employed as a fast-food operative, a factory worker, a bartender, and a telephone salesperson, her real dream is to be a writer. When her twelve-year-old daughter Darlene (brilliantly played by Sara Gilbert) balks at a poetry-writing assignment, Roseanne gives her a little talking-to involving Sylvia Plath:[2] "She inspired quite a few women, including *moi.*" In another episode, a middle-aged friend thanks Roseanne for inspiring her to dump her chauvinist husband and go to college. We have come a long way from the dithering, cowering Edith Bunker.

Most of the time the Connors do the usual sitcom things. They 10 have the little domestic misunderstandings that can be patched up in twenty-four minutes with wisecracks and a round of hugs. But *Roseanne* carries working-class verisimilitude into a new and previously taboo dimension — the workplace. In the world of employment, Roseanne knows exactly where she stands: "All the good power jobs are taken. Vanna turns the letters. Leona's got hotels. Margaret's running England. . . . 'Course she's not doing a very good job. . . .'"

And in the workplace as well as the kitchen, Roseanne knows 11 how to dish it out. A friend of mine, herself a denizen of the low-wage end of the work force, claims to have seen an episode in which Roseanne led an occupational health and safety battle at Wellman Plastics. I missed that one, but I have seen her, on more than one occasion, reduce the boss's ego to rubble. At Chicken Divine, for example, she is ordered to work weekends — an impossibility for a working mother — by an officious teenage boss who confides that he doesn't like working weekends either. In a sequence that could have been crafted by Michael Moore,[3] Roseanne responds: "Well, that's real good 'cause you never do. You sit in your office like a little Napoleon, making up schedules and screwing up people's lives." To which he says, "That's what they pay me for. And you are paid to follow my orders." Blah blah blah. To which she says, staring at him for a long time and then observing with an evil smile: "You know, you got a little prize hanging out of your nose there."

The class conflict continues on other fronts. In one episode, 12 Roseanne arrives late for an appointment with Darlene's history

---

[2]Plath (1932–63) was an influential poet and novelist. — EDS.

[3]Director of *Roger and Me,* a film documenting the effect of General Motors plant closings on the people of Flint, Michigan. — EDS.

teacher, because she has been forced to work overtime at Wellman. The teacher, who is leaning against her desk stretching her quadriceps when Roseanne arrives, wants to postpone the appointment because she has a date to play squash. When Roseanne insists, the teacher tells her that Darlene has been barking in class, "like a dog." This she follows with some psychobabble — on emotional problems and dysfunctional families — that would leave most mothers, whatever their social class, clutched with guilt. Not Roseanne, who calmly informs the yuppie snit that, in the Connor household, everybody barks like dogs.

Now this is the kind of class-militant populism that the Demo-   13
crats, most of them anyway, never seem to get right: up with the little gal; down with the snotty, the pretentious, and the overly paid. At least part of the appeal of *Roseanne* is that it ratifies the resentments of the underdog majority. But this being a sitcom, and Barr being a pacifist, the class-anger never gets too nasty. Even the most loathsome bosses turn out to be human, and in some cases pathetically needy. Rather than hating the bad guys, we end up feeling better about ourselves, which is the function of all good and humanistic humor anyway.

According to high conservative theory, the leftish cast to a show   14
like *Roseanne* must reflect the media manipulations of the alleged "liberal elite." But the politics of *Roseanne* — including its feminist side, which we will get to in a minute — reflects nothing so much as the decidedly un-elite politics of Barr herself. On the Larry King show a few weeks ago, Barr said that she prefers the term "working class" to "blue collar" because (and I paraphrase) it reminds us of the existence of class, a reality that Americans are all too disposed to forget. In her autobiography, right up front in the preface, she tells us that it is a "book about the women's movement . . . a book about the left."

Roseanne: My Life as a Woman traces her journey from alienation   15
to political commitment. It must stand as another one of Barr's commanding oddities. Where you would expect a standard rags-to-riches story, you find a sort of rags-to-revolution tale: more an intellectual and spiritual memoir than the usual chronicle of fearsome obstacles and lucky breaks. She was born the paradigmatic outsider, a jew in Mormon Utah, and a low-income Jew at that. Within the Mormon culture, she was the "Other" (her own term), the "designated Heathen" in school Christmas pageants, always being reminded that "had we been in a Communist country, I would never have been allowed to express my religion, because 'dissent' is not tolerated there." At home she was loved and encouraged, but the emotional

density of the Holocaust-haunted Barr family eventually proved too much for her. After a breakdown and several months of hospitalization, she ran away, at nineteen, to find the sixties, or what was left of them in 1971.

Her hippie phase left Barr with some proto-politics of the peace- 16 and-love variety, three children, and an erratic wage-earner for a husband. It was in this condition that she wandered into the Woman to Woman bookstore on Colfax Avenue in Denver, where she discovered the Movement. Barr seems to have required very little in the way of consciousness-raising. With one gigantic "click," she jumped right in, joined the collective, and was soon occupied giving "seminars on racism, classism, anti-Semitism, pornography, and taking power." If this seems like a rather sudden leap to political leadership, I can attest from my own experience with venues like Woman to Woman that it happens every day.

But even within the ecumenical embrace of feminism, Barr re- 17 mained the Outsider. "We did not agree anymore," she tells us of her collective, "with Betty Friedan, Gloria Steinem, or party politics within the women's movement," which she believes has turned into "a professional, careerist women's thing." When she found her "voice," it spoke in a new tone of working-class existentialism: "I began to speak as a working-class woman who is a mother, a woman who no longer believed in change, progress, growth, or hope." It was this special brand of proletarian feminism that inspired her stand-up comic routine. "I am talking about organizing working-class women and mothers," she tells us, and her comic persona was her way of going about it.

Middle-class feminism has long admitted the possibility of a work- 18 ing-class variant, but the general expectation has been that it would be a diluted version of the "real," or middle-class, thing. According to the conventional wisdom, working-class women would have no truck with the more anti-male aspects of feminism, and would be repelled by the least insult to the nuclear family. They would be comfortable only with the bread-and-butter issues of pay equity, child care, and parental leave. They would be culturally conservative, sensible, dull.

But we had not met Barr. Her stand-up routine was at first almost 19 too vulgar and castrating for Denver's Comedy Works. In her autobiography, Barr offers an example. Heckled by a drunk for not being "feminine," she turned around, stared at her assailant, and said, "Suck my dick." I wish *Roseanne: My Life as a Woman* gave more examples of her early, Denver-era, stand-up style, but the recently released videotape *Roseanne* (made later in a Los Angeles club) may be a fair representation. On it she promotes a product called "Fem-Rage," designed to overcome female conditioning during that "one day of the month when you're free to be yourself," and leaves her female fans with the memorable question: "Ever put those maxi-pads on adhesive side up?"

In *Roseanne*, the sitcom, however, Barr has been considerably 20 tamed. No longer standing bravely, and one must admit massively, alone with the microphone, she comes to us now embedded in the family: overwhelmed by domestic detail, surrounded by children too young for R-rated language, padding back and forth between stove, refrigerator, and kitchen table. Some of the edge is off here. There are no four-letter words, no menstruation jokes; and Roseanne's male-baiting barbs just bounce off her lovable Dan. Still, what better place for the feminist comic than in a family sitcom? Feminist theory, after all, cut its teeth on the critique of the family. Barr continues the process — leaving huge gaping holes where there was sweetness and piety.

All family sitcoms, of course, teach us that wisecracks and swift 21 put-downs are the preferred modes of affectionate discourse. But Roseanne takes the genre a step further — over the edge, some may say. In the era of big weddings and sudden man shortages, she describes marriage as "a life sentence, without parole." And in the era of the biological time clock and the petted yuppie midlife baby, she can tell Darlene to get a fork out of the drawer and "stick it through your tongue." Or she can say, when Dan asks "Are we missing an offspring?" at breakfast, "Yeah. Where do you think I got the bacon?"

It is Barr's narrow-eyed cynicism about the family, even more 22 than her class consciousness, that gives *Roseanne* its special frisson. Archie Bunker got our attention by telling us that we (blacks, Jews, "ethnics," WASPs, etc.) don't really like each other. Barr's message is that even within the family we don't much like each other. We love each other (who else do we have?); but The Family, with its impacted emotions, its lopsided division of labor, and its ancient system of age-graded humiliations, just doesn't work. Or rather, it doesn't work unless the contradictions are smoothed out with irony and the hostilities are periodically blown off as humor. Coming from mom, rather than from a jaded teenager or a bystander dad, this is scary news indeed.

So Barr's theoretical outlook is, in the best left-feminist tradition, 23 dialectical. On the one hand, she presents the family as a zone of intimacy and support, well worth defending against the forces of capitalism, which drive both mothers and fathers out of the home, scratching around for paychecks. On the other hand, the family is hardly a haven, especially for its grown-up females. It is marred from within by — among other things — the patriarchal division of leisure, which makes dad and the kids the "consumers" of mom's cooking, cleaning, nurturing, and (increasingly) her earnings. Mom's job is to keep the whole thing together — to see that the mortgage payments are made, to fend off the viperish teenagers, to find the missing green sock — but mom is no longer interested in being a human sacrifice on the altar of "pro-family values." She's been down to the feminist bookstore; she's been reading Sylvia Plath.

This is a bleak and radical vision. Not given to didacticism, Barr 24 offers no programmatic ways out. Surely, we are led to conclude, pay equity would help, along with child care, and so on. But Barr leaves us hankering for a quality of change that goes beyond mere reform: for a world in which even the lowliest among us — the hash-slinger, the sock-finder, the factory hand — will be recognized as the poet she truly is.

Maybe this is just too radical. The tabloids have taken to stalking 25 Barr as if she were an unsightly blot on the electronic landscape of our collective dreams. The *New York Times* just devoted a quarter of a page to some upscale writer's prissy musings on Roseanne. "Was I just being squeamish" for disliking Barr, she asks herself: "a goody-two-shoes suburban feminist who was used to her icons being chic and sugar-coated instead of this gum-chewing, male-bashing . . . working-class mama with a big mouth?" No, apparently she is not squeamish. Barr is just too, well, unfeminine.

We know what Barr would say to that, and exactly how she would 26 say it. Yeah, she's crude, but so are the realities of pain and exploitation she seeks to remind us of. If middle-class feminism can't claim Roseanne, maybe it's gotten a little too dainty for its own good. We have a long tradition of tough-talking females behind us, after all, including that other great working-class spokesperson, Mary "Mother" Jones, who once advised the troops, "Whatever you do, *don't* be ladylike."

QUESTIONS ON MEANING

1. Briefly restate Ehrenreich's THESIS in this essay.
2. How does Ehrenreich see the characters of Roseanne Connor and Archie Bunker as different? How are they similar?

3. What is the attitude of the character Roseanne Connor toward the family?
4. How was Roseanne's stand-up routine different from the *Roseanne* show?
5. Why might Ehrenreich have chosen Roseanne as the subject of her analysis?

QUESTIONS ON WRITING STRATEGY

1. What is Ehrenreich's principle of analysis in examining Roseanne? How does this principle guide her choice of elements to examine?
2. What GENERALIZATIONS does Ehrenreich make about television and society? What kinds of EXAMPLES does she choose to illustrate them? How do these generalizations help structure her analysis?
3. Why does Ehrenreich discuss the stereotyping in *Roseanne* (para. 7)?
4. OTHER METHODS. Ehrenreich uses COMPARISON AND CONTRAST to distinguish *Roseanne* from several other television shows. How do these comparisons support her claims about the "radical" realism of *Roseanne*?

QUESTIONS ON LANGUAGE

1. In this essay, Ehrenreich uses a number of terms from the social sciences. Make sure you know the meanings of post-feminism (para. 1); underclass (3); class, social strata (5); cognitively disabled (6); psychobabble (12); populism (13); collective (16); existentialism (17); dialectical, patriarchal (23); programmatic (24).
2. How do Ehrenreich's quotations from Roseanne help establish the essay's TONE? What is the EFFECT of the contrast between Ehrenreich's language and Roseanne's? Is Ehrenreich's language appropriate or inappropriate for her subject?
3. Find definitions for these words: eponymous (para. 1); Zeitgeist (2); deconstructions, telegenic (5); modishness, consummate (6); verisimilitude (10); denizen, officious (11); paradigmatic (15); proto-, venues (16); ecumenical (17); frisson (22); viperish (23); didacticism (24).

SUGGESTIONS FOR WRITING

1. Select a television show you know well and write a brief analysis of its political perspective. What ASSUMPTIONS about personal and social rights and responsibilities does the show take for granted? (*Gilligan's Island*, for example, stresses the value of cooperation.) What assumptions does it challenge? (*The Mary Tyler Moore Show*, for instance, presents an unmarried woman as happy and fulfilled.)
2. "The working class," Ehrenreich argues, "does not usually get much of a role in the American entertainment spectacle" (para. 6). Do you agree? In a short essay, support or challenge Ehrenreich's claim. Be sure to use plenty of EVIDENCE to illustrate your point.

3. **CRITICAL WRITING.** "Barr's message," claims Ehrenreich, "is that even within the family we don't much like each other. . . . The Family . . . just doesn't work" (para. 22). What assumptions can be INFERRED from these statements? Write a brief essay analyzing the assumptions behind Ehrenreich's perspective on *Roseanne*. Are these assumptions that you agree with?
4. **CONNECTIONS.** "Madonna," by bell hooks (p. 303), analyzes another and very different figure of popular culture. Drawing on Ehrenreich's and hooks's essays and on your own observations, write an essay on the *similarities* between Madonna and Roseanne. Consider the characters they project both on and off the stage and screen, the ways they use and are used by the media, their power or lack of it, and anything else that occurs to you. Be specific.

BARBARA EHRENREICH ON WRITING

The printed word, in the view of Barbara Ehrenreich, should be a powerful instrument for reform. In an article in *Mother Jones*, though, she complains about a tacit censorship in American magazines that has sometimes prevented her from fulfilling her purpose as a writer. Ehrenreich recalls the difficulties she had in trying to persuade the editor of a national magazine to assign her a story on the plight of Third World women refugees. "Sorry," said the editor, "Third World women have never done anything for me."

Ehrenreich infers that writers who write for such magazines must follow a rule: "You must learn not to stray from your assigned sociodemographic stereotype." She observes, "As a woman, I am generally asked to write on 'women's topics,' such as cooking, divorce, how to succeed in business, diet fads, and the return of the bustle. These are all fine topics and give great scope to my talents, but when I ask, in faltering tones, for an assignment . . . on the trade deficit, I am likely to be told that *anyone* (Bill, Gerry, Bob) could cover that, whereas my 'voice' is *essential* for the aerobic toothbrushing story. This is not, strictly speaking, 'censorship' — just a division of labor in which white men cover politics, foreign policy, and the economy, and the rest of us cover what's left over, such as the bustle."

Over the years Ehrenreich has had many manuscripts rejected by editors who comment, "too angry," "too depressing," and "Where's the bright side?" She agrees with writer Herbert Gold, who once deduced that the American media want only "happy stories about happy people with happy problems." She concludes, "You can write about anything — death squads, AIDS . . . — so long as you make it 'upbeat.'" Despite such discouragements, Ehrenreich continues her battle to "disturb the stupor induced by six straight pages of Calvin Klein ads."

FOR DISCUSSION

1. Is Ehrenreich right about what she calls "a tacit censorship in American magazines"? Check some recent issue of a magazine that prints signed articles. How many of the articles *not* on "women's topics" are written by women? How many are written by men?
2. How many women can you name who write serious newspaper and magazine articles reporting on or arguing matters of general interest, as opposed to those meant to appeal chiefly to women?
3. To what extent do you agree with Ehrenreich — and with Herbert Gold — that the American media are interested only in "upbeat" stories?

BELL HOOKS

BELL HOOKS, the pen name of Gloria Watkins, is well known for her efforts to broaden the feminist movement to include the perspective of African American women. Her book *Ain't I a Woman: Black Women and Feminism* (1981) was named in a *Publishers Weekly* poll as one of the "twenty most influential books of the last twenty years." Her other notable books include *Talking Back: Thinking Feminist, Thinking Black* (1989) and *Yearning: Race, Gender, and Cultural Politics* (1990), both of which won awards. A collection of essays, *Black Looks: Race and Representation* (1992), is hooks's most recent book. Born in 1952, hooks grew up in Kentucky and received her B.A. from Stanford University and her Ph.D. from the University of California, Santa Cruz. At Oberlin College, hooks is a professor of English and women's studies.

Madonna

In this essay from *Black Looks*, hooks takes a serious, steely look at one of the most successful and controversial pop performers of all time. The essay's subtitle, "Plantation Mistress or Soul Sister?" gives a good idea of hooks's approach. For another analysis of a celebrity, this time Roseanne Barr Arnold, see Barbara Ehrenreich's "The Wretched of the Hearth" (p. 292).

Subversion is contextual, historical, and above all social. No matter how exciting the "destabilizing" potential of texts, bodily or otherwise, whether those texts are subversive or recuperative or both or neither cannot be determined by abstraction from actual social practice.

— Susan Bordo

White women "stars" like Madonna, Sandra Bernhard, and many others publicly name their interest in, and appropriation of, black culture as yet another sign of their radical chic. Intimacy with that "nasty" blackness good white girls stay away from is what they seek. To white and other nonblack consumers, this gives them a special flavor, an added spice. After all it is a very recent historical phenomenon for any white girl to be able to get some mileage out of flaunting her fascination with and envy of blackness. The thing about envy is that it is always ready to destroy, erase, take-over, and consume the desired object. That's exactly what Madonna attempts to do when she appropriates and commodifies aspects of black culture. Needless to say this kind of fascination is a threat. It endangers. Perhaps that is why so many of the grown black women I spoke with about Madonna had no interest in her as a cultural icon and said things like, "The bitch can't even sing." It was only among young black females that I could find die-hard Madonna fans. Though I often admire and, yes at times, even envy Madonna because she has created a cultural space where she can invent and reinvent herself and receive public affirmation and material reward, I do not consider myself a Madonna fan.

Once I read an interview with Madonna where she talked about   2
her envy of black culture, where she stated that she wanted to be black as a child. It is a sign of white privilege to be able to "see" blackness and black culture from a standpoint where only the rich culture of opposition black people have created in resistance marks and defines us. Such a perspective enables one to ignore white supremacist domination and the hurt it inflicts *via* oppression, exploitation, and everyday wounds and pains. White folks who do not see black pain never really understand the complexity of black pleasure. And it is no wonder then that when they attempt to imitate the joy in living which they see as the "essence" of soul and blackness, their cultural productions may have an air of sham and falseness that may titillate and even move white audiences yet leave many black folks cold.

Needless to say, if Madonna had to depend on masses of black   3
women to maintain her status as a cultural icon she would have been dethroned some time ago. Many of the black women I spoke with expressed intense disgust at and hatred of Madonna. Most did not respond to my cautious attempts to suggest that underlying those negative feelings might lurk feelings of envy, and dare I say it, desire. No black woman I talked to declared that she wanted to "be Madonna." Yet we have only to look at the number of black women entertainers/stars (Tina Turner, Aretha Franklin, Donna Summer, Vanessa Williams, Yo-Yo, etc.) who gain greater cross-over recognition when they demonstrate that, like Madonna, they too have a healthy dose of "blonde ambition." Clearly their careers have been influenced by Madonna's choices and strategies.

For masses of black women, the political reality that underlies   4
Madonna's and our recognition that this is a society where "blondes" not only "have more fun" but where they are more likely to succeed in any endeavor is white supremacy and racism. We cannot see Madonna's change in hair color as being merely a question of aesthetic choice. I agree with Julie Burchill in her critical work *Girls on Film*,

when she reminds us: "What does it say about racial purity that the best blondes have all been brunettes (Harlow, Monroe, Bardot)? I think it says that we are not as white as we think. I think it says that Pure is a Bore." I also know that it is the expressed desire of the nonblonde Other for those characteristics that are seen as the quintessential markers of racial aesthetic superiority that perpetuate and uphold white supremacy. In this sense Madonna has much in common with the masses of black women who suffer from internalized racism and are forever terrorized by a standard of beauty they feel they can never truly embody.

Like many black women who have stood outside the culture's 5 fascination with the blonde beauty and who have only been able to reach it through imitation and artifice, Madonna often recalls that she was a working-class white-girl who saw herself as ugly, as outside the mainstream beauty standard. And indeed what some of us like about her is the way she deconstructs the myth of "natural" white-girl beauty by exposing the extent to which it can be and is usually artificially constructed and maintained. She mocks the conventional racist defined beauty ideal even as she rigorously strives to embody it. Given her obsession with exposing the reality that the ideal female beauty in this society can be attained by artifice and social construction it should come as no surprise that many of her fans are gay men, and that the majority of nonwhite men, particularly black men, are among that group. Jennie Livingston's film *Paris Is Burning* suggests that many black gay men, especially queens/divas, are as equally driven as Madonna by "blonde ambition." Madonna never lets her audience forget that whatever "look" she acquires is attained by hard work — "it ain't natural." And as Burchill comments in her chapter "Homosexual Girls":

> I have a friend who drives a cab and looks like a Marlboro Man but at night is the second best Jean Harlow I have ever seen. He summed up the kind of film star he adores, brutally and brilliantly, when he said, "I like actresses who look as if they've spent hours putting themselves together — and even then they don't look right."

Certainly no one, not even die-hard Madonna fans, ever insists 6 that her beauty is not attained by skillful artifice. And indeed, a major point of the documentary film *Truth or Dare: In Bed with Madonna* was to demonstrate the amount of work that goes into the construction of her image. Yet when the chips are down, the image Madonna most exploits is that of the quintessential "white girl." To maintain that image she must always position herself as an outsider in relation to black culture. It is that position of outsider that enables her to colonize and appropriate black experience for her own opportunistic ends even as she attempts to mask her acts of racist aggression as affirmation. And no other group sees that as clearly as black females in this society. For we have always known that the socially constructed image of innocent white womanhood relies on the continued production of the racist/sexist sexual myth that black women are not innocent and never can be. Since we are coded always as "fallen" women in the racist cultural iconography we can never, as can Madonna, publicly "work" the image of ourselves as innocent female daring to be bad. Mainstream culture always reads the black female body as a sign of sexual experience. In part, many black women who are disgusted by Madonna's flaunting of sexual experience are enraged because the very image of sexual agency that she is able to project and affirm with material gain has been the stick this society has used to justify its continued beating and assault on the black female body. The vast majority of black women in the United States, more concerned with projecting images of respectability than with the idea of female sexual agency and transgression, do not often feel we have the "freedom" to act in rebellious ways in regards to sexuality without being punished. We have only to contrast the life story of Tina Turner with that of Madonna to see the different connotations "wild" sexual agency has when it is asserted by a black female. Being represented publicly as an active sexual being has only recently enabled Turner to gain control over her life and career. For years the public image of aggressive sexual agency Turner projected belied the degree to which she was sexually abused and exploited privately. She was also materially exploited. Madonna's career could not be all that it is if there were no Tina Turner and yet, unlike her cohort Sandra Bernhard, Madonna never articulates the cultural debt she owes black females.

In her most recent appropriations of blackness, Madonna almost   7 always imitates phallic black masculinity. Although I read many articles which talked about her appropriating male codes, no critic seems to have noticed her emphasis on black male experience. In his *Playboy* profile, "Playgirl of the Western World," Michael Kelly describes Madonna's crotch grabbing as "an eloquent visual put-down of male phallic pride." He points out that she worked with choreographer Vince Paterson to perfect the gesture. Even though Kelly tells readers that Madonna was consciously imitating Michael Jackson, he does not contextualize his interpretation of the gesture to include this act of appropriation from black male culture. And in that specific context the groin grabbing gesture is an assertion of pride and phallic domination that usually takes place in an all male context. Madonna's imitation of this gesture could just as easily be read as an expression of envy.

Throughout much of her autobiographical interviews runs a   8
thread of expressed desire to possess the power she perceives men have. Madonna may hate the phallus, but she longs to possess its power. She is always first and foremost in competition with men to see who has the biggest penis. She longs to assert phallic power, and like every other group in this white supremacist society, she clearly sees black men as embodying a quality of maleness that eludes white men. Hence, they are often the group of men she most seeks to imitate, taunting white males with her own version of "black masculinity." When it comes to entertainment rivals, Madonna clearly perceives black male stars like Prince and Michael Jackson to be the standard against which she must measure herself and that she ultimately hopes to transcend.

Fascinated by yet envious of black style, Madonna appropriates   9
black culture in ways that mock and undermine, making her presentation one that upstages. This is most evident in the video "Like a Prayer." Though I read numerous articles that discussed public outrage at this video, none focused on the issue of race. No article called attention to the fact that Madonna flaunts her sexual agency by suggesting that she is breaking the ties that bind her as a white girl to white patriarchy, and establishing ties with black men. She, however, and not black men, does the choosing. The message is directed at white men. It suggests that they only labeled black men rapists for fear that white girls would choose black partners over them. Cultural critics commenting on the video did not seem at all interested in exploring the reasons Madonna chooses a black cultural backdrop for this video, i.e., black church and religious experience. Clearly, it was this backdrop that added to the video's controversy.

In her commentary in the *Washington Post*, "Madonna: Yuppie   10
Goddess," Brooke Masters writes: "Most descriptions of the controversial video focus on its Catholic imagery: Madonna kisses a black saint, and develops Christ-like markings on her hands. However, the video is also a feminist fairy tale. Sleeping Beauty and Snow White waited for their princes to come along; Madonna finds her own man and wakes him up." Notice that this writer completely overlooks the issue of race and gender. That Madonna's chosen prince was a black man is in part what made the representation potentially shocking and

provocative to a white supremacist audience. Yet her attempt to exploit and transgress traditional racial taboos was rarely commented on. Instead critics concentrated on whether or not she was violating taboos regarding religion and representation.

In the United States, Catholicism is most often seen as a religion 11 that has little or no black followers and Madonna's video certainly perpetuates this stereotype with its juxtaposition of images of black non-Catholic representations with the image of the black saint. Given the importance of religious experience and liberation theology in black life, Madonna's use of this imagery seemed particularly offensive. For she made black characters act in complicity with her as she aggressively flaunted her critique of Catholic manners, her attack on organized religion. Yet, no black voices that I know of came forward in print calling attention to the fact that the realm of the sacred that is mocked in this film is black religious experience, or that this appropriative "use" of that experience was offensive to many black folk. Looking at the video with a group of students in my class on the politics of sexuality where we critically analyze the way race and representations of blackness are used to sell products, we discussed the way in which black people in the video are caricatures reflecting stereotypes. They appear grotesque. The only role black females have in this video is to catch (i.e., rescue) the "angelic" Madonna when she is "falling." This is just a contemporary casting of the black female as Mammy. Made to serve as supportive backdrop for Madonna's drama, black characters in *Like a Prayer* remind one of those early Hollywood depictions of singing black slaves in the great plantation movies or those Shirley Temple films where Bojangles was trotted out to dance with Miss Shirley and spice up her act. Audiences were not supposed to be enamored of Bojangles; they were supposed to see just what a special little old white girl Shirley really was. In her own way Madonna is a modern day Shirley Temple. Certainly her expressed affinity with black culture enhances her value.

Eager to see the documentary *Truth or Dare* because it promised 12 to focus on Madonna's transgressive sexual persona, which I find interesting, I was angered by her visual representation of her domination over not white men (certainly not over Warren Beatty or Alek Keshishian), but people of color and white working-class women. I was too angered by this to appreciate other aspects of the film I might have enjoyed. In *Truth or Dare* Madonna clearly revealed that she can only think of exerting power along very traditional, white supremacist, capitalistic, patriarchal lines. That she made people who were dependent on her for their immediate livelihood submit to her will was neither charming nor seductive to me or the other black folks that I spoke with who saw the film. We thought it tragically ironic that Madonna would choose as her dance partner a black male with dyed blonde hair. Perhaps had he appeared less like a white-identified black male consumed by "blonde ambition" he might have upstaged her. Instead he was positioned as a mirror, into which Madonna and her audience could look and see only a reflection of herself and the worship of "whiteness" she embodies — that white supremacist culture wants everyone to embody. Madonna used her power to ensure that he and the other nonwhite women and men who worked for her, as well as some of the white subordinates, would all serve as the backdrop to her white-girl-makes-good drama. Joking about the film with other black folks, we commented that Madonna must have searched long and hard to find a black female that was not a good dancer, one who would not deflect attention away from her. And it is telling that when the film directly reflects something other than a positive image of Madonna, the camera highlights the rage this black female dancer was suppressing. It surfaces when the "subordinates" have time off and are "relaxing."

As with most Madonna videos, when critics talk about this film 13 they tend to ignore race. Yet no viewer can look at this film and not think about race and representation without engaging in forms of denial. After choosing a cast of characters from marginalized groups — nonwhite folks, heterosexual and gay, and gay white folks — Madonna publicly describes them as "emotional cripples." And of course in the context of the film this description seems borne out by the way they allow her to dominate, exploit, and humiliate them. Those Madonna fans who are determined to see her as politically progressive might ask themselves why it is she completely endorses those racist/sexist/classist stereotypes that almost always attempt to portray marginalized groups as "defective." Let's face it, by doing this, Madonna is not breaking with any white supremacist, patriarchal *status quo;* she is endorsing and perpetuating it.

Some of us do not find it hip or cute for Madonna to brag that 14 she has a "fascistic side," a side well documented in the film. Well, we did not see any of her cute little fascism in action when it was Warren Beatty calling her out in the film. No, there the image of Madonna was the little woman who grins and bears it. No, her "somebody's got to be in charge side," as she names it, was most expressed in her interaction with those representatives from marginalized groups who are most often victimized by the powerful. Why is it there is little or no discussion of Madonna as racist or sexist in her relation to other women? Would audiences be charmed by some rich white male entertainer telling us he must "play father" and oversee the actions of the less powerful, especially women and men of color? So why did so many people find it cute when Madonna asserted that she dominates the inter-racial casts of gay and heterosexual folks in her film because they are crippled and she "like[s] to play mother"? No, this was not a display of feminist power, this was the same old phallic nonsense with white pussy at the center. And many of us watching were not simply unmoved — we were outraged.

Perhaps it is a sign of a collective feeling of powerlessness that 15 many black, nonwhite, and white viewers of this film who were disturbed by the display of racism, sexism, and heterosexism (yes, it's possible to hire gay people, support AIDS projects, and still be biased in the direction of phallic patriarchal heterosexuality) in *Truth or Dare* have said so little. Sometimes it is difficult to find words to make a critique when we find ourselves attracted by some aspect of a performer's act and disturbed by others, or when a performer shows more interest in promoting progressive social causes than is customary. We may see that performer as above critique. Or we may feel our critique will in no way intervene on the worship of them as a cultural icon.

To say nothing, however, is to be complicit with the very forces 16 of domination that make "blonde ambition" necessary to Madonna's success. Tragically, all that is transgressive and potentially empowering to feminist women and men about Madonna's work may be undermined by all that it contains that is reactionary and in no way unconventional or new. It is often the conservative elements in her work converging with the *status quo* that has the most powerful impact. For example: Given the rampant homophobia in this society and the concomitant heterosexist voyeuristic obsession with gay life-styles, to what extent does Madonna progressively seek to challenge this if she insists on primarily representing gays as in some way emotionally handicapped or defective? Or when Madonna responds to the critique that she exploits gay men by cavalierly stating: "What does exploitation mean? . . . In a revolution, some people have to get hurt. To get people to change, you have to turn the table over. Some dishes get broken."

I can only say this doesn't sound like liberation to me. Perhaps 17 when Madonna explores those memories of her white working-class childhood in a troubled family in a way that enables her to understand intimately the politics of exploitation, domination, and submission, she will have a deeper connection with oppositional black culture. If and when this radical critical self-interrogation takes place, she will have the power to create new and different cultural productions, work that will be truly transgressive — acts of resistance that transform rather than simply seduce.

QUESTIONS ON MEANING

1. The THESIS of hooks's essay is stated in the opening paragraph. What is it?
2. What does hooks find most offensive about Madonna's "Like a Prayer" video?
3. How does hooks characterize Madonna's attitude toward employees who are gay people and people of color? Where does hooks get her information?
4. What do you see as hooks's PURPOSE in this essay?

QUESTIONS ON WRITING STRATEGY

1. What elements of the film *Truth or Dare* does hooks single out for examination? What principle of analysis guides her choices?
2. What kinds of EVIDENCE does hooks use to support her analysis of Madonna?
3. Why does hooks begin her essay with the quotation from Susan Bordo? How does the quotation relate to the essay?
4. OTHER METHODS. How does hooks use a CLASSIFICATION of American culture into "white" and "black" as a means of analyzing Madonna's personal conduct and public image?

QUESTIONS ON LANGUAGE

1. Why does hooks put quotation marks around words like "stars," "nasty" (para. 1); "see," "essence" (2); "natural" (5); and "white girl" (6)? How does this help establish her TONE?
2. Is the formality of hooks's language surprising in a discussion of pop music? What is its EFFECT?
3. As an academic theorist, hooks uses some terms in a professionally specific way. Make sure you know the meaning of the following: texts, subversive, recuperative (Bordo quote); appropriation, commodifies (para. 1); culture of opposition, cultural productions (2); deconstructs, social construction (5); iconography, agency (6); phallic (7); patriarchy (9); transgressive, persona (12); marginalized (13).
4. Define any of these words you find unfamiliar: chic (para. 1); titillate

(2); quintessential (4); artifice (5); complicity (11); *status quo* (13); concomitant, voyeuristic, cavalierly (16).

SUGGESTIONS FOR WRITING

1. Write a political analysis of a celebrity familiar to you. What causes does he or she support? Are these causes consistent with his or her performances and life-style? (Many celebrities, for example, enjoy a glamorous jet-set life because of their success at projecting a down-home, no-nonsense image.) What impact do the celebrity's views have on others?
2. In a short essay, summarize hooks's views of white culture as expressed in this selection. Do you agree with her analysis of white culture and its effects on people of color? Use EVIDENCE to support your argument.
3. CRITICAL WRITING. In a short essay, analyze hooks's self-presentation — how she characterizes herself. What does she tell us about herself? What can we INFER? How can she be seen as an alternative role model to Madonna? Which of the two women — hooks or Madonna — presents a greater challenge to mainstream society?
4. CONNECTIONS. In analyzing Roseanne Barr Arnold ("Wretched of the Hearth," p. 292), Barbara Ehrenreich also gives serious attention to an icon of the popular culture. Do Roseanne and Madonna deserve this attention? (As a starting point, you might consider "Mark Crispin Miller on Writing," p. 281, in which Miller explains why he believes that popular culture, especially TV, merits close critical ANALYSIS.) Is it more worthwhile to ignore or to analyze popular culture? Argue your opinion in an essay.

BELL HOOKS ON WRITING

In "Writing from the Darkness," an essay published in *Tri-Quarterly* in 1989, bell hooks traces her development as a writer from early and painful confessions in her diary. "Lost in an inner darkness" during childhood, she writes, "I began to feel uncertain, displaced, estranged even. This was the condition of my spirit when I decided to be a writer, to seek for . . . light in words. . . . Searching for a space where writing could be understood, I asked for a diary. . . . It was for me the space for critical reflection, where I struggled to understand myself and the world around me, that crazy world of family and community, that painful world. I could say there what was hurting me, how I felt about things, what I hoped for. I could be angry there with no threat of punishment. I could 'talk back.' Nothing had to be concealed. I could hold onto myself there."

Yet as hooks filled the pages, she realized that diary writing was often "threatening." "For me the confessions written there were testimony, documenting realities I was not always able to face. My response to this sense of threat was to destroy the diaries. That destruction was linked to my fear that growing up was not supposed to be hard and difficult, a time of anguish and torment. Somehow the diaries were another excusing voice declaring that I was not 'normal.' I destroyed that writing and I wanted to destroy that tormented and struggling self. I did not understand, then, the critical difference between confession as an act of displacement and confession as the beginning stage in the process of self-transformation. . . . Knowledge that the writing could have enabled transformation was blocked by feelings of shame. I was ashamed that I needed this sanctuary in words. . . . Even though acknowledging that self in writing was a necessary anchor enabling me to keep a hold on life, it was not enough. That shame had to be let go before I could fully emerge as a writer because it was there whenever I tried to create, whether the work was confessional or not."

A journal is now, for hooks, "a way to engage in critical self-reflection, confrontation, and challenge." But to arrive at that point, she had to seek out the "shadow-self" of her youth. It "was part of a process of long inward journeying. Much of it took place in writing. I spent more than ten years writing journals, unearthing and restoring memories of that shadow-self, connecting the past with present being. This writing enabled me to look myself over in a new way, without the shame I had experienced earlier. It was no longer an act of displacement. I was not trying to be rid of the shadows, I wanted instead to enter them. That encounter enabled me to learn the self anew in ways that allowed transformation in consciousness and being. . . . Writing was a way of knowing."

FOR DISCUSSION

1. What is the "shadow-self" hooks refers to?
2. What is the critical distinction between "confession as an act of displacement and confession as the beginning stage in the process of self-transformation"?

ADDITIONAL WRITING TOPICS
Division or Analysis

Write an essay by the method of division or analysis using one of the following subjects (or choose your own subject). In your essay, make sure your purpose and your principle of division or analysis are clear to your readers. Explain the parts of your subject so that readers know how each relates to the others and contributes to the whole.

1. The slang or technical terminology of a group such as stand-up comedians or computer hackers
2. An especially bad movie, television show, or book
3. A doll, game, or other toy from childhood
4. A typical TV commercial for a product such as laundry soap, deodorant, beer, or an economy car
5. An appliance or machine, such as a stereo speaker, a motorcycle, a microwave oven, or a camera
6. An organization or association, such as a social club, a sports league, or a support group
7. The characteristic appearance of a rock singer or a classical violinist
8. A year in the life of a student
9. Your favorite poem
10. A short story, essay, or other work that made you think
11. The government of your community
12. The most popular bookstore (or other place of business) in town
13. The Bible
14. A band or orchestra
15. A famous painting or statue

7

CLASSIFICATION
Sorting into Kinds

THE METHOD

To *classify* is to make sense of the world by arranging many units — trucks, chemical elements, wasps, students — into more manageable groups. Zoologists classify animals, botanists classify plants — and their classifications help us to understand a vast and complex subject: life on earth. To help us find books in a library, librarians classify books into categories: fiction, biography, history, psychology, and so forth. For the convenience of readers, newspapers run classified advertising, grouping many small ads into categories such as Help Wanted and Cars for Sale.

The subject of a classification is always a number of things, such as peaches or political systems. (In contrast, DIVISION or ANALYSIS, the topic of the last chapter, usually deals with a solitary subject, a coherent whole, such as *a* peach or *a* political system.) The job of classification is to sort the things into groups or classes based on their similarities and differences. Say, for instance, you're going to write an essay about how people write. After interviewing a lot of writers, you determine that writers' processes differ widely, mainly in the

316 Classification

amount of planning and rewriting they entail. (Notice that this determination involves analyzing the process of writing, separating it into steps. See Chapter 5.) On the basis of your findings, you create groups for planners, one-drafters, and rewriters. Once your groups are defined (and assuming they are valid), your subjects (the writers) almost sort themselves out.

Classification is done for a purpose. In a New York City guide-book, Joan Hamburg and Norma Ketay discuss low-priced hotels. (Notice that already they are examining the members of a group: low-priced as opposed to medium- and high-priced hotels.) They cast the low-priced hotels into categories: Rooms for Singles and Students, Rooms for Families, Rooms for Servicepeople, and Rooms for General Occupancy. Always their purpose is evident: to match up the visitor with a suitable kind of room. When a classification has no purpose, it seems a silly and hollow exercise.

Just as you can analyze a subject (divide a pie) in many ways, you can classify a subject according to many principles. A different New York guidebook might classify all hotels according to price: grand luxury, luxury, commercial, low-priced (Hamburg and Ketay's category), fleabag, and flophouse. The purpose of this classification would be to match visitors to hotels fitting their pocketbooks. The principle you use in classifying things depends on your purpose. A linguist might write an essay classifying the languages of the world according to their origins (Romance languages, Germanic languages, Coptic languages . . .), but a student battling with a college language requirement might write a humorous essay classifying them into three groups: hard to learn, harder to learn, and unlearnable.

The simplest classification is binary (or two-part), in which you sort things out into (1) those with a certain distinguishing feature and (2) those without it. You might classify a number of persons, let's say, into smokers and nonsmokers, Madonna fans and nonfans, runners and nonrunners, believers and nonbelievers. Binary classification is most useful when your subject is easily divisible into positive and negative categories.

Classification can be complex as well. As Jonathan Swift reminds us,

So, naturalists observe, a flea
Hath smaller fleas that on him prey,
And these have smaller yet to bite 'em.
And so proceed *ad infinitum.*

In being faithful to reality, you will sometimes find that you have to sort out the members of categories into subcategories. Hamburg and Ketay did something of the kind when they subclassified the class of low-priced New York hotels. Writing about the varieties of one Germanic language, such as English, a writer could identify the subclasses of British English, North American English, Australian English, and so on.

As readers, we all enjoy watching a clever writer sort things into categories. We like to meet classifications that strike us as true and familiar. This pleasure may account for the appeal of magazine articles that classify things ("The Seven Common Garden Varieties of Moocher," "Five Embarrassing Types of Social Blunder"). Usefulness as well as pleasure may explain the popularity of classifications that evaluate things. In a survey of current movies, a newspaper critic might classify the films into categories: "Don't Miss," "Worth Seeing," "So-So," and "Never Mind." The magazine *Consumer Reports* uses this method of classifying in its comments on different brands of stereo speakers or canned tuna. Products are sorted into groups (excellent, good, fair, poor, and not acceptable), and the merits of each are discussed by the method of description. (Of a frozen pot pie: "Bottom crust gummy, meat spongy when chewed, with nondescript old-poultry and stale-flour flavor.")

THE PROCESS

Classification will usually come into play when you want to impose order on a numerous and unwieldy subject. (In separate essays in this chapter, Ralph Whitehead, Jr., and Robert Reich classify a huge subject, the people of the United States.) Sometimes you may use classification humorously, as Russell Baker and Fran Lebowitz do in other essays in this chapter, to give a charge to familiar experiences. Whichever use you make of classification, though, do it for a reason. The files of composition instructors are littered with student essays in which nothing was ventured and nothing gained by classification.

Things may be classified into categories that reveal truth, or into categories that don't tell us a thing. To sort out ten U.S. cities according to their relative freedom from air pollution, or their cost of living, or the degree of progress they have made in civil rights might prove highly informative and useful. Such a classification might even tell us where we'd want to live. But to sort out the cities according to a superficial feature such as the relative size of their cat and dog populations wouldn't interest anyone, probably, except a veterinarian looking for a job.

Your purpose, your thesis, and your principle of classification will all overlap at the point where you find your interest in your subject. Say you're curious about how other students write. Is your interest primarily in the materials they use (word processor, typewriter, pencil), in where and when they write, or in how much planning and rewriting they do? Any of these could lead to a principle for sorting the students into groups. In the essay itself, let readers in on your principle of classification and explain why you have chosen it.

For a workable classification, make sure that the categories you choose don't overlap. If you were writing a survey of popular magazines for adults and you were sorting your subject into categories that included women's magazines and sports magazines, you might soon run into trouble. Into which category would you place *Women's Sports?* The trouble is that both categories take in the same item. To avoid this problem, you'll need to reorganize your classification on a different principle. You might sort out the magazines by their audiences: magazines mainly for women, magazines mainly for men, magazines for both women and men. Or you might group them according to subject matter: sports magazines, literary magazines, astrology magazines, fashion magazines, TV fan magazines, trade journals, and so on. *Women's Sports* would fit into either of those classification schemes, but into only *one* category in each scheme.

When you draw up a scheme of classification, be sure also that you include all essential categories. Omitting an important category can weaken the effect of your essay, no matter how well written it is. It would be a major oversight, for example, if you were to classify the residents of a dormitory according to their religious affiliations and not include a category for the numerous nonaffiliated. Your reader might wonder if your sloppiness in forgetting a category extended to your thinking about the topic as well.

Some form of outline can be helpful to keep the classes and their members straight as you develop ideas and write. You might experiment with a diagram in which you jot down headings for the groups, with plenty of space around them, and then let each heading accumulate members as you think of them, the way a magnet attracts paperclips. This kind of diagram offers more flexibility than a vertical list or outline, and it may be a better aid for keeping categories from overlapping or disappearing.

CLASSIFICATION IN A PARAGRAPH:
TWO ILLUSTRATIONS

Using Classification
to Write About Television

Most canned laughs produced by laugh machines fall into one of five reliable types. There are *titters,* light vocal laughs with which an imaginary audience responds to a comedian's least wriggle or grimace. Some producers rely heavily on *chuckles,* deeper, more chesty responses. Most profound of all, *belly laughs* are summoned to acclaim broader jokes and sexual innuendos. When provided at full level of sound and in longest duration, the belly laugh becomes the Big Boffola. There are also *wild howls* or *screamers,* extreme responses used not more than three times per show, lest they seem fake. These are crowd laughs, and yet the machine also offers *freaky laughs,* the piercing, eccentric screeches of solitary kooks. With them, a producer affirms that even a canned audience may include one thorny individualist.

COMMENT. This paragraph relates to one in the previous chapter (p. 271) about the laugh machine used by producers of television comedies to make jokes seem funny. In the earlier, analytical paragraph, style was identified as one of the components of the canned laugh. Now in this paragraph the writer classifies the *styles* of canned laughs. (Choosing a different principle of classification, the writer might also have examined different volumes or durations of canned laughs.) The labels for the five categories clearly distinguish them, as do the descriptions and examples. Simple but memorable, the categories register in our minds.

Using Classification
in an Academic Discipline

Sheldon described three types of physical physique: the *endomorph,* who is overweight, with poorly developed bones and muscles; the *mesomorph,* muscular, strong, and athletic; and the thin, fragile *ectomorph.* He then came up with three clusters of personality traits: *viscerotonia* (comfort-loving, food-oriented, sociable, relaxed); *somatotonia* (aggressive, adventure-loving, risk-taking); and *cerebrotonia* (restrained, self-conscious, introverted). When Sheldon rated men according to where they stood with regard to both body types and personality traits, he found high correlations. Extremely endomorphic men were likely to be viscerotonic, mesomorphs tended to be somatotonic, and ectomorphs were cerebrotonic.

COMMENT. In this paragraph from their textbook *Psychology*, the authors Diane E. Papalia and Sally Wendkos Olds are explaining the research of a medical doctor and scholar named William H. Sheldon. Sheldon used two different principles of classification to sort men into groups: physique and personality. The point of the paragraph is that he found correspondences between classes in each scheme. Papalia and Olds go on in a subsequent paragraph to say that later researchers found fewer correlations between body type and personality than Sheldon did; but his classification contains enough of the truth, apparently, to be still worth mentioning.

RUSSELL BAKER

RUSSELL BAKER is one of America's notable humorists and political satirists. He has written his "Observer" column for the *New York Times* for over thirty years, covering topics from the merely bothersome (unreadable menus) to the serious (the Vietnam War). Born in 1925 in Virginia, Baker was raised in New Jersey and Maryland by his widowed mother. After serving in the Navy during World War II, he earned a B.A. from Johns Hopkins University in 1947. He became a reporter for the *Baltimore Sun* that year and then joined the *New York Times* in 1954. He covered the State Department, the White House, and Congress until 1962, when he began the column that is now syndicated in over 400 newspapers. Baker has twice received the Pulitzer Prize, once for distinguished commentary and again for the first volume of his autobiography, *Growing Up* (1982). (The second volume, *The Good Times*, appeared in 1989.) Many of his columns have been collected in books, most recently *There's a Country in My Cellar* (1990). Baker has also written fiction and children's books, and in 1993 he began his television career as host of PBS's *Masterpiece Theatre*.

The Plot Against People

The critic R. Z. Sheppard has commented that Baker can "best be appreciated for doing what a good humorist has always done: writing to preserve his sanity for at least one more day." In this piece from the *New York Times* in 1968, Baker takes aim, as he often does, at things.

Inanimate objects are classified into three major categories — those that don't work, those that break down and those that get lost. 1

The goal of all inanimate objects is to resist man and ultimately to defeat him, and the three major classifications are based on the method each object uses to achieve its purpose. As a general rule, any object capable of breaking down at the moment when it is most needed will do so. The automobile is typical of the category. 2

With the cunning typical of its breed, the automobile never breaks down while entering a filling station with a large staff of idle mechanics. It waits until it reaches a downtown intersection in the middle of the rush hour, or until it is fully loaded with family and luggage on the Ohio Turnpike. 3

Thus it creates maximum misery, inconvenience, frustration and 4
irritability among its human cargo, thereby reducing its owner's life
span.

Washing machines, garbage disposals, lawn mowers, light bulbs, 5
automatic laundry dryers, water pipes, furnaces, electrical fuses, television tubes, hose nozzles, tape recorders, slide projectors — all are
in league with the automobile to take their turn at breaking down
whenever life threatens to flow smoothly for their human enemies.

Many inanimate objects, of course, find it extremely difficult to 6
break down. Pliers, for example, and gloves and keys are almost
totally incapable of breaking down. Therefore, they have had to
evolve a different technique for resisting man.

They get lost. Science has still not solved the mystery of how 7
they do it, and no man has ever caught one of them in the act of
getting lost. The most plausible theory is that they have developed a
secret method of locomotion which they are able to conceal the
instant a human eye falls upon them.

It is not uncommon for a pair of pliers to climb all the way from 8
the cellar to the attic in its single-minded determination to raise its
owner's blood pressure. Keys have been known to burrow three feet
under mattresses. Women's purses, despite their great weight, frequently travel through six or seven rooms to find hiding space under
a couch.

Scientists have been struck by the fact that things that break 9
down virtually never get lost, while things that get lost hardly ever
break down.

A furnace, for example, will invariably break down at the depth 10
of the first winter cold wave, but it will never get lost. A woman's
purse, which after all does have some inherent capacity for breaking
down, hardly ever does; it almost invariably chooses to get lost.

Some persons believe this constitutes evidence that inanimate 11
objects are not entirely hostile to man, and that a negotiated peace
is possible. After all, they point out, a furnace could infuriate a man
even more thoroughly by getting lost than by breaking down, just as
a glove could upset him far more by breaking down than by getting
lost.

Not everyone agrees, however, that this indicates a conciliatory 12
attitude among inanimate objects. Many say it merely proves that
furnaces, gloves and pliers are incredibly stupid.

The third class of objects — those that don't work — is the most 13
curious of all. These include such objects as barometers, car clocks,
cigarette lighters, flashlights and toy-train locomotives. It is inaccu-

rate, of course, to say that they never work. They work once, usually for the first few hours after being brought home, and then quit. Thereafter, they never work again.

In fact, it is widely assumed that they are built for the purpose of 14 not working. Some people have reached advanced ages without ever seeing some of these objects — barometers, for example — in working order.

Science is utterly baffled by the entire category. There are many 15 theories about it. The most interesting holds that the things that don't work have attained the highest state possible for an inanimate object, the state to which things that break down and things that get lost can still only aspire.

They have truly defeated man by conditioning him never to 16 expect anything of them, and in return they have given man the only peace he receives from inanimate society. He does not expect his barometer to work, his electric locomotive to run, his cigarette lighter to light or his flashlight to illuminate, and when they don't it does not raise his blood pressure.

He cannot attain that peace with furnaces and keys and cars and 17 women's purses as long as he demands that they work for their keep.

QUESTIONS ON MEANING

1. What is Baker's THESIS?
2. Why don't things that break down get lost?
3. Does Baker have any PURPOSE other than to make his readers smile?
4. How have inanimate objects "defeated man"?

QUESTIONS ON WRITING STRATEGY

1. Find three places where Baker uses HYPERBOLE. What is the EFFECT of this FIGURE OF SPEECH?
2. How does the essay's INTRODUCTION help set its TONE? How does the CONCLUSION reinforce the tone?
3. What is the effect of Baker's principle of classification? What categories are omitted here, and why?
4. OTHER METHODS. How does Baker use NARRATION to portray inanimate objects in the act of "resisting" people? Discuss how these mini-narratives make his classification more persuasive.

QUESTIONS ON LANGUAGE

1. Look up any of these words that are unfamiliar: plausible, locomotion (para. 7); invariably, inherent (10); conciliatory (12).
2. What are the CONNOTATIONS of the word "cunning" (para. 3)? What is its EFFECT in this context?
3. Why does Baker use such expressions as "man," "some people," and "their human enemies" rather than *I* to describe those who come into conflict with inanimate objects? How might the essay have been different if Baker had relied on *I*?

SUGGESTIONS FOR WRITING

1. Write your own humorous classification of inanimate objects. You could expand on Baker's classification, adding further categories of objects' intentions; or you could use a completely different principle (for example, objects Madonna would own and objects she wouldn't be caught dead with). It may be helpful to use NARRATION or DESCRIPTION in your classification. FIGURES OF SPEECH, especially hyperbole and understatement, can help you to establish a comic TONE.
2. Think of a topic that would not generally be considered appropriate for a serious classification (some examples: game-show winners, body odors, stupid pet tricks, knock-knock jokes). Select a principle of classification and write a brief essay sorting the subject into categories. You may want to use a humorous tone; then again, you may want to approach the topic "seriously," counting on the contrast between subject and treatment to make your IRONY clear.
3. CRITICAL WRITING. In a short essay, discuss the likely AUDIENCE for "The Plot Against People." (Recall that it was first published in the *New York Times.*) What can you INFER from his examples about Baker's own age and economic status? Does he ASSUME his audience is similar? How do the connections between author and audience help establish the essay's humor? Could this humor be seen as excluding some readers?
4. CONNECTIONS. Compare this essay to Fran Lebowitz's "The Sound of Music: Enough Already" (p. 328). How does each writer establish a humorous tone? Which author creates a more persuasive classification? Which essay do you find more amusing?

RUSSELL BAKER ON WRITING

In "Computer Fallout," an essay from the October 11, 1987, *New York Times Magazine*, Baker sets out to prove that computers make a writer's life easier, but he ends up somewhere else entirely. The skillful way he takes us along with him is what makes the journey enjoyable — and perhaps familiar.

"The wonderful thing about writing with a computer instead of a typewriter or a lead pencil is that it's so easy to rewrite that you can make each sentence almost perfect before moving on to the next sentence.

"An impressive aspect of using a computer to write with

"One of the plusses about a computer on which to write

"Happily, the computer is a marked improvement over both the typewriter and the lead pencil for purposes of literary composition, due to the ease with which rewriting can be effectuated, thus enabling

"What a marked improvement the computer is for the writer over the typewriter and lead pencil

"The typewriter and lead pencil were good enough in their day, but if Shakespeare had been able to access a computer with a good writing program

"If writing friends scoff when you sit down at the computer and say, 'The lead pencil was good enough for Shakespeare

"One of the drawbacks of having a computer on which to write is the ease and rapidity with which the writing can be done, thus leading to the inclusion of many superfluous terms like 'lead pencil,' when the single word 'pencil' would be completely, entirely and utterly adequate.

"The ease with which one can rewrite on a computer gives it an advantage over such writing instruments as the pencil and typewriter by enabling the writer to turn an awkward and graceless sentence into one that is practically perfect, although it

"The writer's eternal quest for the practically perfect sentence may be ending at last, thanks to the computer's gift of editing ease and swiftness to those confronting awkward, formless, nasty, illiterate sentences such as

"Man's quest is eternal, but what specifically is it that he quests, and why does he

"Mankind's quest is

"Man's and woman's quest

"Mankind's and womankind's quest

"Humanity's quest for the perfect writing device

"Eternal has been humanity's quest

"Eternal have been many of humanity's quests

"From the earliest cave writing, eternal has been the quest for a device that will forever prevent writers from using the word 'quest,' particularly when modified by such adjectives as 'eternal,' 'endless,' 'tireless' and

"Many people are amazed at the ease

"Many persons are amazed by the ease

"Lots of people are astounded when they see the nearly perfect sentences I write since upgrading my writing instrumentation from pencil and typewriter to

"Listen, folks, there's nothing to writing almost perfect sentences with ease and rapidity provided you've given up the old horse-and-buggy writing mentality that says Shakespeare couldn't have written those great plays if he had enjoyed the convenience of electronic compositional instrumentation.

"Folks, have you ever realized that there's nothing to writing almost

"Have you ever stopped to think, folks, that maybe Shakespeare could have written even better if

"To be or not to be, that is the central focus of the inquiry.

"In the intrapersonal relationships played out within the mind as to the relative merits of continuing to exist as opposed to not continuing to exist

"Live or die, a choice as ancient as humanities' eternal quest, is a tough choice which has confounded mankind as well as womankind ever since the option of dreaming was first perceived as a potentially negating effect of the quiescence assumed to be obtainable through the latter course of action.

"I'm sick and tired of Luddites saying pencils and typewriters are just as good as computers for writing nearly perfect sentences when they — the Luddites, that is — have never experienced the swiftness and ease of computer writing which makes it possible to compose almost perfect sentences in practically no time at

"Folks, are you sick and tired of

"Are you, dear reader

"Good reader, are you

"A lot of you nice folks out there are probably just as sick and tired as I am of hearing people say they are sick and tired of this and that and

"Listen, people, I'm just as sick and tired as you are of having writers and TV commercial performers who oil me in cornpone politician prose addressed to 'you nice folks out

"A curious feature of computers, as opposed to pencils and type-writers, is that when you ought to be writing something more inter-esting than a nearly perfect sentence

"Since it is easier to revise and edit with a computer than with a typewriter or pencil, this amazing machine makes it very hard to stop editing and revising long enough to write a readable sentence, much less an entire newspaper column."

FOR DISCUSSION

1. What is Baker's unstated THESIS? Does he convince you?
2. Do you find yourself ever having the problem Baker finally admits to in the last paragraph?

FRAN LEBOWITZ

Fran Lebowitz is a satirist best known for her witty attacks on contemporary urban life. Born in 1950 in Morristown, New Jersey, Lebowitz finished high school there and skipped college. Instead, she worked in New York City at a series of jobs, including taxi driver and apartment cleaner. A writer since grade school, Lebowitz began publishing in *Changes* magazine — book and movie reviews, mostly — and then in 1972 started a regular column for Andy Warhol's *Interview* magazine. From 1977 to 1979 Lebowitz contributed to *Interview* and also to *Mademoiselle,* but by 1981 she had left both posts to concentrate on fiction writing. Her essays are collected in *Metropolitan Life* (1978) and *Social Studies* (1981). Lebowitz lectures and reads at colleges and universities across the country. She is at work on her first novel, which she once predicted "should be done when I'm about ninety-seven."

The Sound of Music: Enough Already

Lebowitz's reviewers often disagree over her work. "Sour grapes," says one. "Brittle humor, drained of compassion," says another. But still another says, "Lebowitz is . . . a funny, urbane, intelligent one-woman bulwark against ticky-tack, creeping mellowness, and the excesses of what Mencken dubbed 'boobus Americanus.'" See what you think of this essay from *Metropolitan Life.*

First off, I want to say that as far as I am concerned, in instances 1 where I have not personally and deliberately sought it out, the only difference between music and Muzak is the spelling. Pablo Casals practicing across the hall with the door open — being trapped in an elevator, the ceiling of which is broadcasting "Parsley, Sage, Rosemary, and Thyme" — it's all the same to me. Harsh words? Perhaps. But then again these are not gentle times we live in. And they are being made no more gentle by this incessant melody that was once real life.

There was a time when music knew its place. No longer. Possibly 2 this is not music's fault. It may be that music fell in with a bad crowd and lost its sense of common decency. I am willing to consider this. I am willing even to try and help. I would like to do my bit to set music straight in order that it might shape up and leave the mainstream of society. The first thing that music must understand is that there are two kinds of music — good music and bad music. Good music is music that I want to hear. Bad music is music that I don't want to hear.

So that music might more clearly see the error of its ways I offer   3
the following. If you are music and you recognize yourself on this list, you are bad music.

1. Music in Other People's Clock Radios

There are times when I find myself spending the night in the   4
home of another. Frequently the other is in a more reasonable line of work than I and must arise at a specific hour. Ofttimes the other, unbeknownst to me, manipulates an appliance in such a way that I am awakened by Stevie Wonder. On such occasions I announce that if I wished to be awakened by Stevie Wonder I would sleep with Stevie Wonder. I do not, however, wish to be awakened by Stevie Wonder and that is why God invented alarm clocks. Sometimes the other realizes that I am right. Sometimes the other does not. And that is why God invented *many* others.

2. Music Residing in the Hold Buttons of Other People's Business Telephones

I do not under any circumstances enjoy hold buttons. But I am   5
a woman of reason. I can accept reality. I can face the facts. What I cannot face is the music. Just as there are two kinds of music — good and bad — so there are two kinds of hold buttons — good and bad. Good hold buttons are hold buttons that hold one silently. Bad hold buttons are hold buttons that hold one musically. When I hold I want to hold silently. That is the way it was meant to be, for that is what God was talking about when he said, "Forever hold your peace." He would have added, "and quiet," but he thought you were smarter.

3. Music in the Streets

The past few years have seen a steady increase in the number of   6
people playing music in the streets. The past few years have also seen a steady increase in the number of malignant diseases. Are these two facts related? One wonders. But even if they are not — and, as I have pointed out, one cannot be sure — music in the streets has definitely taken its toll. For it is at the very least disorienting. When

one is walking down Fifth Avenue, one does not expect to hear a string quartet playing a Strauss waltz. What one expects to hear while walking down Fifth Avenue is traffic. When one does indeed hear a string quartet playing a Strauss waltz while one is walking down Fifth Avenue, one is apt to become confused and imagine that one is not walking down Fifth Avenue at all but rather that one has somehow wound up in Old Vienna. Should one imagine that one is in Old Vienna one is likely to become upset when one realizes that in Old Vienna there is no sale at Charles Jourdan. And that is why when I walk down Fifth Avenue I want to hear traffic.

4. Music in the Movies

I'm not talking about musicals. Musicals are movies that warn   7
you by saying, "Lots of music here. Take it or leave it." I'm talking about regular movies that extend no such courtesy but allow unsuspecting people to come to see them and then assault them with a barrage of unasked-for tunes. There are two major offenders in this category: black movies and movies set in the fifties. Both types of movies are afflicted with the same misconception. They don't know that movies are supposed to be movies. They think that movies are supposed to be records with pictures. They have failed to understand that if God had wanted records to have pictures, he would not have invented television.

5. Music in Public Places Such as Restaurants, Supermarkets, Hotel Lobbies, Airports, Etc.

When I am in any of the above-mentioned places I am not there   8
to hear music. I am there for whatever reason is appropriate to the respective place. I am no more interested in hearing "Mack the Knife" while waiting for the shuttle to Boston than someone sitting ringside at the Sands Hotel is interested in being forced to choose between sixteen varieties of cottage cheese. If God had meant for everything to happen at once, he would not have invented desk calendars.

Epilogue

Some people talk to themselves. Some people sing to themselves.   9
Is one group better than the other? Did not God create all people equal? Yes, God created all people equal. Only to some he gave the ability to make up their own words.

QUESTIONS ON MEANING

1. What is Lebowitz's PURPOSE: to change the places where we hear music, to express herself, to entertain the reader, or what?
2. What is Lebowitz's THESIS?
3. What does the author admit in the first paragraph? What does this say about her judgments in the essay?

QUESTIONS ON WRITING STRATEGY

1. Lebowitz gives each category a heading. What is the EFFECT of these headings?
2. Lebowitz's categories are actually subcategories of a larger class she identifies early on. What is it?
3. Why does Lebowitz constantly evoke God? Might some readers consider this offensive?
4. How could you characterize the TONE of this essay? Does the author admit to being humorous?
5. **OTHER METHODS.** To what extent is "The Sound of Music" an ARGUMENT?

QUESTIONS ON LANGUAGE

1. Look up any of these words that you do not find familiar: incessant (para. 1); malignant, disorienting (6); barrage, afflicted, misconception (7); respective (8).
2. What ALLUSION does Lebowitz make when she says, "What I cannot face is the music" (para. 5)?
3. How does Lebowitz use PERSONIFICATION in paragraph 2? Why?

SUGGESTIONS FOR WRITING

1. What is your taste in music? Following Lebowitz's example (but not her criteria), classify good and bad music, and subclassify bad music. You can be humorous or serious, as you like.
2. Select some aspect of your life that really irks you, perhaps other people's pets, restaurant servers, customers, bus drivers, car drivers, dorm residents, household pests. Write an essay classifying this irksome thing, being careful to supply details and to indicate your feelings in your TONE.
3. Since Lebowitz wrote "The Sound of Music" in the late 1970s, musical soundtracks have become almost required for nonmusical films. Write an essay agreeing or disagreeing with Lebowitz's contention that such

movies are "records with pictures" rather than movies (para. 7). Use specific examples to support your position.

4. CRITICAL WRITING. From this essay we can INFER much about Fran Lebowitz besides just her taste in music. Write a detailed one- or two-paragraph portrait of the person Lebowitz presents herself to be. (If you like, you may draw on "Fran Lebowitz on Writing" for your portrait, too, but use your own words.)

5. CONNECTIONS. Fran Lebowitz and Suzanne Britt in "Neat People vs. Sloppy People" (p. 174) both use classification for humor. COMPARE AND CONTRAST the two writers' uses of complaint, irritation, exaggeration, and other devices to achieve humor. Which writer is funnier, and why?

FRAN LEBOWITZ ON WRITING

Interviewing Fran Lebowitz in 1983, Jean W. Ross noted that her "very funny writing seems to grow out of a genuine irritation." Lebowitz acknowledged as much: "I've always been enraged. . . . Not only have I always been in a state of rage, but I genuinely don't understand why everyone isn't. I don't think of it as being unusual; I think it's the only logical response to life. I think of my writing as an organized and rarefied form of a tantrum. It's the only thing that keeps me from being a murderer. There is a very thin line that divides the comic writer from the mass murderer, and, you know, I really have that impulse all the time. So I guess writing or making wisecracks and jokes is a way of not ending up in prison.

"People have always told me I'm going to have a heart attack because I get angry and blow up," Lebowitz continued, explaining the source of her attitude. "Every time you get on the subway in New York, it stops between the stations for no reason. You sit there for twenty minutes. No one ever tells you why, and everyone just sits there. But I don't, I walk to the front of the train and start screaming at the conductor. Of course it doesn't get any results. People ask me what I hope to achieve from my writing. I never for a second imagined that I was going to change anyone's mind. And I also never for a second imagined that any complaint I would ever make in writing or talking would have any effect. Which further enrages me. The last writer who managed to move people to action was Thomas Paine, and the time of the pamphleteer is gone. I think of myself as a kind of pamphleteer, though the likelihood of affecting people by writing in a country where people are basically illiterate is not very great."

FOR DISCUSSION

1. How is Lebowitz's behavior in a stalled subway car similar to her attitude about writing?
2. What is a pamphleteer? How is Lebowitz like one?
3. What do you think Lebowitz means by "illiterate"? What do you think of her characterization of the American people as "basically illiterate"?

CAMILO JOSÉ VERGARA

CAMILO JOSÉ VERGARA has had an unusual career: He has a background in sociology and is a writer and architectural photographer specializing in urban poverty. He has organized and shown his work in exhibitions documenting cities, including *Transformed Houses* (1981), *Ruins and Revivals: The Architecture of Urban Devastation* (1983), and *The New American Ghetto* (1992). In addition to photographing urban deterioration, Vergara also writes extensively: *Silent Cities: The Evolution of the American Cemetery* (with Kenneth T. Jackson; 1989); *The New American Ghetto* (1994), based on his exhibition; and articles in *Artforum*, *The Nation*, the *New York Times*, *The Atlantic*, and various design and planning publications. Born in 1944, Vergara received a B.A. from Notre Dame (1968) and an M.A. from Columbia University (1977). He has received many awards, including three fellowships from the National Endowment for the Arts. Vergara lives in New York City.

A Guide to the Ghettos

A student of cities, Vergara has a deeper understanding than most of what poverty and responses to it do to neighborhoods. American ghettos are complex organisms, Vergara maintains, and they come in different varieties. This essay first appeared in *The Nation* in March 1993.

1   If you were among the nearly 11,000 people who lived in two-story row houses in north Camden, New Jersey, in the 1960s, you could walk to work at Esterbrook Pen, at Knox Gelatin, at RCA or at J.R. Evans Leather. You could shop on Broadway, a busy three-mile commercial thoroughfare, nicknamed the Street of Lights because of its five first-run movie theaters, with their bright neon signs.

2   Today, hundreds of those row houses — once counted among the best ordinary urban dwellings in America — have been scooped up by bulldozers, their debris carted to a dump in Delaware. Walking along the narrow streets, one passes entire blocks without a single structure, the empty land crisscrossed by footpaths. The scattered dwellings that remain are faced with iron bars, so that they resemble cages.

3   With nearly half of its overwhelmingly Latino population on some form of public assistance, this once-thriving working-class neighbor-

hood is now the poorest urban community in New Jersey. In 1986, former Mayor Alfred Pierce called Camden a reservation for the destitute. The north section of the city has become the drug center for South Jersey; it also hosts a soup kitchen and a large state prison.

North Camden is not unique. Since the riots of the 1960s,   4 American cities have experienced profound transformations, best revealed in the spatial restructuring of their ghettos and the emergence of new urban forms. During the past decade, however, the "underclass" and homelessness have dominated the study of urban poverty. Meanwhile, the power of the physical surroundings to shape lives, to mirror people's existence and to symbolize social relations has been ignored. When scholars from across the political spectrum discuss the factors that account for the persistence of poverty, they fail to consider its living environments. And when prescribing solutions, they overlook the very elements that define the new ghettos: the ruins and semi-ruins; the medical, warehousing and behavior-modification institutions; the various NIMBYs, fortresses and walls; and, not least, the bitterness and anger resulting from living in these places.

Dismissing the value of information received through sight, taste   5 and smell, or through the emotional overtones of an informant's voice, or from the sensation of moving through the spaces studied, has led to the creation of constructs without character, individuality or a sense of place. And although the limitations of statistical data — particularly when dealing with very poor populations — are widely acknowledged, the dependence on numbers is fiercely defended. Other approaches are dismissed as impressionistic, anecdotal, as poetry or "windshield surveys."

Yet today's ghettos are diverse, rich in public and private re-   6 sponses to the environment, in expressions of cultural identity and in reminders of history. These communities are uncharted territory; to be understood, their forms must be identified, described, inventoried and mapped.

An examination of scores of ghettos across the nation reveals   7 three types: "green ghettos," characterized by depopulation, vacant land overgrown by nature and ruins; "institutional ghettos," publicly financed places of confinement designed mainly for the native-born; and "new immigrant ghettos," deriving their character from an influx of immigrants, mainly Latino and West Indian. Some of these communities have continued to lose population; others have emerged where a quarter-century ago there were white ethnic blue-collar neighborhoods; and sections of older ghettos have remained stable, working neighborhoods or have been rebuilt.

Green ghettos, where little has been done to counter disinvest-   8
ment, abandonment, depopulation and dependency, are the leftovers
of a society. Best exemplified by north Camden, by Detroit's East
Side, Chicago's Lawndale and East St. Louis in Illinois, they are
expanding outward to include poor suburbs such as Robbins, Illinois,
and are even found in small cities such as Benton Harbor, Michigan.

Residents, remembering the businesses that moved to suburban   9
malls, the closed factories, the fires, complain of living in a threatening place bereft of jobs and stores and neglected by City Hall. In
many sections of these ghettos, pheasants and rabbits have regained
the space once settled by humans, yet these are not wilderness retreats
in the heart of the city. "Nothing but weeds are growing there" is a
frequent complaint against vacant lots, expressing no mere distaste
for the vegetation but moral outrage at the attitude that produces
such anomalies.

Vegetation grows wildly on and around the vestiges of the former   10
International Harvester Component plant in West Pullman, Chicago.
Polluted fluids — mixtures of oil, rainwater, solvents and chemicals
used during years of operation — can be seen through the uncapped
sewer holes, their covers stolen by scavengers. Derelict industrial
buildings here and in other ghettos have long ago been sacked of
anything of value. Large parcels of land lie unkempt or paved over,
subtracted from the life of the city. Contradicting a long-held vision
of our country as a place of endless progress, ruins, once unforeseen,
are now ignored.

By contrast, in New York City, Newark and Chicago one finds   11
large and expensive habitats — institutional ghettos — publicly regulated for the weakest and most vulnerable members of society. Institution by institution, facility by facility, these environments have
been assembled in the most drug-infested and devastated parts of
cities. They are the complex poorhouses of the twenty-first century,
places to store a growing marginal population officially certified as
"not employable." Residents are selected from the entire city population for their lack of money or home, for their addictions, for their
diseases and other afflictions. Nonresidents come there to pick up
medications, surplus food and used clothes; to get counseling or job
training; to buy drugs or sex; or to do a stint in prison.

As Greg Turner, the manager of a day shelter on the Near West   12
Side of Chicago, puts it: "They say, 'Let's get them off the streets
and put them together in groups.' It is like the zoo; we are going to
put the birds over here, we are going to put the reptiles over there,
we are going to put the buffalo over here, we are going to put the

seals by the pool. It is doing nothing to work with the root of the problem, just like they do nothing to work with the children, to teach them things so they don't grow up and become more homeless people or substance abusers."

Although individual components — for instance, a homeless 13 shelter or a waste incinerator — may be subject to public debate, the overall consequences of creating such "campuses" of institutions are dismissed. The most important barrier to their growth is cost.

Such sections of the city are not neighborhoods. Along the streets 14 surrounding Lincoln Park in south Newark, an area that includes landmark houses, former public buildings and an elegant hotel was chosen by CURA and Integrity House, two drug-treatment programs, because six of its large mansions would provide inexpensive housing for treatment. On the northwest corner of the park, a shelter for battered women just opened in another mansion, and a block north in a former garage is a men's shelter and soup kitchen. The largest structures overlooking the park, a former hotel and a federal office building, house the elderly, who fear going out by themselves. No children play in the park or travel to and from school; no parents go to or come home from work. This is a no man's land devoted to the contradictory goals of selling drugs, getting high and just surviving, on the one hand, and becoming clean and employed, on the other.

In other parts of New York and Chicago a community of recent 15 immigrants is growing up, but this type of ghetto is most visible in South Central Los Angeles and Compton, where the built environment is more intimate than in older ghettos, the physical structures are more adaptable and it is easier for newcomers to imprint their identity. Here paint goes a long way to transform the appearance of the street.

The new immigrant ghettos are characterized by tiny offices pro- 16 viding numerous services, such as driving instruction, insurance and immigration assistance; by stores that sell imported beer, produce and canned goods; and by restaurants offering home cooking. Notable are the businesses that reflect the busy exchange between the local population and their native country: money transfers, travel agencies, even funeral homes that arrange to have bodies shipped home.

To get by, most residents are forced to resort to exploitative jobs 17 paying minimum wage or less and usually lacking health benefits. For housing they crowd together in small, badly maintained apartments or in cinder-block garages and trailers.

Not being eligible for public housing may in the long run prove 18 to be a blessing for the people. Although forced to pay high rents,

immigrants tend to concentrate in neighborhoods that are part of the
urban economy, thus avoiding the extreme social disorganization,
isolation and violence that characterize other types of ghettos. Because of the huge influx of young people with expectations that life
will be better for their children and grandchildren, these ghettos are
more dynamic and fluid, resembling the foreign-born communities of
a century ago.

No single ghetto is completely green, institutional or immigrant 19
in character. Although the overwhelming trend is toward greater
waste, abandonment and depopulation, these three models are related, channeling people and land to one another. Fires and demo-
litions in the green ghettos provide large tracts of cleared land where
poverty institutions and other facilities can be built. By default the
most desperate people and neighborhoods become wards of the government in communities where, in the words of a Brooklyn organizer,
"all the social disasters of the city are located."

If nothing is done to prevent it, within a decade more working- 20
class communities are likely to belong to one of these types. Con-
versely, some institutional ghettos, such as the Near West Side of
Chicago, are likely to be squeezed out by expanding sports and medical complexes. And the same forces of abandonment that can open
the way for the modern poorhouses can at other times free land for
townhouses built for working families.

These are the "reclaimed ghettos." With their horror stories of 21
violence, public incompetence and waste, ghettos are used to provide
moral justification for privately managed programs of redevelopment.
Under the leadership of churches, community organizations, private
developers and recent immigrants, such ghettos have kicked out most
of the dependent poor and have refused to admit the institutions that
serve them. Instead, they focus on attracting working families, keeping out drug dealers and building guarded enclaves.

These communities are on the verge of melding into mainstream 22
society. But when examining the contribution of community development corporations, we need to ask ourselves whether their efforts
are leading to the elimination of ghettos or toward the creation of
mini-cities of exclusion within a larger wasteland.

For it is at the boundaries that the individual character of ghettos 23
reveals itself most clearly: around embattled clusters of dwellings
where ethnic groups assert themselves, in blocks where strong buildings share a wall with dilapidated crack houses, and along the perimeter of hospitals, universities and other citadels. Borders where white

meets black are stark, presenting a graphic contrast between a seemingly victorious white community and what appears to be a defeated minority community. Along Mack Avenue as it crosses from Detroit's East Side into affluent Grosse Pointe, and along Chicago's East 62nd Street, the border between Woodlawn and Hyde Park (home of the University of Chicago), a history of race relations has been written into the landscape. Security measures, guards, dead-end streets, green grass on one side; vacant land, abandoned buildings, people out of work, hanging out, on the other.

Writers in the mainstream press call ghettos intractable, expressing concern with the public burden they impose. The system works for those who are motivated, many outsiders say, pointing to the presence of minorities in more affluent suburbs, to reclaimed ghettos and to the economic success of recent black, Latino and Asian immigrants. 24

But among many ghetto dwellers, particularly native-born African-Americans, there is growing ideological hardening and a yearning to close ranks, to re-emerge from destitution and to prosper among themselves. A journalist in Gary, Indiana, a city almost completely abandoned by whites, remarked, "I don't know why people have to have white people to succeed." A Chicago construction worker called blacks who moved to the suburbs "imitation white people." A Newark woman suggested that such people have sold out, are living a lie. "They need to take a good look in the mirror," she said. 25

Echoing Malcolm X, most ghetto residents I have encountered see the devastation and violence in their communities as part of a white strategy of domination. Drugs are widely perceived as part of a monstrous plot to destroy and contain poor blacks and Latinos. A Chicago minister states, "White supremacy, a system of oppression that comes out of Western society, is the real problem." A Brooklyn artist declares, "People of color have a right to be paranoid." 26

Within ghetto walls a new generation is growing along with new activities, ideologies, institutions and drugs. Crack sells briskly across the street from drug-treatment centers, and children walk past homeless shelters. An army of men strip cars, and hordes of scavengers push loaded shopping carts along the streets. Houses stand alone like fortresses, enclosed by fences. Dozens of cities are falling into ruin, and along their streets billboards beg people to stop killing one another. 27

Today, there is renewed talk of strategies to bring jobs, to improve education, to build better housing and provide adequate health care for all Americans. Such developments would certainly improve the 28 conditions in poor communities but would not change their isolation, racial composition and fragmentation. Ghettos would continue to expand, new ones to emerge, and the anger of their residents would remain unabated.

Public policy must also address the unique characteristics of our 29 ghettos. A crucial step is to change practices that concentrate in these communities the poor and the institutions that serve them. We need regional and national approaches to population redistribution, such as the building of low-income housing in wealthy suburbs and the elimination of the barriers that define ghettos. And as we once did in the 1960s, we need to convince ourselves that as a nation we have the power not just to improve the ghetto but to abolish it. To do this we need to go beyond the statistics and into the streets, alleys and buildings.

QUESTIONS ON MEANING

1. What are "NIMBYs" (para. 4)? How do they help "define the new ghettos"? Why are they not the solution to the problem of the ghettos? What does Vergara think *is* the solution?
2. What are the "reclaimed ghettos"?
3. What is Vergara's THESIS?
4. What is the PURPOSE of this essay?

QUESTIONS ON WRITING STRATEGY

1. What principle does Vergara use to classify ghettos? Why?
2. Vergara's classification occurs in paragraphs 7–18. What are the purposes of the rather long INTRODUCTION (1–6) and CONCLUSION (19–29)?
3. How would you describe this essay's TONE? Is it in keeping with the subject? Why or why not?
4. **OTHER METHODS.** Vergara uses CAUSE AND EFFECT to explain how the ghettos arrived in their current conditions. List the causes he cites.

QUESTIONS ON LANGUAGE

1. What are the CONNOTATIONS of the word *ghetto*? What other words are used as EUPHEMISMS for it? What is its EFFECT here?
2. What does Vergara mean by "windshield surveys" (para. 5)?
3. Be sure you know the meanings of the following words: anomalies (para.

9); vestiges (10); enclaves (21); melding (22); perimeter, citadels (23); intractable (24); ideological (25).

SUGGESTIONS FOR WRITING

1. Write a brief essay classifying the neighborhoods of your town or city. Choose whatever principle of classification appeals to you: residents' incomes, national origins, professions, ages, or life-styles; population density; age; style of architecture. Give plenty of EXAMPLES to support your classification.
2. Vergara argues that advances in jobs, housing, education, and health care "would certainly improve the conditions in poor communities but would not change their isolation, racial composition and fragmentation" (para. 28). Do you agree? Why or why not? In a short essay, challenge or affirm Vergara's statement.
3. CRITICAL WRITING. In his conclusion (para. 29), Vergara maintains that "we need to convince ourselves that as a nation we have the power not just to improve the ghetto but to abolish it." What are some of the ASSUMPTIONS underlying Vergara's conclusion? (For instance, to whom does "we" refer?) Are these assumptions widely accepted? Do *you* accept them? Why or why not?
4. CONNECTIONS. Consider this essay alongside Stephanie Coontz's "A Nation of Welfare Families" (p. 150). How do the two essays complement each other? (Are their THESES compatible?) Where, if at all, do they diverge?

RALPH WHITEHEAD, JR.

RALPH WHITEHEAD, JR., is a journalist and a professor of journalism at the University of Massachusetts at Amherst. He grew up and attended school in Wisconsin, and in the late 1960s he became a news reporter in Chicago, covering the social tumult of that period for the *Chicago Sun-Times* and *Chicago Today*. He has also reported for the *Newark Star Ledger* and served as both reporter and news anchor on public and commercial television. When Whitehead began teaching at the University of Massachusetts in 1973, he continued writing for various publications, including the *American Scholar*, the *Columbia Journalism Review*, *The New Republic*, and *Psychology Today*. For most of the 1980s, his knack for understanding and articulating social hierarchies and public opinion earned him speaking engagements and consulting work with politicians, political groups, and labor organizations. He now concentrates on teaching and on finishing a book about the changing American class structure.

Class Acts:
America's Changing Middle Class

In this essay from the *Utne Reader* in early 1990, Whitehead outlines changes in the American "social ladder" — the hierarchy of social and economic groups. For a complementary view of American classes, see Robert B. Reich's "Why the Rich Are Getting Richer and the Poor Poorer" (p. 350).

As we enter the 1990s, American society exhibits a vastly differ- 1 ent social and economic makeup from the one that we grew accustomed to in the thirty years that followed World War II. The gap between the top and bottom is far greater now, of course, but the economic position of people in the middle is changing, too. This new social ladder is seen most vividly in the lives of our younger generations, the baby boom and the later baby bust. Because the new ladder is so much steeper than the old one, it's creating an alarming new degree of polarization in American life.

As it held sway for roughly the first three decades after World 2 War II, the old social ladder was shaped largely by the continuing expansion of the middle class. For the first time, many people could afford to buy a house, a car (or two), a washer and dryer, an outdoor grill, adequate health coverage, maybe a motor boat, and possibly college for the kids. And for the first time, a growing number of blacks and Hispanics could enter the middle class.

Within this expanding middle class, there were a couple of fairly well-defined ways of life: white-collar life and blue-collar life. White-collar life was typified by TV characters like Ward and June Cleaver and later Mike and Carol Brady. Blue-collar life was typified by characters like Ralph and Alice Kramden and later Archie and Edith Bunker.   3

At the top of the old social ladder stood a small number of rich people. A larger but declining number of poor people stood at the bottom, and the rest of the ladder was taken up by the middle-class. The old social ladder looked roughly like this: 4

THE RICH

THE EXPANDING MIDDLE CLASS:
White collar
Blue collar

THE POOR

The new social ladder is markedly different. Within the baby boom and baby bust generations, the middle class is no longer expanding. Therefore the new social ladder is shaped by — and at the same time is helping to shape — a new polarization between the haves and the have-nots. The social ladder of the 1990s looks roughly like this: 5

UPSCALE AMERICA:
The Rich
The Overclass

THE DIVERGING MIDDLE CLASS:
Bright collar
New collar
Blue collar

DOWNSCALE AMERICA:
The Poor
The Underclass

The rich are still on top, of course. But the new generation of rich people is typified by Donald Trump, the billionaire developer of luxury buildings for the newly rich, rather than by someone like his father, Fred Trump, a developer who made millions building modestly priced postwar homes and apartments for the expanding middle class — the kinds of homes in which the Kramdens and Bunkers lived.

The poor are still with us, of course, but they're no longer at the   6
bottom. It's not because they've risen to the middle class but rather because some of them have fallen into the underclass. Because definitions of the underclass vary, so do estimates of its size. However, it does include at least two million people who lead lives that aren't typified in America's popular culture. To belong to the underclass is to be without a face and without a voice.

Just as an underclass has emerged, so has an overclass, which   7
occupies the rung just below the rich. Located chiefly in a dozen metropolises and heavily concentrated in lucrative management and professional jobs, the overclass is roughly the same size as the underclass. Its significance lies not in its numbers, however, but in its immense power throughout American society. The overclass holds the highest level positions in the fields of entertainment, media, marketing, advertising, real estate, finance, and politics. It's pursued for its consumption dollars and cajoled for its investment dollars. It is crudely typified by the media stereotype of the yuppie.

What clearly stood out on the old social ladder that shaped   8
American society during the fifties and sixties was the dominant presence of an expanding middle class. What is noticeable about the new social ladder is the unmistakable emergence of distinct upper and lower rungs, and the vast social, economic, and psychological distance between them. Together, the rich and the overclass form Upscale America. Together, the underclass and the poor form Downscale America.

The expanding middle class, with its white and blue collars, has   9
given way in the baby boom and baby bust generations to a diverging middle class. It consists largely of three kinds of workers:

• **Bright collars.** Within the ranks of managerial and professional   10
workers a new category of job has emerged. The white-collar worker is receding and the bright-collar worker is advancing. The bright collars are the 20 million knowledge workers born since 1945: lawyers and teachers, architects and social workers, accountants and budget analysts, engineers and consultants, rising executives and midlevel

administrators. They earn their living by taking intellectual initiatives. They face the luxury and the necessity of making their own decisions on the job and in their personal lives.

Bright-collar people lack the touchstones that guided white-collar 11 workers like Ward Cleaver in the 1950s and 1960s. The white collars believed in institutions; bright collars are skeptical of them. The corporate chain of command, a strong force in white-collar life then, is far weaker for bright collars today. They place a premium on individuality, on standing out rather than fitting in. Although the older white collars knew the rules and played by them, bright collars can't be sure what the rules are and must think up their own. The white collars were organization men and women (mostly men); bright collars are entrepreneurs interested in building careers for themselves outside big corporations.

Three quarters of the managers and professionals of the 1950s 12 were men. Today half are women. Seven percent are black or Hispanic or Asian. Bright collars make up a third of the baby boom work force. They're typified by figures like *L.A. Law's* attorneys.

• **Blue collars.** Within the manufacturing workplace, blue-collar 13 work endures, but on a much smaller scale. Thirty years ago almost 40 percent of the adult work force did blue-collar work. Today, after the relative decline of American heavy industry, it's done by less than 25 percent of baby boom workers. During the fifties and sixties, blue-collar wages rose steadily, thus helping fuel the expansion of the middle class. In the past 15 years these wages have been relatively flat. Young blue collars often must live near the economic margins.

The blue-collar world is still a man's world. Roughly three quarters 14 of today's younger blue collars are men — the same percentage as in the 1950s. Twelve percent are black, Hispanic, or Asian. Within a growing number of innovative manufacturing workplaces, new models of blue-collar work have begun to emerge, but they haven't yet advanced enough to trigger a new category of American worker. In the popular culture the new generation of blue collars finds a voice in Bruce Springsteen, but it still hasn't found a face.

• **New collars.** These people aren't managers and professionals, and 15 they don't do physical labor. Their jobs fall between those two worlds. They're secretaries, clerks, telephone operators, key-punch operators, inside salespeople, police officers. They often avoid the grime and regimentation of blue-collar work. Two thirds of the new collars are women. More than 15 percent are black, Hispanic, or Asian. The new collars make up at least 35 percent of the baby boom work force.

Federal Express truck drivers are typical new-collar workers. They 16 design pickup and delivery routes, explain the company's services and fees, provide mailing supplies, and handle relatively sophisticated information technology in their trucks. They aren't traditional truck drivers so much as sales clerks in offices on wheels.

The rise of the new social ladder has helped to drive a number 17 of changes in American life, but one of them, already evident, should be underscored: the dramatic shift of power within both the middle class and the society as a whole.

As members of the expanding middle class of the postwar years, 18 blue collars once held considerable leverage. In the electorate, for every vote cast by the white collars in 1960, the blue collars cast two. In the workplace, they acted through powerful unions. In the marketplace, they were valued as consumers. As a result, blue collars dealt with white collars as equals. In the fifties and sixties, whatever class lines still divided the two groups seemed to be dissolving.

Within the diverging middle class today, the balance of power is 19 much different. In the electorate, for every vote cast by younger blue collars in 1988, bright collars cast two. In the workplace, younger blue-collar workers are losing union power, while bright collars exert the power of their knowledge and privilege of their status. In the marketplace, blue-collar consumers are written off as too downscale, while the bright-collar consumer is courted as an aspiring member of the overclass. Deep divisions have sprung up between bright collars and blue collars. They look a lot like class lines.

The rise of an overclass throws the decline of blue-collar life into 20 sharper relief, and vice versa. Upscale yuppie haunts spring up: the health club, the gourmet takeout shop, the pricy boutique, the atrium building. Downscale blue-collar haunts wither: the union hall, the lodge, the beauty parlor, the mill. The guys with red suspenders began showing up in the beer commercials right about the time the loggers and guys with air hammers began to disappear. The overclass's stock portfolios began to get fat just as blue-collar families were losing their pensions and health insurance. Condo prices were climbing in Atlanta just as bungalow prices fell in Buffalo. It seems that there's a battle here, a zero-sum game, whereby the rise of one comes at the expense of the other.

The contrast between the rich and the underclass is sharper than 21 ever. If you look at the new social ladder in New York, you see

Donald Trump in his penthouse and the homeless people in the subways.

This situation intensifies the shift of power in society as a whole. With the middle class divided, the center cannot hold. The dominant forces in society become Upscale America and Downscale America — or, more precisely, Upscale America *versus* Downscale America. Upscale America uses its power to secure privileges such as proposed cuts in the capital gains tax. Downscale America strikes back blindly through rising rates of crime. Through the old social ladder, the expanding middle class acted as the nation's glue. With the new social ladder, the diverging middle class is merely caught in the crossfire. 22

QUESTIONS ON MEANING

1. What is Whitehead's THESIS? What does "polarization" mean?
2. What is happening to the American middle class, according to Whitehead?
3. What does Whitehead say is the main result of the change he describes?
4. What do you think is Whitehead's PURPOSE in this essay? To inform? To persuade? Both?

QUESTIONS ON WRITING STRATEGY

1. Whitehead provides a classification within a classification. Why?
2. Why does Whitehead use figures from television and music to illustrate the various classes he identifies (paras. 3, 11, 12, 14, 20)? What is the EFFECT of these examples?
3. What attitudes does Whitehead seem to assume his AUDIENCE will have toward his ideas? (It may help to recall that this essay was first published in the *Utne Reader*, a magazine whose essays and articles take a mainly liberal approach to national and international issues.)
4. OTHER METHODS. How does Whitehead use COMPARISON AND CONTRAST to clarify changes in American society?

QUESTIONS ON LANGUAGE

1. Define the phrases *baby boom* and *baby bust* (para. 1). Do you belong to one of these generations?
2. What is the meaning of the word *collar* to designate classes? What does Whitehead mean by "bright collar"?

3. Use your dictionary to find any of these words that are unfamiliar: lucrative, cajoled (para.7); initiatives (10); touchstones, skeptical, entrepreneurs (11); regimentation (15); leverage (18).

SUGGESTIONS FOR WRITING

1. Write an essay classifying Americans or some part of American society by a principle of classification other than income — for instance, political views, moral values, attitudes toward education. If you like, your essay may be humorous, taking as its principle something like clothing styles, television preferences, or table manners. Draw on your own experiences, observations, and reading, and be sure to give plenty of examples of each class.
2. Whether just as Whitehead outlines it or not, the United States certainly does have a "social and economic makeup," or class structure. What advantages or disadvantages do you see in such a system — or, alternately, what advantages or disadvantages would you see in a system where everyone had the same economic and social position? Be as specific as possible.
3. CRITICAL WRITING. Locate yourself in Whitehead's classification. What ASSUMPTIONS does he make about your class? Do you detect any errors in Whitehead's description? Write an essay agreeing or disagreeing with Whitehead, drawing on EVIDENCE from your own experience, observation, and reading.
4. CONNECTIONS. Both Whitehead's essay and Robert B. Reich's "Why the Rich Are Getting Richer" (p. 350) discuss the classes in American society. When you've read both essays, write an essay of your own that answers the following questions: What are the advantages of such classifications? What are the disadvantages? Where do you see yourself fitting in Reich's and Whitehead's schemes — now and in the future? Does positioning yourself in this way open or close options, do you think?

RALPH WHITEHEAD, JR., ON WRITING

Ralph Whitehead, Jr., has a reputation for translating data about social and economic change into useful ideas for a broad audience. As he told Scott Heller for the *Chronicle of Higher Education*, "I'm a popularizer, a synthesizer, a middlebrow." Unlike many writers on politics and society, Whitehead watches and listens to what's going on outside the narrow circle of journalists, politicians, media consultants, and academics. Such openness and a willingness to say what his research told him led Whitehead in the mid-1980s to articulate the changes outlined in "Class Acts," which had been overlooked by most other observers. "There's a danger," he warns, "that this country will be driven by technocrats who can't get their noses off the sidewalk. Within the world of politics and policy, I'm a guy people like to have in the room. There's always a hunger for a generalizer."

FOR DISCUSSION

1. What does Whitehead mean by "a popularizer, a synthesizer, a middlebrow," and "a generalizer"?
2. Popularizers are often disparaged as less important than the scholars whose work they report. How does Whitehead challenge that view?

ROBERT B. REICH

ROBERT B. REICH is secretary of labor in the administration of President Bill Clinton. Before his appointment, he was already well known as a writer, teacher, and leader of the "neoliberals" — those seeking ways for the United States to achieve economic strength without sacrificing social programs. Reich was born in 1946 in Scranton, Pennsylvania, and attended Dartmouth College, Oxford University (as a Rhodes Scholar), and Yale Law School. He was active in liberal politics in the late 1960s, worked in the federal government for some years, and taught at Harvard University's John F. Kennedy School of Government. Reich has contributed to the *Atlantic*, the *Harvard Business Review*, *The New Republic*, and other periodicals. He has written numerous books, among them *The Next American Frontier* (1983), *Tales of a New America* (1987), *The Power of Public Ideas* (1988), and *The Work of Nations* (1991). A collection of essays, *The Resurgent Liberal (and Other Unfashionable Prophesies)*, was published in 1989.

Why the Rich Are Getting Richer and the Poor Poorer

This essay first appeared in May 1989 in *The New Republic*. Though Reich cites trends from the 1980s, his thesis is not dated: As he says, the changes he discusses are worldwide and far from over. What's needed for our country, Reich has said elsewhere, is a "true patriotism" that is based on "a common concern for, and investment in, the well-being of our future citizens." Reich's classification complements Ralph Whitehead's in the previous essay (p. 342) and was reprinted with it in the January/February 1990 *Utne Reader*.

Between 1978 and 1987, the poorest fifth of American families   1
became 8 percent poorer, and the richest fifth became 13 percent richer. That means the poorest fifth now have less than 5 percent of the nation's income, while the richest fifth have more than 40 percent.

This widening gap can't be blamed on the growth in single-parent   2
lower-income families, which in fact slowed markedly after the late 1970s. Nor is it due mainly to the stingy social policies of the Reagan years. Granted, food stamp benefits have dropped 13 percent since 1981 (in real terms), and many states have failed to raise benefits for

the poor and unemployed to keep up with inflation. But this doesn't come close to accounting for the growing persistence of economic inequality in the United States. Rather, this disturbing trend is connected to a profound change in the American economy as it merges with the global economy. And because the merging is far from complete, this trend will not stop all by itself anytime soon. It is significant that the growth of inequality can be seen most strikingly among Americans who have jobs. Through most of the postwar era, the wages of Americans at different income levels rose at about the same pace. Although different workers occupied different steps on the escalator, everyone moved up together. In those days poverty was the condition of *jobless* Americans, and the major economic challenge was to create enough jobs for everyone. Once people were safely in the work force, their problems were assumed to be over. Thus "full employment" became a liberal rallying cry.

But in recent years Americans with jobs have been traveling on   3
two escalators — one going up, the other going down. In 1987 the average hourly earnings of nonsupervisory workers (adjusted for inflation) were lower than in any year since 1966. Middle-level managers fared much better, although their median real earnings were only slightly above the levels of the 1970s. Executives, however, did spectacularly well. In 1988 alone, CEOs of the 100 largest publicly held industrial corporations received raises averaging almost 12 percent.

Between 1978 and 1987, as the real earnings of unskilled workers   4
were declining, the real incomes of investment bankers and other securities industry workers rose 21 percent. It is not unusual for a run-of-the-mill investment banker to bring home comfortably over a million dollars. Meanwhile, the number of impoverished *working* Americans climbed by nearly two million, or 23 percent, during those same years. Nearly 60 percent of the 20 million people who now fall below the Census Bureau's poverty line are from families with at least one member in full-time or part-time work.

The American economy now exhibits a wider gap between rich   5
and poor than it has at any other time since World War II. The most basic reason, put simply, is that America itself is ceasing to exist as an economic system separate from the rest of the world. One can no more meaningfully speak of an "American economy" than of a "Delaware economy." We are becoming but a region — albeit still a relatively wealthy region — of a global economy. This is a new kind of economy whose technologies, savings, and investments move ef-

fortlessly across borders, making it harder for individual nations to control their economic destinies.

We have yet to come to terms with the rise of the global corpo- 6 ration, whose managers, shareholders, and employees span the world. Our debates over the future of American jobs still focus on topics such as the competitiveness of the American automobile industry or the future of American manufacturing. But these issues are increasingly irrelevant.

New technologies of worldwide communication and transporta- 7 tion have redrawn the economic playing field. American industries no longer compete against Japanese or European industries. Rather, a company with headquarters in the United States, production facilities in Taiwan, and a marketing force spread across many nations competes with another, similarly wide-ranging company. So when General Motors, say, is doing well, that probably is good news for a lot of executives in Detroit, and for GM shareholders across the globe, but it isn't necessarily good news for a lot of assembly-line workers in Detroit, because there may, in fact, be very few GM assembly-line workers in Detroit, or anywhere else in America. The welfare of assembly-line workers in Detroit may depend, instead, on the health of corporations based in Japan or Canada.

More to the point, even if those Canadian and Japanese corpo- 8 rations are doing well, those Detroit workers may be in trouble. For they are increasingly part of an international labor market, encompassing Asia, Africa, Western Europe, and, perhaps before long, Eastern Europe. With relative ease corporations can relocate their production centers to take advantage of low wages. So American workers find themselves settling for low wages in order to hold on to their jobs. More and more, your "competitiveness" as a worker depends not on the fortunes of any American corporation, or of any American industry, but on what function you serve within the global economy.

In order to see in greater detail what is happening to American 9 jobs, it helps to view the work that most Americans do in terms of new categories that reflect how U.S. workers fit into the global economy. Essentially, three broad categories are emerging. I call them: (1) symbolic-analytic services; (2) routine production services; and (3) routine personal services.

1. Symbolic-analytic services are based on the manipulation of in- 10 formation: data, words, and oral and visual symbols. Symbolic analysis comprises some (but by no means all) of the work undertaken by people who call themselves lawyers, investment bankers, commercial bankers, management consultants, research scientists, academics, public-relations executives, real estate developers, and even a few creative accountants. Also, many advertising and marketing specialists, art directors, design engineers, architects, writers and editors, musicians, and television and film producers.

Some of the manipulations of information performed by these 11 symbolic analysts offer ways of more efficiently deploying resources or shifting financial assets, or of otherwise saving time and energy. Other manipulations grab money from people who are too slow or naive to protect themselves. Still others serve to entertain the public.

Most symbolic analysts work alone or in small teams. If they work 12 with others, they often have partners rather than bosses or supervisors. Their work environments tend to be quiet and tastefully decorated, often within tall steel-and-glass buildings. When they are not analyzing, designing, or strategizing, they are in meetings or on the telephone — giving advice or making deals. Many of them spend an inordinate amount of time in jet planes and hotels. They are generally articulate and well groomed. The vast majority are white males.

Symbolic analysis now accounts for more than 40 percent of 13 America's gross national product, and almost 20 percent of our jobs.

The services performed by America's symbolic analysts are in high 14 demand around the world. The Japanese are buying up the insights and inventions of America's scientists and engineers (who are only too happy to sell them at a fat profit). The Europeans, meanwhile, are hiring our management consultants, business strategists, and investment bankers. Developing nations are hiring our civil and design engineers; and almost everyone is buying the output of our pop musicians, television stars, and film producers.

The same thing is happening with the global corporation. The 15 central offices of these sprawling entities, headquartered in America, are filled with symbolic analysts who manipulate information and then export their insights around the world via the corporation's far-flung operations. IBM, for instance, doesn't export machines from the United States; it manufactures its machines in factories all over the globe. IBM world headquarters, in Armonk, New York, exports just strategic planning and related management services.

Thus has the standard of living of America's symbolic analysts 16 risen. They increasingly find themselves part of a global labor market, not a national one. And because the United States has a highly developed economy, and an excellent university system, they find that the services they have to offer are in high demand around the whole world. This ensures that their salaries are quite high.

Those salaries are likely to go even higher in the years ahead, as 17 the world market for symbolic analysis continues to grow. Foreigners are trying to learn these skills and techniques, to be sure, but they still have a long way to go. No other country does a better job of preparing its most fortunate citizens for symbolic analysis than does the United States. None has surpassed America in providing experience and training, often with entire regions specializing in one or another kind of symbolic analysis (New York and Chicago for finance, Los Angeles for music and film, the San Francisco Bay area and greater Boston for science and engineering). In this we can take pride. But for the second major category of American workers — the providers of routine production services — the future doesn't bode well.

2. Routine production services involve tasks that are repeated over 18 and over, as one step in a sequence of steps for producing a finished product. Although we tend to associate these jobs with manufacturing, they are becoming common in banking, insurance, wholesaling, retailing, health care — all industries employing millions of people who spend their days processing data, often putting information into computers or taking it out.

Most people involved in routine production services work with 19 many other people who do similar work, within large, centralized facilities. They are overseen by supervisors, who in turn are monitored by more senior supervisors. They are usually paid an hourly wage. Their jobs are often monotonous. Most of the workers do not have a college education. Those who deal with metal are mostly white males; those who deal with fabrics or information tend to be female and/or minorities.

Decades ago, those kinds of workers were relatively well paid. 20 But in recent years America's providers of routine production services have found themselves in direct competition with millions of foreign workers, most of whom work for a fraction of the pay American workers get. Through the miracle of satellite transmission, even routine data processing can now be undertaken in relatively poor nations, thousands of miles away from the skyscrapers where the data are finally used. This fact has given management ever greater power in bargaining talks. If routine production workers living in America don't agree to reduce their wages, then the work often goes abroad.

And it has. In 1950, routine production services constituted about   21
30 percent of our gross national product and well over half of American jobs. Today such services represent about 20 percent of the GNP
and one fourth of jobs. And the scattering of foreign-owned factories
placed here to circumvent American protectionism isn't going to
reverse the trend. So the standard of living of America's routine
production workers will likely keep declining. The dynamics behind
the wage concessions, plant closings, and union-busting that have
become commonplace won't be stopped without a major turnaround
in labor organizing or political action.

3. Routine personal services also entail simple, repetitive work, but,   22
unlike routine production services, they are provided in person. Included in this employment category are restaurant and hotel workers,
barbers and beauticians, retail sales personnel, cab drivers, household
cleaners, day-care workers, hospital attendants and orderlies, truck
drivers, and — among the fastest-growing of all careers — custodians
and security guards.

Like production workers, providers of personal services are usually   23
paid by the hour. They are also carefully supervised and rarely have
more than a high school education. But unlike people in the other
two categories of work, they are in direct contact with the ultimate
beneficiaries of what they do. And the companies they work for are
often small. In fact, some routine personal-service workers become
entrepreneurs. (Most new businesses and new jobs in America come
from this sector — which now constitutes about 20 percent of GNP
and 30 percent of jobs.) Women and minorities make up the bulk of
routine personal-service workers.

Apart from the small number who strike out on their own, these   24
workers are paid poorly. They are sheltered from the direct effects of
global competition, but not the indirect effects. They often compete
with undocumented workers willing to work for low wages, or with
former or would-be production workers who can't find well-paying
production jobs, or with labor-saving machinery (automated tellers,
self-service gas pumps) dreamed up by symbolic analysts in America and
manufactured in Asia. And because they tend to be unskilled and
dispersed among small businesses, personal-service workers rarely have
a union or a powerful lobby group to stand up for their interests. When
the economy turns sour, they are among the first to feel the effects.

These workers will continue to have jobs in the years ahead and   25
may experience some small increase in real wages. They will have

demographics on their side, as the American work force shrinks. But for all the foregoing reasons, the gap between their earnings and those of the symbolic analysts will continue to grow if present economic trends and labor conditions continue.

These three functional categories — symbolic analysis, routine   26 production services, and routine personal services — cover at least three out of four American jobs. The rest of the nation's work force consists mainly of government employees (including public school teachers), employees in regulated industries (like utility workers), and government-financed workers (engineers working on defense weapons systems), many of whom are sheltered from global competition. One further clarification: Some traditional job categories overlap several of these categories. People called "secretaries," for example, include those who actually spend their time doing symbolic analysis work closely allied to what their bosses do; those who do routine data entry or retrieval of a sort that will eventually be automated or done overseas; and those who provide routine personal services.

The important point is that workers in these three functional   27 categories are coming to have different competitive positions in the world economy. Symbolic analysts hold a commanding position in an increasingly global labor market. Routine production workers hold a relatively weak position in an increasingly global labor market. Routine personal service workers still find themselves in a national labor market, but for various reasons they suffer the indirect effects of competition from workers abroad.

How should we respond to these trends? One response is to accept   28 them as inevitable consequences of change, but to try to offset their polarizing effects through a truly progressive income tax, coupled with more generous income assistance — including health insurance — for poor working Americans. (For a start, we might reverse the extraordinarily regressive Social Security amendments of 1983, through which poor working Americans are now financing the federal budget deficit, often paying more in payroll taxes than in income taxes.)

A more ambitious response would be to guard against class rig-   29 idities by ensuring that any talented American kid can become a symbolic analyst — regardless of family income or race. But America's gifted but poor children can't aspire to such jobs until the government spends substantially more than it does now to ensure excellent public schools in every city and region and ample financial help when they are ready to attend college.

Of course, it isn't clear that even under those circumstances there   30
would be radical growth in the number of Americans who become
research scientists, design engineers, musicians, management consultants, or (even if the world needed them) investment bankers and
lawyers. So other responses are also needed. Perhaps the most ambitious would be to increase the numbers of Americans who could
apply symbolic analysis to production and to personal services.

There is ample evidence, for example, that access to computerized   31
information can enrich production jobs by enabling workers to alter
the flow of materials and components in ways that increase efficiency.
Production workers who have broader responsibilities and more control over how production is organized cease to be "routine" workers —
becoming, in effect, symbolic analysts at a level very close to the
production process. The same transformation can occur in personal-
service jobs. Consider, for example, the checkout clerk whose computer enables her to control inventory and decide when to reorder
items from the factory.

The number of such technologically empowered jobs, of course,   32
is limited by the ability of workers to learn on the job. That means
a far greater number of Americans will need a good grounding in
mathematics, basic science, reading, and communication skills. So
once again, comfortably integrating the American work force into
the new world economy turns out to rest heavily on education. (Better
health care, especially prenatal and pediatric care, would also figure
in here.)

Education and health care for poor children are apt to be costly.   33
Since poorer working Americans, already under a heavy tax load,
can't afford it, the cost would have to be borne by wealthier Americans — who also would have to bear the cost of any income redistribution plans designed to neutralize the polarizing domestic effects
of a globalized economy. Thus a central question is the willingness
of the more fortunate American citizens — especially symbolic analysts, who constitute much of the most fortunate fifth, with 40 percent
of the nation's income — to bear the burden. But here lies a catch-
22. For as our economic fates diverge, the top fifth may be losing its
sense of connectedness with the bottom fifth (or even the bottom
half) that would elicit such generosity.

The conservative tide that has swept the land during the past   34
decade surely has many causes, but the fundamental changes in our
economy should not be discounted as a major factor. It is now possible
for the most fortunate fifth to sell their expertise directly in the global

market, and thus maintain and enhance their standard of living, even
as that of other Americans declines. There is less and less basis for a
strong sense of interclass interdependence in America. Meanwhile,
the fortunate fifth have also been able to insulate themselves from
the less fortunate, by living in suburban enclaves far removed from
the effects of poverty. Neither patriotism nor altruism may be sufficient to overcome these realities. Yet without the active support of
at least some of the fortunate fifth, it will be more difficult to muster
the political will necessary for change. . . .

On withdrawing from the presidential race of 1988, Paul Simon   35
of Illinois said, "Americans instinctively know that we are one nation,
one family, and when anyone in that family hurts, all of us hurt."
Sadly, that is coming to be less and less the case.

QUESTIONS ON MEANING

1. What is Reich's PURPOSE in this essay? Is it the same as his reason for
   classifying the American labor force into three new categories?
2. In paragraphs 28 and 33, Reich speaks of "polarizing effects." What does
   he mean? How would polarization relate to his categories?
3. What responses does the author suggest to the problems he identifies?
   How does he rank these responses?
4. In Reich's opinion, what is needed to implement these responses?

QUESTIONS ON WRITING STRATEGY

1. What EVIDENCE does Reich use to define each of his categories? Does
   each category receive the same attention?
2. How does Reich deal with jobs that don't fit into his categories, or with
   more traditional categories that don't match his?
3. This essay first appeared in *The New Republic* and then in the *Utne
   Reader*, both magazines with a primarily educated, liberal AUDIENCE. In
   what category do his readers most likely belong? How might his audience
   have influenced Reich's purpose?
4. OTHER METHODS. Reich uses classification in the service of ARGUMENT
   AND PERSUASION. What APPEALS (RATIONAL and EMOTIONAL) does the
   author use to bring the reader over to his way of thinking?

QUESTIONS ON LANGUAGE

1. Define these key terms in Reich's essay: global economy (para. 2);
   inflation, median (3); impoverished (4); shareholders (7); symbolic (10);

deploying (11); wholesaling (18); gross national product, protectionism (21); entrepreneurs (23); undocumented workers, lobby (24); demographics (25); progressive income tax, regressive (28); altruism (34).
2. What does the author think of investment bankers? Find language from the essay to support your opinion.
3. What does Reich mean by a *catch-22* (para. 33)? Where does the term come from? What has it come to mean?

SUGGESTIONS FOR WRITING

1. Reich's essay reclassifies a subject (jobs) that has been classified in other ways. Find a traditional classification of something, such as college courses, departments, or schools; staff positions; sections in the college bookstore or local supermarket — classification is everywhere. Reclassify the items according to an alternative principle of classification. You will have to state and perhaps defend your classification, and of course define and illustrate your categories.
2. Reclassify the jobs in the help-wanted or employment section of your local newspaper into Reich's categories: symbolic-analytic, routine production, routine personal, and other (as in para. 26). Give reasons for your inclusion of each job opening in each of Reich's categories.
3. CRITICAL WRITING. What do you think of Reich's assessment of the disconnectedness and responsibilities of the symbolic analysts? Write an essay in which you agree or disagree with Reich, supporting your opinions with EVIDENCE from your own experience and reading as well as from Reich's essay.
4. CONNECTIONS. Both Reich's essay and Ralph Whitehead, Jr.'s "Class Acts" (p. 342) classify American society, and both authors warn of increasing polarization in society. Write an essay comparing and contrasting the two classifications. What is each author's THESIS? What categories does each identify? To what extent do the two classifications overlap? Which essay is more effective, and why?

ROBERT B. REICH ON WRITING

In the introduction to his book *Tales of a New America,* Robert Reich explains why he finds it necessary to "probe the public consciousness and examine the reigning public philosophy": This is the terrain, he insists, "in which public problems are defined and public ideals are forged."

In seeking to map this terrain, Reich makes certain demands on his audience. "I am relying on you, the reader, to be an active explorer as well. You will need to ask yourself: How do these illustrations resonate with my experience? Are these interpretations plausible and meaningful to me? Do they help me better understand my own values, or lead me to question them?" In short, "examining what the prevailing vision has been, and what it might be" is a job not just for political scientists and government officials but for critical thinkers and readers as well.

FOR DISCUSSION

1. Why does writing on "public philosophy" demand critical reading of the sort Reich describes?
2. What other kinds of reading require the critical approach Reich asks of his readers?

ADDITIONAL WRITING TOPICS

Classification

Write an essay by the method of classification, in which you sort one of the following subjects into categories of your own devising. Make clear your PURPOSE in classifying and the basis of your classification. Explain each class with definitions and examples (you may find it helpful to make up a name for each group). Check your classes to be sure they neither gap nor overlap.

1. Commuters, or people who use public transportation
2. Environmental problems
3. Environmental solutions
4. Vegetarians
5. Talk shows
6. The ills or benefits of city life
7. The recordings you own
8. Families
9. Stand-up comedians
10. Present-day styles of marriage
11. Vacations
12. College students today
13. Paperback novels
14. Waiters you'd never tip
15. Comic strips
16. Movie monsters
17. Sports announcers
18. Inconsiderate people
19. Radio stations
20. Mall millers (people who mill around malls)

8

CAUSE AND EFFECT
Asking Why

THE METHOD

Press the button of a doorbell and, inside the house or apartment, chimes sound. Why? Because the touch of your finger on the button closed an electrical circuit. But why did you ring the doorbell? Because you were sent by your dispatcher: You are a bill collector calling on a customer whose payments are three months overdue.

The touch of your finger on the button is the immediate cause of the chimes: the event that precipitates another. That you were ordered by your dispatcher to go ring the doorbell is a remote cause: an underlying, more basic reason for the event, not apparent to an observer. Probably, ringing the doorbell will lead to some results: The door will open, and you may be given a check — or a kick in the teeth.

To figure out reasons and results is to use the method of *cause and effect*. You try to answer the question Why did something happen? or the question What were the consequences? As part of answering either question, you use DIVISION OR ANALYSIS (Chap. 6) to separate the flow of events into causes or effects.

Seeking causes, you can ask, for example, Why did Yugoslavia break apart? For what reason or reasons do birds migrate? What has caused sales of Detroit-made cars to pick up (or decline) lately? Looking for effects, you can ask What have been the effects of the birth-control pill on the typical American family? What impact has the personal computer had on the nursing profession? You can look to a possible future and ask Of what use might a course in psychology be to me if I become an office manager? Suppose a new comet the size of Halley's were to strike Philadelphia — what would be the probable consequences? Essay exams in history and economics courses tend often to ask for either causes or effects: What were the principal causes of America's involvement in the war in Vietnam? What were the immediate effects on the world monetary system of Franklin D. Roosevelt's removing the United States from the gold standard?

Don't, by the way, confuse cause and effect with the method of process analysis (Chap. 5). Some process analysis essays, too, deal with happenings; but they focus more on repeatable events (rather than unique ones) and they explain *how* (rather than why) something happened. If you were explaining the process by which the doorbell rings, you might break the happening into stages — (1) the finger presses the button; (2) the circuit closes; (3) the current travels the wire; (4) the chimes make music — and you'd set forth the process in detail. But why did the finger press the button? What happened because the doorbell rang? To answer those questions, you need cause and effect.

Sometimes one event will appear to trigger another, and it in turn will trigger yet another, and another still, in an order we call a causal chain. A classic example of such a chain is set forth in a Mother Goose rhyme:

> For want of a nail the shoe was lost,
> For want of a shoe the horse was lost,
> For want of a horse the rider was lost,
> For want of a rider the battle was lost,
> For want of a battle the kingdom was lost —
> And all for the want of a nail.

In reality, causes are seldom so easy to find as that missing nail: They tend to be many and complicated. A battle may be lost for more than one reason. Perhaps the losing general had fewer soldiers, and had a blinding hangover the morning he mapped out his battle strategy. Perhaps winter set in, expected reinforcements failed to arrive, and a Joan of Arc inspired the winning army. The downfall of a kingdom is not to be explained as though it were the toppling of the last domino in a file. Still, one event precedes another in time, and in discerning causes you don't ignore chronological order; you pay attention to it.

In trying to account for some public event (a strike, say, or the outcome of an election), in trying to explain a whole trend in today's society (toward nonsmoking, or late marriage), you can expect to find a whole array of causes — interconnected, perhaps, like the strands of a spiderweb. You'll want to do an honest job of unraveling. This may take time. For a jury to acquit or convict an accused slayer, weeks of testimony from witnesses, detectives, and psychiatrists may be required, then days of deliberation. It took a great historian, Jakob Burckhardt, most of his lifetime to set forth a few reasons for the dawn of the Italian Renaissance. To be sure, juries must take great care when a life hangs in the balance; and Burckhardt, after all, was writing an immense book. To produce a college essay, you don't have forty years; but before you start to write, you will need to devote extra time and thought to seeing which facts are the causes, and which matter most.

To answer the questions Why? and What followed as a result? may sometimes be hard, but it can be satisfying — even illuminating. Indeed, to seek causes and effects is one way for the mind to discover order in a reality that otherwise might seem (as life came to seem to Macbeth) "a tale told by an idiot, full of sound and fury, signifying nothing."

THE PROCESS

In writing an essay that seeks causes or one that seeks effects, first make sure that your subject is manageable. Choose a subject you can get to the bottom of, given the time and information you have. For a 500-word essay due Thursday, the causes of teenage rebellion would be a more unwieldy topic than why a certain thirteen-year-old you know ran away from home. Excellent papers may be written on large subjects, and yet they may be written on smaller, more personal subjects as well. You can ask yourself, for instance, why you behaved in a certain way at a certain moment. You can examine the reasons for your current beliefs and attitudes. Such a paper might be rewarding: You might happen upon a truth you hadn't realized before. In fact, both you and your reader may profit from an essay that seeks causes along the lines of these: "Why I Espouse Nudism," or "Why I Quit College and Why I Returned." Such a paper, of course, takes thought. It isn't easy to research your own motivations. A thoughtful, personal paper that discerns *effects* might follow from a topic such as "Where Nudism Led Me" or "What Happened When I Quit College."

When seeking remote causes, look only as far back as necessary. Explaining why a small town has fallen on hard times, you might confine yourself to the immediate cause of the hardship: the closing of a factory. You might explain what caused the shutdown: a dispute between union and management. You might even go back to the cause of the dispute (announced firings) and the cause of the firings (loss of sales to a Japanese competitor). For a short essay, that might be far enough back in time to go; but if you were writing a whole book (*Pottsville in the 1990s: Its Glorious Past and Its Present Agony*), you might look to causes still more remote. You could trace the beginning of the decline of Pottsville back to the discovery, in Kyoto in 1845, of a better carrot grater. A manageable short paper showing effects might work in the other direction, moving from the factory closing to its impact on the town: unemployment, the closing of stores and the only movie house, people packing up and moving away.

When you can see a number of apparent causes, weigh them and assign each a relative importance. Which do you find matter most? Often, you will see that causes are more important or less so: major or minor. If Judd acquires a heavy drug habit and also takes up residence in a video arcade, and as a result finds himself penniless, it is probably safe to assume that the drug habit is the major cause of his going broke and his addiction to video games a minor one. If you were writing about his sad case, you'd probably emphasize the drug habit by giving it most of your space, perhaps touching on video games in a brief sentence.

You can plan out an essay by arranging events in chronological order (or in reverse order: from a recent event back to past events that cause it). If Judd drops out of college, the most immediate cause might be his inability to meet a tuition payment. But his lack of money might have a cause, too: his having earlier acquired a heavy drug habit. The cause of his addiction might be traced back further still: to a period of depression he suffered and — even earlier, more remote — to the death of a friend in a car accident. In writing about Judd, you might begin with the accident, and then step by step work out its consequences; or you could begin with Judd's withdrawal from school, and trace a causal chain back to the accident.

In so doing beware of the logical fallacy "after this, therefore because of this" (in Latin, *post hoc, ergo propter hoc*) — that is, don't expect Event A to cause Event B just because A happened before B.

This is the error of the superstitious man who decides that he lost his job because a black cat walked in front of him. Another error is to oversimplify causes by failing to recognize their full number and complexity — claiming, say, that violent crime is simply a result of "all those gangster shows on TV." Avoid such wrong turns in reasoning by patiently looking for evidence before you write, and by giving it careful thought. (For a fuller list of such LOGICAL FALLACIES, or errors in reasoning, see pp. 469–71.)

To understand the deep-down causes of a person's act takes thought. Before you write, you can ask yourself a few searching questions. These have been suggested by the work of the literary critic Kenneth Burke:

1. *What act am I trying to explain?*
2. *What is the character, personality, or mental state of whoever acted?*
3. *In what scene or location did the act take place, and in what circumstances?*
4. *What instruments or means did the person use?*
5. *For what purpose did the person act?*

Burke calls these elements a *pentad* (or set of five): the *act,* the *actor,* the *scene,* the *agency,* and the *purpose.* If you are trying to explain, for instance, why a person burned down a liquor shop, it will be revealing to ask about his character and mental state. Was the act committed by the shop's worried, debt-ridden owner? A mentally disturbed anti-alcohol crusader? A drunk who had been denied a purchase? The scene of the burning, too, might tell you something. Was the shop near a church, a mental hospital, or a fireworks factory? And what was the agency (or means of the act): a flaming torch or a flipped-away cigarette butt? To learn the purpose might be illuminating, whether it was to collect insurance on the shop, to get revenge, or to work what the actor believed to be the will of the Lord. You can further deepen your inquiry by seeing relationships between the terms of the pentad. Ask, for instance, what does the actor have to do with this scene? (Is he or she the preacher in the church across the street, who has been staring at the liquor shop resentfully for the past twenty years?)[1]

---

[1]If you are interested and care to explore the possibilities of Burke's pentad, you can pair up its five terms in ten different ways: act to actor, actor to scene, actor to agency, actor to purpose, act to scene, act to agency, act to purpose, scene to agency, scene to purpose, agency to purpose. This approach can go profoundly deep. We suggest you try writing ten questions (one for each pair) in the form, What does act have to do with actor? Ask them of some act you'd like to explain.

You can use Burke's pentad to help explain the acts of groups as well as those of individuals. Why, for instance, did the sophomore class revel degenerate into a brawl? Here are some possible answers:

1. *Act:* the brawl
2. *Actors:* the sophs were letting off steam after exams, and a mean, tense spirit prevailed
3. *Scene:* a keg-beer party outdoors in the quad at midnight on a sticky and hot May night
4. *Agencies:* fists and sticks
5. *Purpose:* the brawlers were seeking to punish whoever kicked over the keg

Don't worry if not all the questions apply, if not all the answers are immediately forthcoming. Bring the pentad to bear on the sad case of Judd, and probably only the question about his character and mental state would help you much. Even a single hint, though, can help you write. Burke's pentad isn't meant to be a grim rigmarole; it is a means of discovery, to generate a lot of possible material for you — insights, observations, hunches to pursue. It won't solve each and every human mystery, but sometimes it will helpfully deepen your thought.

In stating what you believe to be causes and effects, don't be afraid to voice a well-considered hunch. Your instructor doesn't expect you to write, in a short time, a definitive account of the causes of an event or a belief or a phenomenon — only to write a coherent and reasonable one. To discern all causes — including remote ones — and all effects is beyond the power of any one human mind. Still, admirable and well-informed writers on matters such as politics, economics, and world and national affairs are often canny guessers and brave drawers of inferences. At times, even the most cautious and responsible writer has to leap boldly over a void to strike firm ground on the far side. Consider your evidence. Think about it hard. Look well before leaping. Then take off.

CAUSE AND EFFECT IN A PARAGRAPH: TWO ILLUSTRATIONS

Using Cause and Effect to Write About Television

Why is it that, despite a growing interest in soccer among American athletes, and despite its ranking as the most popular sport in the world, commercial television ignores it? To see a televised

North American Soccer League game, you have to tune at odd hours to public TV. Part of the reason stems from the basic nature of commercial television, which exists not to inform and entertain but to sell. During most major sporting events on television — football, baseball, basketball, boxing — producers can take advantage of natural interruptions in the action to broadcast sales pitches; or, if the natural breaks occur too infrequently, the producers can contrive time-outs for the sole purpose of airing lucrative commercials. But soccer is played in two solid halves of forty-five minutes each; not even injury to a player is cause for a time-out. How, then, to insert the requisite number of commercial breaks without resorting to false fouls or other questionable tactics? After CBS aired a soccer match, on May 27, 1967, players reported, according to Stanley Frank, that before the game the referee had instructed them "to stay down every nine minutes." The resulting hue and cry rose all the way to the House Communications Subcommittee. From that day to this, no one has been able to figure out how to screen advertising jingles during a televised soccer game. The result is that commercial television has treated the North American Soccer League as if it didn't exist.

COMMENT. In this paragraph, the writer seeks a cause and the opening sentence poses the Why? question to be answered. The middle portion of the paragraph explains one cause — that soccer, unlike other sports, is difficult to adapt to commercial television. The famous case reported by Frank shows what happened when, for a change, a soccer game was telecast, but was artificially orchestrated so as to allow blank moments for commercials. The cause *and* its effect are stated together in the concluding two sentences. Note how the writer illustrates generalizations with examples. The only unillustrated one is the statement that network TV exists for the purpose of selling things, and this seems an apparent truth we all know already.

Using Cause and Effect
in an Academic Discipline

Many factors played a role in Johnson's fateful decision [to escalate the Vietnam War]. But the most obvious explanation is that the new president faced many pressures to expand the American involvement and only a very few to limit it. As the untested successor to a revered and martyred president, he felt obliged to prove his worthiness for the office by continuing the policies of his predecessor. Aid to South Vietnam had been one of the most prominent of those policies. Johnson also felt it necessary to retain in his administration many of the important figures of the Kennedy years. In doing so, he surrounded himself with a group of foreign policy advisers — Secretary of State Dean Rusk, Secretary of Defense Robert McNamara, National Security Adviser McGeorge Bundy — who strongly believed not only that the United States had an important obligation to resist communism in Vietnam, but that it possessed the ability and resources to make that resistance successful. As a result, Johnson seldom had access to information making clear how difficult the new commitment might become. A compliant Congress raised little protest to, and indeed at one point openly endorsed, Johnson's use of executive powers to lead the nation into war. And for several years at least, public opinion remained firmly behind him — in part because Barry Goldwater's bellicose remarks about the war during the 1964 campaign made Johnson seem by comparison to be a moderate on the issue. Above all, intervention in South Vietnam was fully consistent with nearly twenty years of American foreign policy. An anticommunist ally was appealing to the United States for assistance; all the assumptions of the containment doctrine seemed to require the nation to oblige. Johnson seemed unconcerned that the government of South Vietnam existed only because the United States had put it there, and that the regime had never succeeded in acquiring the loyalty of its people. Vietnam, he believed, provided a test of American willingness to fight communist aggression, a test he was determined not to fail.

COMMENT. The ability both to probe causes and to discern effects is fundamental to the study of history, and both are apparent in this paragraph from *American History: A Survey,* by Richard N. Current and others. The authors examine a number of reasons why President Lyndon B. Johnson escalated our country's involvement in Vietnam into "a full-scale American war" during the mid-1960s. The TOPIC SENTENCE, coming right after the transitional sentence that introduces the paragraph, makes clear that not one but many causes resulted in this decision on the part of the president. Succinctly, the authors list and explain the causes.

GORE VIDAL

GORE VIDAL was born in 1925 at the U.S. Military Academy at West Point, where his father was an instructor. At the age of nineteen, he wrote his first novel, *Williwaw* (1946), while serving as a warrant officer aboard an army supply ship. Among the later of his twenty-one novels are *Duluth* (1983), *Lincoln* (1984), *Empire* (1987), and *Hollywood* (1989). He has also written mysteries under the pen name Edgar Box. As a playwright, he is best known for *Visit to a Small Planet* (1957), which was made into a film. The grandson of Senator T. P. Gore, who represented Oklahoma for thirty years, Vidal twice ran unsuccessfully for Congress, but in 1992 he portrayed a senator in the movie *Bob Roberts*. A provocative and perceptive literary and social critic, Vidal is a frequent contributor to *The New York Review of Books* and other magazines, and he has published several collections of essays, most recently *United States Essays, 1951–1991* (1993). Vidal divides his time between Italy and America.

Drugs

Vidal, whom some critics have called America's finest living essayist, first published "Drugs" in 1970 on the *New York Times*'s op-ed page and then included the essay in *Homage to Daniel Shays: Collected Essays 1952–1972*. "Drugs" addresses a problem that has worsened since it was first published. Lately, an increasing number of social scientists, medical professionals, and politicians have urged that we consider just such a radical solution as Vidal proposes. (For an opposing view, see A. M. Rosenthal's "The Case for Slavery," page 376.)

It is possible to stop most drug addiction in the United States 1 within a very short time. Simply make all drugs available and sell them at cost. Label each drug with a precise description of what effect — good and bad — the drug will have on the taker. This will require heroic honesty. Don't say that marijuana is addictive or dangerous when it is neither, as millions of people know — unlike "speed," which kills most unpleasantly, or heroin, which is addictive and difficult to kick.

For the record, I have tried — once — almost every drug and 2 liked none, disproving the popular Fu Manchu theory that a single whiff of opium will enslave the mind. Nevertheless many drugs are bad for certain people to take and they should be told why in a sensible way.

Along with exhortation and warning, it might be good for our   3
citizens to recall (or learn for the first time) that the United States
was the creation of men who believed that each man has the right
to do what he wants with his own life as long as he does not interfere
with his neighbor's pursuit of happiness. (That his neighbor's idea of
happiness is persecuting others does confuse matters a bit.)

This is a startling notion to the current generation of Americans.   4
They reflect a system of public education which has made the Bill of
Rights, literally, unacceptable to a majority of high school graduates
(see the annual Purdue reports) who now form the "silent majority" —
a phrase which that underestimated wit Richard Nixon took from
Homer, who used it to describe the dead.

Now one can hear the warning rumble begin: If everyone is   5
allowed to take drugs everyone will and the GNP will decrease, the
Commies will stop us from making everyone free, and we shall end
up a race of zombies, passively murmuring "groovy" to one another.
Alarming thought. Yet it seems most unlikely that any reasonably
sane person will become a drug addict if he knows in advance what
addiction is going to be like.

Is everyone reasonably sane? No. Some people will always become   6
drug addicts just as some people will always become alcoholics, and
it is just too bad. Every man, however, has the power (and should
have the legal right) to kill himself if he chooses. But since most
men don't, they won't be mainliners either. Nevertheless, forbidding
people things they like or think they might enjoy only makes them
want those things all the more. This psychological insight is, for some
mysterious reason, perennially denied our governors.

It is a lucky thing for the American moralist that our country has   7
always existed in a kind of time-vacuum: We have no public memory
of anything that happened before last Tuesday. No one in Washington
today recalls what happened during the years alcohol was forbidden
to the people by a Congress that thought it had a divine mission to
stamp out Demon Rum — launching, in the process, the greatest
crime wave in the country's history, causing thousands of deaths from
bad alcohol, and creating a general (and persisting) contempt among
the citizenry for the laws of the United States.

The same thing is happening today. But the government has   8
learned nothing from past attempts at prohibition, not to mention
repression.

Last year when the supply of Mexican marijuana was slightly   9 curtailed by the Feds, the pushers got the kids hooked on heroin and deaths increased dramatically, particularly in New York. Whose fault? Evil men like the Mafiosi? Permissive Dr. Spock? Wild-eyed Dr. Leary? No.

The government of the United States was responsible for those 10 deaths. The bureaucratic machine has a vested interest in playing cops and robbers. Both the Bureau of Narcotics and the Mafia want strong laws against the sale and use of drugs because if drugs are sold at cost there would be no money in it for anyone.

If there was no money in it for the Mafia, there would be no 11 friendly playground pushers, and addicts would not commit crimes to pay for the next fix. Finally, if there was no money in it, the Bureau of Narcotics would wither away, something they are not about to do without a struggle.

Will anything sensible be done? Of course not. The American 12 people are as devoted to the idea of sin and its punishment as they are to making money — and fighting drugs is nearly as big a business as pushing them. Since the combination of sin and money is irresistible (particularly to the professional politician), the situation will only grow worse.

QUESTIONS ON MEANING

1. What do you take to be Vidal's main PURPOSE in writing this essay? How well does he accomplish it?
2. For what reasons, according to Vidal, is it unlikely that our drug laws will be eased? Can you suggest other possible reasons why the Bureau of Narcotics favors strict drug laws?
3. Vidal's essay was first published more than two decades ago. Do you find the views expressed in it still timely, or out of date?

QUESTIONS ON WRITING STRATEGY

1. How would you characterize Vidal's humor? Find some examples of it.
2. Where in the essay does Vidal appear to anticipate the response of his AUDIENCE? How can you tell?
3. What function do the essay's RHETORICAL QUESTIONS perform?
4. OTHER METHODS. Study Vidal's use of EXAMPLE in paragraphs 8–10. Does the example of the U.S. government's role in heroin deaths effectively support Vidal's point that restricting drug use does not work? Is Vidal guilty here of oversimplification (p. 367)?

QUESTIONS ON LANGUAGE

1. Know the definitions of the following terms: exhortation (para. 3); GNP (5); mainliners, perennially (6); curtailed (9).
2. How do you interpret Vidal's use of the phrase "underestimated wit" to describe Richard Nixon?

SUGGESTIONS FOR WRITING

1. Write several paragraphs in which you try to predict both the good and the ill effects you think might result from following Vidal's advice to "make all drugs available and sell them at cost."
2. Research the situation reported by Vidal in paragraphs 9 and 10. (Begin with the *New York Times Index* for the years 1969 and 1970.) Write an essay that clearly and objectively analyzes the causes of the situation.
3. CRITICAL WRITING. How readily do you accept Vidal's statement that "each man has a right to do what he wants with his own life" — including, presumably, to be a drug addict — "as long as he does not interfere with his neighbor's pursuit of happiness" (para. 3)? Do you accept Vidal's implicit ASSUMPTION that people with easy access to drugs are not necessarily threats to their neighbors? Back up your answers with EVIDENCE from your experience and reading.
4. CONNECTIONS. In an essay, compare Vidal's essay with A. M. Rosenthal's "The Case for Slavery" (p. 376). Focus especially on the main assertions of each — the advantages and disadvantages of drug legalization — and on the evidence each provides. Conclude with a statement, backed by reasons, about which essay you think is the more effective.

GORE VIDAL ON WRITING

"Do you find writing easy?" Gerald Clark asked Gore Vidal for the *Paris Review.* "Do you enjoy it?"

"Oh, yes, of course I enjoy it," Vidal shot back. "I wouldn't do it if I didn't. Whenever I get up in the morning, I write for about three hours. I write novels in longhand on yellow pads, exactly like the First Criminal Nixon. For some reason I write plays and essays on the typewriter. The first draft usually comes rather fast. One oddity: I never reread a text until I have finished the first draft. Otherwise it's too discouraging. Also, when you have the whole thing in front of you for the first time, you've forgotten most of it and see it fresh. Rewriting, however, is a slow, grinding business.

"When I first started writing, I used to plan everything in advance, not only chapter to chapter but page to page. Terribly constricting — like doing a film from someone else's meticulous treatment. About the time of *The Judgment of Paris* [a novel published in 1952] I started improvising. I began with a mood. A sentence. The first sentence is all-important. [My novel] *Washington, D.C.* began with a dream, a summer storm at night in a garden above the Potomac — that was Merrywood, where I grew up.

"The most interesting thing about writing is the way that it obliterates time. Three hours seem like three minutes. Then there is the business of surprise. I never know what is coming next. The phrase that sounds in the head changes when it appears on the page. Then I start probing it with a pen, finding new meanings. Sometimes I burst out laughing at what is happening as I twist and turn sentences. Strange business, all in all. One never gets to the end of it. That's why I go on, I suppose. To see what the next sentences I write will be."

FOR DISCUSSION

1. What is it that Vidal seems to enjoy most about writing?
2. What advantage does he find in not planning every page in advance?

A. M. ROSENTHAL

ABRAHAM MICHAEL ROSENTHAL, born in 1922 in Ontario, Canada, came to the United States as a child and attended City College in New York City (B.S., 1944). His long association with the *New York Times* began the year he graduated from college. Since then, he has served the newspaper as correspondent at the United Nations and in India, Poland, Switzerland, and Japan; as managing editor; as executive editor; and currently as a regular columnist. Rosenthal is the author of *38 Witnesses* (1964) and coauthor (with Arthur Gelb) of several other books, including those in the series "The Sophisticated Traveller." He has written articles for the *New York Times Magazine*, *Saturday Evening Post*, and *Foreign Affairs*. In 1960 his reporting of international news won him a Pulitzer Prize.

The Case for Slavery

Like Gore Vidal's "Drugs" (p. 371), this essay was first published on the op-ed page of the *New York Times*. But there the similarity ends. Rosenthal's piece appeared in 1989, almost two decades after Vidal's, and it forcefully opposes what Vidal proposes.

1 Across the country, a scattered but influential collection of intellectuals is intensely engaged in making the case for slavery.

2 With considerable passion, these Americans are repeatedly expounding the benefits of not only tolerating slavery but legalizing it:

3 It would make life less dangerous for the free. It would save a great deal of money. And since the economies could be used to improve the lot of the slaves, in the end they would be better off.

4 The new antiabolitionists, like their predecessors in the nineteenth century, concede that those now in bondage do not themselves see the benefits of legalizing their status.

5 But in time they will, we are assured, because the beautiful part of legalization is that slavery would be designed so as to keep slaves pacified with the very thing that enslaves them!

6 The form of slavery under discussion is drug addiction. It does not have every characteristic of more traditional forms of bondage. But they have enough in common to make the comparison morally valid — and the campaign for drug legalization morally disgusting.

7 Like the plantation slavery that was a foundation of American society for so long, drug addiction largely involves specifiable groups

of people. Most of the enchained are children and adolescents of all colors and black and Hispanic adults.

Like plantation slavery, drug addiction is passed on from gener-   8
ation to generation. And this may be the most important similarity: Like plantation slavery, addiction can destroy among its victims the social resources most valuable to free people for their own better-ment — family life, family traditions, family values.

In plantation-time America, mothers were taken from their chil-   9
dren. In drug-time America, mothers abandon their children. Do the children suffer less, or the mothers?

Antiabolitionists argue that legalization would make drugs so   10
cheap and available that the profit for crime would be removed. Well-supplied addicts would be peaceful addicts. We would not waste billions for jails and could spend some of the savings helping the addicted become drug-free.

That would happen at the very time that new millions of Amer-   11
icans were being enticed into addiction by legalization — somehow.

Are we really foolish enough to believe that tens of thousands of   12
drug gang members would meekly steal away, foiled by the marvels of the free market?

Not likely. The pushers would cut prices, making more money   13
than ever from the ever-growing mass market. They would immedi-ately increase the potency and variety beyond anything available at any government-approved narcotics counters.

Crime would increase. Crack produces paranoid violence. More   14
permissiveness equals more use equals more violence.

And what will legalization do to the brains of Americans drawn   15
into drug slavery by easy availability?

Earlier this year, an expert drug pediatrician told me that after   16
only a few months babies born with crack addiction seemed to re-cover. Now we learn that stultifying behavioral effects last at least through early childhood. Will they last forever?

How long will crack affect neurological patterns in the brains of   17
adult crack users? Dr. Gabriel G. Nahas of Columbia University argues in his new book, *Cocaine: The Great White Plague,* that the damage may be irreversible. Would it not be an act of simple intel-ligence to drop the legalization campaign until we find out?

Then why do a number of writers and academicians, left to right,   18
support it? I have discussed this with antidrug leaders like Jesse Jackson, Dr. Mitchell Rosenthal of Phoenix House, and William J. Bennett, who search for answers themselves.

Perhaps the answer is that the legalizers are not dealing with   19
reality in America. I think the reason has to do with class.

Crack is beginning to move into the white middle and upper 20
classes. That is a tragedy for those addicted.

However, it has not yet destroyed the communities around which 21
their lives revolve, not taken over every street and doorway. It has
not passed generation to generation among them, killing the con-
tinuity of family.

But in ghetto communities poverty and drugs come together in a 22
catalytic reaction that is reducing them to social rubble.

The antiabolitionists, virtually all white and well-to-do, do not 23
see or do not care. Either way they show symptoms of the callousness
of class. That can be a particularly dangerous social disorder.

QUESTIONS ON MEANING

1. On what grounds does Rosenthal claim that the ANALOGY between drug
   addiction and slavery is valid? How does he say the two are alike?
2. Rosenthal records two sets of possible results from the legalization of
   drugs: one from those who favor legalization, the other his own. Summarize the two sides.
3. Explain what Rosenthal means when he says that support of drug legalization "has to do with class" (para. 19).
4. What is Rosenthal's PURPOSE in writing this essay? Does he fulfill it?

QUESTIONS ON WRITING STRATEGY

1. Would you say Rosenthal is more interested in the causes and effects of
   drug addiction or in the causes and effects of the legalization argument?
   Why?
2. When does Rosenthal first introduce his topic? Why does he delay it so
   long?
3. Analyze the TONE of this essay. Why do you think Rosenthal takes this
   tone?
4. On what EVIDENCE does Rosenthal's argument principally depend? Is
   his evidence adequate?
5. OTHER METHODS. Rosenthal uses cause and effect to further an AR-
   GUMENT. Examine the APPEALS he relies on: are they mainly rational or
   emotional? Find examples of each.

QUESTIONS ON LANGUAGE

1. What does Rosenthal achieve by repeatedly calling drug legalization
   advocates "antiabolitionists"?

2. Typically for newspaper writers, Rosenthal uses very short paragraphs, some only a sentence. In a newspaper's narrow columns, this approach keeps paragraphs short. What is its EFFECT in the wider columns of a book? As an exercise, connect related paragraphs of Rosenthal's into larger paragraphs.
3. Consult your dictionary for the meanings of any unfamiliar words: expounding (para. 2); concede, predecessors (4); pacified (5); specifiable, enchained (7); enticed (11); foiled (12); paranoid (14); stultifying (16); irreversible (17); academicians (18); catalytic (22); callousness (23).

SUGGESTIONS FOR WRITING

1. In a brief essay, support or refute Rosenthal's assertion that "the callousness of class" causes legalization supporters to disregard the plight of the poor communities destroyed by drugs (paras. 18–23).
2. Choose a controversy that you know something about — it could be local (a college issue such as parking regulations, financial aid, or race relations), national (tax increases, bilingual education), or international (global warming, human rights violations). Take issue with one side in the controversy by analyzing the possible effects of that position.
3. CRITICAL WRITING. ANALYZE Rosenthal's ANALOGY between drug addiction and slavery and, by extension, between legalization and anti-abolition. In your analysis, go beyond Rosenthal to spell out all the similarities and differences you can see. Be specific. All told, how effective do you find the analogy?
4. CONNECTIONS. After reading Gore Vidal's "Drugs" (p. 371) and Rosenthal's "The Case for Slavery," write an essay in which you take sides for or against the legalization of drugs. You may argue from your own experience and observations, using Vidal or Rosenthal as a backup, or you could do some library research to test, extend, and support your opinions.

A. M. ROSENTHAL ON WRITING

In "Learning on the Job," a memoir of his forty years as a newspaper reporter and editor, A. M. Rosenthal has recalled a lesson he learned at the start of his career. "The very first day I was on the job as a reporter — a real reporter, with a press card in my pocket and a light in my heart — I learned all about the First Amendment. It was a Saturday and I was sitting in the *Times*'s newsroom when an assistant editor walked over, told me that there had been a murder or a suicide at the Mayflower Hotel in midtown, and why didn't I go over and see what it was all about. Yes, sir! I rushed out, jumped on a bus, got to the hotel, asked an elevator operator where the trouble was. Ninth floor, he told me, and up I went. A push of the buzzer and the door opened. Standing there was a police detective. He was twelve and a half feet tall. I started to walk in and he put his hand into my face. That hand was just a bit larger than a basketball.

"'Where are you going, kid?' he said.

"'I'm a reporter,' I said. '*Times.* I want to see the body.'

"He looked at me, up and down, slowly. 'Beat it,' he proposed.

"Beat it? I hadn't realized anybody talked to *Times* reporters that way. I knew there had to be some misunderstanding. So I smiled, pulled out my press card, and showed it to him. He took it, read it carefully front and back, handed it back, and said: 'Shove it in your ear.'

"Shove it in my ear? I could not comprehend what was taking place. 'But I'm from the *Times,*' I explained. 'A reporter from the *New York Times.* Don't you want me to get the story right?'

"'Listen, Four Eyes,' he said, 'I don't care if you drop dead.' Then he slammed the door in my face and there I stood, staring at that door. I slunk off to a pay phone in the lobby and called the special reporters' number that had been confided to me — LAckawanna 4-1090, I've never forgotten it — and confessed to the clerk on the city desk that I had not only been unable to crack the case but had never even seen the corpse.

"'Don't worry about it kid,' he said. 'We got it already from the A.P.[1] They called the police headquarters and got the story. Come on in.'

"Right there at the Mayflower I learned my first lesson about the First Amendment. The First Amendment means I have the right to ask anybody any question I wish. And anybody has the right to tell me to shove it in my ear. I have been involved in First Amendment cases for more than twenty years, but when I began as a reporter I was not answering any call to protect and defend the Constitution of the United States. I was not even thinking about the Constitution of the United States. All I was thinking about was the pleasure and joy of newspapering, of the wonderful zest of being able to run around, see things, find out what was going on, write about it. . . . That was what the newspaper business meant to me then and mostly still does — the delight of discovery, the exhilaration of writing a story

---

[1]Associated Press. — EDS.

and the quick gratification of seeing it in the paper; ink, ink, ink, even if it does rub off on your fingers just a tiny bit.

"We newspaper people are given to talking and writing about journalistic philosophy and I certainly have done my share. . . . But newspapering is not a philosophy, it is a way of spending a lifetime, and most of us in it know that if you really don't love it, love the whole mixture of searching, finding, and telling, love the strange daily rhythm where you have to climb higher and higher during the day instead of slackening off as the day goes on as normal people do, if you don't have a sensation of apprehension when you set out to find a story and a swagger when you sit down to write it, you are in the wrong business. You can make more money as a dentist and cops won't tell you to shove it in your ear."

FOR DISCUSSION

1. What is the First Amendment to the Constitution, and exactly what did Rosenthal learn about it?
2. What aspects of being a reporter have the greatest appeal for Rosenthal?
3. As Rosenthal recounts the joys of a reporter's life, he also reveals, directly or indirectly, some of the disadvantages. What are they?

LAWRENCE A. BEYER

LAWRENCE A. BEYER is a scholar, teacher, and musician. Born in New York City in 1958, he has spent almost twenty years in academia, investigating disciplines as varied as computer science, political science, law, linguistics, and philosophy. His writing reflects these broad interests, including scholarly articles and essays on education, ethics, and language. Beyer received a B.A. from Harvard College in 1979 and attended Clare College at Cambridge University as a Frank Knox Memorial Fellow during 1979–80. After receiving a J.D. from Yale Law School in 1984, he served as a law clerk in the U.S. Court of Appeals for the Ninth Circuit, taught law at Tulane Law School, and pursued postdoctoral fellowships in both law and linguistics at Yale University. Beyer is currently completing a Ph.D. in philosophy at Stanford University. Throughout his academic career, he has sung with numerous musical groups, most recently the Chamber Chorale and Early Music Singers at Stanford.

The Highlighter Crisis

This brief and emphatic piece takes aim at a seemingly innocuous target: the felt-tipped highlighter. First appearing in the Summer 1990 issue of the journal *Academic Questions*, the essay was reprinted with the above title in the May 1991 issue of *Harper's* magazine. See if you agree with Beyer's analysis of cause and effect.

The use of highlighters — those marking pens that allow readers 1 to emphasize passages in their books with transparent overlays of bright color — is significantly retarding the education of university students by distorting and cheapening the way many read. Compared to the important issues of academic policy facing education today — government funding, affirmative action, teacher shortages, the role of "the canon" in the humanities — the impact of the humble highlighter might seem trifling. But highlighters, though they appear to be peripheral to educational concerns, are changing the university experience for students in ways that have seriously detrimental consequences.

While some students still read without using any marking imple- 2 ments, and some continue to swear by pens or pencils, most have switched to highlighters. The most common use of highlighters is for simply marking, with a colorful coating over the words, the gist of a text that the student needs to read. While this might seem harmless, such highlighter use in fact encourages passive reading habits in young adults who very much need to learn to read actively, critically, and analytically.

At best, most students who use the highlighter in this fashion are uncritically — almost unthinkingly — ingesting some of the authors' phraseology and gaining sketchy outlines of the texts. At worst, their "reading" consists merely of a skimming sensitivity to those conventional textual indicators that point out which passages are part of the skeletal gists of the texts ("In sum," "The main issue is," etc.). In accenting these passages, students are performing a typographical function that could be accomplished, with the same absence of understanding, by computers. As if seasoning food that will never be eaten, they are coloring pages in vague — but never fulfilled — anticipation of a more serious future review of the now-edited text.

It might be objected, with some validity, that a pencil or pen can be misused in the exact same way. It is nevertheless proper to hold the highlighter responsible for the deterioration in reading skills. When a pencil or pen is used for a highlighting (i.e., underlining) purpose, it is ordinarily used also for writing notes in the margins, a process that greatly enhances the reader's engagement with the text. The highlighter is virtually useless for this purpose.

So, while the highlighter seems to be an inexpensive, helpful minor item in the everyday world of the university student, its size and price tag do not begin to approximate its educational costs. Students, already expert at the simplistic regurgitation of ideas, now have an instrument for applying a pretty coating of color that makes texts even easier to ingest without thoughtful chewing. Reading becomes a mindless swallowing of words that pass through such students without making any lasting impression.

The freedom of inquiry and experimentation that we grant to our university students should not be impeded, but that does not mean universities must adopt laissez-faire attitudes about the nonacademic, but still educationally important, aspects of university life. There are, in fact, participants in the educational process who swim against the laissez-faire tide regarding the university's nonacademic responsibilities toward students: for example, those espousing religious, and particularly Christian fundamentalist, views. There are campuses where kissing, dancing, and drinking are prohibited. Unfortunately, these regulations extend beyond the mere protection of the learning process to an enforcement of certain particular ideas, attitudes, and ways of living. Yet the religious institutions are on the right track in that they show concern for educational issues beyond the narrowly academic. The nature of the *entire* student experience — right down to the simple highlighter — must have an important place in the educational priorities of university administrators.

QUESTIONS ON MEANING

1. Why, in Beyer's opinion, are pencils or pens more helpful than highlighters?
2. What is this essay's PURPOSE? Does Beyer want all highlighter use to stop?
3. How should students read? Why?
4. State Beyer's THESIS. To what extent do you agree with it?

QUESTIONS ON WRITING STRATEGY

1. Describe Beyer's TONE. How does it affect your reaction to the essay?
2. Why does Beyer choose to focus on effects rather than causes?
3. Who do you think was Beyer's intended AUDIENCE? What clues do you have? How might the essay be different if it were aimed at the users of highlighters?
4. OTHER METHODS. Look closely at Beyer's discussion of how a highlighter is used (paras. 2–4). How does he use PROCESS ANALYSIS to show the problems with highlighters? Into what stages does he separate the process of highlighting?

QUESTIONS ON LANGUAGE

1. Consult your dictionary if you are unsure of the meanings of these words: peripheral, detrimental (para. 1); ingesting (3); regurgitation (5); laissez-faire, espousing (6).
2. What is the EFFECT of Beyer's METAPHORS of eating (paras. 3 and 5)?
3. Beyer writes formally — for instance, "It might be argued, with some validity, that a pencil or pen can be misused in the exact same way" (para. 4). Find other examples of formal sentences and words. Is this style appropriate to Beyer's subject and argument?

SUGGESTIONS FOR WRITING

1. Drawing on your own experience, write a brief essay in response to Beyer's argument. You may want to challenge his views on the effects

of highlighter use; or you may wish to examine the causes of highlighters' popularity. PROCESS ANALYSIS and EXAMPLES may help you to support your claims.

2. Choose another popular product or service and trace the effects of its use (some examples: the car radio, the Walkman, the personal computer, electronic bulletin boards, answering machines, fax machines). How has this item changed the ways people interact with each other? What are its positive effects? What are its negative effects? How might the negative effects be counteracted?

3. CRITICAL WRITING. Tease out the ASSUMPTIONS that lie behind Beyer's attack on highlighters — for instance, his views of college students, the goals of education, or how colleges and universities should be run. In an essay, present Beyer's views on education without mentioning highlighters.

4. CONNECTIONS. Compare this essay with Brenda Ueland's "Tell Me More" (p. 233). How is Beyer's careless reader like Ueland's careless listener? How are they different? Are the essays' PURPOSES similar?

JUNE JORDAN

Alice Walker has called JUNE JORDAN's writing the work of a "committed, passionate, revolutionary creative mind that will . . . help deliver us from the deceptions, if not the violence, of American life." Born in 1936 in Harlem, New York City, Jordan attended Barnard College and the University of Chicago. She has taught English at a number of universities and is now professor of Afro-American studies and women's studies at the University of California, Berkeley. Jordan's works of poetry include *Passion* (1980), *Living Room* (1985), and *Naming Our Destiny* (1989). One of her novels for young adults, *His Own Where* (1971), was nominated for the National Book Award. She also writes a political column for *The Progressive* and has published several books of essays, including *Civil Wars* (1981), *On Call* (1986), *Moving Towards Home* (1989), and, most recently, *Technical Difficulties* (1993).

Requiem for the Champ

Originally published in *The Progressive* in 1992, this essay reappeared in Jordan's collection *Technical Difficulties.* Characteristically, Jordan probes deeply into African American experience — this time the experience of Mike Tyson, formerly world heavyweight boxing champion and now a convicted rapist.

Mike Tyson comes from Brooklyn. And so do I. Where he grew up was about a twenty-minute bus ride from my house. I always thought his neighborhood looked like a war zone. It reminded me of Berlin — immediately after World War II. I had never seen Berlin except for black-and-white photos in *Life* magazine, but that was bad enough: Rubble. Barren. Blasted. Everywhere you turned your eyes recoiled from the jagged edges of an office building or a cathedral, shattered, or the tops of apartment houses torn off, and nothing alive even intimated, anywhere. I used to think, "This is what it means to fight and really win or really lose. War means you hurt somebody, or something, until there's nothing soft or sensible left."

For sure I never had a boyfriend who came out of Mike Tyson's territory. Yes, I enjoyed my share of tough guys and/or gang members who walked and talked and fought and loved in quintessential Brooklyn ways: cool, tough, and deadly serious. But there was a code as rigid and as romantic as anything that ever made the pages of traditional English literature. A guy would beat up another guy or, if appropriate, he'd kill him. But a guy talked different to a girl. A guy made other guys clean up their language around "his girl." A guy brought ribbons and candies and earrings and tulips to a girl. He took care of her. He walked her home. And if he got serious about that girl, and even if she was only twelve years old, then she became his "lady." And woe betide any other guy stupid enough to disrespect that particular young black female.

But none of the boys — none of the young men — none of the young Black male inhabitants of my universe and my heart ever came from Mike Tyson's streets or avenues. We didn't live someplace fancy or middle-class, but at least there were ten-cent gardens, front and back, and coin Laundromats, and grocery stores, and soda parlors, and barber shops, and Holy Roller churchfronts, and chicken shacks, and dry cleaners, and bars-and-grills, and a takeout Chinese restaurant, and all of that usable detail that does not survive a war. That kind of seasonal green turf and daily-life supporting pattern of establishments to meet your needs did not exist inside the gelid urban cemetery where Mike Tyson learned what he thought he needed to know.

I remember when the City of New York decided to construct a senior housing project there, in the childhood world of former heavyweight boxing champion Mike Tyson. I remember wondering, "Where in the hell will those old people have to go in order to find food? And how will they get there?"

I'm talking godforsaken. And much of living in Brooklyn was like that. But then it might rain or it might snow and, for example, I could look at the rain forcing forsythia into bloom or watch how snowflakes can tease bare tree limbs into temporary blossoms of snow dissolving into diadems of sunlight. And what did Mike Tyson ever see besides brick walls and garbage in the gutter and disintegrating concrete steps and boarded-up windows and broken car parts blocking the sidewalk and men, bitter, with their hands in their pockets, and women, bitter, with their heads down and their eyes almost closed?

In his neighborhood, where could you buy ribbons for a girl, or tulips?

Mike Tyson comes from Brooklyn. And so do I. In the big picture of America, I never had much going for me. And he had less. I only learned, last year, that I can stop whatever violence starts with me. I only learned, last year, that love is infinitely more interesting, and more exciting, and more powerful, than really winning or really losing a fight. I only learned, last year, that all war leads to death and that all love leads you away from death. I am more than twice Mike Tyson's age. And I'm not stupid. Or slow. But I'm Black. And I come from Brooklyn. And I grew up fighting. And I grew up and I got out of Brooklyn because I got pretty good at fighting. And winning. Or else, intimidating my would-be adversaries with my fists, my feet, and my mouth. And I never wanted to fight. I never wanted anybody to hit me. And I never wanted to hit anybody. But the bell would ring at the end of another dumb day in school and I'd head out with dread and a nervous sweat because I knew some jackass more or less my age and more or less my height would be waiting for me because she or he had nothing better to do than to wait for me and hope to kick my butt or tear up my books or break my pencils or pull hair out of my head.

This is the meaning of poverty: when you have nothing better to 8 do than to hate somebody who, just exactly like yourself, has nothing better to do than to pick on you instead of trying to figure out how come there's nothing better to do. How come there's no gym/no swimming pool/no dirt track/no soccer field/no ice-skating rink/no bike/no bike path/no tennis courts/no language arts workshop/no computer science center/no band practice/no choir rehearsal/no music lessons/no basketball or baseball team? How come neither one of you has his or her own room in a house where you can hang out and dance and make out or get on the telephone or eat and drink up everything in the kitchen that can move? How come nobody on your block and nobody in your class has any of these things?

I'm Black. Mike Tyson is Black. And neither one of us was ever 9 supposed to win anything more than a fight between the two of us. And if you check out the mass-media material on "us," and if you check out the emergency-room reports on "us," you might well believe we're losing the fight to be more than our enemies have decreed. Our enemies would deprive us of everything except each other: hungry and furious and drug-addicted and rejected and ever convinced we can never be beautiful or right or true or different from the beggarly monsters our enemies envision and insist upon, and how should we then stand, Black man and Black woman, face to face?

Way back when I was born, Richard Wright had just published 10 *Native Son* and, thereby, introduced white America to the monstrous product of its racist hatred.

Poverty does not beautify. Poverty does not teach generosity or 11 allow for sucker attributes of tenderness and restraint. In white America, hatred of Blackfolks has imposed horrible poverty upon us.

And so, back in the thirties, Richard Wright's Native Son, Bigger 12
Thomas, did what he thought he had to do: he hideously murdered
a white woman and he viciously murdered his Black girlfriend in
what he conceived as self-defense. He did not perceive any options
to these psychopathic, horrifying deeds. I do not believe he, Bigger
Thomas, had any other choices open to him. Not to him, he who
was meant to die like the rat he, Bigger Thomas, cornered and
smashed to death in his mother's beggarly clean space.

I never thought Bigger Thomas was okay. I never thought he 13
should skate back into my, or anyone's community. But I did and I
do think he is my brother. The choices available to us dehumanize.
And any single one of us, Black in this white country, we may be
defeated, we may become dehumanized, by the monstrous hatred
arrayed against us and our needy dreams.

And so I write this requiem for Mike Tyson: international celeb- 14
rity, millionaire, former heavyweight boxing champion of the world,
a big-time winner, a big-time loser, an African-American male in his
twenties, and, now, a convicted rapist.

Do I believe he is guilty of rape? 15

Yes I do. 16

And what would I propose as appropriate punishment? 17

Whatever will force him to fear the justice of exact retribution, 18
and whatever will force him, for the rest of his damned life, to regret
and to detest the fact that he defiled, he subjugated, and he wounded
somebody helpless to his power.

And do I therefore rejoice in the jury's finding? 19

I do not. 20

Well, would I like to see Mike Tyson a free man again? 21

He was never free! 22

And I do not excuse or condone or forget or minimize or forgive 23
the crime of his violation of the young Black woman he raped!

But did anybody ever tell Mike Tyson that you talk different to 24
a girl? Where would he learn that? Would he learn that from U.S.
Senator Ted Kennedy? Or from hotshot/scot-free movie director Roman Polanski? Or from rap recording star Ice Cube? Or from Ronald
Reagan and the Grenada escapade? Or from George Bush in Panama?
Or from George Bush and Colin Powell in the Persian Gulf? Or from
the military hero flyboys who returned from bombing the shit out of
civilian cities in Iraq and then said, laughing and proud, on international TV: "All I need, now, is a woman"? Or from the hundreds
of thousands of American football fans? Or from the millions of

Americans who would, if they could, pay surrealistic amounts of
money just to witness, up close, somebody like Mike Tyson beat the
brains out of somebody?

And what could which university teach Mike Tyson about the   25
difference between violence and love? Is there any citadel of higher
education in the country that does not pay its football coach at least
three times as much as the chancellor and six times as much as its
professors and ten times as much as its social and psychological
counselors?

In this America where Mike Tyson and I live together and bit-   26
terly, bitterly, apart, I say he became what he felt. He felt the stigma
of a priori hatred and intentional poverty. He was given the choice
of violence or violence: the violence of defeat or the violence of
victory. Who would pay him to rehabilitate inner-city housing or to
refurbish a bridge? Who would pay him what to study the facts of our
collective history? Who would pay him what to plant and nurture
the trees of a forest? And who will write and who will play the songs
that tell a guy like Mike Tyson how to talk to a girl?

What was America willing to love about Mike Tyson? Or any   27
Black man? Or any man's man?

Tyson's neighborhood and my own have become the same no-   28
win battleground. And he has fallen there. And I do not rejoice. I
do not.

QUESTIONS ON MEANING

1. Restate Jordan's THESIS in your own words.
2. How did the neighborhood Jordan grew up in differ from Tyson's? In
   what ways do the differences matter and not matter?
3. Why does Jordan discuss Richard Wright's novel Native Son (paras. 10–
   13)?
4. What is this essay's PURPOSE? Is Jordan attempting to excuse Tyson's
   crime?

QUESTIONS ON WRITING STRATEGY

1. Jordan wrote this essay for The Progressive, a journal of liberal opinion.
   Does Jordan seem to take her AUDIENCE's understanding and agreement
   for granted? Does she seem to be working to change her readers' minds?
2. Does this essay focus primarily on causes or on effects? Why?

3. Identify the causes Jordan sees as leading to Tyson's act of rape.
4. How would you describe the essay's TONE? Is it effective for Jordan's subject and purpose?
5. **OTHER METHODS.** How does Jordan use DESCRIPTION to make her neighborhood and Tyson's vivid to her readers?

QUESTIONS ON LANGUAGE

1. What does Jordan mean by the phrase "man's man" (para. 27)? What are the CONNOTATIONS of this phrase?
2. Do you know the meanings of the following words? Look up any that are unfamiliar: requiem (title); intimated (para. 1); quintessential (2); gelid (3); diadems (5); adversaries (7); defiled, subjugated (18); condone (23); a priori, refurbish (26).
3. How would you characterize Jordan's DICTION? What is its EFFECT?
4. Jordan portrays her neighborhood as richer than Tyson's in "that usable detail that does not survive a war" (para. 3). What does she mean by this METAPHOR? What is its impact?

SUGGESTIONS FOR WRITING

1. Select a recent event that has been widely covered by the media (television, radio, magazines, newspapers). Briefly summarize the event, then detail some of its causes. Try to be as specific as possible. Be sure to include both immediate and remote causes of the event.
2. Research Mike Tyson's trial in the library (consult the *New York Times Index* for 1991). On the basis of trial testimony and editorials, agree or disagree with Jordan's analysis of causes. Does she leave any causes unexamined? Does she give undue attention to some causes? Is she fair? Back up your claims with EVIDENCE from your research.
3. **CRITICAL WRITING.** What ASSUMPTIONS does Jordan seem to make about how white Americans view African Americans? What can you INFER about how she thinks these views should change? (See paras. 9, 13, and 26.) What assumptions does she make about how men view women? Does she seem to imply that these views should change? (See paras. 2, 12, and 26.) Do you accept or reject Jordan's assumptions? Why?
4. **CONNECTIONS.** Look at this essay in conjunction with Brent Staples's "Black Men and Public Space" (p. 159). How does Jordan see Tyson as a victim of the preconceptions Staples describes? How do the authors' views of race relations and male and female social roles compare?

JUNE JORDAN ON WRITING

June Jordan seeks to render African American experience accessible to a wide audience. In a *Publishers Weekly* interview with Stella Dong, she says, "I write for as many different people as I can, acknowledging that in any problem situation you have at least two viewpoints to be reached. I'm also interested in telling the truth as I know it, and in telling people, 'Here's something new that I've just found out about.' I want to share discoveries because other people might never know the thing, and also to get feedback. That's critical."

Perhaps the most striking quality of Jordan's writing is her voice. Writing about Jordan in the *Dictionary of Literary Biography* (1985), Peter B. Erickson observes parallels between her writing and speaking voices: "forthright, resolute, searing, at times explosive and frightening." Quoting from *Soulscript,* a collection of African American poetry edited and introduced by Jordan, Erickson shows how Jordan places this individual voice within a social context. The "struggle to determine and then preserve a particular, human voice," Jordan says, "is closely related to the historic struggling of black life in America."

According to Erickson, Jordan credits religion for her earliest inspiration. "Early on," she recalls, "the scriptural concept that 'in the beginning was the Word and the Word was with God and the Word was God' — the idea that the word could represent and then deliver into reality what the word symbolized — this possibility of language, of writing, seemed to me magical and basic and irresistible. I really do mean 'early on': My mother carried me to the Universal Truth Center on 125th Street, every Sunday, before we moved from Manhattan. I must have been two years old, or three, when the distinctive belief of that congregation began to make sense to me: that 'by declaring the truth, you create the truth.'"

FOR DISCUSSION

1. What attributes create a powerful writing voice? Give other examples of authors who express strength in both the way they write and the things they say.
2. Is it true, in your opinion, that "by declaring the truth, you create the truth"?

STEPHEN JAY GOULD

A paleontologist and collector of snails, STEPHEN JAY GOULD was born in New York City in 1941, went to Antioch College, and took a doctorate from Columbia University. Since the age of twenty-five, Gould has taught biology, geology, and the history of science at Harvard, where his courses are among the most popular. Although he has written for specialists (*Ontogeny and Phylogeny*, 1977), Gould is best known for essays that explore science in prose a layperson can enjoy. He writes a monthly column (called "This View of Life") for *Natural History* magazine, and these and other essays have been collected in *Ever Since Darwin* (1977), *The Panda's Thumb* (1980), *Hens' Teeth and Horses' Toes* (1983), *The Flamingo's Smile* (1985), *An Urchin in the Storm* (1987), *Bully for "Brontosaurus"* (1991), and *Eight Little Piggies* (1993). In 1981, Gould received $200,000 (popularly called a "genius grant") from the MacArthur Foundation, which subsidizes the work of original artists and thinkers.

Sex, Drugs, Disasters, and the Extinction of Dinosaurs

In this essay, Stephen Jay Gould tackles one of the greatest mysteries in the evolution of life on this planet: the extinction of dinosaurs. Working backward from this concrete effect (the fact that dinosaurs are extinct), Gould employs both scholarship and wit to analyze several possible causes. The essay originally appeared in *Discover* magazine in March 1984, and it is included in Gould's fourth collection of essays, *The Flamingo's Smile*.

Science, in its most fundamental definition, is a fruitful mode of 1 inquiry, not a list of enticing conclusions. The conclusions are the consequence, not the essence.

My greatest unhappiness with most popular presentations of sci- 2 ence concerns their failure to separate fascinating claims from the methods that scientists use to establish the facts of nature. Journalists, and the public, thrive on controversial and stunning statements. But science is, basically, a way of knowing — in P. B. Medawar's apt words, "the art of the soluble." If the growing corps of popular science writers would focus on *how* scientists develop and defend those fascinating claims, they would make their greatest possible contribution to public understanding.

393

Consider three ideas, proposed in perfect seriousness to explain   3
that greatest of all titillating puzzles — the extinction of dinosaurs.
Since these three notions invoke the primally fascinating themes of
our culture — sex, drugs, and violence — they surely reside in the
category of fascinating claims. I want to show why two of them rank
as silly speculation, while the other represents science at its grandest
and most useful.

Science works with testable proposals. If, after much compilation   4
and scrutiny of data, new information continues to affirm a hypothesis, we may accept it provisionally and gain confidence as further
evidence mounts. We can never be completely sure that a hypothesis
is right, though we may be able to show with confidence that it is
wrong. The best scientific hypotheses are also generous and expansive:
They suggest extensions and implications that enlighten related, and
even far distant, subjects. Simply consider how the idea of evolution
has influenced virtually every intellectual field.

Useless speculation, on the other hand, is restrictive. It generates   5
no testable hypothesis, and offers no way to obtain potentially refuting
evidence. Please note that I am not speaking of truth or falsity. The
speculation may well be true; still, if it provides, in principle, no
material for affirmation or rejection, we can make nothing of it. It
must simply stand forever as an intriguing idea. Useless speculation
turns in on itself and leads nowhere; good science, containing both
seeds for its potential refutation and implications for more and different testable knowledge, reaches out. But, enough preaching. Let's
move on to dinosaurs, and the three proposals for their extinction.

1. *Sex.* Testes function only in a narrow range of temperature
(those of mammals hang externally in a scrotal sac because internal
body temperatures are too high for their proper function). A worldwide rise in temperature at the close of the Cretaceous period caused
the testes of dinosaurs to stop functioning and led to their extinction
by sterilization of males.

2. *Drugs.* Angiosperms (flowering plants) first evolved toward the
end of the dinosaurs' reign. Many of these plants contain psychoactive agents, avoided by mammals today as a result of their bitter
taste. Dinosaurs had neither means to taste the bitterness nor livers
effective enough to detoxify the substances. They died of massive
overdoses.

3. *Disasters.* A large comet or asteroid struck the earth some 65
million years ago, lofting a cloud of dust into the sky and blocking
sunlight, thereby suppressing photosynthesis and so drastically low-

ering world temperatures that dinosaurs and hosts of other creatures became extinct.

Before analyzing these three tantalizing statements, we must establish a basic ground rule often violated in proposals for the dinosaurs' demise. *There is no separate problem of the extinction of dinosaurs.* Too often we divorce specific events from their wider contexts and systems of cause and effect. The fundamental fact of dinosaur extinction is its synchrony with the demise of so many other groups across a wide range of habitats, from terrestrial to marine.

The history of life has been punctuated by brief episodes of mass   6
extinction. A recent analysis by University of Chicago paleontologists Jack Sepkoski and Dave Raup, based on the best and most exhaustive tabulation of data ever assembled, shows clearly that five episodes of mass dying stand well above the "background" extinctions of normal times (when we consider all mass extinctions, large and small, they seem to fall in a regular 26-million-year cycle.) The Cretaceous debacle, occurring 65 million years ago and separating the Mesozoic and Cenozoic eras of our geological time scale, ranks prominently among the five. Nearly all the marine plankton (single-celled floating creatures) died with geological suddenness; among marine invertebrates, nearly 15 percent of all families perished, including many previously dominant groups, especially the ammonites (relatives of squids in coiled shells). On land, the dinosaurs disappeared after more than 100 million years of unchallenged domination.

In this context, speculations limited to dinosaurs alone ignore   7
the larger phenomenon. We need a coordinated explanation for a system of events that includes the extinction of dinosaurs as one component. Thus it makes little sense, though it may fuel our desire to view mammals as inevitable inheritors of the earth, to guess that dinosaurs died because small mammals ate their eggs (a perennial favorite among untestable speculations). It seems most unlikely that some disaster peculiar to dinosaurs befell these massive beasts — and that the debacle happened to strike just when one of history's five great dyings had enveloped the earth for completely different reasons.

The testicular theory, an old favorite from the 1940s, had its root   8
in an interesting and thoroughly respectable study of temperature tolerances in the American alligator, published in the staid *Bulletin of the American Museum of Natural History* in 1946 by three experts on living and fossil reptiles — E. H. Colbert, my own first teacher in paleontology; R. B. Cowles; and C. M. Bogert.

The first sentence of their summary reveals a purpose beyond   9
alligators: "This report describes an attempt to infer the reactions of
extinct reptiles, especially the dinosaurs, to high temperatures as
based upon reactions observed in the modern alligator." They studied,
by rectal thermometry, the body temperatures of alligators under
changing conditions of heating and cooling. (Well, let's face it, you
wouldn't want to try sticking a thermometer under a 'gator's tongue.)
The predictions under test go way back to an old theory first stated
by Galileo in the 1630s — the unequal scaling of surfaces and volumes. As an animal, or any object, grows (provided its shape doesn't
change), surface areas must increase more slowly than volumes —
since surfaces get larger as length squared, while volumes increase
much more rapidly, as length cubed. Therefore, small animals have
high ratios of surface to volume, while large animals cover themselves
with relatively little surface.

Among cold-blooded animals lacking any physiological mecha-   10
nism for keeping their temperatures constant, small creatures have a
hell of a time keeping warm — because they lose so much heat
through their relatively large surfaces. On the other hand, large
animals, with their relatively small surfaces, may lose heat so slowly
that, once warm, they may maintain effectively constant temperatures
against ordinary fluctuations of climate. (In fact, the resolution of
the "hot-blooded dinosaur" controversy that burned so brightly a few
years back may simply be that, while large dinosaurs possessed no
physiological mechanism for constant temperature, and were not
therefore warm-blooded in the technical sense, their large size and
relatively small surface area kept them warm.)

Colbert, Cowles, and Bogert compared the warming rates of small   11
and large alligators. As predicted, the small fellows heated up (and
cooled down) more quickly. When exposed to a warm sun, a tiny 50-
gram (1.76-ounce) alligator heated up one degree Celsius every minute and a half, while a large alligator, 260 times bigger at 13,000
grams (28.7 pounds), took seven and a half minutes to gain a degree.
Extrapolating up to an adult 10-ton dinosaur, they concluded that a
one-degree rise in body temperature would take eighty-six hours. If
large animals absorb heat so slowly (through their relatively small
surfaces), they will also be unable to shed any excess heat gained
when temperatures rise above a favorable level.

The authors then guessed that large dinosaurs lived at or near   12
their optimum temperatures; Cowles suggested that a rise in global
temperatures just before the Cretaceous extinction caused the dinosaurs to heat up beyond their optimal tolerance — and, being so
large, they couldn't shed the unwanted heat. (In a most unusual

statement within a scientific paper, Colbert and Bogert then explicitly disavowed this speculative extension of their empirical work on alligators.) Cowles conceded that this excess heat probably wasn't enough to kill or even to enervate the great beasts, but since testes often function only within a narrow range of temperature, he proposed that this global rise might have sterilized all the males, causing extinction by natural contraception.

The overdose theory has recently been supported by UCLA psychiatrist Ronald K. Siegel. Siegel has gathered, he claims, more than 2,000 records of animals who, when given access, administer various drugs to themselves — from a mere swig of alcohol to massive doses of the big H. Elephants will swill the equivalent of twenty beers at a time, but do not like alcohol in concentrations greater than 7 percent. In a silly bit of anthropocentric speculation, Siegel states that "elephants drink, perhaps, to forget . . . the anxiety produced by shrinking rangeland and the competition for food." 13

Since fertile imaginations can apply almost any hot idea to the extinction of dinosaurs, Siegel found a way. Flowering plants did not evolve until late in the dinosaurs' reign. These plants also produced an array of aromatic, amino-acid-based alkaloids — the major group of psychoactive agents. Most mammals are "smart" enough to avoid these potential poisons. The alkaloids simply don't taste good (they are bitter); in any case, we mammals have livers happily supplied with the capacity to detoxify them. But, Siegel speculates, perhaps dinosaurs could neither taste the bitterness nor detoxify the substances once ingested. He recently told members of the American Psychological Association: "I'm not suggesting that all dinosaurs OD'd on plant drugs, but it certainly was a factor." He also argued that death by overdose may help explain why so many dinosaur fossils are found in contorted positions. (Do not go gently into that good night.) 14

Extraterrestrial catastrophes have long pedigrees in the popular literature of extinction, but the subject exploded again in 1979, after a long lull, when the father-son, physicist-geologist team of Luis and Walter Alvarez proposed that an asteroid, some 10 km in diameter, struck the earth 65 million years ago (comets, rather than asteroids, have since gained favor. Good science is self-corrective). 15

The force of such a collision would be immense, greater by far than the megatonnage of all the world's nuclear weapons. In trying to reconstruct a scenario that would explain the simultaneous dying of dinosaurs on land and so many creatures in the sea, the Alvarezes proposed that a gigantic dust cloud, generated by particles blown aloft in the impact, would so darken the earth that photosynthesis would cease and temperatures drop precipitously. (Rage, rage against the 16 dying of the light.) The single-celled photosynthetic oceanic plankton, with life cycles measured in weeks, would perish outright, but land plants might survive through the dormancy of their seeds (land plants were not much affected by the Cretaceous extinction, and any adequate theory must account for the curious pattern of differential survival). Dinosaurs would die by starvation and freezing; small, warm-blooded mammals, with more modest requirements for food and better regulation of body temperature, would squeak through. "Let the bastards freeze in the dark," as bumper stickers of our chauvinistic neighbors in sunbelt states proclaimed several years ago during the Northeast's winter oil crisis.

All three theories, testicular malfunction, psychoactive overdos- 17 ing, and asteroidal zapping, grab our attention mightily. As pure phenomenology, they rank about equally high on any hit parade of primal fascination. Yet one represents expansive science, the others restrictive and untestable speculation. The proper criterion lies in evidence and methodology; we must probe behind the superficial fascination of particular claims.

How could we possibly decide whether the hypothesis of testicular 18 frying is right or wrong? We would have to know things that the fossil record cannot provide. What temperatures were optimal for dinosaurs? Could they avoid the absorption of excess heat by staying in the shade, or in caves? At what temperatures did their testicles cease to function? Were late Cretaceous climates ever warm enough to drive the internal temperatures of dinosaurs close to this ceiling? Testicles simply don't fossilize, and how could we infer their temperature tolerances even if they did? In short, Cowles's hypothesis is only an intriguing speculation leading nowhere. The most damning statement against it appeared right in the conclusion of Colbert, Cowles, and Bogert's paper, when they admitted: "It is difficult to advance any definite arguments against this hypothesis." My statement may seem paradoxical — isn't a hypothesis really good if you can't devise any arguments against it? Quite the contrary. It is simply untestable and unusable.

Siegel's overdosing has even less going for it. At least Cowles 19 extrapolated his conclusion from some good data on alligators. And he didn't completely violate the primary guideline of siting dinosaur extinction in the context of a general mass dying — for rise in temperature could be the root cause of a general catastrophe, zapping dinosaurs by testicular malfunction and different groups for other reasons. But Siegel's speculation cannot touch the extinction of ammonites or oceanic plankton (diatoms make their own food with good sweet sunlight; they don't OD on the chemicals of terrestrial plants). It is simply a gratuitous, attention-grabbing guess. It cannot be tested, for how can we know what dinosaurs tasted and what their livers could do? Livers don't fossilize any better than testicles.

The hypothesis doesn't even make any sense in its own context.   20 Angiosperms were in full flower ten million years before dinosaurs went the way of all flesh. Why did it take so long? As for the pains of a chemical death recorded in contortions of fossils, I regret to say (or rather I'm pleased to note for the dinosaurs' sake) that Siegel's knowledge of geology must be a bit deficient: Muscles contract after death and geological strata rise and fall with motions of the earth's crust after burial — more than enough reason to distort a fossil's pristine appearance.

The impact story, on the other hand, has a sound basis in evi-   21 dence. It can be tested, extended, refined, and, if wrong, disproved. The Alvarezes did not just construct an arresting guess for public consumption. They proposed their hypothesis after laborious geochemical studies with Frank Asaro and Helen Michael had revealed a massive increase of iridium in rocks deposited right at the time of extinction. Iridium, a rare metal of the platinum group, is virtually absent from indigenous rocks of the earth's crust; most of our iridium arrives on extraterrestrial objects that strike the earth.

The Alvarez hypothesis bore immediate fruit. Based originally on   22 evidence from two European localities, it led geochemists throughout the world to examine other sediments of the same age. They found abnormally high amounts of iridium everywhere — from continental rocks of the western United States to deep sea cores from the South Atlantic.

Cowles proposed his testicular hypothesis in the mid-1940s.   23 Where has it gone since then? Absolutely nowhere, because scientists can do nothing with it. The hypothesis must stand as a curious appendage to a solid study of alligators. Siegel's overdose scenario will also win a few press notices and fade into oblivion. The Alvarezes' asteroid falls into a different category altogether, and much of the popular commentary has missed this essential distinction by focusing on the impact and its attendant results, and forgetting what really matters to a scientist — the iridium. If you talk just about asteroids, dust, and darkness, you tell stories no better and no more entertaining than fried testicles or terminal trips. It is the iridium — the source of testable evidence — that counts and forges the crucial distinction between speculation and science.

The proof, to twist a phrase, lies in the doing. Cowles's hypothesis   24 has generated nothing in thirty-five years. Since its proposal in 1979, the Alvarez hypothesis has spawned hundreds of studies, a major conference, and attendant publications. Geologists are fired up. They are looking for iridium at all other extinction boundaries. Every week exposes a new wrinkle in the scientific press. Further evidence that the Cretaceous iridium represents extraterrestrial impact and not indigenous volcanism continues to accumulate. As I revise this essay in November 1984 (this paragraph will be out of date when [it] is published), new data include chemical "signatures" of other isotopes indicating unearthly provenance, glass spherules of a size and sort produced by impact and not by volcanic eruptions, and high-pressure varieties of silica formed (so far as we know) only under the tremendous shock of impact.

My point is simply this: Whatever the eventual outcome (I suspect 25 it will be positive), the Alvarez hypothesis is exciting, fruitful science because it generates tests, provides us with things to do, and expands outward. We are having fun, battling back and forth, moving toward a resolution, and extending the hypothesis beyond its original scope.

As just one example of the unexpected, distant cross-fertilization 26 that good science engenders, the Alvarez hypothesis made a major contribution to a theme that has riveted public attention in the past few months — so-called nuclear winter. In a speech delivered in April 1982, Luis Alvarez calculated the energy that a ten-kilometer asteroid would release on impact. He compared such an explosion with a full nuclear exchange and implied that all-out atomic war might unleash similar consequences.

This theme of impact leading to massive dust clouds and falling 27 temperatures formed an important input to the decision of Carl Sagan and a group of colleagues to model the climatic consequences of nuclear holocaust. Full nuclear exchange would probably generate the same kind of dust cloud and darkening that may have wiped out the dinosaurs. Temperatures would drop precipitously and agriculture might become impossible. Avoidance of nuclear war is fundamentally an ethical and political imperative, but we must know the factual consequences to make firm judgments. I am heartened by a final link across disciplines and deep concerns — another criterion, by the way, of science at its best: A recognition of the very phenomenon that made our evolution possible by exterminating the previously dominant dinosaurs and clearing a way for the evolution of large mammals, including us, might actually help to save us from joining those magnificent beasts in contorted poses among the strata of the earth.

QUESTIONS ON MEANING

1. According to Gould, what constitutes a scientific hypothesis? What constitutes useless speculation? Where in the essay do you find his definitions of these terms?
2. State, in your own words, the THESIS of this essay.
3. What does Gould perceive to be the major flaws in the testicular malfunction and drug overdose theories about the extinction of dinosaurs? Cite his specific reasons for discrediting each theory.
4. What is the connection between nuclear holocaust and the extinction of dinosaurs? (See the essay's last paragraph.)

QUESTIONS ON WRITING STRATEGY

1. How do you understand the phrases "hit parade of primal fascination" (para. 17) and "the hypothesis of testicular frying" (18)? Is the TONE here somber, silly, whimsical, ironic, or what?
2. Paragraphs 14 and 16 both contain references to Dylan Thomas's poem "Do Not Go Gentle into That Good Night." (The poem's title is used in para. 14; "Rage, rage against the dying of the light," one of the poem's refrains, appears in para. 16.) If you are not familiar with the poem, look it up. Is it necessary to know the poem to understand Gould's use of these lines? What is the EFFECT of these ALLUSIONS?
3. In explaining the Alvarezes' hypothesis about the dinosaurs, Gould outlines a causal chain. Draw a diagram to illustrate this chain.
4. **OTHER METHODS.** The methods of EXAMPLE, COMPARISON AND CONTRAST, PROCESS ANALYSIS, and DIVISION OR ANALYSIS are all at work in this essay. Identify instances of each, and discuss the function each performs in the essay.

QUESTIONS ON LANGUAGE

1. What do you take the sentence "There is no separate problem of the extinction of dinosaurs" (para. 5) to mean? Separate from what? According to Gould, then, what *is* the problem being discussed?
2. Be sure you can define the following words: enticing (para. 1); hypothesis (4); psychoactive, photosynthesis, synchrony (5); paleontology (8); extrapolating (11); empirical (12); gratuitous (19).

SUGGESTIONS FOR WRITING

1. Write a paragraph addressing either the causes or the effects of a situation or circumstance in which you are directly involved. Possible

situations might include working in the school cafeteria, taking a psychology class offered only on Wednesday evenings, or anything else that interests you. Make sure that you consider the remote causes or effects as well as the immediate.

2. As Gould himself predicts (para. 24), his summary of the research into the Alvarez hypothesis is now dated: more data have accumulated; the hypothesis has been challenged, tested, revised. Consult the *Readers' Guide to Periodical Literature* for the past five or six years to find articles on the extinction of the dinosaurs. Write an essay updating Gould's in which you summarize the significant EVIDENCE for and against the Alvarez hypothesis.

3. CRITICAL WRITING. Apply Gould's distinction between hypothesis and speculation (paras. 4–5) in an area you know well — for instance, Civil War battles, dance, basketball, waste recycling, carpentry, nursing. What, in your area, is the equivalent of the useful hypothesis? What is the equivalent of the useless speculation? Be as specific as possible so that a reader outside the field can understand you.

4. CONNECTIONS. Gould's is one of several essays in this book written by academic specialists for an AUDIENCE of nonspecialists; Marvin Harris's "How Our Skins Got Their Color" (p. 241) and Robert B. Reich's "Why the Rich Are Getting Richer and the Poor Poorer" (p. 350) are others. In an essay, compare Gould's essay with Harris's and Reich's in terms of complexity of material, use and explanation of technical vocabulary, and clarity of explanation. Overall, which essay do you find most effective in explaining a technical subject?

STEPHEN JAY GOULD ON WRITING

In his prologue to *The Flamingo's Smile*, Stephen Jay Gould positions himself in a long and respectable tradition of writers who communicate scientific ideas to a general audience. To popularize, he says, does not mean to trivialize, cheapen, or adulterate. "I follow one cardinal rule in writing these essays," he insists. "No compromises. I will make language accessible by defining or eliminating jargon; I will not simplify concepts. I can state all sorts of highfalutin, moral justifications for this approach (and I do believe in them), but the basic reason is simple and personal. I write these essays primarily to aid my own quest to learn and understand as much as possible about nature in the short time allotted."

In his own view, Gould is lucky: He is a writer carried along by a single, fascinating theme. "If my volumes work at all, they owe their reputation to coherence supplied by the common theme of evolutionary theory. I have a wonderful advantage among essayists because no other theme so beautifully encompasses both the particulars that fascinate and the generalities that instruct. . . . Each essay is both a single long argument and a welding together of particulars."

FOR DISCUSSION

1. What differences would occur naturally between the work of a scientist writing for other scientists and Gould, who writes about science for a general AUDIENCE?
2. How does the author defend himself against the possible charge that, as a popularizer of science, he trivializes his subject?

ADDITIONAL WRITING TOPICS
Cause and Effect

1. In a short essay, explain *either* the causes *or* the effects of a situation that concerns you. Narrow your topic enough to treat it in some detail, and provide more than a mere list of causes or effects. If seeking causes, you will have to decide carefully how far back to go in your search for remote causes. If stating effects, fill your essay with examples. Here are some topics to consider:

    Labor strikes in professional sports
    State laws mandating the use of seat belts in cars (or the wearing of helmets on motorcycles)
    Friction between two roommates, or two friends
    The pressure on students to get good grades
    Some quirk in your personality, or a friend's
    The increasing need for more than one breadwinner per family
    The temptation to do something dishonest to get ahead
    The popularity of a particular television program, comic strip, rock group, or pop singer
    The steady increase in college costs
    The scarcity of people in training for employment as skilled workers: plumbers, tool and die makers, electricians, masons, carpenters, to name a few
    A decision to enter the ministry or a religious order
    The fact that cigarette advertising is banned from television
    The absence of a peacetime draft
    The fact that more couples are choosing to have only one child, or none
    The growing popularity of private elementary and high schools
    The fact that most Americans can communicate in no language other than English
    Being "born again"
    The grim tone of recent novels for young people (such as Robert Cormier's *I Am the Cheese* and other juvenile fiction dealing with violence, madness, and terror)
    The fact that women increasingly are training for jobs formerly regarded as men's only
    The pressure on young people to conform to the standards of their peers
    The emphasis on competitive sports in high school and college
    Children's watching soft-core pornography on cable television

2. In *Blue Highways* (1982), an account of his rambles around America, William Least Heat Moon asserts why Americans, and not the British, settled the vast tract of northern land that lies between the Mississippi

and the Rockies. He traces what he believes to be the major cause in this paragraph:

> Were it not for a web-footed rodent and a haberdashery fad in eighteenth-century Europe, Minnesota might be a Canadian province today. The beaver, almost as much as the horse, helped shape the course of early American history. Some *Mayflower* colonists paid their passage with beaver pelts; and a good fur could bring an Indian three steel knives or a five-foot stack could bring a musket. But even more influential were the trappers and fur traders penetrating the great Northern wilderness between the Mississippi River and the Rocky Mountains, since it was their presence that helped hold the Near West against British expansion from the north; and it was their explorations that opened the heart of the nation to white settlement. These men, by making pelts the currency of the wilds, laid the base for a new economy that quickly overwhelmed the old. And all because European men of mode simply had to wear a beaver hat.

In a Least Heat Moon–like paragraph of your own, explain how a small cause produced a large effect. You might generate ideas by browsing in a history book — where you might find, for instance, that a cow belonging to Mrs. Patrick O'Leary is believed to have started the Great Chicago Fire of 1871 by kicking over a lighted lantern — or in a collection of *Ripley's Believe It or Not*. If some small event in your life has had large consequences, you might care to write instead from personal experience.

9

DEFINITION
Tracing a Boundary

THE METHOD

As a rule, when we hear the word *definition*, we immediately think of a dictionary. In that helpful storehouse — a writer's best friend — we find the literal and specific meaning (or meanings) of a word. The dictionary supplies this information concisely: in a sentence, in a phrase, or even in a synonym — a single word that means the same thing ("**narrative** [năr - e - tǐv] *n.* **1**: story . . .").

Stating such a definition is often a good way to begin an essay when basic terms may be in doubt. A short definition can clarify your subject to your reader, and perhaps help you to limit what you have to say. If, for instance, you are going to discuss a demolition derby, explaining such a spectacle to readers who may never have seen one, you might offer at the outset a short definition of *demolition derby*, your subject and your key term.

In constructing a short definition, the usual procedure is to state the general class to which the subject belongs and then add any particular features that distinguish it. You could say: "A demolition derby is a contest" — that is its general class — "in which drivers ram old cars into one another until only one car is left running."

Short definitions may be useful at *any* moment in an essay, whenever you introduce a technical term that readers may not know. When a term is really central to your essay and likely to be misunderstood, a stipulative definition may be helpful. This fuller explanation stipulates, or specifies, the particular way you are using a term. The paragraph on page 412, defining *TV addiction,* is a stipulative definition from a much longer essay on the causes and cures of the addiction.

In this chapter, we are mainly concerned with extended definition, a kind of expository writing that relies on a variety of other methods. Suppose you wanted to write an essay to make clear what *poetry* means. You would specify its elements — rhythm, images, and so on — by using DIVISION OR ANALYSIS. You'd probably provide EXAMPLES of each element. You might COMPARE AND CONTRAST poetry with prose. You might discuss the EFFECT of poetry on the reader. (Emily Dickinson, a poet herself, once stated the effect that reading a poem had on her: "I feel as if the top of my head were taken off.") In fact, extended definition, unlike other methods of writing discussed in this book, is perhaps less a method in itself than the application of a variety of methods to clarify a purpose. Like DESCRIPTION, extended definition tries to *show* a reader its subject. It does so by establishing boundaries, for its writer tries to differentiate a subject from anything that might be confused with it. When Tom Wolfe, in his essay in this chapter, seeks to define a certain trend he has noticed in newspapers, books, and television, he describes exactly what he sees happening, so that we, too, will understand what he calls "the pornography of violence." In an extended definition, a writer studies the nature of a subject, carefully sums up its chief characteristics, and strives to answer the question What is this? — or What makes this what it is, not something else?

An extended definition can *define* (from the Latin, "to set bounds to") a word, or it can define a thing (a laser beam), a concept (male chauvinism), or a general phenomenon (the popularity of the demolition derby). Unlike a sentence definition, or any you would find in a standard dictionary, an extended definition takes room: at least a paragraph, perhaps an entire volume. The subject may be as large as the concepts of "holocaust" and "pornography."

Outside an English course, how is this method of writing used? In a newspaper feature, a sports writer defines what makes a *great team* great. In a journal article, a physician defines the nature of a previously unknown syndrome or disease. In a written opinion, a judge defines not only a word but a concept, *obscenity.* In a book review, a critic defines a newly prevalent kind of poem. In a letter to a younger brother or sister contemplating college, a student might define a *gut course* and how to recognize one.

Unlike a definition in a dictionary that sets forth the literal meaning of a word in an unimpassioned manner, some definitions imply biases. In his extended definition of *pornoviolence*, Tom Wolfe is biased, even jaundiced, in his view of American media. In defining *patron* to the earl of Chesterfield, who had tried to befriend him after ignoring his petitions for aid during his years of grinding poverty, Samuel Johnson wrote scornfully: "Is not a Patron, my Lord, one who looks with unconcern on a man struggling for life in the water, and, when he has reached the ground, encumbers him with help?" IRONY, METAPHOR, and short definition have rarely been wielded with such crushing power. (*Encumbers,* by the way, is a wonderfully physical word in its context: It means "to burden with dead weight.") In having many methods of writing at their disposal, writers of extended definitions have ample freedom and wide latitude.

THE PROCESS

Writing an extended definition, you'll want to employ whatever method or methods of writing can best answer the question What is the nature of this subject? You will probably find yourself making use of much that you have learned earlier from this book. A short definition like the one for *demolition derby* on page 407 may be a good start for your essay, especially if you think your readers need a quick grounding in the subject or in your view of it. (But feel no duty to place a dictionaryish definition in the INTRODUCTION of every essay you write: The device is overused.) In explaining a demolition derby, if your readers already have at least a vague idea of the meaning of the term and need no short, formal definition of it, you might open your extended definition with the aid of NARRATION. You could relate the events at a typical demolition derby, starting with a description of the lineup of old beat-up vehicles:

> One hundred worthless cars — everything from a 1940 Cadillac to a Dodge Dart to a recently wrecked Thunderbird, their glass removed, their radiators leaking — assemble on a racetrack or an open field. Their drivers, wearing crash helmets, buckle themselves into their seats, some pulling at beer cans to soften the blows to come.

You might proceed by example, listing demolition derbies you have known ("The great destruction of 184 vehicles took place at the Orleans County Fair in Barton, Vermont, in the summer of '91 . . ."). If you have enough examples, you might wish to CLASSIFY them; or perhaps you might analyze a demolition derby, dividing it into its components of cars, drivers, judges, first-aid squad, and spectators, and discussing each. You could compare and contrast a demolition derby with that amusement park ride known as Bumper Cars or Dodge-'ems, in which small cars with rubber bumpers bash one another head-on, but (unlike cars in the derby) harmlessly. A PROCESS ANALYSIS of a demolition derby might help your readers understand the nature of the spectacle: how in round after round, cars are eliminated until one remains. You might ask: What causes the owners of old cars to want to smash them? Or perhaps: What causes people to watch the destruction? Or: What are the consequences? To answer such questions in an essay, you would apply the method of CAUSE AND EFFECT.

Say you're preparing to write an extended definition of anything living or in motion (a basketball superstar, for instance, or a desert, or a comet). To discover points about your subject worth noticing, you may find it useful to ask yourself a series of questions. These questions may be applied both to individual subjects, such as the superstar, and to collective subjects — institutions (like the American family, a typical savings bank, a university, the Church of Jesus Christ of Latter-Day Saints) and organizations (IBM, the Mafia, a heavy-metal band, a Little League baseball team). To illustrate how the questions might work, at least in one instance, let's say you plan to write a paper defining a male chauvinist.[1]

1. *Is this subject unique, or are there others of its kind? If it resembles others, in what ways? How is it different?* As you can see, these last two questions invite you to compare and contrast. Applied to the concept of male chauvinism, these questions might remind you that male chauvinists come in different varieties — middle-aged and college-aged, for instance — and you might care to compare and contrast the two kinds.

---

[1]The six questions that follow are freely adapted from those first stated by Richard E. Young, Alton L. Becker, and Kenneth L. Pike, who have applied insights from psychology and linguistics to the writing process. Their procedure for generating ideas and discovering information is called *tagmemics*. To investigate subjects in greater depth, their own six questions may be used in nine possible combinations, as they explain in detail in *Rhetoric: Discovery and Change* (New York: Harcourt, 1970).

2. *In what different forms does it occur, while keeping its own identity?* Specific examples might occur to you: your Uncle George, who won't hire any "damned females" in his auto repair shop; some college-aged male acquaintance who regards women as nothing but *Penthouse* centerfolds. Each form — Uncle George and the would-be stud — might rate a description.

3. *When and where do we find it? Under what circumstances and in what situations?* Well, where have you been lately? At any parties where male chauvinism reared its ugly head? In any classroom discussions? Consider other areas of your experience: Did you meet any such males while holding a part-time summer job?

4. *What is it at the present moment?* Perhaps you might make the point that a few years ago male chauvinists used to be blatant tyrants and harsh critics of women. Today, wary of being recognized, they appear as ordinary citizens who now and then slip in a little tyranny, or make a nasty remark. You might care to draw examples from life.

5. *What does it do? What are its functions and activities?* Male chauvinists try to keep women in what they imagine to be women's place. These questions might even invite you to reply with a process analysis. You might show how some male chauvinist you know goes about implementing his views: how a personnel director you met, who determines pay scales, systematically eliminates women from better-paying jobs; how the *Penthouse* reader plots a seduction.

6. *How is it put together? What parts make it up? What holds these parts together?* You could apply analysis to the various beliefs and assumptions that, all together, make up a male chauvinist's attitude. This question might work well in writing about some organization: the personnel director's company, for instance, with its unfair hiring policies.

Not all these questions will fit every subject under the sun, and some may lead nowhere, but you will usually find them well worth asking. They can make you aware of points to notice, remind you of facts you already know. They can also suggest interesting points you need to find out more about.

In defining something, you need not try to forge a definition so absolute that it will stand till the mountains turn to plains. Like a mapmaker, the writer of an extended definition draws approximate boundaries, takes in only some of what lies within them, and ignores what lies outside. The boundaries, of course, may be wide; and for this reason, the writing of an extended definition sometimes tempts a writer to sweep across a continent airily and to soar off into abstract

clouds. Like any other method of expository writing, though, definition will work only for the writer who remembers the world of the
senses and supports every generalization with concrete evidence.

There may be no finer illustration of the perils of definition than
the scene, in Charles Dickens's novel *Hard Times*, of the grim schoolroom of a teacher named Gradgrind, who insists on facts but who
completely ignores living realities. When a girl whose father is a horse
trainer is unable to define a horse, Gradgrind blames her for not
knowing what a horse is; and he praises the definition of a horse
supplied by a pet pupil: "Quadruped. Graminivorous. Forty teeth,
namely twenty-four grinders, four eye-teeth, and twelve incisive.
Sheds coat in the spring; in marshy countries, sheds hoofs, too. Hoofs
hard, but requiring to be shod with iron. Age known by marks in
mouth." To anyone who didn't already know what a horse is, this
enumeration of facts would prove of little help. In writing an extended
definition, never lose sight of the reality you are attempting to bound,
even if its frontiers are as inclusive as those of *psychological burnout*
or *human rights*. Give your reader examples, narrate an illustrative
story, bring in specific description — in whatever method you use,
keep coming down to earth. Without your eyes on the world, you
will define no reality. You might define *animal husbandry* till the cows
come home, and never make clear what it means.

DEFINITION IN A PARAGRAPH:
TWO ILLUSTRATIONS

Using Definition to Write About Television

But who is addicted to TV? According to Marie Winn, author
of *The Plug-in Drug: Television, Children, and the Family,* TV addicts
are similar to drug or alcohol addicts: They seek a more pleasurable
experience than they can get from normal life; they depend on the
source of this pleasure; and their lives are damaged by their dependency. TV addicts, says Winn, use TV to screen out the real world
of feelings, worries, demands. They watch compulsively — four,
five, even six hours on a work day. And they reject (usually passively, sometimes actively) interaction with family or friends, diverting or productive work at hobbies or chores, and chances for
change and growth.

COMMENT. This paragraph provides a stipulative definition: Before proceeding with an essay on the causes and cures of TV addition,
the writer pauses to define the malady (drawing on another writer's

ideas). The main method employed here is comparison: TV addicts are like drug and alcohol addicts in specific respects. Following this comparison is a list of the TV addict's characteristics: oblivion, compulsion, rejection. Most of us, alas, know one or two victims.

Using Definition in an Academic Discipline

When the character traits found in any two species owe their resemblance to a common ancestry, taxonomists say the states are *homologous*, or are *homologues* of each other. *Homology* is defined as correspondence between two structures due to inheritance from a common ancestor. Homologous structures can be identical in appearance and can even be based on identical genes. However, such structures can diverge until they become very different in both appearance and function. Nevertheless, homologous structures usually retain certain basic features that betray a common ancestry. Consider the forelimbs of vertebrates. It is easy to make a detailed, bone-by-bone, muscle-by-muscle comparison of the forearm of a person and a monkey and to conclude that the forearms, as well as the various parts of the forearm, are homologous. The forelimb of a dog, however, shows marked differences from those of primates in both structure and function. The forelimb is used for locomotion by dogs but for grasping and manipulation by people and monkeys. Even so, all of the bones can still be matched. The wing of a bird and the flipper of a seal are even more different from each other or from the human forearm, yet they too are constructed around bones that can be matched on a nearly perfect one-to-one basis.

COMMENT. Taken from *Life: The Science of Biology*, by William K. Purves and Gordon H. Orians, this paragraph sets out to define *homology* and also to show how the two related forms of the word, *homologous* and *homologues*, are used. Students need to know the meanings of all three to study biology. The authors begin with a brief definition, then emphasize that not all homologues closely resemble one another on the surface. To show the differences that species can display, as well as what they must have in common to be homologues, Purves and Orians amplify their definition with examples. The forearms of humans closely resemble those of monkeys, and the two are indeed homologous. The forelimbs of dogs, the wings of birds, and the flippers of seals, however, are homologous with the forearms of people even though they appear in many ways different. The examples are valuable here because they help to define the concepts.

TOM WOLFE

Tom Wolfe, author, journalist, and cartoonist, was born in 1931 in Richmond, Virginia, and went to Washington and Lee University. After taking a Ph.D. in American Studies at Yale, he decided against an academic career and instead worked as a reporter for the *Springfield Union* and the *Washington Post*. Early in the 1960s, Wolfe began writing his electrifying, satiric articles on the American scene (with special, mocking attention to subcultures and trendsetters), which have enlivened *New York, Esquire, Rolling Stone, Harper's,* and other magazines. Among his books are *The Electric Kool-Aid Acid Test* (1965), a memoir of LSD-spaced-out hippies; *The Pump House Gang* (1968), a study of California surfers; *The Right Stuff* (1979), a chronicle of America's first astronauts, which was made into a movie; and *From Bauhaus to Our House* (1981), a complaint against modern architecture. Though the movie made from it bombed, Wolfe's first novel, *The Bonfire of the Vanities* (1987), was both controversial and hugely popular.

Pornoviolence

This essay, from a collection raking over the 1970s, *Mauve Gloves & Madmen, Clutter & Vine* (1976), is vintage Tom Wolfe. He played a large part in the invention of "the new journalism" (a brand of reporting that tells the truth excitedly, as if it were fiction), and his essay is marked by certain breathless features of style: long sentences full of parenthetical asides, ellipses (. . .), generous use of italics. Wolfe here coins a term to fit the blend of pornography and pandering to bloodlust that he finds in the media. Although not recent, his remarks have dated little since they first appeared. Compare his ideas about pornography with Gloria Steinem's in the next essay, "Erotica and Pornography" (p. 424).

"*Keeps His Mom-in-law in Chains,* meet *Kills Son and Feeds Corpse* 1
to Pigs."
"Pleased to meet you." 2
"*Teenager Twists Off Corpse's Head . . . to Get Gold Teeth,* meet 3
Strangles Girl Friend, Then Chops Her to Pieces."
"How you doing?" 4
"*Nurse's Aide Sees Fingers Chopped Off in Meat Grinder,* meet *I* 5
Left My Babies in the Deep Freeze."
"It's a pleasure." 6

It's a pleasure! No doubt about that! In all these years of jour- 7
nalism I have covered more conventions than I care to remember.
Podiatrists, theosophists, Professional Budget Finance dentists, oyster
farmers, mathematicians, truckers, dry cleaners, stamp collectors,
Esperantists, nudists, and newspaper editors — I have seen them all,
together, in vast assemblies, sloughing through the wall-to-wall of a
thousand hotel lobbies (the nudists excepted) in their shimmering
gray-metal suits and pajama-stripe shirts with white Plasti-Coat name
cards on their chests, and I have sat through their speeches and
seminars (the nudists included) and attentively endured ear baths
such as you wouldn't believe. And yet none has ever been quite like
the convention of the stringers for the *National Enquirer.*

The *Enquirer* is a weekly newspaper that is probably known by 8
sight to millions more than know it by name. No one who ever came
face-to-face with the *Enquirer* on a newsstand in its wildest days is
likely to have forgotten the sight: a tabloid with great inky shocks of
type all over the front page saying something on the order of *Gouges
Out Wife's Eyes to Make Her Ugly, Dad Hurls Hot Grease in Daughter's
Face, Wife Commits Suicide After 2 Years of Poisoning Fails to Kill
Husband . . .*

The stories themselves were supplied largely by stringers, i.e., 9
correspondents, from all over the country, the world, for that matter,
mostly copy editors and reporters on local newspapers. Every so often
they would come upon a story, usually via the police beat, that was
so grotesque the local sheet would discard it or run it in a highly
glossed form rather than offend or perplex its readers. The stringers
would preserve them for the *Enquirer,* which always rewarded them
well and respectfully.

One year the *Enquirer* convened and feted them at a hotel in 10
Manhattan. This convention was a success in every way. The only
awkward moment was at the outset when the stringers all pulled in.
None of them knew each other. Their hosts got around the problem
by introducing them by the stories they had supplied. The introductions went like this:

"Harry, I want you to meet Frank here. Frank did that story, you 11
remember that story, *Midget Murderer Throws Girl Off Cliff After She
Refuses to Dance with Him.*"

"Pleased to meet you. That was some story." 12

"And Harry did the one about *I Spent Three Days Trapped at* 13
*Bottom of Forty-Foot-Deep Mine Shaft and Was Saved by a Swarm of
Flies.*"

"Likewise, I'm sure." 14

And *Midget Murderer Throws Girl Off Cliff* shakes hands with *I* 15
Spent Three Days Trapped at Bottom of Forty-Foot-Deep Mine Shaft,
and *Buries Her Baby Alive* shakes hands with *Boy, Twelve, Strangles
Two-Year-Old Girl,* and *Kills Son and Feeds Corpse to Pigs* shakes hands
with *He Strangles Old Woman and Smears Corpse with Syrup, Ketchup,
and Oatmeal . . .* and . . .

. . . There was a great deal of esprit about the whole thing. These 16
men were, in fact, the avant-garde of a new genre that since then
has become institutionalized throughout the nation without anyone
knowing its proper name. I speak of the new pornography, the pornography of violence.

Pornography comes from the Greek word *porne,* meaning "harlot," 17
and pornography is literally the depiction of the acts of harlots. In
the new pornography, the theme is not sex. The new pornography
depicts practitioners acting out another, murkier drive: people staving
teeth in, ripping guts open, blowing brains out, and getting even
with all those bastards . . .

The success of the *Enquirer* prompted many imitators to enter the 18
field, *Midnight,* the *Star Chronicle,* the *National Insider, Inside News,*
the *National Close-up,* the *National Tattler,* the *National Examiner.* A
truly competitive free press evolved, and soon a reader could go to
the newspaper of his choice for *Kill the Retarded! (Won't You Join My
Movement?)* and *Unfaithful Wife? Burn Her Bed!, Harem Master's
Mistress Chops Him with Machete, Babe Bites Off Boy's Tongue,* and
Cuts Buddy's Face to Pieces for Stealing His Business and Fiancée.

And yet the last time I surveyed the Violence press, I noticed a 19
curious thing. These pioneering journals seem to have pulled back.
They seem to be regressing to what is by now the Redi-Mix staple of
literate Americans, mere sex. *Ecstasy and Me (by Hedy Lamarr),*[1] says
the *National Enquirer. I Run a Sex Art Gallery,* says the *National Insider.*
What has happened, I think, is something that has happened to
avant-gardes in many fields, from William Morris and the Craftsmen
to the Bauhaus group.[2] Namely, their discoveries have been

---

[1]*Ecstasy,* an early, European-made Hedy Lamarr film, was notorious for its scenes
of soft-core lovemaking. Later, paired with Charles ("Come with me to the Casbah")
Boyer, Lamarr rose to Hollywood stardom in *Algiers* (1938). — EDS.

[2]Morris (1834–96), an English artist, poet, printer, and socialist, founded a
company of craftspeople to bring tasteful design to furniture (the Morris chair) and
other implements of everyday life. The Bauhaus, an influential art school in Germany
(1919–33), taught crafts and brought new ideas of design to architecture and to
goods produced in factories. — EDS.

preempted by the Establishment and so thoroughly dissolved into the mainstream they no longer look original.

Robert Harrison, the former publisher of *Confidential*, and later 20 publisher of the aforementioned *Inside News*, was perhaps the first person to see it coming. I was interviewing Harrison early in January 1964 for a story in *Esquire* about six weeks after the assassination of President Kennedy, and we were in a cab in the West Fifties in Manhattan, at a stoplight, by a newsstand, and Harrison suddenly pointed at the newsstand and said, "Look at that. They're doing the same thing the *Enquirer* does."

There on the stand was a row of slick-paper, magazine-size pub- 21 lications, known in the trade as one-shots, with titles like *Four Days That Shook the World*, *Death of a President*, *An American Tragedy*, or just *John Fitzgerald Kennedy (1921–1963)*. "You want to know why people buy those things?" said Harrison. "People buy those things to see a man get his head blown off."

And, of course, he was right. Only now the publishers were in 22 many cases the pillars of the American press. Invariably, these "special coverages" of the assassination bore introductions piously commemorating the fallen President, exhorting the American people to strength and unity in a time of crisis, urging greater vigilance and safeguards for the new President, and even raising the nice metaphysical question of collective guilt in "an age of violence."

In the years since then, of course, there has been an incessant 23 replay, with every recoverable clinical detail, of those less than five seconds in which a man got his head blown off. And throughout this deluge of words, pictures, and film frames, I have been intrigued with one thing: The point of view, the vantage point, is almost never that of the victim, riding in the Presidential Lincoln Continental. What you get is . . . the view from Oswald's rifle. You can step right up here and look point-blank right through the very hairline cross in Lee Harvey Oswald's Optics Ordinance in weaponry four-power Japanese telescope sight and watch, frame by frame by frame by frame, as that man there's head comes apart. Just a little History there before your very eyes.

The television networks have schooled us in the view from Os- 24 wald's rifle and made it seem a normal pastime. The TV viewpoint is nearly always that of the man who is going to strike. The last time I watched *Gunsmoke*, which was not known as a very violent Western in TV terms, the action went like this: The Wellington agents and the stagecoach driver pull guns on the badlands gang leader's daughter and Kitty, the heart-of-gold saloonkeeper, and kidnap them. Then the badlands gang shoots two Wellington agents. Then they tie up five more and talk about shooting them. Then they desist because they might not be able to get a hotel room in the next town if the word got around. Then one badlands gang gunslinger attempts to rape Kitty while the gang leader's younger daughter looks on. Then Kitty resists, so he slugs her one in the jaw. Then the gang leader slugs him. Then the gang leader slugs Kitty. Then Kitty throws hot stew in a gang member's face and hits him over the back of the head with a revolver. Then he knocks her down with a rock. Then the gang sticks up a bank. Here comes the marshal, Matt Dillon. He shoots a gang member and breaks it up. Then the gang leader shoots the guy who was guarding his daughter and the woman. Then the marshal shoots the gang leader. The final exploding bullet signals The End.

25   It is not the accumulated slayings and bone crushings that make this pornoviolence, however. What makes it pornoviolence is that in almost every case the camera angle, therefore the viewer, is with the gun, the fist, the rock. The pornography of violence has no point of view in the old sense that novels do. You do not live the action through the hero's eyes. You live with the aggressor, whoever he may be. One moment you are the hero. The next you are the villain. No matter whose side you may be on consciously, you are in fact with the muscle, and it is you who disintegrate all comers, villains, lawmen, women, anybody. On the rare occasions in which the gun is emptied into the camera — i.e., into your face — the effect is so startling that the pornography of violence all but loses its fantasy charm. There are not nearly so many masochists as sadists among those little devils whispering into one's ears.

26   In fact, sex — "sadomasochism" — is only a part of the pornography of violence. Violence is much more wrapped up, simply, with status. Violence is the simple, ultimate solution for problems of status competition, just as gambling is the simple, ultimate solution for economic competition. The old pornography was the fantasy of easy sexual delights in a world where sex was kept unavailable. The new pornography is the fantasy of easy triumph in a world where status competition has become so complicated and frustrating.

27   Already the old pornography is losing its kick because of overexposure. In the late thirties, Nathanael West published his last and best-regarded novel, *The Day of the Locust*, and it was a terrible flop commercially, and his publisher said if he ever published another book about Hollywood it would "have to be *My Thirty-nine Ways of Making Love by Hedy Lamarr*." He thought he was saying something

that was funny because it was beyond the realm of possibility. Less than thirty years later, however, Hedy Lamarr's *Ecstasy and Me* was published. Whether she mentions thirty-nine ways, I'm not sure, but she gets off to a flying start: "The men in my life have ranged from a classic case history of impotence, to a whip-brandishing sadist who enjoyed sex only after he tied my arms behind me with the sash of his robe. There was another man who took his pleasure with a girl in my own bed, while he thought I was asleep in it."

Yet she was too late. The book very nearly sank without a trace. 28 The sin itself is wearing out. Pornography cannot exist without certified taboo to violate. And today Lust, like the rest of the Seven Deadly Sins — Pride, Sloth, Envy, Greed, Anger, and Gluttony — is becoming a rather minor vice. The Seven Deadly Sins, after all, are only sins against the self. Theologically, the idea of Lust — well, the idea is that if you seduce some poor girl from Akron, it is not a sin because you are ruining her, but because you are wasting your time and your energies and damaging your own spirit. This goes back to the old work ethic, when the idea was to keep every able-bodied man's shoulder to the wheel. In an age of riches for all, the ethic becomes more nearly: Let him do anything he pleases, as long as he doesn't get in my way. And if he does get in my way, or even if he doesn't . . . well . . . we have *new* fantasies for that. *Put hair on the walls.*

"Hair on the walls" is the invisible subtitle of Truman Capote's 29 book *In Cold Blood.* The book is neither a who-done-it nor a will-they-be-caught, since the answers to both questions are known from the outset. It does ask why-did-they-do-it, but the answer is soon as clear as it is going to be. Instead, the book's suspense is based largely on a totally new idea in detective stories: the promise of gory details, and the withholding of them until the end. Early in the game one of the two murderers, Dick, starts promising to put "plenty of hair on them-those walls" with a shotgun. So read on, gentle readers, and on and on; you are led up to the moment before the crime on page 60 — yet the specifics, what happened, the gory details, are kept out of sight, in grisly dangle, until page 244.

But Dick and Perry, Capote's killers, are only a couple of Low 30 Rent bums. With James Bond the new pornography reached a dead center, the bureaucratic middle class. The appeal of Bond has been explained as the appeal of the lone man who can solve enormously complicated, even world problems through his own bravery and initiative. But Bond is not a lone man at all, of course. He is not the Lone Ranger. He is much easier to identify than that. He is a salaried functionary in a bureaucracy. He is a sport, but a believable one; not a millionaire, but a bureaucrat on an expense account. He is not even a high-level bureaucrat. He is an operative. This point is carefully and repeatedly made by having his superiors dress him down for violations of standard operating procedure. Bond, like the Lone Ranger, solves problems with guns and fists. When it is over, however, the Lone Ranger leaves a silver bullet. Bond, like the rest of us, fills out a report in triplicate.

Marshall McLuhan[3] says we are in a period in which it will   31
become harder and harder to stimulate lust through words and pictures — i.e., the old pornography. In the latest round of pornographic movies the producers have found it necessary to introduce violence, bondage, torture, and aggressive physical destruction to an extraordinary degree. The same sort of bloody escalation may very well happen in the pure pornography of violence. Even such able craftsmen as Truman Capote, Ian Fleming, NBC, and CBS may not suffice. Fortunately, there are historical models to rescue us from this frustration. In the latter days of the Roman Empire, the Emperor Commodus became jealous of the celebrity of the great gladiators. He took to the arena himself, with his sword, and began dispatching suitably screened cripples and hobbled fighters. Audience participation became so popular that soon various *illuminati* of the Commodus set, various boys and girls of the year, were out there, suited up, gaily cutting a sequence of dwarfs and feebles down to short ribs. Ah, swinging generations, what new delights await?

QUESTIONS ON MEANING

1. Which of the following statements comes closest to summing up Tom Wolfe's main PURPOSE in writing "Pornoviolence"?

   Wolfe writes to define a word.
   Wolfe writes to define a trend in society.
   Wolfe writes to define a trend in the media that reflects a trend in society.
   Wolfe writes to explain how John F. Kennedy was assassinated.
   Wolfe writes to entertain us by mocking Americans' latest foolishness.

[3]Canadian English professor, author of *Understanding Media* (1964), *The Medium Is the Message* (1967), and other books, McLuhan (1911–80) analyzed the effects on world society of television and other electronic media. — EDS.

(If you don't find any of these statements adequate, compose your own.)
2. If you have ever read the *National Enquirer* or any of its imitators, test the accuracy of Wolfe's reporting. What is the purpose of a featured article in the *Enquirer*?
3. According to Wolfe, what POINT OF VIEW does the writer or producer of pornoviolence always take? What other examples of this point of view (in violent incidents on films or TV shows) can you supply? (Did you ever see a replay of Jack Ruby's shooting of Oswald, for instance?)
4. "Violence is the simple, ultimate solution for problems of status competition" (para. 26). What does Wolfe mean?
5. Wolfe does not explicitly pass judgment on Truman Capote's book *In Cold Blood* (para. 29). But what is his opinion of it? How can you tell?
6. "No advocate of change for the sake of change, Tom Wolfe writes as a conservative moralist who, like Jonathan Swift, rankles with savage indignation." Does this critical remark fit this particular essay? What, in Wolfe's view, appears to be happening to America and Americans?

QUESTIONS ON WRITING STRATEGY

1. On first reading, what did you make of Wolfe's opening sentence, "'Keeps His Mom-in-Law in Chains, meet Kills Son and Feeds Corpse to Pigs'"? At what point did you first tumble to what the writer was doing? What IRONY do you find in the convention hosts' introducing people by the headlines of their gory stories? What advantage is it to Wolfe's essay that his INTRODUCTION (with its odd introductions) keeps you guessing for a while?
2. What is Wolfe's point in listing (in para. 7) some of the other conventions he has reported — gatherings of nudists, oyster farmers, and others?
3. At what moment does Wolfe give us his short definition of *pornoviolence*, or the new pornography? Do you think he would have done better to introduce his short definition of the word in paragraph 1? Why, or why not?
4. What is the TONE or attitude of Wolfe's CONCLUSION (para. 31)? Note in particular the closing line.
5. **OTHER METHODS.** Typically for a writer of extended definition, Wolfe draws on many methods of development, including NARRATION, DIVISION OR ANALYSIS, and CAUSE AND EFFECT. What is the PURPOSE of the COMPARISON AND CONTRAST in paragraph 30?

QUESTIONS ON LANGUAGE

1. What help to the reader does Wolfe provide by noting the source of the word *pornography* (para. 17)?
2. "The television networks have schooled us in the view from Oswald's rifle" (para. 24). What CONNOTATIONS enlarge the meaning of *schooled*?

3. Define *masochist* and *sadist* (para. 25). What kind of DICTION do you find in these terms? In "plenty of hair on them-those walls" (29)?
4. How much use does Wolfe make of COLLOQUIAL EXPRESSIONS? Point to examples.
5. What does Wolfe mean in noting that the fighters slain by the Emperor Commodus were "hobbled" and the cripples were "suitably screened" (para. 31)? What unflattering connotations does this emperor's very name contain? (If you don't get this, look up *commode* in your desk dictionary.)

SUGGESTIONS FOR WRITING

1. In a paragraph, narrate or describe some recent example of pornoviolence you have seen in the movies or on television or one that you have observed. In a second paragraph, comment on it.
2. Write an essay defining some current trend you've noticed in films or TV, popular music, sports, consumer buying, or some other large arena of life. Like Wolfe, invent a name for it. Use plenty of examples to make your definition clear.
3. CRITICAL WRITING. ANALYZE Wolfe's distinctive journalistic style. In the note on the essay, we mention parenthetical asides (they appear between dashes as well as parentheses), three-dot ellipsis marks, and italics. Consider also his use of *I*, his piling up of detail (as in paras. 7 and 24), his informal DICTION ("losing its kick," "got his head blown off"), his choice of quotations, and any other features that strike you. What is the overall EFFECT of this style? What does it say about Wolfe?
4. CONNECTIONS. Both Tom Wolfe and Gloria Steinem, in "Erotica and Pornography" (p. 424), see violence and assertions of power in today's sexual pornography. What, in your opinion, accounts for this trend? Why would sex and violence become more closely linked in our age? (Draw on Wolfe's and Steinem's explanations to support yours, if you wish.)

TOM WOLFE ON WRITING

"What about your writing techniques and habits?" Tom Wolfe was asked by Joe David Bellamy for *Writer's Digest.* "The actual writing I do very fast," Wolfe said. "I make a very tight outline of everything I write before I write it. And often, as in the case of *The Electric Kool-Aid Acid Test,* the research, the reporting, is going to take me much longer than the writing. By writing an outline you really are writing in a way, because you're creating the structure of what you're going to do. Once I really know what I'm going to write, I don't find the actual writing takes all that long.

"*The Electric Kool-Aid Acid Test* in manuscript form was about 1,100 pages, triple-spaced, typewritten. That means about 200 words a page, and, you know, some of that was thrown out or cut eventually; but I wrote all of that in three and a half months. I had never written a full-length book before, and at first I decided I would treat each chapter as if it were a magazine article — because I *had* done that before. So I would set an artificial deadline, and I'd make myself meet it. And I did that for three chapters.

"But after I had done this three times and then I looked ahead and I saw that there were *twenty-five* more times I was going to have to do this, I couldn't face it anymore. I said, 'I cannot do this, even one more time, because there's no end to it.' So I completely changed my system, and I set up a quota for myself — of ten typewritten pages a day. At 200 words a page that's 2,000 words, which is not, you know, an overwhelming amount. It's a good clip, but it's not overwhelming. And I found this worked much better. I had my outline done, and sometimes ten pages would get me hardly an eighth-of-an-inch along the outline. It didn't bother me. Just like working in a factory — end of ten pages, I'd close my lunch pail."

FOR DISCUSSION

1. In what way is outlining really writing, according to Wolfe? (In answering, consider the implications of his statement about "creating a structure.")
2. What strategy did the author finally settle on to get himself through the toil of his first book? What made this strategy superior to the one he had used earlier?

GLORIA STEINEM

One of the most influential and controversial women of our time, GLORIA STEINEM helped found the modern feminist movement in America. The granddaughter of a leader in the women's suffrage movement, she was born in 1934 in Toledo. She attended Smith College, graduating in 1956, and then traveled through India on a fellowship. On returning to the United States in 1958, Steinem began publishing magazine articles, including her famous "I Was a Playboy Bunny," an exposé of the humiliating job of waitressing in a Playboy Club. In 1968, Steinem began writing a weekly column, "The City Politic," for *New York* magazine. In the early 1970s, she became more involved in political causes and launched the first feminist magazine, *Ms.*, which she edited for over fifteen years. As a political activist, Steinem helped found several feminist organizations. Her books include *Outrageous Acts and Everyday Rebellions* (1983), *Marilyn: Norma Jean* (1986), and *Revolution from Within: A Book of Self-Esteem* (1992).

Erotica and Pornography

A persuasive analyst of contemporary life, Steinem here teases apart two intertwined and often confused aspects of human sexuality. This essay comes from the November 1978 *Ms.*, where it was subtitled "A Clear and Present Difference." In both tone and substance, Steinem's essay complements Tom Wolfe's essay on a related subject, "Pornoviolence" (p. 414).

Human beings are the only animals that experience the same sex 1 drive at times when we can — and cannot — conceive.

Just as we developed uniquely human capacities for language, 2 planning, memory, and invention along our evolutionary path, we also developed sexuality as a form of expression; a way of communicating that is separable from our need for sex as a way of perpetuating ourselves. For humans alone, sexuality can be and often is primarily a way of bonding, of giving and receiving pleasure, bridging differentness, discovering sameness, and communicating emotion.

We developed this and other human gifts through our ability to 3 change our environment, adapt physically, and in the long run, to affect our own evolution. But as an emotional result of this spiraling path away from other animals, we seem to alternate between periods of exploring our unique abilities to change new boundaries, and feelings of loneliness in the unknown that we ourselves have created, a fear that sometimes sends us back to the comfort of the animal world by encouraging us to exaggerate our sameness.

The separation of "play" from "work," for instance, is a problem   4 only in the human world. So is the difference between art and nature, or an intellectual accomplishment and a physical one. As a result, we celebrate play, art, and invention as leaps into the unknown; but any imbalance can send us back to nostalgia for our primate past and the conviction that the basics of work, nature, and physical labor are somehow more worthwhile or even moral.

In the same way, we have explored our sexuality as separable   5 from conception: a pleasurable, empathetic bridge to strangers of the same species. We have even invented contraception — a skill that has probably existed in some form since our ancestors figured out the process of birth — in order to extend this uniquely human difference. Yet we also have times of atavistic suspicion that sex is not complete — or even legal or intended-by-god — if it cannot end in conception.

No wonder the concepts of "erotica" and "pornography" can be   6 so crucially different, and yet so confused. Both assume that sexuality can be separated from conception, and therefore can be used to carry a personal message. That's a major reason why, even in our current culture, both may be called equally "shocking" or legally "obscene," a word whose Latin derivative means "dirty, containing filth." This gross condemnation of all sexuality that isn't harnessed to childbirth and marriage has been increased by the current backlash against women's progress. Out of fear that the whole patriarchal structure might be upset if women really had the autonomous power to decide our reproductive futures (that is, if we controlled the most basic means of production), right-wing groups are not only denouncing pro-choice abortion literature as "pornographic," but are trying to stop the sending of all contraceptive information through the mails by invoking obscenity laws. In fact, Phyllis Schlafly recently denounced the entire Women's Movement as "obscene."

Not surprisingly, this religious, visceral backlash has a secular,   7 intellectual counterpart that relies heavily on applying the "natural" behavior of the animal world to humans. That is questionable in itself, but these Lionel Tiger-ish[1] studies make their political purpose

[1]Tiger (born 1937) is an anthropologist specializing in human evolution. — EDS.

even more clear in the particular animals they select and the habits they choose to emphasize. The message is that females should accept their "destiny" of being sexually dependent and devote themselves to bearing and rearing their young.

Defending against such reaction in turn leads to another temp- 8
tation: to merely reverse the terms, and declare that *all* nonprocreative sex is good. In fact, however, this human activity can be as constructive as destructive, moral or immoral, as any other. Sex as communication can send messages as different as life and death; even the origins of "erotica" and "pornography" reflect that fact. After all, "erotica" is rooted in *eros* or passionate love, and thus in the idea of positive choice, free will, the yearning for a particular person. (Interestingly, the definition of erotica leaves open the question of gender.) "Pornography" begins with a root meaning "prostitution" or "female captives," thus letting us know that the subject is not mutual love, or love at all, but domination and violence against women. (Though, of course, homosexual pornography may imitate this violence by putting a man in the "feminine" role of victim.) It ends with a root meaning "writing about" or "description of" which puts still more distance between subject and object, and replaces a spontaneous yearning for closeness with objectification and a voyeur.

The difference is clear in the words. It becomes even more so by 9
example.

Look at any photo or film of people making love; really making 10
love. The images may be diverse, but there is usually a sensuality and touch and warmth, an acceptance of bodies and nerve endings. There is always a spontaneous sense of people who are there because they *want* to be, out of shared pleasure.

Now look at any depiction of sex in which there is clear force, 11
or an unequal power that spells coercion. It may be very blatant, with weapons or torture or bondage, wounds and bruises, some clear humiliation, or an adult's sexual power being used over a child. It may be much more subtle: a physical attitude of conqueror and victim, the use of race or class difference to imply the same thing, perhaps a very unequal nudity, with one person exposed and vulnerable while the other is clothed. In either case, there is no sense of equal choice or equal power.

The first is erotic: a mutually pleasurable, sexual expression be- 12
tween people who have enough power to be there by positive choice. It may or may not strike a sense-memory in the viewer, or be creative enough to make the unknown seem real; but it doesn't require us to identify with a conqueror or a victim. It is truly sensuous, and may give us a contagion of pleasure.

The second is pornographic: its message is violence, dominance, 13
and conquest. It is sex being used to reinforce some inequality, or to
create one, or to tell us the lie that pain and humiliation (ours or
someone else's) are really the same as pleasure. If we are to feel
anything, we must identify with conqueror or victim. That means we
can only experience pleasure through the adoption of some degree of
sadism or masochism. It also means that we may feel diminished by
the role of conqueror, or enraged, humiliated, and vengeful by sharing
identity with the victim.

Perhaps one could simply say that erotica is about sexuality, but 14
pornography is about power and sex-as-weapon — in the same way
we have come to understand that rape is about violence, and not
really about sexuality at all.

Yes, it's true that there are women who have been forced by 15
violent families and dominating men to confuse love with pain; so
much so that they have become masochists. (A fact that in no way
excuses those who administer such pain.) But the truth is that, for
most women — and for men with enough humanity to imagine themselves into the predicament of women — true pornography could
serve as aversion therapy for sex.

Of course, there will always be personal differences about what is 16
and is not erotic, and there may be cultural differences for a long
time to come. Many women feel that sex makes them vulnerable and
therefore may continue to need more sense of personal connection
and safety before allowing any erotic feelings. We now find competence and erotic expertise in men, but that may pass as we develop
those qualities in ourselves. Men, on the other hand, may continue
to feel less vulnerable, and therefore more open to such potential
danger as sex with strangers. As some men replace the need for
submission from childlike women with the pleasure of cooperation
from equals, they may find a partner's competence to be erotic, too.

Such group changes plus individual differences will continue to 17
be reflected in sexual love between people of the same gender, as well
as between women and men. The point is not to dictate sameness,
but to discover ourselves and each other through sexuality that
is an exploring, pleasurable, empathetic part of our lives; a human
sexuality that is unchained both from unwanted pregnancies and from
violence.

But that is a hope, not a reality. At the moment, fear of change 18
is increasing both the indiscriminate repression of all nonprocreative
sex in the religious and "conservative" male world, and the pornographic vengeance against women's sexuality in the secular world of
"liberal" and "radical" men. It's almost futuristic to debate what is

and is not truly erotic, when many women are again being forced into compulsory motherhood, and the numbers of pornographic murders, tortures, and woman-hating images are on the increase in both popular culture and real life.

It's a familiar division: wife or whore, "good" woman who is 19 constantly vulnerable to pregnancy or "bad" woman who is unprotected from violence. *Both* roles would be upset if we were to control our own sexuality. And that's exactly what we must do.

In spite of all our atavistic suspicions and training for the "natural" 20 role of motherhood, we took up the complicated battle for reproductive freedom. Our bodies had borne the health burden of endless births and poor abortions, and we had a greater motive for separating sexuality and conception.

Now we have to take up the equally complex burden of explaining 21 that all nonprocreative sex is *not* alike. We have a motive: our right to a uniquely human sexuality, and sometimes even to survival. As it is, our bodies have too rarely been enough our own to develop erotica in our own lives, much less in art and literature. And our bodies have too often been the objects of pornography and the woman-hating, violent practice that it preaches. Consider also our spirits that break a little each time we see ourselves in chains or full labial display for the conquering male viewer, bruised or on our knees, screaming a real or pretended pain to delight the sadist, pretending to enjoy what we don't enjoy, to be blind to the images of our sisters that really haunt us — humiliated often enough ourselves by the truly obscene idea that sex and the domination of women must be combined.

Sexuality *is* human, free, separate — and so are we.   22

But until we untangle the lethal confusion of sex with violence, 23 there will be more pornography and less erotica. There will be little murders in our beds — and very little love.

QUESTIONS ON MEANING

1. Why, in Steinem's opinion, do some groups want to censor information on contraception?
2. What are the PURPOSE and THESIS of this essay?
3. What are some of the ways pornography depicts imbalances of power?
4. Does Steinem want pornography to be outlawed?

QUESTIONS ON WRITING STRATEGY

1. In your own words, SUMMARIZE Steinem's definitions of *erotica* and *pornography.*
2. Look closely at paragraphs 1 and 2. How does this INTRODUCTION help set up Steinem's definitions of *erotica* and *pornography?* What does the introduction define?
3. What is Steinem's TONE in this essay? What is its EFFECT?
4. Identify some of Steinem's TRANSITIONS. How do they create bridges between paragraphs?
5. **OTHER METHODS.** Steinem uses COMPARISON AND CONTRAST to help define *pornography* and *erotica.* Is her comparison subject by subject or point by point? What is the EFFECT of this method?

QUESTIONS ON LANGUAGE

1. Look in a dictionary for definitions of the words *erotica* and *pornography.* How do the dictionary definitions differ from Steinem's? What (besides length) accounts for the differences?
2. Why does Steinem use quotation marks around words like "play" and "work" (para. 4), "obscene" (6), and "natural" (7)?
3. Provide meanings for any of these words that are unfamiliar: empathetic, atavistic (para. 5); visceral, secular (7); nonprocreative, objectification, voyeur (8); coercion (11); sensuous (12); sadism, masochism (13); compulsory (18); labial (21).
4. How do the CONNOTATIONS of "making love" (para. 10) and "sex" (11) differ? How does Steinem rely on these connotations in distinguishing erotica and pornography?

SUGGESTIONS FOR WRITING

1. Write an essay that defines *masculine* and *feminine* as expressed on television or in the movies. (You will probably want to make extensive use of COMPARISON AND CONTRAST.) How accurately do television and movie depictions of sex roles match the realities in today's world? Support your ideas with examples from the media and your own experience.
2. Should pornography be banned, in your view? Argue one way or the other, supporting your argument with reasons and examples. Be sure to provide a stipulative definition of *pornography* so that your readers understand your meaning. (Note that the "Connections" question below asks for an extended definition of *pornography.*)
3. **CRITICAL WRITING.** Steinem writes from a feminist's viewpoint about erotica and pornography. What are her ASSUMPTIONS about relations between men and women? What can you INFER about her hopes for the future? Does her viewpoint limit or enlarge her perceptions, in your opinion? Why?

4. **CONNECTIONS.** Both Gloria Steinem and Tom Wolfe, in "Pornovio-lence" (p. 414), define *pornography.* In an essay, offer your own definition of the word, drawing on Steinem's and Wolfe's ideas and the information in a dictionary but focusing on your own ideas and examples. In your definition, you may want to consider Wolfe's statement that "pornog-raphy cannot exist without certified taboo to violate" (para. 28).

GLORIA STEINEM ON WRITING

In her introduction to *Outrageous Acts and Everyday Rebellions,* Gloria Steinem raises the question of why, "after more than twenty years of making a living as a writer, this is the first book I can call my own." Why, that is, has she not been a more productive writer? The answer comes quickly: "Writers are notorious for using any reason to keep from working: over-researching, retyping, going to meetings, waxing the floors — anything. Organizing, fund raising, and working for *Ms.* magazine have given me much better excuses than those, and I've used them. As [newspaper columnist] Jimmy Breslin said when he ran a symbolic campaign for a political office he didn't want, 'Anything that isn't writing is easy.'"

But, hard as she finds it, Steinem does write. Quoting herself in a *Harper's* magazine article twenty years before, she gives some of her reasons why:

" • There is freedom, or the illusion of it. Working in spurts to meet deadlines may be just as restricting as having to show up at the same place every day, but I don't think so. . . . Writing about a disliked person or theory or institution usually turns out to be worth-while, because pride of authorship finally takes over from prejudice. Words in print assume such power and importance that it is impossible not to feel acutely responsible for them.

" • Writing, on the other hand, keeps me from believing every-thing I read. . . .

" • For me, writing is the only thing that passes the three tests of métier: (1) When I'm doing it, I don't feel that I should be doing something else instead; (2) it produces a sense of accomplishment and, once in a while, pride; and (3) it's frightening."

FOR DISCUSSION

1. What does Steinem mean when she says that "pride of authorship finally takes over from prejudice"? How is this pride connected to the sense of responsibility Steinem feels? Do you think it's possible or desirable to

feel such pride and responsibility for one's words even when they aren't published except in the classroom?

2. Why would writing keep Steinem from "believing everything I read"?

3. *Métier* means "occupation or profession." Why do you suppose Steinem wants a "frightening" occupation?

JAMAICA KINCAID

JAMAICA KINCAID was born Elaine Potter Richardson in 1949 on
the Caribbean island of Antigua. She attended school in Antigua
and struggled to become independent of her mother and her place.
"I was supposed to be full of good manners and good speech," she
has recalled. "Where the hell I was going to go with it I don't
know." Kincaid took it to New York, where she went at age 17 to
work as a family helper. She briefly attended Franconia College on
a photography scholarship and did odd jobs in New York. In the
early 1970s, she became friends with George Trow, a writer for *The
New Yorker*. Soon she was contributing to the magazine, and in
1976 she became a staff writer. Soon after, she began writing fiction,
eventually producing a collection of stories, *At the Bottom of the
River* (1983), and two novels, *Annie John* (1985) and *Lucy*
(1990) — all based on her own life on Antigua and as an immigrant. Kincaid now lives in Vermont with her family.

The Tourist

The island of Antigua, where Kincaid was born and raised, was a
British dependency until 1967 and did not become independent
until 1981. In *A Small Place* (1988), Kincaid denounces what she
sees as the ruin of the island and its culture by the colonial rulers
and their political heirs. "The Tourist," an excerpt from the book
(titled by the editors), defines a particularly unattractive island
species.

The thing you have always suspected about yourself the minute   1
you become a tourist is true: A tourist is an ugly human being. You
are not an ugly person all the time; you are not an ugly person
ordinarily; you are not an ugly person day to day. From day to day,
you are a nice person. From day to day, all the people who are
supposed to love you on the whole do. From day to day, as you walk
down a busy street in the large and modern and prosperous city in
which you work and live, dismayed, puzzled (a cliché, but only a
cliché can explain you) at how alone you feel in this crowd, how
awful it is to go unnoticed, how awful it is to go unloved, even as
you are surrounded by more people than you could possibly get to
know in a lifetime that lasted for millennia, and then out of the
corner of your eye you see someone looking at you and absolute

pleasure is written all over that person's face, and then you realize
that you are not as revolting a presence as you think you are (for that
look just told you so). And so, ordinarily, you are a nice person, an
attractive person, a person capable of drawing to yourself the affection
of other people (people just like you), a person at home in your own
skin (sort of; I mean, in a way; I mean, your dismay and puzzlement
are natural to you, because people like you just seem to be like that,
and so many of the things people like you find admirable about
yourselves — the things you think about, the things you think really
define you — seem rooted in these feelings): a person at home in
your own house (and all its nice house things), with its nice back
yard (and its nice backyard things), at home on your street, your
church, in community activities, your job, at home with your family,
your relatives, your friends — you are a whole person. But one day,
when you are sitting somewhere, alone in that crowd, and that awful
feeling of displacedness comes over you, and really, as an ordinary
person you are not well equipped to look too far inward and set
yourself aright, because being ordinary is already so taxing, and being
ordinary takes all you have out of you, and though the words "I must
get away" do not actually pass across your lips, you make a leap from
being that nice blob just sitting like a boob in your amniotic sac of
the modern experience to being a person visiting heaps of death and
ruin and feeling alive and inspired at the sight of it; to being a person
lying on some faraway beach, your stilled body stinking and glistening
in the sand, looking like something first forgotten, then remembered,
then not important enough to go back for; to being a person mar-
velling at the harmony (ordinarily, what you would say is the back-
wardness) and the union these other people (and they are other
people) have with nature. And you look at the things they can do
with a piece of ordinary cloth, the things they fashion out of cheap,
vulgarly colored (to you) twine, the way they squat down over a hole
they have made in the ground, the hole itself is something to marvel
at, and since you are being an ugly person this ugly but joyful thought
will swell inside you: Their ancestors were not clever in the way yours
were and not ruthless in the way yours were, for then would it not
be you who would be in harmony with nature and backwards in that
charming way? An ugly thing, that is what you are when you become
a tourist, an ugly, empty thing, a stupid thing, a piece of rubbish
pausing here and there to gaze at this and taste that, and it will never
occur to you that the people who inhabit the place in which you
have just paused cannot stand you, that behind their closed doors
they laugh at your strangeness (you do not look the way they look);

the physical sight of you does not please them; you have bad manners (it is their custom to eat their food with their hands; you try eating their way, you look silly; you try eating the way you always eat, you look silly); they do not like the way you speak (you have an accent); they collapse helpless from laughter, mimicking the way they imagine you must look as you carry out some everyday bodily function. They do not like you. *They do not like me!* That thought never actually occurs to you. Still, you feel a little uneasy. Still, you feel a little foolish. Still, you feel a little out of place. But the banality of your own life is very real to you; it drove you to this extreme, spending your days and your nights in the company of people who despise you, people you do not like really, people you would not want to have as your actual neighbour. And so you must devote yourself to puzzling out how much of what you are told is really, really true (Is ground-up bottle glass in peanut sauce really a delicacy around here, or will it do just what you think ground-up bottle glass will do? Is this rare, multicoloured, snout-mouthed fish really an aphrodisiac, or will it cause you to fall asleep permanently?). Oh, the hard work all of this is, and is it any wonder, then, that on your return home you feel the need of a long rest, so that you can recover from your life as a tourist?

That the native does not like the tourist is not hard to explain.   2
For every native of every place is a potential tourist, and every tourist is a native of somewhere. Every native everywhere lives a life of overwhelming and crushing banality and boredom and desperation and depression, and every deed, good and bad, is an attempt to forget this. Every native would like to find a way out, every native would like a rest, every native would like a tour. But some natives — most natives in the world — cannot go anywhere. They are too poor. They are too poor to go anywhere. They are too poor to escape the reality of their lives; and they are too poor to live properly in the place where they live, which is the very place you, the tourist, want to go — so when the natives see you, the tourist, they envy you, they envy your ability to leave your own banality and boredom, they envy your ability to turn their own banality and boredom into a source of pleasure for yourself.

QUESTIONS ON MEANING

1. What is this essay's PURPOSE?
2. Why does Kincaid describe being a tourist as "hard work" (para. 1)?

3. What are some of the tourist's motivations?
4. Why does the native dislike the tourist?

QUESTIONS ON WRITING STRATEGY

1. Is Kincaid's intended AUDIENCE more likely "tourists" or "natives"? How do you know?
2. What is the EFFECT of the second-PERSON *you* in this essay? Is it offensive? If so, why would Kincaid want to offend?
3. Discuss the function of the parenthetical asides in this essay. How do they relate to the statements in which they are inserted? What kinds of thoughts do they represent?
4. Why did Kincaid not provide a dictionary-like definition of the word *tourist?*
5. OTHER METHODS. Kincaid uses CLASSIFICATION to distinguish tourists (nonnatives) and natives (nontourists). At what point do the classes overlap? What keeps them separate?

QUESTIONS ON LANGUAGE

1. Kincaid's book *A Small Place,* from which "The Tourist" comes, has been described as "a masterpiece of invective" — that is, of hostile language that denounces or abuses. Find examples of invective in "The Tourist." Do you agree with the quotation?
2. Kincaid describes a tourist on the beach as a "stilled body stinking and glistening in the sand" (para. 1). What is the IMAGE here? What are its CONNOTATIONS?
3. Check your dictionary if any of these words are unfamiliar: millennia, taxing, amniotic, banality, aphrodisiac.

SUGGESTIONS FOR WRITING

1. In a short essay of your own, define what it is to be a *native* of the place you are from. You may want to draw on Kincaid's description of tourists and natives, but your work should rely heavily on your own experience. Provide EXAMPLES to back up your definition. What kinds of experiences are essential to being a native? How can others tell a native from a tourist or a visitor?
2. Taking the POINT OF VIEW of either Kincaid's native or her tourist, write a brief monologue about your opposite (native about tourist, tourist about native). Don't be afraid to be SUBJECTIVE. Match your TONE to your point of view. (It may be helpful to imagine an encounter between native and tourist — say, registering at a hotel, negotiating the price of souvenirs, riding in a taxi or a bus, touring a local landmark.)
3. CRITICAL WRITING. Kincaid writes for *The New Yorker,* and all of her works, with one exception, have been published or excerpted in the magazine. The exception is *A Small Place,* the source of the "The

Tourist." Imagine that you are a *New Yorker* editor responsible for deciding on the basis of "The Tourist" whether or not to publish *A Small Place*. You may make your decision on any reasonable grounds (for instance, literary merit, possible offense to readers, possible offense to advertisers). Write a one-page report of your decision, making your reasons clear and supporting them with examples from the selection.

4. CONNECTIONS. Both Kincaid and Ralph Ellison (in "On Being the Target of Discrimination," p. 55) rely on the second-PERSON *you*. What is the EFFECT of this pronoun in each essay? How does the use of *you* differ? How is it similar? Are there any similarities in the two essays' THESES?

JAMAICA KINCAID ON WRITING

In a 1990 interview with Louise Kennedy in the *Boston Globe*, Jamaica Kincaid says that making sense of life is what motivates her writing. "I started out feeling alone," she remarks. "I grew up in a place where I was very alone. I didn't know then that I wanted to write; I didn't have that thought. But even if I had, I would have had no one to tell it to. They would have laughed before they threw me in a pond or something." With this beginning, Kincaid came to believe that the point of writing is not to please the reader. "Sometimes I feel — 'I'm pushed too far, I don't care, I don't care if you don't like this. I know it and it makes sense to me.'" The point, then, is to understand the world through the self. "I'm trying to discover the secret of myself. . . . For me everything passes through the self."

Kincaid's writing helps her come to terms with the conflicts in her life. "I could be dead or in jail. If you don't know how to make sense of what's happened to you, if you see things but can't express them — it's so painful." Part of Kincaid's pain growing up was the "magic" her mother held over her, a power that fueled Kincaid's rebellion. "That feeling of rebellion is doomed," she says. "You can't succeed. But it's worth trying because you find out that you can't. You have to try, or you die."

Although her native Antigua figures strongly in her writing, Kincaid cannot write there. "When I'm in the place where I'm from, I can't really think. I just absorb it; I take it all in. Then I come back and take it out and unpack it and walk through it." Her need for distance has led her to live in Vermont, "the opposite of where I come from. It changes. It's mountainous. It has seasons." As for

Antigua, Kincaid says, "I don't know how to live there, but I don't know how to live without there."

FOR DISCUSSION

1. How can not caring about the reader's response liberate a writer?
2. What does Kincaid mean by "everything passes through the self"? Do you experience this process from time to time?
3. How does the author view her place of birth? Do you find her last statement contradictory?

BRUNO BETTELHEIM

Described in his *New York Times* obituary as "a psychoanalyst of great impact" and "a gifted writer . . . with a great literary and moral sensibility," BRUNO BETTELHEIM was born in Austria in 1903 and died in the United States in 1990. Growing up in the Vienna of Sigmund Freud, Bettelheim became interested in psychoanalysis as a young teenager and trained as a psychologist at the University of Vienna. He had already earned a wide reputation when he was imprisoned by the Nazis in the Buchenwald and Dachau concentration camps. When released because of American intervention in 1939, Bettelheim emigrated to Chicago. After several research and teaching positions, in 1944 he began teaching at the University of Chicago and continued there until his retirement in 1973. Bettelheim's work concentrated on children with severe emotional disorders such as autism and psychosis, and many of his theories were provocative and controversial. Some of his well-known books, all on children, are *Love Is Not Enough* (1950), *Truants from Life* (1955), *The Children of the Dream* (1969), and *The Uses of Enchantment* (1976).

The Holocaust

In two books, *The Informal Heart* (1960) and *Surviving, and Other Essays* (1979), Bettelheim probed his and others' experiences in the Nazis' concentration camps. What follows is a freestanding slice of a much longer essay, "The Holocaust — One Generation After," from *Surviving*. Here Bettelheim, with cool passion, dissects a loaded word.

To begin with, it was not the hapless victims of the Nazis who 1
named their incomprehensible and totally unmasterable fate the "holocaust." It was the Americans who applied this artificial and highly technical term to the Nazi extermination of the European Jews. But while the event when named as mass murder most foul evokes the most immediate, most powerful revulsion, when it is designated by a rare technical term, we must first in our minds translate it back into emotionally meaningful language. Using technical or specially created terms instead of words from our common vocabulary is one of the best-known and most widely used distancing devices, separating the intellectual from the emotional experience. Talking about "the holocaust" permits us to manage it intellectually where the raw facts,

when given their ordinary names, would overwhelm us emotionally — because it was catastrophe beyond comprehension, beyond the limits of our imagination, unless we force ourselves against our desire to extend it to encompass these terrible events.

This linguistic circumlocution began while it all was only in the planning stage. Even the Nazis — usually given to grossness in language and action — shied away from facing openly what they were up to and called this vile mass murder "the final solution of the Jewish problem." After all, solving a problem can be made to appear like an honorable enterprise, as long as we are not forced to recognize that the solution we are about to embark on consists of the completely unprovoked, vicious murder of millions of helpless men, women, and children. The Nuremberg judges of these Nazi criminals followed their example of circumlocution by coining a neologism out of one Greek and one Latin root: genocide. These artificially created technical terms fail to connect with our strongest feelings. The horror of murder is part of our most common human heritage. From earliest infancy on, it arouses violent abhorrence in us. Therefore in whatever form it appears we should give such an act its true designation and not hide it behind polite, erudite terms created out of classical words.

To call this vile mass murder "the holocaust" is not to give it a special name emphasizing its uniqueness which would permit, over time, the word becoming invested with feelings germane to the event it refers to. The correct definition of *holocaust* is "burnt offering." As such, it is part of the language of the psalmist, a meaningful word to all who have some acquaintance with the Bible, full of the richest emotional connotations. By using the term "holocaust," entirely false associations are established through conscious and unconscious connotations between the most vicious of mass murders and ancient rituals of a deeply religious nature.

Using a word with such strong unconscious religious connotations when speaking of the murder of millions of Jews robs the victims of this abominable mass murder of the only thing left to them: their uniqueness. Calling the most callous, most brutal, most horrid, most heinous mass murder a burnt offering is a sacrilege, a profanation of God and man.

Martyrdom is part of our religious heritage. A martyr, burned at the stake, is a burnt offering to his god. And it is true that after the Jews were asphyxiated, the victims' corpses were burned. But I believe we fool ourselves if we think we are honoring the victims of systematic murder by using this term, which has the highest moral connotations. By doing so, we connect for our own psychological reasons what happened in the extermination camps with historical events we deeply regret, but also greatly admire. We do so because this makes it easier for us to cope; only in doing so we cope with our distorted image of what happened, not with the events the way they did happen.

By calling the victims of the Nazis martyrs, we falsify their fate. 6 The true meaning of *martyr* is: "One who voluntarily undergoes the penalty of death for refusing to renounce his faith" (*Oxford English Dictionary*). The Nazis made sure that nobody could mistakenly think that their victims were murdered for their religious beliefs. Renouncing their faith would have saved none of them. Those who had converted to Christianity were gassed, as were those who were atheists, and those who were deeply religious Jews. They did not die for any conviction, and certainly not out of choice.

Millions of Jews were systematically slaughtered, as were untold 7 other "undesirables," not for any convictions of theirs, but only because they stood in the way of the realization of an illusion. They neither died for their convictions, nor were they slaughtered because of their convictions, but only in consequence of the Nazis' delusional belief about what was required to protect the purity of their assumed superior racial endowment, and what they thought necessary to guarantee them the living space they believed they needed and were entitled to. Thus while these millions were slaughtered for an idea, they did not die for one.

Millions — men, women, and children — were processed after 8 they had been utterly brutalized, their humanity destroyed, their clothes torn from their bodies. Naked, they were sorted into those who were destined to be murdered immediately, and those others who had a short-term usefulness as slave labor. But after a brief interval they, too, were to be herded into the same gas chambers into which the others were immediately piled, there to be asphyxiated so that, in their last moments, they could not prevent themselves from fighting each other in vain for a last breath of air.

To call these most wretched victims of a murderous delusion, of 9 destructive drives run rampant, martyrs or a burnt offering is a distortion invented for our comfort, small as it may be. It pretends that this most vicious of mass murders had some deeper meaning; that in some fashion the victims either offered themselves or at least became sacrifices to a higher cause. It robs them of the last recognition which could be theirs, denies them the last dignity we could accord them: to face and accept what their death was all about, not embellishing it for the small psychological relief this may give us.

We could feel so much better if the victims had acted out of 10 choice. For our emotional relief, therefore, we dwell on the tiny minority who did exercise some choice: the resistance fighters of the Warsaw ghetto, for example, and others like them. We are ready to overlook the fact that these people fought back only at a time when everything was lost, when the overwhelming majority of those who had been forced into the ghettos had already been exterminated without resisting. Certainly those few who finally fought for their survival and their convictions, risking and losing their lives in doing so, deserve our admiration; their deeds give us a moral lift. But the more we dwell on these few, the more unfair are we to the memory of the millions who were slaughtered — who gave in, did not fight back — because we deny them the only thing which up to the very end remained uniquely their own: their fate.

QUESTIONS ON MEANING

1. Why does Bettelheim feel that *holocaust* is an inappropriate term for the mass murder of Jews during World War II? Why does he say this sort of "linguistic circumlocution" is used? (What is a "linguistic circumlocution"?)
2. What is Bettelheim's PURPOSE here?
3. According to Bettelheim, what do we do besides using unemotional terms to distance ourselves from the murder of the Jews?
4. Does Bettelheim suggest an alternative term for *holocaust*?

QUESTIONS ON WRITING STRATEGY

1. Where does Bettelheim stress etymologies, or word histories, and dictionary definitions? What is their EFFECT?
2. What does Bettelheim accomplish with paragraph 8? Why is this paragraph essential?
3. How would you characterize Bettelheim's TONE? What creates it? Is it appropriate, do you think?
4. In several places Bettelheim repeats or restates passages — for instance, "By doing so . . . We do so . . . only in doing so" (para. 5), or "stood in the way of the realization of an illusion . . . in consequence of the Nazis' delusional belief . . . slaughtered for an idea" (7). Do you think such repetition and restatement is deliberate on Bettelheim's part? Why, or why not?
5. OTHER METHODS. Bettelheim's definition is an ARGUMENT. What is the THESIS of his argument? What EVIDENCE supports the thesis?

QUESTIONS ON LANGUAGE

1. Analyze the words Bettelheim uses to refer to the murder of the Jews. How do the words support his argument?
2. What is the effect of Bettelheim's use of *we* — for instance, in paragraphs 5 and 10?
3. Look up any unfamiliar words: hapless (para. 1); neologism, abhorrence, erudite (2); germane, psalmist (3); abominable, callous, heinous, sacrilege, profanation (4); asphyxiated (5); delusional, endowment (7); rampant, embellishing (9).

SUGGESTIONS FOR WRITING

1. For the sake of argument, write an essay in which you defend the use of "technical or specially created terms" — not for the Nazi murders but for an activity or field you're familiar with. For instance, what about the terminology of sports, dance, guitar playing, nursing, business, auto mechanics?
2. Although Bettelheim does not use the term, he is objecting to the use of a EUPHEMISM, or inoffensive word, in place of a word that might wound or offend. Euphemisms abound in the speech of politicians: The economy undergoes a "slowdown" or a "downturn"; lying is "misspeaking." Drawing on Bettelheim's arguments as you see fit, write an essay about one or more euphemisms appearing in a daily newspaper. What do the euphemisms accomplish, and for whom? What do they conceal, and who is hurt?
3. CRITICAL WRITING. Research the word *holocaust* in a dictionary of word histories (an etymological dictionary) and an interpretation of the Bible. (A librarian can direct you to these sources.) On the basis of your research, do you agree or disagree with Bettelheim's rejection of the word? (In your answer, consider whether the word's wide use for the Nazi murders has provided it with new meanings.)
4. CONNECTIONS. Read "I Have a Dream" by Martin Luther King, Jr. (p. 516). Compare it with Bettelheim's essay on the purposeful use of repetition and restatement. How does each author use this device? For what aim? What is the EFFECT? If you like, you can narrow your comparison to one representative passage of each essay. Just be sure to use quotations to support your comparison.

JOSEPH EPSTEIN

JOSEPH EPSTEIN, author, critic, and editor of *The American Scholar*, teaches writing and literature at Northwestern University. He was born in Chicago in 1937. A graduate of the University of Chicago, he served in the army from 1958 to 1960. Epstein's lively, incisive, and independent-minded essays have appeared from time to time in such places as the *New York Times Book Review, Commentary, The New Criterion*, the *New York Times Magazine*, and *Harper's*. He writes regularly for *The American Scholar*. And he is the author of *Divorce in America* (1975), *Familiar Territory* (1980), *Ambition* (1981), *The Middle of My Tether* (1983), *Plausible Prejudices* (1985), *Once More Around the Block* (1987), *Partial Payments* (1989), *A Line Out for a Walk* (1992), and *Pertinent Players* (1993).

What Is Vulgar?

Epstein wrote "What Is Vulgar?" in 1981 for *The American Scholar*, the magazine published by Phi Beta Kappa (the oldest American honor society for college students). Later he included it in *The Middle of My Tether*. In the essay Epstein seems to have a rollicking good time deciding what vulgarity is. He examines the history of both word and concept. He speculates about what vulgarity is *not*. He relishes colorful examples. Some aspects of his definition may surprise you; others may give you a jolt. We're sure they won't bore you.

What's vulgar? Some people might say that the contraction of 1 the words *what* and *is* itself is vulgar. On the other hand, I remember being called a stuffed shirt by a reviewer of a book of mine because I used almost no contractions. I have forgotten the reviewer's name but I have remembered the criticism. Not being of that category of writers who never forget a compliment, I also remember being called a racist by another reviewer for observing that failure to insist on table manners in children was to risk dining with Apaches. The larger criticisms I forget, but, oddly, these goofy little criticisms stick in the teeth like sesame seeds. Yet that last trope — is it, too, vulgar? Ought I really to be picking my teeth in public, even metaphorically?

What, to return to the question in uncontractioned form, is 2 vulgar? Illustrations, obviously, are wanted. Consider a relative of mine, long deceased, my father's Uncle Jake and hence my grand-uncle. I don't wish to brag about bloodlines, but my Uncle Jake was a bootlegger during Prohibition who afterward went into the scrap-iron — that is to say, the junk — business. Think of the archetypal sensitive Jewish intellectual faces: of Spinoza, of Freud, of Einstein, of Oppenheimer.[1] In my uncle's face you would not have found the least trace of any of them. He was completely bald, weighed in at around two hundred fifty pounds, and had a complexion of clear vermilion. I loved him, yet even as a child I knew there was about him something a bit — how shall I put it? — outsized, and I refer not merely to his personal tonnage. When he visited our home he generally greeted me by pressing a ten- or twenty-dollar bill into my hand — an amount of money quite impossible, of course, for a boy of nine or ten, when what was wanted was a quarter or fifty-cent piece. A widower, he would usually bring a lady-friend along; here his tastes ran to Hungarian women in their fifties with operatic bosoms. These women wore large diamond rings, possibly the same rings, which my uncle may have passed from woman to woman. A big spender and a high roller, my uncle was an immigrant version of the sport, a kind of Diamond Chaim Brodsky.

But to see Uncle Jake in action you had to see him at table. He   3
drank whiskey with his meal, the bottle before him on the table along with another of seltzer water, both of which he supplied himself. He ate and drank like a character out of Rabelais.[2] My mother served him his soup course, not in a regular bowl, but in a vessel more on the order of a tureen. He would eat hot soup and drink whiskey and sweat — my Uncle Jake did not, decidedly, do anything so delicate as perspire — and sometimes it seemed that the sweat rolled from his face right into his soup dish, so that, toward the end, he may well have been engaged in an act of liquid auto-cannibalism, consuming his own body fluids with a whiskey chaser.

He was crude, certainly, my Uncle Jake; he was coarse, of course;   4
gross, it goes without saying; uncouth, beyond question. But was he vulgar? I don't think he was. For one thing, he was good-hearted. But more to the point, I don't think that if you had accused him of being vulgar, he would have known what the devil you were talking

---

[1]Benedict (or Baruch) Spinoza (1632–77) was a Dutch philosopher; Sigmund Freud (1856–1939), the Austrian founder of psychoanalysis; Albert Einstein (1879–1955), the eminent physicist; and J. Robert Oppenheimer (1904–67), an American physicist who helped develop the first atomic bomb and then opposed the government's decision to develop the hydrogen bomb. — Eds.

[2]François Rabelais (1494?–1553?), French humorist who in *Gargantua and Pantagruel* (1532–34) depicts two giants with tremendous appetites. — Eds.

about. To be vulgar requires at least a modicum of pretension, and this Uncle Jake sorely lacked. "Wulgar," he might have responded to the accusation that he was vulgar, "so vat's dis wulgar?"

To go from persons to things, and from lack of pretension to a mountain of it, let me tell you about a house I passed one night, in a neighborhood not far from my own, that so filled me with disbelief that I took a hard right turn at the next corner and drove round the block to make certain I had actually seen what I thought I had. I had, but it was no house — it was a bloody edifice! 5

The edifice in question totally fills its rather modest lot, leaving no backyard at all. It is constructed of a white stone, sanded and perhaps even painted, with so much gray-colored mortar that, even though it may be real, the stone looks fake. The roof is red. It has two chimneys, neither of which, I would wager, functions. My confidence here derives from the fact that nothing much else in the structure of the house seems to function. There is, for example, a balcony over a portico — a portico held up by columns — onto which the only possible mode of entry is by pole vault. There is, similarly, over the attached garage, a sun deck whose only access appears to be through a bathroom window. The house seems to have been built on the aesthetic formula of functionlessness follows formlessness. 6

But it is in its details that the true spirit of the house emerges. These details are not minuscule, and neither are they subtle. For starters, outside the house under the portico, there is a chandelier. There are also two torch-shaped lamps on either side of the front door, which is carved in a scallop pattern, giving it the effect of seeming the back door to a much larger house. Along the short walk leading up to this front door stand, on short pillars, two plaster of paris lions — gilded. On each pillar, in gold and black, appears the owner's name. A white chain fence, strung along poles whose tops are painted gold, spans the front of the property; it is the kind of fence that would be more appropriate around, say, the tomb of Lenin. At the curb are two large cars, sheets of plastic covering their grills; there is also a trailer; and, in the summer months, a boat sits in the short driveway leading up to the garage. The lawn disappoints by being not Astro-Turf but, alas, real grass. However, closer inspection reveals two animals, a skunk and a rabbit, both of plastic, in petrified play upon the lawn — a nice, you might almost say a finishing, touch. Sometimes, on long drives or when unable to sleep at night, I have pondered upon the possible decor of this extraordinary house's den and upon the ways of man, which are various beyond imagining. 7

You want vulgar, I am inclined to exclaim, I'll show you vulgar: 8
The house I have just described is vulgar, patently, palpably, pluperfectly vulgar. Forced to live in it for more than three hours, certain
figures of refined sensibility — Edith Wharton or Harold Acton or
Wallace Stevens[3] — might have ended as suicides. Yet as I described
that house, I noted two contradictory feelings in myself: how pleasant
it is to point out someone else's vulgarity, and yet the fear that calling
someone else vulgar may itself be slightly vulgar. After all, the family
that lives in this house no doubt loves it; most probably they feel
that they have a real showplace. Their house, I assume, gives them
a large measure of happiness. Yet why does my calling their home
vulgar also give me such a measure of happiness? I suppose it is because vulgarity can be so amusing — other people's vulgarity, that is.

Here I must insert that I have invariably thought that the people   9
who have called me vulgar were themselves rather vulgar. So far as I
know I have been called vulgar three times, once directly, once
behind my back, and once by association. In each instance the charge
was intellectual vulgarity: On one occasion a contributor to a collection of essays on contemporary writing that I once reviewed called
me vulgar because I didn't find anything good to say about this book
of some six hundred pages; once an old friend, an editor with whom
I had had a falling out over politics, told another friend of mine that
an article I had written seemed to him vulgar; and, finally, having
patched things up with this friend and having begun to write for his
magazine again, yet a third friend asked me why I allowed my writing
to appear in that particular magazine, when it was so patently — you
guessed her, Chester — vulgar.

None of these accusations stung in the least. In intellectual and   10
academic life, vulgar is something one calls people with whom one
disagrees. Like having one's ideas called reductionist, it is nothing to
get worked up about — certainly nothing to take personally. What
would wound me, though, is if word got back to me that someone
had said that my manners at table were so vulgar that it sickened
him to eat with me, or that my clothes were laughable, or that taste
in general wasn't exactly my strong point. In a novel whose author
or title I can no longer remember, I recall a female character who
was described as having vulgar thumbs. I am not sure I have a clear

---

[3]Edith Wharton (1862–1937), American novelist, who frequently wrote of well-
to-do society; Harold Acton (born in 1904), British art critic, historian, and student
of Chinese culture, author of *Memoirs of an Aesthete* (1948) and other works; Wallace
Stevens (1879–1955), American poet and insurance company executive, who wrote
with a philosopher's sensibility. — EDS.

picture of vulgar thumbs, but if it is all the same, I would just as soon not have them.

I prefer not to be thought vulgar in any wise. When not long ago   11
a salesman offered to show me a winter coat that, as he put it, "has been very popular," I told him to stow it — if it has been popular, it is not for me. I comb my speech, as best I am able, of popular phrases: You will not hear an unfundamental "basically" or a flying "whatever" from these chaste lips. I do not utter "bottom line"; I do not mutter "trade-off." I am keen to cut myself out from the herd, at least when I can. In recent years this has not been difficult. Distinction has lain in plain speech, plain dress, clean cheeks. The simple has become rococo, the rococo simple. But now I see that television anchormen, hairdressers, and other leaders in our society have adopted this plainer look. This is discomfiting news. Vulgar is, after all, as vulgar does.

Which returns us yet again to the question: What is vulgar? *The*   12
Oxford English Dictionary, which provides more than two pages on the word, is rather better at telling us what vulgar was than what it is. Its definitions run from "1. The common or usual language of a country; the vernacular. *Obs.*" to "13. Having a common and offensively mean character; coarsely commonplace; lacking in refinement or good taste; uncultured, illbred." Historically, the word *vulgar* was used in fairly neutral description up to the last quarter of the seventeenth century to mean and describe the common people. Vulgar was common but not yet contemned. I noted such a neutral usage as late as a William Hazlitt essay of 1818, "On the Ignorance of the Learned," in which Hazlitt writes: "The vulgar are in the right when they judge for themselves; they are wrong when they trust to their blind guides." Yet, according to the *OED*, in 1797 the *Monthly Magazine* remarked: "So the word *vulgar* now implies something base and groveling in actions."

From the early nineteenth century on, then, vulgar has been   13
purely pejorative, a key term in the lexicon of insult and invective. Its currency as a term of abuse rose with the rise of the middle class; its spread was tied to the spread of capitalism and democracy. Until the rise of the middle class, until the spread of capitalism and democracy, people perhaps hadn't the occasion or the need to call one another vulgar. The rise of the middle class, the spread of capitalism and democracy, opened all sorts of social doors; social classes commingled as never before; plutocracy made possible almost daily strides from stratum to stratum. Still, some people had to be placed outside the pale, some doors had to be locked — and the cry of vulgarity, properly intoned, became a most effective Close Sesame.

Such seems to me roughly the social history of the word *vulgar*.   14

But the history of vulgarity, the thing itself even before it had a name, is much longer. According to the French art historian Albert Dasnoy, aesthetic vulgarity taints Greek art of the fourth and third centuries B.C. "An exhibition of Roman portraits," Dasnoy writes, "shows that, between the Etruscan style of the earliest and the Byzantine style of the latest, vulgarity made its first full-blooded appearance in the academic realism of imperial Rome." Vulgarity, in Dasnoy's view, comes of the shock of philosophic rationalism, when humankind divests itself of belief in the sacred. "Vulgarity seems to be the price of man's liberation," he writes, "one might even say, of his evolution. It is unquestionably the price of the freeing of the individual personality." Certainly it is true that one would never think to call a savage vulgar; a respectable level of civilization has to have been reached to qualify for the dubious distinction of being called vulgar.

"You have surely noticed the curious fact," writes Valéry,[4] "that   15
a certain *word,* which is perfectly clear when you hear or use it in *everyday* speech, and which presents no difficulty when caught up in the rapidity of an ordinary sentence, becomes mysteriously cumbersome, offers a strange resistance, defeats all efforts at definition, the moment you withdraw it from circulation for separate study and try to find its meaning after taking away its temporary function." *Vulgar* presents special difficulties, though: While vulgarity has been often enough on display — may even be a part of the human soul that only the fortunate and the saintly are able to root out — every age has its own notion of what constitutes the vulgar. Riding a bicycle at Oxford in the 1890s, Max Beerbohm reports, "was the earmark of vulgarity." Working further backward, we find that Matthew Arnold frequently links the word *vulgar* with the word *hideous* and hopes that culture "saves the future, as one may hope, from being vulgarized, even if it cannot save the present." "In Jane Austen's novels," Lionel Trilling writes, "vulgarity has these elements: smallness of mind, insufficiency of awareness, assertive self-esteem, the wish to devalue, especially to devalue the human worth of other people." Hazlitt found vulgarity in false feeling among "the herd of pretenders to what they do not feel and to what is not natural to them, whether in high or low life."

Vulgarity, it begins to appear, is often in the eye of the beholder.   16
What is more, it comes in so many forms. It is so multiple and so complex — so multiplex. There are vulgarities of taste, of manner, of mind, of spirit. There are whole vulgar ages — the Gilded Age in

[4]Paul Valéry (1871–1945), French poet and literary critic. — EDS.

the United States, for one, at least to hear Mark Twain and Henry Adams tell it. (Is our own age another?) To compound the complication there is even likeable vulgarity. This is vulgarity of the kind that Cyril Connolly must have had in mind when he wrote, "Vulgarity is the garlic in the salad of life." In the realm of winning vulgarity are the novels of Balzac, the paintings of Frans Hals, some of the music of Tchaikovsky (excluding the cannon fire in the 1812 Overture, which is vulgarity of the unwinning kind).

Rightly used, profanity, normally deemed the epitome of vulgar   17
manners, can be charming. I recently moved to a new apartment, and the person I dealt with at the moving company we employed, a woman whose voice had an almost strident matter-of-factness, instructed me to call back with an inventory of our furniture. When I did, our conversation, starting with my inventory of our living room, began:

"One couch."   18
"One couch."   19
"Two lamp tables, a coffee table, a small gateleg table."   20
"Four tables."   21
"Two wing chairs and an occasional chair."   22
"Three chairs."   23
"One box of bric-a-brac."   24
"One box of shit."   25

Heavy garlic of course is not to every taste; but then again some   26
people do not much care for endive. I attended city schools, where garlic was never in short supply and where profanity, in proper hands, could be a useful craft turned up to the power of fine art. I have since met people so well-mannered, so icily, elegantly correct, that with a mere glance across the table or a word to a waiter they could put a chill on the wine and indeed on the entire evening. Some people have more, some less, in the way of polish, but polish doesn't necessarily cover vulgarity. As there can be diamonds in the rough, so can there be sludge in the smooth.

It would be helpful in drawing a definitional bead on the word   27
vulgar if one could determine its antonym. But I am not sure that it has an antonym. Refined? I think not. Sophisticated? Not really. Elegant? Nope. Charming? Close, but I can think of charming vulgarians — M. Rabelais, please come forth and take a bow. Besides, charm is nearly as difficult to define as vulgarity. Perhaps the only safe thing to be said about charm is that if you think you have it, you can be fairly certain that you don't.

If vulgarity cannot be defined by its antonym, from the rear so   28 to say, examples may be more to the point. I once heard a friend describe a woman thus: "Next to Sam Jensen's prose, she's the vulgarest thing in New York." From this description, I had a fairly firm sense of what the woman was like. Sam Jensen is a writer for one of the newsmagazines; each week on schedule he makes a fresh cultural discovery, writing as if every sentence will be his last, every little movie or play he reviews will change our lives — an exhibitionist with not a great deal to exhibit. Sam Jensen is a fictitious name — made up to protect the guilty — but here are a few sentences that he, not I, made up.

> The great Victorian William Morris combined a practical socialism with a love for the spirit of the King Arthur legends. What these films show is the paradox democracy has forgotten — that the dream of Camelot is the ultimate dream of freedom and order in a difficult but necessary balance.

> The screenplay by Michael Wilson and Richard Maibaum is not from an Ian Fleming novel; it's really a cookbook that throws Roger Moore as Bond into these action recipes like a cucumber tossed into an Osterizer. Osterization is becoming more and more necessary for Moore; he's beginning to look a bit puckered, as if he's been bottled in Bond.

From these sentences — with their false paradoxes, muffed metaphors, obvious puns, and general bloat — I think I can extrapolate the woman who, next to this prose, is the vulgarest thing in New York. I see teeth, I see elaborate hairdo, much jewelry, flamboyant dress, a woman requiring a great deal of attention, who sucks up most of the mental oxygen in any room she is in — a woman, in sum, vastly overdone.

Coming at things from a different angle, I imagine myself in   29
session with a psychologist, playing the word association game. "Vulgar," he says, "quick, name ten items you associate with the word *vulgar*." "Okay," I say, "here goes:

1. Publicity
2. The Oscar awards
3. The Aspen Institute for Humanistic Studies
4. Talk shows
5. Pulitzer Prizes
6. Barbara Walters
7. Interviews with writers
8. Lauren Bacall
9. Dialogue as an ideal
10. Psychology."

This would not, I suspect, be everyone's list. Looking it over, I see that, of the ten items, several are linked with one another. But let me inquire into what made me choose the items I did.

Ladies first. Barbara Walters seems to me vulgar because for a 30 great many years now she has been paid to ask all the vulgar questions, and she seems to do it with such cheerfulness, such competence, such amiable insincerity. "What did you think when you first heard your husband had been killed?" she will ask, just the right hush in her voice. "What went on in your mind when you learned that you had cancer, now for the third time?" The questions that people with imagination do not need to ask, the questions that people with good hearts know they have no right to ask, these questions and others Barbara Walters can be depended upon to ask. "Tell me, Holy Father, have you never regretted not having children of your own?"

Lauren Bacall has only recently graduated to vulgarity, or at least 31 she has only in the past few years revealed herself vulgar. Hers is a double vulgarity: the vulgarity of false candor — the woman who, presumably, tells it straight — and the vulgarity provided by someone who has decided to cash in her chips. In her autobiography, Miss Bacall has supposedly told all her secrets; when interviewed on television — by, for example, Barbara Walters — the tack she takes is that of the ringwise babe over whose eyes no one, kiddo, is going to pull the cashmere. Yet turn the channel or page, and there is Miss Bacall in a commercial or advertisement doing her best to pull the cashmere over ours. Vulgar stuff.

Talk shows are vulgar for the same reason that Pulitzer Prizes and 32 the Aspen Institute for Humanistic Studies are vulgar. All three fail to live up to their pretensions, which are extravagant: talk shows to being serious, Pulitzer Prizes to rewarding true merit, the Aspen Institute to promoting "dialogue" (see item 9), "the bridging of cultures," "the interdisciplinary approach," and nearly every other phony shibboleth that has cropped up in American intellectual life over the past three decades.

Publicity is vulgar because those who seek it — and even those 33 who are sought by it — tend almost without exception to be divested of their dignity. You have to sell yourself, the sales manuals used to advise, in order to sell your product. With publicity, though, one is selling only oneself, which is different. Which is a bit vulgar, really.

The Oscar awards ceremony is the single item on my list least in 34 need of explanation, for it seems vulgar prima facie.[5] It is the air of

---

[5](Latin) "On first sight." — EDS.

self-congratulation — of, a step beyond, self-adulation — that is so splendidly vulgar about the Oscar awards ceremony. Self-congratulation, even on good grounds, is best concealed; on no grounds whatever, it is embarrassing. But then, for vulgarity there's no business like show business.

Unless it be literary business. The only thing worse than false 35 modesty is no modesty at all, and no modesty at all is what interviews with writers generally bring out. "That most vulgar of all crowds the literary," wrote Keats presciently — that is, before the incontestable evidence came in with the advent and subsequent popularity of what is by now that staple of the book review and little magazine and talk show, the interview with the great author. What these interviews generally come down to is an invitation to writers to pontificate upon things for which it is either unseemly for them to speak (the quality of their own work) or upon which they are unfit to judge (the state of the cosmos). Roughly a decade ago I watched Isaac Bashevis Singer,[6] when asked on a television talk show what he thought of the Vietnam War, answer, "I am a writer, and that doesn't mean I have to have an opinion on everything. I'd rather discuss literature." Still, how tempting it is, with an interviewer chirping away at your feet, handing you your own horn and your own drum, to blow it and beat it. As someone who has been interviewed a time or two, I can attest that never have I shifted spiritual gears so quickly from self-importance to self-loathing as during and after an interview. What I felt was, well, vulgar.

Psychology seems to me vulgar because it is too often overbearing 36 in its confidence. Instead of saying, "I don't know," it readily says, "unresolved Oedipus complex" or "manic-depressive syndrome" or "identity crisis." As with other intellectual discoveries before (Marxism) and since (structuralism), psychology acts as if it is holding all the theoretical keys, but then in practice reveals that it doesn't even know where the doors are. As an old *Punch* cartoon once put it, "It's worse than wicked, my dear, it's vulgar."

Reviewing my list and attempting to account for the reasons 37 why I have chosen the items on it, I feel I have a firmer sense of what I think vulgar. Exhibitionism, obviousness, pretentiousness, self-congratulation, self-importance, hypocrisy, overconfidence — these seem to me qualities at the heart of vulgarity in our day. It does, though, leave out common sense, a quality which, like clarity, one

[6]Singer (1904–91), Polish-born American writer of fiction in Yiddish and English, received the Nobel Prize for literature in 1978. — EDS.

might have thought one could never have in overabundance. (On the philosophy table in my local bookstore, a book appeared with the title *Clarity Is Not Enough*; I could never pass it without thinking, "Ah, but it's a start.") Yet too great reliance on common sense can narrow the mind, make meager the imagination. Strict common sense abhors mystery, seldom allows for the attraction of tradition, is intolerant of questions that haven't any answers. The problem that common sense presents is knowing the limits of common sense. The too commonsensical man or woman grows angry at anything that falls outside his or her common sense, and this anger seems to me vulgar.

Vulgarity is not necessarily stupid but it is always insensitive. Its [38] insensitivity invariably extends to itself: The vulgar person seldom knows that he is vulgar, as in the old joke about the young woman whose fiancé reports to her that his parents found her vulgar, and who, enraged, responds, "What's this vulgar crap?" Such obvious vulgarity can be comical, like a nouveau riche man bringing opera glasses to a porno film, or the Chicago politician who, while escorting the then ruling British monarch through City Hall, supposedly introduced him to the assembled aldermen by saying, "King, meet the boys." But such things are contretemps merely, not vulgarity of the insidious kind.

In our age vulgarity does not consist in failing to recognize the [39] fish knife or to know the wine list but in the inability to make distinctions. Not long ago I heard a lecture by a Harvard philosophy professor on a Howard Hawks movie, and thought, as one high reference after another was made in connection with this low subject, "Oh, Santayana,[7] 'tis better you are not alive to see this." A vulgar performance, clearly, yet few people in the audience of professors and graduate students seemed to notice.

A great many people did notice, however, when, in an act of [40] singular moral vulgarity, a publisher, an editor, and a novelist recently sponsored a convicted murderer for parole, and the man, not long after being paroled, murdered again. The reason for these men speaking out on behalf of the convict's parole, they said, was his ability as a writer: His work appeared in the editor's journal; he was to have a book published by the publisher's firm; the novelist had encouraged him from the outset. Distinctions — crucial distinctions — were not made: first, that the man was not a very good writer, but a crudely Marxist one, whose work was filled with hatreds and half-truths;

[7]George Santayana (1863–1952) was a Spanish-born American poet and philosopher. — EDS.

second, and more important, that, having killed before, he might kill again — might just be a pathological killer. Not to have made these distinctions is vulgarity at its most vile. But to adopt a distinction new to our day, the publisher, the editor, and the novelist took responsibility for what they had done — responsibility but no real blame.

Can an entire culture grow vulgar? Matthew Arnold feared such   41 might happen in "the mechanical and material civilization" of the England of his day. Vladimir Nabokov felt it already had happened in the Soviet Union, a country, as he described it, "of moral imbeciles, of smiling slaves and poker-faced bullies," without, as in the old days, "a Gogol, a Tolstoy, a Chekhov in quest of that simplicity of truth [who] easily distinguished the vulgar side of things as well as the trashy systems of pseudo-thought." Moral imbeciles, smiling slaves, poker-faced bullies — the curl of a sneer in those Nabokovian phrases is a sharp reminder of the force that the charge of "vulgar" can have as an insult — as well as a reminder of how deep and pervasive vulgarity can become.

But American vulgarity, if I may put it so, is rather more refined.   42 It is also more piecemeal than pervasive, and more insidious. Creeping vulgarity is how I think of it, the way Taft Republicans[8] used to think of creeping socialism. The insertion of a science fiction course in a major university curriculum, a television commercial by a once-serious actor for a cheap wine, an increased interest in gossip and trivia that is placed under the rubric Style in our most important newspapers: So the vulgar creeps along, while everywhere the third- and fourth-rate — in art, in literature, in intellectual life — is considered good enough, or at any rate highly interesting.

Yet being refined — or at least sophisticated — American vul-   43 garity is vulnerable to the charge of being called vulgar. "As long as war is regarded as wicked," said Oscar Wilde, "it will always have its fascination. When it is looked upon as vulgar, it will cease to be popular." There may be something to this, if not for war then at least for designer jeans, French literary criticism, and other fashions. The one thing the vulgar of our day do not like to be called is vulgar. So crook your little finger, purse your lips, distend your nostrils slightly as you lift your nose in the air the better to look down it, and repeat after me: *Vulgar! Vulgar! Vulgar!* The word might save us all.

---

[8]Robert A. Taft (1889–1953), U.S. senator from Ohio from 1939 to 1953, was a leading spokesperson for Republican conservatives. — Eds.

QUESTIONS ON MEANING

1. On what basis does the author conclude that the house with the portico is vulgar and Uncle Jake is not?
2. To what events in history does Epstein attribute the growth of unfavorable CONNOTATIONS around the word *vulgar*?
3. What are the key words in Epstein's definition of *vulgarity*? Which one seems at first glance the most surprising? In which paragraph does the author most succinctly sum up his definition of vulgarity?
4. What points does Epstein make in paragraph 4 and in paragraph 38? Does he contradict himself? Explain.
5. Look up *vulgar* and *vulgarity* in your desk dictionary. In his essay, what liberties has Epstein taken with the dictionary definition? To what extent are these liberties justified? Do they hint at any PURPOSE besides definition?

QUESTIONS ON WRITING STRATEGY

1. What does Epstein's TONE contribute to his essay?
2. What proportion of Epstein's essay is devoted to illustrating what vulgarity is *not*? Of what value is this material to the essay as a whole?
3. What devices does Epstein use to give his long essay COHERENCE?
4. What segments of Epstein's AUDIENCE might be expected to enjoy his essay the most? Whom might it offend?
5. **OTHER METHODS.** Epstein takes pains to describe the appearance and behavior of Uncle Jake (paras. 2–4). What are the functions of this DESCRIPTION?

QUESTIONS ON LANGUAGE

1. Be sure you know what the following words mean as Epstein uses them: trope (para. 1); archetypal, vermilion, sport (2); modicum, pretension (4); edifice (5); portico (6); minuscule (7); patently, palpably, pluperfectly, sensibility (8); reductionist (10); rococo, discomfiting (11); contemned (12); pejorative, lexicon, invective, commingled, plutocracy, stratum (13); aesthetic, rationalism, divests (14); epitome (17); extrapolate (28); shibboleth (32); presciently, incontestable, advent, pontificate (35); theoretical (36); abhors (37); nouveau riche, contretemps, insidious (38); singular, pathological (40); pervasive (41); piecemeal (42).
2. What does the author mean by "operatic bosoms" (para. 2); "in petrified play" (7); "outside the pale" (13); "diamonds in the rough" (26); "drawing a definitional bead" (27)?
3. What ALLUSION do you find in the name "Diamond Chaim Brodsky"

(para. 2)? In the phrases "functionlessness follows formlessness" (6); "Vulgar is . . . as vulgar does" (11); "Close Sesame" (13); and "pull the cashmere" (31)?

4. Where in the essay does Epstein use COLLOQUIAL EXPRESSIONS? Where does his word choice inject humor into the essay?

5. Identify the METAPHORS in paragraph 26. Do they have any function other than as word play? If so, what?

SUGGESTIONS FOR WRITING

1. Write your own definition of some quality other than vulgarity. Possible subjects might be refinement, prudishness, generosity, classiness, sensitivity, dishonesty, or snobbishness. Try to tell what the quality is *not* as well as what it is. Load your essay with examples.

2. In paragraph 29, Epstein lists ten items he associates with the word *vulgar*. The critic and essayist Paul Fussell is another distinguished writer to ponder the subject of vulgarity. In his book *Class* (1983), in a section of imaginary (and very funny) letters from his readers, he answers the request, "To settle a bet, would you indicate some things that are Vulgar?"

> I'd say these are vulgar, but in no particular order: Jerry Lewis's TV telethon; any "Cultural Center"; beef Wellington; cute words for drinks like *drinky-poos* or *nightcaps;* dinner napkins with high polyester content; colored wineglasses; oil paintings depicting members of the family; display of laminated diplomas.

(Old clothes and paper napkins, he adds, aren't vulgar; neither are fireworks on the Fourth of July.) In two paragraphs, write your own definition of *vulgar* (borrowing from Epstein's if you like, as long as you credit him) and provide your own examples along with your reason(s) for including each one.

3. CRITICAL WRITING. In the nineteenth century, Epstein says, recognizing vulgarity helped prevent too-free movement from one social class to a higher one (para. 13). Does defining and spotting vulgarity serve the same purpose today? In an essay, explain why Epstein may feel the need to make distinctions between *vulgar* and *not vulgar*. (Take into account his statement that today vulgarity is "the inability to make distinctions," para. 39.)

4. CONNECTIONS. How do you think Epstein would characterize the off-color humor defended by David Segal in "Excuuuse Me" (p. 634)? Would Epstein find such humor vulgar or not? Why? Spell out your answers in a brief essay using EVIDENCE from both authors.

JOSEPH EPSTEIN ON WRITING

"As a professional writer, I have this in common with the student writer," says Joseph Epstein in a statement written for *The Bedford Reader*. "I cannot sit around and wait for inspiration to arrive."

Like most of what Epstein writes, "What Is Vulgar?" was written to a deadline. He planned for the essay, following a simple, workable system, which he recommends to students assigned to write a long paper. In a file folder, he notes everything he can think of that has any connection with the proposed subject of his essay: quotations, anecdotes, other books and articles on the subject to look into, stray ideas. On index cards and odd scraps of paper, he jots down any items that occur to him as the days pass; everything swells the folder. "Sometimes, while shopping or driving around, I will think up possible opening sentences for my essay. These, too, go into the folder. When I finally do sit down to the writing of my essay, I don't sit down empty-handed — or, perhaps more precisely, empty-minded. I have a store of material before me, which I find a very great aid to composition."

Epstein never uses an outline. "I am not opposed to outlines in logic or on principle but by temperament. I have never felt comfortable with them. I wonder if many serious essayists do use outlines. Aldous Huxley once described the method of the great French essayist Montaigne as 'free association artistically controlled.' I know something similar occurs in my own writing. We all free-associate easily enough; the trick is in the artistic control. But I know I have given up on outlines because I have discovered that there is no way I can know what will be in the second paragraph of something I write until I have written the first paragraph. My first paragraph may contain a phrase or end on a point I hadn't anticipated, and this phrase or point may send me off into an entirely unexpected direction in my second paragraph."

"When I set out to write the essay 'What Is Vulgar?' I had only a vague notion of what would go into it (apart from some of the scraps in that folder). Certainly, I was not yet clear about my thoughts on vulgarity. The chief point of the essay, for me, was to find out what I really did think about it. The essay itself, now that it is done, shows a writer in the act of thinking.

"Which is a roundabout way of saying that, for me, writing is foremost a mode of thinking and, when it works well, an act of discovery. I write to find out what I believe, what seems logical and sensible to me, what notions, ideas, and views I can live with. I don't mean to say that, when I begin an essay, I don't have some general view or feeling about my subject. I mean instead that, when I begin, I am never altogether sure how I am going to end. Robert Frost once said that whenever he knew how one of his poems was going to end, it almost invariably turned out to be a bad poem. I believe him. Writing for discovery, to find out what one truly thinks of things, may be a bit riskier than writing knowing one's conclusion in advance, but it figures to be much more interesting, more surprising, and, once one gets over one's early apprehension at the prospect of winging it, more fun."

FOR DISCUSSION

1. What makes Epstein skeptical of outlines?
2. Do you agree or disagree with Epstein's view of writing as a way of finding out what you believe? Can you think of any situations for which this approach would not work?

ADDITIONAL WRITING TOPICS
Definition

1. Write an essay in which you define an institution, trend, phenomenon, or abstraction as specifically and concretely as possible. Following are some suggestions designed to stimulate ideas. Before you begin, limit your subject.

   Responsibility
   Fun
   Sorrow
   Unethical behavior
   The environment
   Education
   Progress
   Advertising
   Happiness
   Fads
   Feminism
   Marriage
   Sportsmanship
   Leadership
   Leisure
   Originality
   Character
   Imagination
   Democracy
   A smile
   A classic (of music, literature, art, or film)
   Dieting
   Meditation
   Friendship

2. In a brief essay, define one of the following. In each instance, you have a choice of something good or something bad to talk about.

   A good or bad boss
   A good or bad parent
   A good or bad host
   A good or bad TV newscaster
   A good or bad physician
   A good or bad nurse
   A good or bad minister, priest, or rabbi
   A good or bad roommate
   A good or bad driver
   A good or bad disk jockey

3. In a paragraph, define one of the following for someone who has never heard the term: dis, wigged out, dweeb, awesome, fool around, wimp, druggie, snob, freak, loser, loner, freeloader, burnout, soul, quack, "chill," pig-out, gross out, winging it, "bad," "sweet."

10

ARGUMENT AND PERSUASION
Stating Opinions and Proposals

THE METHOD

Practically every day, we try to persuade ourselves, or someone else. We usually attempt such persuasion without being aware that we follow any special method at all. Often, we'll state an OPINION: We'll tell someone our own way of viewing things. We say to a friend, "I'm starting to like Senator Clark. Look at all she's done to help people with disabilities. Look at her voting record on toxic waste." And, having stated these opinions, we might go on to make a PROPOSAL, to recommend that some action to be taken. Addressing our friend, we might suggest, "Hey, Senator Clark is talking on campus at four thirty. Want to come with me and listen to her?"

Sometimes you try to convince yourself that a certain way of interpreting things is right. You even set forth an opinion in writing — as in a letter to a friend who has asked, "Now that you're at New Age College, how do you like the place?" You may write a letter of protest to a landlord who wants to raise your rent, pointing out that the bathroom hot water faucet doesn't work. As a concerned citizen, you may wish to speak your mind in an occasional letter to a newspaper or to your elected representatives.

If you should enter certain professions, you will be expected to persuade people in writing. Before arguing a case in court, a lawyer prepares briefs setting forth all the points in favor of his or her side. Business executives regularly put in writing their ideas for new products and ventures, for improvements in cost control and job efficiency. Researchers write proposals for grants to obtain money to support their work. Scientists write and publish papers to persuade the scientific community that their findings are valid, often stating hypotheses, or tentative opinions.

Even if you never produce a single persuasive work (which is very unlikely), you will certainly encounter such works directed at you. In truth, we live our lives under a steady rain of opinions and proposals. Organizations that work for causes campaign with posters and direct mail, all hoping that we will see things their way. Moreover, we are bombarded with proposals from people who wish us to act. Religious leaders urge us to lead more virtuous lives. Advertisers urge us to rush right out and buy the large economy size.

Small wonder, then, that argument and persuasion — and CRITICAL READING of argument and persuasion — may be among the most useful skills a college student can acquire. Time and again, your instructors will ask you to criticize or to state opinions, either in class or in writing. You may be asked to state your view of anything from the electoral college to animal experimentation. You may be asked to judge the desirability or undesirability of compulsory testing for AIDS, or the revision of existing immigration laws. On an examination in, say, sociology, you may be asked, "Suggest three practical approaches to the most pressing needs of disadvantaged people in urban areas." Critically reading other people's arguments and composing your own, you will find, helps you discover what you think, refine it, and share what you believe.

Is there a difference between argument and persuasion? It is, admittedly, not always clear. Strictly speaking, PERSUASION aims to influence readers' actions, or their support for an action, by engaging their beliefs and feelings, while ARGUMENT aims to win readers' agreement with an assertion or claim by engaging their powers of reasoning. But most effective persuasion or argument contains elements of both methods; hence the confusion. In this book we tend to use the terms interchangeably. And one other point: We tend to talk here about *writing* argument and persuasion, but most of what we say has to do with *reading* them as well. When we discuss your need, as a writer, to support your assertions, we are also discussing your need, as a reader, to question the support other authors provide for their assertions. In reading arguments critically, you apply the critical reading skills we discussed in the book's Introduction — ANALYSIS, INFERENCE, SYNTHESIS, EVALUATION — to a particular kind of writing.

Basic Considerations

Unlike some television advertisers, responsible writers of argument and persuasion do not try to storm people's minds. In writing a paper for a course, you persuade by gentler means: by sharing your view with a reader willing to consider it. You'll want to learn how to express your view clearly and vigorously. But to be fair and persuasive, it is important to understand your reader's view as well.

In stating your opinion, you present the truth as you see it: "The immigration laws discourage employers from hiring nonnative workers," or, "The immigration laws protect legal aliens." To persuade your readers that your view makes sense, you need not begin by proclaiming that, by Heaven, your view is absolutely right and should prevail. Instead, you might begin by trying to state what your reader probably thinks, as best you can infer it. You don't consider views that differ from your own merely to flatter your reader. You do so to correct your own view and make it more accurate. Regarded in this light, argument and persuasion aren't cynical ways to pull other people's strings. Writer and reader become two sensible people trying to find a common ground. This view will relieve you, whenever you have to state your opinions in writing, of the terrible obligation to be 100 percent right at all times.

In an argument, you champion or defend an assertion, a statement of your view or opinion. This assertion is the THESIS of your argument, or your *claim*. It is a statement of what you believe, and, if you are writing a proposal, it is a statement of an action that you recommend on the basis of what you believe. Sometimes, but not always, you make such a statement at the beginning of your essay: "Welfare funds need to be trimmed from our state budget," or, "To cut back welfare funds now would be a mistake." To support your claim you need EVIDENCE — anything that demonstrates what you're trying to say. Evidence may include facts, statistics (or facts expressed in numbers), expert opinions, illustrations and examples, reported experience.

Often, the writer of an effective argument will appeal both to readers' intelligence and to their feelings. In appealing to reason — a RATIONAL APPEAL — the writer relies on conventional methods of reasoning (see the next page) and supplies facts, figures, and other evidence that may be new to readers. In an EMOTIONAL APPEAL, by contrast, the writer may simply restate what readers already know well. Editorials in publications for special audiences (members of ethnic groups and religious denominations, or people whose political views are far to the left or right) tend to contain few factual surprises for their subscribers, who presumably read to have their views reinforced. In spoken discourse, you can hear this kind of emotional appeal in a commencement day speech or a Fourth of July oration. An impressive example of such emotional appeal is included in this chapter: the speech by Martin Luther King, Jr., "I Have a Dream." Dr. King's speech did not tell its audience anything new to them, for the listeners were mostly African Americans disappointed in the American dream. The speaker appeals not primarily to reason, but to feelings — and to the willingness of his listeners to be inspired.

Emotional argument, to be sure, can sometimes be cynical manipulation. It can mean selling a sucker a bill of shoddy goods by appealing to pride, or shame — "Do you really want to deprive your children of what's best for them?" But emotional argument can also stir readers to constructive action by fair means. It recognizes that we are not intellectual robots, but creatures with feelings. Indeed, in any effective argument, a writer had better engage the feelings of readers or they may reply, "True enough, but who cares?" Argument, to succeed in persuading, makes us feel that a writer's views are close to our own.

Yet another resource in argument is ETHICAL APPEAL: impressing your reader that you are a well-informed person of good will, good sense, and good moral character — and, therefore, to be believed. You make such an appeal by reasoning carefully, writing well, and collecting ample evidence. You can also cite or quote respected authorities. If you don't know whether an authority is respected, you can ask a reference librarian for tips on finding out, or talk to an instructor who is a specialist in that field.

In arguing, you don't prove your assertion in the same irrefutable way in which a chemist demonstrates that hydrogen will burn. If you say, "AIDS should be given first priority among health issues," that kind of claim isn't clearly either true or false. Argument takes place in areas that invite more than one opinion. In writing an argument, you help your reader see and understand just one open-eyed, open-minded view of reality.

Reasoning

When we argue rationally, we reason — that is, we make statements that lead to a conclusion. From the time of the ancient Greeks down to our own day, distinctly different methods of proceeding from statements to conclusions have been devised. This section will tell you of a recent, informal method of reasoning and also of two traditional methods. Understanding these methods, knowing how to use them, and being able to recognize when they are misused will make you a better writer *and* reader.

Data, Claim, and Warrant

In recent decades, a simple, practical method of reasoning has been devised by the British philosopher Stephen Toulmin.[1] Helpfully, Toulmin has divided a typical argument into three parts:

1. The DATA: *the evidence to prove something*
2. The CLAIM: *what you are proving with the data*
3. The WARRANT: *the assumption or principle that connects the data to the claim*

Any clear, explicit argument has to have all three parts. Toulmin's own example of such an argument is this:

Harry was born in Bermuda —┬— Harry is a British subject
(*Data*)   (*Claim*)

Since a man born in Bermuda
will be a British subject
(*Warrant*)

Of course, the data for a larger, more controversial claim will be more extensive. Here are some claims that would call for many more data, perhaps thousands of words.

The war on drugs is not winnable.
The United States must help to destroy drug production in South America.
Drug addiction is a personal matter.

The warrant, that middle term, is often crucially important. It is usually an ASSUMPTION or a GENERALIZATION that explains *why* the claim follows from the data. Often a writer won't bother to state a warrant because it is obvious: "In his bid for reelection, Mayor Perkins

---

[1]*The Uses of Argument* (1969) sets forth Toulmin's system in detail. His views are further explained and applied by Douglas Ehninger and Wayne Brockriede in *Decision by Debate* (2nd ed., 1978) and by Toulmin himself, with Richard Rieke and Allan Janik, in *An Introduction to Reasoning* (2nd ed., 1984).

failed miserably. Out of 5,000 votes cast for both candidates, he received only 200." The warrant might be stated, "To make what I would consider a strong showing, he would have had to receive 2,000 votes or more," but it is clear that 200 out of 5,000 is a small minority, and no further explanation seems necessary.

A flaw in many arguments, though, is that the warrant is not clear. A clear warrant is essential. To be persuaded, a reader needs to understand your assumptions and the thinking that follows from them. If you were to argue, "Drug abuse is a serious problem in the United States. Therefore, the United States must help to destroy drug production in Latin America," then your reader might well be left wondering why the second statement follows from the first. But if you were to add, between the statements, "As long as drugs are manufactured in Latin America, they will be smuggled into the United States, and drug abuse will continue," then you supply a warrant. You show why your claim follows from your data — which, of course, you must also supply to make your case.

The unstated warrant can pitch an argument into trouble — whether your own or another writer's. Since warrants are usually assumptions or generalizations, rather than assertions of fact, they are valid only if readers accept or agree that they are valid. With stated warrants, any weaknesses are more likely to show. Suppose someone asserts that a certain woman should not be elected mayor because women cannot form ideas independently of their husbands and this woman's husband has bad ideas on how to run the city. At least the warrant — that women cannot form ideas independently of their husbands — is out there on the table, exposed for all to inspect. But unstated warrants can be just as absurd, or even just doubtful, and pass unnoticed because they are not exposed. Here's the same argument without its warrant: "She shouldn't be elected mayor because her husband has bad ideas on how to run the city."

Here's another argument with an unstated warrant, this one adapted from a magazine advertisement: "Scientists have no proof, just statistical correlations, linking smoking and heart disease, so you needn't worry about the connection." Now, the fact that this ad was placed by a cigarette manufacturer would tip off any reasonably alert reader to beware of bias in the claim. To discover the slant, we need to examine the unstated warrant, which runs something like this: "Since they are not proof, statistical correlations are worthless as guides to behavior." It is true that statistical correlations are not scientific proof, by which we generally mean repeated results obtained under controlled laboratory conditions — the kind of conditions to which human beings cannot ethically be subjected. But statistical correlations *can* establish connections and in fact inform much of our healthful behavior, such as getting physical exercise, avoiding fatty foods, brushing our teeth, and not driving while intoxicated. The advertiser's unstated warrant isn't valid, so neither is the argument.

Let's look at how Toulmin's scheme can work in constructing an argument. In an assignment for her course in English composition, Maire Flynn was asked to produce a condensed argument in three short paragraphs. The first paragraph was to set forth some data; the second, a claim; and the third, a warrant. The result became a kind of outline that the writer could then expand into a whole essay. Here is Flynn's argument.

> DATA
>
> Over the past five years in the state of Illinois, assistance in the form of food stamps has had the effect of increasing the number of people on welfare instead of reducing it. Despite this help, 95 percent of long-term recipients remain below the poverty line today.

> CLAIM
>
> I maintain that the present system of distributing food stamps is a dismal failure, a less effective way to help the needy than other possible ways.

> WARRANT
>
> No one is happy to receive charity. We need to encourage people to quit the welfare rolls; we need to make sure that government aid goes only to the deserving. More effective than giving out food might be to help untrained young people learn job skills; to help single mothers with small children to obtain child care, freeing them for the job market; and to enlarge and improve our state employment counseling and job-placement services. The problem of poverty will be helped only if more people will find jobs and become self-sufficient.

In her warrant paragraph, Flynn spells out her reasons for holding her opinion — the one she states in her claim. "The warrant," she found, "was the hardest part to write," but hers turned out to be clear. Like any good warrant, hers expresses those thoughts that her data set in motion. Another way of looking at the warrant: It is the thinking that led the writer on to the opinion she holds. In this statement of her warrant, Flynn makes clear her assumptions: that people who can support themselves don't deserve food stamps and that a person is better off (and happier) holding a job than receiving charity. By generating more ideas and evidence, she was easily able to expand both the data paragraph and the warrant paragraph, and the result was a coherent essay of 700 words.

How, by the way, would someone who didn't accept Flynn's warrant argue with her? What about old, infirm, or handicapped persons who cannot work? What quite different assumptions about poverty might be possible?

Deductive and Inductive Reasoning

Stephen Toulmin's method of argument is a fairly recent — and very helpful — way to analyze and construct arguments. Two other reliable methods date back to the Greek philosopher Aristotle, who identified the complementary processes of INDUCTIVE REASONING (induction) and DEDUCTIVE REASONING (deduction). In *Zen and the Art of Motorcycle Maintenance*, Robert M. Pirsig gives examples of deductive and inductive reasoning:

> If the cycle goes over a bump and the engine misfires, and then goes over another bump and the engine misfires, and then goes over another bump and the engine misfires, and then goes over a long smooth stretch of road and there is no misfiring, and then goes over a fourth bump and the engine misfires again, one can logically conclude that the misfiring is caused by the bumps. That is induction: reasoning from particular experiences to general truths.
>
> Deductive inferences do the reverse. They start with general knowledge and predict a specific observation. For example if, from reading the hierarchy of facts about the machine, the mechanic knows the horn of the cycle is powered exclusively by electricity from the battery, then he can logically infer that if the battery is dead the horn will not work. That is deduction.

In inductive reasoning, the method of the sciences, we collect bits of evidence on which to base generalizations. From interviews with a hundred self-identified conservative Republicans (the evidence), you might conclude that conservative Republicans favor less government regulation of business (the generalization). The more evidence you have, the more trustworthy your generalization is, but it would never be airtight unless you talked to every conservative Republican in the country. Since such thoroughness is impractical if not impossible, inductive reasoning involves making a so-called inductive leap from the evidence to the conclusion. The smaller the leap — the more evidence you have — the better.

Deductive reasoning works the other way, from a general statement to particular cases. The basis of deduction is the SYLLOGISM, a three-step form of reasoning practiced by Aristotle:

All men are mortal.
Socrates is a man.
Therefore, Socrates is mortal.

The first statement (the major premise) is a generalization about a large group: It is the result of inductive reasoning. The second statement (the minor premise) says something about a particular member of that large group. The third statement (the conclusion) follows inevitably from the premises and applies the generalization to the particular: If the premises are true, then the conclusion must be true. Here is another syllogism:

Major premise: Conservative Republicans favor less government regulation of business.
Minor premise: William F. Buckley, Jr., is a conservative Republican.
Conclusion: Therefore, William F. Buckley, Jr., favors less government regulation of business.

Problems with deductive reasoning start in the premises. In 1633, Scipio Chiaramonti, professor of philosophy at the University of Pisa, came up with this untrustworthy syllogism: "Animals, which move, have limbs and muscles. The earth has no limbs and muscles. Hence, the earth does not move." This is bad deductive reasoning, and its flaw is to assume that all things need limbs and muscles to move — ignoring raindrops, rivers, and many other moving things. In the next few pages, we'll look at some of the things that can go wrong with any kind of reasoning.

Logical Fallacies

In arguments we read and hear, we often meet LOGICAL FALLACIES: errors in reasoning that lead to wrong conclusions. From the time when you start thinking about your proposition or claim and planning your paper, you'll need to watch out for them. To help you recognize logical fallacies when you see them or hear them, and so guard against them when you write, here is a list of the most common.

Non sequitur (from the Latin, "it does not follow"): stating a conclusion that doesn't follow from the first premise or premises. "I've lived in this town a long time — why, my grandfather was the first mayor — so I'm against putting fluoride in the drinking water."

Oversimplification: supplying neat and easy explanations for large and complicated phenomena. "No wonder drug abuse is out of control. Look at how the courts have hobbled police officers." Oversimplified solutions are also popular: "All these teenage kids that get in trouble with the law — why, they ought to ship 'em over to China. That would straighten 'em out!"

Hasty generalization: leaping to a generalization from inadequate or faulty evidence. The most familiar hasty generalization is the stereotype: "Men aren't sensitive enough to be day-care providers." "Women are too emotional to fight in combat."

Either/or reasoning: assuming that a reality may be divided into only two parts or extremes; assuming that a given problem has only one of two possible solutions. "What's to be done about the trade imbalance with Japan? Either we ban all Japanese imports, or American industry will collapse." Obviously, either/or reasoning is a kind of extreme oversimplification.

Argument from doubtful or unidentified authority: "Certainly we ought to castrate all sex offenders; Uncle Oswald says we should." Or: "According to reliable sources, my opponent is lying."

Argument ad hominem (from the Latin, "to the man"): attacking a person's views by attacking his or her character. "Mayor Burns is divorced and estranged from his family. How can we listen to his pleas for a city nursing home?"

Begging the question: taking for granted from the start what you set out to demonstrate. When you reason in a *logical* way, you state that because something is true, then, as a result, some other truth follows. When you beg the question, however, you repeat that what is true is true. If you argue, for instance, that dogs are a menace to people because they are dangerous, you don't prove a thing, since the idea that dogs are dangerous is already assumed in the statement that they are a menace. Beggars of questions often just repeat what they already believe, only in different words. This fallacy sometimes takes the form of arguing in a circle, or demonstrating a premise by a conclusion and a conclusion by a premise: "I am in college because that is the right thing to do. Going to college is the right thing to do because it is expected of me."

Post hoc, ergo propter hoc (from the Latin, "after this, therefore because of this"): assuming that because B follows A, B was caused by A. "Ever since the city suspended height restrictions on skyscrapers, the city budget has been balanced." (See also pp. 366–67.)

False analogy: the claim of persuasive likeness when no significant likeness exists. An ANALOGY asserts that because two things are comparable in some respects, they are comparable in other respects as well. Analogies cannot serve as evidence in a rational argument because the differences always outweigh the similarities; but analogies can reinforce such arguments *if* the subjects are indeed similar in some ways. If they aren't, the analogy is false. Many observers see the "war on drugs" as a false and damaging analogy because warfare aims for clear victory over a specific, organized enemy, whereas the complete eradication of illegal drugs is probably unrealistic and, in any event, the "enemy" isn't well defined: the drugs themselves? users? sellers? producers? the producing nations? (These critics urge approaching drugs as a social problem to be skillfully managed and reduced.)

THE PROCESS

In stating an opinion, you set forth and support a claim — a truth you believe. You may find such a truth by thinking and feeling, by talking to your instructors or fellow students, by scanning a newspaper or reading books and magazines, by listening to a discussion of some problem or controversy.

In stating a proposal, you already have an opinion in mind, and from there, you go on to urge an action or a solution to a problem. Usually, these two statements will take place within the same piece of writing: A writer will first set forth a view ("Compact disks are grossly overpriced") and then go right on to a proposal ("Compact disks should be discounted in the college store").

Whether your essay states an opinion, a proposal, or both, it is likely to contain similar ingredients. State clearly, if possible at the start of your essay, your thesis — the proposition or claim you are going to defend. If you like, you can explain why you think it worth upholding, showing, perhaps, that it concerns your readers. If you plan to include both an opinion and a proposal in your essay, you may wish to set forth your opinion first, saving your proposal for later, perhaps for your conclusion.

Your thesis stated, introduce your least important point first. Then build in a crescendo to the strongest point you have. This structure will lend emphasis to your essay, and perhaps make your chain of ideas more persuasive as the reader continues to follow it.

For every point, give evidence: facts, figures, examples, expert opinions. If you introduce statistics, make sure that they are up to date and fairly represented. In an essay advocating a law against smoking, it would be unfair to declare that "in Pottsville, Illinois,

last year, 50 percent of all deaths were caused by lung cancer," if only
two people died in Pottsville last year — one of them struck by a car.

If you are arguing fairly, you should be able to face potential
criticisms fairly, and give your critics due credit, by recognizing the
objections you expect your assertion will meet. This is the strategy
H. L. Mencken uses in "The Penalty of Death," and he introduces
it in his essay right at the beginning. (You might also tackle the
opposition at the end of your essay or at relevant points throughout.)
Notice that Mencken takes pains to dispense with his opponents: He
doesn't just dismiss them; he reasons with them.

In your conclusion, briefly restate your claim, if possible in a
fresh, pointed way. (For example, see the concluding sentence in the
essay by William F. Buckley in this chapter.) In emotionally persuasive writing, you may want to end with a strong appeal. (See "I Have
a Dream" by Martin Luther King, Jr.)

Finally, don't forget the power of humor in argument. You don't
have to crack gratuitous jokes, but there is often an advantage in
having a reader or listener who laughs on your side. When Abraham
Lincoln debated Stephen Douglas, he triumphed in his reply to Douglas's snide remark that Lincoln had once been a bartender. "I have
long since quit my side of the bar," Lincoln declared, "while Mr.
Douglas clings to his as tenaciously as ever."

In arguing — doing everything you can to bring your reader
around to your view — you can draw on any method of writing
discussed in this book. Arguing for or against welfare funding, you
might give EXAMPLES of wasteful spending, or of neighborhoods where
welfare funds are needed. You might analyze the CAUSES of social
problems that call for welfare funds, or foresee the likely EFFECTS of
cutting welfare programs, or of keeping them. You might COMPARE
AND CONTRAST the idea of slashing welfare funds with the idea of
increasing them. You could use NARRATION to tell a pointed story;
you could use DESCRIPTION to portray certain welfare recipients and
their neighborhoods. If you wanted to, you could employ several of
these methods in writing a single argument.

You will rarely find, when you begin to write a persuasive paper,
that you have too much evidence to support your claim. But unless
you're writing a term paper and have months to spend on it, you're
limited in how much evidence you can gather. Begin by stating your
claim. Make it narrow enough to support in the time you have
available. For a paper due a week from now, the opinion that "our
city's downtown area has a serious litter problem" can probably be
backed up in part by your own eyewitness reports. But to support the

claim "Litter is one of the worst environmental problems of North American cities," you would surely need to spend time in a library.

In rewriting, you may find yourself tempted to keep all the evidence you have collected with such effort. Of course, some of it may not support your claim; some may seem likely to persuade the reader only to go to sleep. If so, throw it out. A stronger argument will remain.

ARGUMENT AND PERSUASION IN A PARAGRAPH: FOUR ILLUSTRATIONS

Stating an Opinion About Television

Television news has a serious failing: It's show business. Unlike a newspaper, its every image has to entertain the average beer drinker. To score high ratings and win advertisers, the visual medium favors the spectacular: riots, tornados, air crashes. Now that satellite transmission invites live coverage, newscasters go for the fast-breaking story at the expense of thoughtful analysis. "The more you can get data out instantly," says media critic Jeff Greenfield, "the more you rely on instant data to define the news." TV zooms in on people who make news, but, to avoid boredom, won't let them argue or explain. (How can they, in speeches limited to fifteen seconds?) On NBC late news for September 12, 1987, President Reagan blasted a plan to end war in Nicaragua. His address was clipped to sixty seconds, then an anchorwoman digested the opposition in one quick line: "Democrats tonight were critical of the president's remarks." During the 1992 presidential election, all three candidates sometimes deliberately packaged bad news so that it could not be distilled to a sound bite on the evening news — and thus would not make the evening news at all. Americans who rely on television for their news (two-thirds, according to recent polls) exist on a starvation diet.

COMMENT. The writer states an opinion in the opening line, elaborates on it, and then backs it up with evidence: two examples, and a quotation from Jeff Greenfield, a professional critic of the media (and an author represented elsewhere in this book; see p. 199). The bit about President Reagan's condensed address came from the direct experiences of watching TV newscasts. The example of the 1992 election came from newspaper reports. In the last sentence, the writer restates the opening opinion in a fresh way. The next step is to propose a cure.

Stating a Proposal About Television

To make television news more responsible to people who depend on it for full and accurate information, I propose that commercials be banned from televised news programs. This ban would have the effect of freeing newscasters from the obligation to score high ratings. Since 1963, when NBC and CBS began the first thirty-minute evening newscasts, television news has dwindled in integrity. Back then, according to television historian Daniel C. Hallin, the news was designed to earn prestige for the networks, not money. Today the priorities have been reversed. We need a return to the original situation. Eliminating commercials would hurt revenues, it is true, but stations could make up their losses from selling spots on prime-time shows clearly labeled "entertainment." No longer forced to highlight fires, storms, and other violent scenes, no longer tempted to use live coverage (even though the story covered may be trivial), news teams would no longer strive to race with their rivals to break a story. At last there would be time for more analysis, for the thoughtful follow-up story. Television news would become less entertaining, no doubt, and fewer people would watch it. The reader might object that, as a result, the mass of American viewers would be even less well informed. But sheer entertainment that passes for news is, I believe, more insidious than no news at all.

COMMENT. Continuing the argument about television news (begun in the paragraph stating an opinion), the writer makes a radical proposal for greatly improving television news. We get less evidence than in the opinion paragraph, but then, less evidence is available. We do, however, hear from a television historian, and the next sentence ("Today the priorities have been reversed") contrasts present and past. Showing an awareness of skeptical readers, the writer addresses two possible objections to the proposal: (1) stations would suffer losses; and (2) people would be less well informed. (Some readers might object that the writer overlooks, or chooses not to acknowledge, the First Amendment issues in banning ads from TV news. Other readers might defend the omission on the grounds that the writer's proposal just means to get the discussion going.)

Stating an Opinion in an Academic Discipline

We need wilderness, I believe, as an environment of humility. Civilization breeds arrogance. A modern human, armed with checkbook, television, and four-wheel drive, feels like a demigod. It is good to be reminded in wilderness of our true status as member — not master — of the natural world. It is good to rekindle the sense of restraint and limits that has been obscured by technological optimism. It is good to see natural powers and processes greater than our own. The lessons of such experiences are precisely what are needed if human-environment relations are to be harmonious and stable in the long run. Wilderness, then, is a profound educational resource, schooling overcivilized humans in what we once knew but unfortunately forgot.

COMMENT. *Living in the Environment,* by G. Tyler Miller, Jr., is an unusual textbook because many of its chapters contain guest editorials written by respected experts. This paragraph by Roderick Nash, a professor of history and environmental studies at the University of California, Santa Barbara, is taken from one of the editorials. Nash has stated his opinion that wilderness areas are vitally important to all Americans for several reasons. One of those reasons is detailed in the paragraph cited here. Notice how briefly, concretely ("armed with checkbook, television, and four-wheel drive"), and effectively Nash sets it forth. He makes a convincing case for the usefulness of an "environment of humility."

Stating a Proposal in an Academic Discipline

Individual acts of consumption, litter, and so on have contributed to the mess [in our environment]. When you are tempted to say this little bit won't hurt, multiply it by millions of others saying the same thing. Picking up a single beer can, not turning on a light, using a car pool, writing on both sides of a piece of paper, and not buying a grocery product with more packages inside the outer package are all very significant acts. Each small act reminds us of ecological thinking and leads to other ecologically sound practices. Start now with a small concrete personal act and then expand your actions in ever widening circles. Little acts can be used to expand our awareness of the need for fundamental changes in our political, economic, and social systems over the next few decades. These acts also help us to avoid psychological numbness when we realize the magnitude of the job to be done.

COMMENT. Also from *Living in the Environment,* here is a paragraph in which the author of the book, G. Tyler Miller, Jr., makes a proposal. This paragraph in fact is labeled number seven in a whole list of proposals under the title "What Can You Do?" The list is designed to convey a sense that the world's environmental problems are not so overwhelming that individual efforts can't contribute to solving them. "You can do little things" is this paragraph's claim. Notice that almost every sentence gives concrete suggestions for dealing in a small but meaningful way with problems of great magnitude. The paragraph ends effectively, with the author supplying compelling reasons for taking his advice.

H. L. MENCKEN

HENRY LOUIS MENCKEN (1880–1956) was a native of Baltimore, where for four decades he worked as newspaper reporter, editor, and columnist. In the 1920s, his boisterous, cynical observations on American life, appearing regularly in *The Smart Set* and later in *The American Mercury* (which he founded and edited), made him probably the most widely quoted writer in the country. As an editor and literary critic, Mencken championed Sinclair Lewis, Theodore Dreiser, and other realistic writers. As a social critic, he leveled blasts at pomp, hypocrisy, and the middle classes (whom he labeled "the booboisie"). (The publication of *The Diary of H. L. Mencken* in 1989 revealed its author's outspoken opinions and touched off a controversy: Was Mencken a bigot? The debate goes on.) In 1933, when Mencken's attempts to laugh off the Depression began to ring hollow, his magazine died. He then devoted himself to revising and supplementing *The American Language* (4th ed., 1948), a learned and highly entertaining survey of a nation's speech habits and vocabulary. Two dozen of Mencken's books are now in print, including *A Mencken Chrestomathy* (1949), a representative selection of his best writings of various kinds; and *A Choice of Days* (1980), a selection from his memoirs.

The Penalty of Death

Above all, Mencken was a humorist whose thought had a serious core. He argues by first making the reader's jaw drop, then inducing a laugh, and finally causing the reader to ponder, "Hmmmm — what if he's right?" The following still-controversial essay, from *Prejudices, Fifth Series* (1926), shows Mencken the persuader in top form. Alan M. Dershowitz, another renowned advocate, takes a different approach to capital punishment in the essay following Mencken's.

Of the arguments against capital punishment that issue from   1
uplifters, two are commonly heard most often, to wit:

1. That hanging a man (or frying him or gassing him) is a dreadful
   business, degrading to those who have to do it and revolting to
   those who have to witness it.

2. That it is useless, for it does not deter others from the same crime.

The first of these arguments, it seems to me, is plainly too weak   2
to need serious refutation. All it says, in brief, is that the work of
the hangman is unpleasant. Granted. But suppose it is? It may be
quite necessary to society for all that. There are, indeed, many other
jobs that are unpleasant, and yet no one thinks of abolishing them —
that of the plumber, that of the soldier, that of the garbageman, that
of the priest hearing confessions, that of the sandhog, and so on.
Moreover, what evidence is there that any actual hangman complains
of his work? I have heard none. On the contrary, I have known many
who delighted in their ancient art, and practiced it proudly.

In the second argument of the abolitionists there is rather more   3
force, but even here, I believe, the ground under them is shaky. Their
fundamental error consists in assuming that the whole aim of punishing criminals is to deter other (potential) criminals — that we hang
or electrocute A simply in order to so alarm B that he will not kill
C. This, I believe, is an assumption which confuses a part with the
whole. Deterrence, obviously, is *one* of the aims of punishment, but
it is surely not the only one. On the contrary, there are at least a
half dozen, and some are probably quite as important. At least one
of them, practically considered, is *more* important. Commonly, it is
described as revenge, but revenge is really not the word for it. I
borrow a better term from the late Aristotle: *katharsis. Katharsis,* so
used, means a salubrious discharge of emotions, a healthy letting off
of steam. A schoolboy, disliking his teacher, deposits a tack upon the
pedagogical chair; the teacher jumps and the boy laughs. This is
katharsis. What I contend is that one of the prime objects of all
judicial punishments is to afford the same grateful relief (*a*) to the
immediate victims of the criminal punished, and (*b*) to the general
body of moral and timorous men.

These persons, and particularly the first group, are concerned   4
only indirectly with deterring other criminals. The thing they crave
primarily is the satisfaction of seeing the criminal actually before
them suffer as he made them suffer. What they want is the peace of
mind that goes with the feeling that accounts are squared. Until they
get that satisfaction they are in a state of emotional tension, and

hence unhappy. The instant they get it they are comfortable. I do not argue that this yearning is noble; I simply argue that it is almost universal among human beings. In the face of injuries that are unimportant and can be borne without damage it may yield to higher impulses; that is to say, it may yield to what is called Christian charity. But when the injury is serious Christianity is adjourned, and even saints reach for their sidearms. It is plainly asking too much of human nature to expect it to conquer so natural an impulse. A keeps a store and has a bookkeeper, B. B steals $700, employs it in playing at dice or bingo, and is cleaned out. What is A to do? Let B go? If he does so he will be unable to sleep at night. The sense of injury, of injustice, of frustration will haunt him like pruritus. So he turns B over to the police, and they hustle B to prison. Thereafter A can sleep. More, he has pleasant dreams. He pictures B chained to the wall of a dungeon a hundred feet underground, devoured by rats and scorpions. It is so agreeable that it makes him forget his $700. He has got his *katharsis*.

The same thing precisely takes place on a larger scale when there		5
is a crime which destroys a whole community's sense of security. Every law-abiding citizen feels menaced and frustrated until the criminals have been struck down — until the communal capacity to get even with them, and more than even, has been dramatically demonstrated. Here, manifestly, the business of deterring others is no more than an afterthought. The main thing is to destroy the concrete scoundrels whose act has alarmed everyone, and thus made everyone unhappy. Until they are brought to book that unhappiness continues; when the law has been executed upon them there is a sigh of relief. In other words, there is *katharsis*.

I know of no public demand for the death penalty for ordinary		6
crimes, even for ordinary homicides. Its infliction would shock all men of normal decency of feeling. But for crimes involving the deliberate and inexcusable taking of human life, by men openly defiant of all civilized order — for such crimes it seems, to nine men out of ten, a just and proper punishment. Any lesser penalty leaves them feeling that the criminal has got the better of society — that he is free to add insult to injury by laughing. That feeling can be dissipated only by a recourse to *katharsis*, the invention of the aforesaid Aristotle. It is more effectively and economically achieved, as human nature now is, by wafting the criminal to realms of bliss.

The real objection to capital punishment doesn't lie against the		7
actual extermination of the condemned, but against our brutal American habit of putting it off so long. After all, every one of us must die soon or late, and a murderer, it must be assumed, is one who

makes that sad fact the cornerstone of his metaphysic. But it is one thing to die, and quite another thing to lie for long months and even years under the shadow of death. No sane man would choose such a finish. All of us, despite the Prayer Book, long for a swift and unexpected end. Unhappily, a murderer, under the irrational American system, is tortured for what, to him, must seem a whole series of eternities. For months on end he sits in prison while his lawyers carry on their idiotic buffoonery with writs, injunctions, mandamuses, and appeals. In order to get his money (or that of his friends) they have to feed him with hope. Now and then, by the imbecility of a judge or some trick of juridic science, they actually justify it. But let us say that, his money all gone, they finally throw up their hands. Their client is now ready for the rope or the chair. But he must still wait for months before it fetches him.

That wait, I believe, is horribly cruel. I have seen more than one   8
man sitting in the death-house, and I don't want to see any more. Worse, it is wholly useless. Why should he wait at all? Why not hang him the day after the last court dissipates his last hope? Why torture him as not even cannibals would torture their victims? The common answer is that he must have time to make his peace with God. But how long does that take? It may be accomplished, I believe, in two hours quite as comfortably as in two years. There are, indeed, no temporal limitations upon God. He could forgive a whole herd of murderers in a millionth of a second. More, it has been done.

QUESTIONS ON MEANING

1. Identify Mencken's main reasons for his support of capital punishment. What is his THESIS?
2. In paragraph 3, Mencken asserts that there are at least half a dozen reasons for punishing offenders. In his essay, he mentions two, deterrence and revenge. What others can you supply?
3. For which class of offenders does Mencken advocate the death penalty?
4. What is Mencken's "real objection" to capital punishment?

QUESTIONS ON WRITING STRATEGY

1. How would you characterize Mencken's humor? Point to examples of it. In the light of the grim subject, do you find the humor funny?
2. In his first paragraph, Mencken pares his subject down to manageable size. What techniques does he employ for this purpose?

3. At the start of paragraph 7, Mencken shifts his stance from concern for the victims of crime to concern for prisoners awaiting execution. Does the shift help or weaken the effectiveness of his earlier justification for capital punishment?

4. Do you think the author expects his AUDIENCE to agree with him? At what points does he seem to recognize the fact that some readers may see things differently?

5. In paragraphs 2 and 3, Mencken uses ANALOGIES in an apparent attempt to strengthen his argument. What are the analogies? Do they seem false to you? (See pp. 470–71 for a discussion of false analogy.) Do you think Mencken would agree with your judgment?

6. OTHER METHODS. To explain what he sees as the most important aim of capital punishment, Mencken uses DEFINITION. What does he define, and what techniques does he use to make the definition clear?

QUESTIONS ON LANGUAGE

1. Mencken opens his argument by referring to those who reject capital punishment as "uplifters." What CONNOTATIONS does this word have for you? Does the use of this "loaded" word strengthen or weaken Mencken's position? Explain.

2. Be sure you know the meanings of the following words: refutation, sandhog (para. 2); salubrious, pedagogical, timorous (3); pruritus (4); wafting (6); mandamuses, juridic (7).

3. What emotional overtones can you detect in Mencken's reference to the hangman's job as an "ancient art" (para. 2)?

4. Writing at a time when there was no debate over the usage, Mencken often uses "man" and "he" for examples that could be either a man or a woman (such as A in para. 4) and uses "men" to mean people in general ("all men of normal decency of feeling," para. 6). Does this usage date the essay or otherwise weaken it? Why?

SUGGESTIONS FOR WRITING

1. Write a paper in which you state an opinion about one current method of apprehending, trying, or sentencing criminals. Supply EVIDENCE to persuade readers to accept your idea.

2. In a brief essay, argue for or against humor as a technique of argument or persuasion. Use examples from Mencken's essay as EVIDENCE.

3. CRITICAL WRITING. Write an essay refuting Mencken's argument; or take Mencken's side but supply any additional reasons you can think of. In either case, begin your argument with an ANALYSIS of Mencken's argument, and use examples (real or hypothetical) to support your view.

4. CONNECTIONS. In "Don't Pull the Plug on Televised Executions" (p. 484), Alan M. Dershowitz argues that the media have a First Amendment right to televise death-penalty executions, no matter what their possible effects on viewers. Writing in the 1920s, Men-

cken, of course, did not consider televised executions in weighing the cathartic effect of capital punishment. Do you think he would have supported or rejected them? Why?

H. L. MENCKEN ON WRITING

"All my work hangs together," wrote H. L. Mencken in a piece called "Addendum on Aims," "once the main ideas under it are discerned. Those ideas are chiefly of a skeptical character. I believe that nothing is unconditionally true, and hence I am opposed to every statement of positive truth and to every man who states it. Such men seem to me to be either idiots or scoundrels. To one category or the other belong all theologians, professors, editorial writers, right-thinkers, etc. . . . Whether [my work] appears to be burlesque, or serious criticism, or mere casual controversy, it is always directed against one thing: unwarranted pretension."

Mencken cheerfully acknowledged his debts to his teachers: chiefly writers he read as a young man and newspaper editors he worked under. "My style of writing is chiefly grounded upon an early enthusiasm for Huxley,[1] the greatest of all masters of orderly exposition. He taught me the importance of giving to every argument a simple structure. As for the fancy work on the surface, it comes chiefly from an anonymous editorial writer in the *New York Sun*, circa 1900. He taught me the value of apt phrases. My vocabulary is pretty large; it probably runs to 25,000 words. It represents much labor. I am constantly expanding it. I believe that a good phrase is better than a Great Truth — which is usually buncombe. I delight in argument, not because I want to convince, but because argument itself is an end."

In another essay, "The Fringes of Lovely Letters," Mencken wrote that "what is in the head infallibly oozes out of the nub of the pen. If it is sparkling Burgundy the writing is full of life and charm. If it is mush the writing is mush too." He recalls the example of President Warren G. Harding, who once sent a message to Congress that was quite incomprehensible. "Why? Simply because Dr. Harding's thoughts, on the high and grave subjects he discussed, were so muddled that he couldn't understand them himself. But on matters within

---

[1]Thomas Henry Huxley (1825–95), English biologist and educator, who wrote many essays popularizing science. In Victorian England, Huxley was the leading exponent and defender of Charles Darwin's theory of evolution. — EDS.

his range of customary meditation he was clear and even charming, as all of us are. . . . Style cannot go beyond the ideas which lie at the heart of it. If they are clear, it too will be clear. If they are held passionately, it will be eloquent."

FOR DISCUSSION

1. According to Mencken, what PURPOSE animates his writing?
2. What relationship does Mencken see between a writer's thought and his or her STYLE?
3. Where in his views on writing does Mencken use FIGURES OF SPEECH to advantage?

ALAN M. DERSHOWITZ

ALAN M. DERSHOWITZ has built his public reputation defending notorious clients, from pornographic film star Harry Reems to junk bond king Michael Milken to hotel queen Leona Helmsley. His legal reputation rests on his unwavering, often strident, often unpaid support for civil liberties. Born in 1938 in Brooklyn, New York, Dershowitz received a B.A. from Brooklyn College in 1959 and an LL.B. from Yale University in 1962. He joined the faculty of Harvard University Law School in 1964. He is now Felix Frankfurter Professor of Law at that institution. Dershowitz has written law textbooks and several books for the general public, including *The Best Defense* (1982), *Chutzpah* (1991), and *Contrary to Popular Opinion* (1992). *Reversal of Fortune* (1986), about successfully defending Claus Von Bülow against charges that he tried to murder his wealthy wife, was made into a popular movie.

Don't Pull the Plug on Televised Executions

Dershowitz is an adamant defender of the Constitution's First Amendment, which establishes freedom of religion, speech, the press, peaceable assembly, and petition. In this essay from *Contrary to Popular Opinion*, written in May 1991, Dershowitz is guided by the First Amendment in determining whether executions should be televised. Contrast this look at capital punishment with that of H. L. Mencken in the previous essay (p. 477).

So now they want to televise executions. "Snuff films" — movies 1 of actual killings, long rumored to be part of the underground "pornography" industry — may soon become mainstream, as a California public television station demands that its cameras be allowed to transmit the proceeding from the gas chamber. Videotapes of executions, from lethal injections to electrocutions to firing squads to hangings, will become available for rental at the corner video shop. Certain favorites may become cult classics.

Already the political lines are being drawn. Some victims' rights 2 advocates argue against televising executions on the grounds that it will engender sympathy for the condemned. Instead of televising the agony of the criminal, they insist, the agony of the victim should be shown in living color — the wounds, the suffering, the humiliation.

Some defendants' rights advocates would be willing to permit   3
televised executions, but only if the condemned person consented —
as some have already done — to their last moments being telecast to
millions of viewers. Opponents of the death penalty are split, depending on whether they believe that televised execution will be so
traumatic as to generate revulsion, or so crowd-pleasing as to create
new fans for a lethal public spectacle. If the long history of public
executions is any guide to present attitudes, opponents of the death
penalty should not be encouraged to believe that the public will be
repelled by the spectacle of a condemned man being shown suffocating
to death during a televised execution.

First Amendment activists, many of whom are opposed to the   4
death penalty, are also torn, especially those who believe that public
executions will increase the demand for more extensive use of the
death penalty. First Amendment opponents of televised executions
point out that, under our First Amendment, there is a difference
between the government denying the media *access* to an event —
such as an execution, a cabinet meeting, or a military encounter —
and directly *prohibiting* the media from publishing material they have
obtained on their own. (The Pentagon Papers case is a useful example
of that distinction: The press had no right to secure copies of those
classified documents, but once the *New York Times* obtained copies
on its own, the government could not prevent its publication.[1])

But an execution is a quintessential public event in the sense   5
that it involves the controversial use of ultimate governmental force
to achieve a deterrent goal. Moreover, the media are generally allowed
to cover and report on executions, subject, of course, to security
considerations. Although the California legal authorities have raised
the claim that television cameras may compromise security, that is
obviously a makeweight, since it would be a simple matter to arrange
a secure way for a single pool camera to transmit the execution.

Nor is there any real concern that the information itself would   6
pose security problems, as would the precise location of a military
battle. Thus, the argument that justifies controlling the access of the
media to military encounters, cabinet meetings, or classified information doesn't really work when it comes to televising executions.
First Amendment supporters, regardless of their beliefs on capital

---

[1]The Pentagon Papers were secret government documents analyzing U.S. involvement in Southeast Asia. They were leaked to the *New York Times* in June
1971. That same month the Supreme Court allowed their publication on First
Amendment grounds. — EDS.

punishment and the likely impact of televised executions on the future of the death penalty, should favor the right of the media to televise executions and the right of adult citizens to view these spectacles if they choose to. Obviously, discretion would dictate that the telecast be at night when children are unlikely to be watching, and that advance warnings be provided so that only willing adult viewers are exposed.

No First Amendment advocate should be influenced by what he or she believes will be the *effect* of televising executions on the controversial policy and constitutional debates over the death penalty. It is the essence of the First Amendment that decisions about freedom of speech must be content-neutral and must not depend on whether the likely impact of the speech on the open marketplace of ideas is favorable or unfavorable to one's politics. Thus, although I personally suspect that televising executions may well generate a demand for more executions and although I oppose the death penalty, I favor the right of the California public television station to televise executions. 7

If executions are televised, I, for one, will exercise my First Amendment right to turn the channel and watch something else. I might also try to persuade the television station not to exercise its right to televise executions, once that right was recognized by the state. But I would not stand between willing telecasters and willing viewers, even if I disapproved of the reason why the viewers were tuning in, or were afraid of the likely impact of their viewing on the debate over capital punishment. 8

That is what freedom of speech is all about: the right of those with whom you disagree to mount the most effective argument — rational, symbolic, or visual — against your position. My fellow opponents of the death penalty are just going to have to come up with more powerful arguments, if we are to prevail in the highly competitive marketplace of ideas and images. 9

QUESTIONS ON MEANING

1. Why do victims' rights advocates oppose televised executions?
2. In Dershowitz's opinion, would televised executions help or hinder those who oppose the death penalty? Why?
3. What is Dershowitz's THESIS?
4. What is this essay's PURPOSE?

QUESTIONS ON WRITING STRATEGY

1. What, in Toulmin's scheme (pp. 465–68), are Dershowitz's CLAIM, DATA, and WARRANT?
2. What opposing arguments does Dershowitz introduce? How does he deal with them?
3. How would you characterize Dershowitz's TONE? What is his ethical appeal?
4. **OTHER METHODS.** How does Dershowitz use CAUSE AND EFFECT to develop his argument for televised executions? Is he more concerned with causes or effects?

QUESTIONS ON LANGUAGE

1. Who are the "they" who "want to televise executions" (para. 1)? What is this pronoun's EFFECT?
2. Look up the meanings if any of these words are unfamiliar: engender (para. 2); revulsion (3); quintessential, deterrent, makeweight (5); discretion (6).
3. Describe Dershowitz's DICTION in this essay. Is it what you would expect from a law professor? What effect does it have?
4. What are the CONNOTATIONS of words and phrases like "cult classics" (para. 1), "crowd-pleasing," and "fans" (3)? What does Dershowitz accomplish with such words?

SUGGESTIONS FOR WRITING

1. What is your opinion of televised executions? Write an essay making an argument for or against them. Like Dershowitz, you may want to focus on whether they are constitutional, or you may want to imagine the effects of televised executions.
2. Argue for or against televising anything else that interests you — accident victims, say, or hockey fights, or sex or violence in fictional programming. Make your case clear. Support your argument with detailed ANALYSES or other EVIDENCE. Consider opposing arguments.
3. **CRITICAL WRITING.** Look closely at Dershowitz's predictions about what televised executions might lead to (paras. 1, 3, and 7). What ASSUMPTIONS about our society, and human nature in general, can you INFER from these paragraphs? Do you share these assumptions? Why or why not? Do they weaken or strengthen the essay in your eyes?
4. **CONNECTIONS.** As both an advocate of the Constitution and an opponent of capital punishment, Dershowitz would probably cite the Constitution's Eighth Amendment, which prohibits infliction of "cruel and unusual punishments" on convicted persons, as an argument against capital punishment. Imagine a debate between Dershowitz and H. L. Mencken on this issue (see Mencken's "The Penalty of Death," p. 477).

Write this debate into an essay, giving each side fair, objective treatment.

ALAN M. DERSHOWITZ ON WRITING

In 1991 Alan Dershowitz addressed the American Society of Newspaper Editors. "We have an obligation," he said, "to defend the First Amendment. . . . Tell people the First Amendment matters."

It is an obligation Dershowitz himself has not shied from: His writings and his law practice are substantially devoted to defending the amendment's protections of free speech, press, religion, and assembly. "If you must always be right," he admonished the newspaper editors, "you won't publish a great deal of what in the end turns out to be right." Newspapers, he said, "have a constitutional right to be wrong."

Dershowitz is especially concerned about efforts in schools to curtail potentially offensive speech — in his mind a clear violation of the First Amendment. "We are producing a generation of students who do believe in political correctness, who do believe in censorship," he said to the editors. "This is the most serious issue on the university campus today."

FOR DISCUSSION

1. Have you ever censored yourself because you were afraid to be wrong? Or have you ever spoken out and been sorry later? What happened, and what were the results?
2. Do you agree with Dershowitz's concerns about challenges to the First Amendment on college campuses? Why or why not?

A self-described "radical feminist, pacifist, and cripple," NANCY MAIRS aims to "speak the 'unspeakable.'" Her poetry, memoirs, and essays deal with many sensitive subjects, including her struggles with the debilitating disease of multiple sclerosis. Born in Long Beach, California, in 1943, Mairs grew up in New Hampshire and Massachusetts. She received a B.A. from Wheaton College in Massachusetts (1964) and an M.F.A. in creative writing (1975) and a Ph.D. in English literature (1984) from the University of Arizona. While working on her advanced degrees, Mairs taught high school and college writing courses and served as project director at the Southwest Institute for Research on Women. Her second book of poetry, *In All the Rooms of the Yellow House* (1984), received a Western States Arts Foundation book award. Her essays are published in *Plaintext* (1986), *Remembering the Bone-House* (1988), *Carnal Acts* (1990), and *Ordinary Time* (1993).

Disability

As a writer afflicted with multiple sclerosis, Nancy Mairs is in a unique position to examine how the culture responds to people with disabilities. In this essay from *Carnal Acts,* she argues with her usual unsentimental candor that the media must treat disability as normal. The essay was first published in 1987 as a "Hers" column in the *New York Times.*

For months now I've been consciously searching for representa- 1
tions of myself in the media, especially television. I know I'd recognize this self because of certain distinctive, though not unique, features: I am a forty-three-year-old woman crippled by multiple sclerosis; although I can still totter short distances with the aid of a brace and a cane, more and more of the time I ride in a wheelchair. Because of these appliances and my peculiar gait, I'm easy to spot even in a crowd. So when I tell you I haven't noticed any woman like me on television, you can believe me.

Actually, last summer I did see a woman with multiple sclerosis 2
portrayed on one of those medical dramas that offer an illness-of-the-week like the daily special at your local diner. In fact, that was the whole point of the show: that this poor young woman had MS. She was terribly upset (understandably, I assure you) by the diagnosis, and

her response was to plan a trip to Kenya while she was still physically capable of making it, against the advice of the young, fit, handsome doctor who had fallen in love with her. And she almost did make it. At least, she got as far as a taxi to the airport, hotly pursued by the doctor. But at the last she succumbed to his blandishments and fled the taxi into his manly protective embrace. No escape to Kenya for this cripple.

Capitulation into the arms of a man who uses his medical powers 3 to strip one of even the urge toward independence is hardly the sort of representation I had in mind. But even if the situation had been sensitively handled, according the woman her right to her own adventures, it wouldn't have been what I'm looking for. Such a television show, as well as films like *Duet for One* and *Children of a Lesser God*, in taking disability as its major premise, excludes the complexities that round out a character and make her whole. It's not about a woman who happens to be physically disabled; it's about physical disability as the determining factor of a woman's existence.

Take it from me, physical disability looms pretty large in one's 4 life. But it doesn't devour one wholly. I'm not, for instance, Ms. MS, a walking, talking embodiment of a chronic incurable degenerative disease. In most ways I'm just like every other woman of my age, nationality, and socioeconomic background. I menstruate, so I have to buy tampons. I worry about smoker's breath, so I buy mouthwash. I smear my wrinkling skin with lotions. I put bleach in the washer so my family's undies won't be dingy. I drive a car, talk on the telephone, get runs in my pantyhose, eat pizza. In most ways, that is, I'm the advertisers' dream: Ms. Great American Consumer. And yet the advertisers, who determine nowadays who will get represented publicly and who will not, deny the existence of me and my kind absolutely.

I once asked a local advertiser why he didn't include disabled 5 people in his spots. His response seemed direct enough: "We don't want to give people the idea that our product is just for the handicapped." But tell me truly now: If you saw me pouring out puppy biscuits, would you think these kibbles were only for the puppies of cripples? If you saw my blind niece ordering a Coke, would you switch to Pepsi lest you be struck sightless? No, I think the advertiser's excuse masked a deeper and more anxious rationale: To depict disabled people in the ordinary activities of daily life is to admit that there is something ordinary about disability itself, that it may enter anybody's life. If it is effaced completely, or at least isolated as a separate "problem," so that it remains at a safe distance from other human issues, then the viewer won't feel threatened by her or his own physical vulnerability.

This kind of effacement or isolation has painful, even dangerous 6 consequences, however. For the disabled person, these include self-degradation and a subtle kind of self-alienation not unlike that experienced by other minorities. Socialized human beings love to conform, to study others and then to mold themselves to the contours of those whose images, for good reasons or bad, they come to love. Imagine a life in which feasible others — others you can hope to be like — don't exist. At the least you might conclude that there is something queer about you, something ugly or foolish or shameful. In the extreme, you might feel as though you don't exist, in any meaningful social sense, at all. Everyone else is "there," sucking breath mints and splashing on cologne and swigging wine coolers. You're "not there." And if not there, nowhere.

But this denial of disability imperils even you who are able-bodied, 7 and not just by shrinking your insight into the physically and emotionally complex world you live in. Some disabled people call you TAPs, or Temporarily Abled Persons. The fact is that ours is the only minority you can join involuntarily, without warning, at any time. And if you live long enough, as you're increasingly likely to do, you may well join it. The transition will probably be difficult from a physical point of view no matter what. But it will be a good bit easier psychologically if you are accustomed to seeing disability as a normal characteristic, one that complicates but does not ruin human existence. Achieving this integration, for disabled and able-bodied people alike, requires that we insert disability daily into our field of vision: quietly, naturally, in the small and common scenes of our ordinary lives.

QUESTIONS ON MEANING

1. Why does Mairs object to the TV movie about the woman with multiple sclerosis (paras. 2–3)?
2. What does Mairs mean by the phrase "Ms. Great American Consumer"?
3. Why, according to Mairs, should there be images of persons with disabilities on television?
4. Restate Mairs's THESIS in your own words.
5. What is this essay's PURPOSE?

QUESTIONS ON WRITING STRATEGY

1. What key GENERALIZATIONS does Mairs make as part of her argument? Do you find them valid? Why or why not?
2. How does Mairs use her INTRODUCTION to lay the groundwork for her argument? How does she make the TRANSITION from her introduction into her first example?
3. How would you characterize Mairs's TONE in this essay? Point out specific sentences and words that establish it. What is the EFFECT?
4. OTHER METHODS. Discuss how Mairs uses EXAMPLE to help build her case. What kinds of examples does she select? What are their effects?

QUESTIONS ON LANGUAGE

1. What is the function of IRONY in this essay (for example, "If you saw my blind niece ordering a Coke, would you switch to Pepsi lest you be struck sightless?")?
2. Look up *multiple sclerosis* in an encyclopedia or medical dictionary. What is the precise meaning of the term? How might advancing multiple sclerosis affect someone's ease of motion in a world designed for physically able people?
3. Give definitions of the following words: gait (para. 1); blandishments (2); capitulation (3); degenerative (4); rationale, effaced (5); feasible (6).
4. What are the CONNOTATIONS of the words "crippled," "totter," "appliances," and "peculiar gait" (para. 1)? What is the EFFECT of these words in the INTRODUCTION?
5. What do people with disabilities mean when they refer to "Temporarily Abled Persons" (para. 7)? Why might they use this phrase?

SUGGESTIONS FOR WRITING

1. Choose another group you think has been "effaced" in television advertising, and write an argument detailing how and why that group is overlooked. How could representations of these people be incorporated into the media?
2. Write an essay discussing how persons with disabilities are treated in our society. You could NARRATE a day in the life of someone with a disability; you could COMPARE AND CONTRAST the access and facilities your school provides physically average versus disabled students; you could CLASSIFY social attitudes toward disabilities, with EXAMPLES of each.
3. CRITICAL WRITING. Reread this essay carefully, considering Mairs's ETHICAL APPEAL. What does Mairs tell us about herself? What does she reveal through her TONE (for example, through IRONY, intensity, hu-

mor)? Write an essay on how this ethical appeal does or does not help further Mairs's argument.

4. CONNECTIONS. Look at Mairs's essay together with Barbara Ehren-reich's "The Wretched of the Hearth" (p. 292). How are working-class people and people with disabilities similarly excluded from television? How are the authors' assessments of image control in the television industry similar? How do they differ? What kinds of TV images might make people with disabilities more visible, in the way Roseanne Barr Arnold has made working-class women more visible?

NANCY MAIRS ON WRITING

Nancy Mairs frequently writes about the calamities in her life, and she ponders why in an essay appearing in the *New York Times Book Review* in February 1993. Why, for instance, did she record the details of her husband's grave illness? Perhaps because writing about one's misery is a way to overcome the isolation it creates. "There must have been millions keeping bedside vigils, whispering as I whispered over and over, 'Come back. Don't leave me. I need you,' each of us trapped in this profound and irrational solitude, as though walls of black glass had dropped on every side, shutting out the light, deadening all sound but the loved one's morphine-drugged breathing. I was not, in truth, alone."

In addition to this sense of kinship, Mairs also gains personal power from writing about illness. "The impulse, at least for someone of a writerly persuasion, is not to bemoan this condition but to remark on it in detail. Initially, one's motives for translating happenstance into acts of language may be quite private. Catastrophe tends to be composed not of a monolithic event but of a welter of little incidents, many of which bear no apparent relationship to one another, and language, in ordering these into recognizable patterns, counteracts disorientation and disintegration. This process of making sense of a flood of random data also produces the impression — generally quite groundless — of control, which may save one's sanity even though it can't save one's own or anyone else's life."

These therapeutic results, Mairs maintains, provide reason enough for keeping a private journal. However, going public "is an intrinsically social act, 'I' having no reason to speak aloud unless I posit 'you' there listening." The presence of the reader is especially important, Mairs says, "if I am seeking . . . to reconnect my self, now so utterly transformed by events unlike any I've experienced before as to seem a stranger even to myself, to the human community." The human community is no stranger to pain. "All of us who write out of calamity know this above all else: There is nothing exceptional about our lives, however they may differ in their particulars. What we can offer you, when the time comes, is companionship in a common venture. It's not a lot, I know, but it may come in handy. The narrator of personal disaster, I think, wants not to whine, not to boast, but to comfort."

But, Mairs finds, perhaps the most compelling reason of all to record personal affliction is to show "the spiritual maturation that suffering can force." "The writing about personal disaster that functions as literature tends not to be 'about' disaster at all," Mairs observes. Rather, it delineates a "progress toward sympathetic wisdom." The best writers "transcend their separate ordeals to speak generally, and generously, of the human condition." They write about "going on. All the way. To our common destination.

"To which none of us wants to go ignorant and alone. Hence, into the dark, we write."

FOR DISCUSSION

1. Why does Mairs believe that writing about one's own misery is valuable, both for the writer and for readers?
2. How does Mairs distinguish between journal writing and writing with a reader in mind?

CURTIS CHANG

A 1990 graduate of Harvard University, CURTIS CHANG majored in government. He was born in Taiwan and immigrated to the United States in 1971 with his family. He attended public school near Chicago. At Harvard, Chang helped found the Minority Student Alliance, belonged to the debating society, wrote for the *Harvard Political Review*, and was a leader of the Harvard-Radcliffe Christian Fellowship. Winner of the Michael C. Rockefeller Fellowship for Travel Abroad, Chang spent 1992 in Soweto, South Africa, and is writing a book about his experience. He was a teaching fellow in Harvard's government department and is now a campus minister with the Christian Fellowship.

Streets of Gold: The Myth of the Model Minority

This essay, like Linnea Saukko's (p. 659), won a Bedford Prize in Student Writing and was published in *Student Writers at Work* (3rd ed., 1989), edited by Nancy Sommers and Donald McQuade. Written when Chang was a freshman at Harvard, the essay grew out of his friendship with black students, his increasing interest in issues of racial identity, and his realization that Asian Americans had at best an ambiguous position in American society. "Streets of Gold" states and supports an opinion forcefully and, we think, convincingly. And it has something else to recommend it as well: It provides a model of research writing and documentation. The documentation style is that of the Modern Language Association.

Over 100 years ago, an American myth misled many of my ancestors. Seeking cheap labor, railroad companies convinced numerous Chinese that American streets were paved with gold. Today, the media portray Asian-Americans as finally mining those golden streets. Major publications like *Time, Newsweek, U.S. News & World Report, Fortune, The New Republic,* the *Wall Street Journal,* and the *New York Times Magazine* have all recently published congratulatory "Model Minority" headline stories with such titles as

America's Super Minority
An American Success Story
A "Model Minority"
Why They Succeed

The Ultimate Assimilation
The Triumph of Asian-Americans.

But the Model Minority is another "Streets of Gold" tale. It   2
distorts Asian-Americans' true status and ignores our racial handicaps.
And the Model Minority's ideology is even worse than its mythology.
It attempts to justify the existing system of racial inequality by blaming
the victims rather than the system itself.

The Model Minority myth introduces us as an ethnic minority   3
that is finally "making it in America," as stated in *Time* (Doerner
42). The media consistently define "making it" as achieving material
wealth, wealth that flows from our successes in the workplace and
the schoolroom. This economic achievement allegedly proves a minority can, as *Fortune* says, "lay claim to the American dream" (Ramirez 149).

Trying to show how "Asian-Americans present a picture of afflu-   4
ence and economic success," as the *New York Times Magazine* puts it
(Oxnam 72), 9 out of 10 of the major Model Minority stories of the
last four years relied heavily on one statistic: the family median
income. The median Asian-American family income, according to
the U.S. Census Survey of Income and Education data, is $22,713
compared to $20,800 for white Americans. Armed with that figure,
national magazines such as *Newsweek* have trumpeted our "remarkable, ever-mounting achievements" (Kasindorf et al. 51).

Such assertions demonstrate the truth of the aphorism "Statistics   5
are like a bikini. What they reveal is suggestive, but what they conceal
is vital." The family median income statistic conceals the fact that
Asian-American families generally (1) have more children and live-
in relatives and thus have more mouths to feed; (2) are often forced
by necessity to have everyone in the family work, averaging *more*
than two family income earners (whites only have 1.6) (Cabezas
402); and (3) live disproportionately in high cost of living areas (i.e.,
New York, Chicago, Los Angeles, and Honolulu) which artificially
inflate income figures. Dr. Robert S. Mariano, professor of economics
at the University of Pennsylvania, has calculated that

> when such appropriate adjustments and comparisons are made, a
> different and rather disturbing picture emerges, showing indeed a
> clearly disadvantaged group. . . . Filipino and Chinese men *are no
> better off than black men with regard to median incomes.* (55)[1]

[1] The picture becomes even more disturbing when one realizes the higher income
figures do not necessarily equal higher quality of life. For instance, in New York
Chinatown, more than 1 out of 5 residents work more than 57 hours per week,
almost 1 out of 10 elderly must labor more than 55 hours per week (Nishi 503).

Along with other racial minorities, Asian-Americans are still scraping for the crumbs of the economic pie.

Throughout its distortion of our status, the media propagate two 6 crucial assumptions. First, they lump all Asian-Americans into one monolithic, homogeneous, yellow-skinned mass. Such a view ignores the existence of an incredibly disadvantaged Asian-American under-class. Asians work in low-income and low-status jobs two to three times more than whites (Cabezas 438). Recent Vietnamese refugees in California are living like the Appalachian poor. While going to his Manhattan office, multimillionaire architect I. M. Pei's car passes Chinese restaurants and laundries where 72% of all New York Chinese men still work (U.S. Bureau of the Census qtd. in Cabezas 443).

But the media make an even more dangerous assumption. They 7 suggest that (alleged) material success is the same thing as basic racial equality. Citing that venerable family median income figure, maga-zines claim Asian-Americans are "obviously nondisadvantaged folks," as stated in *Fortune* (Seligman 64). Yet a 1979 United States Equal Employment Opportunity Commission study on Asian-Americans discovered widespread anti-Asian hiring and promotion practices. Asian-Americans "in the professional, technical, and managerial oc-cupations" often face "modern racism — the subtle, sophisticated, systemic patterns and practices . . . which function to effect and to obscure the discriminatory outcomes" (Nishi 398). One myth simply does not prove another: Neither our "astonishing economic prosper-ity" (Ramirez 152) nor a racially equal America exist.

An emphasis on material success also pervades the media's stress 8 on Asian-Americans' educational status at "the top of the class" ("Asian Americans" 4). Our "march into the ranks of the educational elite," as *U.S. News & World Report* puts it (McBee et al. 41), is significant, according to *Fortune,* because "all that education is paying off spectacularly" (Ramirez 149). Once again, the same fallacious assumptions plague this "whiz kids" image of Asian-Americans.

The media again ignore the fact that class division accounts for 9 much of the publicized success. Until 1976, the U.S. Immigration Department only admitted Asian immigrants that were termed "skilled" workers. "Skilled" generally meant college educated, usually in the sciences since poor English would not be a handicap. The result was that the vast majority of pre-1976 Asian immigrants came from already well-educated, upper-class backgrounds — the classic "brain drain" syndrome (Hirschman and Wong 507–10).

The post-1976 immigrants, however, come generally from the 10 lower, less educated classes (Kim 24). A study by Professor Elizabeth Ahn Toupin of Tufts University matched similar Asian and non-

Asian students *along class lines* and found that Asian-Americans "did not perform at a superior academic level to non-Asian students. Asian-Americans were more likely to be placed on academic probation than their white counterparts. . . . Twice as many Asian-American students withdrew from the university" (12).

Thus, it is doubtful whether the perceived widespread educational 11 success will continue as the Asian-American population eventually balances out along class lines. When 16.2% of all Chinese have less than four years of schooling (*four times* the percentage of whites) (Azores 73), it seems many future Asian-Americans will worry more about being able to read a newspaper rather than a Harvard acceptance letter.

Most important, the media assume once again that achieving a 12 certain level of material or educational success means achieving real equality. People easily forget that to begin with, Asians invest heavily in education since other means of upward mobility are barred to them by race. Until recently, for instance, Asian-Americans were barred from unions and traditional lines of credit (Yun 23–24).[2] Other "white" avenues to success, such as the "old boy network," are still closed to Asian-Americans.

When *Time* claims "as a result of their academic achievement 13 Asians are climbing the economic ladder with remarkable speed," it glosses over an inescapable fact: There is a white ladder and then there is a yellow one. Almost all of the academic studies on the *actual returns Asians receive* from their education point to prevalent discrimination. A striking example of this was found in a City University of New York research project which constructed résumés with equivalent educational backgrounds. Applications were then sent to employers, one group under an Asian name and a similar group under a Caucasian name. Whites received interviews five times more than Asians (Nishi 399). The media never headline even more shocking data that can be easily found in the U.S. Census. For instance, Chinese and Filipino males only earned respectively 74% and 52% as much as their *equally educated* white counterparts. Asian females fared even worse. Their salaries were only 44% to 54% as large as equivalent white males' paychecks (Cabezas 391). Blacks suffer from this same statistical disparity. We Asian-Americans are indeed a Model Minority — a perfect model of racial discrimination in America.

Yet this media myth encourages neglect of our pressing needs. 14

[2]For further analysis on the role racism plays in Asian-Americans' stress on education and certain technical and scientific fields, see Suzuki 44.

"Clearly, many Asian-Americans and Pacific peoples are invisible to the governmental agencies," reported the California State Advisory Committee to the U.S. Commission on Civil Rights. "Discrimination against Asian-Americans and Pacific peoples is as much the result of omission as commission" (qtd. in Chun 7). In 1979, while the president praised Asian-Americans' "successful integration into American society," his administration revoked Asian-Americans' eligibility for minority small business loans, devastating thousands of struggling, newly arrived small businessmen. Hosts of other minority issues, ranging from reparations for the Japanese-American internment to the ominous rise of anti-Asian violence, are widely ignored by the general public.

The media, in fact, insist to the general populace that we are not   15
a true racial minority. In an attack on affirmative action, the *Boston Globe* pointed out that universities, like many people, "obviously feel that Asian-Americans, especially those of Chinese and Japanese descent, are brilliant, privileged, and wrongly classified as minorities" ("Affirmative Non-actions" 10). Harvard Dean Henry Rosovsky remarked in the same article that "It does not seem to me that as a group, they are disadvantaged. . . . Asian-Americans appear to be in an odd category among other protected minorities."

The image that we Asians aren't like "other minorities" is fun-   16
damental to the Model Minority ideology. Any elementary-school student knows that the teacher designates one student the model, the "teacher's pet," in order to set an example for others to follow. One only sets up a "model minority" in order to communicate to the other "students," the blacks and Hispanics, "Why can't you be like that?" The media, in fact, almost admit to "grading" minorities as they headline Model Minority stories "Asian-Americans: Are They Making the Grade?" (McBee et al.). And Asians have earned the highest grade by fulfilling one important assignment: identifying with the white majority, with its values and wishes.

Unlike blacks, for instance, we Asian-Americans have not vig-   17
orously asserted our ethnic identity (a.k.a. Black Power). And the American public has historically demanded assimilation over racial pluralism.[3] Over the years, *Newsweek* has published titles from "Suc-

---

[3]A full discussion of racial pluralism versus assimilation is impossible here. But suffice it to say that pluralism accepts ethnic cultures as equally different; assimilation asks for a "melting" into the majority. An example of the assimilation philosophy is the massive "Americanization" programs of the late 1880s, which successfully erased Eastern Europe immigrants' customs in favor of Anglo-Saxon ones.

cess Story: Outwhiting the Whites" to "The Ultimate Assimilation," which lauded the increasing number of Asian-white marriages as evidence of Asian-Americans' "acceptance into American society" (Kantrowitz et al. 80).

Even more significant is the public's approval of how we have 18 succeeded in the "American tradition" (Ramirez 164). Unlike the blacks and Hispanics, we "Puritan-like" Asians (Oxnam 72) disdain governmental assistance. A *New Republic* piece, "The Triumph of Asian-Americans," similarly applauded how "Asian-Americans pose no problems at all" (Bell 30). The media consistently compare the crime-ridden image of other minorities with the picture of law-abiding Asian parents whose "well-behaved kids" hit books and not the streets ("Asian Americans" 4).

Some insist there is nothing terrible about whites conjuring up 19 our "tremendous" success, divining from it model American traits, then preaching, "Why can't you blacks and Hispanics be like that?" After all, one might argue, aren't those traits desirable?

Such a view, as mentioned, neglects Asian-Americans' true and 20 pressing needs. Moreover, this view completely misses the Model Minority image's fundamental ideology, an ideology meant to falsely grant America absolution from its racial barriers.

David O. Sears and Donald R. Kinder, two social scientists, have 21 recently published significant empirical studies on the underpinnings of American racial attitudes. They consistently discovered that Americans' stress on "values, such as 'individualism and self-reliance, the work ethic, obedience, and discipline' . . . can be invoked, however perversely, to feed racist appetites" (qtd. in Kennedy 88). In other words, the Model Minority image lets Americans' consciences rest easy. They can think: "It's not our fault those blacks and Hispanics can't make it. They're just too lazy. After all, look at the Asians."[4] Consequently, American society never confronts the systemic racial and economic factors underlying such inequality. The victims instead bear the blame.

This ideology behind the Model Minority image is best seen when 22

_____

[4]This phenomenon of blaming the victim for racial inequality is as old as America itself. For instance, southerners once eased their consciences over slavery by labeling blacks as animals lacking humanity. Today, America does it by labeling them as inferior people lacking "desirable" traits. For an excellent further analysis of this ideology, actually widespread among American intellectuals, see *Iron Cages: Race and Culture in 19th-Century America* by Ronald T. Takaki.

we examine one of the first Model Minority stories, which suddenly appeared in the mid-1960s. It is important to note that the period was marked by newfound, strident black demands for equality and power.

> At a time when it is being proposed that hundreds of billions be spent to uplift Negroes and other minorities, the nation's 300,000 Chinese-Americans are moving ahead on their own — with no help from anyone else. . . . Few Chinese-Americans are getting welfare handouts — or even want them. . . . They don't sit around moaning. ("Success Story of One Minority Group" 73)

The same article then concludes that the Chinese-American history and accomplishment "would shock those now complaining about the hardships endured by today's Negroes."

Not surprisingly, the dunce-capped blacks and Hispanics resent 23 us apple-polishing, "well-behaved" teacher's pets. Black comedian Richard Pryor performs a revealing routine in which new Asian immigrants learn from whites their first English word: "Nigger." And Asian-Americans themselves succumb to the Model Minority's deceptive mythology and racist ideology.[5] "I made it without help," one often hears among Asian circles; "why can't they?" In a 1986 nationwide poll, only 27% of Asian-American students rated "racial understanding" as "essential." The figure plunged 9% in the last year alone (a year marked by a torrent of Model Minority stories) (Hune). We "whitewashed" Asians have simply lost our identity as a fellow, disadvantaged minority.

But we don't even need to look beyond the Model Minority 24 stories themselves to realize that whites see us as "whiter" than blacks — but not quite white enough. For instance, citing that familiar median family income figure, *Fortune* magazine of 17 May 1982 complained that the Asian-American community is in fact "getting *more* than its share of the pie" (Seligman 64). For decades, when white Americans were leading the nation in every single economic measure, editorials arguing that whites were getting more than *their* share of the pie were rather rare.

[5]America has a long history of playing off one minority against the other. During the early 1900s, for instance, mining companies in the west often hired Asians solely as scabs against striking black miners. Black versus Asian hostility and violence usually followed. This pattern was repeated in numerous industries. In a larger historical sense, almost every immigrant group has assimilated, to some degree, the culture of antiblack racism.

No matter how "well-behaved" we are, Asian-Americans are still   25
excluded from the real pie, the "positions of institutional power and
political power" (Kuo 289). Professor Harry Kitano of UCLA has
written extensively on the plight of Asian-Americans as the "middle-
man minority," a minority supposedly satisfied materially but forever
racially barred from a true, *significant* role in society. Empirical studies
indicate that Asian-Americans "have been channeled into lower-
echelon white-collar jobs having little or no decision making authority" (Suzuki 38). For example, in *Fortune's* 1,000 largest companies,
Asian-American nameplates rest on a mere half of one percent of all
officers' and directors' desks (a statistical disparity worsened by the
fact that most of the Asians founded their companies) (Ramirez 152).
While the education of the upper-class Asians may save them from
the bread lines, their race still keeps them from the boardroom.

Our docile acceptance of such exclusion is actually one of our   26
"model" traits. When Asian-Americans in San Francisco showed their
first hint of political activism and protested Asian exclusion from city
boards, the *Washington Monthly* warned in a long Asian-American
article, "Watch out, here comes another group to pander to" ("The
Wrong Way" 21). *The New Republic* praised Asian-American political
movements because

> Unlike blacks or Hispanics, Asian-American politicians have the
> luxury of not having to devote the bulk of their time to an "Asian-
> American agenda," and thus escape becoming prisoners of such an
> agenda. . . . The most important thing for Asian-Americans . . .
> is simply "being part of the process." (Bell 31)

This is strikingly reminiscent of another of the first Model Mi-   27
nority stories:

> As the Black and Brown communities push for changes in the
> present system, the Oriental is set forth as an example to be fol-
> lowed — a minority group that has achieved success through ad-
> aptation rather than confrontation. (*Gidra* qtd. in Chun 7)

But it is precisely this "present system," this system of subtle,   28
persistent racism that we all must confront, not adapt to. For example,
we Asians gained our right to vote from the 1964 Civil Rights Act
that blacks marched, bled, died, and, in the words of that original
Model Minority story, "sat around moaning for." Unless we assert our
true identity as a minority and challenge racial misconceptions and
inequalities, we will be nothing more than techno-coolies — collecting our wages but silently enduring basic political and economic
inequality.

This country perpetuated a myth once. Today, no one can afford 29
to dreamily chase after that gold in the streets, oblivious to the
genuine treasure of racial equality. When racism persists, can one
really call any minority a "model"?

Works Cited

"Affirmative Non-actions." Op-ed. *The Boston Globe* 14 Jan. 1985: 10.

"Asian Americans, The Drive to Excel." *Newsweek on Campus* April 1984:
4–13.

Asian American Studies: Contemporary Issues. Proc. from East Coast Asian
American Scholars Conference. 1986.

Azores, Fortunata M. "Census Methodology and the Development of Social
Indicators for Asian and Pacific Americans." United States Commission
on Civil Rights 70–79.

Bell, David A. "The Triumph of Asian-Americans." *The New Republic* 15
& 22 July 1985: 24–31.

Cabezas, Armado. "Employment Issues of Asian Americans." United States
Commission on Civil Rights.

Chun, Ki-Taek. "The Myth of Asian American Success and Its Educational
Ramifications." *IRCD Bulletin* Winter/Spring 1980.

Doerner, William R. "To America with Skills." *Time* 8 July 1985: 42–44.

Dutta, Manoranjan. "Asian/Pacific American Employment Profile: Myth and
Reality — Issues and Answers." The United States Commission on
Civil Rights 445–489.

Hirschman, Charles, and Morrison G. Wong. "Trends in Socioeconomic
Achievement Among Immigrants and Native-Born Asian-Americans,
1960–1976." *Sociological Quarterly* 22.4 (1981): 495–513.

Hune, Shirley. Keynote address. East Coast Asian Student Union Conference. Boston University. 14 Feb. 1987.

Kahng, Anthony. "Employment Issues." The United States Commission on
Civil Rights 1980.

Kantrowitz, Barbara, et al. "The Ultimate Assimilation." *Newsweek* 24 Nov.
1986: 80.

Kasindorf, Martin, et al. "Asian-Americans: A 'Model Minority.'" *Newsweek*
6 Dec. 1982: 39–51.

Kennedy, David M. "The Making of a Classic. Gunnar Myrdal and Black-
White Relations: The Use and Abuse of *An American Dilemma.*" *Atlantic*
May 1987: 86–89.

Kiang, Peter. Personal interview. 1 May 1987.

Kim, Illsoo. "Class Division Among Asian Immigrants: Its Implications for
Social Welfare Policy." *Asian American Studies* 24–25.

Kuo, Wen H. "On the Study of Asian-Americans: Its Current State and
Agenda." *Sociological Quarterly* 20.2 (1979): 279–90.

Mariano, Robert S. "Census Issues." United States Commission on Civil
Rights 54–59.

McBee, Susanna, et al. "Asian-Americans: Are They Making the Grade?" *U.S. News & World Report* 2 Apr. 1984: 41–47.

Nishi, Setsuko Matsunaga. "Asian American Employment Issues: Myths and Realities." United States Commission on Civil Rights 397–99, 495–507.

Oxnam, Robert B. "Why Asians Succeed Here." *New York Times Magazine* 30 Nov. 1986: 72+.

Ramirez, Anthony. "America's Super Minority." *Fortune* 24 Nov. 1986: 148–49.

Seligman, Daniel. "Keeping Up: Working Smarter." *Fortune* 17 May 1982: 64.

"Success Story of One Minority Group in the US." *U.S. News & World Report* 26 Dec. 1966: 73–76.

"Success Story: Outwhiting the Whites." *Newsweek* 21 June 1971: 24–25.

Sung, Betty Lee. *A Survey of Chinese American Manpower and Employment.* NY: Praeger, 1976.

Suzuki, Bob H. "Education and the Socialization of Asian Americans: A Revisionist Analysis of the 'Model Minority' Thesis." *Amerasia Journal* 4.2 (1977): 23–51.

Toupin, Elizabeth Ahn. "A Model University for a Model Minority." *Asian American Studies* 10–12.

"The Wrong Way to Court Ethnics." *Washington Monthly* May 1986: 21–26.

United States Commission on Civil Rights. *Civil Rights Issues of Asian and Pacific Americans: Myths and Realities.* 1980.

Yun, Grace. "Notes from Discussions on Asian American Education." *Asian American Studies* 20–24.

QUESTIONS ON MEANING

1. What is Chang's THESIS? Why does he introduce it where he does?
2. What "two crucial assumptions" do the media mistakenly propagate about Asian Americans?
3. What exactly does Chang mean by the "pressing needs" of Asian Americans?
4. SUMMARIZE Chang's ideas about the "Model Minority ideology" (beginning in para. 16). What is an *ideology*? What does this one do?

QUESTIONS ON WRITING STRATEGY

1. Is Chang's argument based more on EMOTIONAL APPEAL or on RATIONAL APPEAL? Why do you say so?

2. Try to summarize Chang's argument in a SYLLOGISM (as demonstrated on p. 469). What part of the syllogism corresponds to Chang's thesis?
3. What types of EVIDENCE does Chang base his argument on? Is the evidence adequate?
4. Analyze Chang's POINT OF VIEW. With whom does he ally himself? How does his position affect the essay?
5. Where does Chang acknowledge and address possible objections to his argument?
6. **OTHER METHODS.** How does Chang use DIVISION OR ANALYSIS to develop his argument?

QUESTIONS ON LANGUAGE

1. What is the "old boy network" (para. 12)? What are the implications of this phrase?
2. In paragraph 28, Chang uses the term "techno-coolies." What ALLUSION is he making? Why is it especially suitable at this point in the essay?
3. Chang refers in paragraphs 5, 24, and 25 to an "economic pie." What images does this METAPHOR evoke?
4. Consult your dictionary if any of the following words are unfamiliar: allegedly (para. 3); median (4); aphorism (5); propagates, monolithic (6); venerable, systemic (7); fallacious (8); prevalent, disparity (13); reparations, internment (14); assimilation, lauded (17); absolution (20); empirical (21); succumb, torrent (23); lower-echelon (25); docile, pander (26); perpetuated (29).

SUGGESTIONS FOR WRITING

1. Do you know of an issue or an incident when the media have distorted or omitted facts? (The subject could be a local fire, a demonstration, an arrest, a legislative debate, anything.) Write an argument in which you ANALYZE and correct the media record.
2. Take Chang's essay further: Write a concrete proposal for correcting the situation he describes.
3. **CRITICAL WRITING.** Number 4 under "Questions on Meaning" asked you to SUMMARIZE Chang's assertions about the "Model Minority ideology" (paras. 16–29). In an essay, ANALYZE and EVALUATE these assertions. What ASSUMPTIONS is Chang making — for instance, about the existence or denial of racial barriers in the United States? Do you agree or disagree with Chang's assumptions and with his argument about Model Minority ideology? Why?
4. **CONNECTIONS.** In "The Cult of Ethnicity, Good and Bad" (p. 689), Arthur M. Schlesinger, Jr., warns of the "unhealthy consequences" of ethnic cohesion and political consciousness. After reading Schlesinger's essay, write an essay of your own in which you draw on Schlesinger's ideas to refute Chang's, or vice versa.

CURTIS CHANG ON WRITING

For Curtis Chang, a word processor is an "essential" writing tool. Once he completes and outlines his research, he explains in *Student Writers at Work*, "I must see my thoughts on the computer screen. I find it difficult to manipulate thoughts unless I can physically manipulate the words that represent them."

But the word processor can be a mixed blessing, for it supports Chang's "urge to perfect each sentence as I am writing. One is especially vulnerable when working on a word processor. I often have to force myself to continue getting the basic facts out first." Once he does have his thoughts on screen, Chang turns to global revision, an important part of his writing process. Although he strives for perfect sentences, Chang thinks of revision as "more than just the usual forms of correcting grammar and spelling and using one adjective instead of another." For Chang, "Revising means acting as devil's advocate and trying to pick apart my paper's argument. Then I have to answer to those criticisms."

Like many writers, Chang is rarely satisfied with his work. For each paper, he reports, "I average about three drafts, but it is usually determined by time constraints. I never really finish an essay; I just tire of tinkering with it."

FOR DISCUSSION

1. Why does Chang try not to perfect his sentences until the entire essay is written? What is the advantage of "getting the basic facts out first"?
2. Chang considers the word processor essential for writing. Would his extensive revisions be possible without one?

WILLIAM F. BUCKLEY, JR.

Born in New York in 1925, WILLIAM FRANK BUCKLEY, JR., is one of the most articulate proponents of American conservatism. Shortly after his graduation from Yale, he published *God and Man at Yale* (1951), a memoir espousing conservative political values and traditional Christian principles. Since then, he has written more than twenty works on politics and government, published a syndicated newspaper column, and founded and edited *The National Review*, a magazine of conservative opinion. His most recent work, *Happy Days Were Here Again: Reflections of a Libertarian Journalist* (1993), is a collection of essays. In addition, Buckley has written several books on sailing and many spy novels. With all his publications, however, Buckley is probably best known for his weekly television debate program, *Firing Line*. As the program's several million viewers know, he is a man of wry charm. When he was half-seriously running for mayor of New York City in 1965, someone asked him what he would do if elected. "Demand a recount," he replied.

Why Don't We Complain?

Most people riding in an overheated commuter train would perspire quietly. For Buckley, this excess of warmth sparks an indignant essay, first published in *Esquire* in 1961, in which he takes to task both himself and his fellow Americans. Does the essay appeal mainly to reason or to emotion? And what would happen if everyone were to do as Buckley urges?

It was the very last coach and the only empty seat on the entire train, so there was no turning back. The problem was to breathe. Outside, the temperature was below freezing. Inside the railroad car the temperature must have been about 85 degrees. I took off my overcoat, and a few minutes later my jacket, and noticed that the car was flecked with the white shirts of the passengers. I soon found my hand moving to loosen my tie. From one end of the car to the other, as we rattled through Westchester County, we sweated; but we did not moan.

I watched the train conductor appear at the head of the car. 2
"Tickets, all tickets, please!" In a more virile age, I thought, the
passengers would seize the conductor and strap him down on a seat
over the radiator to share the fate of his patrons. He shuffled down
the aisle, picking up tickets, punching commutation cards. *No one
addressed a word to him.* He approached my seat, and I drew a deep
breath of resolution. "Conductor," I began with a considerable
edge to my voice. . . . Instantly the doleful eyes of my seatmate
turned tiredly from his newspaper to fix me with a resentful stare:
What question could be so important as to justify my sibilant in-
trusion into his stupor? I was shaken by those eyes. I am incapable
of making a discreet fuss, so I mumbled a question about what
time we were due in Stamford (I didn't even ask whether it would
be before or after dehydration could be expected to set in), got my
reply, and went back to my newspaper and to wiping my brow.

The conductor had nonchalantly walked down the gauntlet of 3
eighty sweating American freemen, and not one of them had
asked him to explain why the passengers in that car had been consigned to suffer. There is nothing to be done when the temperature *outdoors* is 85 degrees, and indoors the air conditioner has
broken down; obviously when that happens there is nothing to do,
except perhaps curse the day that one was born. But when the
temperature outdoors is below freezing, it takes a positive act of
will on somebody's part to set the temperature *indoors* at 85.
Somewhere a valve was turned too far, a furnace overstocked, a
thermostat maladjusted: something that could easily be remedied
by turning off the heat and allowing the great outdoors to come
indoors. All this is so obvious. What is not obvious is what has
happened to the American people.

It isn't just the commuters, whom we have come to visualize 4
as a supine breed who have got on to the trick of suspending their
sensory faculties twice a day while they submit to the creeping dissolution of the railroad industry. It isn't just they who have given
up trying to rectify irrational vexations. It is the American people
everywhere.

A few weeks ago at a large movie theater I turned to my wife 5
and said, "The picture is out of focus." "Be quiet," she answered. I
obeyed. But a few minutes later I raised the point again, with
mounting impatience. "It will be all right in a minute," she said
apprehensively. (She would rather lose her eyesight than be around
when I make one of my infrequent scenes.) I waited. It was *just*
out of focus — not glaringly out, but out. My vision is 20–20, and

I assume that is the vision, adjusted, for most people in the movie house. So, after hectoring my wife throughout the first reel, I finally prevailed upon her to admit that it *was* off, and very annoying. We then settled down, coming to rest on the presumption that: a) someone connected with the management of the theater must soon notice the blur and make the correction; or b) that someone seated near the rear of the house would make the complaint in behalf of those of us up front; or c) that — any minute now — the entire house would explode into catcalls and foot stamping, calling dramatic attention to the irksome distortion.

What happened was nothing. The movie ended, as it had begun *just* out of focus, and as we trooped out, we stretched our faces in a variety of contortions to accustom the eye to the shock of normal focus.

I think it is safe to say that everybody suffered on that occasion. And I think it is safe to assume that everyone was expecting someone else to take the initiative in going back to speak to the manager. And it is probably true even that if we had supposed the movie would run right through the blurred image, someone surely would have summoned up the purposive indignation to get up out of his seat and file his complaint.

But notice that no one did. And the reason no one did is because we are all increasingly anxious in America to be unobtrusive, we are reluctant to make our voices heard, hesitant about claiming our rights; we are afraid that our cause is unjust, or that if it is not unjust, that it is ambiguous; or if not even that, that it is too trivial to justify the horrors of a confrontation with Authority; we will sit in an oven or endure a racking headache before undertaking a head-on, I'm-here-to-tell-you complaint. That tendency to passive compliance, to a heedless endurance, is something to keep one's eyes on — in sharp focus.

I myself can occasionally summon the courage to complain, but I cannot, as I have intimated, complain softly. My own instinct is so strong to let the thing ride, to forget about it — to expect that someone will take the matter up, when the grievance is collective, in my behalf — that it is only when the provocation is at a very special key, whose vibrations touch simultaneously a complexus of nerves, allergies, and passions, that I catch fire and find the reserves of courage and assertiveness to speak up. When that happens, I get quite carried away. My blood gets hot, my brow wet, I become unbearably and unconscionably sarcastic and bellicose; I am girded for a total showdown.

Why should that be? Why could not I (or anyone else) on   10
that railroad coach have said simply to the conductor, "Sir" — I
take that back: that sounds sarcastic — "Conductor, would you be
good enough to turn down the heat? I am extremely hot. In fact,
I tend to get hot every time the temperature reaches 85 degr — ."
Strike that last sentence. Just end it with the simple statement
that you are extremely hot, and let the conductor infer the cause.

Every New Year's Eve I resolve to do something about the   11
Milquetoast in me and vow to speak up, calmly, for my rights, and
for the betterment of our society, on every appropriate occasion.
Entering last New Year's Eve I was fortified in my resolve because
that morning at breakfast I had had to ask the waitress three times
for a glass of milk. She finally brought it — after I had finished my
eggs, which is when I don't want it any more. I did not have the
manliness to order her to take the milk back, but settled instead
for a cowardly sulk, and ostentatiously refused to drink the milk —
though I later paid for it — rather than state plainly to the hostess, as I should have, why I had not drunk it, and would not pay
for it.

So by the time the New Year ushered out the Old, riding in on   12
my morning's indignation and stimulated by the gastric juices of
resolution that flow so faithfully on New Year's Eve, I rendered my
vow. Henceforward I would conquer my shyness, my despicable disposition to supineness. I would speak out like a man against the
unnecessary annoyances of our time.

Forty-eight hours later, I was standing in line at the ski repair   13
store in Pico Peak, Vermont. All I needed, to get on with my
skiing, was the loan, for one minute, of a small screwdriver, to
tighten a loose binding. Behind the counter in the workshop were
two men. One was industriously engaged in servicing the complicated requirements of a young lady at the head of the line, and
obviously he would be tied up for quite a while. The other —
"Jiggs," his workmate called him — was a middle-aged man, who
sat in a chair puffing a pipe, exchanging small talk with his working partner. My pulse began its telltale acceleration. The minutes
ticked on. I stared at the idle shopkeeper, hoping to shame him
into action, but he was impervious to my telepathic reproof and
continued his small talk with his friend, brazenly insensitive to the
nervous demands of six good men who were raring to ski.

Suddenly my New Year's Eve resolution struck me. It was now   14
or never. I broke from my place in line and marched to the
counter. I was going to control myself. I dug my nails into my
palms. My effort was only partially successful.

"If you are not too busy," I said icily, "would you mind hand-   15
ing me a screwdriver?"

Work stopped and everyone turned his eyes on me, and I ex-   16
perienced that mortification I always feel when I am the center of
centripetal shafts of curiosity, resentment, perplexity.

But the worst was yet to come. "I am sorry, sir," said Jiggs def-   17
erentially, moving the pipe from his mouth. "I am not supposed to
move. I have just had a heart attack." That was the signal for a
great whirring noise that descended from heaven. We looked,
stricken, out the window, and it appeared as though a cyclone had
suddenly focused on the snowy courtyard between the shop and
the ski lift. Suddenly a gigantic army helicopter materialized, and
hovered down to a landing. Two men jumped out of the plane
carrying a stretcher, tore into the ski shop, and lifted the shopkeeper
onto the stretcher. Jiggs bade his companion good-bye and was
whisked out the door, into the plane, up to the heavens, down —
we learned — to a nearby army hospital. I looked up manfully —
into a score of man-eating eyes. I put the experience down as a
reversal.

As I write this, on an airplane, I have run out of paper and   18
need to reach into my briefcase under my legs for more. I cannot
do this until my empty lunch tray is removed from my lap. I ar-
rested the stewardess as she passed empty-handed down the aisle
on the way to the kitchen to fetch the lunch trays for the passengers up forward who haven't been served yet. "Would you please
take my tray?" "Just a *moment, sir!*" she said, and marched on
sternly. Shall I tell her that since she is headed for the kitchen
anyway, it could not delay the feeding of the other passengers by
more than two seconds necessary to stash away my empty tray? Or
remind her that not fifteen minutes ago she spoke unctuously into
the loudspeaker the words undoubtedly devised by the airline's
highly paid public relations counselor: "If there is anything I or
Miss French can do for you to make your trip more enjoyable,
please let us — " I have run out of paper.

I think the observable reluctance of the majority of Americans   19
to assert themselves in minor matters is related to our increased
sense of helplessness in an age of technology and centralized political and economic power. For generations, Americans who were too
hot, or too cold, got up and did something about it. Now we call
the plumber, or the electrician, or the furnace man. The habit of
looking after our own needs obviously had something to do with
the assertiveness that characterized the American family familiar to
readers of American literature. With the technification of life goes

our direct responsibility for our material environment, and we are conditioned to adopt a position of helplessness not only as regards the broken air conditioner, but as regards the overheated train. It takes an expert to fix the former, but not the latter; yet these distinctions, as we withdraw into helplessness, tend to fade away.

Our notorious political apathy is a related phenomenon. Every 20 year, whether the Republican or the Democratic Party is in office, more and more power drains away from the individual to feed vast reservoirs in far-off places; and we have less and less say about the shape of events which shape our future. From this alienation of personal power comes the sense of resignation with which we accept the political dispensations of a powerful government whose hold upon us continues to increase.

An editor of a national weekly news magazine told me a few 21 years ago that as few as a dozen letters of protest against an editorial stance of his magazine was enough to convene a plenipotentiary meeting of the board of editors to review policy. "So few people complain, or make their voices heard," he explained to me, "that we assume a dozen letters represent the inarticulated views of thousands of readers." In the past ten years, he said, the volume of mail has noticeably decreased, even though the circulation of his magazine has risen.

When our voices are finally mute, when we have finally sup- 22 pressed the natural instinct to complain, whether the vexation is trivial or grave, we shall have become automatons, incapable of feeling. When Premier Khrushchev first came to this country late in 1959 he was primed, we are informed, to experience the bitter resentment of the American people against his tyranny, against his persecutions, against the movement which is responsible for the great number of American deaths in Korea, for billions in taxes every year, and for life everlasting on the brink of disaster; but Khrushchev was pleasantly surprised, and reported back to the Russian people that he had been met with overwhelming cordiality (read: apathy), except, to be sure, for "a few fascists who followed me around with their wretched posters, and should be horse-whipped."

I may be crazy, but I say there would have been lots more 23 posters in a society where train temperatures in the dead of winter are not allowed to climb to 85 degrees without complaint.

QUESTIONS ON MEANING

1. How does Buckley account for his failure to complain to the train conductor? What reasons does he give for not taking action when he notices that the movie he is watching is out of focus?
2. Where does Buckley finally place the blame for the average American's reluctance to try to "rectify irrational vexations"?
3. By what means does the author bring his argument around to the subject of political apathy?
4. What THESIS does Buckley attempt to support? How would you state it?

QUESTIONS ON WRITING STRATEGY

1. In taking to task not only his fellow Americans but also himself, does Buckley strengthen or weaken his charge that, as a people, Americans do not complain enough?
2. Judging from the vocabulary displayed in this essay, would you say that Buckley is writing for a highly specialized AUDIENCE or an educated but nonspecialized general audience?
3. As a whole, is Buckley's essay an example of appeal to emotion or of reasoned argument? Give EVIDENCE for your answer.
4. OTHER METHODS. Buckley includes as evidence four NARRATIVES of his personal experiences. What is the point of the narrative about Jiggs (paras. 13–17)?

QUESTIONS ON LANGUAGE

1. Define the following words: virile, doleful, sibilant (para. 2); supine (4); hectoring (5); unobtrusive, ambiguous (8); intimated, unconscionably, bellicose (9); ostentatiously (11); despicable (12); impervious (13); mortification, centripetal (16); deferentially (17); unctuously (18); notorious, dispensations (20); plenipotentiary, inarticulated (21); automatons (22).
2. What does Buckley's use of the capital A in *Authority* (para. 8) contribute to the sentence in which he uses it?
3. What is Buckley talking about when he alludes to "the Milquetoast in me" (para. 11)? (Notice how well the ALLUSION fits into the paragraph, with its emphasis on breakfast and a glass of milk.)

SUGGESTIONS FOR WRITING

1. Write about an occasion when you should have registered a complaint and did not; or recount what happened when you did in fact protest against one of "the unnecessary annoyances of our time."
2. Think of some disturbing incident you have witnessed, or some annoying treatment you have received in a store or other public place, and write a letter of complaint to whomever you believe responsible. Be specific in your evidence, be temperate in your language, make clear what you would like to come of your complaint (your proposal), and be sure to put your letter in the mail.
3. CRITICAL WRITING. Write a paper in which you ANALYZE and EVALUATE any one of Buckley's ideas. For instance: Do we feel as helpless as Buckley says (para. 19)? Are we politically apathetic, and if so should the government be blamed (para. 20)? For that matter, do we not complain? Support your view with EVIDENCE from your experience, observation, or reading.
4. CONNECTIONS. The "speakers" in both Buckley's "Why Don't We Complain?" and Jonathan Swift's "A Modest Proposal" (p. 522) make a strong ethical appeal, going out of their way to convince readers of their good will, reasonableness, and authority. Write an essay in which you analyze the "speaker" created by each writer, its character, its functions, and its EFFECT. Use quotations, PARAPHRASES, and SUMMARIES from both essays to support your analysis.

WILLIAM F. BUCKLEY, JR., ON WRITING

In the autobiographical *Overdrive*, Buckley recalls a conversation with a friend and fellow columnist: "George Will once told me how deeply he loves to write. 'I wake in the morning,' he explained to me, 'and I ask myself: Is this one of the days I have to write a column? And if the answer is yes, I rise a happy man.' I, on the other hand, wake neither particularly happy nor unhappy, but to the extent that my mood is affected by the question whether I need to write a column that morning, the impact of Monday-Wednesday-Friday" — the days when he must write a newspaper column — "is definitely negative. Because I do not like to write, for the simple reason that writing is extremely hard work, and I do not 'like' extremely hard work."

Still, in the course of a "typical year," Buckley estimates that he produces not only 150 newspaper columns, but also a dozen longer articles, eight or ten speeches, fifty introductions for his television program, various editorial pieces for the magazine he edits, *The National Review,* and a book or two. "Why do I do so much? . . . It is easier to stay up late working for hours than to take one tenth the time to inquire into the question whether the work is worth performing."

In the introduction to another book, *A Hymnal: The Controversial Arts,* Buckley states an attitude toward writing that most other writers would not share. "I have discovered, in sixteen years of writing columns," he declares, "that there is no observable difference in the quality of that which is written at very great speed (twenty minutes, say), and that which takes three or four times as long. . . . Pieces that take longer to write sometimes, on revisiting them, move along grumpily."

FOR DISCUSSION

1. Given that he so dislikes writing, why does Buckley do it?
2. Buckley's attitude toward giving time to writing is unusual. What is the more usual view of writing?

MARTIN LUTHER KING, JR.

MARTIN LUTHER KING, JR., (1929–68) was born in Atlanta, the son of a Baptist minister, and was himself ordained in the same denomination. Stepping to the forefront of the civil rights movement in 1955, King led African Americans in a boycott of segregated city buses in Montgomery, Alabama; became first president of the Southern Christian Leadership Conference; and staged sit-ins and mass marches that helped bring about the Civil Rights Act passed by Congress in 1964 and the Voting Rights Act of 1965. He received the Nobel Peace Prize in 1964. In view of the fact that King preached "nonviolent resistance," it is particularly ironic that he was himself the target of violence. He was stabbed in New York, pelted with stones in Chicago; his home in Montgomery was bombed; and finally in Memphis he was assassinated by a sniper. On his tombstone near Atlanta's Ebenezer Baptist Church are these words from the spiritual he quotes at the conclusion of "I Have a Dream": "Free at last, free at last, thank God almighty, I'm free at last." Martin Luther King's birthday, January 15, is now a national holiday.

I Have a Dream

In Washington, D.C., on August 28, 1963, King's campaign of nonviolent resistance reached its historic climax. On that date, commemorating the centennial of Lincoln's Emancipation Proclamation freeing the slaves, King led a march of 200,000 persons, black and white, from the Washington Monument to the Lincoln Memorial. Before this throng, and to millions who watched on television, he delivered this unforgettable speech.

Five score years ago, a great American, in whose symbolic shadow 1 we stand, signed the Emancipation Proclamation. This momentous decree came as a great beacon light of hope to millions of Negro slaves who had been seared in the flames of withering injustice. It came as a joyous daybreak to end the long night of captivity.

But one hundred years later, we must face the tragic fact that the 2 Negro is still not free. One hundred years later, the life of the Negro is still sadly crippled by the manacles of segregation and the chains of discrimination. One hundred years later, the Negro lives on a lonely island of poverty in the midst of a vast ocean of material prosperity. One hundred years later, the Negro is still languishing in the corners of American society and finds himself in exile in his own land. So we have come here today to dramatize an appalling condition.

In a sense we have come to our nation's capital to cash a check.   3
When the architects of our republic wrote the magnificent words of the Constitution and the Declaration of Independence, they were signing a promissory note to which every American was to fall heir. This note was a promise that all men would be guaranteed the unalienable rights of life, liberty, and the pursuit of happiness.

It is obvious today that America has defaulted on this promissory   4
note insofar as her citizens of color are concerned. Instead of honoring this sacred obligation, America has given the Negro people a bad check; a check which has come back marked "insufficient funds." But we refuse to believe that the bank of justice is bankrupt. We refuse to believe that there are insufficient funds in the great vaults of opportunity of this nation. So we have come to cash this check — a check that will give us upon demand the riches of freedom and the security of justice. We have also come to this hallowed spot to remind America of the fierce urgency of *now*. This is no time to engage in the luxury of cooling off or to take the tranquilizing drugs of gradualism. *Now* is the time to make real the promises of Democracy. *Now* is the time to rise from the dark and desolate valley of segregation to the sunlit path of racial justice. *Now* is the time to open the doors of opportunity to all of God's children. *Now* is the time to lift our nation from the quicksands of racial injustice to the solid rock of brotherhood.

It would be fatal for the nation to overlook the urgency of the   5
moment and to underestimate the determination of the Negro. This sweltering summer of the Negro's legitimate discontent will not pass until there is an invigorating autumn of freedom and equality; 1963 is not an end, but a beginning. Those who hope that the Negro needed to blow off steam and will now be content will have a rude awakening if the nation returns to business as usual. There will be neither rest nor tranquillity in America until the Negro is granted his citizenship rights. The whirlwinds of revolt will continue to shake the foundations of our nation until the bright day of justice emerges.

But there is something that I must say to my people who stand   6
on the warm threshold which leads into the palace of justice. In the process of gaining our rightful place we must not be guilty of wrongful deeds. Let us not seek to satisfy our thirst for freedom by drinking from the cup of bitterness and hatred. We must forever conduct our struggle on the high plane of dignity and discipline. We must not

allow our creative protest to degenerate into physical violence. Again and again we must rise to the majestic heights of meeting physical force with soul force. The marvelous new militancy which has engulfed the Negro community must not lead us to a distrust of all white people, for many of our white brothers, as evidenced by their presence here today, have come to realize that their destiny is tied up with our destiny and their freedom is inextricably bound to our freedom. We cannot walk alone.

And as we walk, we must make the pledge that we shall march 7 ahead. We cannot turn back. There are those who are asking the devotees of civil rights, "When will you be satisfied?" We can never be satisfied as long as the Negro is the victim of the unspeakable horrors of police brutality. We can never be satisfied as long as our bodies, heavy with the fatigue of travel, cannot gain lodging in the motels of the highways and the hotels of the cities. We cannot be satisfied as long as the Negro's basic mobility is from a smaller ghetto to a larger one. We can never be satisfied as long as a Negro in Mississippi cannot vote and a Negro in New York believes he has nothing for which to vote. No, no, we are not satisfied, and we will not be satisfied until justice rolls down like waters and righteousness like a mighty stream.

I am not unmindful that some of you have come here out of great 8 trials and tribulations. Some of you have come fresh from narrow jail cells. Some of you have come from areas where your quest for freedom left you battered by the storms of persecution and staggered by the winds of police brutality. You have been the veterans of creative suffering. Continue to work with the faith that unearned suffering is redemptive.

Go back to Mississippi, go back to Alabama, go back to South 9 Carolina, go back to Georgia, go back to Louisiana, go back to the slums and ghettos of our northern cities, knowing that somehow this situation can and will be changed. Let us not wallow in the valley of despair.

I say to you today, my friends, that in spite of the difficulties and 10 frustrations of the moment I still have a dream. It is a dream deeply rooted in the American dream.

I have a dream that one day this nation will rise up and live out 11 the true meaning of its creed: "We hold these truths to be self-evident; that all men are created equal."

I have a dream that one day on the red hills of Georgia the sons 12 of former slaves and the sons of former slaveowners will be able to sit down together at the table of brotherhood.

I have a dream that one day even the state of Mississippi, a desert 13
state sweltering with the heat of injustice and oppression, will be
transformed into an oasis of freedom and justice.

I have a dream that my four little children will one day live in a 14
nation where they will not be judged by the color of their skin but
by the content of their character.

I have a dream today. 15

I have a dream that one day the state of Alabama, whose gov- 16
ernor's lips are presently dripping with the words of interposition and
nullification, will be transformed into a situation where little black
boys and black girls will be able to join hands with little white boys
and white girls and walk together as sisters and brothers.

I have a dream today. 17

I have a dream that one day every valley shall be exalted, every 18
hill and mountain shall be made low, the rough places will be made
plain, and the crooked places will be made straight, and the glory of
the Lord shall be revealed, and all flesh shall see it together.

This is our hope. This is the faith with which I return to the 19
South. With this faith we will be able to hew out of the mountain
of despair a stone of hope. With this faith we will be able to transform
the jangling discords of our nation into a beautiful symphony of
brotherhood. With this faith we will be able to work together, to
pray together, to struggle together, to go to jail together, to stand up
for freedom together, knowing that we will be free one day.

This will be the day when all of God's children will be able to 20
sing with new meaning

> My country, 'tis of thee,
> Sweet land of liberty,
>   Of thee I sing:
> Land where my fathers died,
> Land of the pilgrims' pride,
> From every mountainside
>   Let freedom ring.

And if America is to be a great nation this must become true. 21
So let freedom ring from the prodigious hilltops of New Hampshire.
Let freedom ring from the mighty mountains of New York. Let free-
dom ring from the heightening Alleghenies of Pennsylvania!

Let freedom ring from the snowcapped Rockies of Colorado! 22

Let freedom ring from the curvaceous peaks of California! 23

But not only that; let freedom ring from Stone Mountain of 24
Georgia!

Let freedom ring from Lookout Mountain of Tennessee! 25

Let freedom ring from every hill and molehill of Mississippi. From 26
every mountainside, let freedom ring.

When we let freedom ring, when we let it ring from every village 27
and every hamlet, from every state and every city, we will be able to
speed up that day when all of God's children, black men and white
men, Jews and Gentiles, Protestants and Catholics, will be able to
join hands and sing in the words of the old Negro spiritual, "Free at
last! free at last! thank God almighty, we are free at last!"

QUESTIONS ON MEANING

1. What is the apparent PURPOSE of this speech?
2. What THESIS does King develop in his first four paragraphs?
3. What does King mean by the "marvelous new militancy which has
   engulfed the Negro community" (para. 6)? Does this contradict King's
   nonviolent philosophy?
4. In what passages of his speech does King notice events of history? Where
   does he acknowledge the historic occasion on which he is speaking?

QUESTIONS ON WRITING STRATEGY

1. Analyze King's ETHICAL APPEAL (see p. 464). Where in the speech, for
   instance, does he present himself as reasonable despite his passion? To
   what extent does his personal authority lend power to his words?
2. What indicates that King's words were meant primarily for an AUDIENCE
   of listeners, and only secondarily for a reading audience? To hear these
   indications, try reading the speech aloud. What use of PARALLELISM do
   you notice?
3. Where in the speech does King acknowledge that not all of his listeners
   are African American?
4. How much EMPHASIS does King place on the past? How much does he
   place on the future?
5. OTHER METHODS. What EXAMPLES does King offer of particular injus-
   tices (para. 7)? In his speech as a whole, do his observations tend to
   be GENERAL or SPECIFIC?

QUESTIONS ON LANGUAGE

1. In general, is the language of King's speech ABSTRACT or CONCRETE?
   How is this level appropriate to the speaker's message and to the span
   of history with which he deals?

2. Point to memorable FIGURES OF SPEECH.
3. Define momentous (para. 1); manacles, languishing (2); promissory note (3); defaulted, hallowed, gradualism (4); inextricably (6); mobility, ghetto (7); tribulations, redemptive (8); interposition, nullification (16); prodigious (21); curvaceous (23); hamlet (27).

SUGGESTIONS FOR WRITING

1. Has America (or your locality) today moved closer in any respects to the fulfillment of King's dream? Discuss this question in an essay, giving specific examples.
2. Propose some course of action in a situation that you consider an injustice. Racial injustice is one possible area, or unfairness to any minority, or to women, children, the old, ex-convicts, the handicapped, the poor. If possible, narrow your subject to a particular incident or a local situation on which you can write knowledgeably.
3. CRITICAL WRITING. What can you INFER from this speech about King's own attitudes toward oppression and injustice? Does he follow his own injunction not "to satisfy our thirst for freedom by drinking from the cup of bitterness and hatred" (para. 6)? Explain your answer, using EVIDENCE from the speech.
4. CONNECTIONS. King's "I Have a Dream" and Jonathan Swift's "A Modest Proposal" (the following essay) both seek to arouse an AUDIENCE to action, and yet they take very different approaches to achieve this PURPOSE. COMPARE AND CONTRAST the authors' persuasive strategies, considering especially their effectiveness for the situation each writes about and the audience each addresses.

JONATHAN SWIFT

JONATHAN SWIFT (1667–1745), the son of English parents who had settled in Ireland, divided his energies among literature, politics, and the Church of England. Dissatisfied with the quiet life of an Anglican parish priest, Swift spent much of his time in London hobnobbing with writers and producing pamphlets in support of the Tory Party. In 1713 Queen Anne rewarded his political services with an assignment the London-loving Swift didn't want: to supervise St. Patrick's Cathedral in Dublin. There, as Dean Swift, he ended his days — beloved by the Irish, whose interests he defended against the English government. Although Swift's chief works include the remarkable satires *The Battle of the Books* and *A Tale of a Tub* (both 1704) and scores of fine poems, he is best remembered for *Gulliver's Travels* (1726), an account of four imaginary voyages. This classic is always abridged when it is given to children because of its frank descriptions of human filth and viciousness. In *Gulliver's Travels*, Swift pays tribute to the reasoning portion of "that animal called man," and delivers a stinging rebuke to the rest of him.

A Modest Proposal

Three consecutive years of drought and sparse crops had worked hardship upon the Irish when Swift wrote this ferocious essay in the summer of 1729. At the time, there were said to be 35,000 wandering beggars in the country: Whole families had quit their farms and had taken to the roads. Large landowners, of English ancestry, preferred to ignore their tenants' sufferings and lived abroad to dodge taxes and payment of church duties. Swift had no special fondness for the Irish, but he hated the inhumanity he witnessed.

Although printed as a pamphlet in Dublin, Swift's essay is clearly meant for English readers as well as Irish ones. When circulated, the pamphlet caused a sensation in both Ireland and England and had to be reprinted seven times in the same year. Swift is an expert with plain, vigorous English prose, and "A Modest Proposal" is a masterpiece of satire and irony. (If you are uncertain what Swift argues for, see the discussion of SATIRE and IRONY in Useful Terms.)

*For Preventing the Children of Poor People in Ireland
from Being a Burden to Their Parents or Country,
and for Making Them Beneficial to the Public*

It is a melancholy object to those who walk through this great   1
town[1] or travel in the country, when they see the streets, the roads,
and cabin doors, crowded with beggars of the female sex, followed
by three, four, or six children, all in rags and importuning every
passenger for an alms. These mothers, instead of being able to work
for their honest livelihood, are forced to employ all their time in
strolling to beg sustenance for their helpless infants, who, as they
grow up, either turn thieves for want of work, or leave their dear
native country to fight for the Pretender in Spain, or sell themselves
to the Barbados.[2]

I think it is agreed by all parties that this prodigious number of   2
children in the arms, or on the backs, or at the heels of their mothers,
and frequently of their fathers, is in the present deplorable state of
the kingdom a very great additional grievance; and therefore whoever
could find out a fair, cheap, and easy method of making these children
sound, useful members of the commonwealth would deserve so well
of the public as to have his statue set up for a preserver of the nation.

But my intention is very far from being confined to provide only   3
for the children of professed beggars; it is of a much greater extent,
and shall take in the whole number of infants at a certain age who
are born of parents in effect as little able to support them as those
who demand our charity in the streets.

As to my own part, having turned my thoughts for many years   4
upon this important subject, and maturely weighed the several
schemes of other projectors,[3] I have always found them grossly mistaken in their computation. It is true, a child just dropped from its
dam may be supported by her milk for a solar year, with little other
nourishment; at most not above the value of two shillings, which the
mother may certainly get, or the value in scraps, by her lawful
occupation of begging; and it is exactly at one year that I propose to
provide for them in such a manner as instead of being a charge upon
their parents or the parish, or wanting food and raiment for the rest

---

[1]Dublin. — EDS.

[2]The Pretender was James Stuart, exiled in Spain; in 1718 many Irishmen had
joined an army seeking to restore him to the English throne. Others wishing to
emigrate had signed papers as indentured servants, agreeing to work for a number of
years in the Barbados or other British colonies in exchange for their ocean passage. —
EDS.

[3]Planners. — EDS.

of their lives, they shall on the contrary contribute to the feeding, and partly to the clothing, of many thousands.

There is likewise another great advantage in my scheme, that it will prevent those voluntary abortions, and that horrid practice of women murdering their bastard children, alas, too frequent among us, sacrificing the poor innocent babes, I doubt, more to avoid the expense than the shame, which would move tears and pity in the most savage and inhuman breast.

The number of souls in this kingdom being usually reckoned one million and a half, of these I calculate there may be about two hundred thousand couples whose wives are breeders; from which number I subtract thirty thousand couples who are able to maintain their own children, although I apprehend there cannot be so many under the present distress of the kingdom; but this being granted, there will remain an hundred and seventy thousand breeders. I again subtract fifty thousand for those women who miscarry, or whose children die by accident or disease within the year. There only remain an hundred and twenty thousand children of poor parents annually born. The question therefore is, how this number shall be reared and provided for, which, as I have already said, under the present situation of affairs, is utterly impossible by all the methods hitherto proposed. For we can neither employ them in handicraft or agriculture; we neither build houses (I mean in the country) nor cultivate land. They can very seldom pick up a livelihood stealing till they arrive at six years old, except where they are of towardly parts;[4] although I confess they learn the rudiments much earlier, during which time they can however be looked upon only as probationers, as I have been informed by a principal gentleman in the country of Cavan, who protested to me that he never knew above one or two instances under the age of six, even in a part of the kingdom so renowned for the quickest proficiency in that art.

I am assured by our merchants that a boy or a girl before twelve years old is no salable commodity; and even when they come to this age they will not yield above three pounds, or three pounds and half a crown at most on the Exchange; which cannot turn to account either to the parents or the kingdom, the charge of nutriment and rags having been at least four times that value.

I shall now therefore humbly propose my own thoughts, which I hope will not be liable to the least objection.

I have been assured by a very knowing American of my acquaintance in London, that a young healthy child well nursed is at a year

---

[4]Teachable wits, innate abilities. — Eds.

old a most delicious, nourishing, and wholesome food, whether stewed, roasted, baked, or boiled; and I make no doubt that it will equally serve in a fricassee or a ragout.[5]

I do therefore humbly offer it to public consideration that of the [10] hundred and twenty thousand children, already computed, twenty thousand may be reserved for breed, whereof only one fourth part to be males, which is more than we allow to sheep, black cattle, or swine; and my reason is that these children are seldom the fruits of marriage, a circumstance not much regarded by our savages, therefore one male will be sufficient to serve four females. That the remaining hundred thousand may at a year old be offered in sale to the persons of quality and fortune through the kingdom, always advising the mother to let them suck plentifully in the last month, so as to render them plump and fat for a good table. A child will make two dishes at an entertainment for friends; and when the family dines alone, the fore or hind quarter will make a reasonable dish, and seasoned with a little pepper or salt will be very good boiled on the fourth day, especially in winter.

I have reckoned upon a medium that a child just born will weigh [11] twelve pounds, and in a solar year it tolerably nursed increaseth to twenty-eight pounds.

I grant this food will be somewhat dear, and therefore very proper [12] for landlords, who, as they have already devoured most of the parents, seem to have the best title to the children.

Infant's flesh will be in season throughout the year, but more [13] plentiful in March, and a little before and after. For we are told by a grave author, an eminent French physician,[6] that fish being a prolific diet, there are more children born in Roman Catholic countries about nine months after Lent than at any other season; therefore, reckoning a year after Lent, the markets will be more glutted than usual, because the number of popish infants is at least three to one in this kingdom; and therefore it will have one other collateral advantage, by lessening the number of Papists among us.

I have already computed the charge of nursing a beggar's child [14] (in which list I reckon all cottagers, laborers, and four-fifths of the farmers) to be about two shillings per annum, rags included; and I believe no gentleman would repine to give ten shillings for the carcass of a good fat child, which, as I have said, will make four dishes of excellent nutritive meat, when he hath only some particular friend

[5]Stew. — Eds.

[6]Swift's favorite French writer, François Rabelais, sixteenth-century author; not "grave" at all, but a broad humorist. — Eds.

or his own family to dine with him. Thus the squire will learn to be a good landlord, and grow people among the tenants; the mother will have eight shillings net profit, and be fit for work till she produces another child.

Those who are more thrifty (as I must confess the times require)   15 may flay the carcass; the skin of which artificially[7] dressed will make admirable gloves for ladies, and summer boots for fine gentlemen.

As to our city of Dublin, shambles[8] may be appointed for this   16 purpose in the most convenient parts of it, and butchers we may be assured will not be wanting; although I rather recommend buying the children alive, and dressing them hot from the knife as we do roasting pigs.

A very worthy person, a true lover of his country, and whose   17 virtues I highly esteem, was lately pleased in discoursing on this matter to offer a refinement upon my scheme. He said that many gentlemen of his kingdom, having of late destroyed their deer, he conceived that the want of venison might be well supplied by the bodies of young lads and maidens, not exceeding fourteen years of age nor under twelve, so great a number of both sexes in every county being now ready to starve for want of work and service; and these to be disposed of by their parents, if alive, or otherwise by their nearest relations. But with due deference to so excellent a friend and so deserving a patriot, I cannot be altogether in his sentiments; for as to the males, my American acquaintance assured me from frequent experience that their flesh was generally tough and lean, like that of our schoolboys, by continual exercise, and their taste disagreeable; and to fatten them would not answer the charge. Then as to the females, it would, I think with humble submission, be a loss to the public, because they soon would become breeders themselves; and besides, it is not improbable that some scrupulous people might be apt to censure such a practice (although indeed very unjustly) as a little bordering upon cruelty; which, I confess, hath always been with me the strongest objection against any project, how well soever intended.

But in order to justify my friend, he confessed that this expedient   18 was put into his head by the famous Psalmanazar,[9] a native of the

[7]With art or craft. — Eds.

[8]Butcher shops or slaughterhouses. — Eds.

[9]Georges Psalmanazar, a Frenchman who pretended to be Japanese, author of a completely imaginary *Description of the Isle Formosa* (1705), had become a well-known figure in gullible London society. — Eds.

island Formosa, who came from thence to London above twenty years ago, and in conversation told my friend that in his country when any young person happened to be put to death, the executioner sold the carcass to persons of quality as a prime dainty; and that in his time the body of a plump girl of fifteen, who was crucified for an attempt to poison the emperor, was sold to his Imperial Majesty's prime minister of state, and other great mandarins of the court, in joints from the gibbet, at four hundred crowns. Neither indeed can I deny that if the same use were made of several plump young girls in this town, who without one single groat to their fortunes cannot stir abroad without a chair, and appear at the playhouse and assemblies in foreign fineries which they never will pay for, the kingdom would not be the worse.

Some persons of a desponding spirit are in great concern about   19
that vast number of poor people who are aged, diseased, or maimed, and I have been desired to employ my thoughts what course may be taken to ease the nation of so grievous an encumbrance. But I am not in the least pain upon that matter, because it is very well known that they are every day dying and rotting by cold and famine, and filth and vermin, as fast as can be reasonably expected. And as to the younger laborers, they are now in almost as hopeful a condition. They cannot get work, and consequently pine away for want of nourishment to a degree that if any time they are accidentally hired to common labor, they have not strength to perform it; and thus the country and themselves are happily delivered from the evils to come.

I have too long digressed, and therefore shall return to my subject.   20
I think the advantages by the proposal which I have made are obvious and many, as well as of the highest importance.

For first, as I have already observed, it would greatly lessen the   21
number of Papists, with whom we are yearly overrun, being the principal breeders of the nation as well as our most dangerous enemies; and who stay at home on purpose to deliver the kingdom to the Pretender, hoping to take their advantage by the absence of so many good Protestants, who have chosen rather to leave their country than to stay at home and pay tithes against their conscience to an Episcopal curate.

Secondly, the poorer tenants will have something valuable of   22
their own, which by law may be made liable to distress,[10] and help to pay their landlord's rent, their corn and cattle being already seized and money a thing unknown.

[10]Subject to seizure by creditors. — EDS.

Thirdly, whereas the maintenance of an hundred thousand chil- 23
dren, from two years old and upwards, cannot be computed at less
than ten shillings a piece per annum, the nation's stock will be
thereby increased fifty thousand pounds per annum, besides the profit
of a new dish introduced to the tables of all gentlemen of fortune in
the kingdom who have any refinement in taste. And the money will
circulate among ourselves, the goods being entirely of our own growth
and manufacture.

Fourthly, the constant breeders, besides the gain of eight shillings 24
sterling per annum by the sale of their children, will be rid of the
charge of maintaining them after the first year.

Fifthly, this food would likewise bring great custom to taverns, 25
where the vintners will certainly be so prudent as to procure the best
receipts for dressing it to perfection, and consequently have their
houses frequented by all the fine gentlemen, who justly value themselves upon their knowledge in good eating; and a skillful cook, who
understands how to oblige his guests, will contrive to make it as
expensive as they please.

Sixthly, this would be a great inducement to marriage, which all 26
wise nations have either encouraged by rewards or enforced by laws
and penalties. It would increase the care and tenderness of mothers
toward their children, when they were sure of a settlement for life to
the poor babes, provided in some sort by the public, to their annual
profit instead of expense. We should see an honest emulation among
the married women, which of them could bring the fattest child to
the market. Men would become as fond of their wives during the
time of their pregnancy as they are now of their mares in foal, their
cows in calf, or sows when they are ready to farrow; nor offer to beat
or kick them (as is too frequent a practice) for fear of a miscarriage.

Many other advantages might be enumerated. For instance, the 27
addition of some thousand carcasses in our exportation of barreled
beef, the propagation of swine's flesh, and improvements in the art
of making good bacon, so much wanted among us by the great
destruction of pigs, too frequent at our tables, which are no way
comparable in taste or magnificence to a well-grown, fat, yearling
child, which roasted whole will make a considerable figure at a lord
mayor's feast or any other public entertainment. But this and many
others I omit, being studious of brevity.

Supposing that one thousand families in this city would be con- 28
stant customers for infants' flesh, besides others who might have it at
merry meetings, particularly weddings and christenings, I compute
that Dublin would take off annually about twenty thousand carcasses,

and the rest of the kingdom (where probably they will be sold somewhat cheaper) the remaining eighty thousand.

I can think of no one objection that will possibly be raised against   29
this proposal, unless it should be urged that the number of people
will be thereby much lessened in the kingdom. This I freely own,
and it was indeed one principal design in offering it to the world. I
desire the reader will observe, that I calculate my remedy for this one
individual kingdom of Ireland and for no other that ever was, is, or
I think ever can be upon earth. Therefore let no man talk to me of
other expedients: of taxing our absentees at five shillings a pound: of
using neither clothes nor household furniture except what is of our
own growth and manufacture: of utterly rejecting the materials and
instruments that promote foreign luxury: of curing the expensiveness
of pride, vanity, idleness, and gaming in our women: of introducing
a vein of parsimony, prudence, and temperance: of learning to love
our country, in the want of which we differ even from Laplanders
and the inhabitants of Topinamboo:[11] of quitting our animosities and
factions, nor acting any longer like the Jews, who were murdering
one another at the very moment their city was taken:[12] of being a
little cautious not to sell our country and conscience for nothing: of
teaching landlords to have at least one degree of mercy toward their
tenants: lastly, of putting a spirit of honesty, industry, and skill into
our shopkeepers; who, if a resolution could now be taken to buy only
our native goods, would immediately unite to cheat and exact upon
us in the price, the measure, and the goodness, nor could ever yet
be brought to make one fair proposal of just dealing, though often
and earnestly invited to it.

Therefore I repeat, let no man talk to me of these and the like   30
expedients, till he hath at least some glimpse of hope that there will
ever be some hearty and sincere attempt to put them in practice.

But as to myself, having been wearied out for many years with   31
offering vain, idle, visionary thoughts, and at length utterly despairing
of success, I fortunately fell upon this proposal, which, as it is wholly
new, so it hath something solid and real, of no expense and little
trouble, full in our own power, and whereby we can incur no danger
in disobliging England. For this kind of commodity will not bear
exportation, the flesh being of too tender a consistence to admit a

---

[11]District of Brazil inhabited by primitive tribes. — EDS.
[12]During the Roman siege of Jerusalem (A.D. 70), prominent Jews were executed
on the charge of being in league with the enemy. — EDS.

long continuance in salt, although perhaps I could name a country which would be glad to eat up our whole nation without it.

After all, I am not so violently bent upon my own opinion as to 32 reject any offer proposed by wise men, which shall be found equally innocent, cheap, easy, and effectual. But before something of that kind shall be advanced in contradiction to my scheme, and offering a better, I desire the author or authors will be pleased maturely to consider two points. First, as things now stand, how they will be able to find food and raiment for an hundred thousand useless mouths and backs. And secondly, there being a round million of creatures in human figure throughout this kingdom, whose sole subsistence put into a common stock would leave them in debt two millions of pounds sterling, adding those who are beggars by profession to the bulk of farmers, cottagers, and laborers, with their wives and children who are beggars in effect; i desire those politicians who dislike my overture, and may perhaps be so bold to attempt an answer, that they will first ask the parents of these mortals whether they would not at this day think it a great happiness to have been sold for food at a year old in this manner I prescribe, and thereby have avoided such a perpetual scene of misfortunes as they have since gone through by the oppression of landlords, the impossibility of paying rent without money or trade, the want of common sustenance, with neither house nor clothes to cover them from the inclemencies of the weather, and the most inevitable prospect of entailing the like or greater miseries upon their breed forever.

I profess, in the sincerity of my heart, that I have not the least 33 personal interest in endeavoring to promote this necessary work, having no other motive than the public good of my country, by advancing our trade, providing for infants, relieving the poor, and giving some pleasure to the rich. I have no children by which I can propose to get a single penny; the youngest being nine years old, and my wife past childbearing.

QUESTIONS ON MEANING

1. On the surface, what is Swift proposing?
2. Beneath his IRONY, what is Swift's argument?
3. What do you take to be the PURPOSE of Swift's essay?
4. How does the introductory paragraph serve Swift's purpose?

5. Comment on the statement, "I can think of no one objection that will possibly be raised against this proposal" (para. 29). What objections can you think of?

QUESTIONS ON WRITING STRATEGY

1. Describe the mask of the personage through whom Swift writes.
2. By what means does the writer attest to his reasonableness?
3. At what point in the essay did it become clear to you that the proposal isn't modest but horrible?
4. As an essay in argument, does "A Modest Proposal" appeal primarily to reason or to emotion?
5. OTHER METHODS. Although not serious, Swift's proposal is worked out in detailed paragraphs of PROCESS ANALYSIS. What is the EFFECT of paragraphs 10–16? Why do you think Swift took such trouble with the process?

QUESTIONS ON LANGUAGE

1. How does Swift's choice of words enforce the monstrousness of his proposal? Note especially words from the vocabulary of breeding and butchery.
2. Consult your dictionary for the meanings of any of the following words not yet in your vocabulary: importuning, sustenance (para. 1); prodigious, commonwealth (2); computation, raiment (4); apprehend, rudiments, probationers (6); nutriment (7); fricassee (9); repine (14); flay (15); scrupulous, censure (17); mandarins (18); desponding, encumbrance (19); per annum (23); vintners (25); emulation, foal, farrow (26); expedients, parsimony, animosities (29); disobliging, consistence (31); overture, inclemencies (32).

SUGGESTIONS FOR WRITING

1. Consider a group of people whom you regard as mistreated or victimized. (If none come immediately to mind, see today's newspaper — or write, less seriously, about college freshmen.) Then write either:

   a. A straight argument, giving EVIDENCE, in which you set forth possible solutions to their plight.
   b. An IRONIC proposal in the manner of Swift. If you do this one, find a device other than cannibalism to eliminate the victims or their problems. You don't want to imitate Swift too closely; he is probably inimitable.

2. In an encyclopedia, look into what has happened in Ireland since Swift wrote. Choose a specific contemporary aspect of Irish-English relations, research it in books and periodicals, and write a report on it.
3. CRITICAL WRITING. Choose several examples of irony in "A Modest

Proposal" that you find particularly effective. In a brief essay, ANALYZE Swift's use of irony. Do your examples of irony depend on understating, overstating, or saying the opposite of what is meant? How do they improve on literal statements? What is the value of irony in argument?

4. CONNECTIONS. Analyze the ways Swift and Martin Luther King, Jr. (in "I Have A Dream," p. 516), create sympathy for the oppressed groups they are concerned about. Concentrate not only on what they say but on the words they use and their TONE. Then write a PROCESS ANALYSIS explaining techniques for portraying oppression so as to win the reader's sympathy. Use quotations or PARAPHRASES from Swift's and King's essays as examples. If you can think of other techniques that neither author uses, by all means include and illustrate them as well.

JONATHAN SWIFT ON WRITING

Although surely one of the most inventive writers in English literature, Swift voiced his contempt for writers of his day who bragged of their newness and originality. In *The Battle of the Books*, he compares such a self-professed original to a spider who "spins and spits wholly from himself, and scorns to own any obligation or assistance from without." Swift has the fable-writer Aesop praise that writer who, like a bee gathering nectar, draws from many sources.

> Erect your schemes with as much method and skill as you please; yet if the materials be nothing but dirt, spun out of your own entrails (the guts of modern brains), the edifice will conclude at last in a cobweb. . . . As for us Ancients, we are content, with the bee, to pretend to nothing of our own beyond our wings and our voice, that is to say, our flights and our language. For the rest, whatever we have got has been by infinite labor and search and ranging through every corner of nature; the difference is, that, instead of dirt and poison, we have rather chosen to fill our hives with honey and wax, thus furnishing mankind with the two noblest of things, which are sweetness and light.

Swift's advice for a writer would seem to be: Don't just invent things out of thin air; read the best writers of the past. Observe and converse. Do legwork.

Interestingly, when in *Gulliver's Travels* Swift portrays his ideal beings, the Houyhnhnms, a race of noble and intelligent horses, he includes no writers at all in their society. "The Houyhnhnms have no letters," Gulliver observes, "and consequently their knowledge is all traditional." Still, "in poetry they must be allowed to excel all other mortals; wherein the justness of their description are indeed inimitable." (Those very traits — striking comparisons and detailed descriptions — make much of Swift's own writing memorable.)

In his great book, in "A Modest Proposal," and in virtually all he wrote, Swift's purpose was forthright and evident. He declared in "Verses on the Death of Dr. Swift,"

> As with a moral view designed
> To cure the vices of mankind: . . .
> Yet malice never was his aim;
> He lashed the vice but spared the name.
> No individual could resent,
> Where thousands equally were meant.
> His satire points at no defect
> But what all mortals may correct.

FOR DISCUSSION

1. Try applying Swift's parable of the spider and the bee to our own day. How much truth is left in it?
2. Reread thoughtfully the quotation from Swift's poem. According to the poet, what faults or abuses can a satiric writer fall into? How may these be avoided?
3. What do you take to be Swift's main PURPOSE as a writer? In your own words, summarize it.

ADDITIONAL WRITING TOPICS

Argument and Persuasion

1. Write a persuasive essay in which you express a deeply felt opinion. In it, address a particular person or audience. For instance, you might direct your essay:

   To a friend unwilling to attend a ballet performance (or a wrestling match) with you on the grounds that such an event is for the birds
   To a teacher who asserts that more term papers, and longer ones, are necessary
   To a state trooper who intends to give you a ticket for speeding
   To a male employer skeptical of hiring women
   To a developer who plans to tear down a historic house
   To someone who sees no purpose in studying a foreign language
   To a high-school class whose members don't want to go to college
   To an older generation skeptical of the value of "all that noise" (meaning current popular music)
   To an atheist who asserts that religion is a lot of pie-in-the-sky
   To the members of a library board who want to ban a certain book

2. Write a letter to your campus newspaper, or to a city newspaper, in which you argue for or against a certain cause or view. You may wish to object to a particular feature, column, or editorial in the paper. Send your letter and see if it is published.

3. Write a short letter to your congressional or state representative, arguing in favor of (or against) the passage of some pending legislation. See a news magazine or a newspaper for a worthwhile bill to champion. Or else write in favor of some continuing cause: for instance, saving whales, reducing (or increasing) armaments, or providing aid to the arts.

4. Write an essay arguing that something you feel strongly about should be changed, removed, abolished, enforced, repeated, revised, reinstated, or reconsidered. Be sure to propose some plan for carrying out whatever suggestions you make. Possible topics, listed to start you thinking, are:

   The drinking age
   Gun laws
   Low-income housing
   Graduation requirements
   The mandatory retirement age
   ROTC programs in schools and colleges
   The voting age
   Movie ratings (G, PG, PG-13, R, NC-17, X)
   School prayer
   Fraternities and sororities

Dress codes
TV advertising

5. On the model of Maire Flynn's three-part condensed argument on page 467, write a condensed argument in three paragraphs demonstrating data, claim, and warrant. For a topic, consider any problem or controversy in this morning's newspaper and form an opinion on it.

PART TWO

MIXING THE METHODS

$\mathbf{E}$verywhere in this book, we've tried to prove how flexible the methods of development are. All the preceding essays offer superb examples of DESCRIPTION or CLASSIFICATION or DEFINITION or ARGUMENT, but every one also illustrates other methods, too — description in PROCESS ANALYSIS, ANALYSIS and NARRATION in COMPARISON, EXAMPLES and CAUSE AND EFFECT in argument.

In the next four chapters, we take this point even further: We abandon the individual methods and instead focus on how writers choose from all the methods to achieve their purpose. Each chapter's essays center on a common theme: the power of family, language and truth, our place in the environment, diversity in the curriculum. Yet, as you will see, while several authors write on the same subject, their approaches, including their use of methods, could not be more varied. Each writer draws on whatever methods, at whatever length, will help him or her get a point across to readers.

You have already begun to attain this same command by focusing on the individual methods, making each a part of your kit of writing tools. Now, when you face a writing assignment, you can consider whether and how each method may help you develop your subject. Indeed, one way to approach a subject is to pose a series of questions derived from the methods. We have listed these questions below, along with some examples from George Orwell's "Politics and the English Language," an essay appearing in Chapter 12 (p. 606). This long and powerful essay is about the degraded condition of the English language and thus of thought and truth. In it, Orwell uses every single method of development.

1. *Narration: Can you tell a story about the subject?* Orwell tells several brief stories about real and imaginary abuses of the language.

2. *Description: Can you use your senses to illuminate the subject?* Using vivid IMAGES of people and the effect of their words, Orwell freshens his narratives and other passages.

3. *Example: Can you point to instances that will make the subject concrete and specific?* Orwell uses innumerable specific examples — passages of prose, particular phrases, dishonest people, political lies.

4. *Comparison and contrast: Will setting the subject alongside another generate useful information?* Comparison lets Orwell show concrete differences between the prose he despises and the prose he trusts.

5. *Process analysis: Will a step-by-step explanation add to the reader's understanding?* Orwell explains several processes, most notably how to defend the English language by writing freshly, concretely, simply.

6. *Division or analysis: Can slicing the subject into its parts produce a clearer vision of it?* "Politics and the English Language" is studded with analyses of prose passages by other writers.

7. *Classification: Is it worthwhile to sort the subject into kinds or groups?* A key section of Orwell's essay classifies the "tricks" of bad prose writers, such as "pretentious diction" and "meaningless words."

8. *Cause and effect: Does it add to the subject to ask why it happened or what its results are?* Orwell answers both of these questions, examining the causes and the effects of the language's decline.

9. *Definition: Can you trace a boundary that will clarify the subject's meaning?* In one definition after another, Orwell pins down exactly what he means by terms such as "dying metaphor" and "false verbal limb."

10. *Argument and persuasion: Can you state an opinion or make a proposal about the subject?* "Politics and the English Language" is an extended argument against one kind of writing and in favor of another. Orwell states his opinion early on and supports it with the kinds of EVIDENCE we've noted above.

Rarely will every one of these questions produce fruit for a given essay, but inevitably two or three or four will. Try the whole list when you're stuck at the beginning of an assignment, or when you're snagged in the middle of a draft. You'll find they are as good at removing obstacles as they are at generating ideas.

11

THE POWER OF FAMILY

What is the hold, for good or ill, that family members have on one another? The essays in this chapter can only begin to answer such a question, but they are so varied that just about everyone will hear in them a familiar chord or two. In "Mama Went to Work," Vivian Gornick tells of her adolescent struggles with her mother's obsessive grief and severe depression. In "My Brother on the Shoulder of the Road," Clifford Chase probes his relationship with his brother, who died of AIDS. In "Aria: A Memoir of a Bilingual Childhood," Richard Rodriguez recalls the loss he experienced when English supplanted Spanish in his Mexican American family. In "The Colorings of Childhood," David Updike contemplates his son's advantages as the offspring of a white American father and a black Kenyan mother. And finally, in "No Name Woman," Maxine Hong Kingston tries to imagine what pressures of family led her Chinese aunt to drown herself in the household well.

VIVIAN GORNICK

VIVIAN GORNICK was born in 1935 in New York City to working-class Jewish parents. Her father died when she was thirteen, a loss that possessed her mother, who in turn stifled Gornick. Their relationship is the subject of Gornick's intense memoir, *Fierce Attachments* (1987). Gornick left her mother's home to attend the City College of New York, earning a B.A. in 1957, and New York University, earning an M.A. in 1960. She was a staff writer on the *Village Voice* from 1969 to 1977 and has contributed articles and reviews, many of them dealing with women's issues, to *The Nation*, the *New York Times Magazine*, *The Atlantic*, the *Washington Post*, and other periodicals. Gornick has taught creative writing at several schools, most recently the University of Arizona. Her books, in addition to *Fierce Attachments*, are *In Search of Ali Mahmoud: An American Woman in Egypt* (1973), *The Romance of American Communism* (1978), *Essays in Feminism* (1979), and *Women in Science: Portraits from a World in Transition* (1983).

Mama Went to Work

This excerpt from *Fierce Attachments* was reprinted and titled in *Calling Home: Working-Class Women's Writings* (1990). As an adolescent, Gornick recalls, she occupied a world defined by her mother's determined, miserable widowhood.

While reading this reminiscence, notice the way Gornick uses at least five methods of development: NARRATION structures her story. DESCRIPTION vivifies her feelings. EXAMPLE pins down specifics. ANALYSIS makes sense of her experience. And, overall, CAUSE AND EFFECT explains her mother's reaction to her father's death and her own reaction to her mother.

Mama went to work five weeks after my father died. He had left 1 us two thousand dollars. To work or not to work was not a debatable question. But it's hard to imagine what would have happened if economic necessity had not forced her out of the house. As it was, it seemed to me that she lay on a couch in a half-darkened room for twenty-five years with her hand across her forehead murmuring, "I can't." Even though she could, and did.

She pulled on her girdle and her old gray suit, stepped into her 2 black suede chunky heels, applied powder and lipstick to her face, and took the subway downtown to an employment agency where she got a job clerking in an office for twenty-eight dollars a week. After that, she rose each morning, got dressed and drank coffee, made out a grocery list for me, left it together with money on the kitchen table, walked four blocks to the subway station, bought the *Times*, read it on the train, got off at Forty-second Street, entered her office building, sat down at her desk, put in a day's work, made the trip home at five o'clock, came in the apartment door, slumped onto the kitchen bench for supper, then onto the couch where she instantly sank into a depression she welcomed like a warm bath. It was as though she had worked all day to earn the despair waiting faithfully for her at the end of her unwilling journey into daily life.

Weekends, of course, the depression was unremitting. A black and wordless pall hung over the apartment all of Saturday and all of Sunday. Mama neither cooked, cleaned, nor shopped. She took no part in idle chatter: the exchange of banalities that fills a room with human presence, declares an interest in being alive. She would not laugh, respond, or participate in any of the compulsive kitchen talk that went on among the rest of us: me, my aunt Sarah, Nettie,[1] my brother. She spoke minimally, and when she did speak her voice was uniformly tight and miserable, always pulling her listener back to a proper recollection of her "condition." If she answered the phone her voice dropped a full octave when she said hello; she could not trust that the caller would otherwise gauge properly the abiding nature of her pain. For five years she did not go to a movie, a concert, a public meeting. She worked, and she suffered.

Widowhood provided Mama with a higher form of being. In refusing to recover from my father's death she had discovered that her life was endowed with a seriousness her years in the kitchen had denied her. She remained devoted to this seriousness for thirty years. She never tired of it, never grew bored or restless in its company, found new ways to keep alive the interest it deserved and had so undeniably earned.

Mourning Papa became her profession, her identity, her persona. Years later, when I was thinking about the piece of politics inside of which we had all lived (Marxism and the Communist Party), and I realized that people who worked as plumbers, bakers, or sewing-machine operators had thought of themselves as thinkers, poets, and scholars because they were members of the Communist Party, I saw that Mama had assumed her widowhood in much the same way. It elevated her in her own eyes, made of her a spiritually significant

3

4

5

[1]Nettie was a neighbor and a friend of the family. — EDS.

person, lent richness to her gloom and rhetoric to her speech. Papa's death became a religion that provided ceremony and doctrine. A woman-who-has-lost-the-love-of-her-life was now her orthodoxy: She paid it Talmudic attention.

Papa had never been so real to me in life as he was in death.   6
Always a somewhat shadowy figure, benign and smiling, standing there behind Mama's dramatics about married love, he became and remained what felt like the necessary instrument of her permanent devastation. It was almost as though she had lived with Papa in order that she might arrive at this moment. Her distress was so all-consuming it seemed ordained. For me, surely, it ordered the world anew.

The air I breathed was soaked in her desperation, made thick and   7
heady by it, exciting and dangerous. Her pain became my element, the country in which I lived, the rule beneath which I bowed. It commanded me, made me respond against my will. I longed endlessly to get away from her, but I could not leave the room when she was in it. I dreaded her return from work, but I was never not there when she came home. In her presence anxiety swelled my lungs (I suffered constrictions of the chest and sometimes felt an iron-ring clamped across my skull), but I locked myself in the bathroom and wept buckets on her behalf. On Friday I prepared myself for two solid days of weeping and sighing and the mysterious reproof that depression leaks into the air like the steady escape of gas when the pilot light is extinguished. I woke up guilty and went to bed guilty, and on weekends the guilt accumulated into low-grade infection.

She made me sleep with her for a year, and for twenty years   8
afterward I could not bear a woman's hand on me. Afraid to sleep alone, she slung an arm across my stomach, pulled me toward her, fingered my flesh nervously, inattentively. I shrank from her touch: she never noticed. I yearned toward the wall, couldn't get close enough, was always being pulled back. My body became a column of aching stiffness. I must have been excited. Certainly I was repelled.

For two years she dragged me to the cemetery every second or   9
third Sunday morning. The cemetery was in Queens. This meant taking three buses and traveling an hour and fifteen minutes each way. When we climbed onto the third bus she'd begin to cry. Helplessly, I would embrace her. Her cries would grow louder. Inflamed with discomfort, my arm would stiffen around her shoulder and I would stare at the black rubber floor. The bus would arrive at the last stop just as she reached the verge of convulsion.

"We have to get off, Ma," I'd plead in a whisper.   10

She would shake herself reluctantly (she hated to lose momentum   11 once she'd started on a real wail) and slowly climb down off the bus. As we went through the gates of the cemetery, however, she'd rally to her own cause. She would clutch my arm and pull me across miles of tombstones (neither of us ever seemed to remember the exact location of the grave), stumbling like a drunk, lurching about and shrieking, "Where's Papa? Help me find Papa! They've lost Papa. Beloved! I'm coming. Wait, only wait, I'm coming!" Then we would find the grave and she would fling herself across it, arrived at last in a storm of climatic release. On the way home she was a rag doll. And I? Numb and dumb, only grateful to have survived the terror of the earlier hours.

One night when I was fifteen I dreamed that the entire apartment   12 was empty, stripped of furniture and brilliantly whitewashed, the rooms gleaming with sun and the whiteness of the walls. A long rope extended the length of the apartment, winding at waist-level through all the rooms. I followed the rope from my room to the front door. There in the open doorway stood my dead father, gray-faced, surrounded by mist and darkness, the rope tied around the middle of his body. I laid my hands on the rope and began to pull, but try as I might I could not lift him across the threshold. Suddenly my mother appeared. She laid her hands over mine and began to pull also. I tried to shake her off, enraged at her interference, but she would not desist, and I did so want to pull him in I said to myself, "All right, I'll even let her have him, if we can just get him inside."

For years I thought the dream needed no interpretation, but now   13 I think I longed to get my father across the threshold not out of guilt and sexual competition but so that I could get free of Mama. My skin crawled with her. She was everywhere, all over me, inside and out. Her influence clung, membrane-like, to my nostrils, my eyelids, my open mouth. I drew her into me with every breath I took. I drowsed in her etherizing atmosphere, could not escape the rich and claustrophobic character of her presence, her being, her suffocating suffering femaleness.

I didn't know the half of it.   14

One afternoon, in the year of the dream, I was sitting with Nettie.   15 She was making lace, and I was drinking tea. She began to dream out loud. "I think you'll meet a really nice boy this year," she said. "Someone older than yourself. Almost out of college. Ready to get a good job. He'll fall in love with you, and soon you'll be married."

"That's ridiculous," I said sharply.   16

Nettie let her hands, with the lace still in them, fall to her lap.   17 "You sound just like your mother," she said softly.

QUESTIONS ON MEANING

1. Why does Gornick answer "sharply" when Nettie predicts that Gornick will soon marry?
2. Who is the AUDIENCE for this essay? How familiar does Gornick assume her readers are with the behavior of depressed persons?
3. Does Gornick seem to think readers will sympathize with her or with her mother?
4. Does Gornick seem to have any PURPOSE in mind besides depicting her troubled childhood? If so, what?

QUESTIONS ON WRITING STRATEGY

1. Why does Gornick rely so heavily on the first-PERSON *I* and *me*? What is the EFFECT of this usage?
2. Gornick's organization is partly chronological, but a number of events are not specifically placed in the sequence (paras. 7, 8, 9–11, 12, 15–17). Why isn't Gornick clearer about when these incidents occurred?
3. What is the effect of Gornick's last line, the observation from Nettie?
4. MIXED METHODS. How does Gornick combine NARRATION, DESCRIPTION, and EXAMPLE to open a window into her adolescence? Point out instances of each method and discuss what each contributes to the essay. How do the methods interact to create a vivid characterization?
5. MIXED METHODS. Gornick uses ANALYSIS, particularly analysis of CAUSE AND EFFECT, to explain her situation. What were the effects her mother had on her?

QUESTIONS ON LANGUAGE

1. How does Gornick use FIGURES OF SPEECH to make her descriptions more arresting? (Look at para. 7, for instance, where she describes her mother's pain as "my element, the country in which I lived, the rule beneath which I bowed.") Identify at least two other figures of speech and discuss their EFFECT.
2. Be sure you can define the following words: unremitting, pall, banalities, octave, gauge (para. 3); persona, rhetoric, orthodoxy, Talmudic (5); benign, ordained (6); etherizing, claustrophobic (13).
3. Throughout the essay, Gornick uses the language of the senses to communicate emotion. Locate at least three examples appealing to the sense of touch and three that appeal to the sense of hearing. How does this language help Gornick accomplish her PURPOSE?

SUGGESTIONS FOR WRITING

1. In an essay, use the first-PERSON *I* to relate an important moment between you and one of your parents. (It may be a conflict, a resolution, a recognition.) Relate your memory as vividly as possible.
2. At the end of this essay, Gornick realizes something troubling about herself. Write an essay that tells about an incident in which you learned something about yourself that upset or challenged you.
3. CRITICAL WRITING. Consider Gornick's ASSUMPTIONS about her mother. How does Gornick's ANALYSIS of her mother's feelings and behavior differ from her mother's own presentation of her motives and thoughts? Do you find Gornick's analysis persuasive? Why or why not?
4. CONNECTIONS. Both Gornick's essay and Maxine Hong Kingston's "No Name Woman" (p. 589) probe the authors' difficult relationships with their mothers. Which mother is described more fully? Which portrayal seems more realistic? With which mother do we sympathize more? In an essay, COMPARE AND CONTRAST the mothers and their function in each selection.

VIVIAN GORNICK ON WRITING

In her autobiography, *Fierce Attachments* (1987), Vivian Gornick describes her experiences trying to be a writer, enduring the fatiguing toil of working without inspiration and reveling in the exciting release when inspiration struck.

For Gornick, writing without inspiration was half-seeing. "I sat at the desk and struggled to think. . . . I sat with my eyelids nailed open against the fog, the vapor, the mist, straining to see through to my thoughts, trapped inside the murk. Once every few weeks the air cleared for half a second, and quick! I'd get down two paragraphs of readable prose. Time passed. Much time. Much dead time. Finally, a page. Then two pages. When there were ten pages I rushed to print. I looked at my paragraphs in print: really looked at them. How small, I thought. How small it all is."

Then once Gornick's perseverance led her to an internal place where inspiration arrived in the form of an open space, a "rectangle," within the fog. "I was writing an essay, a piece of graduate-student criticism that had flowered without warning into thought, radiant shapely thought. The sentences began pushing up in me, struggling to get out, each one moving swiftly to add itself to the one that preceded it. I realized suddenly that an image had taken control of me: I saw its shape and its outline clearly. The sentences were trying to fill in the shape. The image was the wholeness of my thought. . . . In the middle of the rectangle only my image, waiting patiently to clarify itself." The writing poured out.

Sometimes the writing had to be abandoned, or the rectangle failed to make its appearance. Even then, however, Gornick "felt strengthened by the sustained effort of the work."

FOR DISCUSSION

1. Have you ever suffered from the lack of inspiration? If so, what did it feel like? How did you handle the crisis?
2. Have you ever received inspiration? Can you describe it?
3. What does Gornick mean by the "rectangle" and the "image"? Are these purely personal symbols, or do they touch on your own experience?
4. If writing is difficult for many writers, why do you think they slog away at it?

CLIFFORD CHASE

Born in 1958 in Connecticut, CLIFFORD CHASE grew up in San Jose, California. He received a B.A. from the University of California at Santa Cruz (1980) and a graduate degree from the City College of New York (1987), where he studied creative writing. In the public relations department of *Newsweek* magazine since 1985, Chase writes the company newsletter. He also writes short fiction and has published stories in *The Yale Review, Threepenny Review, Boulevard,* and other magazines. His work has been selected by the PEN Syndicated Fiction Project for broadcast on National Public Radio's *Sound of Writing.* His book *On the Shoulder of the Road* (1994) is a memoir of his brother and the rest of his family. Chase lives in Brooklyn, New York.

My Brother
on the Shoulder of the Road

This essay, the seed of Chase's memoir, was first published in *A Member of the Family* (1992), a collection of essays by gay men on their relationships to mothers, fathers, siblings, and other kin. Chase's complex reminiscence draws on discrete incidents to portray his bond with his brother Ken.

"My Brother on the Shoulder of the Road" is predominantly a work of NARRATION, but that is not its only method. Chase also DESCRIBES, notably the people in his story and the puppets he and his brother played with. He COMPARES AND CONTRASTS the puppets. He uses PROCESS ANALYSIS to explain how he and his brother worked with the puppets. He gives EXAMPLES of incidents and conversations that make his experiences immediate and concrete. He tries to find a pattern of CAUSE AND EFFECT in his brother's life and death.

My brother Ken, who died of AIDS at thirty-seven, almost died 1 in a car accident when he was three. My mother almost ran him over.

This was in Illinois, before I was born. So for me the accident 2 takes place in a mythical prehistory that shapes everything to come. For me it's almost as if it takes place in the womb.

It was on a family trip. My father and Uncle Pete were driving 3 in one car, with Ken and my oldest brother, Paul, in the wide backseat. Following in the next car was my mother, who was driving, and Aunt Helen and my two sisters. My father and uncle got involved in conversation and weren't watching the boys. Nor did the men

notice that the doors were unlocked. Apparently Ken grew restless
and decided to experiment with the door handle.

So, driving along a two-lane highway at sixty miles an hour, my   4
mother sees my two brothers fly out of the car ahead of her. She
swerved, only narrowly avoiding the boys as they rolled onto the
pavement.

My brothers and the two cars all came to rest on the shoulder of   5
the road. I imagine the cars were black or dark green, with tiny
rounded windows, and there were light green wheat fields off to the
right.

Miraculously, neither of my brothers was badly hurt: a chipped   6
elbow for Paul, a broken leg for Ken. But this became one of the
cautionary stories that ruled the family. After that, my father wouldn't
pull an inch out of the driveway without making certain the car was
secure. I remember we'd be all ready for a pleasant drive, and suddenly
the air would be filled with tension. Urgently, sometimes angrily, my
father would ask: "Did you lock your doors, boys?" To me, who came
years after the near-tragedy, his caution seemed ridiculous. And to
this day, when any of us comes for a visit, my father continues the
drill, even though obviously we're all adults, and no one is going to
decide to just open the door when the car is hurtling down the
highway.

Ken was in a sense my only sibling. The others are much older   7
and were all out of the house by the time I was seven. My sisters,
born fourteen and sixteen years before me, are more like beloved
aunts. And when I say "my brother," without using a name, I don't
mean my oldest brother, Paul. I could only mean Ken.

My family moved a lot, so Ken and I spent a lot of time together   8
despite an age difference of six years. By the time we got to California,
the two of us played and fought on surprisingly equal terms. Paul had
been left in college in the last state, and my mother started working,
so now just Ken and I were at home. And we moved across town
only six months later, when my parents bought a house, so Ken and
I had to change schools just as we were making friends; the two of
us were thrown together again. I was nine and he was fifteen. We
started playing a lot with a dozen or so hand puppets given to me by
our Uncle John. First we told stories about them, then we started
making props and clothing, and eventually, over the next few years,
we created a whole world with them.

They were made of molded plastic and were painted either blue   9
or yellow. We called them muppets. The blue ones frowned and had

bulbous green noses, and the yellow ones smiled with big red mouths. They came in pairs, stuffed in small corrugated boxes, and each of them had distinctive features depending on how he had been packed with his partner. To adults they all looked the same, but Ken and I had no trouble telling them apart. For instance, one of the yellow ones had been smashed so flat in his box that his smile was completely gone, and Ken called him Dead Codfish. He was a gangster.

We made the frowning blue ones female, which may have re- 10 flected my mother's temper, and perhaps an underlying sadness or fragility that we sensed in her. The yellow smiling ones were always male, and they had high voices. One of them could play either Ken or me, or sometimes my father, in his amiable, accommodating mode. But my father could also be represented by a blue muppet. In our cartoons, if you were a yellow muppet and you got really angry, you'd turn into a blue muppet. But if you were a blue muppet you were always a blue muppet, and if you were angry you simply grew ten feet tall.

In fact, we made up a special word for the blue muppets to express 11 their anger: "Dih." It could be either a swear word or like "blah-blah" for rage. Usually the blue muppets resorted to strings of "Dih" when reason failed them, pummeling the yellow ones into submission. I think my mother's moods made about as much sense to me when I was growing up: "Dih, dih" — Die, die.

The muppets were my opportunity for revenge and conspiracy. 12 Whenever Ken and I were in trouble, we could go into my room, shut the door, and reenact the scolding scene with my parents completely in the wrong. We drew cartoons or set up scenes in the muppets' houses, and the parent muppets would rant and rave ridiculously. (Perhaps the muppets prefigured a later conspiracy, when Ken and I were out only to each other, or still later when, at least until he was gravely ill, I was the only one in the family who knew Ken was HIV positive.)

Even my best friends at school never quite entered fully into the 13 muppets' world: It was Ken's and mine. We used to say "Dih" to each other even as adults, which expressed both a particular kind of exasperation — that is, that we knew it was futile to be so mad — and the intimacy between us.

Ken made up countries for them, and each pair was a king and 14 queen. They lived in suburban houses, open-topped corrugated boxes, and their furniture and clothes were mostly construction paper. I sat on the floor in my room for hours with the glue and scissors and Scotch tape. I wanted them to have everything on *Let's Make a Deal:*

kitchen ranges, refrigerators, cars, boats, minks. My mother sewed them royal robes that tied around the neck, with terrycloth fur trim. Ken and I cut up bits of paper and made money.

All the muppets were mine except one pair, which was Ken's. 15 Harold and Victoria were rulers of the smallest but most powerful country, Heere. Harold owned the casino where all the others lost their money. Victoria owned the Beauty Baths, which we set up every once in a while in the bathroom — some lounging in the sink and others sitting to dry up on the plastic decorative shelves above the toilet, next to the fake fish bowl. This was the analog of the wig and beauty shop where my mother was bookkeeper and about which she complained nightly at dinner. We soon discovered that the tap water actually helped chip their paint, which for the muppets was a sign of aging. "So really they're ugly baths!" Ken cried.

(It was Harold and Victoria that I would search for most desper- 16 ately in Ken's house in San Diego after he died. I couldn't find them, and so I took other childhood objects: Matchbox cars, a worn stuffed dog, and two early hand puppets, Tiger and Ruff, a furry tiger and puppy whom I remembered but had never really played with. As it turned out, Harold and Victoria were still at my parents' house up in San Jose; I found them the following Christmas, staring up out of a box in the garage.)

For a time we took delight in making the muppets the most 17 outlandish clothing and furniture because Ken said they had a mental disease called "opposit-itis." It meant they liked ugly things. I'd make a green-checked bedspread and then put black-and-pink snowflake wrapping paper up on the walls. "How lovely!" Ken would exclaim, speaking in the high voice of the yellow muppet. "How elegant!" They had "bad taste," Ken said. Later they all got over it and had to redecorate.

Besides the obvious, is there something inherently gay about these 18 games? Could two straight brothers have constructed the same world? Or one straight and one queer? Somehow the answer is no, and lately I like to think of my time spent playing with the muppets as the height of a gay childhood.

As if to prove this, at school that world soon became suspect. It 19 was said that Cliff *played with dolls.* For I made them clothes and furniture. "They're not dolls, they're *puppets,*" I would reply. The muppets hardly resembled people, I reasoned, and their clothing and houses weren't at all realistic. Besides, I thought, everything was made out of construction paper, and I didn't buy anything, the way a girl would buy Barbie clothes; I made everything myself.

Early in sixth grade I made the mistake of bringing a pair of 20
muppets to math class one day, setting them up in the corner of my
desk so I could look at their faces. Mr. Lang said I had to put them
away, and then began asking pointed questions. *Do you play with them
all the time? Do you sew them clothes? Do you make them doll houses?*
Like a doctor he nodded a short "uh-huh" to each answer, and then
he turned in his gray suit back to the blackboard.

The year before, it had been Mr. Lang who wouldn't let me give 21
a puppet show to his regular class. Perhaps my own teacher said
something to me about his not approving. In any case, somehow I
knew Mr. Lang's refusal wasn't because he thought my show would
disrupt his curriculum, but because of me.

It was also about then that the other kids began calling me names: 22
girl, fem, fag. My friend Chipper had moved away the year before,
and my new friend, David Vickers, called me a fem all the time.

But at home in my room I still had my own, safe world if I 23
wanted. Here there was nothing wrong with me. "The other kids
play with GI Joe, don't they?" Ken would point out. "GI Joe is a
doll."

Even as the year went by and I began to move on from the 24
muppets, it was always a world to return to — as Ken and I knelt on
the floor beside the cardboard houses and each took a puppet in hand.
It might be a fight with my parents, or just plain boredom, that
brought him into my room. But then we could draw a cartoon or
take the muppets and move them about in their open-roofed houses,
which were growing dusty now, and act out a story.

So it was a refuge, but a betrayal was coming. 25

It was the summer before Ken went away to college. My mother, 26
who worked full-time, was paying him to clean house for her, and
babysit for me. I had a cruel streak, and I teased Ken mercilessly
when he was vacuuming or dusting. Like my parents, he had a terrible
temper. It was easy even for me, six years younger, to get his goat. I
would stand in the path of the vacuum cleaner and make faces, or
I'd follow him around while he was dusting and make farting noises.
Sometimes I'd just lean in the doorway of the bathroom and stare at
him until he turned from his cleaning and said, "Do you mind!"

I also defied him as much as possible that summer. Perhaps I was 27
angry that he was going away to college in the fall. Perhaps I had
simply reached the age to rebel, and Ken was more available than
either of my parents.

David Vickers and I had set up the train table in the living room 28
for the summer. In self-defense I had put the muppets aside and now

played with trains every day, a more boyish activity. David and I had built bridges from the train table to the two steps into the sunken living room — and this was the cause of perhaps the worst fight I ever had with Ken.

It was hot, and the sunlight pressed against all the windows of 29 the house. I had no doubt been teasing Ken all day, and now he wanted to vacuum the steps. I remember he came into my room and asked me to move the bridges.

"No," I said, fingering the curtains. "I don't feel like it." 30

He grabbed my arm, I began to scream, and things went on from 31 there. He managed to drag me out into the entryway above the living room, and he hit me a few times on the shoulder. Still I refused to help him. "Cleaning is your job," I said. By now he had pinned me to the cold tile floor and was kneeling over me, his face and arms red with fury. I struggled, and then came his worst blow:

"Stupid little faggot!" 32

He had never called me that before. Or if he had, somehow it 33 had never hit me in quite the same way. We stared at each other a moment, and I think my face must have changed its shape. Perhaps I screamed. What I felt, and could not find words for, was this: *Not you, too.*

I tore myself from his grasp and ran down the hall, an incredible 34 and shameful grief pushing up behind my eyes. It was one of the last times until adulthood that I would really cry. Once in my room with the door closed behind me, that privacy did not seem enough either, and, as if to confirm the power of a future metaphor, I ran and shut myself in the closet.

Ken came into my room after me. Somehow I had known he 35 would see the seriousness of the situation and not open the closet as well. He stood outside the sliding door, and I sat fingering the opaque plastic door handle, a cap over a hole in the door and the only light that came in. "Come on," he said. "I hardly touched you."

But I kept still. My head hurt with trying not to cry, and it was 36 hot in there. Ken waited a moment longer. "What's the matter?" he asked.

As much as we fought, and as often as Ken hit me, he was 37 sensitive and he knew when he had really hurt me. I think he was sorry now, but still I didn't speak. I couldn't have explained it anyway, and at that moment I just wanted to be left alone to cry.

"Okay, be that way," he said, and I heard him go out. 38

The following spring, it was a chance remark by Ken that made 39 me understand that I was gay.

He came home one weekend from college with his girlfriend, 40
Kathleen. This was Ken's first girlfriend, and I don't remember my
oldest brother, Paul, ever bringing anyone home, so this was new to
me too. The air seemed charged with sexuality. My mother approached Kathleen gingerly, as if on tiptoe; my father teased her. On
Saturday afternoon Kathleen and Ken sunbathed on lawn chairs in
the backyard. I followed my mother out with the tray of iced tea,
and as Kathleen walked barefoot to the patio in her yellow bikini,
her browned hips and breasts flowing out, my mother exclaimed, as
she always did during sexy scenes in movies on TV, imitating a huffy
matron: "Well!"

I had been lonely since Ken went away to college, and I wanted 41
to sunbathe myself now in his and Kathleen's brief presence. I wanted
to know them, their private jokes, their world together. They called
each other "Rabbit." They surfed. They smoked pot. They had a
communal way of talking, Southern Californian and ironic, with
certain phrases that seemed unusual and hip to me: "How odd," they'd
say. Or, "Mr. Meat says, 'Make a mess!'" I didn't know where the
phrases came from or even what some of them meant.

Saturday night I went to the movies with them. Or maybe we 42
went miniature golfing, I don't remember. By the end of the evening
it was like I was drunk on their company. As we drove home, in the
darkness of the backseat I grew more and more vivacious, trying to
imitate them and their phrases as much as possible. Maybe I was
really imitating Kathleen. Anyway, after seven months of junior high
constraint, I let go completely.

I like to think of that utterly fluid moment in seventh grade, 43
before I quite knew the names of things, the proper boundaries
between masculine and feminine, gay and straight — where my personality was so unformed and changeable that I could, with a little
encouragement and excitement, let my guard down and emerge as a
flaming queen of a child.

"Oh, how odd!" I cried, giggling. "Make a mess!"   44

I was scarcely aware of whether Ken and Kathleen were listening 45
or not, so happy was I to be with my brother and his girlfriend, this
wonderful alternative to my hate-filled life at school.

"Why are you acting so strangely?" Ken asked as we turned onto 46
our block. All the houses were dark.

I stopped and thought. I was so happy, I wasn't even offended by 47
his question. "I don't know," I said. "I usually don't act this way.
How am I acting?"

"Really femmy," was his reply. Maybe he was embarrassed in front 48

of Kathleen. And yet I like to think there was a strangely nonjudgmental quality in his voice, as if he were simply describing a fact.

"Really?" I said.   49

"Yeah, femmy," agreed Kathleen genially. She didn't seem to   50
care.

"Hmm," I said. I looked for a reason. "I am acting differently.   51
Maybe it's because of being with you two."

Then Ken said something very strange. I'll never forget it, though   52
I don't remember his exact words, and it was only a joke. He said
something like, "Maybe you're a *contact homosexual.*"

"What's that?" I asked.   53

And he explained that it was someone who was homosexual only   54
in contact with certain people, or in certain situations. It was a
phrase he and Kathleen had learned in psychology class.

Shame began to ring in my head like a bell. We had pulled up   55
in the drive a few minutes ago, and now we got out of the car. As I
followed them up the dark walk to the house, in the California night
air, I was beginning to put it together — what homosexual was, what
fag was, and what I was. Inside, I said goodnight to my parents, who
were getting ready for bed. Ken and Kathleen went to their rooms —
they had to sleep separately — and I went to my own room quickly,
as if holding my discovery close to my breast. I closed the door and
looked up the "H" word in the *Encyclopaedia Britannica* and confirmed
that I really was what the other boys at school said I was.

Ken came out to me when I was twenty-one. He had been living   56
with Kathleen nearly six years when he started seeing men. He had
moved with her to the East Coast, where she was getting her Ph.D.,
but he couldn't find work in Vermont and had to move to Boston.
Now, a year and a half later, they had broken up and he had just
moved back to California. He was staying with my parents while he
looked for a job, and so now it was I who came home from college
to visit one weekend.

Saturday night we went to a ferny, brightly lit bar in the next   57
town where you could play backgammon. We sat down and had
beers.

I didn't know Ken had something to tell me. His initial strategy   58
was to remark on how other men in the bar were cute. I was so far
from letting myself look at men that I had no idea what he was
talking about. I remember at one point a stocky blond guy came in

the door, at the far end of the room. Ken pointed discreetly. "Oh, there's a cute one," he said.

I turned. "Uh-huh," I said vaguely, guardedly. 59

I must have been frowning. 60

"Do you think it's strange for me to say that?" Ken asked. 61

"I don't know. I guess you're scoping out the competition, huh?" 62
I meant his competition for the women in the bar. I genuinely thought this was some sort of "swinging singles" technique.

Ken did one of his joking double takes, a fidgety gesture he had. 63
He was always very nervous, his hands shaky and his eyes darting, in the manner of everyone in the family, to your face and shyly away again. He had ruddy skin and a high forehead that furrowed easily. "Not exactly," he said. Then he just blurted it out: "I'm trying to tell you that I'm gay."

I almost think I had the same feeling of fear as that night when 64
I was thirteen, when Ken made that chance remark — only now the feeling was more like elation. "Really?" I said. I saw him fidgeting with his beer, waiting for my reaction. It was as much to put him at ease as to satisfy any desire to talk about these things that I told him about myself too. "I've had those feelings," I said, faltering. Then I was a little more honest: "Actually I've had them a lot."

Ken did another one of his false double takes. But he was happy 65
now.

We talked first about our mutual surprise. "I guess I always thought 66
you were basically straight," Ken said.

"No . . . I thought that about you, too." And I have a particular 67
image in my mind of Ken as a straight man, which was perhaps my model for any straight man: Ken washing his red Ford Falcon in the drive. His teenager's manly persona was, in fact, part of my own ideal self-image, nurtured throughout high school — that of the kind of guy who fixes things, who swears, who smartly ruffles the newspaper before he starts to read. I wonder at how we had fooled each other all that time with these personas, or rather with the idea that such a persona could not be gay. We each believed in this "basically straight" guy, and we each fooled ourselves with him.

So it was that we began to compare notes. I had had no experience 68
and was still too scared to be planning any, so I had little to tell. I did manage to say I had felt this way since I was five. Ken countered that he had had no sexuality at all until after high school. In the back of my mind, I attributed this to the family's moving constantly, which meant that Ken went to three elementary schools, two junior

highs, and three high schools. It seemed logical that he might protect himself by feeling nothing sexually. But I wonder now just how much to believe him, or just what he really meant. Anyway, he explained that it was in graduate school in San Diego (the city where he would later settle, and where he would die) that he started looking at men: "On the beach, when I used to go surfing," he said. "The other guys."

I think this probably seemed a little too real to me at that   69
moment: sitting on the beach; surfers in wet bathing suits; looking at them. . . . But the story continued.

Back East, he and Kathleen had had to live apart and they began   70
to fight. In Boston Ken started seeing a guy from work on the side. Within a few months Kathleen figured out something was up. Ken had never hinted to her anything about being attracted to men, so she assumed he was seeing another woman. There was the expected confrontation. "I told her, no, I'm seeing a man," Ken explained, smiling angrily now, seeming to take a certain pleasure in that exchange — the kind of scene where you're holding all the cards, and you lay them all on the table at once.

"So what happened?" I asked.   71

There were more fights, he said, and he and Kathleen stopped   72
speaking altogether for a while. Then Kathleen started seeing someone else, in Burlington, and she and Ken decided finally to break up.

There was a pause. Ken was upset, and I imagine him frowning   73
and staring down at the table, the same frown he'd had since childhood.

Then began the most curious part of the conversation.   74

"Why do you think you're gay?" I asked.   75

Ken waited a minute and said, "I think it was because of the   76
accident." He meant when he was three.

I knit my brow. "How is that related?"   77

Then he said, "I could have died, you know. . . . I think after   78
that, Mom clung to me too much."

Now, how did those fifties shrinks propagate that dominating-   79
mother story so effectively? I think it was even in the *Encyclopaedia Britannica*. Anyway, even then I didn't put much stock in what Ken was saying, or maybe I was just jealous of the idea of his being so close to my mother — so I tried to make a joke of it all. "Well," I said. "I wasn't in any accident. So how does that explain me?"

But now I want to make connections to that accident as a means   80
of creating some kind of order from my brother's life. I want for a moment to see a random event, Ken's illness, as part of some pattern.

For instance: It was always said that when Ken was three, after 81
he returned from the hospital, he never complained about the cast
on his leg. Similarly, my mother says, he never complained as she
and my father cared for him in the last months of his life.

But more important: Two and a half years ago, it was a car 82
accident that marked the onset of my brother's final illness. Suffering
from dementia, he ran his car off the road one day and was found
wandering like a three-year-old along the banks of the freeway. Para-
medics took him to the hospital, but this time there was no miracle.
His moments of lucidity were less and less frequent, he was in great
pain, and he died, more quickly than expected, just two months later.
So I lost him by the side of the road. I wasn't present at his first
accident, which was before I was born, nor at this last one, which
took place three thousand miles away, and I was on my way to visit
him when he died.

QUESTIONS ON MEANING

1. What is Chase's PURPOSE in this essay? Is there only one?
2. What functions did playing with puppets serve for Clifford and Ken?
3. What does Chase mean when he describes his childhood as "gay" (para. 18)?
4. How would you state Chase's THESIS?

QUESTIONS ON WRITING STRATEGY

1. Why does Chase tell us in his first sentence that his brother died of AIDS at thirty-seven?
2. What is the function of the parenthetical asides Chase inserts in paragraphs 12 and 16?
3. What TRANSITIONS does Chase use to tie together the incidents he reports?
4. MIXED METHODS. Within Chase's overall NARRATIVE, each incident is in essence an EXAMPLE of something. What do paragraphs 18–25 illustrate?
5. MIXED METHODS. Chase mingles DESCRIPTION, COMPARISON, and PROCESS ANALYSIS in relating how he and his brother played with puppets (paras. 8–17). What does each of these methods contribute to this part of Chase's story?

QUESTIONS ON LANGUAGE

1. What are the CONNOTATIONS of these words: gay, queer (para. 18); fem, fag (22); faggot (32); queen (43); homosexual (52)? Which does Chase use to describe himself? Which do others use of him?
2. Use a dictionary to find the meanings of these words: amiable, accommodating (para. 10); pummeling (11); prefigured (12); analog (15); inherently (18); curriculum (21); huffy (40); persona (67); propagate (79); dementia, lucidity (82).
3. How would you characterize Chase's DICTION in this selection? How is it suited to the essay's subject?
4. Why does Chase describe his brother's accident as part of "a mythical prehistory" (para. 2)?

SUGGESTIONS FOR WRITING

1. Chase sees the games he and his brother played with their puppets as an anticipation of the way they would live their lives. In an essay, describe one of the favorite games of your childhood. How could it be seen as a preview of your life today? What did you learn from the game? With whom did you share it? How was it different from others' games?
2. Write a brief essay analyzing your relationship with a sibling or a childhood friend. Use NARRATION and EXAMPLE to give a vivid characterization of that person and your interaction with him or her. How has your relationship with that person changed over the years? What has been lost? What has been gained? How do you predict your relationship will develop in the future?
3. CRITICAL WRITING. Throughout his essay, Chase tries to show a pattern in his life and his brother's. Locate at least three places where Chase sees childhood predicting adulthood. Why might Chase emphasize such a pattern? What ASSUMPTIONS does it reveal? Do you perceive your own life in this way? Why or why not?
4. CONNECTIONS. In "Aria: A Memoir of a Bilingual Childhood" (p. 563), Richard Rodriguez describes how he and his family "transformed the knowledge of our public separateness into a consoling reminder of our intimacy" (para. 18). How might this description apply to Chase and his brother? Compare the feelings of alienation expressed by Rodriguez and Chase. How were the two authors made to feel different from their peers? How were the authors' responses similar or dissimilar?

CLIFFORD CHASE ON WRITING

In comments written especially for *The Bedford Reader,* Clifford Chase muses about disorderliness and inspiration in the writing process. (Grace Paley, whom Chase mentions in the first sentence, is a fiction writer, author of *Later the Same Day* and other works.)

"One day when I was in graduate school, Grace Paley, who was my teacher, asked me what I was working on at the moment. She was giving me a lift home from City College. As we sped down the West Side Highway, I told her I had just started writing a short story. I shook my head: 'But I have no idea what I'm doing.'

"'Oh, I never know what I'm doing,' she replied, waving her hand. Her little Toyota swerved. 'It's no fun if you do.'

"That was one of the best things a teacher ever said to me. Until then I thought that my chaotic and intuitive approach to writing was a problem I would someday solve, when I became a 'real' writer. But here was a famous writer saying that she, too, was in the dark. I saw that my own process was already real, that I had already found a valid way to go about writing.

"The poet John Keats called it 'Negative Capability' — 'when man is capable of being in uncertainties, Mysteries, doubts, without any irritable reaching after fact & reason.' Working intuitively requires most of all the tolerance for uncertainty — Will this turn out? What's it about? Am I a complete idiot? — and a willingness to live with a mess for at least a little while. Whenever I begin to write, I long for the order that comes only at the end of the process. Each time I have to tell myself: Make a mess; explore; you can organize and plan later.

"Usually, wandering in a forest of scenes and ideas, I turn some corner and there it is: insight. It may be simply a matter of assembling the pieces and seeing what they add up to, what they look like next to one another. Before I gathered up the memories for 'My Brother on the Shoulder of the Road,' for example, I had no idea just how much my sense of myself as a gay man had its roots in my relationship to my brother Ken. But there it was on the page, and for the first time the pattern was perfectly clear.

"Through autobiography I place myself out in the world, as a character on the page, and I can see things in myself that I wouldn't otherwise. It's a way of being smarter than myself, more insightful than I really am. Sometimes I don't see the connections even after they're staring right up at me. I'll give someone a story or an essay to read, and she'll laugh or raise one eyebrow unexpectedly, grasping some point I had completely missed. The sentences did it for me.

"I've always believed in writing not so much what I know, but what I barely know or almost know. I like getting ahead of myself. For me, the best kind of writing isn't putting down what I've always understood; it's an experiment, full of surprise. In *The Writing Life*, Annie Dillard characterizes the writing process as first a wonderful vision of the work and then an imperfect, disappointing realization of that vision. I disagree. I prefer to begin with only the barest idea — a tone of voice, a stray memory, a quotation — and then let the vision and inspiration emerge as I write. I don't see any difference between creative inspiration and the act of creation. What is inspiration apart from creation? As the sentences and paragraphs unfold, they are, in themselves, inspiring."

FOR DISCUSSION

1. What, in your own words, is Chase's "valid way to go about writing"?
2. Why does writing, for Chase, require something like John Keats's "Negative Capability"?
3. Where does Chase get inspiration?

RICHARD RODRIGUEZ

The son of Spanish-speaking Mexican Americans, RICHARD RODRI-
GUEZ was born in 1944 in San Francisco. After graduation from
Stanford in 1967, he earned an M.A. from Columbia, studied at
the Warburg Institute in London, and received a Ph.D. in English
literature from the University of California at Berkeley. He once
taught but now devotes himself to writing and lecturing. Rodriguez's
essays have appeared in *The American Scholar, Change, Harper's,*
and many other magazines. In 1982 he published *Hunger of Memory,*
a widely discussed book of autobiographical essays. *Mexico's Children*
(1991) is a study of Mexicans in America, and *Days of Obligation:
An Argument with My Father* (1992) is also a memoir.

Aria: A Memoir of a Bilingual Childhood

"Aria: A Memoir of a Bilingual Childhood" is taken from *Hunger
of Memory.* First published in *The American Scholar* in 1981, this
poignant memoir sets forth the author's views of bilingual education. To the child Rodriguez, Spanish was a private language,
English a public one. Would the boy have learned faster and better
if his teachers had allowed him the use of his native language in
school?

In this essay, four methods of development predominate. Rodriguez uses NARRATION and DESCRIPTION to evoke his childhood experiences with language. He uses COMPARISON AND CONTRAST to
distinguish home and school, Spanish and English, the private and
the public realms. And the whole essay is an ARGUMENT against
bilingual education.

I remember, to start with, that day in Sacramento, in a California   1
now nearly thirty years past, when I first entered a classroom — able
to understand about fifty stray English words. The third of four children, I had been preceded by my older brother and sister to a neighborhood Roman Catholic school. But neither of them had revealed
very much about their classroom experiences. They left each morning
and returned each afternoon, always together, speaking Spanish as
they climbed the five steps to the porch. And their mysterious books,
wrapped in brown shopping-bag paper, remained on the table next
to the door, closed firmly behind them.

An accident of geography sent me to a school where all my   2
classmates were white and many were the children of doctors and

lawyers and business executives. On that first day of school, my classmates must certainly have been uneasy to find themselves apart from their families, in the first institution of their lives. But I was astonished. I was fated to be the "problem student" in class.

The nun said, in a friendly but oddly impersonal voice: "Boys   3
and girls, this is Richard Rodriguez." (I heard her sound it out: *Rich-heard Road-ree-guess.*) It was the first time I had heard anyone say my name in English. "Richard," the nun repeated more slowly, writing my name down in her book. Quickly I turned to see my mother's face dissolve in a watery blur behind the pebbled-glass door.

Now, many years later, I hear of something called "bilingual   4
education" — a scheme proposed in the late 1960s by Hispanic-American social activists, later endorsed by a congressional vote. It is a program that seeks to permit non–English-speaking children (many from lower class homes) to use their "family language" as the language of school. Such, at least, is the aim its supporters announce. I hear them, and am forced to say no: It is not possible for a child, any child, ever to use his family's language in school. Not to understand this is to misunderstand the public uses of schooling and to trivialize the nature of intimate life.

Memory teaches me what I know of these matters. The boy   5
reminds the adult. I was a bilingual child, but of a certain kind: "socially disadvantaged," the son of working-class parents, both Mexican immigrants.

In the early years of my boyhood, my parents coped very well in   6
America. My father had steady work. My mother managed at home. They were nobody's victims. When we moved to a house many blocks from the Mexican-American section of town, they were not intimidated by those two or three neighbors who initially tried to make us unwelcome. ("Keep your brats away from my sidewalk!") But despite all they achieved, or perhaps because they had so much to achieve, they lacked any deep feeling of ease, of belonging in public. They regarded the people at work or in crowds as being very distant from us. Those were the others, *los gringos.* That term was interchangeable in their speech with another, even more telling: *los americanos.*

I grew up in a house where the only regular guests were my   7
relations. On a certain day, enormous families of relatives would visit us, and there would be so many people that the noise and the bodies would spill out to the backyard and onto the front porch. Then for weeks no one would come. (If the doorbell rang, it was usually a salesman.) Our house stood apart — gaudy yellow in a row of white

bungalows. We were the people with the noisy dog, the people who raised chickens. We were the foreigners on the block. A few neighbors would smile and wave at us. We waved back. But until I was seven years old, I did not know the name of the old couple living next door or the names of the kids living across the street.

In public, my father and mother spoke a hesitant, accented, and not always grammatical English. And then they would have to strain, their bodies tense, to catch the sense of what was rapidly said by *los gringos*. At home, they returned to Spanish. The language of their Mexican past sounded in counterpoint to the English spoken in public. The words would come quickly, with ease. Conveyed through those sounds was the pleasing, soothing, consoling reminder that one was at home. 8

During those years when I was first learning to speak, my mother and father addressed me only in Spanish; in Spanish I learned to reply. By contrast, English (*inglés*) was the language I came to associate with gringos, rarely heard in the house. I learned my first words of English overhearing my parents speaking to strangers. At six years of age, I knew just enough words for my mother to trust me on errands to stores one block away — but no more. 9

I was then a listening child, careful to hear the very different sounds of Spanish and English. Wide-eyed with hearing, I'd listen to sounds more than to words. First, there were English (gringo) sounds. So many words still were unknown to me that when the butcher or the lady at the drugstore said something, exotic polysyllabic sounds would bloom in the midst of their sentences. Often the speech of people in public seemed to me very loud, booming with confidence. The man behind the counter would literally ask, "What can I do for you?" But by being so firm and clear, the sound of his voice said that he was a gringo; he belonged in public society. There were also the high, nasal notes of middle-class American speech — which I rarely am conscious of hearing today because I hear them so often, but could not stop hearing when I was a boy. Crowds at Safeway or at bus stops were noisy with the birdlike sounds of *los gringos*. I'd move away from them all — all the chirping chatter above me. 10

My own sounds I was unable to hear, but I knew that I spoke English poorly. My words could not extend to form complete thoughts. And the words I did speak I didn't know well enough to make distinct sounds. (Listeners would usually lower their heads to hear better what I was trying to say.) But it was one thing for *me* to speak English with difficulty; it was more troubling to hear my parents speaking in public: their high-whining vowels and guttural conso- 11 nants; their sentences that got stuck with "eh" and "ah" sounds; the confused syntax; the hesitant rhythm of sounds so different from the way gringos spoke. I'd notice, moreover, that my parents' voices were softer than those of gringos we would meet.

I am tempted to say now that none of this mattered. (In adulthood 12 I am embarrassed by childhood fears.) And, in a way, it didn't matter very much that my parents could not speak English with ease. Their linguistic difficulties had no serious consequences. My mother and father made themselves understood at the county hospital clinic and at government offices. And yet, in another way, it mattered very much. It was unsettling to hear my parents struggle with English. Hearing them, I'd grow nervous, and my clutching trust in their protection and power would be weakened.

There were many times like the night at a brightly lit gasoline 13 station (a blaring white memory) when I stood uneasily hearing my father talk to a teenage attendant. I do not recall what they were saying, but I cannot forget the sounds my father made as he spoke. At one point his words slid together to form one long word — sounds as confused as the threads of blue and green oil in the puddle next to my shoes. His voice rushed through what he had left to say. Toward the end, he reached falsetto notes, appealing to his listener's understanding. I looked away at the lights of passing automobiles. I tried not to hear any more. But I heard only too well the attendant's reply, his calm, easy tones. Shortly afterward, headed for home, I shivered when my father put his hand on my shoulder. The very first chance that I got, I evaded his grasp and ran on ahead into the dark, skipping with feigned boyish exuberance.

But then there was Spanish: *español*, the language rarely heard 14 away from the house; *español*, the language which seemed to me therefore a private language, my family's language. To hear its sounds was to feel myself specially recognized as one of the family, apart from *los otros*. A simple remark, an inconsequential comment could convey that assurance. My parents would say something to me and I would feel embraced by the sounds of their words. Those sounds said: *I am speaking with ease in Spanish. I am addressing you in words I never use with los gringos. I recognize you as someone special, close, like no one outside. You belong with us. In the family. Ricardo.*

At the age of six, well past the time when most middle-class 15 children no longer notice the difference between sounds uttered at home and words spoken in public, I had a different experience. I lived in a world compounded of sounds. I was a child longer than most. I lived in a magical world, surrounded by sounds both pleasing and fearful. I shared with my family a language enchantingly private — different from that used in the city around us.

Just opening or closing the screen door behind me was an important experience. I'd rarely leave home all alone or without feeling reluctance. Walking down the sidewalk, under the canopy of tall trees, I'd warily notice the (suddenly) silent neighborhood kids who stood warily watching me. Nervously, I'd arrive at the grocery store to hear there the sounds of the gringo, reminding me that in this so-big world I was a foreigner. But if leaving home was never routine, neither was coming back. Walking toward our house, climbing the steps from the sidewalk, in summer when the front door was open, I'd hear voices beyond the screen door talking in Spanish. For a second or two I'd stay, linger there listening. Smiling, I'd hear my mother call out, saying in Spanish, "Is that you, Richard?" Those were her words, but all the while her sounds would assure me: *You are home now. Come close inside. With us.* "Sí," I'd reply.

Once more inside the house, I would resume my place in the family. The sounds would grow harder to hear. Once more at home, I would grow less conscious of them. It required, however, no more than the blurt of the doorbell to alert me all over again to listen to sounds. The house would turn instantly quiet while my mother went to the door. I'd hear her hard English sounds. I'd wait to hear her voice turn to soft-sounding Spanish, which assured me, as surely as did the clicking tongue of the lock on the door, that the stranger was gone.

Plainly it is not healthy to hear such sounds so often. It is not healthy to distinguish public from private sounds so easily. I remained cloistered by sounds, timid and shy in public, too dependent on the voices at home. I remember many nights when my father would come back from work, and I'd hear him call out to my mother in Spanish, sounding relieved. In Spanish, his voice would sound the light and free notes that he never could manage in English. Some nights I'd jump up just hearing his voice. My brother and I would come running into the room where he was with our mother. Our laughing (so deep was the pleasure!) became screaming. Like others who feel the pain of public alienation, we transformed the knowledge of our public separateness into a consoling reminder of our intimacy. Excited, our voices joined in a celebration of sounds. *We are speaking now the way we never speak out in public — we are together,* the sounds told me. Some nights no one seemed willing to loosen the hold that sounds had on us. At dinner we invented new words that sounded Spanish, but made sense only to us. We pieced together new words by taking, say, an English verb and giving it Spanish endings. My mother's instructions at bedtime would be lacquered with mock-urgent tones. Or a word like *sí*, sounded in several notes, would convey added measures of feeling. Tongues lingered around the edges of words, especially fat vowels, and we happily sounded that military drum roll, the twirling roar of the Spanish *r*. Family language, my family's sounds: the voices of my parents and sisters and brother. Their voices insisting: *You belong here. We are family members. Related. Special to one another. Listen!* Voices singing and sighing, rising and straining, then surging, teeming with pleasure which burst syllables into fragments of laughter. At times it seemed there was steady quiet only when, from another room, the rustling whispers of my parents faded and I edged closer to sleep.

Supporters of bilingual education imply today that students like me miss a great deal by not being taught in their family's language. What they seem not to recognize is that, as a socially disadvantaged child, I regarded Spanish as a private language. It was a ghetto language that deepened and strengthened my feeling of separateness. What I needed to learn in school was that I had the right, and the obligation, to speak the public language. The odd truth is that my first-grade classmates could have become bilingual, in the conventional sense of the word, more easily than I. Had they been taught early (as upper-middle-class children often are taught) a "second language" like Spanish or French, they could have regarded it simply as another public language. In my case, such bilingualism could not have been so quickly achieved. What I did not believe was that I could speak a single public language. 19

Without question, it would have pleased me to have heard my teachers address me in Spanish when I entered the classroom. I would have felt much less afraid. I would have imagined that my instructors were somehow "related" to me; I would indeed have heard their Spanish as my family's language. I would have trusted them and responded with ease. But I would have delayed — postponed for how long? — having to learn the language of public society. I would have evaded — and for how long? — learning the great lesson of school: that I had a public identity. 20

Fortunately, my teachers were unsentimental about their responsibility. What they understood was that I needed to speak public English. So their voices would search me out, asking me questions. Each time I heard them I'd look up in surprise to see a nun's face frowning at me. I'd mumble, not really meaning to answer. The nun 21 would persist. "Richard, stand up. Don't look at the floor. Speak up. Speak to the entire class, not just to me!" But I couldn't believe English could be my language to use. (In part, I did not want to believe it.) I continued to mumble. I resisted the teacher's demands. (Did I somehow suspect that once I learned this public language my family life would be changed?) Silent, waiting for the bell to sound, I remained dazed, different, afraid.

Because I wrongly imagined that English was intrinsically a public   22 language and Spanish was intrinsically private, I easily noted the difference between classroom language and the language at home. At school, words were directed to a general audience of listeners. ("Boys and girls . . .") Words were meaningfully ordered. And the point was not self-expression alone, but to make oneself understood by many others. The teacher quizzed: "Boys and girls, why do we use that word in this sentence? Could we think of a better word to use there? Would the sentence change its meaning if the words were differently arranged? Isn't there a better way of saying much the same thing?" (I couldn't say. I wouldn't try to say.)

Three months passed. Five. A half year. Unsmiling, ever watch-   23 ful, my teachers noted my silence. They began to connect my behavior with the slow progress my brother and sisters were making. Until, one Saturday morning, three nuns arrived at the house to talk to our parents. Stiffly they sat on the blue living-room sofa. From the doorway of another room, spying on the visitors, I noted the incongruity, the clash of two worlds, the faces and voices of school intruding upon the familiar setting of home. I overheard one voice gently wondering, "Do your children speak only Spanish at home, Mrs. Rodriguez?" While another voice added, "That Richard especially seems so timid and shy."

That Rich-heard!   24

With great tact, the visitors continued, "Is it possible for you and   25 your husband to encourage your children to practice their English when they are home?" Of course my parents complied. What would they not do for their children's well-being? And how could they question the Church's authority which those women represented? In an instant they agreed to give up the language (the sounds) which had revealed and accentuated our family's closeness. The moment after the visitors left, the change was observed. "*Ahora*, speak to us only *en inglés*," my father and mother told us.

At first, it seemed a kind of game. After dinner each night, the   26 family gathered together to practice "our" English. It was still then *inglés*, a language foreign to us, so we felt drawn to it as strangers.

Laughing, we would try to define words we could not pronounce. We played with strange English sounds, often overanglicizing our pronunciations. And we filled the smiling gaps of our sentences with familiar Spanish sounds. But that was cheating, somebody shouted, and everyone laughed.

In school, meanwhile, like my brother and sisters, I was required 27 to attend a daily tutoring session. I needed a full year of this special work. I also needed my teachers to keep my attention from straying in class by calling out, *"Rich-heard"* — their English voices slowly loosening the ties to my other name, with its three notes, *Ri-car-do*. Most of all, I needed to hear my mother and father speak to me in a moment of seriousness in "broken" — suddenly heartbreaking — English. This scene was inevitable. One Saturday morning I entered the kitchen where my parents were talking, but I did not realize that they were talking in Spanish until, the moment they saw me, their voices changed and they began speaking English. The gringo sounds they uttered startled me. Pushed me away. In that moment of trivial misunderstanding and profound insight, I felt my throat twisted by unsounded grief. I simply turned and left the room. But I had no place to escape to where I could grieve in Spanish. My brother and sisters were speaking English in another part of the house.

Again and again in the days following, as I grew increasingly 28 angry, I was obliged to hear my mother and father encouraging me: "Speak to us *en inglés.*" Only then did I determine to learn classroom English. Thus, sometime afterward it happened: One day in school, I raised my hand to volunteer an answer to a question. I spoke out in a loud voice and I did not think it remarkable when the entire class understood. That day I moved very far from being the disadvantaged child I had been only days earlier. Taken hold at last was the belief, the calming assurance, that I *belonged* in public.

Shortly after, I stopped hearing the high, troubling sounds of *los* 29 *gringos*. A more and more confident speaker of English, I didn't listen to how strangers sounded when they talked to me. With so many English-speaking people around me, I no longer heard American accents. Conversations quickened. Listening to persons whose voices sounded eccentrically pitched, I might note their sounds for a few seconds, but then I'd concentrate on what they were saying. Now when I heard someone's tone of voice — angry or questioning or sarcastic or happy or sad — I didn't distinguish it from the words it expressed. Sound and word were thus tightly wedded. At the end of each day I was often bemused, and always relieved, to realize how "soundless," though crowded with words, my day in public had been. An eight-year-old boy, I finally came to accept what had been technically true since my birth: I was an American citizen.

But diminished by then was the special feeling of closeness at home. Gone was the desperate, urgent, intense feeling of being at home among those with whom I felt intimate. Our family remained a loving family, but one greatly changed. We were no longer so close, no longer bound tightly together by the knowledge of our separateness from *los gringos*. Neither my older brother nor my sisters rushed home after school any more. Nor did I. When I arrived home, often there would be neighborhood kids in the house. Or the house would be empty of sounds.

Following the dramatic Americanization of their children, even my parents grew more publicly confident — especially my mother. First she learned the names of all the people on the block. Then she decided we needed to have a telephone in our house. My father, for his part, continued to use the word gringo, but it was no longer charged with bitterness or distrust. Stripped of any emotional content, the word simply became a name for those Americans not of Hispanic descent. Hearing him, sometimes, I wasn't sure if he was pronouncing the Spanish word *gringo,* or saying gringo in English.

There was a new silence at home. As we children learned more and more English, we shared fewer and fewer words with our parents. Sentences needed to be spoken slowly when one of us addressed our mother or father. Often the parent wouldn't understand. The child would need to repeat himself. Still the parent misunderstood. The young voice, frustrated, would end up saying, "Never mind" — the subject was closed. Dinners would be noisy with the clinking of knives and forks against dishes. My mother would smile softly between her remarks; my father, at the other end of the table, would chew and chew his food while he stared over the heads of his children.

My mother! My father! After English became my primary language, I no longer knew what words to use in addressing my parents. The old Spanish words (those tender accents of sound) I had earlier used — *mamá* and *papá* — I couldn't use any more. They would have been all-too-painful reminders of how much had changed in my life. On the other hand, the words I heard neighborhood kids call their parents seemed equally unsatisfactory. "Mother" and "father," "ma," "pa," "dad," "pop" (how I hated the all-American sound of that last word) — all these I felt were unsuitable terms of address for *my* parents. As a result, I never used them at home. Whenever I'd speak to my parents, I would try to get their attention by looking at them.

In public conversations, I'd refer to them as my "parents" or my "mother" and "father."

My mother and father, for their part, responded differently, as 34 their children spoke to them less. My mother grew restless, seemed troubled and anxious at the scarceness of words exchanged in the house. She would question me about my day when I came home from school. She smiled at my small talk. She pried at the edges of my sentences to get me to say something more. ("What . . . ?") She'd join conversations she overheard, but her intrusions often stopped her children's talking. By contrast, my father seemed to grow reconciled to the new quiet. Though his English somewhat improved, he tended more and more to retire into silence. At dinner he spoke very little. One night his children and even his wife helplessly giggled at his garbled English pronunciation of the Catholic "Grace Before Meals." Thereafter he made his wife recite the prayer at the start of each meal, even on formal occasions when there were guests in the house.

Hers became the public voice of the family. On official business 35 it was she, not my father, who would usually talk to strangers on the phone or in stores. We children grew so accustomed to his silence that years later we would routinely refer to his "shyness." (My mother often tried to explain: Both of his parents died when he was eight. He was raised by an uncle who treated him as little more than a menial servant. He was never encouraged to speak. He grew up alone — a man of few words.) But I realized my father was not shy whenever I'd watch him speaking Spanish with relatives. Using Spanish, he was quickly effusive. Especially when talking with other men, his voice would spark, flicker, flare alive with varied sounds. In Spanish he expressed ideas and feelings he rarely revealed when speaking English. With firm Spanish sounds he conveyed a confidence and authority that English would never allow him.

The silence at home, however, was not simply the result of fewer 36 words passing between parents and children. More profound for me was the silence created by my inattention to sounds. At about the time I no longer bothered to listen with care to the sounds of English in public, I grew careless about listening to the sounds made by the family when they spoke. Most of the time I would hear someone speaking at home and didn't distinguish his sounds from the words people uttered in public. I didn't even pay much attention to my parents' accented and ungrammatical speech — at least not at home. Only when I was with them in public would I become alert to their accents. But even then their sounds caused me less and less concern. For I was growing increasingly confident of my own public identity.

I would have been happier about my public success had I not 37
recalled, sometimes, what it had been like earlier, when my family
conveyed its intimacy through a set of conveniently private sounds.
Sometimes in public, hearing a stranger, I'd hark back to my lost
past. A Mexican farm worker approached me one day downtown. He
wanted directions to some place. "*Hijito*, . . ." he said. And his voice
stirred old longings. Another time I was standing beside my mother
in the visiting room of a Carmelite convent, before the dense screen
which rendered the nuns shadowy figures. I heard several of them
speaking Spanish in their busy, singsong, overlapping voices, assuring
my mother that, yes, yes, we were remembered, all our family was
remembered, in their prayers. Those voices echoed faraway family
sounds. Another day a dark-faced old woman touched my shoulder
lightly to steady herself as she boarded a bus. She murmured something to me I couldn't quite comprehend. Her Spanish voice came
near, like the face of a never-before-seen relative in the instant before
I was kissed. That voice, like so many of the Spanish voices I'd hear
in public, recalled the golden age of my childhood.

Bilingual educators say today that children lose a degree of "in- 38
dividuality" by becoming assimilated into public society. (Bilingual
schooling is a program popularized in the seventies, that decade when
middle-class "ethnics" began to resist the process of assimilation —
the "American melting pot.") But the bilingualists oversimplify when
they scorn the value and necessity of assimilation. They do not seem
to realize that a person is individualized in two ways. So they do not
realize that, while one suffers a diminished sense of *private* individuality by being assimilated into public society, such assimilation makes
possible the achievement of *public* individuality.

Simplistically again, the bilingualists insist that a student should 39
be reminded of his difference from others in mass society, of his
"heritage." But they equate mere separateness with individuality. The
fact is that only in private — with intimates — is separateness from
the crowd a prerequisite for individuality; an intimate "tells" me that
I am unique, unlike all others, apart from the crowd. In public, by
contrast, full individuality is achieved, paradoxically, by those who
are able to consider themselves members of the crowd. Thus it happened for me. Only when I was able to think of myself as an American, no longer an alien in gringo society, could I seek the rights and
opportunities necessary for full public individuality. The social and
political advantages I enjoy as a man began on the day I came to
believe that my name is indeed *Rich-heard Road-ree-guess*. It is true
that my public society today is often impersonal; in fact, my public

society is usually mass society. But despite the anonymity of the crowd, and despite the fact that the individuality I achieve in public is often tenuous — because it depends on my being one in a crowd — I celebrate the day I acquired my new name. Those middle-class ethnics who scorn assimilation seem to me filled with decadent self-pity, obsessed by the burden of public life. Dangerously, they romanticize public separateness and trivialize the dilemma of those who are truly socially disadvantaged.

If I rehearse here the changes in my private life after my Amer-   40
icanization, it is finally to emphasize a public gain. The loss implies the gain. The house I returned to each afternoon was quiet. Intimate sounds no longer greeted me at the door. Inside there were other noises. The telephone rang. Neighborhood kids ran past the door of the bedroom where I was reading my schoolbooks — covered with brown shopping-bag paper. Once I learned the public language, it would never again be easy for me to hear intimate family voices. More and more of my day was spent hearing words, not sounds. But that may only be a way of saying that on the day I raised my hand in class and spoke loudly to an entire roomful of faces, my childhood started to end.

QUESTIONS ON MEANING

1. Rodriguez's essay is both memoir and argument. What is the thrust of the author's argument? Where in the essay does he set it forth?
2. How did the child Rodriguez react when, in his presence, his parents had to struggle to make themselves understood by "*los gringos*"?
3. What does the author mean when he says, "I was a child longer than most" (para. 15)?
4. According to the author, what impact did the Rodriguez children's use of English have on relationships within the family?
5. Contrast the child Rodriguez's view of the nuns who insisted he speak English with his adult view.

QUESTIONS ON WRITING STRATEGY

1. How effective an INTRODUCTION is Rodriguez's first paragraph?
2. Several times in his essay Rodriguez shifts from memoir to argument and back again. What is the overall EFFECT of these shifts? Do they strengthen or weaken the author's stance against bilingual education?

3. Twice in his essay (in paras. 1 and 40) the author mentions schoolbooks wrapped in shopping-bag paper. How does the use of this detail enhance his argument?

4. What AUDIENCE probably would not like this essay? Why would they not like it?

5. MIXED METHODS. Examine how Rodriguez uses DESCRIPTION to COMPARE AND CONTRAST the sounds of Spanish and English (paras. 10, 11, 13, 14, 18, 33, 37). What sounds does he evoke? What are the differences in them?

6. MIXED METHODS. Rodriguez's essay is an ARGUMENT supported mainly by personal NARRATIVE — Rodriguez's own experience. What kind of ETHICAL APPEAL does the narrative make? What can we INFER about Rodriguez's personality, intellect, fairness, and trustworthiness?

QUESTIONS ON LANGUAGE

1. Consult the dictionary if you need help defining these words: counterpoint (para. 8); polysyllabic (10); guttural, syntax (11); falsetto, exuberance (13); inconsequential (14); cloistered, lacquered (18); diffident (21); intrinsically (22); incongruity (23); bemused (29); effusive (35); assimilated (38); paradoxically, tenuous, decadent (39).

2. In Rodriguez's essay, how do the words *public* and *private* relate to the issue of bilingual education? What important distinction does the author make between *individuality* and *separateness* (para. 39)?

3. What exactly does the author mean when he says, "More and more of my day was spent hearing words, not sounds" (para. 40)?

SUGGESTIONS FOR WRITING

1. Try to define the distinctive quality of the language spoken in your home when you were a child. Explain any ways in which this language differed from what you heard in school. How has the difference mattered to you? (This language need not be a foreign language; it might include any words used in your family but not in the world at large: a dialect, slang, ALLUSIONS, sayings, FIGURES OF SPEECH, or a special vocabulary.)

2. Bilingual education is a controversial issue with evidence and strong feelings on both sides. In a page or so of preliminary writing, respond to Rodriguez's essay with your own gut feelings on the issue. Then do some library research to extend, support, or refute your views. (Consult the *Readers' Guide to Periodical Literature* as a first step.) In a well-reasoned and well-supported essay, give your opinion on whether or not public schools should teach children in their "family language."

3. CRITICAL WRITING. In his ARGUMENT against bilingual education, Rodriguez offers no data from studies, no testimony from education experts, indeed no EVIDENCE at all except his personal experience. In an essay, ANALYZE and EVALUATE this evidence: How convincing do you find it?

Is it adequate to support the argument? (In your essay consider Rodriguez's ETHICAL APPEAL, the topic of the sixth question on writing strategy, above.)

4. CONNECTIONS. Richard Rodriguez and Vivian Gornick (in "Mama Went to Work," p. 542) convey nearly opposite experiences of being with their families. In an essay, analyze the language each author uses to DESCRIBE the "family feeling."

RICHARD RODRIGUEZ ON WRITING

For *The Bedford Reader,* Richard Rodriguez has described the writing of "Aria":

"From grammar school to college, my teachers offered perennial encouragement: 'Write about what you know.' Every year I would respond with the student's complaint: 'I have nothing to write about . . . I haven't done anything.' (Writers, real writers, I thought, lived in New York or Paris; they smoked on the back jackets of library books, their chores done.)

"Stories die for not being told. . . . My story got told because I had received an education; my teachers had given me the skill of stringing words together in a coherent line. But it was not until I was a man that I felt any need to write my story. A few years ago I left graduate school, quit teaching for political reasons (to protest affirmative action). But after leaving the classroom, as the months passed, I grew desperate to talk to serious people about serious things. In the great journals of the world, I noticed, there was conversation of a sort, glamorous company of a sort, and I determined to join it. I began writing to stay alive — not as a job, but to stay alive.

"Even as you see my essay now, in cool printer's type, I look at some pages and cannot remember having written them. Or else I can remember earlier versions — unused incident, character, description (rooms, faces) — crumbled and discarded. Flung from possibility. They hit the wastebasket, those pages, and yet, defying gravity with a scratchy, starchy resilience, tried to reopen themselves. Then they fell silent. I read certain other sentences now and they recall the very day they were composed — the afternoon of rain or the telephone call that was to come a few moments after, the house, the room where these sentences were composed, the pattern of the rug, the wastebasket. (In all there were about thirty or forty versions that preceded this final 'Aria.') I tried to describe my experiences exactly, at once to discover myself and to reveal myself. Always I had to write against the fear I felt that no one would be able to understand what I was saying.

"As a reader, I have been struck by the way those novels and essays that are most particular, most particularly about one other life and time (Hannibal, Missouri; one summer; a slave; the loveliness of a muddy river) most fully achieve universality and call to be cherished. It is a paradox apparently: The more a writer unearths the detail that makes a life singular, the more a reader is led to feel a kind of sharing. Perhaps the reason we are able to respond to the life that is so different is because we all, each of us, think privately that we are different from one another. And the more closely we examine another life in its misery or wisdom or foolishness, the more it seems we take some version of ourselves.

"It is, in any case, finally you that I end up having to trust not to laugh, not to snicker. Even as you regard me in these lines, I try to imagine your face as you read. You who read 'Aria,' especially those of you with your theme-divining yellow felt pen poised in your hand, you for whom this essay is yet another assignment, please do not forget that it is my life I am handing you in these pages — memories that are as personal for me as family photographs in an old cigar box."

FOR DISCUSSION

1. What seems to be Rodriguez's attitude toward his AUDIENCE when he writes? Do you think he writes chiefly for his readers, or for himself? Defend your answer.
2. Rodriguez tells us what he said when, as a student, he was told, "Write about what you know." What do you think he would say now?

DAVID UPDIKE

DAVID UPDIKE is best known for his short stories and his children's books. His stories have appeared in *The New Yorker* and are collected in *Out on the Marsh* (1988). His children's books number five: *A Winter Journey* (1985), *An Autumn Tale* (1988), *A Spring Story* (1989), *Seven Times Eight* (1990), and *The Sounds of Summer* (1993). He is currently at work with his father, the writer John Updike, on a children's alphabet book. Born in New York City in 1957, Updike earned a B.A. from Harvard College (1980) and an M.A.T. from Teachers College, Columbia University (1985). He has taught writing at City College of New York, Bunker Hill Community College, Massachusetts Institute of Technology, and, most recently, Middlesex Community College. Updike and his family live in Cambridge, Massachusetts.

The Colorings of Childhood

Updike is a white American; he is married to a black African, a Kenyan; his son is an African American and American African. Thus Updike is in an unusual position to consider the divisiveness of race in American and African culture and the effect it may or may not have on his mixed-race son. This essay, first published in *Harper's* magazine in 1992, was then collected in *Voices in Black and White* (1993).

No one method of development dominates Updike's essay: He draws on whatever helps him make and demonstrate his points. In passages of NARRATION, he reports encounters with others. Many EXAMPLES illustrate the way different people feel about race. Extensive COMPARISON AND CONTRAST illuminates the ideas of race held by Americans and Africans and by black and white Americans. ANALYSIS of these ideas and dissection of their CAUSES AND EFFECTS occur throughout the essay.

Five or six years ago, when my older sister revealed to the rest of   1
our family her intention of marrying her boyfriend, from Ghana, I remember that my reaction, as a nervous and somewhat protective younger brother, was something like "Well, that's fine for them — I just wonder about the children." I'm not sure what I was wondering, exactly, but it no doubt had to do with the thorny questions of race and identity, of having parents of different complexions, and a child,

presumably, of some intermediate shade, and what that would mean for a child growing up here, in the United States of America.

I had no idea, at the time, that I, too, would one day marry an African, or that soon thereafter we would have a child, or that I would hear my own apprehensions of several years before echoed in the words of one of my wife's friends. She was a white American of a classic liberal mold — wearer of Guatemalan shawls, befriender of Africans, espouser of worthy causes — but she was made uneasy by the thought of Njoki, her friend from Kenya, marrying me, a white person. She first asked Njoki what my "politics" were and, having been assured that they were okay, went on to say, "Well, I'm sure he's a very nice person, but before you get married I just hope you'll think about the children." 2

I recognized in her remarks the shadow of my own, but when it is one's own marriage that is being worried about, one's children, not yet conceived, one tends to ponder such comments more closely. By this time, too, I was the uncle of two handsome, happy boys, Ghanian-American, who, as far as I could tell, were suffering no side effects for having parents of different colors. Njoki, too, was displeased. 3

"What is she trying to say, exactly — that *my* child will be disadvantaged because he looks like me?" my wife asked. "So what does she think about me? Does she think *I'm* disadvantaged because I'm African?" 4

I responded that our liberal friend was trying to get at the complicated question of identity, knowing, as she did, that the child, in a country that simplifies complicated, racial equations to either "black" or "white," wouldn't know to which group he "belonged." 5

"To both of them," Njoki answered, "or to neither. He will be Kenyan-American. The ridiculous part is that if I was marrying an African she wouldn't mind at all — she wouldn't say, 'Think of the children,' because the child would just be black, like me, and it wouldn't be her problem. She wouldn't have to worry about it. Honestly," she finally said, her head bowed into her hand in resignation, "this country is so complicated." 6

But her friend's reaction is not, I suspect, an uncommon one, even among those who think of themselves as progressive and ideologically unfettered: They don't mind, in principle, the idea of interracial unions, but the prospect of children clouds the issue, so to speak, and raises the identity issue — if not for the child, the *beheld,* then for us, the beholders. For as I slowly pondered the woman's remarks, it occurred to me that she was not saying "He won't know 7 who he is," but something closer to "*I* won't know who he is — I won't know to which group this child belongs, the black people or the white." Added to this is the suppressed, looming understanding that, however the child sees himself, however we see the child, the country at large will perceive the child as "black," and, consequently, this son or daughter of a friend, this child to whom we might actually be an aunt or uncle, parent or grandparent, cousin or friend, this person whom we love and wish the best for in life, will grow up on the opposite side of the color line from us and, as such, will be privy to a whole new realm of the American Experience, which we, by virtue of our skin color, have previously avoided; and this — for the vast majority of white Americans — is a new and not altogether comforting experience.

Harlem, Anacostia, Roxbury, Watts: in every major city in America, and most minor ones, there is a neighborhood that most whites have never been to, will never go to, and regard, from a distance, with an almost primordial fear, akin to the child's apprehension of the bogeyman. They have read about this place in the paper and heard on the nightly news of the crime and violence there, but the thought of actually going there for a visit is almost unthinkable; if they ever found themselves there — got off at the wrong subway stop or took an ill-fated wrong turn — they imagine they would be set upon by hordes of angry, dark people with nothing better to do than sit around waiting for hapless white people to amble into their lair. Most white Americans, I suspect, would be more comfortable walking through the streets of Lagos, or Nairobi, or Kingston, than they would be walking through any predominantly black neighborhood in America. 8

For a couple of years Njoki lived in Harlem, on Riverside Drive and 145th Street, and was visited there one evening by a couple of our friends and their one-year-old child. When it came time to leave, after dark, the woman asked Njoki if she would walk them to the corner, to hail a cab — as if the presence of a black person would grant them free passage and protect them from the perils of the neighborhood. Njoki explained that it was okay, that the neighborhood was quite safe and they wouldn't be singled out for special attention because they were white. 9

"It's okay for us," the friend explained. "I just wouldn't want anything to happen to the baby." 10

Njoki relented and walked them over to Broadway, but as they went she wondered what made her friends think the residents of 11

Harlem wanted to attack a couple with a baby, or why she, an African and a stranger to this country, was called upon to somehow protect her American friends from their own countrymen. At the corner they hailed a cab, and they were whisked off to some safer corner of the city, leaving Njoki to walk back alone to her apartment, at far greater risk, as a single woman, than any group of people, white or black, would ever be.

Which is not to say that I myself felt at perfect ease walking   12
through the streets of Harlem, but simply that the more time I spent there the more I realized that no one was particularly interested, or concerned, that a pale man in collegiate tweeds was walking through the neighborhood. During the two years that my wife lived there, I walked often from her apartment down to City College, where I taught, and from there to Columbia University, and I was never bothered or heckled by anyone. As a friend of mine, a resident of Harlem, said to me once, "Black people are around white people all the time."

But as a child growing up in a small New England town, I was   13
almost never around black people. My impressions of the world beyond, or of African-Americans, were mostly gleaned from television and magazines and movies, from which, it seems to me, it is nearly impossible not to acquire certain racist assumptions about people, however slight and subtle; and even when one has become aware of them they are nearly impossible to shed entirely. Like astronomers who can hear the "background radiation" that marks the beginning of the universe, so can one hear, in the background of one's own thoughts, the persistent, static hiss of American history.

By the time my second nephew was born I had written two   14
children's books, both about a boy and his dog and their various adventures in the small New England town where they lived. As I began to think about a third book in this series, it occurred to me that the boy could now have a friend, and if he was to have a friend it might be nice if his complexion was somewhat closer to that of my two nephews, so that when they read the book they would find a character who, in this regard, looked somewhat like themselves. I wrote such a book and sent in the manuscript with a letter explaining that, although there was no reference to race in the book, I would like the second boy to appear darker than his friend in the illustrations.

A few weeks later I received the editor's response: He liked the   15
plot and story line, he said, but was confused by this new character,

which seemed underdeveloped and vague. The editor didn't understand what this character was doing in a small New England town. I
ran the risk, too, of being accused of "tokenism" by some of the
members of the library association — black women especially, he
pointed out — who were on the lookout for such things.

I wrote back and, among other things, suggested that children   16
are less encumbered by problems of race and ethnicity than their
parents or teachers, and I thought it unlikely they would worry what
he was doing in a small New England town. I was willing to run the
risk of being accused of tokenism either by reviewers or watchdogs of
the children's-book world. In the end, we agreed on a few small
editorial changes, when the book came out the character in question
was indeed of brown skin, and I never heard another word about it
either from teachers or reviewers or disgruntled children. But this
editorial skirmish gave me a taste of the children's-world book world
I had not quite imagined, and I've since had dealings with several
other publishers, most of whom, it seemed to me, exhibited a kind
of heightened vigilance when it came to books about "children of
color," so wrought were editors with anxieties about tokenism and
marketing and whatever other obstacles lie between them and a
slightly broader vision of what constitutes suitable subject matter for
children.

Njoki is often asked what my family thinks of my being married   17
to an African woman, a black woman, but she is almost never asked
what her family thinks of her being married to a "mzungu" — a white
person. Her interviewers are surprised to learn that my parents don't
mind and that hers don't either, and that her parents regret much
more that neither she nor I is a practicing Catholic. They are also
surprised to learn that there would be much more apprehension and
mutual suspicion had she married a Kenyan of another ethnic group,
or an African of another country. And I am married to an African,
not an African-American, and in my case, too, the suspicions and
animosities of history are diffused by the absence of a common and
adversarial past. And, similarly, for Njoki, the thought of her being
married to a white Kenyan — the descendants of Karen Blixen (more
commonly known as Isak Dinesen[1]) and her ilk — is almost laughable.

Several summers ago we spent six weeks in Kenya and passed   18

---

[1]Dinesen (1885–1962) was a Danish writer, the author of *Out of Africa* (1938),
who for many years ran a farm in what is now Kenya. — EDS.

much of our time there in a middle-class suburb of Nairobi called Karen, named after this same Karen Blixen, who once lived here in the shadow of the Ngong Hills. One night we were invited to dinner at the house of a neighbor — a couple in the tourist industry who had invited a group of traveling Americans over to their house for dinner. Their home was in the typically grand style of the Kenyan middle class, the "grounds" surrounded by a tall barbed-wire and electrified fence, and further protected by an all-night watchman and several roaming dogs. But inside the floors were polished wood parquet, the furniture was tasteful, and, aside from a few African prints, we could have been in an upper-middle-class dwelling in Los Angeles, or Buenos Aires, or Rome. The other guests had already arrived, and sat on couches eating and drinking and talking with their hosts. As it turned out, all of the guests were African-American, mostly from New Jersey and New York; we were introduced, and joined them, but it became clear that some were not very happy to find me, a white American, here in the home of an African, 8,000 miles from the country they and I so uneasily shared. When I tried to speak to one of the African-American women, she would answer in clipped monosyllables and stare into distant corners of the room; another woman had brought a tape recorder, with which to record some of the conversations, but whenever I spoke, it was observed, she would turn off the machine and wait for my polluting commentary to pass. I did find one woman who was not, outwardly, troubled by my presence, and spent much of the evening talking with her, but my otherwise chilly reception had not been lost on Njoki's sister and brother-in-law and niece, who were both mystified and amused. On the car ride home we tried to explain — about the history of the United States, and slavery, and about African-Americans' identification with Africa as the place from which their ancestors were taken, stolen, for hundreds of years. Njoki tried to explain how their visit here was a kind of homecoming, a return to the continent they probably would have never left, were it not for the unpleasant fact of slavery.

"Yes, but that was West Africa — it has nothing to do with here. 19 And besides, they're Americans now — and you're American, too."

"Yes, but . . ." 20

"And you're a guest. You have as much right to be here as they 21 do."

"Yes, but . . ." 22

It is difficult to accurately convey the complexities of race in 23 America to someone who has never been here, and they remained unconvinced. Our American dinner companions, I suspect, would have been saddened, if not maddened, by our sour postmortem of the evening, and I was sorry to have been, as far as they were concerned, in the wrong place at the wrong time, was sorry to have diminished their enjoyment of their visit. But I still felt that I had more in common with my fellow African-American guests than either of us did with our Kenyan hosts — an idea to which they might have heartily objected. They shared with our hosts a genetic and, to some extent, cultural "Africanness," and the experience of being mistreated by peoples of European ancestry; I shared with my hosts the experience of growing up in a place where people of one's own ethnicity, or color, were in the majority; but with my fellow guests I shared the more immediate experience of having grown up in America, where our experiences have been rather different, where we also live, as uneasy acquaintances, on opposing sides of the same, American coin.

I am asked, sometimes, either directly or by implication, how it 24 is that both my sister and I — New Englanders of northern European extraction — came to marry Africans, people of another culture and color and continent. I have never had much of an answer for these people, except to say that both my sister and I are compatible with our respective spouses in ways neither of us had been with previous companions, all of whom were far closer to our own complexions. When I was five or so, and my sister seven, my family lived for two months on a small island in the Caribbean, and it is my mother's rather whimsical theory that it was from impressions gleaned during this trip — for my sister from the somewhat older boys she played with in an old, rusty model T that sat beside our house, and for me from the long-limbed, beautiful baby-sitters who used to take care of us — that led us both, thirty years later, to marry Africans. Nor do I think that it was any strain of "jungle fever" that caused us to marry who we did. More likely, my sister and I both married Africans because, as children, we were not conditioned not to, were not told that this was not one of life's options, and so, when the opportunity arose, there were no barriers — neither our own nor our parents'. And in the "white liberal" world in which I grew up, it would have been uncouth to make any outward show of disapproval — though I suspect some amused speculation went on behind closed doors about my sister's and my choice of mates, and I believe some of my parents' friends expressed quiet concern, but I have never personally received any negative commentary, neither from friends nor passersby. It had been more of an issue for Njoki, who has some friends who believe marrying a white man is a "sellout" of some kind, a "betrayal" of the race, and that with it comes the loss of some strain of political correctness. But such friends either tend to adjust or to fade away into a world more cleanly divided between black and white, where they will be irritated and confused no more.

By some unexpected confluence of genes our son Wesley's hair 25 is, to our surprise, relatively straight — long, looping curls that tighten slightly when it rains — and this, too, will mean something in America, means something already to the elderly neighborhood women who tell us, with a smile, that he has "good" hair, and to other people, friends and strangers both, who tell us he looks like he is from Central America, or India, or the Middle East, implicitly meaning *rather than black.* Children, however, are less circumspect in their observations, and I have no doubt my son will be called a few names while growing up, both by white children and by brown; he may be told that he is really "black," and he may be told that he thinks he's "white"; in Kenya, I have been assured, he will be considered "half-caste" — an unpleasant linguistic relic from colonial days. He may also be treated badly by teachers prone to impatience, or a lack of empathy, with students of lighter, or darker, complexions than their own. He may be embarrassed by the sound of his mother's language; he may be embarrassed by my whiteness. He may go through a time when he is, indeed, confused about his "identity," but in this respect I don't think he will be much different from other children, or teenagers, or adults. There is no way of my knowing, really, what his experience as a multiracial child will be, or, for that matter, how helpful I or his mother will be to him along the way. We can only tell him what we think and know, and hope, as all parents do, that our words will be of some use.

We are not bothered by mothers in the park who seem to get a 26 little nervous, overly vigilant, when their children begin to commiserate with other, darker children, as if their children are in some sort of subtle, ineffable danger — too close for comfort. Their fears seem laughable, absurd, and one comes to almost pity the children who will grow up in the shadow of such fearful, narrow people, from whom they will inherit the same nervous bundle of apprehensions and pathologies. Many of them will be sent to private schools, not because the public schools in our city are not very good but because of the subconscious assumption that schools with so many children of other races *can't* be that good: Such schools and students will hold their own children back somehow. But in the end, these people tend to recede, not disappear, exactly, but shrink before the simple, overwhelming presence of your child, who shrieks with joy at something as simple as the sound of your key turning in the door.

Wesley will visit Africa and live there for a time, and will know 27 the Kenyan half of his family there and the American half here, and into the bargain will know his Ghanian uncle and his Ghanian-American cousins and a whole West African branch of his extended family. And it may just be that, contrary to the assumptions of concerned friends, this child of a "mixed" marriage will suffer no great disadvantages at all, but rather will enjoy advantages denied the rest of us; for as the child of two cultures he will "belong" to neither of them exclusively but both of them collectively, will be a part of my Americanness and Njoki's Africanness, and will be something neither she nor I ever will be — African-American — and as such will be a part of a rich and varied culture that will always hold me at arm's length. And in these layers of identity lies an opportunity for a kind of expansion of the world, a dissolution of the boundaries and obstacles that hold us all in a kind of skittish, social obeisance, and he thus may be spared the suspicions and apprehensions that plague those of us who have grown up with an exclusive, clearly defined sense of belonging. In the end, my son will be, simply, an American child, an American adult. His will be a wider, more complicated world than mine was, and to him will fall the privilege and burden, as it falls to us all, of making of it what he will.

QUESTIONS ON MEANING

1. Why is Njoki offended when her white friends ask her to escort them to a cab (paras. 9–11)?
2. Why, in Updike's opinion, do Americans feel threatened by the children of interracial marriages? Is it only white Americans who seem to feel threatened?
3. What, briefly, is Updike's THESIS? Consider what he says about both the disadvantages and the advantages for children of interracial marriages.
4. What main reason does Updike give for his and his sister's interracial marriages?
5. How would you characterize this essay's PURPOSE?

QUESTIONS ON WRITING STRATEGY

1. Updike makes his structure visual with blank lines between sections of the essay. What does each section contribute to Updike's THESIS?
2. *Harper's* magazine, where Updike's essay first appeared, is a journal of opinion and literature aimed at a mostly affluent, liberal AUDIENCE. Where do you see Updike addressing this audience? Where does his idea of his audience seem wider?
3. MIXED METHODS. Using NARRATION, EXAMPLE, and ANALYSIS, Updike COMPARES AND CONTRASTS the attitudes toward race of black and white Americans and of Americans and Africans. SUMMARIZE these comparisons.
4. MIXED METHODS. Updike's comparisons serve his attempt to analyze the CAUSES of bias against interracial children in America. Summarize these causes. What EFFECTS does Updike predict for his son, Wesley?

QUESTIONS ON LANGUAGE

1. Where does Updike use "black" in this essay to describe people of color? Where does he use "brown"? Why does he differentiate between these words?
2. Describe Updike's TONE. How appropriate is it for his PURPOSE?
3. ANALYZE the long final sentence of paragraph 7. What do its structure and length contribute to its content?
4. Consult your dictionary if you are unsure of these words: ideologically, privy (para. 7); primordial (8); gleaned (13); tokenism (15); disgruntled, vigilance (16); animosities, adversarial (17); parquet, monosyllables (18); postmortem (23); confluence, circumspect (25); pathologies (26); obeisance (27).

SUGGESTIONS FOR WRITING

1. "In the end," writes Updike, "my son will be, simply, an American child, an American adult" (para. 27). Do you agree? In an essay, state and defend your opinion on the future of race relations in the United States. Consider whether interracial children such as Updike's son will have an easier or harder time than they had in the past. Provide EVIDENCE from your own experiences, observation, and reading.
2. Updike says that his "impressions . . . of African-Americans" came from "television and magazines and movies, from which, it seems to me, it is nearly impossible not to acquire certain racist assumptions about people, however slight and subtle" (para. 13). In an essay, detail some media images of your own ethnic group or another group that have made an impression on you. How have these images affected you? How do they stack up against reality? Do you think they have helped or hurt our society?

3. **CRITICAL WRITING.** Closely ANALYZE the ideas about race in two or three paragraphs of Updike's essay. (Some likely candidates are paras. 7, 8, 17, 18, 23, 24, 25, 26, 27.) What conventional ASSUMPTIONS about "blackness" and "whiteness" does Updike challenge? What assumptions does he leave undisturbed? Present your analysis in an essay of your own.

4. **CONNECTIONS.** Compare this essay to Richard Rodriguez's "Aria: A Memoir of a Bilingual Childhood" (p. 563). Both writers view cultural assimilation as a necessary and worthwhile goal. How does each writer depict the process of assimilation differently? Which author do you think has a more realistic view of the problems involved?

MAXINE HONG KINGSTON

Maxine Hong Kingston grew up caught between two complex and very different cultures: the China of her parents and the America of her surroundings. In her first two books, *The Woman Warrior: Memoirs of a Girlhood Among Ghosts* (1979) and *China Men* (1980), Kingston combines Chinese myth and history with family tales to create a dreamlike world that shifts between reality and fantasy. Born in 1940 in Stockton, California, Kingston was the first American-born child of a scholar and a medical practitioner who became laundry workers in this country. After graduating from the University of California at Berkeley (B.A., 1962), Kingston taught English at California and Hawaii high schools and at the University of Hawaii. She has contributed essays, poems, and stories to *The New Yorker*, the *New York Times Magazine*, *Ms.*, and other periodicals. In Kingston's most recent book, the novel *Tripmaster Monkey: His Fake Book* (1989), the Chinese American Wittman Ah Sing relates wild and comical adventures in a distinctive voice. Kingston lives in Oakland, California.

No Name Woman

"No Name Woman" is part of *The Woman Warrior*. Like much of Kingston's writing, it blends the "talk-stories" of Kingston's elders, her own vivid imaginings, and the reality of her experience — this time to discover why her Chinese aunt drowned herself in the family well.

"No Name Woman" thus seeks CAUSES, and it does so by COMPARING TWO NARRATIVES — that told by Kingston's mother and that invented by Kingston herself. Besides these three methods of development, DESCRIPTION and EXAMPLE are also pervasive.

"You must not tell anyone," my mother said, "what I am about to tell you. In China your father had a sister who killed herself. She jumped into the family well. We say that your father has all brothers because it is as if she had never been born.

"In 1924 just a few days after our village celebrated seventeen hurry-up weddings — to make sure that every young man who went 'out on the road' would responsibly come home — your father and his brothers and your grandfather and his brothers and your aunt's new husband sailed for America, the Gold Mountain. It was your grandfather's last trip. Those lucky enough to get contracts waved good-bye from the decks. They fed and guarded the stowaways and helped them off in Cuba, New York, Bali, Hawaii. 'We'll meet in California next year,' they said. All of them sent money home.

"I remember looking at your aunt one day when she and I were   3
dressing; I had not noticed before that she had such a protruding melon of a stomach. But I did not think, 'She's pregnant,' until she began to look like other pregnant women, her shirt pulling and the white tops of her black pants showing. She could not have been pregnant, you see, because her husband had been gone for years. No one said anything. We did not discuss it. In early summer she was ready to have the child, long after the time when it could have been possible.

"The village had also been counting. On the night the baby was   4
to be born the villagers raided our house. Some were crying. Like a great saw, teeth strung with lights, files of people walked zigzag across our land, tearing the rice. Their lanterns doubled in the disturbed black water, which drained away through the broken bunds. As the villagers closed in, we could see that some of them, probably men and women we knew well, wore white masks. The people with long hair hung it over their faces. Women with short hair made it stand up on end. Some had tied white bands around their foreheads, arms, and legs.

"At first they threw mud and rocks at the house. Then they threw   5
eggs and began slaughtering our stock. We could hear the animals scream their deaths — the roosters, the pigs, a last great roar from the ox. Familiar wild heads flared in our night windows; the villagers encircled us. Some of the faces stopped to peer at us, their eyes rushing like searchlights. The hands flattened against the panes, framed heads, and left red prints.

"The villagers broke in the front and the back doors at the same   6
time, even though we had not locked the doors against them. Their knives dripped with the blood of our animals. They smeared blood on the doors and walls. One woman swung a chicken, whose throat she had slit, splattering blood in red arcs about her. We stood together in the middle of our house, in the family hall with the pictures and tables of the ancestors around us, and looked straight ahead.

"At that time the house had only two wings. When the men   7
came back, we would build two more to enclose our courtyard and a third one to begin a second courtyard. The villagers pushed through both wings, even your grandparents' rooms, to find your aunt's, which was also mine until the men returned. From this room a new wing for one of the younger families would grow. They ripped up her clothes

and shoes and broke her combs, grinding them underfoot. They tore her work from the loom. They scattered the cooking fire and rolled the new weaving in it. We could hear them in the kitchen breaking our bowls and banging the pots. They overturned the great waist-high earthenware jugs; duck eggs, pickled fruits, vegetables burst out and mixed in acrid torrents. The old woman from the next field swept a broom through the air and loosed the spirits-of-the-broom over our heads. 'Pig.' 'Ghost.' 'Pig,' they sobbed and scolded while they ruined our house.

"When they left, they took sugar and oranges to bless themselves. 8 They cut pieces from the dead animals. Some of them took bowls that were not broken and clothes that were not torn. Afterward we swept up the rice and sewed it back up into sacks. But the smells from the spilled preserves lasted. Your aunt gave birth in the pigsty that night. The next morning when I went up for the water, I found her and the baby plugging up the family well.

"Don't let your father know that I told you. He denies her. Now 9 that you have started to menstruate, what happened to her could happen to you. Don't humiliate us. You wouldn't like to be forgotten as if you had never been born. The villagers are watchful."

Whenever she had to warn us about life, my mother told stories 10 that ran like this one, a story to grow up on. She tested our strength to establish realities. Those in the emigrant generations who could not reassert brute survival died young and far from home. Those of us in the first American generations have had to figure out how the invisible world the emigrants built around our childhoods fit in solid America.

The emigrants confused the gods by diverting their curses, mis- 11 leading them with crooked streets and false names. They must try to confuse their offspring as well, who, I suppose, threaten them in similar ways — always trying to get things straight, always trying to name the unspeakable. The Chinese I know hide their names; so-journers take new names when their lives change and guard their real names with silence.

Chinese-Americans, when you try to understand what things in 12 you are Chinese, how do you separate what is peculiar to childhood, to poverty, insanities, one family, your mother who marked your growing with stories, from what is Chinese? What is Chinese tradition and what is the movies?

If I want to learn what clothes my aunt wore, whether flashy or 13 ordinary, I would have to begin, "Remember Father's drowned-in-the-well sister?" I cannot ask that. My mother has told me once and for all the useful parts. She will add nothing unless powered by Necessity, a riverbank that guides her life. She plants vegetable gardens rather than lawns; she carries the odd-shaped tomatoes home from the fields and eats food left for the gods.

Whenever we did frivolous things, we used up energy; we flew high kites. We children came up off the ground over the melting cones our parents brought home from work and the American movie on New Year's Day — *Oh, You Beautiful Doll* with Betty Grable one year, and *She Wore a Yellow Ribbon* with John Wayne another year. After the one carnival ride each, we paid in guilt; our tired father counted his change on the dark walk home.

Adultery is extravagance. Could people who hatch their own chicks and eat the embryos and the heads for delicacies and boil the feet in vinegar for party food, leaving only the gravel, eating even the gizzard lining — could such people engender a prodigal aunt? To be a woman, to have a daughter in starvation time was a waste enough. My aunt could not have been the lone romantic who gave up everything for sex. Women in the old China did not choose. Some man had commanded her to lie with him and be his secret evil. I wonder whether he masked himself when he joined the raid on her family.

Perhaps she encountered him in the fields or on the mountain where the daughters-in-law collected fuel. Or perhaps he first noticed her in the marketplace. He was not a stranger because the village housed no strangers. She had to have dealings with him other than sex. Perhaps he worked an adjoining field, or he sold her the cloth for the dress she sewed and wore. His demand must have surprised, then terrified her. She obeyed him; she always did as she was told.

When the family found a young man in the next village to be her husband, she stood tractably beside the best rooster, his proxy, and promised before they met that she would be his forever. She was lucky that he was her age and she would be the first wife, an advantage secure now. The night she first saw him, he had sex with her. Then he left for America. She had almost forgotten what he looked like. When she tried to envision him, she only saw the black and white face in the group photograph the men had had taken before leaving.

The other man was not, after all, much different from her husband. They both gave orders: she followed. "If you tell your family, I'll beat you. I'll kill you. Be here again next week." No one talked sex, ever. And she might have separated the rapes from the rest of living if only she did not have to buy her oil from him or gather wood in the same forest. I want her fear to have lasted just as long as rape lasted so that the fear could have been contained. No drawn-out fear. But women at sex hazarded birth and hence lifetimes. The fear did not stop but permeated everywhere. She told the man, "I think I'm pregnant." He organized the raid against her.

On nights when my mother and father talked about their life 19 back home, sometimes they mentioned an "outcast table" whose business they still seemed to be settling, their voices tight. In a commensal tradition, where food is precious, the powerful older people made wrongdoers eat alone. Instead of letting them start separate new lives like the Japanese, who could become samurais and geishas, the Chinese family, faces averted but eyes glowering sideways, hung on to the offenders and fed them leftovers. My aunt must have lived in the same house as my parents and eaten at an outcast table. My mother spoke about the raid as if she had seen it, when she and my aunt, a daughter-in-law to a different household, should not have been living together at all. Daughters-in-law lived with their husbands' parents, not their own; a synonym for marriage in Chinese is "taking a daughter-in-law." Her husband's parents could have sold her, mortgaged her, stoned her. But they had sent her back to her own mother and father, a mysterious act hinting at disgraces not told me. Perhaps they had thrown her out to deflect the avengers.

She was the only daughter; her four brothers went with her father, 20 husband, and uncles "out on the road" and for some years became western men. When the goods were divided among the family, three of the brothers took land, and the youngest, my father, chose an education. After my grandparents gave their daughter away to her husband's family, they had dispensed all the adventure and all the property. They expected her alone to keep the traditional ways, which her brothers, now among the barbarians, could fumble without detection. The heavy, deep-rooted women were to maintain the past against the flood, safe for returning. But the rare urge west had fixed upon our family, and so my aunt crossed boundaries not delineated in space.

The work of preservation demands that the feelings playing about 21 in one's guts not be turned into action. Just watch their passing like cherry blossoms. But perhaps my aunt, my forerunner, caught in a slow life, let dreams grow and fade and after some months or years went toward what persisted. Fear at the enormities of the forbidden kept her desires delicate, wire and bone. She looked at a man because she liked the way the hair was tucked behind his ears, or she liked the question-mark line of a long torso curving at the shoulder and

straight at the hip. For warm eyes or a soft voice or a slow walk —
that's all — a few hairs, a line, a brightness, a sound, a pace, she
gave up family. She offered us up for a charm that vanished with
tiredness, a pigtail that didn't toss when the wind died. Why, the
wrong lighting could erase the dearest thing about him.

It could very well have been, however, that my aunt did not take   22
subtle enjoyment of her friend, but, a wild woman, kept rollicking
company. Imagining her free with sex doesn't fit, though. I don't
know any women like that, or men either. Unless I see her life
branching into mine, she gives me no ancestral help.

To sustain her being in love, she often worked at herself in the   23
mirror, guessing at the colors and shapes that would interest him,
changing them frequently in order to hit on the right combination.
She wanted him to look back.

On a farm near the sea, a woman who tended her appearance   24
reaped a reputation for eccentricity. All the married women blunt-
cut their hair in flaps about their ears or pulled it back in tight buns.
No nonsense. Neither style blew easily into heart-catching tangles.
And at their weddings they displayed themselves in their long hair
for the last time. "It brushed the backs of my knees," my mother tells
me. "It was braided, and even so, it brushed the backs of my knees."

At the mirror my aunt combed individuality into her bob. A bun   25
could have been contrived to escape into black streamers blowing in
the wind or in quiet wisps about her face, but only the older women
in our picture album wear buns. She brushed her hair back from her
forehead, tucking the flaps behind her ears. She looped a piece of
thread, knotted into a circle between her index fingers and thumbs,
and ran the double strand across her forehead. When she closed her
fingers as if she were making a pair of shadow geese bite, the string
twisted together catching the little hairs. Then she pulled the thread
away from her skin, ripping the hairs out neatly, her eyes watering
from the needles of pain. Opening her fingers, she cleaned the thread,
then rolled it along her hairline and the tops of her eyebrows. My
mother did the same to me and my sisters and herself. I used to
believe that the expression "caught by the short hairs" meant a captive
held with a depilatory string. It especially hurt at the temples, but
my mother said we were lucky we didn't have to have our feet bound
when we were seven. Sisters used to sit on their beds and cry together,
she said, as their mothers or their slave removed the bandages for a
few minutes each night and let the blood gush back into their veins.
I hope that the man my aunt loved appreciated a smooth brow, that
he wasn't just a tits-and-ass man.

Once my aunt found a freckle on her chin, at a spot that the 26
almanac said predestined her for unhappiness. She dug it out with a
hot needle and washed the wound with peroxide.

More attention to her looks than these pullings of hairs and 27
pickings at spots would have caused gossip among the villagers. They
owned work clothes and good clothes, and they wore good clothes
for feasting the new seasons. But since a woman combing her hair
hexes beginnings, my aunt rarely found an occasion to look her best.
Women looked like great sea snails — the corded wood, babies, and
laundry they carried were the whorls on their backs. The Chinese
did not admire a bent back; goddesses and warriors stood straight.
Still there must have been a marvelous freeing of beauty when a
worker laid down her burden and stretched and arched.

Such commonplace loveliness, however, was not enough for my 28
aunt. She dreamed of a lover for the fifteen days of New Year's, the
time for families to exchange visits, money, and food. She plied her
secret comb. And sure enough she cursed the year, the family, the
village, and herself.

Even as her hair lured her imminent lover, many other men 29
looked at her. Uncles, cousins, nephews, brothers would have looked,
too, had they been home between journeys. Perhaps they had already
been restraining their curiosity, and they left, fearful that their
glances, like a field of nesting birds, might be startled and caught.
Poverty hurt, and that was their first reason for leaving. But another,
final reason for leaving the crowded house was the never-said.

She may have been unusually beloved, the precious only daughter, 30
spoiled and mirror gazing because of the affection the family lavished
on her. When her husband left, they welcomed the chance to take
her back from the in-laws; she could live like the little daughter for
just a while longer. There are stories that my grandfather was different
from other people, "crazy ever since the little Jap bayoneted him in
the head." He used to put his naked penis on the dinner table,
laughing. And one day he brought home a baby girl, wrapped up
inside his brown western-style greatcoat. He had traded one of his
sons, probably my father, the youngest, for her. My grandmother
made him trade back. When he finally got a daughter of his own, he
doted on her. They must have all loved her, except perhaps my
father, the only brother who never went back to China, having once
been traded for a girl.

Brothers and sisters, newly men and women, had to efface their 31
sexual color and present plain miens. Disturbing hair and eyes, a
smile like no other, threatened the ideal of five generations living

under one roof. To focus blurs, people shouted face to face and yelled from room to room. The immigrants I know have loud voices, un-modulated to American tones even after years away from the village where they called their friendships out across the fields. I have not been able to stop my mother's screams in public libraries or over telephones. Walking erect (knees straight, toes pointed forward, not pigeon-toed, which is Chinese-feminine) and speaking in an inaudible voice, I have tried to turn myself American-feminine. Chinese com-munication was loud, public. Only sick people had to whisper. But at the dinner table, where the family members came nearest one another, no one could talk, not the outcasts nor any eaters. Every word that falls from the mouth is a coin lost. Silently they gave and accepted food with both hands. A preoccupied child who took his bowl with one hand got a sideways glare. A complete moment of total attention is due everyone alike. Children and lovers have no singularity here, but my aunt used a secret voice, a separate atten-tiveness.

She kept the man's name to herself throughout her labor and   32
dying; she did not accuse him that he be punished with her. To save her inseminator's name she gave silent birth.

He may have been somebody in her own household, but inter-   33
course with a man outside the family would have been no less abhor-rent. All the village were kinsmen, and the titles shouted in loud country voices never let kinship be forgotten. Any man within vis-iting distance would have been neutralized as a lover — "brother," "younger brother," "older brother" — one hundred and fifteen rela-tionship titles. Parents researched birth charts probably not so much to assure good fortune as to circumvent incest in a population that has but one hundred surnames. Everybody has eight million relatives. How useless then sexual mannerisms, how dangerous.

As if it came from an atavism deeper than fear, I used to add   34
"brother" silently to boys' names. It hexed the boys, who would or would not ask me to dance, and made them less scary and as familiar and deserving of benevolence as girls.

But, of course, I hexed myself also — no dates. I should have   35
stood up, both arms waving, and shouted out across libraries, "Hey, you! Love me back." I had no idea, though, how to make attraction selective, how to control its direction and magnitude. If I made myself American-pretty so that the five or six Chinese boys in the class fell in love with me, everyone else — the Caucasian, Negro, and Japa-nese boys — would too. Sisterliness, dignified and honorable, made much more sense.

Attraction eludes control so stubbornly that whole societies de-   36
signed to organize relationships among people cannot keep order, not
even when they bind people to one another from childhood and raise
them together. Among the very poor and the wealthy, brothers married their adopted sisters, like doves. Our family allowed some romance, paying adult brides' prices and providing dowries so that their
sons and daughters could marry strangers. Marriage promises to turn
strangers into friendly relatives — a nation of siblings.

In the village structure, spirits shimmered among the live crea-   37
tures, balanced and held in equilibrium by time and land. But one
human being flaring up into violence could open up a black hole, a
maelstrom that pulled in the sky. The frightened villagers, who depended on one another to maintain the real, went to my aunt to
show her a personal, physical representation of the break she made
in the "roundness." Misallying couples snapped off the future, which
was to be embodied in true offspring. The villagers punished her for
acting as if she could have a private life, secret and apart from them.

If my aunt had betrayed the family at a time of large grain yields   38
and peace, when many boys were born, and wings were being built
on many houses, perhaps she might have escaped such severe punishment. But the men — hungry, greedy, tired of planting in dry soil,
cuckolded — had been forced to leave the village in order to send
food-money home. There were ghost plagues, bandit plagues, wars
with the Japanese, floods. My Chinese brother and sister had died of
an unknown sickness. Adultery, perhaps only a mistake during good
times, became a crime when the village needed food.

The round moon cakes and round doorways, the round tables of   39
graduated size that fit one roundness inside another, round windows
and rice bowls — these talismans had lost their power to warn this
family of the law: A family must be whole, faithfully keeping the
descent line by having sons to feed the old and the dead who in turn
look after the family. The villagers came to show my aunt and lover-
in-hiding a broken house. The villagers were speeding up the circling
of events because she was too shortsighted to see that her infidelity
had already harmed the village, that waves of consequences would
return unpredictably, sometimes in disguise, as now, to hurt her. This
roundness had to be made coin-sized so that she would see its circum-
ference: punish her at the birth of her baby. Awaken her to the
inexorable. People who refused fatalism because they could invent
small resources insisted on culpability. Deny accidents and wrest fault
from the stars.

After the villagers left, their lanterns now scattering in various   40 directions toward home, the family broke their silence and cursed her. "Aiaa, we're going to die. Death is coming. Death is coming. Look what you've done. You've killed us. Ghost! Dead Ghost! Ghost! You've never been born." She ran out into the fields, far enough from the house so that she could no longer hear their voices, and pressed herself against the earth, her own land no more. When she felt the birth coming, she thought that she had been hurt. Her body seized together. "They've hurt me too much," she thought. "This is gall, and it will kill me." With forehead and knees against the earth, her body convulsed and then relaxed. She turned on her back, lay on the ground. The black well of sky and stars went out and out and out forever; her body and her complexity seemed to disappear. She was one of the stars, a bright dot in blackness, without home, without a companion, in eternal cold and silence. An agoraphobia rose in her, speeding higher and higher, bigger and bigger; she would not be able to contain it; there would be no end to fear.

Flayed, unprotected against space, she felt pain return, focusing 41 her body. This pain chilled her — a cold, steady kind of surface pain. Inside, spasmodically, the other pain, the pain of the child, heated her. For hours she lay on the ground, alternately body and space. Sometimes a vision of normal comfort obliterated reality: she saw the family in the evening gambling at the dinner table, the young people massaging their elders' backs. She saw them congratulating one another, high joy on the mornings the rice shoots came up. When these pictures burst, the stars drew out further apart. Black space opened.

She got to her feet to fight better and remembered that old- 42 fashioned women gave birth in their pigsties to fool the jealous, pain-dealing gods, who do not snatch piglets. Before the next spasms could stop her, she ran to the pigsty, each step a rushing out into emptiness. She climbed over the fence and knelt in the dirt. It was good to have a fence enclosing her, a tribal person alone.

Laboring, this woman who had carried her child as a foreign 43 growth that sickened her every day, expelled it at last. She reached down to touch the hot, wet, moving mass, surely smaller than anything human, and could feel that it was human after all — fingers, toes, nails, nose. She pulled it up on to her belly, and it lay curled there, butt in the air, feet precisely tucked one under the other. She opened her loose shirt and buttoned the child inside. After resting, it squirmed and thrashed and she pushed it up to her breast. It turned its head this way and that until it found her nipple. There, it made little snuffling noises. She clenched her teeth at its preciousness, lovely as a young calf, a piglet, a little dog.

She may have gone to the pigsty as a last act of responsibility: 44
she would protect this child as she had protected its father. It would
look after her soul, leaving supplies on her grave. But how would this
tiny child without family find her grave when there would be no
marker for her anywhere, neither in the earth nor the family hall?
No one would give her a family hall name. She had taken the child
with her into the wastes. At its birth the two of them had felt the
same raw pain of separation, a wound that only the family pressing
tight could close. A child with no descent line would not soften her
life but only trail after her, ghost-like, begging her to give it purpose.
At dawn the villagers on their way to the fields would stand around
the fence and look.

Full of milk, the little ghost slept. When it awoke, she hardened 45
her breasts against the milk that crying loosens. Toward morning she
picked up the baby and walked to the well.

Carrying the baby to the well shows loving. Otherwise abandon 46
it. Turn its face into the mud. Mothers who love their children take
them along. It was probably a girl; there is some hope of forgiveness
for boys.

"Don't tell anyone you had an aunt. Your father does not want 47
to hear her name. She has never been born." I have believed that
sex was unspeakable and words so strong and fathers so frail that
"aunt" would do my father mysterious harm. I have thought that my
family, having settled among immigrants who had also been their
neighbors in the ancestral land, needed to clean their name, and a
wrong word would incite the kinspeople even here. But there is more
to this silence: they want me to participate in her punishment. And
I have.

In the twenty years since I heard this story I have not asked for 48
details nor said my aunt's name; I do not know it. People who comfort
the dead can also chase after them to hurt them further — a reverse
ancestor worship. The real punishment was not the raid swiftly inflicted by the villagers, but the family's deliberately forgetting her.
Her betrayal so maddened them, they saw to it that she would suffer
forever, even after death. Always hungry, always needing, she would
have to beg food from other ghosts, snatch and steal it from those
whose living descendants give them gifts. She would have to fight
the ghosts massed at crossroads for the buns a few thoughtful citizens
leave to decoy her away from village and home so that the ancestral
spirits could feast unharassed. At peace, they could act like gods, not
ghosts, their descent lines providing them with paper suits and dresses,

spirit money, paper houses, paper automobiles, chicken, meat, and rice into eternity — essences delivered up in smoke and flames, steam and incense rising from each rice bowl. In an attempt to make the Chinese care for people outside the family, Chairman Mao encourages us now to give our paper replicas to the spirits of outstanding soldiers and workers, no matter whose ancestors they may be. My aunt remains forever hungry. Goods are not distributed evenly among the dead.

My aunt haunts me — her ghost drawn to me because now, after 49 fifty years of neglect, I alone devote pages of paper to her, though not origamied into houses and clothes. I do not think she always means me well. I am telling on her, and she was a spite suicide, drowning herself in the drinking water. The Chinese are always very frightened of the drowned one, whose weeping ghost, wet hair hanging and skin bloated, waits silently by the water to pull down a substitute.

QUESTIONS ON MEANING

1. What PURPOSE does Kingston have in telling her aunt's story? How does this differ from her mother's purpose in relating the tale?
2. According to Kingston, who could have been the father of her aunt's child? Who could not?
3. Kingston says that her mother told them stories "to warn us about life." What warning does this story provide?
4. Why is Kingston so fascinated by her aunt's life and death?

QUESTIONS ON WRITING STRATEGY

1. Whom does Kingston seem to include in her AUDIENCE: her family and other older Chinese? second-generation Chinese Americans like herself? other Americans? How might she expect each of these groups to respond to her essay?
2. Why is Kingston's opening line — her mother's "You must not tell anyone" — especially fitting for this essay? What secrets are being told? Why does Kingston divulge them?
3. As Kingston tells her tale of her aunt, some events are based on her mother's story or her knowledge of Chinese customs, and some are wholly imaginary. What is the EFFECT of blending these several threads of reality, perception, and imagination?
4. MIXED METHODS. Kingston COMPARES AND CONTRASTS various versions of her aunt's story, trying to find the CAUSES that led her aunt to drown in the well. In the end, what causes does Kingston seem to accept?

5. MIXED METHODS. Examine the DESCRIPTION in the two contrasting NARRATIVES of how Kingston's aunt became pregnant: one in paragraphs 15–18 and the other in paragraphs 21–28. How do the details create different realities? Which version does Kingston seem more committed to? Why?

QUESTIONS ON LANGUAGE

1. How does Kingston's language — lyrical, poetic, full of IMAGES and METAPHORS — reveal her relationship to her Chinese heritage? Find phrases that are especially striking.
2. Look up any of these words you do not know: bunds (para. 4); acrid (7); frivolous (14); tractably, proxy (17); hazarded (18); commensal (19); delineated (20); depilatory (25); plied (28); miens (31); abhorrent, circumvent (33); atavism (34); maelstrom (37); talismans, inexorable, fatalism, culpability (39); gall, agoraphobia (40); spasmodically (41).
3. Sometimes Kingston indicates that she is reconstructing or imagining events through verbs like "would have" and words like "maybe" and "perhaps" ("Perhaps she encountered him in the fields," para. 16). Other times she presents obviously imaginary events as if they actually happened ("Once my aunt found a freckle on her chin," 26). What EFFECT does Kingston achieve with these apparent inconsistencies?

SUGGESTIONS FOR WRITING

1. In an essay, tell a family story that has had a significant effect on you. (It may, like Kingston's, be a ghost story; it could also be a superstition, a tradition, or the life of an ancestor.) Who told you the story? What purpose did he or she have in telling it to you? How does it illustrate your family's beliefs and values?
2. Write an essay explaining the role of ancestors in Chinese family and religious life, supplementing what Kingston says with research in the library or (if you are Chinese American) drawing on your own experiences.
3. CRITICAL WRITING. ANALYZE the ideas about gender roles revealed in "No Name Woman," both in China and in the Chinese American culture Kingston grew up in. How have these ideas affected Kingston? Do you perceive any semblance of them in contemporary American culture?
4. CONNECTIONS. Kingston is both allied with and haunted by her deceased aunt. Similarly, Clifford Chase, in "My Brother by the Shoulder of the Road" (p. 549), has both a fulfilled and an unfinished relationship with his deceased brother Ken. Starting from these essays, write an essay of your own about how the dead stay with us. Your essay could compare Kingston's and Chase's visions of their relatives, or it could be more personal, drawing on your own experience.

MAXINE HONG KINGSTON ON WRITING

In an interview with Jean W. Ross published in *Contemporary Authors* in 1984, Maxine Hong Kingston discusses the writing and revising of *The Woman Warrior*. Ross asks Kingston to clarify an earlier statement that she had "no idea how people who don't write endure their lives." Kingston replies: "When I said that, I was thinking about how words and stories create order. Some of the things that happen to us in life seem to have no meaning, but when you write them down you find the meanings for them; or, as you translate life into words, you force a meaning. Meaning is intrinsic in words and stories."

Ross then asks if Kingston used an outline and planned to blend fact with legend in *The Woman Warrior*. "Oh no, no," Kingston answers. "What I have at the beginning of a book is not an outline. I have no idea of how stories will end or where the beginning will lead. Sometimes I draw pictures. I draw a blob and then I have a little arrow and it goes to this other blob, if you want to call that an outline. It's hardly even words; it's like a doodle. Then when it turns into words, I find the words lead me to various scenes and stories which I don't know about until I get there. I don't see the order until very late in the writing and sometimes the ending just comes. I just run up against it. All of a sudden the book's over and I didn't know it would be over."

A question from Ross about whether her emotions enter her writing leads Kingston to talk about revision. "Well, when I first set something down I feel the emotions I write about. But when I do a second draft, third draft, ninth draft, then I don't feel very emotional. The rewriting is very intellectual; all my education and reading and intellect are involved. The mechanics of sentences, how one phrase or word goes with another one — all that happens in later drafts. There's a very emotional first draft and a very technical last draft."

FOR DISCUSSION

1. Do you agree with Kingston that when you write things down you find their meaning? Give examples of when the writing process has or hasn't clarified an experience for you.
2. Kingston doodles as a way to discover her material. How do you discover what you have to say?
3. What does Kingston mean by "the mechanics of sentences"? Do you consider this element as you revise?

ADDITIONAL WRITING TOPICS

The Power of Family

1. Compare Maxine Hong Kingston's "No Name Woman" (p. 589) and Judith Ortiz Cofer's "*Casa*: A Partial Remembrance of a Puerto Rican Childhood" (p. 73). Both essays are about a family story and its telling. How are the two stories similar? How are their tellers similar? Do the stories serve the same function in Kingston's and Cofer's lives? What are the significant differences between the two essays?

2. How does a mixed cultural identity affect a family? Several essays in this book examine this issue, including Judith Ortiz Cofer's "*Casa*" (p. 73), Amy Tan's "The Language of Discretion" (p. 187), Richard Rodriguez's "Aria: A Memoir of a Bilingual Childhood" (p. 563), David Updike's "The Colorings of Childhood" (p. 578), and Maxine Hong Kingston's "No Name Woman" (p. 589). You may have a mixed identity yourself. How can such a mixed identity unite a family? How can it drive a family apart?

3. A number of essays in this book deal with memory of family. See, for instance, M. F. K. Fisher's "The Broken Chain" (p. 10), Ralph Ellison's "On Being the Target of Discrimination" (p. 55), Judith Ortiz Cofer's "*Casa*" (p. 73), E. B. White's "Once More to the Lake" (p. 120), and, of course, all the essays in this chapter. Drawing on as many of these essays as you like and on your own experiences, write an essay about how our families live in us even when we are not among them. What can memory of family do to help us? What can it do to hurt us? Use specific EXAMPLES.

12

LANGUAGE AND TRUTH

How many ways can we lie to each other? Why don't we just tell the truth? The authors in this chapter grapple with such questions. George Orwell, in his famous diatribe "Politics and the English Language," rails against abuses of the language that, he believes, undermine the way we think and even threaten our liberty. Stephanie Ericsson, in "The Ways We Lie," takes on the humble deceptions and evasions of everyday life — some perhaps desirable and even essential, but all regrettable and possibly dangerous. In "Excuuuse Me," David Segal bemoans the eclipse of ethnic and other "off-color" humor, a necessary form of truth telling, he thinks, that releases tension in a diverse culture. And finally, in "The Word Police," Michiko Kakutani evokes Orwell in arguing that today's "political correctness" obscures the truth of injustice and infringes on freedom.

GEORGE ORWELL

GEORGE ORWELL was the pen name of Eric Blair (1903–50), born in Bengal, India, the son of an English civil servant. After attending Eton on a scholarship, he joined the British police in Burma, where he acquired a distrust for the methods of the empire. Then followed years of tramping, odd jobs, and near-starvation — recalled in *Down and Out in Paris and London* (1933). From living on the fringe of society and from his reportorial writing about English miners and factory workers, Orwell deepened his sympathy with underdogs. Severely wounded while fighting in the Spanish Civil War, he wrote a memoir, *Homage to Catalonia* (1938), voicing disillusionment with Loyalists who, he claimed, sought not to free Spain but to exterminate their political enemies. A socialist by conviction, Orwell kept pointing to the dangers of a collective state run by totalitarians. In *Animal Farm* (1945), he satirized Soviet bureaucracy; and in his famous novel *1984* (1949), he foresaw a regimented England whose government perverts truth and spies on citizens by two-way television. (The motto of the state and its leader: Big Brother Is Watching You.)

Politics and
the English Language

In Orwell's novel *1984*, a dictatorship tries to replace spoken and written English with Newspeak, an official language that limits thought by reducing its users' vocabulary. (The words *light* and *bad*, for instance, are suppressed in favor of *unlight* and *unbad*.) This concern with language and with its importance to society is constant in George Orwell's work. First published in 1946, "Politics and the English Language" still stands as one of the most devastating attacks on muddy writing and thinking ever penned. Orwell's six short rules for writing responsible prose are well worth remembering.

As we noted in the introduction to this part of the book (pp. 538–539), Orwell draws on every method of development in constructing his case. Perhaps more than any other essay in this book, Orwell's shows the flexibility and the power of the methods in concert.

Most people who bother with the matter at all would admit that the English language is in a bad way, but it is generally assumed that we cannot by conscious action do anything about it. Our civilization is decadent and our language — so the argument runs — must inevitably share in the general collapse. It follows that any struggle against the abuse of language is a sentimental archaism, like preferring candles to electric light or hansom cabs to airplanes. Underneath this lies the half-conscious belief that language is a natural growth and not an instrument which we shape for our own purposes.

Now, it is clear that the decline of a language must ultimately 2 have political and economic causes: It is not due simply to the bad influence of this or that individual writer. But an effect can become a cause, reinforcing the original cause and producing the same effect in an intensified form, and so on indefinitely. A man may take a drink because he feels himself to be a failure, and then fail all the more completely because he drinks. It is rather the same thing that is happening to the English language. It becomes ugly and inaccurate because our thoughts are foolish, but the slovenliness of our language makes it easier for us to have foolish thoughts. The point is that the process is reversible. Modern English, especially written English, is full of bad habits which spread by imitation and which can be avoided if one is willing to take the necessary trouble. If one gets rid of these habits one can think more clearly, and to think clearly is a necessary first step toward political regeneration: so that the fight against bad English is not frivolous and is not the exclusive concern of professional writers. I will come back to this presently, and I hope that by that time the meaning of what I have said here will have become clearer. Meanwhile, here are five specimens of the English language as it is now habitually written.

These five passages have not been picked out because they are 3 especially bad — I could have quoted far worse if I had chosen — but because they illustrate various of the mental vices from which we now suffer. They are a little below the average, but are fairly representative samples. I number them so that I can refer back to them when necessary:

> (1) I am not, indeed, sure whether it is not true to say that the Milton who once seemed not unlike a seventeenth-century Shelley had not become, out of an experience ever more bitter in each year, more alien [sic] to the founder of that Jesuit sect which nothing could induce him to tolerate.
> Professor Harold Laski (Essay in *Freedom of Expression*).

> (2) Above all, we cannot play ducks and drakes with a native battery of idioms which prescribes such egregious collocations of

vocables as the Basic *put up with* for *tolerate* or *put at a loss* for
bewilder.   Professor Lancelot Hogben (*Interglossa*).

(3) On the one side we have the free personality: By definition
it is not neurotic, for it has neither conflict nor dream. Its desires,
such as they are, are transparent, for they are just what institutional
approval keeps in the forefront of consciousness; another institutional pattern would alter their number and intensity; there is little
in them that is natural, irreducible, or culturally dangerous. But *on
the other side*, the social bond itself is nothing but the mutual
reflection of these self-secure integrities. Recall the definition of
love. Is not this the very picture of a small academic? Where is
there a place in this hall of mirrors for either personality or
fraternity?   Essay on psychology in *Politics* (New York).

(4) All the "best people" from the gentlemen's clubs, and all
the frantic fascist captains, united in common hatred of Socialism
and bestial horror of the rising tide of the mass revolutionary movement, have turned to acts of provocation, to foul incendiarism, to
medieval legends of poisoned wells, to legalize their own destruction
of proletarian organizations, and rouse the agitated petty-bourgeoisie
to chauvinistic fervor on behalf of the fight against the revolutionary
way out of the crisis.   Communist pamphlet.

(5) If a new spirit *is* to be infused into this old country, there
is one thorny and contentious reform which must be tackled, and
that is the humanization and galvanization of the B.B.C. Timidity
here will bespeak cancer and atrophy of the soul. The heart of
Britain may be sound and of strong beat, for instance, but the
British lion's roar at present is like that of Bottom in Shakespeare's
Midsummer Night's Dream — as gentle as any sucking dove. A virile
new Britain cannot continue indefinitely to be traduced in the eyes
or rather ears, of the world by the effete languors of Langham Place,
brazenly masquerading as "standard English." When the Voice of
Britain is heard at nine o'clock, better far and infinitely less ludicrous to hear aitches honestly dropped than the present priggish,
inflated, inhibited, school-ma'amish arch braying of blameless bash-
ful mewing maidens!   Letter in *Tribune*.

Each of these passages has faults of its own, but, quite apart from   4
avoidable ugliness, two qualities are common to all of them. The first
is staleness of imagery: The other is lack of precision. The writer
either has a meaning and cannot express it, or he inadvertently says
something else, or he is almost indifferent as to whether his words
mean anything or not. The mixture of vagueness and sheer incom-

petence is the most marked characteristic of modern English prose, and especially of any kind of political writing. As soon as certain topics are raised, the concrete melts into the abstract and no one seems to think of turns of speech that are not hackneyed: Prose consists less and less of *words* chosen for the sake of their meaning, and more and more of *phrases* tacked together like the sections of a prefabricated hen-house. I list below, with notes and examples, various of the tricks by means of which the work of prose-construction is habitually dodged:

Dying Metaphors. A newly invented metaphor assists thought by   5
evoking a visual image, while on the other hand a metaphor which is technically "dead" (e.g., *iron resolution*) has in effect reverted to being an ordinary word and can generally be used without loss of vividness. But in between these two classes there is a huge dump of worn-out metaphors which have lost all evocative power and are merely used because they save people the trouble of inventing phrases for themselves. Examples are: *Ring the changes on, take up the cudgels for, toe the line, ride roughshod over, stand shoulder to shoulder with, play into the hands of, no axe to grind, grist to the mill, fishing in troubled waters, rift within the lute, on the order of the day, Achilles' heel, swan song, hotbed.* Many of these are used without knowledge of their meaning (what is a "rift," for instance?), and incompatible metaphors are frequently mixed, a sure sign that the writer is not interested in what he is saying. Some metaphors now current have been twisted out of their original meaning without those who use them even being aware of the fact. For example, *toe the line* is sometimes written *tow the line.* Another example is *the hammer and the anvil,* now always used with the implication that the anvil gets the worst of it. In real life it is always the anvil that breaks the hammer, never the other way about: A writer who stopped to think what he was saying would be aware of this, and would avoid perverting the original phrase.

Operators or Verbal False Limbs. These save the trouble of picking   6
out appropriate verbs and nouns, and at the same time pad each sentence with extra syllables which give it an appearance of symmetry. Characteristic phrases are: *render inoperative, militate against, make contact with, be subjected to, give rise to, give grounds for, have the effect of, play a leading part (role) in, make itself felt, take effect, exhibit a tendency to, serve the purpose of,* etc., etc. The keynote is the elimination of simple verbs. Instead of being a single word, such as *break, stop, spoil, mend, kill,* a verb becomes a *phrase,* made up of a noun or

adjective tacked on to some general-purpose verb such as *prove, serve, form, play, render*. In addition, the passive voice is wherever possible used in preference to the active, and noun constructions are used instead of gerunds (*by examination of* instead of *by examining*). The range of verbs is further cut down by means of the *-ize* and *de-* formation, and the banal statements are given an appearance of profundity by means of the *not un-* formation. Simple conjunctions and prepositions are replaced by such phrases as *with respect to, having regard to, the fact that, by dint of, in view of, in the interests of, on the hypothesis that;* and the ends of sentences are saved from anticlimax by such resounding commonplaces as *greatly to be desired, cannot be left out of account, a development to be expected in the near future, deserving of serious consideration, brought to a satisfactory conclusion,* and so on and so forth.

Pretentious Diction. Words like *phenomenon, element, individual* (as 7 noun), *objective, categorical, effective, virtual, basic, primary, promote, constitute, exhibit, exploit, utilize, eliminate, liquidate,* are used to dress up simple statements and give an air of scientific impartiality to biased judgments. Adjectives like *epoch-making, epic, historic, unforgettable, triumphant, age-old, inevitable, inexorable, veritable,* are used to dignify the sordid processes of international politics, while writing that aims at glorifying war usually takes on an archaic color, its characteristic words being: *realm, throne, chariot, mailed fist, trident, sword, shield, buckler, banner, jackboot, clarion.* Foreign words and expressions such as *cul de sac, ancien régime, deus ex machina, mutatis mutandis, status quo, gleichschaltung, weltanschauung,* are used to give an air of culture and elegance. Except for the useful abbreviations *i.e., e.g.,* and *etc.,* there is no real need for any of the hundreds of foreign phrases now current in English. Bad writers, and especially scientific, political, and sociological writers, are nearly always haunted by the notion that Latin or Greek words are grander than Saxon ones, and unnecessary words like *expedite, ameliorate, predict, extraneous, deracinated, clandestine, subaqueous* and hundreds of others constantly gain ground from their Anglo-Saxon opposite numbers.[1] The jargon peculiar to Marxist writing (*hyena, hangman, cannibal, petty bourgeois, these gentry, lackey,*

---

[1]An interesting illustration of this is the way in which the English flower names which were in use till very recently are being ousted by Greek ones, *snapdragon* becoming *antirrhinum, forget-me-not* becoming *myosotis,* etc. It is hard to see any practical reason for this change of fashion: It is probably due to an instinctive turning-away from the more homely word and a vague feeling that the Greek word is scientific.

flunkey, mad dog, White Guard, etc.) consists largely of words and phrases translated from Russian, German, or French; but the normal way of coining a new word is to use a Latin or Greek root with the appropriate affix and, where necessary, the *-ize* formation. It is often easier to make up words of this kind (*deregionalize, impermissible, extramarital, nonfragmentatory,* and so forth) than to think up the English words that will cover one's meaning. The result, in general, is an increase in slovenliness and vagueness.

Meaningless Words. In certain kinds of writing, particularly in art 8 criticism and literary criticism, it is normal to come across long passages which are almost completely lacking in meaning.[2] Words like *romantic, plastic, values, human, dead, sentimental, natural, vitality,* as used in art criticism, are strictly meaningless in the sense that they not only do not point to any discoverable object, but are hardly ever expected to do so by the reader. When one critic writes, "The outstanding feature of Mr. X's work is its living quality," while another writes, "The immediately striking thing about Mr. X's work is its peculiar deadness," the reader accepts this as a simple difference of opinion. If words like *black* and *white* were involved, instead of the jargon words *dead* and *living,* he would see at once that language was being used in an improper way. Many political words are similarly abused. The word *fascism* has now no meaning except in so far as it signifies "something not desirable." The words *democracy, socialism, freedom, patriotic, realistic, justice,* have each of them several different meanings which cannot be reconciled with one another. In the case of a word like *democracy,* not only is there no agreed definition, but the attempt to make one is resisted from all sides. It is almost universally felt that when we call a country democratic we are praising it: Consequently the defenders of every kind of regime claim that it is a democracy, and fear that they might have to stop using the word if it were tied down to any one meaning. Words of this kind are often used in a consciously dishonest way. That is, the person who uses them has his own private definition, but allows his hearer to think he means something quite different. Statements like *Marshal Pétain was a true patriot, The Soviet Press is the freest in the world, The Catholic*

---

[2]Example: "Comfort's catholicity of perception and image, strangely Whitman-esque in range, almost the exact opposite in aesthetic compulsion, continues to evoke that trembling atmospheric accumulative hinting at a cruel, an inexorably serene timelessness. . . . Wrey Gardiner scores by aiming at simple bull's-eyes with precision. Only they are not so simple, and through this contented sadness runs more than the surface bitter-sweet of resignation." (*Poetry Quarterly.*)

Church is opposed to persecution, are almost always made with intent to deceive. Other words used in variable meanings, in most cases more or less dishonestly, are: *class, totalitarian, science, progressive, reactionary, bourgeois, equality.*

Now that I have made this catalog of swindles and perversions, 9 let me give another example of the kind of writing that they lead to. This time it must of its nature be an imaginary one. I am going to translate a passage of good English into modern English of the worst sort. Here is a well-known verse from *Ecclesiastes*:

> I returned and saw under the sun, that the race is not to the swift, nor the battle to the strong, neither yet bread to the wise, nor yet riches to men of understanding, nor yet favor to men of skill; but time and chance happeneth to them all.

Here it is in modern English:

> Objective consideration of contemporary phenomena compels the conclusion that success or failure in competitive activities exhibits no tendency to be commensurate with innate capacity, but that a considerable element of the unpredictable must invariably be taken into account.

This is a parody, but not a very gross one. Exhibit (3), above, 10 for instance, contains several patches of the same kind of English. It will be seen that I have not made a full translation. The beginning and ending of the sentence follow the original meaning fairly closely, but in the middle the concrete illustrations — race, battle, bread — dissolve into the vague phrase "success or failure in competitive activities." This had to be so, because no modern writer of the kind I am discussing — no one capable of using phrases like "objective consideration of contemporary phenomena" — would ever tabulate his thoughts in that precise and detailed way. The whole tendency of modern prose is away from concreteness. Now analyze these two sentences a little more closely. The first contains forty-nine words but only sixty syllables, and all its words are those of everyday life. The second contains thirty-eight words of ninety syllables: eighteen of its words are from Latin roots, and one from Greek. The first sentence contains six vivid images, and only one phrase ("time and chance") that could be called vague. The second contains not a single fresh, arresting phrase, and in spite of its ninety syllables it gives only a shortened version of the meaning contained in the first. Yet without a doubt it is the second kind of sentence that is gaining ground in modern English. I do not want to exaggerate. This kind of writing is not yet universal, and outcrops of simplicity will occur here and there in the worst-written page. Still, if you or I were told to write a few lines on the uncertainty of human fortunes, we should probably come much nearer to my imaginary sentence than to the one from *Ecclesiastes.*

As I have tried to show, modern writing at its worst does not 11 consist in picking out words for the sake of their meaning and inventing images in order to make the meaning clearer. It consists in gumming together long strips of words which have already been set in order by someone else, and making the results presentable by sheer humbug. The attraction of this way of writing is that it is easy. It is easier — even quicker once you have the habit — to say *In my opinion it is a not unjustifiable assumption that* than to say *I think.* If you use ready-made phrases, you not only don't have to hunt about for words; you also don't have to bother with the rhythms of your sentences, since these phrases are generally so arranged as to be more or less euphonious. When you are composing in a hurry — when you are dictating to a stenographer, for instance, or making a public speech — it is natural to fall into a pretentious, Latinized style. Tags like *a consideration which we should do well to bear in mind* or *a conclusion to which all of us would readily assent* will save many a sentence from coming down with a bump. By using stale metaphors, similes, and idioms, you save much mental effort, at the cost of leaving your meaning vague, not only for your reader but for yourself. This is the significance of mixed metaphors. The sole aim of a metaphor is to call up a visual image. When these images clash — as in *The Fascist octopus has sung its swan song, the jackboot is thrown into the melting pot* — it can be taken as certain that the writer is not seeing a mental image of the objects he is naming; in other words he is not really thinking. Look again at the examples I gave at the beginning of this essay. Professor Laski (1) uses five negatives in fifty-three words. One of these is superfluous, making nonsense of the whole passage, and in addition there is the slip *alien* for akin, making further nonsense, and several avoidable pieces of clumsiness which increase the general vagueness. Professor Hogben (2) plays ducks and drakes with a battery which is able to write prescriptions, and, while disapproving of the everyday phrase *put up with,* is unwilling to look *egregious* up in the dictionary and see what it means. (3), if one takes an uncharitable attitude toward it, is simply meaningless: Probably one could work out its intended meaning by reading the whole of the article in which it occurs. In (4), the writer knows more or less what he wants to say, but an accumulation of stale phrases chokes him like tea leaves blocking a sink. In (5), words and meaning have almost parted company. People who write in this manner usually have a general emotional meaning — they dislike one thing and want to express solidarity with another — but they are not interested in the detail of what they are saying. A scrupulous writer, in every sentence that he writes, will ask himself at least four questions, thus: What am I trying to say? What words will express it? What image or idiom will make it clearer? Is this image fresh enough to have an effect? And he will probably ask himself two more: Could I put it more shortly? Have I said anything that is avoidably ugly? But you are not obliged to go to all this trouble. You can shirk it by simply throwing your mind open and letting the ready-made phrases come crowding in. They will construct your sentences for you — even think your thoughts for you, to a certain extent — and at need they will perform the important service of partially concealing your meaning even from yourself. It is at this point that the special connection between politics and the debasement of language becomes clear.

In our time it is broadly true that political writing is bad writing. 12 Where it is not true, it will generally be found that the writer is some kind of rebel, expressing his private opinions and not a "party line." Orthodoxy, of whatever color, seems to demand a lifeless, imitative style. The political dialects to be found in pamphlets, leading articles, manifestos, White Papers, and the speeches of under-secretaries do, of course, vary from party to party, but they are all alike in that one almost never finds in them a fresh, vivid, homemade turn of speech. When one watches some tired hack on the platform mechanically repeating the familiar phrases — *bestial atrocities, iron heel, bloodstained tyranny, free peoples of the world, stand shoulder to shoulder* — one often has a curious feeling that one is not watching a live human being but some kind of dummy; a feeling which suddenly becomes stronger at moments when the light catches the speaker's spectacles and turns them into blank discs which seem to have no eyes behind them. And this is not altogether fanciful. A speaker who uses that kind of phraseology has gone some distance toward turning himself into a machine. The appropriate noises are coming out of his larynx, but his brain is not involved as it would be if he were choosing his words for himself. If the speech he is making is one that he is accustomed to make over and over again, he may be almost unconscious of what he is saying, as one is when one utters the responses in church. And this reduced state of consciousness, if not indispensable, is at any rate favorably to political conformity.

In our time, political speech and writing are largely the defense 13 of the indefensible. Things like the continuance of British rule in

India, the Russian purges and deportations, the dropping of the atom bombs on Japan, can indeed be defended, but only by arguments which are too brutal for most people to face, and which do not square with the professed aims of political parties. Thus political language has to consist largely of euphemism, question-begging and sheer cloudy vagueness. Defenseless villages are bombarded from the air, the inhabitants driven out into the countryside, the cattle machine-gunned, the huts set on fire with incendiary bullets: This is called *pacification*. Millions of peasants are robbed of their farms and sent trudging along the roads with no more than they can carry: This is called *transfer of population* or *rectification of frontiers*. People are imprisoned for years without trial, or shot in the back of the neck or sent to die of scurvy in Arctic lumber camps: This is called *elimination of unreliable elements*. Such phraseology is needed if one wants to name things without calling up mental pictures of them. Consider for instance some comfortable English professor defending Russian totalitarianism. He cannot say outright, "I believe in killing off your opponents when you can get good results by doing so." Probably, therefore, he will say something like this:

"While freely conceding that the Soviet régime exhibits certain   14
features which the humanitarian may be inclined to deplore, we must, I think, agree that a certain curtailment of the right to political opposition is an unavoidable concomitant of transitional periods, and that the rigors which the Russian people have been called upon to undergo have been amply justified in the sphere of concrete achievement."

The inflated style is itself a kind of euphemism. A mass of Latin   15
words fall upon the facts like soft snow, blurring the outlines and covering up all the details. The great enemy of clear language is insincerity. When there is a gap between one's real and one's declared aims, one turns as it were instinctively to long words and exhausted idioms, like a cuttlefish squirting out ink. In our age there is no such thing as "keeping out of politics." All issues are political issues, and politics itself is a mass of lies, evasions, folly, hatred, and schizophrenia. When the general atmosphere is bad, language must suffer. I should expect to find — this is a guess which I have not sufficient knowledge to verify — that the German, Russian, and Italian languages have all deteriorated in the last ten or fifteen years, as a result of dictatorship.

But if thought corrupts language, language can also corrupt   16
thought. A bad usage can spread by tradition and imitation, even among people who should and do know better. The debased language that I have been discussing is in some ways very convenient. Phrases

like *a not unjustifiable assumption, leaves much to be desired, would serve no good purpose, a consideration which we should do well to bear in mind,* are a continuous temptation, a packet of aspirins always at one's elbow. Look back through this essay, and for certain you will find that I have again and again committed the very faults I am protesting against. By this morning's post I have received a pamphlet dealing with conditions in Germany. The author tells me that he "felt impelled" to write it. I open it at random, and here is almost the first sentence that I see: "(The Allies) have an opportunity not only of achieving a radical transformation of Germany's social and political structure in such a way as to avoid a nationalistic reaction in Germany itself, but at the same time of laying the foundations of a co-operative and unified Europe." You see, he "feels impelled" to write — feels, presumably, that he has something new to say — and yet his words, like cavalry horses answering the bugle, group themselves automatically into the familiar dreary pattern. This invasion of one's mind by ready-made phrases (*lay the foundations, achieve a radical transformation*) can only be prevented if one is constantly on guard against them, and every such phrase anesthetizes a portion of one's brain.

I said earlier that the decadence of our language is probably 17 curable. Those who deny this would argue, if they produced an argument at all, that language merely reflects existing social conditions, and that we cannot influence its development by any direct tinkering with words and constructions. So far as the general tone or spirit of a language goes, this may be true, but it is not true in detail. Silly words and expressions have often disappeared, not through any evolutionary process but owing to the conscious action of a minority. Two recent examples were *explore every avenue* and *leave no stone unturned,* which were killed by the jeers of a few journalists. There is a long list of flyblown metaphors which could similarly be got rid of if enough people would interest themselves in the job; and it should also be possible to laugh the *not un-* formation out of existence,[3] to reduce the amount of Latin and Greek in the average sentence, to drive out foreign phrases and strayed scientific words, and, in general, to make pretentiousness unfashionable. But all these are minor points. The defense of the English language implies more than this, and perhaps it is best to start by saying what it does *not* imply.

To begin with it has nothing to do with archaism, with the 18

[3]One can cure oneself of the *not un-* formation by memorizing this sentence: *A not unblack dog was chasing a not unsmall rabbit across a not ungreen field.*

salvaging of obsolete words and turns of speech, or with the setting up of a "standard English" which must never be departed from. On the contrary, it is especially concerned with the scrapping of every word or idiom which has outworn its usefulness. It has nothing to do with correct grammar and syntax, which are of no importance so long as one makes one's meaning clear, or with the avoidance of Americanisms, or with having what is called a "good prose style." On the other hand it is not concerned with fake simplicity and the attempt to make written English colloquial. Nor does it even imply in every case preferring the Saxon word to the Latin one, though it does imply using the fewest and shortest words that will cover one's meaning. What is above all needed is to let the meaning choose the word, and not the other way about. In prose, the worst thing one can do with words is to surrender to them. When you think of a concrete object, you think wordlessly, and then, if you want to describe the thing you have been visualizing you probably hunt about till you find the exact words that seem to fit. When you think of something abstract you are more inclined to use words from the start, and unless you make a conscious effort to prevent it, the existing dialect will come rushing in and do the job for you, at the expense of blurring or even changing your meaning. Probably it is better to put off using words as long as possible and get one's meaning as clear as one can through pictures or sensations. Afterwards one can choose — not simply *accept* — the phrases that will best cover the meaning, and then switch round and decide what impression one's words are likely to make on another person. This last effort of the mind cuts out all stale or mixed images, all prefabricated phrases, needless repetitions, and humbug and vagueness generally. But one can often be in doubt about the effect of a word or phrase, and one needs rules that one can rely on when instinct fails. I think the following rules will cover most cases:

(i) Never use a metaphor, simile, or other figure of speech which you are used to seeing in print.
(ii) Never use a long word where a short one will do.
(iii) If it is possible to cut a word out, always cut it out.
(iv) Never use the passive where you can use the active.
(v) Never use a foreign phrase, a scientific word or a jargon word if you can think of an everyday English equivalent.
(vi) Break any of these rules sooner than say anything outright barbarous.

These rules sound elementary, and so they are, but they demand a deep change in attitude in anyone who has grown used to writing in the style now fashionable. One could keep all of them and still write bad English, but one could not write the kind of stuff that I quoted in those five specimens at the beginning of this article.

I have not here been considering the literary use of language, but   19 merely language as an instrument for expressing and not for concealing or preventing thought. Stuart Chase and others have come near to claiming that all abstract words are meaningless, and have used this as a pretext for advocating a kind of political quietism. Since you don't know what Fascism is, how can you struggle against Fascism? One need not swallow such absurdities as this, but one ought to recognize that the present political chaos is connected with the decay of language, and that one can probably bring about some improvement by starting at the verbal end. If you simplify your English, you are freed from the worst follies of orthodoxy. You cannot speak any of the necessary dialects, and when you make a stupid remark its stupidity will be obvious, even to yourself. Political language — and with variations this is true of all political parties, from Conservatives to Anarchists — is designed to make lies sound truthful and murder respectable, and to give an appearance of solidity to pure wind. One cannot change this all in a moment, but one can at least change one's own habits, and from time to time one can even, if one jeers loudly enough, send some worn-out and useless phrase — some *jackboot, Achilles' heel, hotbed, melting pot, acid test, veritable inferno,* or other lump of verbal refuse — into the dustbin where it belongs.

QUESTIONS ON MEANING

1. Orwell states his THESIS early in his essay. What is it?
2. What two common faults does Orwell find in all five of his horrible examples (para. 3)?
3. What questions does Orwell provide for scrupulous writers to ask themselves?
4. How does Orwell support his contention that there is a direct relationship between bad writing and political injustice? Why, in his view, is vague and misleading language necessary to describe acts of oppression?
5. What, according to Orwell, can *you* do to combat the decay of the English language?

QUESTIONS ON WRITING STRATEGY

1. Identify Orwell's AUDIENCE.
2. Taking his own advice, Orwell seeks fresh phrases and colorful, concrete FIGURES OF SPEECH. Point to some of these.
3. Examine the organization of this essay. (Following the order of the essay, list the topics covered.) Is the structure clear to you? Why or why not?
4. MIXED METHODS. Orwell makes his case with many, many EXAMPLES of bad prose, some of which he ANALYZES to show just what is wrong (see especially paras. 3–4, 9–11). Some of Orwell's examples are dated, such as a few dying metaphors (5) that have mercifully disappeared or the British rule of India (13), which ended in 1947. Does the age of the essay weaken it? Can you think of examples (and corresponding analysis) to replace any of Orwell's that are dated?
5. MIXED METHODS. Orwell musters not only example and analysis but also every other method to develop his ARGUMENT. Locate uses of CLASSIFICATION and PROCESS ANALYSIS. What do these contribute to the essay?

QUESTIONS ON LANGUAGE

1. In plainer words than Lancelot Hogben's, what are "egregious collocations of vocables" (in Orwell's second example in para. 3)?
2. Mixed METAPHORS, such as "the fascist octopus has sung its swan song" (para. 11), can be unintentionally funny. Recall or invent some more examples. What, according to Orwell, is the cause of such verbal snafus?
3. Does Orwell agree that "all abstract words are meaningless" (para. 20)?
4. Define decadent, archaism (para. 1); slovenliness, regeneration, frivolous (2); inadvertently, hackneyed, prefabricated (4); evocative (5); symmetry, banal, profundity (6); sordid (7); reconciled (8); parody, tabulate (10); euphonious, superfluous, scrupulous, debasement (11); orthodoxy, phraseology (12); purges, euphemism, totalitarianism (13); curtailment, concomitant (14); impelled (16); colloquial, barbarous (18); quietism (19).

SUGGESTIONS FOR WRITING

1. From browsing in current newspapers and magazines, find a few passages of writing as bad as the ones George Orwell quotes and condemns in "Politics and the English Language." ANALYZE what you find wrong with them.
2. Like Orwell, who in "Politics and the English Language" deliberately worsens a verse from Ecclesiastes (para. 9), take a passage of excellent prose and try rewriting it in words as abstract and colorless as possible.

For passages to work on, try paragraph 14 from Bruce Catton's "Grant and Lee" (p. 183), paragraph 12 from Martin Luther King's "I Have a Dream" (p. 518), or any other passage you admire. If you choose an unfamiliar passage, supply a copy of it along with your finished paper. What does your experiment demonstrate?

3. **CRITICAL WRITING.** Does Orwell do as Orwell says? Apply his *do*'s and *don't*'s to his own writing, choosing one or two paragraphs to analyze. Use quotations from the essay to explain and support your analysis.

4. **CONNECTIONS.** Orwell points out that much political speech and writing is deliberately vague because blunt, truthful words would reveal arguments "too brutal for most people to face" (para. 13). Stephanie Ericsson, in "The Ways We Lie" (p. 623), proposes that some lying seems justified to protect ourselves from exposure or to avoid offending people or hurting their feelings. Is this the kind of lying Orwell means? Write an essay discussing the harm or harmlessness of political evasions, using EXAMPLES from Orwell, if you like, and from recent news. (It may help to work with some classmates to generate examples that you can all use.)

GEORGE ORWELL ON WRITING

Orwell explains the motives for his own writing in the essay "Why I Write" (1946):

"What I have most wanted to do throughout the past ten years is to make political writing into an art. My starting point is always a feeling of partisanship, a sense of injustice. When I sit down to write a book, I do not say to myself, 'I am going to produce a work of art.' I write it because there is some lie that I want to expose, some fact to which I want to draw attention, and my initial concern is to get a hearing. But I could not do the work of writing a book, or even a long magazine article, if it were not also an esthetic experience. Anyone who cares to examine my work will see that even when it is downright propaganda it contains much that a full-time politician would consider irrelevant. I am not able, and I do not want, completely to abandon the worldview that I acquired in childhood. So long as I remain alive and well I shall continue to feel strongly about prose style, to love the surface of the earth, and to take a pleasure in solid objects and scraps of useless information. It is no use trying to suppress that side of myself. The job is to reconcile my ingrained likes and dislikes with the essentially public, nonindividual activities that this age forces on all of us.

"It is not easy. It raises problems of construction and of language, and it raises in a new way the problem of truthfulness. Let me give just one example of the cruder kind of difficulty that arises. My book about the Spanish civil war, *Homage to Catalonia,* is, of course, a frankly political book, but in the main it is written with a certain detachment and regard for form. I did try very hard in it to tell the whole truth without violating my literary instincts. But among other things it contains a long chapter, full of newspaper quotations and the like, defending the Trotskyists who were accused of plotting with Franco. Clearly such a chapter, which after a year or two would lose its interest for any ordinary reader, must ruin the book. A critic whom I respect read me a lecture about it. 'Why did you put in all that stuff?' he said. 'You've turned what might have been a good book into journalism.' What he said was true, but I could not have done otherwise. I happened to know, what very few people in England had been allowed to know, that innocent men were being falsely accused. If I had not been angry about that I should never have written the book.

"In one form or another this problem comes up again. The problem of language is subtler and would take too long to discuss. I will only say that of late years I have tried to write less picturesquely and more exactly. In any case I find that by the time you have perfected any style of writing, you have always outgrown it. *Animal Farm* was the first book in which I tried, with full consciousness of what I was doing, a fuse political purpose and artistic purpose into the whole. . . .

"Looking back through the last page or two, I see that I have made it appear as though my motives in writing were wholly public-spirited. I don't want to leave that as the final impression. All writers are vain, selfish, and lazy, and at the very bottom of their motives there lies a mystery. Writing a book is a horrible, exhausting struggle, like a long bout of some painful illness. One would never undertake such a thing if one were not driven on by some demon whom one can neither resist nor understand. For all one knows that demon is simply the same instinct that makes a baby squall for attention. And yet it is also true that one can write nothing readable unless one constantly struggles to efface one's own personality. Good prose is like a windowpane. I cannot say with certainty which of my motives are the strongest, but I know which of them deserve to be followed. And looking back through my work, I see that it is invariably where I lacked a *political* purpose that I wrote lifeless books and was betrayed into purple passages, sentences without meaning, decorative adjectives, and humbug generally."

FOR DISCUSSION

1. What does Orwell mean by his "political purpose" in writing? By his "artistic purpose"? How did he sometimes find it hard to fulfill both purposes?

2. Think about Orwell's remark that "one can write nothing readable unless one constantly struggles to efface one's own personality." From your own experience, have you found any truth in this observation, or any reason to think otherwise?

STEPHANIE ERICSSON

Stephanie Ericsson is an insightful and frank writer who composes out of her own life. Her book on loss, *Companion Through the Darkness: Inner Dialogues on Grief* (1993), grew out of journal entries and extensive research into the grieving process following the sudden death of her husband while she was pregnant. Ericsson was born in 1953, grew up in San Francisco, and began writing at the age of fifteen. After studying filmmaking in college, she became a screenwriter's assistant and later a writer of situation comedies and advertising. During these years she struggled with substance abuse; after her recovery in 1980 she published *Shamefaced* and *Women of AA: Recovering Together* (both 1985). *Companion into the Dawn: Inner Dialogues on Loving* (1994) is Ericsson's latest book. She lives in Minneapolis with her partner and two children.

The Ways We Lie

Ericsson wrote this essay from notes for *Companion into the Dawn*, and it was published in the *Utne Reader* for November/December 1992. We all lie, Ericsson finds; indeed, lying may be unavoidable and even sometimes beneficial. But then how do we know when to stop?

This essay is most notably a CLASSIFICATION of lies: Ericsson identifies ten all-too-common types. Within this classification scheme, however, Ericsson draws on several other methods of development, DEFINING each class, giving EXAMPLES of it, and COMPARING its pros and cons. And the classification itself serves a larger goal of analyzing the CAUSES AND EFFECTS of lying.

The bank called today and I told them my deposit was in the mail, even though I hadn't written a check yet. It'd been a rough day. The baby I'm pregnant with decided to do aerobics on my lungs for two hours, our three-year-old daughter painted the living-room couch with lipstick, the IRS put me on hold for an hour, and I was late to a business meeting because I was tired. 1

I told my client that traffic had been bad. When my partner came home, his haggard face told me his day hadn't gone any better than mine, so when he asked, "How was your day?" I said, "Oh, fine," knowing that one more straw might break his back. A friend called and wanted to take me to lunch. I said I was busy. Four lies in the course of a day, none of which I felt the least bit guilty about. 2

We lie. We all do. We exaggerate, we minimize, we avoid con-   3
frontation, we spare people's feelings, we conveniently forget, we
keep secrets, we justify lying to the big-guy institutions. Like most
people, I indulge in small falsehoods and still think of myself as an
honest person. Sure I lie, but it doesn't hurt anything. Or does it?

I once tried going a whole week without telling a lie, and it was   4
paralyzing. I discovered that telling the truth all the time is nearly
impossible. It means living with some serious consequences: The bank
charges me $60 in overdraft fees, my partner keels over when I tell
him about my travails, my client fires me for telling her I didn't feel
like being on time, and my friend takes it personally when I say I'm
not hungry. There must be some merit to lying.

But if I justify lying, what makes me any different from slick   5
politicians or the corporate robbers who raided the S&L industry?
Saying it's okay to lie one way and not another is hedging. I cannot
seem to escape the voice deep inside me that tells me: When someone
lies, someone loses.

What far-reaching consequences will I, or others, pay as a result   6
of my lie? Will someone's trust be destroyed? Will someone else pay
my penance because I ducked out? We must consider the *meaning of
our actions.* Deception, lies, capital crimes, and misdemeanors all
carry meanings. *Webster's* definition of *lie* is specific:

> 1: a false statement or action especially made with the intent to
> deceive; 2: anything that gives or is meant to give a false impression.

A definition like this implies that there are many, many ways to   7
tell a lie. Here are just a few.

The White Lie

*A man who won't lie to a woman has very little consideration for her
feelings.*

— Bergen Evans

The white lie assumes that the truth will cause more damage than   8
a simple, harmless untruth. Telling a friend he looks great when he
looks like hell can be based on a decision that the friend needs a
compliment more than a frank opinion. But, in effect, it is the liar
deciding what is best for the lied to. Ultimately, it is a vote of no
confidence. It is an act of subtle arrogance for anyone to decide what
is best for someone else.

Yet not all circumstances are quite so cut-and-dried. Take, for   9
instance, the sergeant in Vietnam who knew one of his men was

killed in action but listed him as missing so that the man's family would receive indefinite compensation instead of the lump-sum pittance the military gives widows and children. His intent was honorable. Yet for twenty years this family kept their hopes alive, unable to move on to a new life.

Façades

Et tu, Brute?
— Caesar

We all put up façades to one degree or another. When I put on   10
a suit to go to see a client, I feel as though I am putting on another face, obeying the expectation that serious businesspeople wear suits rather than sweatpants. But I'm a writer. Normally, I get up, get the kid off to school, and sit at my computer in my pajamas until four in the afternoon. When I answer the phone, the caller thinks I'm wearing a suit (though the UPS man knows better).

But façades can be destructive because they are used to seduce   11
others into an illusion. For instance, I recently realized that a former friend was a liar. He presented himself with all the right looks and the right words and offered lots of new consciousness theories, fabulous books to read, and fascinating insights. Then I did some business with him, and the time came for him to pay me. He turned out to be all talk and no walk. I heard a plethora of reasonable excuses, including in-depth descriptions of the big break around the corner. In six months of work, I saw less than a hundred bucks. When I confronted him, he raised both eyebrows and tried to convince me that I'd heard him wrong, that he'd made no commitment to me. A simple investigation into his past revealed a crowded graveyard of disenchanted former friends.

Ignoring the Plain Facts

Well, you must understand that Father Porter is only human
— A Massachusetts priest

In the '60s, the Catholic Church in Massachusetts began hearing   12
complaints that Father James Porter was sexually molesting children. Rather than relieving him of his duties, the ecclesiastical authorities simply moved him from one parish to another between 1960 and 1967, actually providing him with a fresh supply of unsuspecting families and innocent children to abuse. After treatment in 1967 for

pedophilia, he went back to work, this time in Minnesota. The new diocese was aware of Father Porter's obsession with children, but they needed priests and recklessly believed treatment had cured him. More children were abused until he was relieved of his duties a year later. By his own admission, Porter may have abused as many as a hundred children.

Ignoring the facts may not in and of itself be a form of lying, but consider the context of this situation. If a lie is *a false action done with the intent to deceive,* then the Catholic Church's conscious covering for Porter created irreparable consequences. The church became a co-perpetrator with Porter. 13

Deflecting

When you have no basis for an argument, abuse the plaintiff.
— Cicero

I've discovered that I can keep anyone from seeing the true me by being selectively blatant. I set a precedent of being up-front about intimate issues, but I never bring up the things I truly want to hide; I just let people assume I'm revealing everything. It's an effective way of hiding. 14

Any good liar knows that the way to perpetuate an untruth is to deflect attention from it. When Clarence Thomas exploded with accusations that the Senate hearings were a "high-tech lynching," he simply switched the focus from a highly charged subject to a radioactive subject.[1] Rather than defending himself, he took the offensive and accused the country of racism. It was a brilliant maneuver. Racism is now politically incorrect in official circles — unlike sexual harassment, which still rewards those who can get away with it. 15

Some of the most skillful deflectors are passive-aggressive people who, when accused of inappropriate behavior, refuse to respond to the accusations. This you-don't-exist stance infuriates the accuser, who, understandably, screams something obscene out of frustration. The trap is sprung and the act of deflection successful, because now the passive-aggressive person can indignantly say, "Who can talk to someone as unreasonable as you?" The real issue is forgotten and the sins of the original victim become the focus. Feeling guilty of name-calling, the victim is fully tamed and crawls into a hole, ashamed. I have watched this fighting technique work thousands of times in 16

[1]Ericsson refers to the 1991 hearings to confirm Thomas for the Supreme Court, at which Thomas was accused by Anita Hill of sexual harassment. — EDS.

disputes between men and women, and what I've learned is that the real culprit is not necessarily the one who swears the loudest.

Omission

The cruelest lies are often told in silence.
— R. L. Stevenson

Omission involves telling most of the truth minus one or two key   17
facts whose absence changes the story completely. You break a pair of glasses that are guaranteed under normal use and get a new pair, without mentioning that the first pair broke during a rowdy game of basketball. Who hasn't tried something like that? But what about omission of information that could make a difference in how a person lives his or her life?

For instance, one day I found out that rabbinical legends tell of   18
another woman in the Garden of Eden before Eve. I was stunned. The omission of the Sumerian goddess Lilith from Genesis — as well as her demonization by ancient misogynists as an embodiment of female evil — felt like spiritual robbery. I felt like I'd just found out my mother was really my stepmother. To take seriously the tradition that Adam was created out of the same mud as his equal counterpart, Lilith, redefines all of Judeo-Christian history.

Some renegade Catholic feminists introduced me to a view of   19
Lilith that had been suppressed during the many centuries when this strong goddess was seen only as a spirit of evil. Lilith was a proud goddess who defied Adam's need to control her, attempted negotiations, and when this failed, said adios and left the Garden of Eden.

This omission of Lilith from the Bible was a patriarchal strategy   20
to keep women weak. Omitting the strong-woman archetype of Lilith from Western religions and starting the story with Eve the Rib has helped keep Christian and Jewish women believing they were the lesser sex for thousands of years.

Stereotypes and Clichés

Where opinion does not exist, the status quo becomes stereotyped and all originality is discouraged.
— Bertrand Russell

Stereotype and cliché serve a purpose as a form of shorthand.   21
Our need for vast amounts of information in nanoseconds has made

the stereotype vital to modern communication. Unfortunately, it often shuts down original thinking, giving those hungry for the truth a candy bar of misinformation instead of a balanced meal. The stereotype explains a situation with just enough truth to seem unquestionable.

All the "isms" — racism, sexism, ageism, et al. — are founded 22 on and fueled by the stereotype and the cliché, which are lies of exaggeration, omission, and ignorance. They are always dangerous. They take a single tree and make it a landscape. They destroy curiosity. They close minds and separate people. The single mother on welfare is assumed to be cheating. Any black male could tell you how much of his identity is obliterated daily by stereotypes. Fat people, ugly people, beautiful people, old people, large-breasted women, short men, the mentally ill, and the homeless all could tell you how much more they are like us than we want to think. I once admitted to a group of people that I had a mouth like a truck driver. Much to my surprise, a man stood up and said, "I'm a truck driver, and I never cuss." Needless to say, I was humbled.

Groupthink

Who is more foolish, the child afraid of the dark, or the man afraid of the light?

— Maurice Freehill

Irving Janis, in *Victims of Group Think,* defines this sort of lie as 23 a psychological phenomenon within decision-making groups in which loyalty to the group has become more important than any other value, with the result that dissent and the appraisal of alternatives are suppressed. If you've ever worked on a committee or in a corporation, you've encountered groupthink. It requires a combination of other forms of lying — ignoring facts, selective memory, omission, and denial, to name a few.

The textbook example of groupthink came on December 7, 1941. 24 From as early as the fall of 1941, the warnings came in, one after another, that Japan was preparing for a massive military operation. The Navy command in Hawaii assumed Pearl Harbor was invulnerable — the Japanese weren't stupid enough to attack the United States' most important base. On the other hand, racist stereotypes said the Japanese weren't smart enough to invent a torpedo effective in less than 60 feet of water (the fleet was docked in 30 feet); after all, U.S. technology hadn't been able to do it.

On Friday, December 5, normal weekend leave was granted to   25
all the commanders at Pearl Harbor, even though the Japanese con-
sulate in Hawaii was busy burning papers. Within the tight, good-
ole-boy cohesiveness of the U.S. command in Hawaii, the myth of
invulnerability stayed well entrenched. No one in the group considered the alternatives. The rest is history.

Out-and-Out Lies

The only form of lying that is beyond reproach is lying for its own sake.
                                                    — Oscar Wilde

Of all the ways to lie, I like this one the best, probably because   26
I get tired of trying to figure out the real meanings behind things. At
least I can trust the bald-faced lie. I once asked my five-year-old
nephew, "Who broke the fence?" (I had seen him do it.) He answered,
"The murderers." Who could argue?

At least when this sort of lie is told it can be easily confronted.   27
As the person who is lied to, I know where I stand. The bald-faced
lie doesn't toy with my perceptions — it argues with them. It doesn't
try to refashion reality, it tries to refute it. *Read my lips . . .* No
sleight of hand. No guessing. If this were the only form of lying,
there would be no such things as floating anxiety or the adult-
children-of-alcoholics movement.

Dismissal

Pay no attention to that man behind the curtain! I am the Great Oz!
                                                    — The Wizard of Oz

Dismissal is perhaps the slipperiest of all lies. Dismissing feelings,   28
perceptions, or even the raw facts of a situation ranks as a kind of lie
that can do as much damage to a person as any other kind of lie.

The roots of many mental disorders can be traced back to the   29
dismissal of reality. Imagine that a person is told from the time she
is a tot that her perceptions are inaccurate. "*Mommy, I'm scared.*"
"No you're not, darling." "*I don't like that man next door, he makes me
feel icky.*" "Johnny, that's a terrible thing to say, of course you like
him. You go over there right now and be nice to him."

I've often mused over the idea that madness is actually a sane   30
reaction to an insane world. Psychologist R. D. Laing supports this
hypothesis in *Sanity, Madness and the Family,* an account of his investigations into the families of schizophrenics. The common thread

that ran through all of the families he studied was a deliberate, staunch dismissal of the patient's perceptions from a very early age. Each of the patients started out with an accurate grasp of reality, which, through meticulous and methodical dismissal, was demolished until the only reality the patient could trust was catatonia.

Dismissal runs the gamut. Mild dismissal can be quite handy for 31 forgiving the foibles of others in our day-to-day lives. Toddlers who have just learned to manipulate their parents' attention sometimes are dismissed out of necessity. Absolute attention from the parents would require so much energy that no one would get to eat dinner. But we must be careful and attentive about how far we take our "necessary" dismissals. Dismissal is a dangerous tool, because it's nothing less than a lie.

Delusion

We lie loudest when we lie to ourselves.
— Eric Hoffer

I could write the book on this one. Delusion, a cousin of dismissal, 32 is the tendency to see excuses as facts. It's a powerful lying tool because it filters out information that contradicts what we want to believe. Alcoholics who believe that the problems in their lives are legitimate reasons for drinking rather than results of the drinking offer the classic example of deluded thinking. Delusion uses the mind's ability to see things in myriad ways to support what it wants to be the truth.

But delusion is also a survival mechanism we all use. If we were 33 to fully contemplate the consequences of our stockpiles of nuclear weapons or global warming, we could hardly function on a day-to-day level. We don't want to incorporate that much reality into our lives because to do so would be paralyzing.

Delusion acts as an adhesive to keep the status quo intact. It 34 shamelessly employs dismissal, omission, and amnesia, among other sorts of lies. Its most cunning defense is that it cannot see itself.

• • •

The liar's punishment . . . is that he cannot believe anyone else.
— George Bernard Shaw

These are only a few of the ways we lie. Or are lied to. As I said 35 earlier, it's not easy to entirely eliminate lies from our lives. No matter how pious we may try to be, we will still embellish, hedge, and omit to lubricate the daily machinery of living. But there is a world of difference between telling functional lies and living a lie. Martin Buber once said, "The lie is the spirit committing treason against itself." Our acceptance of lies becomes a cultural cancer that eventually shrouds and reorders reality until moral garbage becomes as invisible to us as water is to a fish.

How much do we tolerate before we become sick and tired of 36 being sick and tired? When will we stand up and declare our *right* to trust? When do we stop accepting that the real truth is in the fine print? Whose lips do we read this year when we vote for president? When will we stop being so reticent about making judgments? When do we stop turning over our personal power and responsibility to liars?

Maybe if I don't tell the bank the check's in the mail I'll be less 37 tolerant of the lies told me every day. A country song I once heard said it all for me: "You've got to stand for something or you'll fall for anything."

QUESTIONS ON MEANING

1. What is Ericsson's THESIS?
2. Does Ericsson think it's possible to eliminate lies from our lives? What EVIDENCE does she offer?
3. If it were possible to eliminate lies from our lives, why would that be desirable?
4. What is this essay's PURPOSE?

QUESTIONS ON WRITING STRATEGY

1. Ericsson starts out by recounting her own four-lie day (paras. 1–2). What is the EFFECT of this INTRODUCTION?
2. At the beginning of each kind of lie, Ericsson provides an epigraph, a short quotation that forecasts a theme. Which of these epigraphs work best, do you think? What are your criteria for judgment?
3. What is the message of Ericsson's CONCLUSION? Does the conclusion work well? Why or why not?
4. MIXED METHODS. Examine the way Ericsson uses DEFINITION and EX-AMPLE to support her CLASSIFICATION. Which definitions are clearest? Which examples are the most effective? Why?
5. MIXED METHODS. Ericsson uses CLASSIFICATION to work out CAUSES AND EFFECTS — why we lie, and what the consequences are. Does it weaken her explanation that her classification is not exhaustive? (Er-

icsson twice says she is providing "a few" kinds of lies.) Do her ten categories provide enough range to support her conclusion about the effects of lying?

QUESTIONS ON LANGUAGE

1. In paragraph 35, Ericsson writes, "Our acceptance of lies becomes a cultural cancer that eventually shrouds and reorders reality until moral garbage becomes as invisible to us as water is to a fish." How do the two METAPHORS in this sentence — cancer and garbage — relate to each other?
2. Occasionally Ericsson's anger shows through, as in paragraphs 12–13 and 18–20. Is the TONE appropriate in these cases? Why or why not?
3. Look up any of these words you do not know: haggard (para. 2); travails (4); façades (10); plethora (11); ecclesiastical, pedophilia (12); irreparable, co-perpetrator (13); misogynists (18); patriarchal, archetype (20); gamut (31); myriad (32); reticent (36).
4. Ericsson uses several words and phrases from the fields of psychology and sociology. Define: passive-aggressive (para. 16); floating anxiety, adult-children-of-alcoholics movement (27); schizophrenics, catatonia (30).

SUGGESTIONS FOR WRITING

1. In an essay, probe lies you have told. You may want to use CLASSIFICATION as your primary method, or you may want to NARRATE the story of a lie and how it turned out. What were the CAUSES of your lie or lies? What were the EFFECTS?
2. Ericsson writes, "All the 'isms' — racism, sexism, ageism, et al. — are founded on and fueled by the stereotype and the cliché, which are lies of exaggeration, omission, and ignorance. They are always dangerous. They take a single tree and make it a landscape" (para. 22). Write an essay discussing stereotypes and how they work to encourage prejudice. Use Ericsson's definition as a base, and expand it to include stereotypes you find particularly injurious. How do these stereotypes oversimplify? How are they "dangerous"?
3. CRITICAL WRITING. EVALUATE the success of Ericsson's essay, considering especially how effectively her EVIDENCE supports her GENERALIZATIONS. Are there important categories she overlooks, exceptions she neglects to account for, gaps in DEFINITIONS or EXAMPLES? Offer specific evidence for your own view, whether positive or negative.
4. CONNECTIONS. In "Excuuuse Me" (p. 634), David Segal asserts that the suppression of ethnic and other "off-color" humor is part of a general trend toward "impeding frank talk about race, sex, class, and sexuality"

(para. 3). After reading Segal's essay, write an essay of your own in which you examine such humor in Ericsson's terms. Is its suppression a way to "lubricate the daily machinery of existence" (para. 35), or is it just another demonstration that we are unwholesomely "reticent about making judgments" (36)? Draw on Segal's examples, or use your own.

DAVID SEGAL

Born in Boston in 1964, DAVID SEGAL graduated from Harvard University in 1986 and received a master's degree in politics from Oxford University in 1989. His journalism and essays have appeared in *The New Republic*, the *Washington Post*, and the *Wall Street Journal*. He has worked as a speechwriter for the Israeli ambassador to the United States and is now an editor of *The Washington Monthly*, a journal of politics. Segal reports being "happiest," however, "when singing and playing rhythm guitar for the Bremmers, a D.C.-based rock and blues band which makes up in enthusiasm what it lacks in precision."

Excuuuse Me

In this essay for *The New Republic* in May 1992, Segal argues that exaggerated efforts not to offend people's feelings — what has been called "political correctness" — are robbing our tense multicultural society of an essential "safety valve": ethnic and other off-color humor.

"Excuuuse Me" is a strong ARGUMENT for reviving such humor, an argument backed by ANALYSIS of off-color jokes and an examination of their CAUSES AND EFFECTS. Throughout, Segal peppers his essay with EXAMPLES of the kind of humor he has in mind.

It was inevitable that the chill of sensitivity now felt in public discourse and academic life would eventually come to comedy. But P.C.[1] humor has arrived more swiftly — and completely — than even ardent activists could have hoped. Take three films written and directed by David and Jerry Zucker and Jim Abrahams. *Airplane*, released in 1980, has a slew of gay bits, two black men speaking indecipherable jive over subtitles, close to a minyan of Jewish jokes, drug gags, references to bestiality, nun jokes, five obscenities, and one gratuitous front shot of a naked woman. *Naked Gun*, released in 1989, contains only one drug joke, one obscenity, no nudity, not a single Jewish joke, and three gay lines. In 1991 and *Naked Gun 2½*, there were no obscenities, no frontal nudity, just two ethnic slurs, three tentative gay jokes, and one muttered "mazel-tov." Moreover, an earnest stripe of environmentalism is painted down the movie's

[1]Politically correct. — EDS.

middle. At the end of the film the protagonist says, "Love is like the ozone layer: you only miss it once it's gone" without a hint of irony.

It's been a long slide downhill. Like the deficit, off-color humor touches everyone but has no constituency, and neither politicians nor pundits will be clamoring for its return anytime soon. But there are good reasons to lament its passing. Let me count the ways.

Risqué humor defuses tensions. Lenny Bruce used to do a stand-up routine in which he'd gesture to each ethnic minority in the room and call them the most offensive names in the book: "I got a nigger here, two spics there. . . ." When his audience was ready to assault him, he'd reveal his point: that epithets get at least part of their sting precisely by being placed off-limits. By spreading the abuse about, you take the sting out of it. (The caveat, of course, is that if you're going to use ethnic humor, you should avoid singling out any particular group for derision.) Today's puritans, in contrast, are a drag on our culture, impeding frank talk about race, sex, class, and sexuality, and deadening our public wit at the same time. It's no coincidence that in the 1980s, before multiculturalism killed racial jokes, productive discussions of race were more common.

Risqué humor educates. The experience of American Jews in this country may be the best example of how this works. For decades the capacity of Jewish comedians to poke fun at the peculiar tics of their people helped make Jewish otherness, a quality that aroused suspicion and hatred in bygone eras, something disarming. It's a safe bet that the films of Mel Brooks and Woody Allen did more to stymie anti-Semitism in the past twenty years than all the wide-eyed vigilance and arm-waving of the Anti-Defamation League. When a quick cutaway shot in *Annie Hall* reveals that the grandmother of Allen's WASPY girlfriend sees him as a bearded and yarmulked rabbi, we laugh even as we empathize with his discomfort. Gays have used humor the same way. You'd be hard-pressed to watch *La Cage Aux Folles,* a musical about a troupe of mincing gay entertainers, and have your homophobia strengthened. *Airplane* had a character — John, an air traffic controller — whose jokes, improvised by gay actor and activist Steve Stucco, made fun of gay sensibility without attacking it. When someone hands him a piece of paper and asks what he can make of it, Stucco begins folding it and says, "Oh a brooch, or a hat, or a pterodactyl."

Risqué humor disarms. A classic — and rare — modern example is *In Living Color,* which showcases merciless skits about black culture. (The reason it survives the P.C. police is that it's largely written and acted by blacks.) Witness a *Star Trek* spoof, "The Wrath of Farrakhan," a vicious lampoon of the black Muslim leader; or a sketch making fun of West Indians' hard-work habits. The feature "Men on Films," starring Damon Wayans and David Alan Grier (a.k.a. Antoine and Blaine), breaks taboos and wows both gay and straight audiences — while enraging the humorless activists. One regular skit centers on "Handi Man," a caped, spastic superhero who foils villains with his dwarf sidekick. To believe this hardens prejudice against people with disabilities is to believe that people are fundamentally barbaric; and assuming the handicapped are too tender a subject for humor is more patronizing than outright disdain. Indeed, there may be no better way to perpetrate a myth of disabled otherness than coming up with euphemisms like "the differently abled" and making irreverent utterances off-limits.

Risqué humor undermines prejudices. A black comic I recently saw   6
had the right idea: He said he got so mad when a grocery clerk snickered about his purchase of frozen fried chicken that "I just grabbed my watermelon and tap danced on out of there." The joke both played with stereotypes and ridiculed them: Sometimes the best offense is offense. The major problem with ethnic humor — that it is often deployed by the powerful against the powerless — is best answered not by silencing the powerful (that hardly takes away their power) but by unleashing the humorous abilities of the powerless. Allowing ethnic humor means that blacks are allowed to make fun of whites (Eddie Murphy), gays are allowed to make fun of straights (Harvey Fierstein), and women are allowed to make fun of men (Roseanne Barr). In today's more ethnically and sexually diverse media, little of this opportunity for humor is being realized. Diversity is being achieved; and the result, ironically, is more piety. This is not only a bore, but an insult to the rich traditions of gay, black, Jewish, female, fat, ugly, disabled humor — and a boon to society's wealthy, powerful, and largely unfunny elites.

Risqué humor is funny. Ethnic humor's final defense is that it makes   7
people laugh. In a free society, this is an irrepressible — and admirable — activity, and one I suspect we did more of some years back. Ask yourself: Were you laughing harder a decade ago? When Buck Henry hosted *Saturday Night Live* in the 1970s he'd do a skit in which he played a pedophilic baby sitter who got his jollies by playing games with his two nieces, like "find the pocket with the treat" and "show me your dirty laundry." In 1967 Mel Brooks won a best screenplay Academy Award for *The Producers,* which was full of Jewish, gay, and Nazi jokes and is now a confirmed classic. Brooks's 1991 offering was *Life Stinks,* which was bereft of anything off-color and was rightly panned.

As we've pushed the risqué off-stage, we've brought violent slap-   8
stick back on as a means of keeping the audience's attention. *Saturday
Night Live* has abandoned racy material in favor of skits like "Horrible
Headwound Harry," which features Dana Carvey as a party guest
bleeding from the head. And last year *Home Alone*, the story of a
little boy, played by Macaulay Culkin, who fends off two burglars
from his house by, among other things, dropping a hot iron on their
heads, became the most lucrative comedy of movie history, grossing
more than $285 million. The violence was far more explicit than
anything the Three Stooges ever came up with, and all of it was done
by a 12-year-old. Compare this with *Animal House*, which used to be
the top-grossing comedy; it was filled with sexist — and hilarious —
moments like the one in which the conscience of Tom Hulce's
character advises him to take advantage of his passed-out, underage
date.

In a multicultural society like ours, humor is not a threat, it's a   9
critical support. It keeps us sane, and it's a useful safety valve. If we
can't be cruel about each other in jest, we might end up being cruel
to each other in deadly seriousness. The politically correct war against
insensitive humor might end up generating the very social and racial
tension it is trying to defuse.

QUESTIONS ON MEANING

1. What does Segal mean by the "chill of sensitivity" that he feels has
   "come to comedy"?
2. Why does Segal believe comedy has become more physically violent?
3. Why does Segal say that "political correctness" in humor is a "boon to
   society's wealthy, powerful, and largely unfunny elites"?
4. What is Segal's THESIS? Where does he state it?
5. What is Segal's PURPOSE?

QUESTIONS ON WRITING STRATEGY

1. From the EVIDENCE of the essay itself, whom does Segal see as his
   AUDIENCE? How old are they? What are their attitudes toward his
   subject?
2. What is Segal's TONE? In this essay on humor, does he try to be funny?
   Why or why not?
3. MIXED METHODS. Segal's ARGUMENT is supported mainly by ANALYSIS
   of off-color humor and of its EFFECTS. List the elements he identifies in
   such humor and the effects of each.

4. MIXED METHODS. Consider the EXAMPLES Segal uses to support his argument. Do they convince you? Can you think of other examples that might undermine Segal's THESIS?

QUESTIONS ON LANGUAGE

1. Segal uses several words and phrases from show business. Can you give meanings for these: bits (para. 1); routine (3); cut-away shot, improvised (4); skits (5); panned (7); slapstick, grossing (8)?
2. What are the CONNOTATIONS of the word "puritans" (para. 3)? Why does Segal apply it to advocates of "political correctness"? How is its use IRONIC here?
3. What does Segal mean by "a myth of disabled otherness" (para. 5)?
4. Supply definitions for the following words: gratuitous (para. 1); pundits (2); risqué, epithets, caveat (3); tics, stymie (4); piety (6); pedophilic, bereft (7).

SUGGESTIONS FOR WRITING

1. Almost everyone has been the butt of someone else's joke. Think of a time when you heard a joke based on a stereotype of a group you belong to. Did you find it funny? Why or why not? NARRATE your experience so that the reader understands it. Use EXAMPLES from Segal's essay *and* from your own experience to support your claims.
2. Argue in favor of some widely criticized media content. Examples: religious television programming, "feelings"-oriented children's songs and videos, violent horror movies, sexy music videos. Why are the critics wrong? How does this entertainment contribute to society?
3. CRITICAL WRITING. Write an essay in which you agree or disagree with Segal. If you agree with him, extend his ARGUMENT in some way, such as discussing how other supposed insensitivities actually benefit our culture. If you disagree with Segal, refute his claims one by one. In either case, be as careful as Segal is to supply clear reasons and specific EXAMPLES.
4. CONNECTIONS. Compare this essay to Michiko Kakutani's "The Word Police" (p. 640). How do the authors conceive of "political correctness" in similar ways? How do their conceptions differ? Which author would give free speech greater leeway? What do *you* think of their arguments?

DAVID SEGAL ON WRITING

For *The Bedford Reader*, David Segal provided some good pointers on writing arguments.

"Every opinion essay, like a springboard dive, comes with a degree-of-difficulty factor — the more outrageous the argument, the more points you get for simply trying to make it. 'What's Right with Mother Theresa' would no doubt be a tale of noble sentiments and heart-warming anecdotes, but it promises all the flair of a pool-side two-hand cannonball. 'The Case Against Mother Teresa,' on the other hand, is a full-twisting triple back flip off the three-meter board. And probably a lot of fun to read.

"Ideally, a piece like 'Excuuuse Me' convinces a reader of something that he or she didn't believe at the start, and that means some finesse work is necessary. I like to imagine when I write an argument like 'Excuuuse Me' that I have my arm slung chummily around a friend — a college roommate perhaps — and I'm quietly and earnestly talking as we walk.

"Usually my strategy is to make an argument that carries him along a seamless path. 'You believe this, right?' 'Well, yeah,' I hear back. 'Then you also have to believe this,' I reply. 'I guess,' he replies. 'In that case you also agree that . . .' And so on until by the end of our walk he's in some place that he never thought he'd be, allowing, with a hint of resignation, that we actually are of one mind on an issue he thought we disagreed about.

"For 'Excuuuse Me' I used a variant of that strategy: Instead of linking the ideas, I simply piled one on top of the other. In this case, I'm saying to my reader, 'Look, here's a mass of evidence to support my idea. You might not buy all the evidence, but you'll probably buy some of it.' When your reader agrees with enough of what you've written, you win. And if your point is sufficiently outlandish, winning is just like nailing that triple back flip and getting a 9.9 from the competitor's toughest judge."

FOR DISCUSSION

1. How does Segal conceive of his AUDIENCE? What does he have to do to achieve his PURPOSE with this audience?
2. Segal doesn't mention whether he cares about his subject in addition to finding it challenging. Judging from "Excuuuse Me," do you think he does? Why?
3. Consider Segal's comments about the structure and the use of EVIDENCE in "Excuuuse Me." Were you aware of these strategies when reading the essay?
4. Out of ten possible points, what score would *you* give Segal's essay? Why?

MICHIKO KAKUTANI

MICHIKO KAKUTANI is a reporter covering cultural news for the *New York Times,* a position she has held since 1979. She is the paper's principal book reviewer and also writes criticism and feature stories on literary and cultural issues. She has published one book, a collection of interviews she conducted at the *Times* titled *The Poet at the Piano: Portraits of Writers, Filmmakers, Playwrights, and Other Artists at Work* (1988). Kakutani was born in 1955 in New Haven, Connecticut, and earned a B.A. from Yale University in 1976. After graduation she worked at the *Washington Post* and then served as a staff writer for *Time* magazine until joining the *New York Times.* She lives in Manhattan.

The Word Police

"The Word Police" is a kind of book review in which Kakutani goes beyond particular books to comment on the entire cultural trend they represent — in this case, efforts by some to rid the language of its biases. The essay first appeared in the *New York Times* in January 1993.

Like David Segal's "Excuuuse Me" (p. 634), Kakutani's essay is predominantly an ARGUMENT against "political correctness," the controversial stance that language and behavior should be modified or even restricted to avoid offending feelings. Two other methods do much of the work to support this argument: CAUSE AND EFFECT and EXAMPLE.

This month's inaugural festivities,[1] with their celebration, in Maya Angelou's words, of "humankind" — "the Asian, the Hispanic, the Jew / The African, the Native American, the Sioux, / The Catholic, the Muslim, the French, the Greek / The Irish, the Rabbi, the Priest, the Sheik, / The Gay, the Straight, the Preacher, / The privileged, the homeless, the Teacher" — constituted a kind of official embrace of multiculturalism and a new politics of inclusion.

The mood of political correctness, however, has already made firm inroads into popular culture. Washington boasts a store called Politically Correct that sells pro-whale, anti-meat, ban-the-bomb T-shirts, bumper stickers and buttons, as well as a local cable tele-

---

[1] The inauguration of President Bill Clinton, at which Angelou read the poem quoted. — EDS.

vision show called *Politically Correct Cooking* that features interviews in the kitchen with representatives from groups like People for the Ethical Treatment of Animals. The Coppertone suntan lotion people are planning to give their longtime cover girl, Little Miss (Ms?) Coppertone, a male equivalent, Little Mr. Coppertone. And even Superman (Superperson?) is rumored to be returning this spring, reincarnated as four ethnically diverse clones: an African-American, an Asian, a Caucasian and a Latino.

Nowhere is this P.C. mood more striking than in the increasingly   3
noisy debate over language that has moved from university campuses to the country at large — a development that both underscores Americans' puritanical zeal for reform and their unwavering faith in the talismanic power of words.

Certainly no decent person can quarrel with the underlying im-   4
pulse behind political correctness: a vision of a more just, inclusive society in which racism, sexism and prejudice of all sorts have been erased. But the methods and fervor of the self-appointed language police can lead to a rigid orthodoxy — and unintentional self-parody — opening the movement to the scorn of conservative opponents and the mockery of cartoonists and late-night television hosts.

It's hard to imagine women earning points for political correctness   5
by saying *ovarimony* instead of *testimony* — as one participant at the recent Modern Language Association convention was overheard to suggest. It's equally hard to imagine people wanting to flaunt their lack of prejudice by giving up such words and phrases as *bull market*, *kaiser roll*, *Lazy Susan*, and *charley horse*.

Several books on bias-free language have already appeared, and   6
the 1991 edition of the Random House *Webster's College Dictionary* boasts an appendix titled "Avoiding Sexist Language." The dictionary also includes such linguistic mutations as *womyn* (women, "used as an alternative spelling to avoid the suggestion of sexism perceived in the sequence m-e-n") and *waitron* (a gender-blind term for waiter or waitress).

Many of these dictionaries and guides not only warn the reader   7
against offensive racial and sexual slurs, but also try to establish and enforce a whole new set of usage rules. Take, for instance, *The Bias-Free Word Finder, a Dictionary of Nondiscriminatory Language* by Rosalie Maggio (Beacon Press) — a volume often indistinguishable, in its meticulous solemnity, from the tongue-in-cheek *Official Politically Correct Dictionary and Handbook* put out last year by Henry Beard and Christopher Cerf (Villard Books). Ms. Maggio's book supplies the reader intent on using kinder, gentler language with writing guidelines

as well as a detailed listing of more than 5,000 "biased words and phrases."

Whom are these guidelines for? Somehow one has a tough time 8 picturing them replacing *Fowler's Modern English Usage* in the classroom, or being adopted by the average man (sorry, individual) in the street.

The "pseudogeneric *he*," we learn from Ms. Maggio, is to be 9 avoided like the plague, as is the use of the word *man* to refer to humanity. *Fellow, king, lord* and *master* are bad because they're "male-oriented words," and *king, lord* and *master* are especially bad because they're also "hierarchical, dominator society terms." The politically correct lion becomes the "monarch of the jungle," new-age children play "someone on the top of the heap," and the *Mona Lisa* goes down in history as Leonardo's "acme of perfection."

As for the word *black*, Ms. Maggio says it should be excised from 10 terms with a negative spin: She recommends substituting words like *mouse* for *black eye, ostracize* for *blackball, payola* for *blackmail,* and *outcast* for *black sheep.* Clearly, some of these substitutions work better than others: Somehow the "sinister humor" of Kurt Vonnegut or *Saturday Night Live* doesn't quite make it; nor does the "denouncing" of the Hollywood 10.

For the dedicated user of politically correct language, all these 11 rules can make for some messy moral dilemmas. Whereas *battered wife* is a gender-biased term, the gender-free term *battered spouse,* Ms. Maggio notes, incorrectly implies "that men and women are equally battered."

On one hand, say Francine Wattman Frank and Paula A. Treich- 12 ler in their book *Language, Gender, and Professional Writing* (Modern Language Association), *he or she* is an appropriate construction for talking about an individual (like a jockey, say) who belongs to a profession that's predominantly male — it's a way of emphasizing "that such occupations are not barred to women or that women's concerns need to be kept in mind." On the other hand, they add, using masculine pronouns rhetorically can underscore ongoing male dominance in those fields, implying the need for change.

And what about the speech codes adopted by some universities 13 in recent years? Although they were designed to prohibit students from uttering sexist and racist slurs, they would extend, by logic, to blacks who want to use the word *nigger* to strip the term of its racist connotations, or homosexuals who want to use the word *queer* to reclaim it from bigots.

In her book, Ms. Maggio recommends applying bias-free usage 14 retroactively: She suggests paraphrasing politically incorrect quotations, or replacing "the sexist words or phrases with ellipsis dots and/or bracketed substitutes," or using *sic* "to show that the sexist words come from the original quotation and to call attention to the fact that they are incorrect."

Which leads the skeptical reader of *The Bias-Free Word Finder* to   15
wonder whether *All the King's Men* should be retitled *All the Ruler's People*; *Pet Sematary*, *Animal Companion Graves*; *Birdman of Alcatraz*, *Birdperson of Alcatraz*; and *The Iceman Cometh*, *The Ice Route Driver Cometh*?

Will making such changes remove the prejudice in people's   16
minds? Should we really spend time trying to come up with non-male-based alternatives to *Midas touch*, *Achilles' heel*, and *Montezuma's revenge*? Will tossing out Santa Claus — whom Ms. Maggio accuses of reinforcing "the cultural male-as-norm system" — in favor of Belfana, his Italian female alter ego, truly help banish sexism? Can the avoidance of "violent expressions and metaphors" like *kill two birds with one stone*, *sock it to 'em* or *kick an idea around* actually promote a more harmonious world?

The point isn't that the excesses of the word police are comical.   17
The point is that their intolerance (in the name of tolerance) has disturbing implications. In the first place, getting upset by phrases like *bullish on America* or *the City of Brotherly Love* tends to distract attention from the real problems of prejudice and injustice that exist in society at large, turning them into mere questions of semantics. Indeed, the emphasis currently put on politically correct usage has uncanny parallels with the academic movement of deconstruction — a method of textual analysis that focuses on language and linguistic pyrotechnics — which has become firmly established on university campuses.

In both cases, attention is focused on surfaces, on words and   18
metaphors; in both cases, signs and symbols are accorded more importance than content. Hence, the attempt by some radical advocates to remove *The Adventures of Huckleberry Finn* from curriculums on the grounds that Twain's use of the word *nigger* makes the book a racist text — never mind the fact that this American classic (written in 1884) depicts the spiritual kinship achieved between a white boy and a runaway slave, never mind the fact that the "nigger" Jim emerges as the novel's most honorable, decent character.

Ironically enough, the P.C. movement's obsession with language   19
is accompanied by a strange Orwellian willingness to warp the meaning of words by placing them under a high-powered ideological lens.

For instance, the *Dictionary of Cautionary Words and Phrases* — a pamphlet issued by the University of Missouri's Multicultural Management Program to help turn "today's journalists into tomorrow's multicultural newsroom managers" — warns that using the word *articulate* to describe members of a minority group can suggest the opposite, "that 'those people' are not considered well educated, articulate and the like."

The pamphlet patronizes minority groups, by cautioning the reader against using the words *lazy* and *burly* to describe any member of such groups; and it issues a similar warning against using words like *gorgeous* and *petite* to describe women.

As euphemism proliferates with the rise of political correctness, there is a spread of the sort of sloppy, abstract language that Orwell said is "designed to make lies sound truthful and murder respectable, and to give an appearance of solidity to pure wind." *Fat* becomes *big boned* or *differently sized; stupid* becomes *exceptional; stoned* becomes *chemically inconvenienced.*

Wait a minute here! Aren't such phrases eerily reminiscent of the euphemisms coined by the government during Vietnam and Watergate? Remember how the military used to speak of "pacification," or how President Richard M. Nixon's press secretary, Ronald L. Ziegler, tried to get away with calling a lie an "inoperative statement"?

Calling the homeless "the underhoused" doesn't give them a place to live; calling the poor "the economically marginalized" doesn't help them pay the bills. Rather, by playing down their plight, such language might even make it easier to shrug off the seriousness of their situation.

Instead of allowing free discussion and debate to occur, many gung-ho advocates of politically correct language seem to think that simple suppression of a word or concept will magically make the problem disappear. In the *Bias-Free Word Finder,* Ms. Maggio entreats the reader not to perpetuate the negative stereotype of Eve. "Be extremely cautious in referring to the biblical Eve," she writes; "this story has profoundly contributed to negative attitudes toward women throughout history, largely because of misogynistic and patriarchal interpretations that labeled her evil, inferior, and seductive."

The story of Bluebeard, the rake (whoops! — the libertine) who killed his seven wives, she says, is also to be avoided, as is the biblical story of Jezebel. Of Jesus Christ, Ms. Maggio writes: "There have been few individuals in history as completely androgynous as Christ, and it does his message a disservice to overinsist on his maleness." She doesn't give the reader any hints on how this might be accomplished; presumably, one is supposed to avoid describing him as the Son of God.

Of course the P.C. police aren't the only ones who want to pro- 26 scribe what people should say or give them guidelines for how they may use an idea; Jesse Helms and his supporters are up to exactly the same thing when they propose to patrol the boundaries of the permissible in art. In each case, the would-be censor aspires to suppress what he or she finds distasteful — all, of course, in the name of the public good.

In the case of the politically correct, the prohibition of certain 27 words, phrases and ideas is advanced in the cause of building a brave new world free of racism and hate, but this vision of harmony clashes with the very ideals of diversity and inclusion that the multicultural movement holds dear, and it's purchased at the cost of freedom of speech.

In fact, the utopian world envisioned by the language police 28 would be bought at the expense of the ideals of individualism and democracy articulated in the "Gettysburg Address": "Four score and seven years ago our fathers brought forth on this continent a new nation, conceived in liberty and dedicated to the proposition that all men are created equal."

Of course, the P.C. police have already found Lincoln's words 29 hopelessly "phallocentric." No doubt they would rewrite the passage: "Four score and seven years ago our foremothers and forefathers brought forth on this continent a new nation, formulated with liberty, and dedicated to the proposition that all humankind is created equal."

QUESTIONS ON MEANING

1. Why is *The Bias-Free Word Finder* "indistinguishable" from the satiric *Official Politically Correct Dictionary and Handbook* (para. 7)?
2. In your own words, restate Kakutani's THESIS. What is her PURPOSE?
3. Why, in Kakutani's opinion, do the "word police" hurt the cause they are trying to help?
4. How are advocates of "political correctness" like advocates of right-wing censorship?

QUESTIONS ON WRITING STRATEGY

1. The *New York Times*, where this essay was first published, is one of the nation's most widely read newspapers. Who in the paper's vast AUDIENCE does Kakutani seem to ASSUME will read the essay?

2. What is Kakutani's TONE? (Look, for instance, at paras. 7–8, 14–15, and 24–25.) How might it affect her audience? How does it affect *you*?

3. MIXED METHODS. Kakutani's ARGUMENT develops from her ANALYSIS of CAUSES AND EFFECTS. What does she think causes "political correctness"? What are its consequences?

4. MIXED METHODS. The EVIDENCE for Kakutani's argument is mainly EXAMPLES. Which ones do you think are the most effective? Which are least effective? Why?

QUESTIONS ON LANGUAGE

1. Give meanings for any of these words that are unfamiliar: puritanical, talismanic (para. 3); fervor, orthodoxy (4); meticulous (7); pseudo-, generic, hierarchical (9); excised (10); semantics, pyrotechnics (17); ideological (19); misogynistic, patriarchal (24); androgynous (25); proscribe (26); phallocentric (29).

2. Locate some words and phrases of Kakutani's that might be seen as unacceptable by the "word police." Do they offend or disturb you?

3. What are some of the CONNOTATIONS of the phrase "politically correct"?

4. What does Kakutani mean by the phrase "Orwellian willingness to warp the meaning of words" (para. 19)?

SUGGESTIONS FOR WRITING

1. Do you agree or disagree with Kakutani's argument that "politically correct" language "might even make it easier to shrug off the seriousness" of excluded groups' problems (para. 23)? Answer with EXAMPLES from your own experience. Have you seen careless language hurt groups or individuals? Have you seen individuals or groups hurt by too-careful language?

2. Kakutani writes, "The mood of political correctness . . . has already made firm inroads into popular culture" (para. 2), and gives examples from television, suntan-lotion ads, and comic books to support her claim. Do you agree or disagree? Write a short essay arguing that popular culture has, or has not, become more "politically correct." Support your claims with EVIDENCE. You may want to COMPARE AND CONTRAST past movies, comics, pop songs, or television shows with their present-day counterparts as a way of making your case.

3. CRITICAL WRITING. In an essay, ANALYZE Kakutani's ASSUMPTIONS about the connections between language and action. How do they compare with the assumptions Kakutani attributes to the advocates of "political correctness"? With whose assumptions are you more comfortable, and why?

4. CONNECTIONS. Although in paragraph 21 Kakutani quotes from George Orwell's "Politics and the English Language" (p. 606), she and

Orwell appear to disagree over the connections between language and thought and social change. In an essay, compare Kakutani's paragraphs 16–18 and 23–24 with Orwell's paragraphs 13–17. SUMMARIZE each writer's position, and then analyze each. Which position do you find more convincing? Why?

ADDITIONAL WRITING TOPICS
Language and Truth

1. "If thought corrupts language, language can also corrupt thought," says George Orwell (p. 615). What does he mean by this statement? How might Amy Tan ("The Language of Discretion," p. 187) apply it to stereotypes of Chinese and Chinese American people? How might Stephanie Ericsson ("The Ways We Lie," p. 623) apply it to our daily untruths? Draw on Tan's and Ericsson's essays and your own experiences and observations to support or challenge Orwell's claims about the connections between language and thought.

2. David Segal argues in "Excuuuse Me" (p. 634) that when it comes to dealing with stereotypes in popular culture, "sometimes the best offense is offense." How might Barbara Ehrenreich ("The Wretched of the Hearth," p. 292) respond to this statement? How might Nancy Mairs ("Disability," p. 489) respond? Write an essay discussing all three authors' views of how popular culture presents non-mainstream groups. What do *you* think of this issue?

3. Write an essay on the issue of "political correctness," supporting your own views as appropriate with those of George Orwell in "Politics and the English Language" (p. 606), David Segal in "Excuuuse Me" (p. 634), Michiko Kakutani in "The Word Police" (p. 640), Arthur M. Schlesinger, Jr., in "The Cult of Ethnicity, Good and Bad" (p. 689), and Katha Pollitt in "Why Do We Read?" (p. 695). Consider: Is there a need to make the language fairer and more inclusive? Should "hate speech" be restricted? Do any or all corrections or restrictions of other people's language violate their First Amendment rights? Why is language so controversial, anyway?

13

OUR PLACE
IN THE ENVIRONMENT

Just what is our place in the earthly environment? For centuries, it seemed beyond question: Human beings, the earth's smart inhabitants, had unlimited rights to inexhaustible resources. Now, of course, there are plenty of questions: What have we done to the earth's ecosystem and what may we still do? What habits of mind and behavior do we need to change? What are our responsibilities to the earth, its other creatures, and ourselves?

The essays in this chapter approach our place in the environment from very different directions. In "Ships in the Desert," Albert Gore, Jr., now the vice president of the United States, vividly portrays the injuries inflicted on the earth by humankind. In "How to Poison the Earth," Linnea Saukko, an environmentalist, uses her sharp wit to skewer polluters of all stripes. In "Some Doubts About Fur Coats," the Croatian writer Slavenka Drakulić introduces needed complexity into the debate over who, if anyone, has the right to use animal pelts to clothe themselves. And finally, in "Waking Up the Rake," Linda Hogan brings a Native American perspective to the search for a reunion of humans and the earth.

ALBERT GORE, JR.

ALBERT GORE, JR., was elected vice president of the United States in 1992, the same year he published *Earth in the Balance*, a best-selling manifesto about environmental problems and solutions. Born in 1948, Gore was familiar with public service: His father, Albert Gore, Sr., represented Tennessee in the U.S. House and Senate, and Gore grew up in Washington, D.C. He graduated from Harvard College in 1969 with a B.A. in government and was soon drafted into the army, serving as an army reporter in Vietnam. On release, he wrote for the Nashville *Tennessean* and studied philosophy and law at Vanderbilt University. Gore entered politics in 1976 as a U.S. Representative from Tennessee. In the House, he gained considerable expertise on environmental issues, helping to develop the 1980 "Superfund" bill to clean up hazardous waste sites and promoting nuclear disarmament. Gore entered the U.S. Senate in 1984 and served there until his election as vice president.

Ships in the Desert

Following are the opening pages of Gore's book, *Earth in the Balance*; "Ships in the Desert" is the title of the first chapter. Moving from sea to earth to sky, Gore depicts the range and extent of environmental destruction. This introduction to the book raises an alarm; the rest of the book fills in the details and proposes solutions.

To grip his readers, Gore relies heavily on EXAMPLES — one after another illustrating how the earth has changed. For several of these changes, Gore ANALYZES CAUSES or a PROCESS. Throughout, he uses NARRATION and DESCRIPTION to make his examples immediate and concrete.

1 I was standing in the sun on the hot steel deck of a fishing ship capable of processing a fifty-ton catch on a good day. But it wasn't a good day. We were anchored in what used to be the most productive fishing site in all of central Asia, but as I looked out over the bow, the prospects of a good catch looked bleak. Where there should have been gentle blue-green waves lapping against the side of the ship, there was nothing but hot dry sand — as far as I could see in all directions. The other ships of the fleet were also at rest in the sand, scattered in the dunes that stretched all the way to the horizon.

2 Oddly enough, it made me think of a fried egg I had seen back in the United States on television the week before. It was sizzling

and popping the way a fried egg should in a pan, but it was in the middle of a sidewalk in downtown Phoenix. I guess it sprang to mind because, like the ship on which I was standing, there was nothing wrong with the egg itself. Instead, the world beneath it had changed in an unexpected way that made the egg seem — through no fault of its own — out of place. It was illustrating the newsworthy point that at the time Arizona wasn't having an especially good day, either, because for the second day in a row temperatures had reached a record 122 degrees.

As a camel walked by on the dead bottom of the Aral Sea, my   3
thoughts returned to the unlikely ship of the desert on which I stood, which also seemed to be illustrating the point that its world had changed out from underneath it with sudden cruelty. Ten years ago the Aral was the fourth-largest inland sea in the world, comparable to the largest of North America's Great Lakes. Now it is disappearing because the water that used to feed it has been diverted in an ill-considered irrigation scheme to grow cotton in the desert. The new shoreline was almost forty kilometers across the sand from where the fishing fleet was now permanently docked. Meanwhile, in the nearby town of Muynak the people were still canning fish — brought not from the Aral Sea but shipped by rail through Siberia from the Pacific Ocean, more than a thousand miles away.

I had come to the Aral Sea in August 1990 to witness at first   4
hand the destruction taking place there on an almost biblical scale. But during the trip I encountered other images that also alarmed me. For example, the day I returned to Moscow from Muynak, my friend Alexei Yablokov, possibly the leading environmentalist in the Soviet Union, was returning from an emergency expedition to the White Sea, where he had investigated the mysterious and unprecedented death of several *million* starfish, washed up into a knee-deep mass covering many miles of beach. That night, in his apartment, he talked of what it was like for the residents to wade through the starfish in hip boots, trying to explain their death.

Later investigations identified radioactive military waste as the   5
likely culprit in the White Sea deaths. But what about all of the other mysterious mass deaths washing up on beaches around the world? French scientists recently concluded that the explanation for the growing number of dead dolphins washing up along the Riviera was accumulated environmental stress, which, over time, rendered the animals too weak to fight off a virus. This same phenomenon may also explain the sudden increase in dolphin deaths along the Gulf Coast in Texas as well as the mysterious deaths of 12,000 seals whose

corpses washed up on the shores of the North Sea in the summer of 1988. Of course, the oil-covered otters and seabirds of Prince William Sound a year later presented less of a mystery to science, if no less an indictment of our civilization.

As soon as one of these troubling images fades, another takes its 6 place, provoking new questions. What does it mean, for example, that children playing in the morning surf must now dodge not only the occasional jellyfish but the occasional hypodermic needle washing in with the waves? Needles, dead dolphins, and oil-soaked birds — are all these signs that the shores of our familiar world are fast eroding, that we are now standing on some new beach, facing dangers beyond the edge of what we are capable of imagining?

With our backs turned to the place in nature from which we 7 came, we sense an unfamiliar tide rising and swirling around our ankles, pulling at the sand beneath our feet. Each time this strange new tide goes out, it leaves behind the flotsam and jetsam of some giant shipwreck far out at sea, startling images washed up on the sands of our time, each a fresh warning of hidden dangers that lie ahead if we continue on our present course.

My search for the underlying causes of the environmental crisis 8 has led me to travel around the world to examine and study many of these images of destruction. At the very bottom of the earth, high in the Trans-Antarctic Mountains, with the sun glaring at midnight through a hole in the sky, I stood in the unbelievable coldness and talked with a scientist in the late fall of 1988 about the tunnel he was digging through time. Slipping his parka back to reveal a badly burned face that was cracked and peeling, he pointed to the annual layers of ice in a core sample dug from the glacier on which we were standing. He moved his finger back in time to the ice of two decades ago. "Here's where the U.S. Congress passed the Clean Air Act," he said. At the bottom of the world, two continents away from Washington, D.C., even a small reduction in one country's emissions had changed the amount of pollution found in the remotest and least accessible place on earth.

But the most significant change thus far in the earth's atmosphere 9 is the one that began with the industrial revolution early in the last century and has picked up speed ever since. Industry meant coal, and later oil, and we began to burn lots of it — bringing rising levels of carbon dioxide (CO_2), with its ability to trap more heat in the atmosphere and slowly warm the earth. Fewer than a hundred yards from the South Pole, upwind from the ice runway where the ski plane lands and keeps its engines running to prevent the metal parts from freeze-locking together, scientists monitor the air several times every day to chart the course of that inexorable change. During my visit, I watched one scientist draw the results of that day's measurements, pushing the end of a steep line still higher on the graph. He told me how easy it is — there at the end of the earth — to see that this enormous change in the global atmosphere is still picking up speed.

Two and a half years later I slept under the midnight sun at the   10 other end of our planet, in a small tent pitched on a twelve-foot-thick slab of ice floating in the frigid Arctic Ocean. After a hearty breakfast, my companions and I traveled by snowmobiles a few miles farther north to a rendezvous point where the ice was thinner — only three and a half feet thick — and a nuclear submarine hovered in the water below. After it crashed through the ice, took on its new passengers, and resubmerged, I talked with scientists who were trying to measure more accurately the thickness of the polar ice cap, which many believe is thinning as a result of global warming. I had just negotiated an agreement between ice scientists and the U.S. Navy to secure the release of previously top secret data from submarine sonar tracks, data that could help them learn what is happening to the north polar cap. Now, I wanted to see the pole itself, and some eight hours after we met the submarine, we were crashing through that ice, surfacing, and then I was standing in an eerily beautiful snowscape, windswept and sparkling white, with the horizon defined by little hummocks, or "pressure ridges" of ice that are pushed up like tiny mountain ranges when separate sheets collide. But here too, CO_2 levels are rising just as rapidly, and ultimately temperatures will rise with them — indeed, global warming is expected to push temperatures up much more rapidly in the polar regions than in the rest of the world. As the polar air warms, the ice here will thin; and since the polar cap plays such a crucial role in the world's weather system, the consequences of a thinning cap could be disastrous.

Considering such scenarios is not a purely speculative exercise.   11 Six months after I returned from the North Pole, a team of scientists reported dramatic changes in the pattern of ice distribution in the Arctic, and a second team reported a still controversial claim (which a variety of data now suggest) that, overall, the north polar cap has thinned by 2 percent in just the last decade. Moreover, scientists established several years ago that in many land areas north of the Arctic Circle, the spring snowmelt now comes earlier every year, and deep in the tundra below, the temperature of the earth is steadily rising.

As it happens, some of the most disturbing images of environ-   12
mental destruction can be found exactly halfway between the North
and South poles — precisely at the equator in Brazil — where billowing clouds of smoke regularly blacken the sky above the immense
but now threatened Amazon rain forest. Acre by acre, the rain forest
is being burned to create fast pasture for fast-food beef; as I learned
when I went there in early 1989, the fires are set earlier and earlier
in the dry season now, with more than one Tennessee's worth of rain
forest being slashed and burned each year. According to our guide,
the biologist Tom Lovejoy, there are more different species of birds
in each square mile of the Amazon than exist in all of North
America — which means we are silencing thousands of songs we
have never even heard.

But for most of us the Amazon is a distant place, and we scarcely   13
notice the disappearance of these and other vulnerable species. We
ignore these losses at our peril, however. They're like the proverbial
miners' canaries, silent alarms whose message in this case is that
living species of animals and plants are now vanishing around the
world *one thousand times faster* than at any time in the past 65 million
years.

To be sure, the deaths of some of the larger and more spectacular   14
animal species now under siege do occasionally capture our attention.
I have also visited another place along the equator, East Africa, where
I encountered the grotesquely horrible image of a dead elephant, its
head mutilated by poachers who had dug out its valuable tusks with
chain saws. Clearly, we need to change our purely aesthetic consideration of ivory, since its source is now so threatened. To me, its
translucent whiteness seems different now, like evidence of the
ghostly presence of a troubled spirit, a beautiful but chill apparition,
inspiring both wonder and dread.

A similar apparition lies just beneath the ocean. While scuba   15
diving in the Caribbean, I have seen and touched the white bones
of a dead coral reef. All over the earth, coral reefs have suddenly
started to "bleach" as warmer ocean temperatures put unaccustomed
stress on the tiny organisms that normally live in the skin of the coral
and give the reef its natural coloration. As these organisms — nicknamed "zooks" — leave the membrane of the coral, the coral itself
becomes transparent, allowing its white limestone skeleton to shine
through — hence its bleached appearance. In the past, bleaching was
almost always an occasional and temporary phenomenon, but repeated episodes can exhaust the coral. In the last few years, scientists
have been shocked at the sudden occurrence of extensive worldwide

bleaching episodes from which increasing numbers of coral reefs have failed to recover. Though dead, they shine more brightly than before, haunted perhaps by the same ghost that gives spectral light to an elephant's tusk.

But one doesn't have to travel around the world to witness humankind's assault on the earth. Images that signal the distress of our global environment are now commonly seen almost anywhere. A few miles from the Capitol, for example, I encountered another startling image of nature out of place. Driving in the Arlington, Virginia, neighborhood where my family and I live when the Senate is in session, I stepped on the brake to avoid hitting a large pheasant walking across the street. It darted between the parked cars, across the sidewalk, and into a neighbor's backyard. Then it was gone. But this apparition of wildness persisted in my memory as a puzzle: Why would a pheasant, let alone such a large and beautiful mature specimen, be out for a walk in my neighborhood? Was it a much wilder place than I had noticed? Were pheasants, like the trendy Vietnamese potbellied pigs, becoming the latest fashion in unusual pets? I didn't solve the mystery until weeks later, when I remembered that about three miles away, along the edge of the river, developers were bulldozing the last hundred acres of untouched forest in the entire area. As the woods fell to make way for more concrete, more buildings, parking lots, and streets, the wild things that lived there were forced to flee. Most of the deer were hit by cars; other creatures — like the pheasant that darted into my neighbor's backyard — made it a little farther. 16

Ironically, before I understood the mystery, I felt vaguely comforted to imagine that perhaps this urban environment, so similar to the one in which many Americans live, was not so hostile to wild things after all. I briefly supposed that, like the resourceful raccoons and possums and squirrels and pigeons, all of whom have adapted to life in the suburbs, creatures as wild as pheasants might have a fighting chance. Now I remember that pheasant when I take my children to the zoo and see an elephant or a rhinoceros. They too inspire wonder and sadness. They too remind me that we are creating a world that is hostile to wildness, that seems to prefer concrete to natural landscapes. We are encountering these creatures on a path we have paved — one that ultimately leads to their extinction. 17

On some nights, in high northern latitudes, the sky itself offers another ghostly image that signals the loss of ecological balance now in progress. If the sky is clear after sunset — and if you are watching 18 from a place where pollution hasn't blotted out the night sky alto-gether — you can sometimes see a strange kind of cloud high in the sky. This "noctilucent cloud" occasionally appears when the earth is first cloaked in the evening darkness; shimmering above us with a translucent whiteness, these clouds seem quite unnatural. And they should: Noctilucent clouds have begun to appear more often because of a huge buildup of methane gas in the atmosphere. (Also called natural gas, methane is released from landfills, from coal mines and rice paddies, from billions of termites that swarm through the freshly cut forestland, from the burning of biomass and from a variety of other human activities.) Even though noctilucent clouds were some-times seen in the past, all this extra methane carries more water vapor into the upper atmosphere, where it condenses at much higher alti-tudes to form more clouds that the sun's rays still strike long after sunset has brought the beginning of night to the surface far beneath them.

What should we feel toward these ghosts in the sky? Simple 19 wonder or the mix of emotions we feel at the zoo? Perhaps we should feel awe for our own power: Just as men tear tusks from elephants' heads in such quantity as to threaten the beast with extinction, we are ripping matter from its place in the earth in such volume as to upset the balance between daylight and darkness. In the process, we are once again adding to the threat of global warming, because methane has been one of the fastest-growing greenhouse gases, and is third only to carbon dioxide and water vapor in total volume, changing the chemistry of the upper atmosphere. But, without even considering that threat, shouldn't it startle us that we have now put these clouds in the evening sky which glisten with a spectral light? Or have our eyes adjusted so completely to the bright lights of civilization that we can't see these clouds for what they are — a physical manifestation of the violent collision between human civi-lization and the earth?

QUESTIONS ON MEANING

1. This part of Gore's book has a THESIS of its own. What is it?
2. If you don't already know where they are, look up the places Gore mentions on a map or globe. Why might he have chosen to discuss these sites?

3. Why might the consequences of thinning polar caps be "disastrous" (para. 10)?
4. Why are coral reefs "bleaching" in ever-increasing numbers?

QUESTIONS ON WRITING STRATEGY

1. Why do you think Gore opens with the disappearing Aral Sea? How effective do you find this INTRODUCTION?
2. What is Gore's TONE? How is it affected by his frequent use of the first-person *I*?
3. MIXED METHODS. Both NARRATION and DESCRIPTION enliven many of Gore's EXAMPLES. Which example did you find most vivid? Why?
4. MIXED METHODS. Gore often examines CAUSE AND EFFECT, as in paragraphs 9 and 12. From the examples he cites, what are the chief causes of the environmental crisis?

QUESTIONS ON LANGUAGE

1. How is Gore's title a PARADOX? How does it function as a METAPHOR?
2. Gore's DICTION is straightforward, neither informal nor formal, and he uses little scientific terminology. Why, do you think?
3. Locate definitions in your dictionary if any of these words are unfamiliar: indictment (para. 5); flotsam, jetsam (7); inexorable (9); rendezvous (10); tundra (11); aesthetic, translucent (14); spectral (15); biomass (18).
4. In paragraph 4, Gore describes the destruction of the Aral Sea as occurring "on an almost biblical scale." What does he mean by this phrase?

SUGGESTIONS FOR WRITING

1. In an essay, outline the steps you and your family, school, and community are taking to preserve the environment. What prompted these steps? How are they helping? How are they inadequate? What further steps might be taken?
2. Do you agree with Gore's assessment of the earth's health? Why or why not? If you agree, extend Gore's essay with examples of your own. If you disagree, refute one or more of Gore's examples point by point. Whatever your position, conclude by saying what, if anything, we should do about the environment.
3. CRITICAL WRITING. Picking up from Writing Strategy question 2, ANALYZE Gore's POINT OF VIEW. Reread the essay closely, noting shifts between *I* and *we*. Is the *I* inviting or off-putting? Who is meant by *we*? Do you feel included or excluded by this *we*? Is the shift of pronouns appropriate? Why?

4. CONNECTIONS. Compare Gore's essay with Linnea Saukko's "How to Poison the Earth," beginning on the next page. Which environmental problems do both authors address? Which problems are addressed by only one author, and why? How do their TONES differ? Which essay do you find more effective, and why?

LINNEA SAUKKO

LINNEA SAUKKO was born in Warren, Ohio, in 1956. After receiving a degree in environmental quality control from Muskingum Area Technical College, she spent three years as an environmental technician, developing hazardous waste programs and acting as adviser on chemical safety at a large corporation. Concerned about the lack of safe methods for disposing of hazardous waste, Saukko went back to school to earn a B.A. in geology (Ohio State University, 1985) so that she could help address this issue. She currently lives in Hilliard, Ohio, and works as supervisor of the Groundwater Division of the Ohio Environmental Protection Division, evaluating various sites for possible contamination of the groundwater.

How to Poison the Earth

Like Curtis Chang's "Streets of Gold" (p. 495), "How to Poison the Earth" was written in response to an assignment given in a freshman composition class and was awarded a Bedford Prize in Student Writing. It was subsequently published in *Student Writers at Work: The Bedford Prizes*, edited by Nancy Sommers and Donald McQuade (1984). In this satire, Saukko shares with readers some of what she has learned on the job and suggests one way we can guarantee the fate of the earth.

"How to Poison the Earth" is first and foremost a PROCESS ANALYSIS, providing step-by-step instructions. But other methods of development also play a role: Saukko does not list every known means of pollution but gives EXAMPLES. Through DESCRIPTION, she introduces many specific details. And she frequently pauses to DEFINE key terms.

Poisoning the earth can be difficult because the earth is always   1
trying to cleanse and renew itself. Keeping this in mind, we should generate as much waste as possible from substances such as uranium-238, which has a half-life (the time it takes for half of the substance to decay) of one million years, or plutonium, which has a half-life of only 0.5 million years but is so toxic that if distributed evenly, ten pounds of it could kill every person on the earth. Because the United States generates about eighteen tons of plutonium per year, it is about the best substance for long-term poisoning of the earth. It would help if we would build more nuclear power plants because each one generates only 500 pounds of plutonium each year. Of course, we must

include persistent toxic chemicals such as polychlorinated biphenyl (PCB) and dichlorodiphenyl trichloroethane (DDT) to make sure we have enough toxins to poison the earth from the core to the outer atmosphere. First, we must develop many different ways of putting the waste from these nuclear and chemical substances in, on, and around the earth.

Putting these substances in the earth is a most important step in   2 the poisoning process. With deep-well injection we can ensure that the earth is poisoned all the way to the core. Deep-well injection involves drilling a hole that is a few thousand feet deep and injecting toxic substances at extremely high pressures so they will penetrate deep into the earth. According to the Environmental Protection Agency (EPA), there are about 360 such deep injection wells in the United States. We cannot forget the groundwater aquifers that are closer to the surface. These must also be contaminated. This is easily done by shallow-well injection, which operates on the same principle as deep-well injection, only closer to the surface. The groundwater that has been injected with toxins will spread contamination beneath the earth. The EPA estimates that there are approximately 500,000 shallow injection wells in the United States.

Burying the toxins in the earth is the next best method. The   3 toxins from landfills, dumps, and lagoons slowly seep into the earth, guaranteeing that contamination will last a long time. Because the EPA estimates there are only about 50,000 of these dumps in the United States, they should be located in areas where they will leak to the surrounding ground and surface water.

Applying pesticides and other poisons on the earth is another   4 part of the poisoning process. This is good for coating the earth's surface so that the poisons will be absorbed by plants, will seep into the ground, and will run off into surface water.

Surface water is very important to contaminate because it will   5 transport the poisons to places that cannot be contaminated directly. Lakes are good for long-term storage of pollutants while they release some of their contamination to rivers. The only trouble with rivers is that they act as a natural cleansing system for the earth. No matter how much poison is dumped into them, they will try to transport it away to reach the ocean eventually.

The ocean is very hard to contaminate because it has such a large   6 volume and a natural buffering capacity that tends to neutralize some of the contamination. So in addition to the pollution from rivers, we must use the ocean as a dumping place for as many toxins as possible. The ocean currents will help transport the pollution to places that cannot otherwise be reached.

Now make sure that the air around the earth is very polluted. ⁷
Combustion and evaporation are major mechanisms for doing this.
We must continuously pollute because the wind will disperse the
toxins while rain washes them from the air. But this is good because
a few lakes are stripped of all living animals each year from acid rain.
Because the lower atmosphere can cleanse itself fairly easily, we must
explode nuclear test bombs that shoot radioactive particles high into
the upper atmosphere where they will circle the earth for years.
Gravity must pull some of the particles to earth, so we must continue
exploding these bombs.

So it is that easy. Just be sure to generate as many poisonous ⁸
substances as possible and be sure they are distributed in, on, and
around the entire earth at a greater rate than it can cleanse itself. By
following these easy steps we can guarantee the poisoning of the
earth.

QUESTIONS ON MEANING

1. Is the author's main PURPOSE to amuse and entertain, to inform readers
   of ways they can make better use of natural resources, to warn readers
   about threats to the future of our planet, or to make fun of scientists?
   Support your answer with EVIDENCE from the essay.
2. Describe at least three of the earth's mechanisms for cleansing its land,
   water, and atmosphere, as presented in this essay.
3. According to Saukko, many of our actions are detrimental, if not
   outright destructive, to our environment. Identify these practices and
   discuss them. If these activities are harmful to the earth, why are they
   permitted? Do they serve some other important goal or purpose? If so,
   what? Are there other ways that these goals might be reached?

QUESTIONS ON WRITING STRATEGY

1. How is Saukko's essay organized? Follow the process carefully to determine whether it happens chronologically, with each step depending on
   the one before it, or whether it follows another order. How effective is
   this method of organization and presentation?
2. For what AUDIENCE is this essay intended? How can you tell?
3. What is the TONE of this essay? Consider especially the title and the
   last paragraph as well as examples from the body of the essay. How does
   the tone contribute to Saukko's SATIRE?
4. **MIXED METHODS.** In this PROCESS ANALYSIS, how detailed and specific
   are Saukko's instructions for poisoning the earth? Which steps in this

process would you be able to carry out, once you finished reading the essay? In what instances might an author choose not to provide concrete, comprehensive instructions for a procedure? Relate your answer to the tone and purpose of this essay.

5. MIXED METHODS. Saukko doesn't mention every possible pollutant but instead focuses on certain EXAMPLES. Why do you think she chooses these particular examples? What serious pollutants can you think of that Saukko doesn't mention specifically?

QUESTIONS ON LANGUAGE

1. How do the phrases "next best method" (para. 3), "another part of the poisoning process" (4), and "lakes are good for long-term storage of pollutants" (5) signal the tone of this essay? Should they be read literally, ironically, metaphorically, or some other way?

2. Be sure you know how to define the following words: generate, nuclear, toxins (para. 1); lagoons, contamination (3); buffering, neutralize (6); combustion (7).

SUGGESTIONS FOR WRITING

1. Write a satirical essay in which you propose the solution to a problem or the means to an end. Make sure your tone signals your satiric intent. Describe your solution in detail, using time-markers to indicate the order of steps or events.

2. Write an essay defending and justifying the use of nuclear power plants, pesticides, or another pollutant Saukko mentions. This essay will require some research because you will need to argue that the benefits of these methods outweigh their hazardous and destructive effects. Be sure to support your claims with factual information and statistics. Or, approach the issue from the same point of view that Saukko did, and argue against the use of nuclear power plants or pesticides. Substantiate your argument with data and facts, and be sure to propose alternative sources of power or alternative methods of insect control.

3. CRITICAL WRITING. Albert Gore, Jr. (in "Ships in the Desert," p. 650), and Linnea Saukko make essentially the same point, but in very different ways. In an essay, COMPARE AND CONTRAST these two essays' TONES, uses of EVIDENCE, and effectiveness. (Be sure to address Saukko's use of IRONY.) Which is the more successful piece? Why?

4. CONNECTIONS. Saukko addresses a global problem, but it is one for which the United States and other prosperous industrial nations bear large responsibility. Consider Slavenka Drakulić's concern, in "Some Doubts About Fur Coats" (p. 664), that "the Third World will have to pay the price for the 'development' and high standard of living of the First World" (para. 9) — in other words, that the Third World will have to forgo such a standard of living for the sake of the environment,

while the First World may even continue on its polluting path. What might Saukko make of Drakulić's concern? Would she exempt any group or region from change? Should the desires of Third World peoples for a higher standard of living be subordinated to the need to clean up the environment? What do you think about this issue?

LINNEA SAUKKO ON WRITING

"After I have chosen a topic," says Linnea Saukko, "the easiest thing for me to do is to write about how I really feel about it. The goal of 'How to Poison the Earth' was to inform people, or more specifically, to open their eyes.

"As soon as I decided on my topic, I made a list of all the types of pollution and I sat down and basically wrote the paper in less than two hours. The information seemed to pour from me onto the page. Of course I did a lot of editing afterward, but I never changed the idea and the tone that I started with."

FOR DISCUSSION

When have you had the experience of writing on a subject that compelled your words to pour forth with little effort? What was the subject? What did you learn from this experience?

SLAVENKA DRAKULIĆ

SLAVENKA DRAKULIĆ is a journalist, commentator, and novelist in Croatia, one of the states of the former communist Yugoslavia. The daughter of Croats and once married to a Serb, she writes from a war-torn land, personalizing and humanizing conflicts that have dominated the news. Her most recent book of essays, *The Balkan Express: Fragments from the Other Side of War* (1993), fits, in Drakulić's words, "somewhere in between hard facts and analysis and personal stories, because the war is happening not only at the front, but everywhere and to us all." Her previous nonfiction work in English, *How We Survived Communism and Even Laughed* (1991), details the physical and emotional deprivations of life under decades of communism. Drakulić is a contributor to *The Nation* and *The New Republic*, a member of the advisory board of *Ms.* magazine, and a columnist for the magazine *Danas* in Zagreb, Croatia. She has also published two novels, *Holograms of Fear* (1992) and *Marble Skin* (1994).

Some Doubts About Fur Coats

For people throughout the world who are deprived of meat, automobiles, and other goods we consider necessities, environmentalism can seem a luxury. This is Drakulić's point in the following essay from *How We Survived Communism and Even Laughed.* In the West, a fur coat is a badge of wealth or a trophy of senseless cruelty. In Eastern Europe, it is these and more.

"Some Doubts About Fur Coats" is an ARGUMENT about environmentalism built mainly on EXAMPLES that are brief NARRATIVES and on Drakulić's ANALYSIS of their significance. Besides these methods, be alert for DESCRIPTION, CAUSE AND EFFECT, and COMPARISON AND CONTRAST.

Whether winter or summer, streetcar 14 never comes. They say   1
it is because it was produced in Czechoslovakia. PRAHA, OBOROVY PODNIK, it says on a small metal plate inside. You know, a communist product — what can you expect from it? Our experience tells us that it can't stand either too much rain or too much sunshine; it runs only on nice days when the temperature is between 17 and 22 degrees Celsius and you are not in a hurry. But because it was December — the middle of winter — just before Christmas, drizzling, and incidentally I was in a hurry, number 14 was naturally nowhere in sight.

Instead, in my sight was a lady, a lady in a splendid long fur coat —
a silver fox, a wolf, a bear, or some other poor animal. Because of
that coat, I couldn't miss her, even if I wanted to. There was a time
when I'd wanted such a thing myself.

Years ago, I fell into the trap of buying a fur coat. It was winter   2
and a cold wind was blowing from the harbor as I spotted it walking
through the Church Street flea market in Cambridge, Massachusetts.
It was an old-fashioned mink coat that caught my eye from a distance,
like something from a thirties Hollywood movie. I knew it was just
waiting for me, for the right alibi to buy it. It didn't take me long to
make one up: It was so cheap, compared to the prices in my country,
where you can't buy a second-hand fur and therefore new ones are
very expensive. Perhaps I can finally afford it, I thought. I put it on.
In the little mirror that a young woman held up for me, I didn't look
like a sick, divorced, single mother, or an East European woman at
all, but like the person I wanted to be. That's what I liked so much
about it: It turned me instantly into another person.

I was very well aware that for that money — I remember it cost   3
$90, but the woman reduced it to $75 — I could buy books, something that I definitely needed much more. I also was aware that that
had been my plan before I saw the coat. I was on my way to the
Reading International Bookstore right there, at the corner of that
very street. On the other hand, I knew that buying a fur coat for
such an amount back home was absolutely out of the question; it
would have cost me at least twice my monthly income. For a moment — but only a moment — I thought about the carefully composed book list in my purse — then I looked in the mirror again and
took out $80. Somewhere at the back of my mind there was one last
argument left. As if someone was whispering in my ear, I heard that
tiny little voice: "What about dead animals? Do you really want to
wear their furs — you, the vegetarian, animal lover, ecologist?" As
artificial fur was not yet in vogue and the animals in question were
long dead, I simply ignored the weak voice of conscience in my head.
It just couldn't match my whole Eastern European background, which
was urging: Take it, take it, here's your chance.

I have worn the coat, forgetting the whole episode. It was while   4
I was in New York in early 1989 that I remembered it again. Another
episode reminded me of it. It happened in Beograd that winter, when
a young girl, J. Simović, climbed onto bus number 26. It was cold
and she had on an old mink coat. At eleven o'clock in the morning
the bus was almost empty, only a few old people, a housewife or two,
and two young couples. "Where did you get your mink coat, pussy-

cat?" asked one young man. "Did your father buy it for you?" The girl didn't answer. She stood by the door, with her back to him. Then the four of them became more aggressive. They surrounded her, one took out his lighter, lit it, and grabbed her sleeve, as if he wanted to test whether it was a real fur or not. The girl withdrew, looking helplessly around the bus. But people in the bus — even the driver — pretended not to notice what was going on. Then the bus stopped and J. Simović was kicked out in the street. "Out!" yelled one of the girls. "If you can afford a mink coat, you can afford a taxi!"

I read this episode in an article from the newspaper *Politika* that 5 a friend from Beograd sent me, as an example of what is going on back home: growing poverty and frustration, leading to the revival of the egalitarian syndrome. I noticed that the reporter chose to stress that the girl was wearing an *old* fur coat. What he meant by that, using it as an argument in her defense, was that she didn't deserve what happened to her because she wasn't really rich, she was as poor as the aggressors, and therefore she was not to blame. But by saying that, he justified the same logic of equal distribution of poverty that the two young couples from the bus used in molesting her. Yet the word "old" in that context had more than one meaning: Perhaps the fur coat was inherited? Then, if it belonged to her grandmother, it meant that she came from a prewar, wealthy bourgeois family — one more reason to be hostile toward her. But if the reporter, in his wish to protect the girl, wasn't accurate in his reporting, and she was wearing a *new* mink coat, then perhaps her father really did buy it for her. In that case, she was a daughter of a new class, the so-called red bourgeoisie, and again despised as a symbol. But in spite of a profound, decade-long indoctrination, much as it was hated, a fur coat was an object of envy at the same time. A fur coat, whether old or new, is a visible symbol of wealth and luxury everywhere — the only difference is that in Yugoslavia and Eastern Europe wealth and luxury were for a long time illegal (and they become illegal every time the country sinks into a deep economic and political crisis, when, for a moment, postrevolutionary egalitarianism replaces a real solution). And even those who would like to believe in egalitarianism must ask themselves why we have to be equal only in poverty.

That same winter my friend Jasmina from Zagreb visited New 6 York, and one afternoon we went downtown for some windowshopping in SoHo. It was cold — five degrees below zero — and we were wandering around the stores. Due to the fact that we had no money, we were enjoying the expensive clothes just as someone would enjoy an exhibition of modern art. We had such a good feeling of detachment, like when you are looking at a Van Gogh painting: You love it, no matter that you know you won't be able to buy it in your lifetime. An American acquaintance advised Jasmina to go to the museums — MOMA or the Metropolitan — that she had not seen yet. "Sure I will," she answered, "but we, too, have museums. It's the beautiful shops that we don't have, and I need to see them first." We laughed at the prices, amusing ourselves by converting them into dinars. We browsed through delicate silk blouses and crazy, glittering evening dresses. We tried on Italian shoes, pretending that we were going to buy them, but they were just too little or too big or we wanted another, nonexistent color, or . . . We loved playing those "buying games," choosing endlessly, behaving as if we could buy if only we wanted to, discovering an element of playfulness, of fun in consumerism.

Either that day was too cold — like the day in Cambridge — or   7
else at some point Jasmina lost her sense of humor. As we entered the Canal Jean Company on Broadway at Canal Street, she stopped in the fur department, looking at the coats there as if she was drawn to them by some magic power. "Look, Jasmina, you don't need a coat," I tried to convince her, as if need has anything to do with buying, especially in New York. "No, no, I'm just looking at how unbelievably cheap they are," she answered, hesitatingly. It was all so familiar, her argument, her wish to have one . . . She was right, of course, they were cheap second-hand fur coats, ranging from $20 to about $100. And she didn't need one, she wanted one. She looked at me seriously. "Why shouldn't I buy such a coat? You know I could never afford it back home." By now, all the fun of our shopping spree was gone; I realized this was not a game anymore. She had on a $50 astrakhan that looked as if it was made for her. Her red lips, her pale face, her long curly brown hair looked gorgeous as she spun around in front of the mirror. "You look lovely," I admitted halfheartedly.

We stood there, amid racks and racks of coats — foxes, wolves,   8
ermines, minks, real tigers, sheep — smelling of old fur, mothballs, dry-cleaning chemicals, and stagnant, unaired cupboards. And we both knew what it was about. This was an opportunity to buy something more than a simple fur coat: It was an opportunity to buy an image, a soft, warm wrapping that will protect you from the terrible vulgar gray Varteks or Standard konfekcija coats you have been wearing all your life, an illusory ticket to your dreams. While we could easily toy with expensive dresses or shoes, the affordable fur coat was just too big a challenge. Of course, I tried the same last argument that years ago hadn't worked with me: "Remember a poster we saw

in some English newspaper, a woman dragging her bleeding fur coat? It says: 'It takes thirty dumb animals to make this coat, and only one to wear it,' or something like that." Jasmina stood still for a while, then she said: "Yes, I remember, but I don't think that you can apply First World ecological philosophy to Third World women." With that, she bought the astrakhan coat.

Her words made me remember a TV interview by an Italian 9 journalist with Fidel Castro, back in 1987. Surprisingly enough, they touched on ecology. Castro said he won't let his people have one car each. It is simply not possible — not only for economical but for ecological reasons. There are too many cars in the world anyway, he said, the whole of Europe is suffocating in cars. I was sitting in a small rented apartment in Perugia. It was early evening, the air was still hot, and sweat was pouring down my temples. But as Castro uttered that sentence, I shivered with cold. At that very moment, I detected for the first time in his words a frightening totalitarian idea in ecology — or better, the totalitarian use of ecology. He was asking his people to give up a better standard of living, even before they tasted it, in order to save the planet, to renounce in advance something that was glorified as the idea of progress. It seemed to me that asking for postconsumer ecological consciousness in a poor, preconsumer society was nothing but an act of the totalitarian mind. We do live on the same planet, I thought, as his voice faded away, but not in the same world. It is precisely the Third World people who have every right to demand that the Western European and American white middle class give up *their* standard of living and redistribute wealth so we can all survive. Otherwise, the Third World will have to pay the price for the "development" and high standard of living of the First World in the way Castro proposed, and he definitely won't be the only one to blame.

For obvious reasons, Castro didn't mention furs in his interview, 10 but the idea is the same, particularly because the ecological way of seeing the world is forced upon Third World people — in this case, women — in the name of "higher goals," a very familiar notion in the communist part of the world. And I can hardly think of anything more repulsive than that. So, what are women expected to do, when they see it as just an old ideological trick? Before they give up fur coats, they certainly want to have them, at least for a while; and I'm afraid that no propaganda about poor little animals will help before fur coats have become at least a choice.

This very winter I stumbled into the same situation again, this 11 time not in New York and not with a friend, but in my own house with my mother. She had decided to buy a fur. She was saving money for it, calculating carefully where and how to buy it, and even found a shop that gives three months' credit. I felt like a character in a classic, well-rehearsed play. "Mother," I told her, in an over-rational, highly pedagogical tone of voice, "you live on the coast, it's not even cold enough there." Mother looked at me as if I were speaking a foreign language. And I was: There she was, an old lady now. Fifty years ago, she was a young beauty from a wealthy family who was to marry a factory owner's son. Then she met a partisan, Tito's warrior, "a man from the woods," as my grandfather used to say.[1] Not only was he a People's Army officer, but he was hopelessly poor. But my mother married him against her parents' will, leaving her rich fiancé behind (not a bad move, in fact, because soon enough he wasn't rich anymore; his factory was nationalized by the same partisans and communists, "men from the woods," that my father belonged to). Her whole life she not only could not, but was afraid to buy a fur coat because of my father's true communist morals. Now he was dead. She was too old really to enjoy it. Nevertheless, she had decided to buy one. What right did I have to tell her not to? What did I know of her life, of her frustrations and renunciations — of the clothes bought with a monthly ration card, of her desire to be a woman, not just the sexless human being propaganda was teaching her to become? It seemed to me that I just couldn't find the right words and arguments to fight her will to buy a fur coat. I felt helpless — and guilty of the same desire, too. Sitting at the kitchen table, this is what she finally said: "You know, I have wanted to buy a fur like this for forty years." She said that as if it was the ultimate argument, the final judgment, her last word about it.

Standing at the streetcar stop and looking at the lady dressed in foxes (I finally recognized the fur), I remembered all those doubts about fur coats. I hardly noticed two teen-agers, a boy and a girl of about fifteen, standing there, holding hands, and giggling. At first they whispered, pointing at the fox lady. Then they deliberately raised their voices. "Just imagine," the girl said, "that this fur coat starts bleeding somewhere near the collar. Do you think the lady would notice?" The boy chuckled. "Oh, yes, I'd like to see that — a tiny red stream of blood dripping from each animal that was killed to make this stupid coat." She heard them — she must have, they wanted to be heard. But her face was stone. They were not egalitarian-

12

---

[1]Marshal Tito led partisan troops in Yugoslavia during World War II and led the Yugoslavian government until his death in 1980. — Eds.

minded, for sure; they were too well dressed for that. Even if they were the same age as the two couples in the Beograd bus, these kids were of an entirely different breed — a new breed around here, I dare say — real ecologists. Perhaps to them and their peers their ecological consciousness is a bigger sign of prestige than a fur coat. Perhaps they feel on more equal terms with the world. I admit I saw the future in them. But they were aggressive and I didn't like it, in spite of their concern for animals. On the other hand, perhaps they are too young to understand that human beings are an endangered species and that they too have a right to protection — particularly in some parts of the world. I hope they learn this soon.

QUESTIONS ON MEANING

1. What is the function of the "buying games" Drakulić and her friend play (para. 6)? How do you explain their fascination with consumerism?
2. Drakulić's friend Jasmina says that one can't "apply First World ecological philosophy to Third World women" (para. 8). What does she mean by "First World" and "Third World"? Why can't the philosophy of one place be applied to the other?
3. What does Drakulić mean when she says that "human beings are an endangered species" (para. 12)? What does this assertion have to do with her ARGUMENT?
4. Drakulić's THESIS is complex. Can you state it in one or two sentences?
5. What do you think is this essay's PURPOSE?

QUESTIONS ON WRITING STRATEGY

1. How familiar does Drakulić require her AUDIENCE to be with conditions in the former Yugoslavia? What does she tell readers about those conditions?
2. Drakulić frames her essay with one story involving a woman in a fur coat on a corner. Why do you think she chooses this particular story for her INTRODUCTION and CONCLUSION?
3. When Drakulić wrote this essay, Yugoslavia, like the rest of Eastern Europe, had already begun to turn away from communism. Is the essay dated, then, or are the issues Drakulić raises still current? Why?
4. MIXED METHODS. Drakulić uses EXAMPLES to support her ARGUMENT about fur coats. But fur coats are themselves an example. What of?
5. MIXED METHODS. What does each of Drakulić's NARRATIVE examples contribute to her argument? Examine her ANALYSIS of each one in formulating your answer.

QUESTIONS ON LANGUAGE

1. What is the meaning of the phrase "totalitarian use of ecology" (para. 9)? Consult a dictionary if you need to, and study Drakulić's discussion. Why does Drakulić find the concept "frightening"? Do you?
2. Give definitions of these other key words in Drakulić's essay: egalitarian, bourgeois, indoctrination (para. 5); illusory (8); ideological, propaganda (10); pedagogical, partisan, renunciations (11).
3. Describe Drakulić's TONE in paragraphs 9–10. How does her choice of words create the tone? Do you find it effective?
4. What is the EFFECT of the many place names Drakulić mentions? If you do not know where all these places are, consult an atlas.

SUGGESTIONS FOR WRITING

1. Drakulić describes "the element of playfulness, of fun in consumerism" (para. 6). To what extent is this feeling experienced by Americans as well? Why? Do you perceive any downside to consumerism, on either a personal or a societal level? Consider these questions in writing an essay on consumerism in America.
2. Argue for or against the right to wear a fur coat without being verbally attacked. Direct your argument to someone of the opposite persuasion.
3. CRITICAL WRITING. "It is precisely the Third World people who have every right to demand that the Western European and American white middle class give up *their* standard of living and redistribute wealth so we can all survive," argues Drakulić (para. 9). What ASSUMPTIONS is this statement based on? Do you agree or disagree? In an essay, spell out your ANALYSIS and support your own opinion.
4. CONNECTIONS. In "Waking Up the Rake" (p. 672), Linda Hogan says that "in whatever we do, the brushing of hair, the cleaning of cages, we begin to see the larger order of things . . . the natural laws that exist apart from our own written ones" (para. 18). Do you think Drakulić is sensitive to this order, too? Taking Drakulić's paragraphs 9–10 as a point of departure, write an essay on what you perceive to be Drakulić's own ecological vision.

LINDA HOGAN

Linda Hogan draws on Native American traditions to write about the interconnectedness of humankind and nature. She was born in 1947 in Denver and received a B.A. (1973) and an M.A. (1978) from the University of Colorado. Her published works include *Calling Myself Home* (poetry, 1979); *A Piece of the Moon* (play, 1981), which won the Five Civilized Tribes Playwriting Award; *Eclipse* (poetry, 1983); *Seeing Through the Sun* (poetry, 1985), which received the American Book Award from the Before Columbus Foundation; *The Big Woman* (stories, 1987); and *Mean Spirit* (novel, 1990). In addition, Hogan has edited collections of stories, written several screenplays, and contributed to many anthologies and literary magazines. She has taught English at the University of Minnesota and Colorado College and is now an associate professor at the University of Colorado.

Waking Up the Rake

Hogan finds large meanings in the smallest manifestations, here the healing of an owl, the decaying of a mouse, the raking of the ground. This essay first appeared in *Parabola* magazine in 1988 and then was reprinted in *Sisters of the Earth* (1991), an anthology of women's writings about nature.

Reading "Waking Up the Rake," you will probably be struck most by the author's powers of DESCRIPTION: Details of sound, sight, and touch abound. But the essay is also largely NARRATIVE, and Hogan uses both these methods in the service of CAUSE AND EFFECT: What does work do for us, and why? She also draws significantly on DEFINITION.

In the still dark mornings, my grandmother would rise up from 1 her bed and put wood in the stove. When the fire began to burn, she would sit in front of its warmth and let down her hair. It had never been cut and it knotted down in two long braids. When I was fortunate enough to be there, in those red Oklahoma mornings, I would wake up with her, stand behind her chair, and pull the brush through the long strands of her hair. It cascaded down her back, down over the chair, and touched the floor.

We were the old and the new, bound together in front of the 2 snapping fire, woven like a lifetime's tangled growth of hair. I saw my future in her body and face, and her past was alive in me. We

were morning people, and in all of earth's mornings the new inter-
twines with the old. Even new, a day itself is ancient, old with earth's
habit of turning over and over again.

Years later, I was sick, and I went to a traditional healer. The   3
healer was dark and thin and radiant. The first night I was there, she
also lit a fire. We sat before it, smelling the juniper smoke. She asked
me to tell her everything, my life spoken in words, a case history of
living, with its dreams and losses, the scars and wounds we all bear
from being in the world. She smoked me with cedar smoke, wrapped
a sheet around me, and put me to bed, gently, like a mother caring
for her child.

The next morning she nudged me awake and took me outside to   4
pray. We faced east where the sun was beginning its journey on our
side of earth.

The following morning in red dawn, we went outside and prayed.   5
The sun was a full orange eye rising up the air. The morning after
that we did the same, and on Sunday we did likewise.

The next time I visited her it was a year later, and again we went   6
through the same prayers, standing outside facing the early sun. On
the last morning I was there, she left for her job in town. Before
leaving, she said, "Our work is our altar."

Those words have remained with me.   7

Now I am a disciple of birds. The birds that I mean are eagles,   8
owls, and hawks. I clean cages at the Birds of Prey Rehabilitation
Foundation. It is the work I wanted to do, in order to spend time
inside the gentle presence of the birds.

There is a Sufi saying that goes something like this: "Yes, worship   9
God, go to church, sing praises, but first tie your camel to the post."
This cleaning is the work of tying the camel to a post.

I pick up the carcasses and skin of rats, mice, and of rabbits.   10
Some of them have been turned inside out by the sharp-beaked eaters,
so that the leathery flesh becomes a delicately veined coat for the
inner fur. It is a boneyard. I rake the smooth fragments of bones.
Sometimes there is a leg or shank of deer to be picked up.

In this boneyard, the still-red vertebrae lie on the ground beside   11
an open rib cage. The remains of a rabbit, a small intestinal casing,
holds excrement like beads in a necklace. And there are the clean,
oval pellets the birds spit out, filled with fur, bone fragments and now
and then, a delicate sharp claw that looks as if it were woven inside.
A feather, light and soft, floats down a current of air, and it is also
picked up.

Over time, the narrow human perspective from which we view   12
things expands. A deer carcass begins to look beautiful and rich in
its torn redness, the muscle and bone exposed in the shape life took
on for a while as it walked through meadows and drank at creeks.

And the bone fragments have their own stark beauty, the clean   13
white jaw bones with ivory teeth small as the head of a pin still in
them. I think of medieval physicians trying to learn about our private,
hidden bodies by cutting open the stolen dead and finding the splen-
dor inside, the grace of every red organ, and the smooth, gleaming
bone.

This work is an apprenticeship, and the birds are the teachers.   14
Sweet-eyed barn owls, such taskmasters, asking us to be still and slow
and to move in time with their rhythms, not our own. The short-
eared owls with their startling yellow eyes require the full presence
of a human. The marsh hawks, behind their branches, watch our
every move.

There is a silence needed here before a person enters the bordered   15
world the birds inhabit, so we stop and compose ourselves before
entering their doors, and we listen to the musical calls of the eagles,
the sound of wings in air, the way their feet with sharp claws, many
larger than our own hands, grab hold of a perch. Then we know we
are ready to enter, and they are ready for us.

The most difficult task the birds demand is that we learn to be   16
equal to them, to feel our way into an intelligence that is different
from our own. A friend, awed at the thought of working with eagles,
said, "Imagine knowing an eagle." I answered her honestly, "It isn't
so much that we know the eagles. It's that they know us."

And they know that we are apart from them, that as humans we   17
have somehow fallen from our animal grace, and because of that we
maintain a distance from them, though it is not always a distance of
heart. The places we inhabit, even sharing a common earth, must
remain distinct and separate. It was our presence that brought most
of them here in the first place, nearly all of them injured in a clash
with the human world. They have been shot, or hit by cars, trapped
in leg hold traps, poisoned, ensnared in wire fences. To ensure their
survival, they must remember us as the enemies that we are. We are
the embodiment of a paradox; we are the wounders and we are the
healers.

There are human lessons to be learned here, in the work. Fritjof   18
Capra wrote: "Doing work that has to be done over and over again

helps us to recognize the natural cycles of growth and decay, of birth and death, and thus become aware of the dynamic order of the universe." And it is true, in whatever we do, the brushing of hair, the cleaning of cages, we begin to see the larger order of things. In this place, there is a constant coming to terms with both the sacred place life occupies, and with death. Like one of those early physicians who discovered the strange, inner secrets of our human bodies, I'm filled with awe at the very presence of life, not just the birds, but a horse contained in its living fur, a dog alive and running. What a marvel it is, the fine shape life takes in all of us. It is equally marvelous that life is quickly turned back to the earth-colored ants and the soft white maggots that are time's best and closest companions. To sit with the eagles and their flute-like songs, listening to the longer flute of wind sweep through the lush grasslands, is to begin to know the natural laws that exist apart from our own written ones.

One of those laws, that we carry deep inside us, is intuition. It 19 is lodged in a place even the grave-robbing doctors could not discover. It's a blood-written code that directs us through life. The founder of this healing center, Sigrid Ueblacker, depends on this inner knowing. She watches, listens, and feels her way to an understanding of each eagle and owl. This vision, as I call it, directs her own daily work at healing the injured birds and returning them to the wild.

"Sweep the snow away," she tells me. "The Swainson's hawks 20 should be in Argentina this time of year and should not have to stand in the snow."

I sweep. 21

And that is in the winter when the hands ache from the cold, 22 and the water freezes solid and has to be broken out for the birds, fresh buckets carried over icy earth from the well. In summer, it's another story. After only a few hours the food begins to move again, as if resurrected to life. A rabbit shifts a bit. A mouse turns. You could say that they have been resurrected, only with a life other than the one that left them. The moving skin swarms with flies and their offspring, ants, and a few wasps, busy at their own daily labor.

Even aside from the expected rewards for this work, such as seeing 23 an eagle healed and winging across the sky it fell from, there are others. An occasional snake, beautiful and sleek, finds its way into the cage one day, eats a mouse and is too fat to leave, so we watch its long muscular life stretched out in the tall grasses. Or, another summer day, taking branches to be burned with a pile of wood near the little creek, a large turtle with a dark and shining shell slips soundlessly into the water, its presence a reminder of all the lives beyond these that occupy us.

One green morning, an orphaned owl perches nervously above   24
me while I clean. Its downy feathers are roughed out. It appears to
be twice its size as it clacks its beak at me, warning me: Stay back.
Then, fearing me the way we want it to, it bolts off the perch and
flies, landing by accident onto the wooden end of my rake, before it
sees that a human is an extension of the tool, and it flies again to a
safer place, while I return to raking.

The word *rake* means to gather or heap up, to smooth the broken   25
ground. And that's what this work is, all of it, the smoothing over
of broken ground, the healing of the severed trust we humans hold
with earth. We gather it back together again with great care, take
the broken pieces and fragments and return them to the sky. It is
work at the borderland between species, at the boundary between
injury and healing.

There is an art to raking, a very fine art, one with rhythm in it,   26
and life. On the days I do it well, the rake wakes up. Wood that
came from dark dense forests seems to return to life. The water that
rose up through the rings of that wood, the minerals of earth mined
upward by the burrowing tree roots, all come alive. My own fragile
hand touches the wood, a hand full of my own life, including that
which rose each morning early to watch the sun return from the
other side of the planet. Over time, these hands will smooth the
rake's wooden handle down to a sheen.

Raking. It is a labor round and complete, smooth and new as an   27
egg, and the rounding seasons of the world revolving in time and
space. All things, even our own heartbeats and sweat, are in it, part
of it. And that work, that watching the turning over of life, becomes
a road into what is essential. Work is the country of hands, and they
want to live there in the dailiness of it, the repetition that is time's
language of prayer, a common tongue. Everything is there, in that
language, in the humblest of labor. The rake wakes up and the healing
is in it. The shadows of leaves that once fell beneath the tree the
handle came from are in that labor, and the rabbits that passed this
way, on the altar of our work. And when the rake wakes up, all
earth's gods are reborn and they dance and sing in the dusty air
around us.

QUESTIONS ON MEANING

1. What does the healer mean when she says, "Our work is our altar" (para. 6)?
2. Hogan says that the owl fears her "the way we want it to" (para. 24). What does she mean? Whom does she mean by "we" here?
3. What are some of the "lessons to be learned" from Hogan's work with the birds?
4. What is Hogan's THESIS? Her PURPOSE?

QUESTIONS ON WRITING STRATEGY

1. How do the events in the INTRODUCTION (paras. 1–6) relate to the rest of the essay? Why do you think Hogan did not opt for a more straight-forward, conventional introduction?
2. Hogan quotes several sources: the healer (para. 6); a Sufi saying (9); a friend (16); Fritjof Capra, a physicist (18); and Sigrid Ueblacker, who runs the rehabilitation center (20). What does each quotation contribute to the essay?
3. MIXED METHODS. Hogan combines NARRATION with DESCRIPTION to convey her feelings and experiences. Choose three descriptive IMAGES that seem to you particularly effective. What kinds of information do they convey? Why do they work so well?
4. MIXED METHODS. As part of her examination of the EFFECTS of work, Hogan introduces a DEFINITION of *rake* (para. 25). To what extent is this definition literal? (Can you find all of it in your dictionary?) How does this definition function for Hogan?

QUESTIONS ON LANGUAGE

1. How does Hogan use repetition to create a mood?
2. Supply definitions of the following words: prey (para. 8); Sufi (9); vertebrae, excrement (11).
3. Why is the phrase "gentle presence of the birds" (para. 8) surprising when applied to hawks, eagles, and owls? In what ways are these birds "gentle"?
4. Where does Hogan use PERSONIFICATION to depict the birds? What does she accomplish with it?

SUGGESTIONS FOR WRITING

1. Describe a familiar small task that, as Hogan says of raking, involves "a very fine art, one with rhythm in it, and life" (para. 26). It could be

weeding, mowing, tuning a guitar, ironing, chopping vegetables, tuning a car engine, or any other work. What does it take to do the task well? What feelings do you have about it? Consider following Hogan's example by using FIGURES OF SPEECH to describe the work and your feelings.

2. "This work is an apprenticeship, and the birds are the teachers," writes Hogan (para. 14). Discuss the roles animals play in our understanding of the world. What can we learn from animals? How is our observation of animals inadequate for understanding our own, human experience? Use many EXAMPLES to support your essay, or, if you prefer, use a single detailed example of an animal you know well.

3. CRITICAL WRITING. What ASSUMPTIONS underlie the statement "Our work is our altar" (para. 6) and Hogan's use of it (27)? Do Hogan's claims for work apply to all physical labor or all work of any kind (such as desk jobs and service jobs)? Could Hogan's ideas help anyone get more out of any job, or are they limited to raking in a bird-rehabilitation center? Write an essay considering these questions, supporting your own ideas with EVIDENCE from your experience, observation, and reading.

4. CONNECTIONS. COMPARE AND CONTRAST Hogan's essay and Albert Gore's "Ships in the Desert" (p. 650). Both authors use the first-PERSON *I* in their essays. How do their self-presentations differ? In what ways are they similar? What are the differences and similarities in their relationships to nature? In their understanding of ecology? Whose argument do you find more convincing?

LINDA HOGAN ON WRITING

For the biographical reference work *Contemporary Authors,* Linda Hogan gave simple voice to her motivation as a writer: "My writing comes from and goes back to the community, both the human and the global community. I am interested in the deepest questions, those of spirit, of shelter, of growth and movement toward peace and liberation. My main interest at the moment is in wildlife rehabilitation and studying the relationship between humans and other species, and trying to create world survival skills out of what I learn from this."

FOR DISCUSSION

This statement is quite abstract. Judging from "Waking Up the Rake," what occurs during Hogan's writing process to help her realize her goals?

ADDITIONAL WRITING TOPICS

Our Place in the Environment

1. In his essay "Ships in the Desert" (p. 650), Albert Gore, Jr., describes the environmental crisis as a "violent collision between human civilization and the earth." Who does Gore seem to think is responsible for this collision? Business and industry? Government? Individuals? To whom do Mark Crispin Miller ("Dow Recycles Reality," p. 277), Linnea Saukko ("How to Poison the Earth," p. 659), and Slavenka Drakulić ("Some Doubts About Fur Coats," p. 664) seem to assign the blame? Who do you think is responsible? Why?

2. Linda Hogan's "Waking Up the Rake" offers one person's view of our relationship to the natural world. In a short essay, compare Hogan's essay with Virginia Woolf's "The Death of the Moth" (p. 101) and Annie Dillard's "Death of a Moth" (p. 107). What, in each writer's view, is the essence of that relationship? How does each writer's use of language reinforce her view?

3. What *is* our place in the environment? What are our limitations? What frontiers may we yet cross? What are our rights and responsibilities? Explain your own view, but support it as you see fit by drawing on other essays in this book that address this question directly or indirectly: Virginia Woolf's "The Death of the Moth" (p. 101); Annie Dillard's "Death of a Moth" (p. 107); E. B. White's "Once More to the Lake" (p. 120); Emily Dickinson's "A narrow Fellow in the Grass" (p. 129); Marvin Harris's "How Our Skins Got Their Color" (p. 241); Stephen Jay Gould's "Sex, Drugs, Disasters, and the Extinction of Dinosaurs" (p. 393); and Gore's, Saukko's, Drakulić's, and Hogan's essays in this chapter.

14

DIVERSITY IN THE CURRICULUM

In recent years, it's been one of the most hotly debated questions in American education: Should courses of study be modified to reflect the increasingly diverse backgrounds and interests of students? As the authors in this chapter remind us, the stakes are high: liberal education, national unity, justice, truth. We have found three calm voices among the raucous noise of the controversy. Ishmael Reed, in "America: The Multinational Society," argues that cultural pluralism is nothing to fear — is, indeed, a source of strength. Arthur M. Schlesinger, Jr., in "The Cult of Ethnicity, Good and Bad," warns that pluralism could undermine the nation's identity. And Katha Pollitt, striking a balance in "Why Do We Read?," finds much to be said for either side but a big problem left unexamined by them both.

ISHMAEL REED

Born in Chattanooga, Tennessee, in 1938 and raised in Buffalo, New York, ISHMAEL REED began writing in elementary school and as a teenager had work published. He attended the State University of New York at Buffalo. In the years since, Reed has become known as a writer given to experimentation and provocation. He has produced nine novels, four volumes of poetry, three plays, and countless songs. Some notable works include the poetry collections *catechism of d neoamerican hoodoo church* (1971) and *Conjure* (1972); the novels *The Free-Lance Pallbearers* (1967), *Mumbo Jumbo* (1972), *The Terrible Threes* (1989), and *Japanese by Spring* (1993); and the essay collection *Writin' Is Fightin'* (1988). A supporter of young writers from all cultures through his publishing imprint, I. Reed Books, Reed has also taught writing at many colleges and universities. He now lives in California and teaches at the University of California at Berkeley.

America:
The Multinational Society

As its title suggests, this essay holds that Americans need not be afraid of immigrants and others who may seem to threaten unity and stability: The transformation to a multicultural society is already occurring, and, Reed thinks, it is making us a stronger nation. Reed's opinion is perhaps unsurprising from one whose own ancestry is part African American, part Native American, part French, and part Irish. The essay was first published in a periodical, *San Francisco Focus*, and was then collected in *Writin' Is Fightin'*.

"America: The Multinational Society" is an ARGUMENT in favor of a certain way of viewing cultural pluralism. Two other methods figure prominently in Reed's argument: numerous EXAMPLES, some extended, some very brief, and CAUSE AND EFFECT, especially in the influence of the Puritans.

At the annual Lower East Side Jewish Festival yesterday, a Chinese woman ate a pizza slice in front of Ty Thuan Duc's Vietnamese grocery store. Beside her a Spanish-speaking family patronized a cart with two signs: "Italian Ices" and "Kosher by Rabbi Alper." And after the pastrami ran out, everybody ate knishes.

— *New York Times*, 23 June 1983

On the day before Memorial Day, 1983, a poet called me to describe a city he had just visited. He said that one section included mosques, built by the Islamic people who dwelled there. Attending his reading, he said, were large numbers of Hispanic people, forty thousand of whom lived in the same city. He was not talking about a fabled city located in some mysterious region of the world. The city he'd visited was Detroit.

A few months before, as I was leaving Houston, Texas, I heard 2 it announced on the radio that Texas's largest minority was Mexican-American, and though a foundation recently issued a report critical of bilingual education, the taped voice used to guide the passengers on the air trams connecting terminals in Dallas Airport is in both Spanish and English. If the trend continues, a day will come when it will be difficult to travel through some sections of the country without hearing commands in both English and Spanish; after all, for some western states, Spanish was the first written language and the Spanish style lives on in the western way of life.

Shortly after my Texas trip, I sat in an auditorium located on the 3 campus of the University of Wisconsin at Milwaukee as a Yale professor — whose original work on the influence of African cultures upon those of the Americas has led to his ostracism from some monocultural intellectual circles — walked up and down the aisle, like an old-time southern evangelist, dancing and drumming the top of the lectern, illustrating his points before some serious Afro-American intellectuals and artists who cheered and applauded his performance and his mastery of information. The professor was "white." After his lecture, he joined a group of Milwaukeeans in a conversation. All of the participants spoke Yoruban, though only the professor had ever traveled to Africa.

One of the artists told me that his paintings, which included 4 African and Afro-American mythological symbols and imagery, were hanging in the local McDonald's restaurant. The next day I went to McDonald's and snapped pictures of smiling youngsters eating hamburgers below paintings that could grace the walls of any of the country's leading museums. The manager of the local McDonald's said, "I don't know what you boys are doing, but I like it," as he commissioned the local painters to exhibit in his restaurant.

Such blurring of cultural styles occurs in everyday life in the 5 United States to a greater extent than anyone can imagine and is probably more prevalent than the sensational conflict between people of different backgrounds that is played up and often encouraged by the media. The result is what the Yale professor Robert Thompson referred to as a cultural bouillabaisse, yet members of the nation's present educational and cultural Elect still cling to the notion that the United States belongs to some vaguely defined entity they refer to as "Western civilization," by which they mean, presumably, a civilization created by the people of Europe, as if Europe can be viewed in monolithic terms. Is Beethoven's Ninth Symphony, which includes Turkish marches, a part of Western civilization, or the late nineteenth- and twentieth-century French paintings, whose creators were influenced by Japanese art? And what of the Cubists, through whom the influence of African art changed modern painting, or the Surrealists, who were so impressed with the art of the Pacific Northwest Indians that, in their map of North America, Alaska dwarfs the lower forty-eight in size?

Are the Russians, who are often criticized for their adoption of   6
"Western" ways by Tsarist dissidents in exile, members of Western civilization? And what of the millions of Europeans who have black African and Asian ancestry, black Africans having occupied several countries for hundreds of years? Are these "Europeans" members of Western civilization, or the Hungarians, who originated across the Urals in a place called Greater Hungary, or the Irish, who came from the Iberian Peninsula?

Even the notion that North America is part of Western civiliza-   7
tion because our "system of government" is derived from Europe is being challenged by Native American historians who say that the founding fathers, Benjamin Franklin especially, were actually influenced by the system of government that had been adopted by the Iroquois hundreds of years prior to the arrival of large numbers of Europeans.

Western civilization, then, becomes another confusing category   8
like Third World, or Judeo-Christian culture, as man attempts to impose his small-screen view of political and cultural reality upon a complex world. Our most publicized novelist recently said that Western civilization was the greatest achievement of mankind, an attitude that flourishes on the street level as scribbles in public restrooms: "White Power," "Niggers and Spics Suck," or "Hitler was a prophet," the latter being the most telling, for wasn't Adolf Hitler the archetypal monoculturalist who, in his pigheaded arrogance, believed that one way and one blood was so pure that it had to be protected from alien strains at all costs? Where did such an attitude, which has caused so much misery and depression in our national life, which has tainted even our noblest achievements, begin? An attitude that caused the incarceration of Japanese-American citizens during World War II, the persecution of Chicanos and Chinese-Americans, the near-extermination of the Indians, and the murder and lynchings of thousands of Afro-Americans.

Virtuous, hardworking, pious, even though they occasionally   9
would wander off after some fancy clothes, or rendezvous in the woods
with the town prostitute, the Puritans are idealized in our schoolbooks
as "a hardy band" of no-nonsense patriarchs whose discipline razed
the forest and brought order to the New World (a term that annoys
Native American historians). Industrious, responsible, it was their
"Yankee ingenuity" and practicality that created the work ethic. They
were simple folk who produced a number of good poets, and they set
the tone for the American writing style, of lean and spare lines, long
before Hemingway. They worshiped in churches whose colors blended
in with the New England snow, churches with simple structures and
ornate lecterns.

The Puritans were a daring lot, but they had a mean streak. They   10
hated the theater and banned Christmas. They punished people in a
cruel and inhuman manner. They killed children who disobeyed their
parents. When they came in contact with those whom they considered heathens or aliens, they behaved in such a bizarre and irrational
manner that this chapter in the American history comes down to us
as a late-movie horror film. They exterminated the Indians, who
taught them how to survive in a world unknown to them, and their
encounter with the calypso culture of Barbados resulted in what the
tourist guide in Salem's Witches' House refers to as the Witchcraft
Hysteria.

The Puritan legacy of hard work and meticulous accounting led   11
to the establishment of a great industrial society; it is no wonder that
the American industrial revolution began in Lowell, Massachusetts.
But there was the other side, the strange and paranoid attitudes
toward those different from the Elect.

The cultural attitudes of that early Elect continue to be voiced   12
in everyday life in the United States: the president of a distinguished
university, writing a letter to the *Times*, belittling the study of African
civilizations; the television network that promoted its show on the
Vatican art with the boast that this art represented "the finest achievements of the human spirit." A modern up-tempo state of complex
rhythms that depends upon contacts with an international community
can no longer behave as if it dwelled in a "Zion Wilderness" surrounded by beasts and pagans.

When I heard a schoolteacher warn the other night about the   13
invasion of the American educational system by foreign curriculums,
I wanted to yell at the television set, "Lady, they're already here." It
has already begun because the world is here. The world has been
arriving at these shores for at least ten thousand years from Europe,

Africa, and Asia. In the late nineteenth and early twentieth centuries, large numbers of Europeans arrived, adding their cultures to those of the European, African, and Asian settlers who were already here, and recently millions have been entering the country from South America and the Caribbean, making Yale Professor Bob Thompson's bouillabaisse richer and thicker.

One of our most visionary politicians said that he envisioned a   14
time when the United States could become the brain of the world, by which he meant the repository of all of the latest advanced information systems. I thought of that remark when an enterprising poet friend of mine called to say that he had just sold a poem to a computer magazine and that the editors were delighted to get it because they didn't carry fiction or poetry. Is that the kind of world we desire? A humdrum homogeneous world of all brains and no heart, no fiction, no poetry; a world of robots with human attendants bereft of imagination, of culture? Or does North America deserve a more exciting destiny? To become a place where the cultures of the world crisscross. This is possible because the United States is unique in the world: The world is here.

QUESTIONS ON MEANING

1. How does Reed see *Western civilization* being defined by those who champion it as the dominant culture? In his eyes, what is wrong with this definition?
2. What do you take to be Reed's PURPOSE in this essay?
3. What does Reed mean by the two key and contrasting terms *monocultural* (paras. 3, 8) and *bouillabaisse* (5, 13)?
4. How does Reed interpret the notion that "the United States could become the brain of the world" (para. 14)? What is his objection?

QUESTIONS ON WRITING STRATEGY

1. Why does Reed wait until the fifth paragraph to present his THESIS? Does he arrive at it through INDUCTION or DEDUCTION?
2. How does Reed's CONCLUSION promote his ARGUMENT?
3. What ASSUMPTIONS does the author make about the attitudes and beliefs of his AUDIENCE? How do his use of evidence and his TONE support your answer?

4. MIXED METHODS. Reed's argument rests largely on EXAMPLES. Where do most of the examples come from? Are they adequate as EVIDENCE? Why or why not?
5. MIXED METHODS. In paragraphs 8–12, Reed examines CAUSES AND EFFECTS. What is the point of this ANALYSIS in his argument?

QUESTIONS ON LANGUAGE

1. Look up the definitions of any words below that you are unfamiliar with: mosques (para. 1); ostracism (3); Elect (noun), Cubists, Surrealists (5); dissidents (6); archetypal, incarceration, lynchings (8); razed (9); repository, bereft (14).
2. What is the EFFECT of the "scribbles in public restrooms" (para. 8)? What do they represent to Reed?
3. Analyze Reed's use of language in discussing the Puritans (paras. 9–11). What attitude(s) toward the Puritans does the language convey?

SUGGESTIONS FOR WRITING

1. "The dreams and fears of a community can be found written on the walls of its restrooms." Check out some restrooms in your community and write an essay that supports or rejects the above statement.
2. Reed calls Western civilization "another confusing category like Third World, or Judeo-Christian culture" (para. 8). How confusing are these other terms? In social-science encyclopedias, dictionaries of culture, and other library references (but not abridged dictionaries), find at least three definitions of either term. Write a brief essay that specifies the similarities and differences in the definitions.
3. CRITICAL WRITING. Reed asserts that a "blurring of cultural styles . . . is probably more prevalent [in the United States] than the sensational conflict between people of different backgrounds that is played up and often encouraged by the media." Is this true in your experience? Support or refute Reed's assertion by COMPARING AND CONTRASTING the image and reality of a community you either live in or visit. Support your essay with EXAMPLES.
4. CONNECTIONS. COMPARE Reed's essay with "The Cult of Ethnicity, Good and Bad," by Arthur M. Schlesinger, Jr. (p. 689). Where do the authors agree? Where do they disagree? As clearly as possible, SUMMARIZE and ANALYZE the two arguments, using quotations and PARAPHRASES from them to support your ideas.

ISHMAEL REED ON WRITING

Ishmael Reed describes himself as someone with a "prolific writing jab" — a knack for starting fights, or at least stirring up controversy, with his pen. In fiction and nonfiction, he has taken on governments, literary intellectuals, the media, feminists — any person or any group he felt needed correcting. As he told the writer William C. Brisick, he sees himself as part "trickster," a term he learned from Native Americans for a figure common to many folk traditions who exposes pretension and dishonesty. Essays for Reed are a means of "talking back, a way of including in the national dialogue another point of view, one not present in the media."

Reed does not disdain using his talents for even more practical purposes. To publicize the deterioration of his crack-infested neighborhood in Oakland, California, Reed wrote an article for a local newspaper that gained wide attention, both pro and con. In addition to this piece, Reed composed press releases for the neighborhood association — writing that "really moved the community," he says. "It's become functional art."

FOR DISCUSSION

1. Would you say that writing that has a practical goal (a press release, for instance) can be valued for its own sake as writing? Is it art?
2. What of the "trickster" do you see in Reed's essay "America: The Multinational Society"?

ARTHUR M. SCHLESINGER, JR.

"History is to a nation the way memory is to an individual. . . . A nation that has forgotten its history may become disoriented." These words reflect the serious purpose behind the prolific and celebrated work of the historian ARTHUR MEIER SCHLESINGER, JR. Born in 1917 in Columbus, Ohio, Schlesinger graduated from Harvard University in 1938. He pursued fellowships at Cambridge and Harvard universities and then served during World War II in the offices of War Information and Strategic Services. Right after the war he published *The Age of Jackson* (1945), which won a Pulitzer Prize, and entered Harvard's history department, where he taught until 1962. That year he became a special assistant to President John F. Kennedy, continuing with President Lyndon B. Johnson after Kennedy's assassination. Schlesinger's memoir of the Kennedy years, *A Thousand Days* (1965), won both the National Book Award and the Pulitzer Prize. In 1966 Schlesinger became the Albert Schweitzer Professor of the Humanities at the City University of New York. Among his more than fifteen other books, *Robert Kennedy and His Times* (1979) also won the National Book Award.

The Cult of Ethnicity, Good and Bad

In 1992, Schlesinger published a controversial book, *The Disunity of America*, that makes a case against what Schlesinger sees as separatism among American racial and ethnic groups. The following essay from *Time* magazine in 1991 anticipates the book. In a few pages, Schlesinger outlines the pros and the worrisome cons of contemporary multiculturalism.

"The Cult of Ethnicity" is an ARGUMENT based mainly on ANALYSIS of CAUSES AND EFFECTS. For support, Schlesinger offers a number of EXAMPLES.

The history of the world has been in great part the history of the mixing of peoples. Modern communication and transport accelerate mass migrations from one continent to another. Ethnic and racial diversity is more than ever a salient fact of the age.

But what happens when people of different origins, speaking different languages and professing different religions, inhabit the same locality and live under the same political sovereignty? Ethnic and racial conflict — far more than ideological conflict — is the explosive problem of our times.

On every side today ethnicity is breaking up nations. The Soviet   3
Union, India, Yugoslavia, Ethiopia are all in crisis. Ethnic tensions
disturb and divide Sri Lanka, Burma, Indonesia, Iraq, Cyprus, Ni-
geria, Angola, Lebanon, Guyana, Trinidad — you name it. Even
nations as stable and civilized as Britain and France, Belgium and
Spain, face growing ethnic troubles. Is there any large multiethnic
state that can be made to work?

The answer to that question has been, until recently, the United   4
States. "No other nation," Margaret Thatcher[1] has said, "has so
successfully combined people of different races and nations within a
single culture." How have Americans succeeded in pulling off this
almost unprecedented trick?

We have always been a multiethnic country. Hector St. John de   5
Crèvecoeur, who came from France in the eighteenth century, mar-
veled at the astonishing diversity of the settlers — "a mixture of
English, Scotch, Irish, French, Dutch, Germans, and Swedes . . .
this promiscuous breed." He propounded a famous question: "What
then is the American, this new man?" And he gave a famous answer:
"Here individuals of all nations are melted into a new race of men."
E pluribus unum.

The United States escaped the divisiveness of a multiethnic so-   6
ciety by a brilliant solution: the creation of a brand-new national
identity. The point of America was not to preserve old cultures but
to forge a new, *American* culture. "By an intermixture with our
people," President George Washington told Vice President John
Adams, immigrants will "get assimilated to our customs, measures
and laws: in a word, soon become one people." This was the ideal
that a century later Israel Zangwill crystallized in the title of his
popular 1908 play *The Melting Pot.* And no institution was more
potent in molding Crèvecoeur's "promiscuous breed" into Washington's "one people" than the American public school.

The new American nationality was inescapably English in lan-   7
guage, ideas, and institutions. The pot did not melt everybody, not
even all the white immigrants; deeply bred racism put black Americans, yellow Americans, red Americans, and brown Americans well
outside the pale. Still, the infusion of other stocks, even of nonwhite
stocks, and the experience of the New World reconfigured the British
legacy and made the United States, as we all know, a very different
country from Britain.

In the twentieth century, new immigration laws altered the com-   8

[1]Thatcher (born 1925) was Britain's prime minister 1979–90. — Eds.

position of the American people, and a cult of ethnicity erupted both among non-Anglo whites and among nonwhite minorities. This had many healthy consequences. The American culture at last began to give shamefully overdue recognition to the achievements of groups subordinated and spurned during the high noon of Anglo dominance, and it began to acknowledge the great swirling world beyond Europe. Americans acquired a more complex and invigorating sense of their world — and of themselves.

But, pressed too far, the cult of ethnicity has unhealthy conse-   9
quences. It gives rise, for example, to the conception of the United States as a nation composed not of individuals making their own choices but of inviolable ethnic and racial groups. It rejects the historic American goals of assimilation and integration. And, in an excess of zeal, well-intentioned people seek to transform our system of education from a means of creating "one people" into a means of promoting, celebrating, and perpetuating separate ethnic origins and identities. The balance is shifting from *unum* to *pluribus*.

That is the issue that lies behind the hullabaloo over "multicul-   10
turalism" and "political correctness," the attack on the "Eurocentric" curriculum and the rise of the notion that history and literature should be taught not as disciplines but as therapies whose function is to raise minority self-esteem. Group separatism crystallizes the differences, magnifies tensions, intensifies hostilities. Europe — the unique source of the liberating ideas of democracy, civil liberties, and human rights — is portrayed as the root of all evil, and non-European cultures, their own many crimes deleted, are presented as the means of redemption.

I don't want to sound apocalyptic about these developments.   11
Education is always in ferment, and a good thing too. The situation in our universities, I am confident, will soon right itself. But the impact of separatist pressures on our public schools is more troubling. If a Kleagle of the Ku Klux Klan wanted to use the schools to disable and handicap black Americans, he could hardly come up with anything more effective than the "Afrocentric" curriculum. And if separatist tendencies go unchecked, the result can only be the fragmentation, resegregation, and tribalization of American life.

I remain optimistic. My impression is that the historic forces   12
driving toward "one people" have not lost their power. The eruption of ethnicity is, I believe, a rather superficial enthusiasm stirred by romantic ideologues on the one hand and by unscrupulous con men on the other: self-appointed spokesmen whose claim to represent their minority groups is carelessly accepted by the media. Most American-

born members of minority groups, white or nonwhite, see themselves primarily as Americans rather than primarily as members of one or another ethnic group. A notable indicator today is the rate of inter-marriage across ethnic lines, across religion lines, even (increasingly) across racial lines. "We Americans," said Theodore Roosevelt, "are children of the crucible."

The growing diversity of the American population makes the 13 quest for unifying ideals and a common culture all the more urgent. In a world savagely rent by ethnic and racial antagonisms, the United States must continue as an example of how a highly differentiated society holds itself together.

QUESTIONS ON MEANING

1. What does *E pluribus unum* mean (paras. 5, 9)? Where do we encounter this phrase? How does the phrase serve Schlesinger's ARGUMENT?
2. What does Schlesinger mean by the phrase "cult of ethnicity"?
3. Why, in Schlesinger's opinion, is "group separatism" bad for the nation?
4. Where does Schlesinger state his THESIS? Restate it in your own words.

QUESTIONS ON WRITING STRATEGY

1. What is the EFFECT of paragraphs 2–3? Why does Schlesinger put these paragraphs up front?
2. Why does Schlesinger devote several paragraphs to a history lesson (paras. 5–8)?
3. What does Schlesinger accomplish with quotations from Margaret Thatcher (para. 4), Hector St. John de Crèvecoeur (5), George Washington (6), and Theodore Roosevelt (12)?
4. MIXED METHODS. SUMMARIZE Schlesinger's ANALYSIS of CAUSES AND EFFECTS. Is it reasonable? Fair? Does it support Schlesinger's ARGUMENT to your satisfaction?

QUESTIONS ON LANGUAGE

1. Provide definitions of the following words: salient (para. 1); sovereignty, ideological (2); stocks (7); spurned (8); Eurocentric (10); apocalyptic, ferment (11); crucible (12); rent, antagonisms (13).
2. Crèvecoeur called eighteenth-century Americans a "promiscuous breed." Look up the word *promiscuous* in the dictionary. Which of the meanings seems closest to Crèvecoeur's?

3. What does the phrase "outside the pale" (para. 7) mean?
4. How does Schlesinger use language to further his argument? For instance, what are the CONNOTATIONS of "cult" (title); "excess," "promoting" (para. 9); "hullabaloo" (10); "superficial," "romantic" (12)? How does Schlesinger use these words?

SUGGESTIONS FOR WRITING

1. In a personal essay, discuss your own ethnic heritage and its place in contemporary American culture. What are some preconceptions and stereotypes about people of your ancestry and their culture(s)? What are some notable achievements by people who share your background? How have you been made to feel about your cultural inheritance?
2. Write an ARGUMENT agreeing or disagreeing with Schlesinger. Do you think there is too much emphasis on racial and ethnic identification in education today? Not enough? How has your own experience in school and college contributed to your opinion on this issue? Support your claims with EVIDENCE.
3. CRITICAL WRITING. Examine Schlesinger's argument closely for its underlying ASSUMPTIONS about American culture. What assumptions does Schlesinger challenge? What does he leave unquestioned? Does the essay endorse or challenge mainstream American values? Defend your ANALYSIS with specific EXAMPLES from the essay.
4. CONNECTIONS. Schlesinger and Ishmael Reed, in "America: The Multinational Society" (p. 682), approach American history from different directions: Schlesinger acknowledges that the "pot did not melt everybody" but implies that minority groups are now recognized (paras. 9–10). Reed finds the "paranoid" stance of the Puritans still figuring strongly in contemporary attitudes toward minorities (paras. 9–12). With which of these authors do you agree? Support your answer with EXAMPLES from your experience or reading.

ARTHUR M. SCHLESINGER, JR., ON WRITING

In an interview in *Contemporary Authors* in 1988, Arthur Schlesinger credited a Harvard professor, the writer Bernard De Voto, with teaching him to write award-winning prose. "For some years at Harvard he gave an advanced course in composition," Schlesinger recalls. "He was a merciless critic. You would write a paper for him, and it would come back with savage, insulting remarks. His general technique was to goad his students into an awareness of the falsity and excess in their writing, and the obscurity of thought that lies behind muddiness of expression. I learned a lot in that course, and I've been

a great champion ever since of courses in English composition."
There, Schlesinger says, at least students will write. Objective tests,
he thinks, are "a great mistake." "Often the only way people know
what they think is when they are forced to write it down."

FOR DISCUSSION

1. What does Schlesinger mean by "the obscurity of thought that lies
   behind muddiness of expression"? Can you think of times when your
   own prose betrayed "obscurity of thought"? What did you do about it?
2. Do you find it odd that Schlesinger would praise a teacher who savagely
   attacked students' work? Have you benefited from a guiding hand —
   whether harsh or gentle — in your own writing?

KATHA POLLITT

KATHA POLLITT is a poet and essayist. Her poetry has been praised
for its "serious charm" and "spare delicacy" in capturing thought
and feeling. Her essays have contained strong and convincing commentary on such topics as surrogate motherhood and women in the
media. Pollitt was born in New York City in 1949 and earned a
B.A. from Radcliffe College in 1972. Her verse began appearing in
the 1970s in such magazines as *The New Yorker* and *Atlantic Monthly;*
it was collected in the book *Antarctic Traveler* (1982), which won
the National Book Critics Circle award in 1983. Pollitt has received
several other awards as well, including a grant from the National
Endowment for the Arts and a Guggenheim fellowship. Her essays
and criticism have appeared in *Mother Jones,* the *New York Times
Book Review,* and *The Nation,* where she is currently an associate
editor. Pollitt lives in New York City.

Why Do We Read?

This essay first appeared in *The Nation* in September 1991 and won
a National Magazine Award that year. It was then reprinted with
the title here in *Debating P.C.* (1992), an anthology of writings on
issues of "political correctness" and diversity in the curriculum.
Pollitt examines the arguments in one of the curriculum debates:
Should the literary canon, the body of literature considered "great,"
be enlarged to include works by women and members of minorities
who have previously been omitted? Pollitt finds merit in many sides
of the debate but thinks it obscures the real question: Do we read
enough?

Pollitt's essay draws on many of the methods of development.
She CLASSIFIES the debaters, COMPARES AND CONTRASTS their positions, examines the CAUSES of their debate. Throughout, she gives
EXAMPLES of the issues and the literary works in question. She
constantly ANALYZES the debate, seeking its ASSUMPTIONS. And,
overall, her essay is an ARGUMENT for a certain way of viewing the
debate.

For the past couple of years, we've all been witnesses to a furious   1
debate about the literary canon. What books should be assigned to
students? What books should critics discuss? What books should the
rest of us read — and who are *we,* anyway? Like everyone else, I've
given these questions some thought and, when an invitation came

my way, leaped to produce my own manifesto. But to my surprise, when I sat down to write — in order to discover, as E. M. Forster once said, what I really think — I found that I agreed with all sides in the debate at once.

Take the conservatives. Now, this rather dour collection of schol-   2
ars and diatribists — Allan Bloom, Hilton Kramer, John Silber, and so on — are not, to my mind, a particularly appealing group of people. They are arrogant, they are rude, they are gloomy, they do not suffer fools gladly — and everywhere they look, fools are what they see. All good reasons not to elect them to public office, as the voters of Massachusetts recently decided.[1] But what is so terrible, really, about what they are saying? I too believe that some books are profounder, more complex, more essential to an understanding of our culture than others; I too am appalled to think of students graduating from college not having read Homer, Plato, Virgil, Milton, Tolstoy — all writers, dead white Western men though they be, whose works have meant a great deal to me. As a teacher of literature and of writing, I too have seen at first hand how ill-educated many students are and how little aware they are of this important fact about them- selves. Last year, for instance, I taught a graduate seminar in the writing of poetry. None of my students had read more than a smat- tering of poems by anyone, male or female, published more than ten years ago. Robert Lowell was as far outside their frame of reference as Alexander Pope. When I gently suggested to one students that it might benefit her to read some poetry if she planned to spend her life writing it, she told me that yes, she knew she should read more, but when she encountered a really good poem it only made her depressed. That contemporary writing has a history which it profits us to know in some depth, that we ourselves were not born yesterday, seems too obvious even to argue.

But ah, say the liberals, the canon exalted by the conservatives   3
is itself an artifact of history. Sure, some books are more rewarding than others, but why can't we revise the list of which books those are? The canon itself was not always the list we know today: Until the 1920s, *Moby-Dick* was shelved with the boys' adventure stories. If T. S. Eliot could singlehandedly dethrone the Romantic poets in favor of the neglected Metaphysicals and place John Webster along- side Shakespeare, why can't we dip into the sea of stories and pluck out Edith Wharton or Virginia Woolf? And this position too makes

[1]John Silber, the president of Boston University, ran unsuccessfully for governor of Massachusetts in 1991. — EDS.

a great deal of sense to me. After all, alongside the many good reasons why a book might end up on the required reading shelf are some rather suspect reasons why it might be excluded — because it was written by a woman and therefore presumed to be too slight; because it was written by a black person and therefore presumed to be too unsophisticated or, in any case, to reflect too special an instance. By all means, say the liberals, let's have great books and a shared culture. But let's make sure that all the different kinds of greatness are represented and that the culture we share reflects the true range of human experience.

If we leave the broadening of the canon up to the conservatives,   4
it will never happen because, to them, change only means defeat. Look at the recent fuss over the latest edition of the Great Books series published by the Encyclopaedia Britannica, headed by that old snake-oil salesman Mortimer Adler. Four women have now been added to the series: Virginia Woolf, Willa Cather, Jane Austen, and George Eliot. That's nice, I suppose, but really! Jane Austen has been a certified great writer for a hundred years! Lionel Trilling said so! There's something truly absurd about the conservatives, earnestly sitting in judgment on the illustrious dead as though up in Writers' Heaven Jane and George and Willa and Virginia were breathlessly waiting to hear if they'd finally made it into the club, while Henry Fielding, newly dropped from the list, howls in outer darkness and the Brontës, presumably, stamp their feet in frustration and hope for better luck in twenty years, when *Jane Eyre* and *Wuthering Heights* will suddenly turn out to have qualities of greatness never before detected in their pages. It's like Poets' Corner over at Manhattan's Cathedral of St. John the Divine, where mortal men — and a woman or two — of letters actually vote on which immortals to put up a plaque to — complete, no doubt, with electoral campaigns, compromise candidates, and all the rest of the underside of the literary life. "No, I'm sorry, I just can't vote for Whitman. I'm a Washington Irving man myself."

Well, being a liberal is not a very exciting thing to be, and so   5
we have the radicals, who attack the concepts of "greatness," "shared," "culture," and "lists." (I'm overlooking here the ultra-radicals, who attack the "privileging," horrible word, of "texts," as they insist on calling books, and think one might as well spend one's college years "deconstructing," i.e., watching reruns of *Leave It to Beaver.*) Who is to say, ask the radicals, what is a great book? What's so terrific about complexity, ambiguity, historical centrality, and high seriousness? If *The Color Purple*, say, gets students thinking about

their own experience, maybe they ought to read it and forget about — and here you can fill in the name of whatever classic work you yourself found dry and tedious and never got around to finishing. For the radicals, the notion of a shared culture is a lie, because it means presenting as universally meaningful and politically neutral books that reflect the interests and experiences and values of privileged white men at the expense of those of others — women, blacks, Hispanics, Asians, the working class, whatever. Why not scrap the one-list-for-everyone idea and let people connect with books that are written by people like themselves about people like themselves? It will be a more accurate reflection of a multifaceted and conflict-ridden society and do wonders for everyone's self-esteem, except, of course, for living white men — but they have too much self-esteem already.

Now, I have to say that I dislike the radicals' vision intensely. 6 How foolish to argue that Chekhov has nothing to say to a black woman — or, for that matter, myself — merely because he is Russian, long dead, a man. The notion that one reads to increase one's self-esteem sounds to me like more snake oil: Literature is not a session at the therapist's. But then I think of myself as a child, leafing through anthologies of poetry for the names of women. I never would have admitted that I needed a role model, even if that awful term had existed back in the prehistory of which I speak, but why was I so excited to find a female name, even when, as was often the case, it was attached to a poem of no interest to me whatsoever? Anna Laetitia Barbauld, author of "Life! I know not what thou art / But know that thou and I must part!," Lady Anne Lindsay, writer of languid ballads in incomprehensible Scots dialect, and the other minor female poets included by chivalrous Sir Arthur Quiller-Couch in the old *Oxford Anthology of English Verse* — I have to admit it, just by their presence in that august volume they did something for me. And although it had nothing to do with reading or writing, it was an important thing they did.

Now, what are we to make of this spluttering debate, in which 7 charges of imperialism are met by equally passionate accusations of vandalism, in which each side hates the others, and yet each seems to have its share of reason? It occurs to me that perhaps what we have here is one of those debates in which the opposing sides, unbeknownst to themselves, share a myopia that will turn out to be the most interesting and important feature of the whole discussion, a debate, for instance, like that of our Founding Fathers over the nature of the franchise. Think of all the energy and passion spent debating the question of property qualifications, or direct versus legislative elections, while all along, unmentioned and unimagined, was the fact — to us so central — that women and slaves were never considered for any kind of vote.

Something is being overlooked. That is the state of reading, and 8 books, and literature in our country, at this time. Why, ask yourself, is everyone so hot under the collar about what to put on the required-reading shelf? It is because, while we have been arguing so fiercely about which books make the best medicine, the patient has been slipping deeper and deeper into a coma.

Let us imagine a country in which reading was a popular voluntary 9 activity. There, parents read books for their own edification and pleasure and are seen by their children at this silent and mysterious pastime. These parents also read to their children, give them books for presents, talk to them about books, and underwrite, with their taxes, a public library system that is open all day, every day. In school — where an attractive library is invariably to be found — the children study certain books together but also have an active reading life of their own. Years later, it may even be hard for them to remember if they read *Jane Eyre* at home and Judy Blume in class or the other way around. In college, young people continue to be assigned certain books, but far more important are the books they discover for themselves browsing in the library, in bookstores, on the shelves of friends, one book leading to another, back and forth in history and across languages and cultures. After graduation, they continue to read and in the fullness of time produce a new generation of readers. Oh happy land! I wish we all lived there.

In that other country of real readers — voluntary, active, self- 10 determined readers — a debate like the current one over the canon would not be taking place. Or if it did, it would be as a kind of parlor game: What books would *you* take to a desert island? Everyone would know that the top-ten list was merely a tiny fraction of the books one would read in a lifetime. It would not seem racist or sexist or hopelessly hidebound to put Hawthorne on the list and not Toni Morrison. It would be more like putting oatmeal and not noodles on the breakfast menu — a choice part arbitrary, part a nod to the national past, part, dare one say it, a kind of reverse affirmative action: School might frankly *be* the place where one reads the books that are a little off-putting, that have gone a little cold, that you might overlook because they do not address, in reader-friendly contemporary fashion, the issues most immediately at stake in modern life but that, with a little study, turn out to have a great deal to say. Being on the list wouldn't mean so much. It might even add to a writer's cachet *not* to be on the list, to be in one way or another too heady, too daring, too exciting to be ground up into institutional fodder for teenagers. Generations of high-school kids have been turned off to George Eliot by being forced to read *Silas Marner* at a tender age. One can imagine a whole new readership for her if grownups were left to approach *Middlemarch* and *Daniel Deronda* with open minds, at their leisure.

Of course, they rarely do. In America today, the assumption 11 underlying the canon debate is that the books on the list are the only books that are going to be read and if the list is dropped, *no* books are going to be read. Becoming a textbook is a book's only chance; all sides take that for granted. And so all agree not to mention certain things that they themselves, as highly educated people and, one assumes, devoted readers, know perfectly well. For example, that if you read only twenty-five, or fifty, or a hundred books, you can't understand them, however well-chosen they are. And that if you don't have an independent reading life — and very few students do — you won't *like* reading the books on the list and will forget them the minute you finish them. And that books have, or should have, other lives than as items in a syllabus — which is why there is now a totally misguided attempt to put current literature in the classroom. How strange to think that people need professorial help to read John Updike or Alice Walker, writers people actually *do* read for fun. But all sides agree, if it isn't taught, it doesn't count.

Let's look at the canon question from another angle. Instead of 12 asking what books we want others to read, let's ask why we read books ourselves. I think it will become clear very quickly that the canon debaters are being a little disingenuous here, are suppressing, in the interest of their own positions, their own experience of reading. Sure, we read to understand our own American culture and history, and we also read to recover neglected masterpieces, and to learn more about the accomplishments of our subgroup and thereby, as I've admitted about myself, increase our self-esteem. But what about reading for the aesthetic pleasures of language, form, image? What about reading to learn something new, to have a vicarious adventure, to follow the workings of an interesting, if possibly skewed, narrow and ill-tempered, mind? What about reading for the story? For an expanded sense of sheer human variety? There are a thousand reasons why a book might have a claim on our time and attention, other than its canonization. I once infuriated an acquaintance by asserting that Trollope, although in many ways a lesser writer than Dickens, possessed some wonderful qualities Dickens lacked: a more realistic view of women, a more skeptical view of good intentions, a subtler sense of humor — a drier vision of life that I myself found congenial. You'd think I'd advocated throwing Dickens out and replacing him with a toaster. Because Dickens is a certified Great Writer, and Trollope is not.

Am I saying anything different than what Randall Jarrell said in   13
his great 1953 essay, "The Age of Criticism"? Not really, so I'll quote him. Speaking of the literary social gatherings of the era, Jarrell wrote:

> If, at such parties, you wanted to talk about *Ulysses* or *The Castle* or *The Brothers Karamazov* or *The Great Gatsby* or Graham Greene's last novel — Important books — you were at the right place. (Though you weren't so well off if you wanted to talk about *Remembrance of Things Past*. Important, but too long.) But if you wanted to talk about Turgenev's novelettes, or *The House of the Dead*, or *Lavengro*, or *Life on the Mississippi*, or *The Old Wives' Tale*, or *The Golovlyov Family*, or Cunningham-Grahame's stories, or Saint-Simon's memoirs, or *Lost Illusions*, or *The Beggar's Opera*, or *Eugene Onegin*, or *Little Dorrit*, or the *Burnt Njal Saga*, or *Persuasion*, or *The Inspector-General*, or *Oblomov*, or *Peer Gynt*, or *Far From the Madding Crowd*, or *Out of Africa*, or the *Parallel Lives*, or *A Dreary Story*, or *Debits and Credits*, or *Arabia Deserta*, or *Elective Affinities*, or *Schweik*, or — any of a thousand good or interesting but Unimportant books, you couldn't expect a very ready knowledge or sympathy from most of the readers there. They had looked at the big sights, the current sights, hard, with guides and glasses; and those walks in the country, over unfrequented or thrice-familiar territory, all alone — those walks from which most of the joy and good of reading come — were walks that they hadn't gone on very often.

I suspect that most canon debaters have taken those solitary   14
rambles, if only out of boredom — how many times, after all, can you reread the *Aeneid*, or *Mrs. Dalloway*, or *Cotton Comes to Harlem* (to pick one book from each column)? But those walks don't count, because of another assumption all sides hold in common. And that is that the purpose of reading is not the many varied and delicious satisfactions I've mentioned; it's medicinal. The chief end of reading is to produce a desirable kind of person and a desirable kind of society — a respectful high-minded citizen of a unified society for the

conservatives, an up-to-date and flexible sort for the liberals, a subgroup-identified, robustly confident one for the radicals. How pragmatic, how moralistic, how American! The culture debaters turn out to share a secret suspicion of culture itself, as well as the anti-pornographer's belief that there is a simple, one-to-one correlation between books and behavior. Read the conservatives' list and produce a nation of sexists and racists — or a nation of philosopher kings. Read the liberals' list and produce a nation of spineless relativists — or a nation of open-minded world citizens. Read the radicals' list, and produce a nation of psychobabblers and ancestor-worshippers — or a nation of stalwart proud-to-be-me pluralists.

But is there any list of a few dozen books that can have such a   15
magical effect, for good or for ill? Of course not. It's like arguing that the perfectly nutritional breakfast cereal is enough food for the whole day. And so the canon debate is really an argument about what books to cram down the resistant throats of a resentful captive populace of students — and the trick is never to mention the fact that, under such circumstances, one book is as good, or as bad, as another. Because, as the debaters know from their own experience as readers but never acknowledge because it would count against all sides equally, books are not pills that produce health when ingested in measured doses. Books do not shape character in any simple way, if indeed they do so at all, or the most literate would be the most virtuous instead of just the ordinary run of humanity with larger vocabularies. Books cannot mold a common national purpose when, in fact, people are honestly divided about what kind of country they want — and are divided, moreover, for very good and practical reasons, as they always have been.

For these burly and energetic purposes, books are all but useless.   16
The way books affect us is an altogether more subtle, delicate, wayward, and individual, not to say private, affair. And that reading, at the present moment, is being made to bear such an inappropriate and simplistic burden speaks to the poverty both of culture and of frank political discussion in our time.

On his deathbed, Dr. Johnson — once canonical, now more   17
admired than read — is supposed to have said to a friend who was energetically rearranging his bedclothes, "Thank you, this will do all that a pillow can do." One might say that the canon debaters are all asking of their handful of chosen books that they do a great deal more than any handful of books can do.

QUESTIONS ON MEANING

1. Why was Pollitt, when young, "so excited to find a female name" in poetry anthologies (para. 6)?
2. What does Pollitt mean by "reverse affirmative action" for noncontemporary books (para. 10)?
3. What unspoken ASSUMPTIONS does Pollitt believe the canon debate is based on?
4. What is Pollitt's THESIS? Where does she state it? Why there, do you think?
5. Is Pollitt's PURPOSE to stop the canon debate, or something else? Explain.

QUESTIONS ON WRITING STRATEGY

1. *The Nation,* where this essay first appeared, is a magazine with a predominantly liberal AUDIENCE. How might its readers have been surprised by Pollitt's ideas?
2. When Pollitt mentions "students" in paragraphs 11 and 15, it's evident that she is not addressing them. Do you feel excluded from Pollitt's audience? Do you think what she says about students is fair?
3. Pollitt's essay is full of ALLUSIONS to specific literary works. Did you find these helpful or off-putting? If there were some you didn't understand, could you nonetheless understand Pollitt's point? Explain.
4. MIXED METHODS. Pollitt's ARGUMENT is based on her ANALYSIS of the debate. SUMMARIZE her analysis of each side's position.
5. MIXED METHODS. Pollitt's analysis uncovers several unspoken ASSUMPTIONS in the canon debate. What pattern of CAUSES AND EFFECTS does she dispute in these assumptions?

QUESTIONS ON LANGUAGE

1. What are the CONNOTATIONS of the phrase "snake oil" (paras. 4 and 6)? What does Pollitt mean by it each time she uses it?
2. In paragraph 4, Pollitt refers to Jane Austen as "a certified great writer." What clues tell us this is IRONY? Is the irony at the expense of Austen, or of Austen's critics?
3. Pollitt uses three breakfast IMAGES: oatmeal versus noodles (para. 10), a toaster (12), and nutritional cereal (15). Aside from the possibility that Pollitt was hungry or was sitting at her breakfast table when writing, what do these images convey? Do they help clarify her meaning?
4. If any of these words are unfamiliar, look them up in your dictionary: manifesto (para. 1); dour, diatribists (2); artifact (3); ambiguity (5); languid, chivalrous, august (6); myopia, franchise (7); edification (9); cachet (10); disingenuous, vicarious (12); stalwart (14).

SUGGESTIONS FOR WRITING

1. Pollitt describes, in paragraphs 8 and 9, her vision of an ideal world of readers. In an essay, discuss your own ideas of how reading should work. How does your current reading life measure up to Pollitt's ideal? Does anything keep you from reading as much, or as well, as you would like? How have your experiences reading for school affected the way you read on your own? Do you agree with Pollitt that "becoming a textbook is a book's only chance" of getting read (para. 11)?

2. "Books cannot mold a common national purpose when, in fact, people are honestly divided about what kind of country they want," writes Pollitt (para. 15). Do you agree? Write a brief ARGUMENT expressing your views. How can the selection of books to be taught in schools influence our society's attitudes? How is "the canon" irrelevant? Draw on your own experience for EXAMPLES that reinforce your argument.

3. CRITICAL WRITING. Pollitt teases out the unspoken ASSUMPTIONS in the canon debate. What are *her* spoken and unspoken assumptions about reading? For instance, what does she think reading can do? Under what circumstances? For whom? What does the last sentence in paragraph 15 imply about her position in the debate? Write an essay in which you characterize Pollitt the way she characterizes the conservatives, liberals, and radicals.

4. CONNECTIONS. COMPARE Pollitt's essay with Ishmael Reed's "America: The Multinational Society" (p. 682) and Arthur M. Schlesinger's "The Cult of Ethnicity, Good and Bad" (p. 689). In an essay, EVALUATE the three essays on the strength of their ARGUMENTS. Which essay do you find most convincing, and why? (Or, if you found none convincing, why?)

ADDITIONAL WRITING TOPICS

Diversity in the Curriculum

1. In "The Cult of Ethnicity, Good and Bad" (p. 689), Arthur M. Schlesinger, Jr., argues that, taken too far, ethnic and racial identification "rejects the historic American goals of assimilation and integration." Consider Schlesinger's essay in light of Ralph Ellison's "On Being the Target of Discrimination" (p. 55), bell hooks's "Madonna" (p. 303), and Curtis Chang's "Streets of Gold" (p. 495). Would Ellison, hooks, and Chang agree with Schlesinger's optimistic view of minorities' "assimilation and integration" into white America? How do the writers differ in their assessments of the need for, and consequences of, identification with a racial or ethnic group?

2. Katha Pollitt, in "Why Do We Read?" (p. 695), and Lawrence A. Beyer, in "The Highlighter Crisis" (p. 382), both assert that students' reading is deteriorating. Do you accept this judgment? If students with little ability and interest in reading are increasing in number, is this just another way in which student bodies are becoming more diversified? What should the schools do about the problem of reading, if it is one? (Is it a problem for you?)

3. Should America's school curriculums be changed to reflect the ethnic and racial identity of the nation's students? If not, why? If so, how far should the change go? (Should dead white males like Shakespeare and Hemingway still be taught in literature classes? Should the experiences of assimilated, predominantly European immigrants still be emphasized in American history courses?) In developing your essay, consider the ideas of Amy Tan ("The Language of Discretion," p. 187), Richard Rodriguez ("Aria: A Memoir of a Bilingual Childhood," p. 563), and the three authors represented in this chapter, Ishmael Reed, Arthur M. Schlesinger, Jr., and Katha Pollitt.

USEFUL TERMS

Abstract and concrete   Two kinds of language. *Abstract* words refer to ideas, conditions, and qualities we cannot directly perceive: *truth, love, courage, evil, wealth, poverty, progressive, reactionary.* *Concrete* words indicate things we can know with our senses: *tree, chair, bird, pen, motorcycle, perfume, thunderclap, cheeseburger.* The use of concrete words lends vigor and clarity to writing, for such words help a reader to picture things. See IMAGE.

Writers of expository essays tend to shift back and forth from one kind of language to the other. They often begin a paragraph with a general statement full of abstract words ("There is *hope* for the *future* of *motoring*"). Then they usually go on to give examples and present evidence in sentences full of concrete words ("Inventor *Jones* claims his *car* will go from *Fresno* to *Los Angeles* on a *gallon* of *peanut oil*"). Beginning writers often use too many abstract words and not enough concrete ones.

Allude, allusion   To refer to a person, place, or thing believed to be common knowledge (*allude*), or the act or result of doing so (*allusion*). An allusion may point to a famous event, a familiar saying, a noted personality, a well-known story or song. Usually brief, an allusion is a space-saving way to convey much meaning. For example, the statement "The game was Coach Johnson's Waterloo" informs the reader that, like Napoleon meeting defeat in a celebrated battle, the coach led a confrontation resulting in his downfall and that of his team. If the writer is also showing Johnson's character, the allusion might further tell us that the coach is a man of Napoleonic ambition and pride. To make an effective allusion, you have to be aware of your audience. If your readers do not recognize the allusion, it will only confuse. Not everyone, for example, would understand you if you alluded to a neighbor, to a seventeenth-century Russian harpsichordist, or to a little-known stock car driver.

Analogy   An extended comparison based on the like features of two unlike things: one familiar or easily understood, the other unfamiliar, abstract, or complicated. For instance, most people know at least vaguely how the human eye works: The pupil adjusts to admit light, which registers as an image on the retina at the back of the eye. You might use this familiar information to explain something less familiar to many people, such as how a camera works: The aperture (like the pupil) adjusts to admit light, which registers as an image on the film (like the retina) at the back of the camera. Analogies are especially helpful for explaining technical information in a way that is nontechnical, more easily grasped. In August 1981, for example, the spacecraft *Voyager 2* transmitted spectacular pictures of Saturn to Earth. To explain the difficulty of their achievement, NASA scientists compared their feat to a golfer sinking a putt from five hundred miles away. Because it can make abstract ideas vivid and memorable, analogy is also a favorite device of philosophers, politicians, and preachers. In his his celebrated speech "I Have a Dream" (p. 516), Martin Luther King, Jr., draws a remarkable analogy to express the anger and disappointment of African Americans that, one hundred years after Lincoln's Emancipation Proclamation, their full freedom has yet to be achieved. "It is obvious today," declares King, "that America has defaulted on this promissory note"; and he compares the founding fathers' written guarantee — of the rights of life, liberty, and the pursuit of happiness — to a bad check returned for insufficient funds.

Analogy is similar to the method of COMPARISON AND CONTRAST. Both use DIVISION OR ANALYSIS to identify the distinctive features of two things and then set the features side by side. But a comparison explains two obviously similar things — two Civil War generals, two styles of basketball play — and considers both their differences and their similarities. An analogy yokes two apparently unlike things (eye and camera, spaceflight and golf, guaranteed human rights and bad checks) and focuses only on their major similarities. Analogy is thus an extended METAPHOR, the FIGURE OF SPEECH that declares one thing to be another — even though it isn't, in a strictly literal sense — for the purpose of making us aware of similarity: "Hope," says the poet Emily Dickinson, "is the thing with feathers / That perches in the soul."

In an ARGUMENT, analogy can make readers more receptive to a point or inspire them, but it can't prove anything because in the end the subjects are dissimilar. A false analogy is a LOGICAL FALLACY that claims a fundamental likeness when none exists. See pages 470–71.

Analyze, analysis   To separate a subject into its parts (*analyze*), or the act or result of doing so (*analysis*, also called *division*). Analysis is a key skill in CRITICAL THINKING, READING, AND WRITING; see pages 16–17. It is also considered a method of development; see Chapter 6.

Anecdote   A brief narrative, or retelling of a story or event. Anecdotes have many uses: as essay openers or closers, as examples, as sheer entertainment. See Chapter 1.

Appeals   Resources writers draw on to connect with and persuade readers.

A **rational appeal** asks readers to use their intellects and their powers of reasoning. It relies on established conventions of logic and evidence.

An **emotional appeal** asks readers to respond out of their beliefs, values, or feelings. It inspires, affirms, frightens, angers.

An **ethical appeal** asks readers to look favorably on the writer. It stresses the writer's intelligence, competence, fairness, morality, and other qualities desirable in a trustworthy debater or teacher.

See also pages 463–64.

Argument   A mode of writing intended to win readers' agreement with an assertion by engaging their powers of reasoning. Argument often overlaps PERSUASION. See Chapter 10.

Assume, assumption   To take something for granted (*assume*), or a belief or opinion taken for granted (*assumption*). Whether stated or unstated, assumptions influence a writer's choices of subject, viewpoint, evidence, and even language. See also page 17.

Audience   A writer's readers. Having in mind a particular audience helps the writer in choosing strategies. Imagine, for instance, that you are writing two reviews of the movie *In the Line of Fire:* one for the students who read the campus newspaper, the other for amateur and professional filmmakers who read *Millimeter*. For the first audience, you might write about the actors, the plot, and especially dramatic scenes. You might judge the picture and urge your readers to see it — or to avoid it. Writing for *Millimeter*, you might discuss special effects, shooting techniques, problems in editing and in mixing picture and sound. In this review, you might use more specialized and technical terms. Obviously, an awareness of the interests and knowledge of your readers, in each case, would help you decide how to write. If you told readers of the campus paper too much about filming techniques, you would lose most of them. If you told *Millimeter*'s readers the plot of the film in detail and how you liked its opening scene, probably you would put them to sleep.

You can increase your awareness of your audience by asking yourself a few questions before you begin to write. Who are to be your readers? What is their age level? Background? Education? Where do they live? What are their beliefs and attitudes? What interests them? What, if anything, sets them apart from most people? How familiar are they with your subject? Knowing your audience can help you write so that your readers will not only understand you better, but more deeply care about what you say.

Cause and effect   A method of development in which a writer ANALYZES reasons for an action, event, or decision, or analyzes its consequences. See Chapter 8. See also EFFECT.

Chronological order   The arrangement of events as they occurred or occur in time, first to last. Most NARRATIVES and PROCESS ANALYSES use chronological order.

Claim   The proposition that an ARGUMENT demonstrates. Stephen Toulmin favors this term in his system of reasoning. See page 465. In some discussions of argument, the term THESIS is used instead.

Classification   A method of development in which a writer sorts out plural things (contact sports, college students, kinds of music) into categories. See Chapter 7.

Cliché   A worn-out, trite expression that a writer employs thoughtlessly. Although at one time the expression may have been colorful, from heavy use it has lost its luster. It is now "old as the hills." In conversation, most of us sometimes use clichés, but in writing they "stick out like sore thumbs." Alert writers, when they revise, replace a cliché with a fresh, concrete expression. Writers who have trouble recognizing clichés should be suspicious of any phrase they've heard before and should try to read more widely. Their problem is that, so many expressions being new to them, they do not know which ones are full of moths.

Coherence   The clear connection of the parts in a piece of effective writing. This quality exists when the reader can easily follow the flow of ideas between sentences, paragraphs, and larger divisions, and can see how they relate successively to one another.

   In making your essay coherent, you may find certain devices useful. TRANSITIONS, for instance, can bridge ideas. Reminders of points you have stated earlier are helpful to a reader who may have forgotten them — as readers tend to do sometimes, particularly if your essay is long. However, a coherent essay is not one merely pasted together with transitions and reminders. It derives its coherence from the clear relationship between its THESIS (or central idea) and all its parts.

Colloquial expressions   Words and phrases occurring primarily in speech and informal writing that seeks a relaxed, conversational tone. "My favorite chow is a burger and a shake" or "This math exam has me wired" may be acceptable in talking to a roommate, in corresponding with a friend, or in writing a humorous essay for general readers. Such choices of words, however, would be out of place in formal writing — in, say, a laboratory report or a letter to your senator. Contractions (*let's, don't, we'll*) and abbreviated words (*photo, sales rep, TV*) are the shorthand of spoken language. Good writers use such expressions with an awareness that they produce an effect of casualness.

Comparison and contrast   Two methods of development usually found together. Using them, a writer examines the similarities and differences between two things to reveal their natures. See Chapter 4.

Conclusion   The sentences or paragraphs that bring an essay to a satisfying and logical end. A conclusion is purposefully crafted to give a sense of unity and completeness to the whole essay. The best conclusions evolve naturally out of what has gone before and convince the reader that the essay is indeed at an end, not that the writer has run out of steam.

Conclusions vary in type and length depending on the nature and scope of the essay. A long research paper may require several paragraphs of summary to review and emphasize the main points. A short essay, however, may benefit from a few brief closing sentences.

In concluding an essay, beware of diminishing the impact of your writing by finishing on a weak note. Don't apologize for what you have or have not written, or cram in a final detail that would have been better placed elsewhere.

Although there are no set formulas for closing, the following list presents several options:

1. Restate the thesis of your essay, and perhaps your main points.
2. Mention the broader implications or significance of your topic.
3. Give a final example that pulls all the parts of your discussion together.
4. Offer a prediction.
5. End with the most important point as the culmination of your essay's development.
6. Suggest how the reader can apply the information you have just imparted.
7. End with a bit of drama or flourish. Tell an ANECDOTE, offer an appropriate quotation, ask a question, make a final insightful remark. Keep in mind, however, that an ending shouldn't sound false and gimmicky. It truly has to conclude.

Concrete   See ABSTRACT AND CONCRETE.

Connotation and denotation   Two types of meanings most words have. *Denotation* is the explicit, literal, dictionary definition of a word. *Connotation* refers to the implied meaning, resonant with associations, of a word. The denotation of *blood* is "the fluid that circulates in the vascular system." The word's connotations range from *life force* to *gore* to *family bond.* A doctor might use the word *blood* for its denotation, and a mystery writer might rely on the rich connotations of the word to heighten a scene.

Because people have different experiences, they bring to the same word different associations. A conservative's emotional response to the word *welfare* is not likely to be the same as a liberal's. And referring to your senator as a *diplomat* evokes a different response, from the senator and from others, than would *baby-kisser, political hack,* or even *politician.* The effective use of words involves knowing both what they mean literally and what they are likely to suggest.

Critical thinking, reading, and writing   A group of interlocking skills that are essential for college work and beyond. Each seeks the meaning beneath the surface of a statement, poem, editorial, picture, advertisement, or other "text." Using ANALYSIS, INFERENCE, SYNTHESIS, and often EVALUATION, the critical thinker, reader, and writer separates this text into its elements in order to see and judge meanings, relations, and ASSUMPTIONS that might otherwise remain buried. See also pages 16–18 and 269.

Data The name for EVIDENCE favored by logician Stephen Toulmin in his system of reasoning. See page 465.

Deductive reasoning, deduction The method of reasoning from the general to the particular: From information about what we already know, we deduce what we need or want to know. See Chapter 10, pages 468–69.

Definition A statement of the literal and specific meaning or meanings of a word, or a method of developing an essay. In the latter, the writer usually explains the nature of a word, a thing, a concept, or a phenomenon; in doing so the writer may employ NARRATION, DESCRIPTION, or any other method. See Chapter 9.

Denotation See CONNOTATION AND DENOTATION.

Description A mode of writing that conveys the evidence of the senses: sight, hearing, touch, taste, smell. See Chapter 2.

Diction The choice of words. Every written or spoken statement contains diction of some kind. To describe certain aspects of diction, the following terms may be useful:

Standard English: words and grammatical forms that native speakers of the language use in formal writing.

Nonstandard English: words and grammatical forms such as *theirselves* and *ain't* that occur mainly in the speech of people from a particular area or social background.

Slang: certain words in highly informal speech or writing, or in the speech of a particular group. For example, *blow off, dis, dweeb.*

Colloquial expressions: words and phrases from conversation. See COLLOQUIAL EXPRESSIONS for examples.

Regional terms: words heard in a certain locality, such as *spritzing* for "raining" in Pennsylvania Dutch country.

Dialect: a variety of English based on differences in geography, education, or social background. Dialect is usually spoken, but may be written. Maya Angelou's essay in Chapter 1 transcribes the words of dialect speakers: people waiting for the fight broadcast ("He gone whip him till that white boy call him Momma").

Technical terms: words and phrases that form the vocabulary of a particular discipline (*monocotyledon* from botany), occupation (*drawplate* from die-making), or avocation (*interval training* from running). See also JARGON.

Archaisms: old-fashioned expressions, once common but now used to suggest an earlier style, such as *ere, yon,* and *forsooth.* (Actually, *yon* is still current in the expression *hither and yon;* but if you say "Behold yon glass of beer!" it is an archaism.)

Obsolete diction: words that have passed out of use (such as the verb *werien,* "to protect or defend," and the noun *isetnesses,* "agreements"). *Obsolete* may also refer to certain meanings of words no longer current (*fond* for foolish, *clipping* for hugging or embracing).

 Pretentious diction: use of words more numerous and elaborate than necessary, such as *institution of higher learning* for college, and *partake of solid nourishment* for eat.

 Archaic, obsolete, and pretentious diction usually has no place in good writing unless a writer deliberately uses it for ironic or humorous effect: H. L. Mencken delighted in the hifalutin use of *tonsorial studio* instead of barber shop. Still, any diction may be the right diction for a certain occasion: The choice of words depends on a writer's purpose and audience.

Discovery The stage of the writing process before the first draft. It may include deciding on a topic, narrowing the topic, creating or finding ideas, doing reading and other research, defining PURPOSE and AUDIENCE, planning and arranging material. Discovery may follow from daydreaming or meditation, reading, or perhaps carefully ransacking memory. In practice, though, it usually involves considerable writing and is aided by the act of writing. The operations of discovery — reading, research, further idea-creation, and refinement of subject, purpose, and audience — may all continue well into drafting as well. See also pages 25, 27–28.

Division See ANALYSIS.

Dominant impression The main idea a writer conveys about a subject through DESCRIPTION — that an elephant is gigantic, for example, or an experience scary. See also Chapter 2.

Drafting The stage of the writing process during which a writer expresses ideas in complete sentences, links them, and arranges them in a sequence. See also pages 25–26, 29–30.

Effect The result of an event or action, usually considered together with CAUSE as a method of development. See the discussion of cause and effect in Chapter 8. In discussing writing, the term *effect* also refers to the impression a word, sentence, paragraph, or entire work makes on the reader: how convincing it is, whether it elicits an emotional response, what associations it conjures up, and so on.

Emotional appeal See APPEALS.

Emphasis The stress or special importance given to a certain point or element to make it stand out. A skillful writer draws attention to what is most important in a sentence, paragraph, or essay by controlling emphasis in any of the following ways:

 Proportion: Important ideas are given greater coverage than minor points.

 Position: The beginnings and ends of sentences, paragraphs, and larger divisions are the strongest positions. Placing key ideas in these spots helps draw attention to their importance. The end is the stronger position, for what stands last stands out. A sentence in which less important details precede the main point is called a **periodic sentence:** "Having disguised himself as a guard and walked through the courtyard to the side gate, the prisoner made his escape." A sentence in which the main point precedes less important details is a **loose sentence:** "Autumn is orange: gourds in baskets at roadside stands, the harvest moon hanging like a pumpkin, and oak and beech leaves flashing like goldfish."

   Repetition: Careful repetition of key words or phrases can give them greater importance. (Careless repetition, however, can cause boredom.)

   Mechanical devices: Italics (underlining), capital letters, and exclamation points can make words or sentences stand out. Writers sometimes fall back on these devices, however, after failing to show significance by other means. Italics and exclamation points can be useful in reporting speech, but excessive use sounds exaggerated or bombastic.

Essay   A short nonfiction composition on one central theme or subject in which the writer may offer personal views. Essays are sometimes classified as either formal or informal. In general, a **formal essay** is one whose diction is that of the written language (not colloquial speech), serious in tone, and usually focused on a subject the writer believes is important. (For example, see Bruce Catton's "Grant and Lee.") An **informal essay,** in contrast, is more likely to admit colloquial expressions; the writer's tone tends to be lighter, perhaps humorous, and the subject is likely to be personal, sometimes even trivial. (See James Thurber's "University Days.") These distinctions, however, are rough ones: An essay such as Judy Brady's "I Want a Wife" may use colloquial language and speak of personal experience, though it is serious in tone and has an undeniably important subject.

Ethical appeal   See APPEALS.

Euphemism   The use of inoffensive language in place of language that readers or listeners may find hurtful, distasteful, frightening, or otherwise objectionable — for instance, a police officer's announcing that someone *passed on* rather than *died*, or a politician's calling for *revenue enhancement* rather than *taxation*. Writers sometimes use euphemism out of consideration for readers' feelings, but just as often they use it to deceive readers or shirk responsibility.

Evaluate, evaluation   To judge the merits of something (*evaluate*), or the act or result of doing so (*evaluation*). Evaluation is often part of CRITICAL THINKING, READING, AND WRITING. In evaluating a work of writing, you base your judgment on your ANALYSIS of it and your sense of its quality or value. See also pages 17–18.

Evidence   The factual basis for an argument or an explanation. In a courtroom, an attorney's case is only as good as the evidence marshaled to support it. In an essay, a writer's OPINIONS and GENERALIZATIONS also must rest upon evidence. The common forms of evidence are **facts,** verifiable statements; **statistics,** facts stated numerically; **examples,** specific instances of a generalization; **reported experience,** usually eyewitness accounts; **expert testimony,** the opinions of people considered very skilled or knowledgeable in the field; and, in CRITICAL WRITING about other writing, **quotations** or **paraphrases** from the work being discussed. (See PARAPHRASE.)

Example   Also called **exemplification** or **illustration,** a method of development in which the writer provides instances of a general idea. See Chapter 3. An *example* is a verbal illustration.

Exposition   The mode of prose writing that explains (or exposes) its subject. Its function is to inform, to instruct, or to set forth ideas: the major trade routes in the Middle East, how to make a dulcimer, why the United States consumes more energy than it needs. Exposition may call various methods to its service: EXAMPLE, COMPARISON AND CONTRAST, PROCESS ANALYSIS, and so on. Most college writing is at least partly exposition, and so are most of the essays in this book.

Fallacies   Errors in reasoning. See pages 469–71 for a list and examples.

Figures of speech   Expressions that depart from the literal meanings of words for the sake of emphasis or vividness. To say "She's a jewel" doesn't mean that the subject of praise is literally a kind of shining stone; the statement makes sense because its CONNOTATIONS come to mind: rare, priceless, worth cherishing. Some figures of speech involve comparisons of two objects apparently unlike. A **simile** (from the Latin, "likeness") states the comparison directly, usually connecting the two things using *like, as,* or *than:* "The moon is like a snowball," "He's lazy as a cat full of cream," "My feet are flatter than flyswatters." A **metaphor** (from the Greek, "transfer") declares one thing to *be* another: "A mighty fortress is our God," "The sheep were bolls of cotton on the hill." (A **dead metaphor** is a word or phrase that, originally a figure of speech, has come to be literal through common usage: "the *hands* of a clock.") **Personification** is a simile or metaphor that assigns human traits to inanimate objects or abstractions: "A stoop-shouldered refrigerator hummed quietly to itself," "All of a sudden the solution to the math problem sat there winking at me."

Other figures of speech consist of deliberate misrepresentations. **Hyperbole** (from the Greek, "throwing beyond") is a conscious exaggeration: "I'm so hungry I could eat a horse and saddle," "I'd wait for you a thousand years." Its opposite, **understatement,** creates an ironic or humorous effect: "I accepted the ride. At the moment, I didn't much feel like walking across the Mojave Desert." A **paradox** is a seemingly self-contradictory statement that, on reflection, makes sense: "Children are the poor person's wealth" (wealth can be monetary, or it can be spiritual). *Paradox* may also refer to a situation that is inexplicable or contradictory, such as the restriction of one group's rights in order to secure the rights of another group.

Flashback   A technique of NARRATIVE in which the sequence of events is interrupted to recall an earlier period.

Focus   The narrowing of a subject to make it manageable. Beginning with a general subject, you concentrate on a certain aspect of it. For instance, you may select crafts as a general subject, then decide your main interest lies in weaving. You could focus your essay still further by narrowing it to operating a hand loom. You can also focus your writing according to who will read it (AUDIENCE) or what you want it to achieve (PURPOSE).

General and specific   Terms that describe the relative number of instances or objects included in the group signified by a word. *General* words name a group or class (*flowers*); *specific* words limit the class by naming its individual members (*rose, violet, dahlia, marigold*). Words may be arranged in a series from more general to more specific: *clothes, pants, jeans, Levis*. The word *cat* is more specific than *animal*, but less specific than *tiger cat*, or *Garfield*. See also ABSTRACT AND CONCRETE.

Generalization   A statement about a class based on an examination of some of its members: "Lions are fierce." The more members examined and the more representative they are of the class, the sturdier the generalization. The statement "Solar heat saves homeowners money" would be challenged by homeowners who have yet to recover their installation costs. "Solar heat can save homeowners money in the long run" would be a sounder generalization. Insufficient or nonrepresentative evidence often leads to a hasty generalization, such as "All freshmen hate their roommates" or "Men never express their feelings." Words such as *all, every, only, never,* and *always* have to be used with care. "Some men don't express their feelings" is more credible than the statement above. Making a trustworthy generalization involves the use of INDUCTIVE REASONING (discussed on p. 468).

Hyperbole   See FIGURES OF SPEECH.

Illustration   Another name for EXAMPLE. See Chapter 3.

Image   A word or word sequence that evokes a sensory experience. Whether literal ("We picked two red apples") or figurative ("His cheeks looked like two red apples, buffed and shining"), an image appeals to the reader's memory of seeing, hearing, smelling, touching, or tasting. Images add concreteness to fiction — "The farm looked as tiny and still as a seashell, with the little knob of a house surrounded by its curved furrows of tomato plants" (Eudora Welty in a short story, "The Whistle") — and are an important element in poetry. But writers of essays, too, find images valuable to bring ideas down to earth. See also FIGURES OF SPEECH.

Inductive reasoning, induction   The process of reasoning to a conclusion about an entire class by examining some of its members. See page 468.

Infer, inference   To draw a conclusion (*infer*), or the act or result of doing so (*inference*). In CRITICAL THINKING, READING, AND WRITING, inference is the means to understanding a writer's meaning, ASSUMPTIONS, PURPOSE, fairness, and other attributes. See also page 17.

Introduction   The opening of a written work. Often it states the writer's subject, narrows it, and communicates an attitude toward it (TONE). Introductions vary in length, depending on their purposes. A research paper may need several paragraphs to set forth its central idea and its plan of organization; a brief, informal essay may need only a sentence or two for an introduction. Whether long or short, good introductions tell readers no more than they need to know when they begin reading. Here are a few possible ways to open an essay effectively:

1. State your central idea, or THESIS, perhaps showing why you care about it.

2. Present startling facts about your subject.

3. Tell an illustrative ANECDOTE.

4. Give background information that will help your reader understand your subject, or see why it is important.

5. Begin with an arresting quotation.

6. Ask a challenging question. (In your essay, you'll go on to answer it.)

Irony   A manner of speaking or writing that does not directly state a discrepancy, but implies one. **Verbal irony** is the intentional use of words to suggest a meaning other than literal: "What a mansion!" (said of a shack); "There's nothing like sunshine" (said on a foggy morning). (For more examples, see the essays by James Thurber, Jessica Mitford, Judy Brady, and Fran Lebowitz.) If irony is delivered contemptuously with an intent to hurt, we call it **sarcasm:** "Oh, you're a real friend!" (said to someone who refuses to lend the speaker a quarter to make a phone call). With **situational irony,** the circumstances themselves are incongruous, run contrary to expectations, or twist fate: Juliet regains consciousness only to find that Romeo, believing her dead, has stabbed himself. See also SATIRE.

Jargon   Strictly speaking, the special vocabulary of a trade or profession. The term has also come to mean inflated, vague, meaningless language of any kind. It is characterized by wordiness, ABSTRACTIONS galore, pretentious DICTION, and needlessly complicated word order. Whenever you meet a sentence that obviously could express its idea in fewer words and shorter ones, chances are that it is jargon. For instance: "The motivating force compelling her to opt continually for the most labor-intensive mode of operation in performing her functions was consistently observed to be the single constant and regular factor in her behavior patterns." Translation: "She did everything the hard way."

Metaphor   See FIGURES OF SPEECH.

Narration   The mode of writing that tells a story. See Chapter 1.

Narrator   The teller of a story, either in the first PERSON (*I*) or in the third (*he, she, it, they*). See pages 41–42.

Nonstandard English   See DICTION.

Objective and subjective   Kinds of writing that differ in emphasis. In *objective* writing, the emphasis falls on the topic; in *subjective* writing, it falls on the writer's view of the topic. Objective writing occurs in factual journalism, science reports, certain PROCESS ANALYSES (such as recipes, directions, and instructions), and logical arguments in which the writer attempts to downplay personal feelings and opinions. Subjective writing sets forth the writer's feelings, opinions, and interpretations. It occurs in friendly letters, journals, editorials, bylined feature stories and columns in newspapers, personal essays, and arguments that appeal to emotion. Very few essays, however, contain one kind of writing exclusive of the other.

Opinion   A view backed by EVIDENCE, or an essay expressing such a view. See pages 461, 473, and 474–75.

Paradox   See FIGURES OF SPEECH.

Paragraph   A group of closely related sentences that develop a central idea. In an essay, a paragraph is the most important unit of thought because it is both self-contained and part of the larger whole. Paragraphs separate long and involved ideas into smaller parts that are more manageable for the writer and easier for the reader to take in. Good paragraphs, like good essays, possess UNITY and COHERENCE. The central idea is usually stated in the TOPIC SENTENCE, often found at the beginning of the paragraph. All other sentences in the paragraph relate to this topic sentence, defining it, explaining it, illustrating it, providing it with evidence and support. Sometimes you will meet a unified and coherent paragraph that has no topic sentence. It usually contains a central idea that no sentence in it explicitly states, but that every sentence in it clearly implies.

Parallelism, parallel structure   A habit of good writers: keeping ideas of equal importance in similar grammatical form. A writer may place nouns side by side ("*Trees* and *streams* are my weekend tonic") or in a series ("Give me *wind*, *sea*, and *stars*"). Phrases, too, may be arranged in parallel structure ("*Out of my bed, into my shoes, up to my classroom* — that's my life"); or clauses ("Ask not what your country can do for you; ask what you can do for your country").

   Parallelism may be found not only in single sentences, but in larger units as well. A paragraph might read: "Rhythm is everywhere. It throbs in the rain forests of Brazil. It vibrates ballroom floors in Vienna. It snaps its fingers on street corners in Chicago." In a whole essay, parallelism may be the principle used to arrange ideas in a balanced or harmonious structure. See the famous speech given by Martin Luther King, Jr. (p. 516), in which each paragraph in a series (paragraphs 11 through 18) begins with the words "I have a dream" and goes on to describe an imagined future. Not only does such a parallel structure organize ideas, but it also lends them force.

Paraphrase   Putting another writer's thoughts into your own words. In writing a research paper or an essay containing EVIDENCE gathered from your reading, you will find it necessary to paraphrase — unless you are using another writer's very words with quotation marks around them. In paraphrasing, you rethink what the other writer has said, decide what is essential, and determine how you would say it otherwise. (Of course, you still acknowledge your source.) The purpose of paraphrasing is not merely to avoid copying word for word, but to adapt material to the needs of your own paper.

   Although a paraphrase sometimes makes material briefer, it does not always do so; in principle, it rewrites and restates, sometimes in the same number of words, if not more. A condensation of longer material that renders it more concise is a SUMMARY: for instance, a statement of the plot of a whole novel in a few sentences.

Person   A grammatical distinction made between the speaker, the one spoken to, and the one spoken about. In the first person (*I, we*), the subject is speaking. In the second person (*you*), the subject is being spoken to. In the third person (*he, she, it*), the subject is being spoken about. The point of view of an essay or work of fiction is often specified according to person: "This short story is told from a first-person point of view." See POINT OF VIEW.

Personification   See FIGURES OF SPEECH.

Persuasion   A mode of writing intended to influence people's actions by engaging their beliefs and feelings. Persuasion often overlaps ARGUMENT. See Chapter 10.

Point of view   In an essay, the physical position or the mental angle from which a writer beholds a subject. Assuming the subject is starlings, the following three writers have different points of view. An ornithologist might write OBJECTIVELY about the introduction of these birds into North America. A farmer might advise others farmers how to prevent the birds from eating seed. A bird-watcher might SUBJECTIVELY describe a first glad sighting of an unusual species. Furthermore, the PERSON of each essay would probably differ: The scientist might present a scholarly paper in the third person; the farmer might offer advice in the second; the bird-watcher might recount the experience in the first.

Premise   A proposition or ASSUMPTION that supports a conclusion. See page 469 for examples.

Process analysis   A method of development that most often explains step by step how something is done or how to do something. See Chapter 5.

Proposal   A recommendation that an action be taken. In an ARGUMENT essay, a proposal is backed by EVIDENCE. See Chapter 10.

Purpose   A writer's reason for trying to convey a particular idea (THESIS) about a particular subject to a particular AUDIENCE of readers. Though it may emerge gradually during the writing process, in the end purpose should govern every element of a piece of writing.

In trying to define the purpose of an essay you read, ask yourself, Why did the writer write this? or, What was this writer trying to achieve? Even though you cannot know the writer's intentions with absolute certainty, an effective essay generally makes some purpose clear.

Rational appeal   See APPEALS.

Revision   The stage of the writing process during which a writer "re-sees" a draft from the viewpoint of a reader. Revision usually involves two steps, first considering fundamental matters such as purpose and organization, and then editing for surface matters such as smooth transitions and error-free sentences. See pages 26–27, 31–34.

Rhetoric   The study (and the art) of using language effectively. *Rhetoric* also has a negative connotation of empty or pretentious language meant to waffle, stall, or even deceive. This is the meaning in "The president had nothing substantial to say about taxes. Just the usual rhetoric."

Rhetorical question   A question posed for effect, one that requires no answer. Instead, it often provokes thought, lends emphasis to a point, asserts or denies something without making a direct statement, launches further discussion, introduces an opinion, or leads the reader where the writer intends. Sometimes a writer throws one in to introduce variety in a paragraph full of declarative sentences. The following questions are rhetorical: "When will the United States learn that sending people to the moon does not feed them on the earth?" "Shall I compare thee to a summer's day?" "What is the point of making money if you've no one but yourself to spend it on?" Both reader and writer know what the answers are supposed to be. (1) Someday, if the United States ever wises up. (2) Yes. (3) None.

Sarcasm   See IRONY.

Satire   A form of writing that employs wit to attack folly. Unlike most comedy, the purpose of satire is not merely to entertain, but to bring about enlightenment — even reform. Usually, satire employs irony — as in Jonathan Swift's "A Modest Proposal" (p. 522). See also IRONY.

Scene   In a NARRATIVE, an event retold in detail to re-create an experience. See Chapter 1.

Sentimentality   A quality sometimes found in writing that fails to communicate. Such writing calls for an extreme emotional response on the part of an AUDIENCE, although its writer fails to supply adequate reason for any such reaction. A sentimental writer delights in waxing teary over certain objects: great-grandmother's portrait, the first stick of chewing gum baby chewed (now a shapeless wad), an empty popcorn box saved from the World Series of 1952. Sentimental writing usually results when writers shut their eyes to the actual world, preferring to snuffle the sweet scents of remembrance.

Simile   See FIGURES OF SPEECH.

Slang   See DICTION.

Specific   See GENERAL AND SPECIFIC.

Standard English   See DICTION.

Strategy   Whatever means a writer employs to write effectively. The methods set forth in this book are strategies; but so are narrowing a subject, organizing ideas clearly, using TRANSITIONS, writing with an awareness of your reader, and other effective writing practices.

Style   The distinctive manner in which a writer writes. Style may be seen especially in the writer's choice of words and sentence structure. Two writers may write on the same subject, even express similar ideas, but it is style that gives each writer's work a personality.

Subjective   See OBJECTIVE AND SUBJECTIVE.

Summarize, summary   To condense a work (essay, movie, news story) to its essence (*summarize*), or the act or result of doing so (*summary*). Summarizing a piece of writing in one's own words is an effective way to understand it. See pages 15–16.

Suspense   Often an element in narration: the pleasurable expectation or anxiety we feel that keeps us reading a story. In an exciting mystery story, suspense is constant: How will it all turn out? Will the detective get to the scene in time to prevent another murder? But there can be suspense in less melodramatic accounts as well.

Syllogism   A three-step form of reasoning that employs DEDUCTION. See page 469 for an illustration.

Symbol   A visible object or action that suggests some further meaning. The flag suggests country, the crown suggests royalty — these are conventional symbols familiar to us. Life abounds in such relatively clear-cut symbols. Football teams use dolphins and rams for easy identification; married couples symbolize their union with a ring.

In writing, symbols usually do not have such a one-to-one correspondence, but evoke a whole constellation of associations. In Herman Melville's *Moby-Dick,* the whale suggests more than the large mammal it is. It hints at evil, obsession, and the untamable forces of nature. Such a symbol carries meanings too complex or elusive to be neatly defined.

Although more common in fiction and poetry, symbols can be used to good purpose in nonfiction because they often communicate an idea in a compact and concrete way.

Synthesize, synthesis   To link elements into a whole (*synthesize*), or the act or result of doing so (*synthesis*). In CRITICAL THINKING, READING, AND WRITING, synthesis is the key step during which you reassemble a work you have ANALYZED or connect the work with others. See page 17.

Thesis   The central idea in a work of writing, to which everything else in the work refers. In some way, each sentence and PARAGRAPH in an effective essay serves to support the thesis and to make it clear and explicit to readers. Good writers, while writing, often set down a **thesis sentence** or **thesis statement** to help them define their purpose. They may also include this statement in their essay as a promise and a guide to readers.

Tone   The way a writer expresses his or her regard for subject, audience, or self. Through word choice, sentence structures, and what is actually said, the writer conveys an attitude and sets a prevailing spirit. Tone in writing varies as greatly as tone of voice varies in conversation. It can be serious, distant, flippant, angry, enthusiastic, sincere, sympathetic. Whatever tone a writer chooses, usually it informs an entire essay and helps a reader decide how to respond. For works of strong tone, see the essays by Joan Didion, Annie Dillard, Jessica Mitford, Judy Brady, A. M. Rosenthal, and Martin Luther King, Jr.

Topic sentence   The statement of the central idea in a PARAGRAPH. Often it will appear at (or near) the beginning of the paragraph, announcing the idea and beginning its development. Because all other sentences in the paragraph explain and support this central idea, the topic sentence is a way to create UNITY.

Transitions   Words, phrases, sentences, or even paragraphs that relate ideas. In moving from one topic to the next, a writer has to bring the reader along by showing how the ideas are developing, what bearing a new thought or detail has on an earlier discussion, or why a new topic is being introduced. A clear purpose, strong ideas, and logical development certainly aid COHERENCE, but to ensure that the reader is following along, good writers provide signals, or transitions.

To bridge paragraphs and to point out relationships within them, you can use some of the following devices of transition:

1. Repeat words or phrases to produce an echo in the reader's mind.

2. Use PARALLEL STRUCTURES to produce a rhythm that moves the reader forward.

3. Use pronouns to refer back to nouns in earlier passages.

4. Use transitional words and phrases. These may indicate a relationship of time (*right away, later, soon, meanwhile, in a few minutes, that night*), proximity (*beside, close to, distant from, nearby, facing*), effect (*therefore, for this reason, as a result, consequently*), comparison (*similarly, in the same way, likewise*), or contrast (*yet, but, nevertheless, however, despite*). Some words and phrases of transition simply add on: *besides, too, also, moreover, in addition to, second, last, in the end.*

Understatement   See FIGURES OF SPEECH.

Unity   The quality of good writing in which all parts relate to the THESIS. In a unified essay, all words, sentences, and PARAGRAPHS support the single central idea. Your first step in achieving unity is to state your thesis; your next step is to organize your thoughts so that they make your thesis clear.

Voice   In writing, the sense of the author's character, personality, and attitude that comes through the words. See TONE.

Warrant   The name in Stephen Toulmin's system of reasoning for the thinking, or ASSUMPTION, that links DATA and CLAIM. See pages 465–68.

M. F. K. Fisher. "The Broken Chain." From *To Begin Again* by M. F. K. Fisher. Copyright © 1992 the M. F. K. Fisher Literary Trust. Reprinted by permission of Pantheon Books, a division of Random House, Inc.

Robert Francis. Excerpt from "Teacher" from *Pot Shots at Poetry* (1980). Reprinted by permission of the University of Michigan Press.

Albert Gore, Jr. "Ships in the Desert." From *Earth in the Balance* by Albert Gore, Jr. Copyright © 1992 by Senator Al Gore. Reprinted by permission of Houghton Mifflin Co. All rights reserved.

Vivian Gornick. "Mama Went to Work." Excerpt (re-titled) and "Vivian Gornick on Writing" from *Fierce Attachments* by Vivian Gornick. Copyright © 1987 by Vivian Gornick.

Stephen Jay Gould. "Sex, Drugs, Disasters, and the Extinction of Dinosaurs." Reprinted from *The Flamingo's Smile: Reflections in Natural History* by Stephen Jay Gould, by permission of W. W. Norton & Company, Inc. Copyright © 1985 by Stephen Jay Gould. In "Stephen Jay Gould on Writing," Prologue excerpts are reprinted from *The Flamingo's Smile: Reflections in Natural History* by Stephen Jay Gould, by permission of W. W. Norton & Company, Inc. Copyright © 1985 by Stephen Jay Gould.

Jeff Greenfield. "The Black and White Truth about Basketball." Copyright © 1975 by Jeff Greenfield. Reprinted by permission of Sterling Lord Literistic. "Jeff Greenfield on Writing," copyright © 1984 by St. Martin's Press, Inc.

Marvin Harris. "How Our Skins Got Their Color." Reprinted from *Our Kind* by Marvin Harris, by permission of HarperCollins Publishers Inc. Copyright © 1989 by Marvin Harris.

Linda Hogan. "Waking Up the Rake." Reprinted from *Parabola*, The Magazine of Myth and Tradition, Vol. XIII, No. 2 (Summer, 1988). Reprinted by permission of the author. "Linda Hogan on Writing," from *Contemporary Authors*, vol. 120.

bell hooks. "Madonna." From *Black Looks*. Reprinted by permission of South End Press. In "bell hooks on Writing," excerpts from "Writing in the Darkness," which appeared originally in *TriQuarterly*, Spring–Summer 1989.

Shirley Jackson. "The Lottery." From *The Lottery* by Shirley Jackson. Copyright © 1948, 1949 by Shirley Jackson. Renewed © 1976, 1977 by Laurence Hyman, Barry Hyman, Mrs. Sarah Webster and Mrs. Joanne Schnurer. In "Shirley Jackson on Writing," excerpts from "Biography of a Story" from *Come Along with Me* by Shirley Jackson. Copyright © 1948, 1952, © 1960 by Shirley Jackson. Used by permission of Viking Penguin, a division of Penguin Books USA Inc.

H. W. Janson. Excerpt from *History of Art*, 2nd ed., by H. W. Janson, published in 1977 by Harry N. Abrams, Inc., New York. All rights reserved.

Laurie Johnston and Suzanne Daley. Excerpt from an article that appeared in *The New York Times* on July 23, 1983. Copyright © 1983 by The New York Times Company. Reprinted by permission.

June Jordan. "Requiem for the Champ." From *Technical Difficulties* by June Jordan. Copyright © 1992 by June Jordan. Reprinted by permission of the author. In "June Jordan on Writing," excerpts from the May 1, 1981, issue of *Publisher's Weekly*, published by R. R. Bowker and Company. Copyright © 1981 by Xerox Corporation.

Michiko Kakutani. "The Word Police." Copyright © 1993 by The New York Times Company. Reprinted by permission.

Jamaica Kincaid. "The Tourist." Excerpt re-titled from *A Small Place* by Jamaica Kincaid. Copyright © 1988 by Jamaica Kincaid. In "Jamaica Kincaid on Writing," excerpt from Louise Kennedy, "A Writer Retraces Her Steps" from *The Boston Globe*, 11/7/90. Reprinted by permission.

Martin Luther King, Jr. "I Have a Dream." Reprinted by arrangement with The Heirs to the Estate of Martin Luther King, Jr., c/o Joan Daves Agency as agent for the proprietor. Copyright © 1963 by Martin Luther King, Jr., copyright renewed © 1991 by Coretta Scott King.

Maxine Hong Kingston. "No Name Woman." From *The Woman Warrior* by Maxine Hong Kingston. Copyright © 1975, 1976 by Maxine Hong Kingston. Reprinted by permission of Alfred A. Knopf, Inc. "Maxine Hong Kingston on Writing" from *Contemporary Authors*, vol. 13.

Spiro Kostof. Excerpt from *A History of Architecture: Settings and Rituals* by Spiro Kostof. Copyright © 1985 by Oxford University Press, Inc. Reprinted by permission.

William Least Heat Moon. Excerpt reprinted from *Blue Highways: A Journey into America* by William Least Heat Moon, by permission of the publisher, Little, Brown and Company. Copyright © 1982 by William Least Heat Moon.

Fran Lebowitz. "The Sound of Music: Enough Already." From *Metropolitan Life* by Fran Lebowitz. Copyright © 1974, 1975, 1976, 1977, 1978 by Fran Lebowitz. In "Fran Lebowitz on Writing," excerpt from Jean W. Ross's interview with Fran Lebowitz in *Contemporary Authors, New Revision Series*, vol. 14, edited by Linda Metzger. Copyright © 1985 by Gale Research Inc. All rights reserved. Reprinted by permission of the publisher.

Nancy Mairs. "Disability." Reprinted form *Carnal Acts* by Nancy Mairs, by permission of HarperCollins Publishers Inc. Copyright © 1991 by Nancy Mairs. In "Nancy Mairs on Writing," excerpts from "When Bad Things Happen to Good Writers" by Nancy Mairs, *The New York Times Book Review*, February 21, 1993. Copyright © 1993 by The New York Times Company. Reprinted by permission.

Merrill Markoe. "Conversation Piece." From *What the Dogs Have Taught Me* by Merrill Markoe. Copyright © 1992 by Merrill Markoe. Reprinted by permission of Viking Penguin, a division of Penguin Books USA Inc.

H. L. Mencken. "The Penalty of Death" from *A Mencken Chrestomathy* by H. L. Mencken, copyright © 1923 by Alfred A. Knopf, Inc. and renewed 1954 by H. L. Mencken, reprinted by permission of Alfred A. Knopf, Inc. In "H. L. Mencken on Writing," excerpts from "Addendum on Aims" by H. L. Mencken in *American Scene* and from "The Fringes of Lovely Letters" by H. L. Mencken in *Prejudices: Fifth Series*, all copyright © by Alfred A. Knopf, Inc. and reprinted by permission of Alfred A. Knopf, Inc.

Mark Crispin Miller. "Dow Recycles Reality." Reprinted by permission of the author.

G. Tyler Miller. Excerpts from *Living in the Environment*, second edition. Copyright © 1979 by Wadsworth, Inc. Reprinted by permission of the publisher.

Jessica Mitford. "Behind the Formaldehyde Curtain." Reprinted by permission of Jessica Mitford. All rights reserved. Copyright © 1963, 1978 by Jessica Mitford. In "Jessica Mitford on Writing," excerpts from *Poison Penmanship* by Jessica

Mitford, copyright © 1979 and from *A Fine Old Conflict* by Jessica Mitford, copyright © 1977, both reprinted by permission of Alfred A. Knopf.

Robert A. Muller and Theodore M. Oberlander. Excerpt from *Physical Geography Today: A Portrait of a Planet*, 3rd ed. (1984). Reprinted by permission of McGraw-Hill, Inc.

George Orwell. "Politics and the English Language." Reprinted from *Shooting an Elephant and Other Essays*, by George Orwell. Copyright © 1946 by George Orwell and renewed 1974 by Sonia Orwell. Reprinted by permission of Harcourt Brace & Company and the estate of the late Sonia Bronwell Orwell and Martin Secker & Warburg Ltd.

Diane E. Papalia and Sally Wendkos Olds. Excerpts from *Psychology* (1985). Reprinted by permission of the publisher, McGraw-Hill, Inc.

Robert Pirsig. Excerpt from *Zen and the Art of Motorcycle Maintenance* by Robert Pirsig. Copyright © 1974 by Robert Pirsig.

Katha Pollitt. "Why Do We Read?" Reprinted from *The Nation* magazine, September 23, 1991, where it appeared as "Why We Read: Canon to the Right of Me." Copyright © The Nation Company, Inc.

William K. Purves and Gordon H. Orians. Excerpt from *Life: The Science of Biology*. Copyright © 1983 by Sinauer Associates, Inc. Reprinted by permission of the publisher.

Anna Quindlen. "Homeless." From *Living Out Loud* by Anna Quindlen. In "Anna Quindlen on Writing," excerpts from "In the Beginning" from *Living Out Loud* by Anna Quindlen. Copyright © 1987 by Anna Quindlen. Reprinted by permission of Random House, Inc.

Ishmael Reed. "America: The Multinational Society." Reprinted by permission of Atheneum Publishers, an imprint of Macmillan Publishing Company, from *Writin' Is Fightin'* by Ishmael Reed. Copyright © 1983 by Ishmael Reed. In "Ishmael Reed on Writing," excerpts from William C. Brisick, "Ishmael Reed," *Publishers Weekly*, July 1, 1988.

Robert B. Reich. "Why the Rich Are Getting Richer and the Poor Poorer." Excerpted from *The New Republic*, May 1, 1989. Reprinted by permission of *The New Republic*, Copyright © 1989 by The New Republic, Inc. In "Robert B. Reich on Writing," excerpts from Introduction to *Tales of America* by Robert B. Reich. Copyright © 1987 by Robert B. Reich. Reprinted by permission of Times Books, a division of Random House, Inc.

Richard Rodriguez. "Aria: A Memoir of a Bilingual Childhood." Copyright © 1980 by Richard Rodriguez. Reprinted by permission of Georges Borchardt, Inc. for the author. First appeared in *The American Scholar*. "Richard Rodriguez on Writing," copyright © 1985 by St. Martin's Press, Inc.

A. M. Rosenthal. "The Case for Slavery." Copyright © 1990 by The New York Times Company. Reprinted by permission. In "A. M. Rosenthal on Writing," excepts from "Learning on the Job," by A. M. Rosenthal. Copyright © 1986 by The New York Times Company. Reprinted by permission.

Murray Ross. "Football Red and Baseball Green." Copyright © 1991 by Murray Ross. An earlier version of this article appeared in *Chicago Review*, January/February 1971. "Murray Ross on Writing," copyright © 1994 by St. Martin's Press, Inc.

Edward Sapir. Excerpt from *Selected Writings of Edward Sapir in Language, Culture and*

Personality. Edited/translated by David Mandelbaum. Copyright © 1949 The Regents of the University of California.

Linnea Saukko. "How to Poison the Earth" (and in "Linnea Saukko on Writing") excerpts from *Student Writers at Work and in the Company of Other Writers.* Copyright © 1984 by St. Martin's Press, Inc. Reprinted by permission.

Arthur M. Schlesinger, Jr. "The Cult of Ethnicity, Good and Bad." Copyright © 1991 Time, Inc. Reprinted by permission. "Arthur M. Schlesinger, Jr., on Writing," from *Contemporary Authors,* vol. 28.

David Segal. "Excuuuse Me." From *The New Republic,* May 11, 1990. Reprinted by permission of the author. "David Segal on Writing," copyright © 1994 by St. Martin's Press, Inc.

Gail Sheehy. "Predictable Crises of Adulthood." From *Passages* by Gail Sheehy. Copyright © 1974, 1976 by Gail Sheehy. Used by permission of Dutton Signet, a division of Penguin Books USA Inc.

Lewis C. Solmon. *Microeconomics, 3rd edition* (excerpt from page 198), copyright © 1980 by Addison-Wesley Publishing Company, Inc. Reprinted by permission of the publisher.

Michael Sorkin. Excerpt from "Faking It" from *Watching Television* by Todd Gitlin. Copyright © 1986 by Mark Crispin Miller. Reprinted by permission of Pantheon Books, a division of Random House, Inc.

Brent Staples. "Black Men and Public Space." From *Harper's* Magazine, December 1986. Reprinted by permission of the author. "Brent Staples on Writing," copyright © 1991 by St. Martin's Press, Inc.

Gloria Steinem. "Erotica and Pornography" and "Gloria Steinem on Writing." Excerpts from *Outrageous Acts and Everyday Rebellions* by Gloria Steinem. Copyright © 1983 by East Toledo Productions, Inc. Reprinted by permission of Henry Holt and Company, Inc.

Amy Tan. "The Language of Discretion." Copyright © 1989 by Amy Tan. Reprinted by permission of the author. In "Amy Tan on Writing," excerpts from "Mother Tongue," copyright © 1989 by Amy Tan. As first appeared in *Threepenny Review.*

James Thurber. "University Days" by James Thurber. From *My Life and Hard Times,* published by HarperCollins. Copyright © 1933, 1961 by James Thurber. Reprinted by permission. In "James Thurber on Writing," excerpts from *Writers at Work, First Series* by Malcolm Cowley, Editor. Copyright © 1957, 1958 by The Paris Review, renewed © 1985 by Malcolm Cowley, © 1986 by The Paris Review. Reprinted by permission of Viking Penguin, a division of Penguin Books USA Inc. Excerpt from *Thurber Country,* published by Simon and Schuster. Copyright © 1953 by James Thurber, © 1981 by Helen Thurber and Rosemary A. Thurber. Reprinted by permission.

Alice Trillin. Excerpt from "A Writer's Process: A Conversation with Calvin Trillin." Copyright © 1982 *Journal of Basic Writing,* Instructional Resource Center, Office of Academic Affairs, The City University of New York.

Brenda Ueland. "Tell Me More." From *Strength to Your Sword Arm: Selected Writings* by Brenda Ueland. Copyright © 1993 by the Estate of Brenda Ueland. Reprinted by permission of Holy Cow! Press, P. O. Box 3170, Mt. Royal Station, Duluth, Minnesota 55803. In "Brenda Ueland on Writing," excerpt reprinted from *If*

You Want to Write, copyright © 1987 by the Estate of Brenda Ueland, with the permission of Graywolf Press, Saint Paul, Minnesota.

David Updike. "The Colorings of Childhood." Reprinted by permission of Wylie, Aitken and Stone.

Robert M. Veatch. Excerpt from "Models for Medicine in a Revolutionary Age," *Hastings Center Report,* June 1972. Reprinted by permission.

Camilo José Vergara. "A Guide to the Ghettos." Reprinted from *The Nation* magazine, March 15, 1993, in which it appeared as "Down Our Mean Streets: A Guide to the Ghettos." Copyright © The Nation Company, Inc.

Gore Vidal. "Drugs." From *Homage to Daniel Shays: Collected Essays 1952–1972* by Gore Vidal. Copyright © 1970 by Gore Vidal. Reprinted by permission of Random House, Inc. In "Gore Vidal on Writing," excerpt from *Writers at Work, Fifth Series,* by George Plimpton, ed. Introduction by Francine du Plessix Gray. Copyright © 1981 by The Paris Review. Used by permission of Viking Penguin, a division of Penguin Books USA Inc.

E. B. White. "Once More to the Lake." Reprinted from *One Man's Meat* by E. B. White. By permission of HarperCollins, Publishers, Inc. Copyright © 1941, by E. B. White. In "E. B. White on Writing," excerpt reprinted from *Letters of E. B. White,* collected and edited by Dorothy Lobrano Guth, by permission of HarperCollins Publishers Inc. Copyright © 1976 by E. B. White.

Ralph Whitehead, Jr. "Class Acts: America's Changing Middle Class," from *Utne Reader,* January/February 1990. Reprinted by permission of the author. In "Ralph Whitehead, Jr., on Writing," excerpts from an interview with the author in Scott Heller, "Appealing to the 'New-Collar' Voter," in *The Chronicle of Higher Education,* November 21, 1987. Reprinted by permission.

William Carlos Williams. Excerpt from *The Collected Poems of William Carlos Williams, 1909–1939, vol. 1.* Copyright © 1938 by New Directions Publishing Corporation.

Linda Wolfe. Excerpt from *The Literary Gourmet: Menus from Masterpieces.* Copyright ©1962, 1985 by Linda Wolfe. Reprinted by permission of Simon and Schuster, Inc.

Tom Wolfe. "Pornoviolence." From *Mauve Gloves and Madmen, Cutter and Vine* by Tom Wolfe. Copyright © 1976 by Tom Wolfe. In "Tom Wolfe on Writing," excerpt from David Bellamy, *New Fiction: Interviews with Innovative American Authors.* Copyright © 1974 by The Trustees of the University of Illinois. Reprinted by permission of the author and the University of Illinois Press.

Virginia Woolf. "The Death of the Moth." From *The Death of the Moth and Other Essays* by Virginia Woolf. Reprinted by permission of the Estate of the Author and The Hogarth Press. In "Virginia Woolf on Writing," excerpts from "A Letter to a Young Poet" from *The Death of the Moth and Other Essays* by Virginia Woolf, copyright © 1942 by Harcourt Brace and Company and renewed in 1970 by Marjorie T. Parsons, Executrix, reprinted by permission of the publisher, and from "Sunday (Easter) 20 April" in *The Diary of Virginia Woolf,* Vol. 1, 1915–1919, edited by Anne Olivier Bell, copyright © 1977 by Quentin Bell and Angelica Garnett, reprinted by permission of Harcourt Brace & Company.

INDEX

Page numbers in bold type refer to
definitions in the glossary.

Abstract language, **707**
 definition and, 411–12
 Didion on, 118
Act (in Burke's pentad), 367
Actor (in Burke's pentad), 367
Agency (in Burke's pentad), 367
Allusion, **707**
"America: The Multinational Society"
  (Reed), 681, 682–86
Analogy, 169, 470, **708**
 argument and persuasion and, 470–
  71
 false, 470–71
 process analysis and, 224
Analysis, **709**. *See also* Cause and effect; Division or analysis; Process
  analysis
 critical reading with, 17, 19–20,
  463, 711, 714
 mixing other methods with, 537
Anecdote, **709,** 717
 conclusion with, 711
 example and, 138

narration and, 40–41
 Staples on, 163, 164
Angelou, Maya, 3, 49
 "Champion of the World," 41, 43,
  45, 46, 49–52
 "Maya Angelou on Writing," 53–54
Appeals, **709**
 emotional, 463–64
 ethical, 464
 rational, 463
Archaisms, **712**
Argument ad hominem, 470
Argument and persuasion, 461–76, **709**
 authority and, 470
 circular, 470
 comparison and contrast in, 167–68
 data, claim, and warrant in, 465–68
 deductive reasoning in, 468–69
 description and, 95
 emotional appeal in, 463–64
 ethical appeal in, 464
 evidence and, 463, 471–72, 472–73
 flawed, 466

Argument and persuasion (*cont.*)
  inductive reasoning in, 468
  logical fallacies and, 469–71
  Mencken on, 482–83
  method of, 461–71
  mixing other methods with, 537
  paragraph illustrations of, 473–76
  process of, 471–73
  professions and, 462
  rational appeal in, 463
  Segal on, 648–49
  thesis and, 19, 463, 471
  Toulmin method of, 465–68
Argument from doubtful or unidentified
    authority, 470
"Aria: A Memoir of a Bilingual Child-
    hood" (Rodriguez), 541, 563–74
Aristotle, 468, 469
Ascher, Barbara Lazear, 140
  "On Compassion," 140–42
Assumption, 17, 20, 269, 465, 467,
    709
Audience, **709**
  argument and persuasion and, 462,
    463–64, 465, 466, 472
  chronological order and, 45
  classification and, 317
  Coontz on, 157–58
  description and, 95–96
  discovery and, 713
  division or analysis and, 222–23
  Elbow on, 250–52
  example and, 138
  humor and, 472
  Jackson on, 90–91
  Jordan on, 392
  narrative and, 41–42, 43, 44
  process analysis and, 222–23
  proposals and, 474
  questions about, 709
  Reich on, 359–60
  sentimentality and, 720
  Tan on, 198
  Whitehead on, 348–49
  writing strategy and, 21
Authority, argument from, 470
Autobiography, Chase on, 561–62

Baker, Russell, 321
  "The Plot Against People," 317,
    321–23
  "Russell Baker on Writing," 324–26
Bate, W. Jackson, 40, 43
Begging the question, 470
"Behind the Formaldehyde Curtain"
    (Mitford), 222, 253–61
Bettelheim, Bruno, 438
  "The Holocaust," 438–41
Beyer, Lawrence A., 382
  "The Highlighter Crisis," 15, 382–84
Bilingualism, 197–98
Binary classification, 316
"Black and White Truth About Basket-
    ball, The" (Greenfield), 4, 168,
    199–204
"Black Men and Public Space" (Sta-
    ples), 159–62
Brady, Judy, 273, 717, 721
  "I Want a Wife," 268, 270, 273–75
Breslin, Jimmy, 430
Britt, Suzanne, 174
  "Neat People vs. Sloppy People,"
    174–76
  "Suzanne Britt on Writing," 178–79
"Broken Chain, The" (Fisher), 4, 6, 7,
    8, 9, 10–13, 15–16, 18, 19–23,
    24, 25, 27
Buckley, William F., Jr., 507
  "Why Don't We Complain?" 40, 95,
    472, 507–12
  "William F. Buckley, Jr., on Writ-
    ing," 514–15
Burckhardt, Jakob, 365
Burke, Kenneth, 367–68

"*Casa:* A Partial Remembrance of a
    Puerto Rican Childhood" (Cofer),
    73–78
"Case for Slavery, The" (Rosenthal),
    376–78
Categories in classification, 316–17,
    318, 319
Catton, Bruce, 180
  "Bruce Catton on Writing," 186

"Grant and Lee: A Study in Contrasts," 7, 169, 180–83
Causal chain, 364–65, 366
Cause and effect, 4, 21, 363–70, **710**
  argument and persuasion and, 472
  chain in, 364–65, 366
  definition and, 408, 410
  Greenfield's use of, 5
  historical studies and, 365, 370
  immediate cause in, 363
  logical fallacies and, 366–67
  major or minor cause in, 366
  mixing other methods with, 537
  paragraph illustrations of, 368–70
  process of, 365–68
  questions in, 363–64, 365, 367, 368, 369, 538
  remote cause in, 363, 366, 368
  subject and, 365–66
Censorship
  Dershowitz on, 488
  Ehrenreich on, 301–2
"Champion of the World" (Angelou), 41, 43, 45, 46, 49–52
Chang, Curtis, 3, 495
  "Curtis Chang on Writing," 506
  "Streets of Gold: The Myth of the Model Minority," 495–504
Chase, Clifford, 549
  "Clifford Chase on Writing," 561–62
  "My Brother on the Shoulder of the Road," 541, 549–59
Chayevsky, Paddy, 172
Chiaramonti, Scipio, 469
Chronological order, 22, **710**
  cause and effect and, 365
  narration and, 45
  process analysis and, 223
  Trillin on, 45–46
Claim, in argument and persuasion, 463, 465, 467, 471, 472–73, **710**
"Class Acts: America's Changing Middle Class" (Whitehead), 317, 342–47
Classification, 315–20, **710**
  binary, 316
  categories in, 316–17, 318, 319

complex, 316–17
  definition and, 410
  evaluation and, 317
  method of, 315–17
  mixing other methods with, 537
  paragraph illustrations of, 319–20
  principles of, 316, 317, 319, 320
  process analysis and, 223
  process of, 317–18
  purpose of, 316, 317
  subject of, 315–16, 318
Cliché, **710**
Cofer, Judith Ortiz, 42, 45, 73
  "*Casa:* A Partial Remembrance of a Puerto Rican Childhood," 73–78
Coherence, **710**, 718, 722
Colloquial expressions, **710**, **712**
"Colorings of Childhood, The" (Updike), 541, 578–86
Comic writing. *See* Humor
Comparison and contrast, 3–4, 167–73, 708, **710**
  argument and persuasion and, 472, 474
  definition and, 408, 410, 413
  description and, 95
  division or analysis and, 268
  Greenfield's use of, 5
  method of, 167–68
  organization of, 169–71, 172–73
  paragraph illustrations of, 172–73
  process of, 169–71
  purposes of, 168
  writing strategy with, 21
Complex classification, 316–17
Composition, Schlesinger on, 693–94
Computers
  Baker on, 324–26
  Chang on, 506
Conciseness
  Dillard on, 111
  opinion and, 475
Conclusion, **710–11**
  argument and persuasion and, 472
  Epstein on, 458
  narration and, 46

Conclusion (*cont.*)
  options for, 711
  reasoning with, 469, 472
Concrete language, 475, **707**
Connotation, **711,** 715
Contrast. *See* Comparison and contrast
"Conversation Piece" (Markoe), 222,
  227–31
Coontz, Stephanie, 150
  "A Nation of Welfare Families," 150–
  55
  "Stephanie Coontz on Writing,"
  156–58
Creative process
  Chase on, 561, 562
  Jackson on, 90–91
  Ueland on, 240
  Vidal on, 375
Critical thinking, reading, and writing,
  16–18, **711–12**
  analysis in, 17, 269, 709
  argument and persuasion and, 462
  assumptions and, 17
  critical reading of an essay in, 6–9
  Epstein on, 457–58
  evaluation in, 17–18, 714
  first reading in, 8–9
  inference in, 17, 716
  language and, 22–24
  meaning and, 18–20
  Miller on, 281–82
  operations in, 17–18
  preliminaries in, 6–8
  rereadings in, 14–24
  summarizing during, 15–16
  synthesis in, 17
  taking notes during, 14–15
  writing strategy and, 20–22
Criticism, 269
"Cult of Ethnicity, Good and Bad,
  The" (Schlesinger), 681, 689–92
Current, Richard N., 369–70

D'Angelo, Christine, 3, 5, 14
  "Has the Chain Been Broken? Two
  Ideas of Violence in 'The Broken
  Chain,'" 25, 27–35

Daniels, Josephus, 41
Data, in reasoning, 465, 467, 468,
  712
Deadlines
  Epstein on, 457
  Steinem on, 430
  Wolfe on, 423
Dead metaphor, 715
"Death of a Moth" (Dillard), 107–10
"Death of the Moth, The" (Woolf),
  101–4
Deductive reasoning, 468–69, **712**
Definition, 407–13, **712**
  construction of, 407–8
  extended, 408, 410, 411
  Greenfield and, 4
  method of, 407–9
  mixing other methods with, 537
  paragraph illustrations of, 412–13
  process of, 409–12
  questions used for, 409, 410–11, 538
  stipulative, 408, 412
  uses of, 408–409
Denotation, **711**
Dershowitz, Alan M., 484
  "Alan M. Dershowitz on Writing,"
  488
  "Don't Pull the Plug on Televised
  Executions," 484–86
Description, 93–100, **712**
  argument and persuasion and, 472
  definition and, 408, 712
  Dillard on, 111
  dominant impression in, 96
  example and, 138
  method of, 93–95
  mixing other methods with, 537
  narration and, 43–44, 95
  objective, 94, 95
  organization of, 96–98
  paragraph illustrations of, 98–100
  point of view in, 96
  process of, 95–98
  purpose of, 93
  questions in, 96, 538
  subjective, 94
  as teaching aid, 100
  writing strategy with, 21

"Desperation Writing" (Elbow),
246–49
Details
description and, 96, 97, 98–99
Didion on, 117–18
Staples on, 164
De Voto, Bernard, 693
Dialect, **712**
Dialogue, Jackson's use of, 45
Diary writing
hooks on, 312–13
Woolf on, 105–6
Dickens, Charles, 94–95, 96, 97, 412
Dickinson, Emily, 129, 408
"Emily Dickinson on Writing," 131–
32
"A narrow Fellow in the Grass,"
129–30
Diction, **712–13**
Dictionary, 23, 407
Didion, Joan, 113, 721
"Joan Didion on Writing," 117–18
"Marrying Absurd," 113–16
Dillard, Annie, 107, 562, 721
"Annie Dillard on Writing," 111
"Death of a Moth," 107–10
"Disability" (Mairs), 489–91
Discovery, **713**
Division or analysis, 167, 267–72
analogy and, 708
cause and effect and, 364
critical thinking, reading, and writ-
ing, 17, 19–20, 269
definition and, 408
method of, 267–69
paragraph illustrations of, 271–72
principle of, 271–72
process analysis and, 221–22
process of, 270–71
questions for writers of, 270, 363,
538
subject of, 268, 270, 271, 315
Dominant impression, 96, **713**
"Don't Pull the Plug on Televised
Executions" (Dershowitz), 484–86
Douglas, Stephen, 472
"Dow Recycles Reality" (Miller), 269,
277–80

Drafts and drafting, **713**
Chang on, 506
D'Angelo example of, 34–35
Dickinson on, 131–32
Elbow on, 251
example of changes during,
27–34
Kingston on, 602
process analysis and, 224
Vidal on, 374
Wolfe on, 423
writing process and, 25–26
Drakulić, Slavenka, 664
"Some Doubts About Fur Coats,"
649, 664–70
"Drugs" (Vidal), 371–73

Editing of work. *See* Revision
Education, Schlesinger on, 693–94
Effect, 408, **713**. *See also* Cause and ef-
fect
Ehrenreich, Barbara, 292
"Barbara Ehrenreich on Writing,"
301–2
"The Wretched of the Hearth," 269,
292–99
Either/or reasoning, 470
Elbow, Peter, 246
"Desperation Writing," 246–49
"Peter Elbow on Writing," 250–52
Eliot, T. S., 268
Ellison, Ralph, 41, 45, 55
"On Being the Target of Discrimina-
tion," 55–61
"Ralph Ellison on Writing," 63
Emotional appeal, 463–64, **709**
Emphasis, 44, **713–14**
Environment, our place in, 537, 649
Epstein, Joseph, 443
"Joseph Epstein on Writing," 457–58
"What Is Vulgar?" 443–54
Ericsson, Stephanie, 623
"The Ways We Lie," 605, 623–31
"Erotica and Pornography" (Steinem),
424–28
Essays, **714**
Epstein on, 457–58

Essays (*cont.*)
 formal, 714
 Gould on, 402–3
 informal, 714
 Reed on, 688
 Segal on, 648–49
 Staples on, 163, 164–65
 White on, 128
Ethical appeal, 464, **709**
Euphemisms, **714**
 Mitford on, 264
Evaluation, **714**
 classification and, 317
 comparison and contrast and, 168
 critical reading and, 17–18, 463, 712
Evidence, 21, **714–15**
 argument and persuasion and, 463,
  467, 471–72, 472–73, 539
 definition and, 412
 division or analysis and, 270–71
 examples and, 156
 inductive reasoning with, 468
 opinion and, 474
 paraphrase of, 718
 proposals and, 474
 Staples on, 164
Examples, 21, 26, 135–39, 714, **715**
 argument and persuasion with, 472
 cause and effect and, 369
 classification and, 319
 Coontz and, 156
 definition and, 410, 411, 413
 experience and, 136–37
 Greenfield and, 4
 hypothetical, 137
 method of, 135–36
 mixing other methods with, 537
 paragraph illustrations of, 138–39
 process of, 136–38
"Excuuuse Me" (Segal), 605, 634–37
Exposition, **715**
Extended definition, 408, 410, 411

Facts, 128, 164, 714. *See also* Evidence
Fallacies, **715**. *See also* Logical fallacies
False analogy, 470–71

Family, power of, 537, 541
Figures of speech, 708, **715**
 in Fisher, 23
 in White, 97
First person, 42, 719
Fisher, M. F. K., 10
 "The Broken Chain," 4, 6, 7, 8, 9,
  10–13, 15–16, 18, 19–23, 24, 25,
  27
Flashback, 45, **715**
Flynn, Maire, 467–68
Focus, **715–16**
"Football Red and Baseball Green"
 (Ross), 209–16
Form
 Angelou on, 54
 White on, 128
Formal essay, 714
Forster, E. M., 20
Francis, Robert, 268
Free association, Epstein on, 457
Freewriting, 105
Frost, Robert, 2, 458

General and specific, **716**
Generalization, **716**
 cause and effect and, 369
 definition and, 412
 example and, 135–36, 156
 reasoning and, 465, 468, 469, 470,
  714
Gore, Albert, Jr., 650
 "Ships in the Desert," 650–56
Gornick, Vivian, 542
 "Mama Went to Work," 541, 542–45
 "Vivian Gornick on Writing," 546–
  47
Gould, Stephen Jay, 393
 "Sex, Drugs, Disasters, and the Ex-
  tinction of Dinosaurs," 393–400
 "Stephen Jay Gould on Writing,"
  402–3
Grammar, 27
 Didion on, 118
"Grant and Lee: A Study in Contrasts"
 (Catton), 7, 169, 180–83

Greenfield, Jeff, 199, 473
"The Black and White Truth About Basketball," 4, 168, 199–204
"Jeff Greenfield on Writing," 206–7
"Guide to the Ghettos, A" (Vergara), 334–40
Guttmacher, Alan F., 224

Hamburg, Joan, 316
Harding, Warren G., 483
Harris, Marvin, 241
"How Our Skins Got Their Color," 7, 241–44
"Has the Chain Been Broken? Two Ideas of Violence in 'The Broken Chain' " (D'Angelo), 25, 34–35
drafts of, 27–34
Hasty generalization, 470
Hayakawa, S. I., 138
Higginson, Thomas Wentworth, 132
"Highlighter Crisis, The" (Beyer), 15, 382–84
Historical studies, cause and effect in, 365, 370
Hogan, Linda, 672
"Linda Hogan on Writing," 678
"Waking Up the Rake," 649, 672–76
"Holocaust, The" (Bettelheim), 438–41
"Homeless" (Quindlen), 145–47
hooks, bell, 303
"bell hooks on Writing," 269, 312–13
"Madonna," 303–11
"How Our Skins Got Their Color" (Harris), 7, 241–44
"How to Poison the Earth" (Saukko), 649, 659–61
Humor
argument and, 472
classification and, 317
Greenfield on, 206–7
Lebowitz on, 332
Mitford and, 264
Thurber on, 71–72
Huxley, Aldous, 457

Huxley, Thomas Henry, 482
Hyperbole, 715

"I Have a Dream" (King), 464, 472, 516–20, 708, 718
Illiteracy, Lebowitz on, 332
Image, 716
in Orwell, 538
in White, 97
Imitation, Woolf on, 106
Immediate cause, 363
Imperative mood, 226
Improvising, Vidal on, 375
Indifference, Britt on, 178
Inductive leap, 468
Inductive reasoning, 468, 716
Inference, 716
critical reading with, 17, 463, 711
division or analysis with, 268
Informal essay, 714
Inspiration
Chase on, 561, 562
Epstein on, 457
Gornick on, 546–47
Jackson on, 90
Jordan on, 392
Ueland on, 240
Introduction, 716–17
argument and persuasion and, 463
definition in, 409
Dillard on, 111
narration and, 45–46
Vidal on, 375
Irony, 409, 717, 720
"I Want a Wife" (Brady), 268, 270, 273–75

Jackson, Shirley, 80
"The Lottery," 42, 45, 80–88
"Shirley Jackson on Writing," 90–91
Janson, H. W., 99–100
Jargon, 224, 717
Gould on, 402
Mitford on, 264
Johnson, Samuel, 18, 40, 43, 409

Jokes. *See* Humor
Jordan, June, 386
  "June Jordan on Writing," 392
  "Requiem for the Champ," 386–90
Journalism
  chronological order and, 46
  definition in, 408
  Dershowitz on, 488
  Ehrenreich on, 301
  essential questions in, 42–43
  Greenfield on, 206–7
  Orwell on, 621
  process analysis in, 223
  Quindlen on, 148–149
  Rosenthal on, 379–81
  Staples on, 164
  women and, 301
Journal writing
  Elbow on, 251
  hooks on, 313
  Mairs on, 493–94
  White on, 127

Kakutani, Michiko, 640
  "The Word Police," 605, 640–45
Keats, John, 561
Keta, Norma, 316
Kincaid, Jamaica, 432
  "Jamaica Kincaid on Writing," 436–
    37
  "The Tourist," 432–34
King, Martin Luther, Jr., 516, 721
  "I Have a Dream," 464, 472, 516–
    20, 708, 718
Kingston, Maxine Hong, 589
  "Maxine Hong Kingston on Writ-
    ing," 602
  "No Name Woman," 541, 589–600
Kostof, Spiro, 173

Language
  critical reading and, 22–24
  Dickinson on, 132
  Didion on, 117–18
  Fisher and, 22–23
    Gould on, 402
    Mencken on, 482–83
    Orwell on, 620–21
    revision and, 26–27
    Tan on, 197
    truth and, 537, 605
  "Language of Discretion, The" (Tan),
    187–95
Lead, in journalism, 46
Lebowitz, Fran, 328, 717
  "Fran Lebowitz on Writing," 332
  "The Sound of Music: Enough Al-
    ready," 7, 317, 328–30
Lincoln, Abraham, 472
Literacy, uses of, 1–2
Logical fallacies, 708
  cause and effect and, 366–67
  list of, 469–71
  reasoning and, 469–71
Loose sentence, 714
"Lottery, The" (Jackson), 42, 45, 80–
    88
Lutgens, Frederick K., 48

"Madonna" (hooks), 269, 303–11
Mairs, Nancy, 489
  "Disability," 489–91
  "Nancy Mairs on Writing,"
    493–94
Major cause, 366
Major premise, 469
"Mama Went to Work" (Gornick),
    541, 542–45
Markoe, Merrill, 227
  "Conversation Piece," 222, 227–31
"Marrying Absurd" (Didion), 113–16
Meaning
  critical reading for, 16, 18–20
  Kingston on, 602
Melville, Herman, 721
Mencken, H. L., 477
  "H. L. Mencken on Writing," 482–
    83
  "The Penalty of Death," 7, 472,
    477–80
Metaphor, 409, 708, 715

in Fisher, 23
in White, 98
Miller, G. Tyler, Jr., 475
Miller, Mark Crispin, 277
    "Dow Recycles Reality," 269, 277–80
    "Mark Crispin Miller on Writing,"
      281–82
Minor cause, 366
Minor premise, 469
Mitford, Jessica, 253, 717, 721
    "Behind the Formaldehyde Curtain,"
      222, 253–61
    "Jessica Mitford on Writing," 263–64
Mixed methods of development, 537–39
"Modest Proposal, A" (Swift), 522–30,
    720
Motives for writing
    Didion on, 117–18
    Ellison on, 63
    Gould on, 402
    Greenfield on, 207
    Hogan on, 678
    Kincaid on, 436
    Lebowitz on, 332
    Orwell on, 620, 621
    Quindlen on, 148–49
    Reich on, 359
    Rodriguez on, 576
    Staples on, 163, 164–65
    Vidal on, 375
Muller, Robert A., 226
"My Brother on the Shoulder of the
    Road" (Chase), 541, 549–59

Narration, 39–48, **717**
    Angelou and, 3
    argument and persuasion and, 472
    chronological order in, 710
    definition and, 409, 712
    description and, 43–44, 95
    example and, 138
    Fisher and, 22
    method of, 39–41
    mixing other methods with, 537
    oral, 40, 46
    paragraph illustrations of, 47–48

    point of view and, 42
    process of, 41–46
    questions for writers of, 42–43, 44,
      538
    writing strategy with, 21
Narrator, 41–42, **717**
"narrow Fellow in the Grass, A" (Dick-
    inson), 129–30
Nash, Roderick, 475
"Nation of Welfare Families, A"
    (Coontz), 150–55
"Neat People vs. Sloppy People"
    (Britt), 174–76
News stories. *See* Journalism
"No Name Woman" (Kingston), 541,
    589–600
Nonparticipant in narrative, 42
Non sequitur, 469
Nonstandard English, **712**

Oberlander, Theodore M., 226
Objective writing, 42, 94, **717–18,**
    719
Obsolete diction, **712–13**
Olds, Sally Wendkos, 319–20
"On Being the Target of Discrimina-
    tion" (Ellison), 55–61
"Once More to the Lake" (White), 97–
    98, 120–26
"On Compassion" (Ascher), 140–42
Opinion, **718**
    argument and, 463, 471, 473, 474,
      477–506, 539, 714
    Segal on, 648–49
Orians, Gordon H., 413
Originality, Swift on, 532
Orwell, George, 117, 606
    "George Orwell on Writing," 620–21
    "Politics and the English Language,"
      19, 538–39, 605, 606–18
Outline
    classification with, 318
    comparison and contrast and, 171,
      172–73
    division or analysis and, 270
    Epstein on, 457

Outline (*cont.*)
  Kingston on, 602
  paragraph building with, 172–73
  Wolfe on, 422, 423
Oversimplification, 470

Paine, Thomas, 332
Paley, Grace, 561
Papalia, Diane E., 319–20
Paradox, 715
Paragraph, **718**
  Epstein on, 457
  outline for building, 172–73
  revision and, 26
  thesis and, 721
Parallelism, **718,** 722
Paraphrase, 715, **718–19**
"Penalty of Death, The" (Mencken), 7,
    472, 477–80
Pentad of Burke, 367–68
Perelman, S. J., 98
Periodic sentence, 714–15
Person, **719**
  first person, 42, 719
  narration and, 42
  process analysis and, 226
  second person, 226, 719
  third person, 42, 719
Personification, 715
Persuasion, 18, 462, **719.** *See also* Ar-
    gument and persuasion
Pirsig, Robert M., 468
"Plot Against People, The" (Baker),
    317, 321–23
Poetry
  analysis of, 281
  Dickinson on, 131–32
Point-by-point organization, 170–71
Point of view, **719**
  argument and persuasion and, 463,
    471
  description and, 96–98
  Epstein on, 458
  narration and, 4
  Reed on, 688
Political writing
  Dershowitz on, 488

Greenfield on, 206
Orwell on, 620–21
Reed on, 688
Reich on, 359–60
Whitehead on, 348–49
"Politics and the English Language"
    (Orwell), 19, 538–39, 605, 606–
    18
Pollitt, Katha, 695
  "Why Do We Read?" 681, 695–
    702
Popularizer
  Gould as, 402
  Whitehead as, 348–49
"Pornoviolence" (Wolfe), 408, 409,
    414–20
Position, **713–14**
Post hoc, ergo propter hoc, 470
"Predictable Crises of Adulthood"
    (Sheehy), 283–90
Premise, 469, **719**
Present tense, 44–45
Pretentious diction, **713**
Process analysis, 221–26, **719**
  audience and, 222–23
  cause and, 364
  chronological order in, 710
  definition and, 410
  directive, 222, 223, 225–26
  division or analysis in, 268
  informative, 222, 226, 264
  method of, 221–23
  Mitford on, 264
  mixing other methods with, 537
  paragraph illustrations of, 225–26
  process of, 223–25
  questions in, 223–24, 538
  scientists' use of, 222, 224, 226
Pronouns, 719
  first person, 42, 719
  second person, 226, 719
  third person, 42, 719
Proportion, **713**
Proposal, 471, 507–33, **719**
Publication information, 8
Purpose, 26, 45, **719**
  in Burke's pentad, 367
  chronological order and, 45

classification and, 316, 317
comparison and contrast and, 168
critical reading for, 18–19
description and, 94, 95, 97, 98
discovery for, 25, 713
Ehrenreich on, 301
Fisher and, 19–20
Mencken and, 482
narration and, 41, 43, 44
Orwell on, 621
Reed on, 688
Saukko on, 663
Swift on, 533
Whitehead on, 348–49
Purves, William K., 413

Questions, 538
audience awareness through, 709
cause and effect and, 363–64, 365,
367, 368, 369
comparison and contrast and, 167
definition and, 409, 410–11
description and, 96
division or analysis and, 270, 363
Ellison on use of, 63
narration and, 42–43, 44
process analysis and, 223–24
readers and, 16, 18, 23–24
revision and, 26–27
Quindlen, Anna, 145
"Anna Quindlen on Writing," 148–
49
"Homeless," 145–47
Quotations, 715

Rational appeal, 463, **709**
Readers. *See* Audience
Reading
critical, 16–20
Ellison on, 63
first, 8–9
notes during, 14–15
prereading, 6–8
questions to ask when, 16, 18,
23–24
summarizing, 15–16

Reading and writing. *See also* Critical
thinking, reading, and writing
Ellison on, 63
Mencken on, 482–83
reasons for, 1–2
Reasoning, 464–71
deductive, 468–68
inductive, 468
logical fallacies and, 469–71
Toulmin's method of, 465–69
Reed, Ishmael, 682
"America: The Multinational Soci-
ety," 681, 682–86
"Ishmael Reed on Writing," 688
Regional terms, **712**
Reich, Robert B., 350
"Robert B. Reich on Writing," 359–
60
"Why the Rich Are Getting Richer
and the Poor Poorer," 7, 317,
350–58
Remote cause, 363, 366, 368
Repetition, **714**
"Requiem for the Champ" (Jordan),
386–90
Research
examples and, 137–38
Mitford on, 263–64
Wolfe on, 422
Revision, **719**
Baker on, 325–26
Catton on, 186
Chang on, 506
Coontz on, 156
D'Angelo examples of, 31–34
Dickinson on, 131–32
Dillard on, 111
Jackson on, 90
Kingston on, 602
process analysis and, 225
questions for, 26
Rodriguez on, 576–77
Ross on, 219
Saukko on, 663
Thurber on, 71
Vidal on, 374
writing process with, 26–27
Rhetorical forms, 4, **719**

Rhetorical question, **720**
Rhythm, Angelou on, 53–54
Rodriguez, Richard, 563
  "Aria: A Memoir of a Bilingual
    Childhood," 541, 563–74
  "Richard Rodriguez on Writing,"
    576–77
Rosenthal, A. M., 376, 721
  "A. M. Rosenthal on Writing," 379–
    81
  "The Case for Slavery," 376–78
Ross, Murray, 209
  "Football Red and Baseball Green,"
    209–16
  "Murray Ross on Writing," 218–19
Rules, Woolf on, 105–6

Satire, **720**
Saukko, Linnea, 3, 659
  "How to Poison the Earth," 649,
    659–61
  "Linnea Saukko on Writing," 663
Scene, **720**
  in Burke's pentad, 367
  narration and, 43, 44
Schlesinger, Arthur M., Jr., 689
  "Arthur M. Schlesinger, Jr., on
    Writing," 693–94
  "The Cult of Ethnicity, Good and
    Bad," 681, 689–92
Scientific writing
  Gould on, 402–3
  process analysis in, 222, 224, 226
Second person, 226, 719
Segal, David, 634
  "David Segal on Writing," 638–39
  "Excuuuse Me," 605, 634–37
Sensory experience
  definition and, 412
  description and, 94, 95, 97, 98
  Didion on, 117
  Dillard on, 111
Sentence
  Angelou on, 54
  Baker on, 325–26
  Chang on, 506

conclusion with, 472
Didion on, 118
Dillard on, 111
Gornick on, 546–47
Kingston on, 602
loose, 714
periodic, 714–15
purpose and, 19
revisions of, 26
Staples on, 163–64
summary, 15
Tan on, 198
thesis, **721**
topic, 136, 370, 718, **721**
transitional, 370
Vidal on, 375
Sentimentality, **720**
"Sex, Drugs, Disasters, and the Extinc-
  tion of Dinosaurs" (Gould), 393–
  400
Sheehy, Gail, 283
  "Predictable Crises of Adulthood,"
    283–90
"Ships in the Desert" (Gore), 650–56
Simile, 715
  in White, 98
Slang, **712**
Solmon, Lewis C., 139
"Some Doubts About Fur Coats"
  (Drakulić), 649, 664–70
Sorkin, Michael, 139
"Sound of Music, The: Enough Al-
  ready" (Lebowitz), 7, 317,
  328–30
Sports writing
  Greenfield on, 206–7
  Ross on, 218–19
Standard English, **712**
Staples, Brent, 159
  "Black Men and Public Space," 159–
    62
  "Brent Staples on Writing," 163–65
Steinem, Gloria, 424
  "Erotica and Pornography," 424–28
  "Gloria Steinem on Writing," 430
Stipulative definition, 408, 412
Storytelling. *See* Narration

Strategy, 20–22, **720**
  methods used in, 21–22
  Segal on, 649
  Wolfe on, 422–23
"Streets of Gold: The Myth of the
    Model Minority" (Chang), 495–
    504
Structure
  analysis of, 267
  Angelou on, 54
  comparison and contrast and, 169–
    71, 172–73
  description and, 99
  Fisher and, 22
  White on, 127–28
  Wolfe on, 423
Style, **720**
  Dickinson on, 132
  Mencken on, 482, 483
  Tan on, 197
Subject
  Angelou on, 53–54
  cause and effect and, 365–66
  classification and, 315–16, 318
  comparison and contrast and, 169–71
  definition and, 408
  division or analysis and, 268, 270,
    271, 315
  Ehrenreich on, 301
  Mitford on, 263
  Saukko on, 663
  Steinem on, 430
  White on, 128
Subject-by-subject organization, 169–
    70, 171
Subjective writing, 94, **717–18,** 719
Subjectivism
  Britt on, 178–79
  Saukko on, 663
Summarizing, in critical reading,
    15–16
Summary, **720**
  narration and, 43, 44
Summary sentence, 15
Surprise
  Trillin on, 46
  Vidal on, 375

Suspense, **720–21**
Swift, Jonathan, 18, 316, 522
  "Jonathan Swift on Writing," 532–33
  "A Modest Proposal," 522–30, 720
Syllogism, 469, **721**
Syntax, Didion on, 117–18
Synthesis, **721**
  critical reading with, 17, 463, 711
  division or analysis with, 269

Tan, Amy, 187
  "Amy Tan on Writing," 197–98
  "The Language of Discretion," 187–95
Tarbuck, Edward J., 48
Technical terms, 223–24, **712.** See also
    Jargon
Television, critical approach to, 281–82
"Tell Me More" (Ueland), 233–38
Tense, 44–45
Theme, Gould on, 402–3
Thesis, 7, 19, 26, 710, 717, **721**
  argument and persuasion and, 463,
    471
  classification and, 317
  division or analysis and, 271
  narration and, 47
  sentence, **721**
Thinking. See Critical thinking, read-
    ing, and writing
Third person, 42, 719
Thoreau, Henry David, 128, 137
Thurber, James, 42, 45, 64, 717
  "James Thurber on Writing," 71–72
  "University Days," 64–69
Time-markers, 224, 225
Title, 7
Tone, 7, 23, 26, 715, **721**
  Ehrenreich on, 301–2
Topic sentence, 136, 370, 718, **721**
Toulmin, Stephen, 465, 467, 710, 712
"Tourist, The" (Kincaid), 432–34
Transitions, 26, 46, **721–22**
  coherence and, 710
  process analysis and, 224
  in time, 46
Trillin, Calvin, 45–46

Truth
    Jordan on, 392
    language and, 537, 605
    Mencken on, 482
    Orwell on, 620–21
    White on, 128
Twain, Mark, 46

Ueland, Brenda, 233
    "Brenda Ueland on Writing," 240
    "Tell Me More," 233–38
Understatement, 715
Unity, 718, 721, **722**
"University Days" (Thurber), 64–69
Updike, David, 578
    "The Colorings of Childhood," 541,
        578–86

Values of author, Greenfield on, 207
Veatch, Robert M., 272
Verbal irony, 717
Verbs
    Dillard on voice of, 111
    imperative mood in process analysis,
        226
    tenses in narration, 44–45
Vergara, Camilo José, 334
    "A Guide to the Ghettos," 334–40
Vidal, Gore, 371
    "Drugs," 371–373
    "Gore Vidal on Writing," 374–75
Viewpoint. *See* Point of view
Vocabulary
    Fisher and, 22–23
    Mencken on, 482
Voice, **722**
    Ehrenreich on, 301
    Jordan on, 392
    Ross on, 219

"Waking Up the Rake" (Hogan), 649,
    672–76
Warrant, in reasoning, 465–67, **722**
"Ways We Lie, The" (Ericsson), 605,
    623–31

Welty, Eudora, 716
"What Is Vulgar?" (Epstein), 443–54
White, E. B., 3, 120
    "E. B. White on Writing," 127–28
    "Once More to the Lake," 97–98,
        120–26
Whitehead, Ralph, Jr., 342
    "Class Acts: America's Changing
        Middle Class," 317, 342–47
    "Ralph Whitehead, Jr., on Writing,"
        348–49
"Why Don't We Complain?" (Buckley),
    40, 95, 472, 507–12
"Why Do We Read?" (Pollitt), 681,
    695–702
"Why the Rich Are Getting Richer and
    the Poor Poorer" (Reich), 7, 317,
    350–58
Wilder, Thornton, 2
Will, George, 514
Wilson, Woodrow, 41, 42
Wolfe, Linda, 135–36, 138
Wolfe, Tom, 3, 414
    "Pornoviolence," 408, 409, 414–20
    "Tom Wolfe on Writing," 422–23
Woolf, Virginia, 101
    "The Death of the Moth," 101–4
    "Virginia Woolf on Writing," 105–6
"Word Police, The" (Kakutani), 605,
    640–45
Word processors. *See* Computers
Words. *See* Language; Vocabulary
"Wretched of the Hearth, The"
    (Ehrenreich), 269, 292–99
Writer
    Catton on purpose of, 186
    Chase on, 561
    Didion on, 118
    reading and knowledge about, 7–8
    as trickster, 688
Writer and society
    Ehrenreich on, 301–2
    Ellison on, 63
    Hogan on, 678
    hooks on, 312
    Jordan on, 392
    Lebowitz on, 332
    Mairs on, 493–94

Orwell on, 620–21
Reed on, 687–88
Reich on, 359–60
Rodriguez on, 576–77
Saukko on, 663
Swift on, 532–33
Whitehead on, 348–49
Writer's block
  Elbow on, 251
  Steinem on, 430
Writing. *See also* Political writing; Sci-
  entific writing; Sports writing
  attitude toward, Buckley on, 514
  craft of
    Baker on, 324–26
    Ellison on, 63
  discovery in
    Epstein on, 457–58
    Gould on, 402
    Vidal on, 375
  emotional health and, Lebowitz on,
    332
  as functional art, Reed on, 688
  inspiration for
    Chase on, 561, 562
    Epstein on, 457
    Gornick on, 546–47
    Jackson on, 90
    Jordan on, 392
    Ueland on, 240
  liveliness of, 132
  methods of, 3–4
    Baker on, 324–26
    mixing of, 537–38
    writing strategy with, 21–22
  as a mode of thinking, Epstein on,
    457–58
  motivation for
    Didion on, 117–18
    Ellison on, 63
    Gould on, 402
    Greenfield on, 207
    Hogan on, 678
    Kincaid on, 436
    Lebowitz on, 332
    Orwell on, 620, 621
    Quindlen on, 148–49
    Reich on, 359

Rodriguez on, 576
Staples on, 163, 164–65
Vidal on, 375
and observation, Britt on, 178–79
place for, Kincaid on, 436–37
pleasures of
  Buckley on, 514
  Ellison on, 63
  Rosenthal on, 380–81
  Ross on, 218–19
  Steinem on, 430
  Vidal on, 374
preparation for
  Angelou on, 53–54
  Catton on, 186
  Epstein on, 457–58
  Vidal on, 374–75
process of, 25–27
  Baker on, 324–26
  Britt on, 178
  Chang on, 506
  Chase on, 561–62
  Dillard on, 562
  D'Angelo example of, 34–35
  Epstein on, 457
  Kingston on, 602
  Rodriguez on, 576–77
  Rosenthal on, 381
  stages of, 25–26
  Steinem on, 430
  Vidal on, 374–75
  White on, 128
  Woolf on, 105–6
productivity of
  Buckley on, 514–15
  Steinem on, 430
  Wolfe on, 106
and self-discovery
  Britt on, 178–79
  Didion on, 117–18
  Ellison on, 63
  hooks on, 313
  Kincaid on, 436
  Mairs on, 493–94
  Quindlen on, 148–49
  Rodriguez on, 576–77
  Staples on, 163, 164
  Steinem on, 430

Writing (*cont.*)
  strategy for, 20–22
  surprise in, Vidal on, 375
  work habits in
    Coontz on, 156–57
    Jackson on, 90

  Ross on, 218–19
  Thurber on, 71
  Wolfe on, 422–23
writers on, 5